JUSTICE LEAGUE OF AMERICA

ARCHIVES ▾ VOLUME 8

ARCHIVE EDITIONS

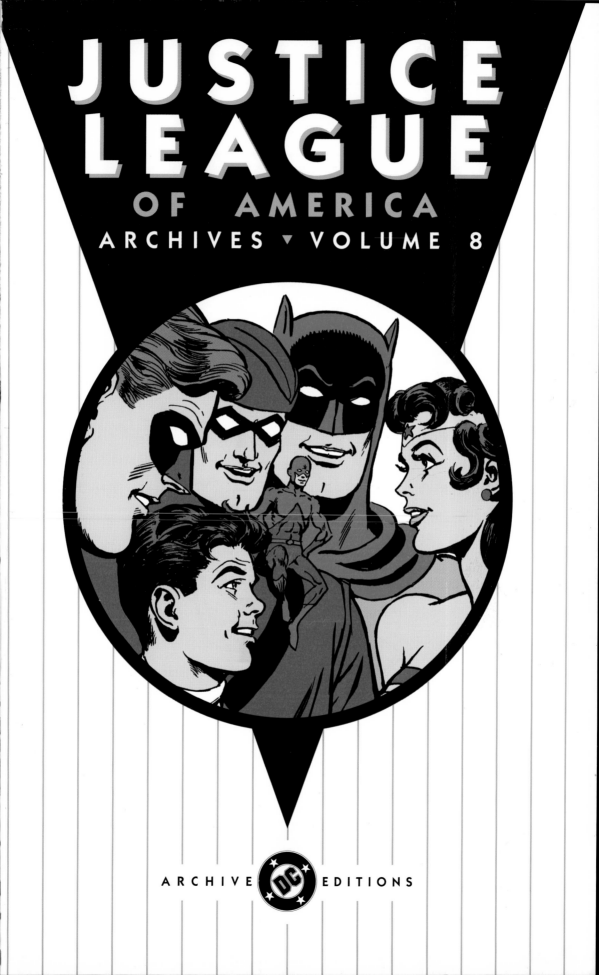

DC COMICS

DALE CRAIN
SENIOR EDITOR-COLLECTED
EDITIONS

ROBBIN BROSTERMAN
SENIOR ART DIRECTOR

PAUL LEVITZ
PRESIDENT & PUBLISHER

GEORG BREWER
VP-DESIGN & RETAIL PRODUCT
DEVELOPMENT

RICHARD BRUNING
VP-CREATIVE DIRECTOR

PATRICK CALDON
SENIOR VP-FINANCE &
OPERATIONS

CHRIS CARAMALIS
VP-FINANCE

TERRI CUNNINGHAM
VP-MANAGING EDITOR

DAN DIDIO
VP-EDITORIAL

JOEL EHRLICH
SENIOR VP-ADVERTISING &
PROMOTIONS

ALISON GILL
VP-MANUFACTURING

LILLIAN LASERSON
SENIOR VP & GENERAL COUNSEL

DAVID MCKILLIPS
VP-ADVERTISING

JOHN NEE
VP-BUSINESS
DEVELOPMENT

CHERYL RUBIN
VP-LICENSING &
MERCHANDISING

BOB WAYNE
VP-SALES & MARKETING

JUSTICE LEAGUE OF AMERICA ARCHIVES
VOLUME EIGHT

ISBN: 1-56389-977-9

PUBLISHED BY DC COMICS
COVER, INTRODUCTION AND COMPILATION
COPYRIGHT © 2003 DC COMICS

ORIGINALLY PUBLISHED IN SINGLE MAGAZINE
FORM IN JUSTICE LEAGUE OF AMERICA 61-70.
COPYRIGHT © 1968, 1969 DC COMICS.
ALL RIGHTS RESERVED.

THE JUSTICE LEAGUE OF AMERICA AND
ALL RELATED CHARACTERS, THE DISTINCTIVE
LIKENESSES THEREOF AND RELATED
INDICIA ARE TRADEMARKS OF DC COMICS.
THE STORIES, CHARACTERS, AND INCIDENTS
FEATURED IN THIS PUBLICATION ARE
ENTIRELY FICTIONAL. DC COMICS DOES NOT
READ OR ACCEPT UNSOLICITED SUBMISSIONS
OF IDEAS, STORIES OR ARTWORK.

DC COMICS
1700 BROADWAY
NEW YORK, NY 10019

A DIVISION OF WARNER BROS. –
AN AOL TIME WARNER COMPANY
PRINTED IN HONG KONG.
FIRST PRINTING.

THE DC ARCHIVE EDITIONS

COVER ILLUSTRATION BY MIKE SEKOWSKY.
COVER BLACK-AND-WHITE RECONSTRUCTION
BY JERRY ORDWAY

COVER COLOR BY JAMISON

SERIES DESIGN BY ALEX JAY/STUDIO J

PUBLICATION DESIGN BY LOUIS PRANDI

BLACK AND WHITE RECONSTRUCTION ON
SELECTED INTERIOR PAGES BY RICK KEENE

COLOR RECONSTRUCTION BY JAMISON

12/16/05
B+T
$49.95

TABLE OF CONTENTS

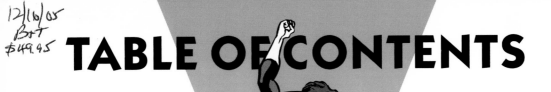

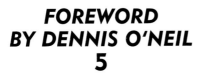

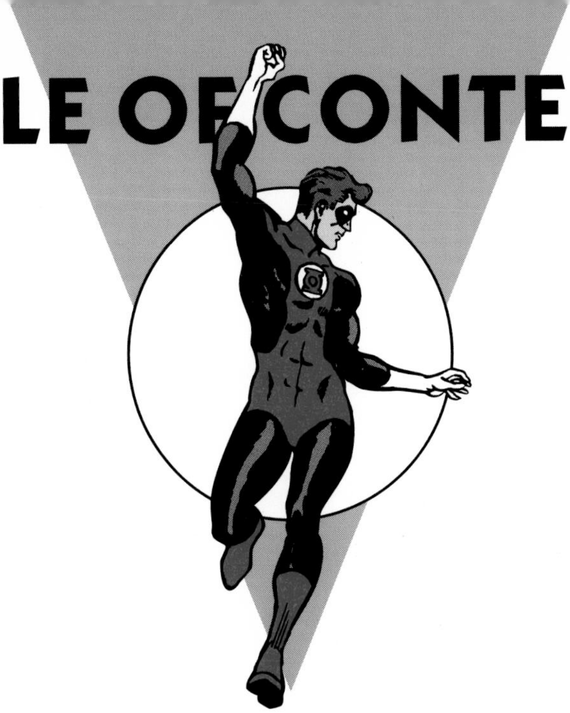

TABLE OF CONTENTS

FOREWORD

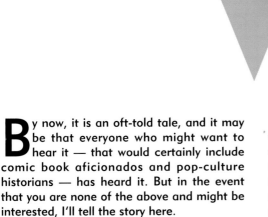

By now, it is an oft-told tale, and it may be that everyone who might want to hear it — that would certainly include comic book aficionados and pop-culture historians — has heard it. But in the event that you are none of the above and might be interested, I'll tell the story here.

Very briefly: Two comic-book publishers were playing golf. Their names were Irwin Donenfeld and Martin Goodman. Donenfeld told Goodman that he was making a nice profit with a new super-hero title, THE JUSTICE LEAGUE OF AMERICA, which featured a whole bunch of costumed heroes instead of the usual one. Soon thereafter, Goodman went to his editor-in-chief and suggested, perhaps strongly, that their company emulate the competition and publish a title featuring a group of super-doers.

The editor was Stan Lee and the comic book he and the superb artist Jack Kirby created was *The Fantastic Four*, which is generally credited with being the first true Marvel comic and hence launching an empire.

Is the story about Messrs. Donenfeld and Goodman true? Well, I wasn't there, but I suspect it is. But there's another story, equally important in the history of comics, that *hasn't* been told, at least as far as I know. Let us assume that the success of the Justice League prompted the creation of *The Fantastic Four* — okay. But where did the Justice League come from?

Julie Schwartz was happy to tell me when, a few days ago, I mentioned that I was going to write this introduction. Julie is retired now, but he still comes into his office at DC Comics about once a week and I always enjoy talking to him, my former and most valued editor. He remembered exactly how he and writer Gardner Fox came to do the Justice League and he was happy to share his memories. I'll be happy to share his memories, too, with you, in just a few hundred words. But first, we might do well to establish a little historical context.

From the debut of Superman in ACTION COMICS in 1938 until, approximately, the end of the 1940s, comic books were a vigorous and profitable medium. Then, in the early years of the '50s — the Eisenhower era — comics' fortunes waned, drastically. There were a number of reasons. The one most comics fans know best is the blame comics incurred for juvenile delinquency, prompted by the writings of Frederic Wertham, a New York psychiatrist, and the Congressional hearings held by Estes Kefauver, an ambitious senator from Kentucky. It's almost certainly true that the accusations of Dr. Wertham and Senator Kefauver harmed comics — they were authority figures, after all, and in those lost, innocent days we tended to believe in the sagacity of people whose names were preceded by titles. But other factors may have harmed the comic-book business more than any of the Wertham/Kefauver denouncements. These were the changing retail patterns of post-war America. Owners of the small retail establishments which had been comics' main venue — drug stores and candy stores, chiefly — were discovering that the space they had been devoting to comics might generate more profit used for something else. That was one problem. Another was that these small shops were, in fact, vanishing as urban neighborhoods fragmented and the middle class migrated to the suburbs, where neighborhood stores were rare. Finally, there was the Glowing Blue Devil that was beginning to dominate the nation's living rooms: television, which was a technological curiosity before the war and became our primary source of entertainment after it. The tube provided low-common-denominator amusement at negligible cost and, in so doing, competed devastatingly with comics and their first cousins, pulp magazines. Of course, comics and the pulps hadn't had a monopoly on entertaining the masses before the war; there were radio and the movies, both enormously popular. (There were also a lot of other things, like live theater and concert halls at one end of the entertainment spectrum and smoky jazz clubs at the other, but these were for the urban few, the cognoscenti and the hepsters, not the guy who sold mom pork chops.) However, movies involved an investment of time and money: you had to leave the house and go somewhere and pay to sit with strangers in a darkened chamber. And radio did not demand as much of the audience's attention as television — and comics, and magazines. Yet it was, oddly, more user-friendly than the print media; you had to watch it, yes, but that's *all* you had to do: switch that sucker on and sink into the couch and be entertained — the perfect antidote to a rotten day at the office, or store, or school, or kitchen. Who needed to *read* when all you had to do was *stare?*

To say the answer is "nobody" would be to exaggerate. There were still people who loved to read, but maybe they gravitated away from periodicals — including comics — and toward the paperback books which could be had for a quarter, the price of a magazine. So the magazine business declined. In wholesale lots, magazines

stopped publishing: all *kinds* of magazines, from middlebrow slicks like the venerable *Saturday Evening Post* to the raunchiest crime pulps.

And comics — comics declined, too. Several dozen comic-book purveyors either stopped publishing or, like Fawcett, went into other businesses. By 1955 there were only a few comic-book companies left, and even fewer super-heroes. The reading public had apparently lost interest in comic books' great contribution to popular culture, the costumed super-doers. DC Comics, then called National Periodical Publications, continued to issue new stories about the Big Three, the super-heroes, Superman, Batman and Wonder Woman. But only those three. Mostly, the comic books of the era were about funny animals or cowboys or comedians or frolicsome teens.

That was the situation in 1956 when the editors of the aforementioned National Periodical Publications decided to revive one of the more popular heroes of the '40s, The Flash. As Julie Schwartz tells the story, the editors were sitting around a conference table discussing who should edit the new Flash adventures and everyone looked at him. I can imagine him shrugging and saying "okay" and getting up from the table to go to work, perhaps hiding any enthusiasm he might be feeling.

I could use a lot of words relating just *how* Julie revived the Flash and, in the process, created a method for revitalizing old characters in general and super-heroes in particular, and the story is worth telling and retelling, both as history and as an example for young editorial types, but this introduction isn't about that. (It's about The Justice League — remember?) For now, all we need to know is that Julie's revamp of the Flash was a success which led him to revamp another '40s favorite, Green Lantern, and when the new version of the Green Lantern also succeeded, Julie was asked what he wanted to do next. His reply: The Justice Society.

The Justice Society's ALL-STAR COMICS had been a popular title from 1940 to 1950 and you don't need to be a publishing genius to understand why. In a way, it's only reasonable: if readers like *one* costumed hero, isn't it logical that they'll like a *bunch* of costumed heroes even more? Someone must have thought so because The Justice Society, which first appeared in 1940, featured a super-hero *team*. The story rationale went like this: most, if not all, of the costumed fraternity were acquainted, as people in the same profession tend to be, and they got together and formed a club. At regular intervals the club met and undertook to solve a problem, often involving a miscreant who wanted to cause great consternation. The group dealt with the situation, or situations, and then presumably separated to pursue their own lives, which generally meant dealing with miscreants who wanted to cause great consternation. The idea was sound and, for a time, The Justice Society's comic was a money-making title. In 1959 Julie Schwartz thought it might become so again and, once more, began the process of revivification. His first decision was to change the name. "To me, *'society'* means 'social club'," he remembered recently. "I wanted something stronger." The word he settled on was — you've already guessed it — "league," and so the new super-hero club was christened The Justice League of America.

The newly dubbed "Justice League of America" was given a three-issue tryout in THE BRAVE AND THE BOLD, a title that didn't feature a regular hero. It sent the circulation figures for the comic climbing, and so Julie put the League into their own monthly magazine.

If we believe the story about Messrs. Donenfeld and Goodman on the links — and I'm pretty sure we do — we know that the JUSTICE LEAGUE OF AMERICA did well and Julius Schwartz had another winner, which was getting to be a habit with him. We are also remembering that it prompted Stan Lee to create his own group-of-heroes book and in doing so launch what became the Marvel empire.

About that empire: Although today it is a mighty entertainment conglomerate, it began with not much more than a single man's ideas of how to do comic books a bit differently. The man, of course, was Stan Lee and he has influenced, in one way or another, virtually every English-speaking comics writer who has come after him. It seems to me that Stan demonstrated two new approaches. The first was to give characters different personalities. (We in the professional wordsmith dodge call this "characterization"; you may have heard of it, maybe in a classroom somewhere.) Though now it's high on some comics writers' lists of priorities, it was pretty rare in the comics I grew up reading in the '40s and it continued to be rare in the '50s. Julie told me that he and his writers never fretted about characterization much; their main concern was plot, and if you read the work you can see what he means. Characterization was fairly rudimentary and the good guys were identifiable mostly by their powers: Hawkman was the one with the wings, the Flash ran fast, Green Lantern had a magic ring, *et al*. This was not wrong or bad or inadequate. Let me repeat that in italics: *this was not wrong*. Rather, it was just how comics were written. The medium was evolving (along with everything else, all the time) and this kind of story was a step in that evolution. It was what people knew to do. And as a narrative strategy it had merits, among them a virtual guarantee that stories had some kind of structure — at least a beginning, a middle, and an end — and so were understandable. You didn't need to read the first 64 issues of THE JUSTICE LEAGUE to comprehend the story in number 65; everything you needed was there, on the pages. But maybe stories that were completely plot-driven were, by 1968, passé without editors, writers and even readers being *aware* that they were passé. In any case, the comics audience responded with both disposable income and enthusiasm to Stan Lee's writing, which featured characters full of idiosyncrasies and rough edges.

Stan's approach to characterization was one of his early contributions to comics writing. The other, seldom recognized, was that he, the writer, didn't seem to be taking the stuff seriously. His letters pages and sometimes copy-heavy captions seemed to be gently mocking his heroes, his company, his competition, and himself. So, we thought, he recognized that these are just comic books — not literature, not art, not even serious pop culture like movies: just comic books. And *his* not taking them seriously gave *us* license not to take them seriously and, ironically, *that* gave us permission to read them. Just comic books. Just a goof, right? Okay for sophisticated beings like ourselves to indulge in a goof now and then, right? It's not like anybody might think we were actually comic-book readers, right?

We were, of course. We enjoyed comics for a lot of reasons, probably the least of which were and are their goofy/campy aspects. Some of us were tempted to do something far, far goofier than merely *reading* comics; we considered *working* on them.

And that almost brings us to the Justice League stories reprinted in this volume. Almost.

Before we actually consider them, you should be aware that when the powers-that-were decided to let Julie Schwartz edit a monthly Justice League title, Julie chose as his writer one of the reliable pros and, some would say, one of the greats: Gardner Fox. Fox, who had been working in comics almost from their beginning and had created dozens of the characters who were the mainstays of the super-hero pantheon, produced 65 highly readable, plot-driven issues of THE JUSTICE LEAGUE OF AMERICA. Then, Julie thought, it was time for a change. As Fox's replacement, he chose an ex-journalist in his mid-20s from the Midwest who was new to both publishing and comics. This newcomer — let's not call him a "usurper" — wrote the last four stories in the collection you're holding. I am not about to venture even the most timid opinion as to their merit, but I will stop writing about myself in the third person. I was the young ex-newspaper guy who replaced Gardner Fox as the Justice League scripter. Before declaring myself a freelance writer, I'd worked, briefly, as an editorial assistant and writer at Marvel Comics and so most of what I knew about the business I'd learned from Stan Lee.

This might be a good place for a glowing reminiscence about the Grand Old Days of Comics. Might be, but won't be. Sorry. My memory is lousy. I don't even recall how I came to get the Justice League gig, just that I did and went on to script the next 16 issues. Eventually I established a first for myself by leaving the assignment, surely an act of hubris coming from someone who a) was still pretty much a neophyte, especially when compared to guys like Gardner Fox, and b) had mouths to feed. But I did quit THE JUSTICE LEAGUE and I guess Julie wasn't too mad because I continued to work for him for years. As noted above, my memory is awful, but I do remember why I felt I had to walk away from THE JUSTICE LEAGUE: there were too many of them and they were too powerful. I was having trouble thinking of situations that presented them with any significant problems, much less put them in peril. Stories without problems and/or danger often aren't terribly absorbing, another thing you may have heard somewhere.

Maybe I didn't appreciate Gardner Fox's achievement in producing those 65 plot-driven adventures when I was first offered THE JUSTICE LEAGUE OF AMERICA, but I do now.

Both Fox's and my Justice League are represented in these pages, and that makes this volume more than a collection. It is, in a way, a document that lets us look at two different approaches to a certain creative endeavor at a certain time in its existence. And it presents us with an odd kind of symmetry: if we believe the story of the golf-playing publishers, The Justice League of America led to the creation of *The Fantastic Four* and the techniques Stan Lee developed in creating *The Fantastic Four* eventually influenced The Justice League of America.

You can ponder that, if you like. But you don't have to. Instead, you can just flip a few pages and read the stories. If we all did our jobs, all those years ago, you'll enjoy them.

— Dennis O'Neil
December 2002

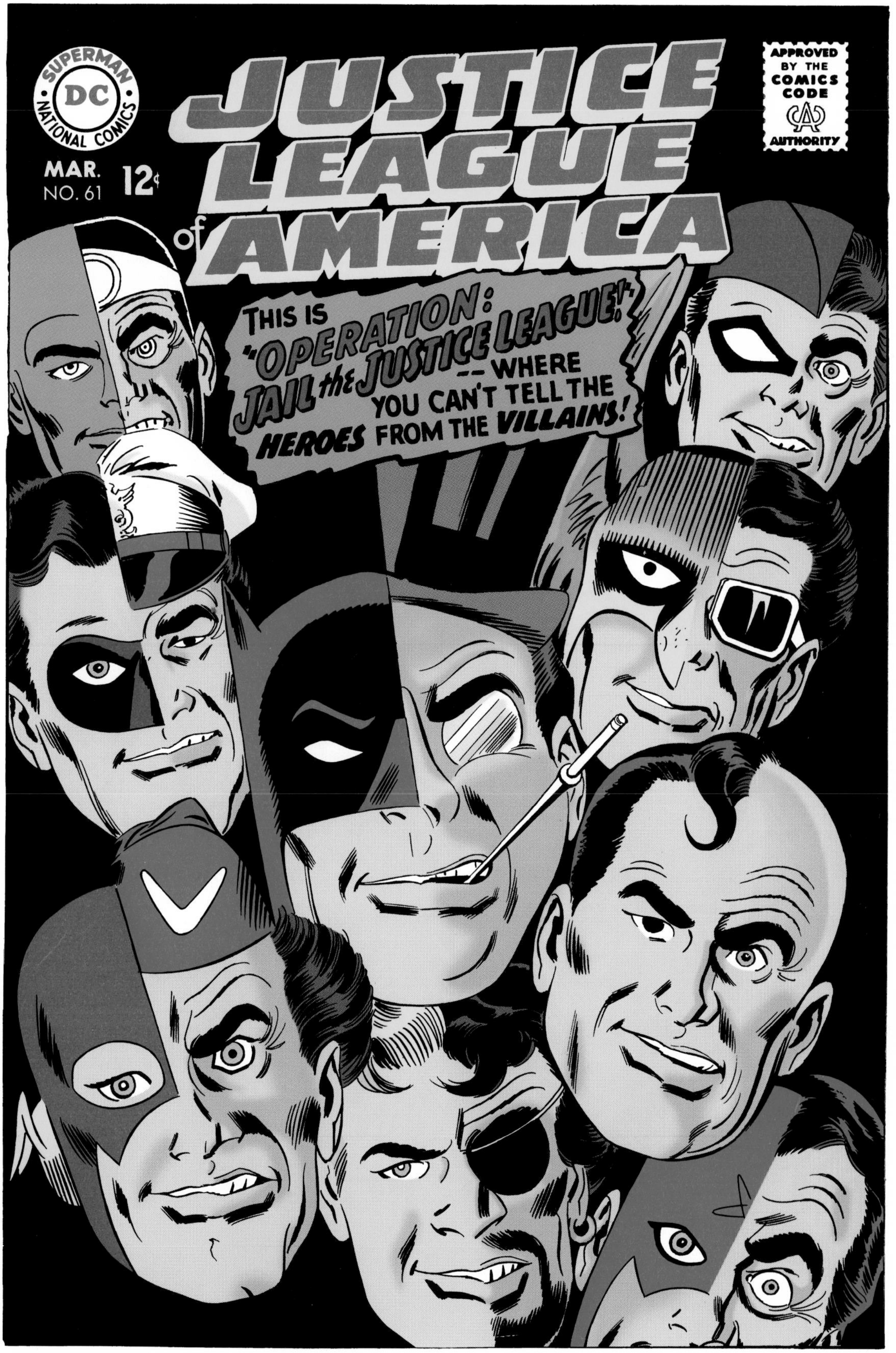
SUPERMAN DC NATIONAL COMICS
MAR. NO. 61 12¢
JUSTICE LEAGUE of AMERICA
APPROVED BY THE COMICS CODE AUTHORITY
THIS IS "OPERATION: JAIL the JUSTICE LEAGUE!" -- WHERE YOU CAN'T TELL THE HEROES FROM THE VILLAINS!

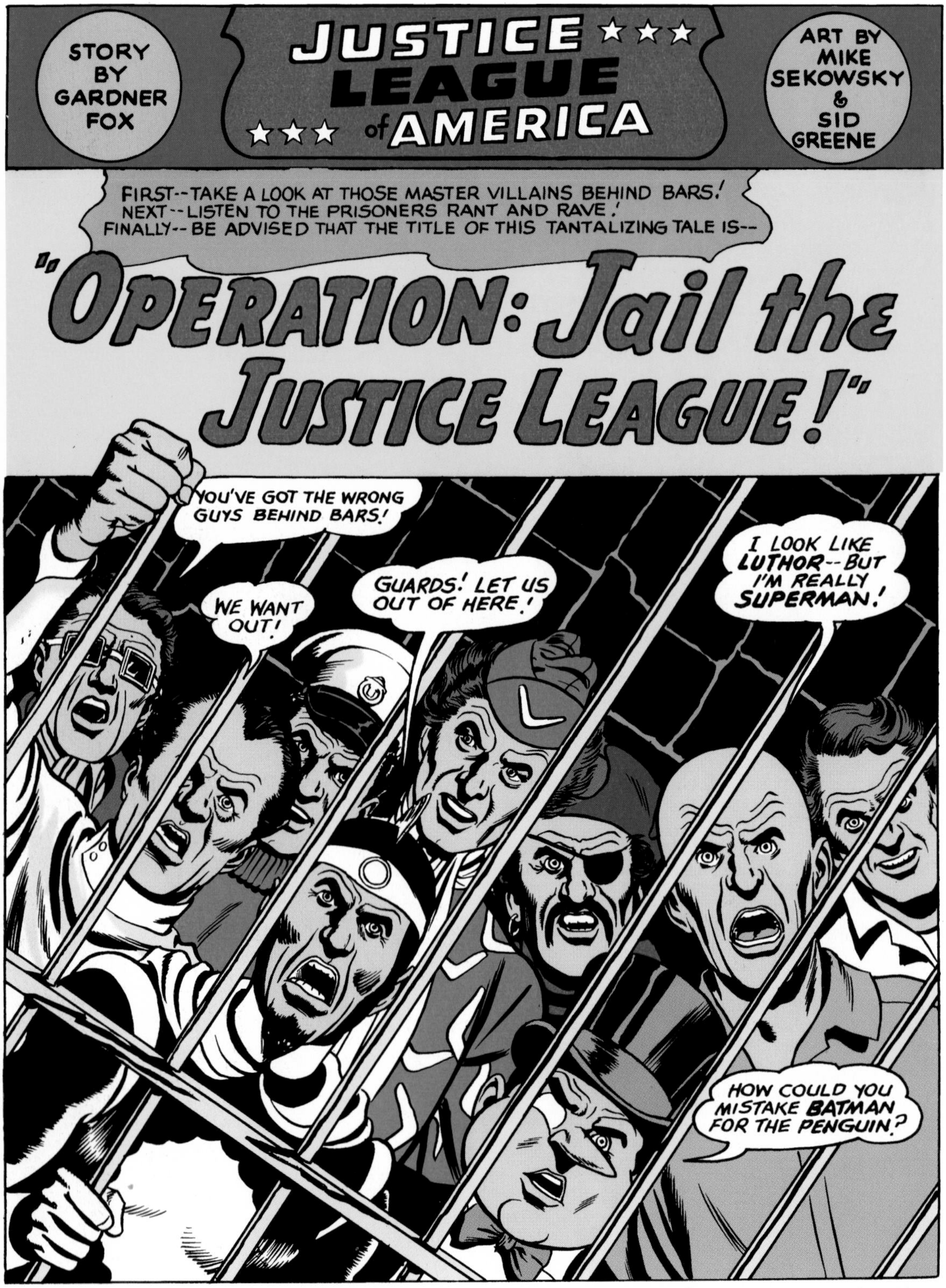
STORY BY GARDNER FOX
JUSTICE LEAGUE of AMERICA
ART BY MIKE SEKOWSKY & SID GREENE
FIRST--TAKE A LOOK AT THOSE MASTER VILLAINS BEHIND BARS! NEXT--LISTEN TO THE PRISONERS RANT AND RAVE! FINALLY--BE ADVISED THAT THE TITLE OF THIS TANTALIZING TALE IS--
"OPERATION: Jail the JUSTICE LEAGUE!"
YOU'VE GOT THE WRONG GUYS BEHIND BARS!
WE WANT OUT!
GUARDS! LET US OUT OF HERE!
I LOOK LIKE LUTHOR--BUT I'M REALLY SUPERMAN!
HOW COULD YOU MISTAKE BATMAN FOR THE PENGUIN?

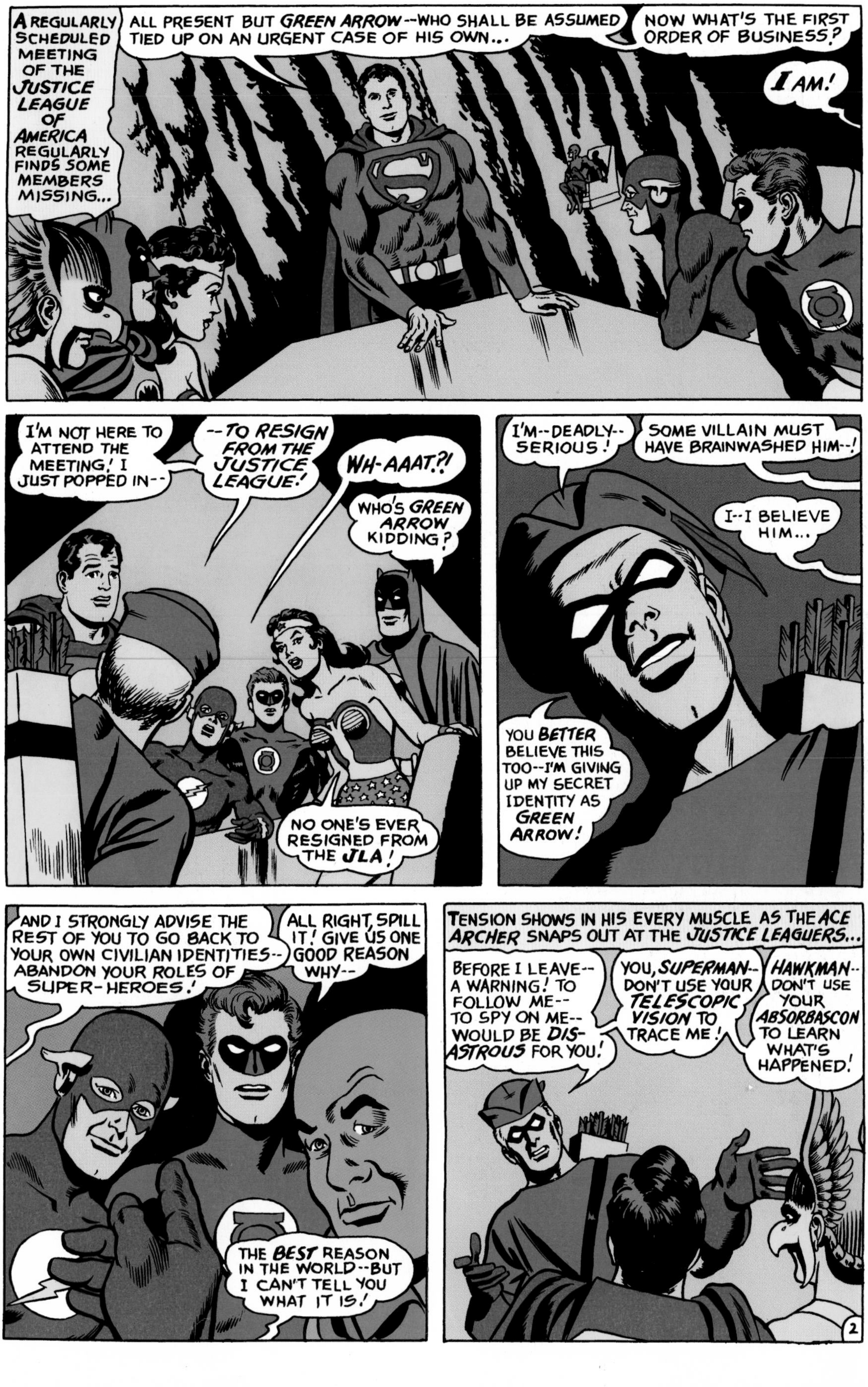
A REGULARLY SCHEDULED MEETING OF THE JUSTICE LEAGUE OF AMERICA REGULARLY FINDS SOME MEMBERS MISSING...
ALL PRESENT BUT GREEN ARROW--WHO SHALL BE ASSUMED TIED UP ON AN URGENT CASE OF HIS OWN...
NOW WHAT'S THE FIRST ORDER OF BUSINESS?
I AM!
I'M NOT HERE TO ATTEND THE MEETING! I JUST POPPED IN--
--TO RESIGN FROM THE JUSTICE LEAGUE!
WH-AAAT?!
WHO'S GREEN ARROW KIDDING?
NO ONE'S EVER RESIGNED FROM THE JLA!
I'M--DEADLY--SERIOUS!
SOME VILLAIN MUST HAVE BRAINWASHED HIM--!
I--I BELIEVE HIM...
YOU BETTER BELIEVE THIS TOO--I'M GIVING UP MY SECRET IDENTITY AS GREEN ARROW!
AND I STRONGLY ADVISE THE REST OF YOU TO GO BACK TO YOUR OWN CIVILIAN IDENTITIES--ABANDON YOUR ROLES OF SUPER-HEROES!
ALL RIGHT, SPILL IT! GIVE US ONE GOOD REASON WHY--
THE BEST REASON IN THE WORLD--BUT I CAN'T TELL YOU WHAT IT IS!
TENSION SHOWS IN HIS EVERY MUSCLE AS THE ACE ARCHER SNAPS OUT AT THE JUSTICE LEAGUERS...
BEFORE I LEAVE--A WARNING! TO FOLLOW ME--TO SPY ON ME--WOULD BE DISASTROUS FOR YOU!
YOU, SUPERMAN--DON'T USE YOUR TELESCOPIC VISION TO TRACE ME!
HAWKMAN--DON'T USE YOUR ABSORBASCON TO LEARN WHAT'S HAPPENED!
2

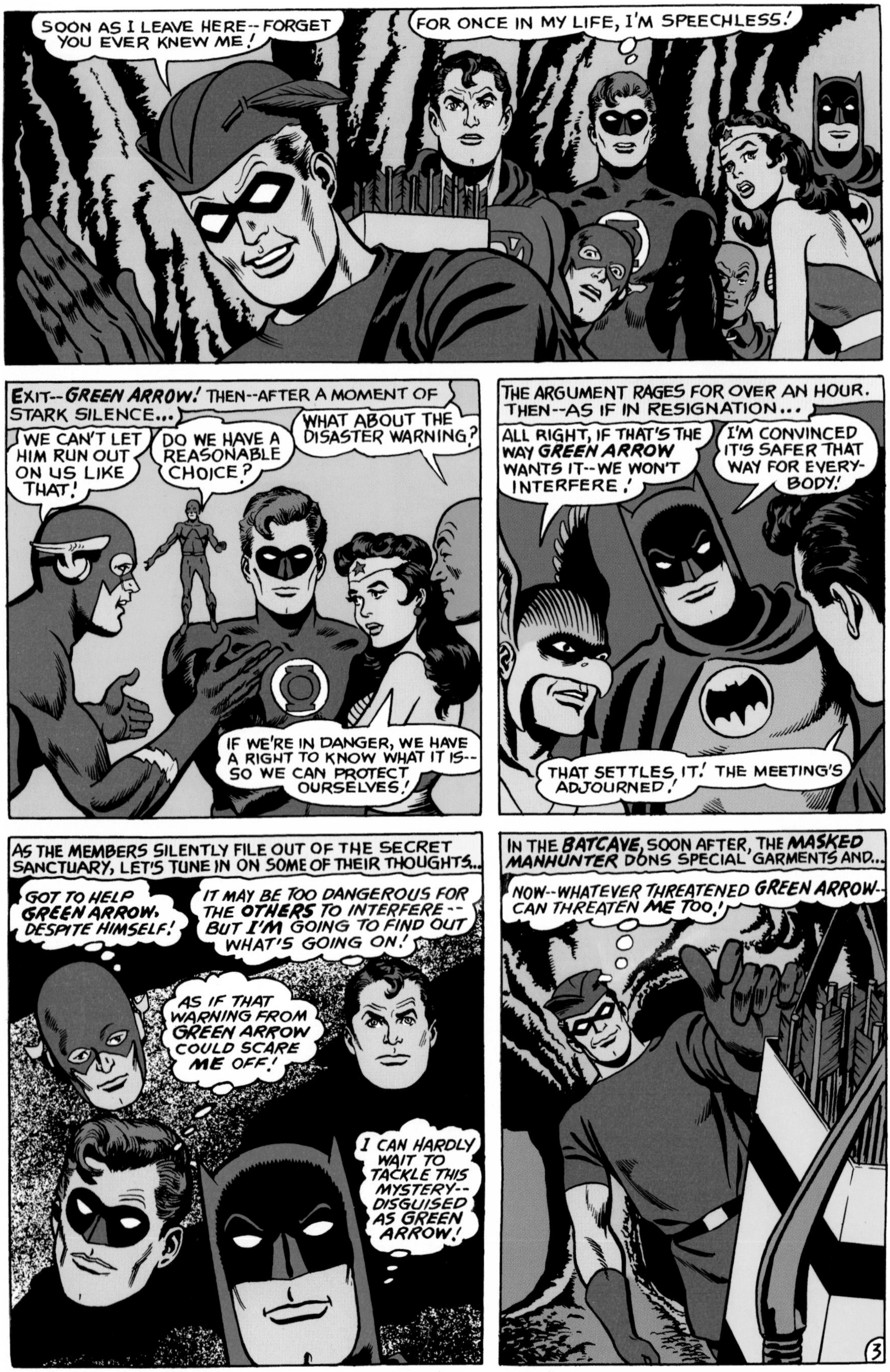
SOON AS I LEAVE HERE--FORGET YOU EVER KNEW ME!
FOR ONCE IN MY LIFE, I'M SPEECHLESS!
EXIT--GREEN ARROW! THEN--AFTER A MOMENT OF STARK SILENCE...
WE CAN'T LET HIM RUN OUT ON US LIKE THAT!
DO WE HAVE A REASONABLE CHOICE?
WHAT ABOUT THE DISASTER WARNING?
IF WE'RE IN DANGER, WE HAVE A RIGHT TO KNOW WHAT IT IS--SO WE CAN PROTECT OURSELVES!
THE ARGUMENT RAGES FOR OVER AN HOUR. THEN--AS IF IN RESIGNATION...
ALL RIGHT, IF THAT'S THE WAY GREEN ARROW WANTS IT--WE WON'T INTERFERE!
I'M CONVINCED IT'S SAFER THAT WAY FOR EVERYBODY!
THAT SETTLES IT! THE MEETING'S ADJOURNED!
AS THE MEMBERS SILENTLY FILE OUT OF THE SECRET SANCTUARY, LET'S TUNE IN ON SOME OF THEIR THOUGHTS...
GOT TO HELP GREEN ARROW, DESPITE HIMSELF!
IT MAY BE TOO DANGEROUS FOR THE OTHERS TO INTERFERE--BUT I'M GOING TO FIND OUT WHAT'S GOING ON!
AS IF THAT WARNING FROM GREEN ARROW COULD SCARE ME OFF!
I CAN HARDLY WAIT TO TACKLE THIS MYSTERY--DISGUISED AS GREEN ARROW!
IN THE BATCAVE, SOON AFTER, THE MASKED MANHUNTER DONS SPECIAL GARMENTS AND...
NOW--WHATEVER THREATENED GREEN ARROW--CAN THREATEN ME TOO!
3

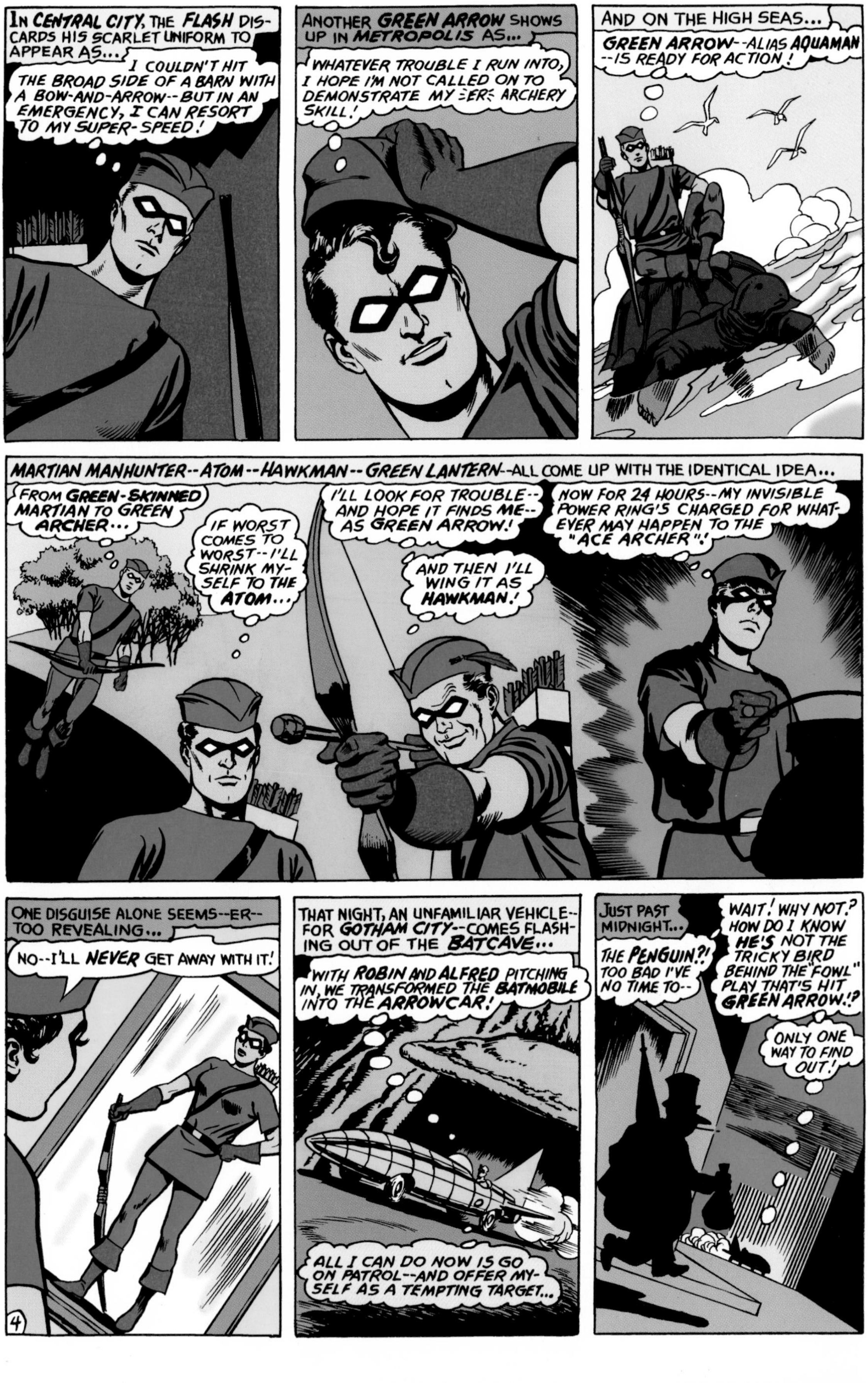

IN CENTRAL CITY, THE FLASH DISCARDS HIS SCARLET UNIFORM TO APPEAR AS...
I COULDN'T HIT THE BROAD SIDE OF A BARN WITH A BOW-AND-ARROW--BUT IN AN EMERGENCY, I CAN RESORT TO MY SUPER-SPEED!
ANOTHER GREEN ARROW SHOWS UP IN METROPOLIS AS...
WHATEVER TROUBLE I RUN INTO, I HOPE I'M NOT CALLED ON TO DEMONSTRATE MY -ER- ARCHERY SKILL!
AND ON THE HIGH SEAS...
GREEN ARROW--ALIAS AQUAMAN--IS READY FOR ACTION!
MARTIAN MANHUNTER--ATOM--HAWKMAN--GREEN LANTERN--ALL COME UP WITH THE IDENTICAL IDEA...
FROM GREEN-SKINNED MARTIAN TO GREEN ARCHER...
IF WORST COMES TO WORST--I'LL SHRINK MYSELF TO THE ATOM...
I'LL LOOK FOR TROUBLE--AND HOPE IT FINDS ME--AS GREEN ARROW!
AND THEN I'LL WING IT AS HAWKMAN!
NOW FOR 24 HOURS--MY INVISIBLE POWER RING'S CHARGED FOR WHATEVER MAY HAPPEN TO THE "ACE ARCHER"!
ONE DISGUISE ALONE SEEMS--ER--TOO REVEALING...
NO--I'LL NEVER GET AWAY WITH IT!
4
THAT NIGHT, AN UNFAMILIAR VEHICLE--FOR GOTHAM CITY--COMES FLASHING OUT OF THE BATCAVE...
WITH ROBIN AND ALFRED PITCHING IN, WE TRANSFORMED THE BATMOBILE INTO THE ARROWCAR!
ALL I CAN DO NOW IS GO ON PATROL--AND OFFER MYSELF AS A TEMPTING TARGET...
JUST PAST MIDNIGHT...
THE PENGUIN?! TOO BAD I'VE NO TIME TO--
WAIT! WHY NOT? HOW DO I KNOW HE'S NOT THE TRICKY BIRD BEHIND THE "FOWL" PLAY THAT'S HIT GREEN ARROW!?
ONLY ONE WAY TO FIND OUT!

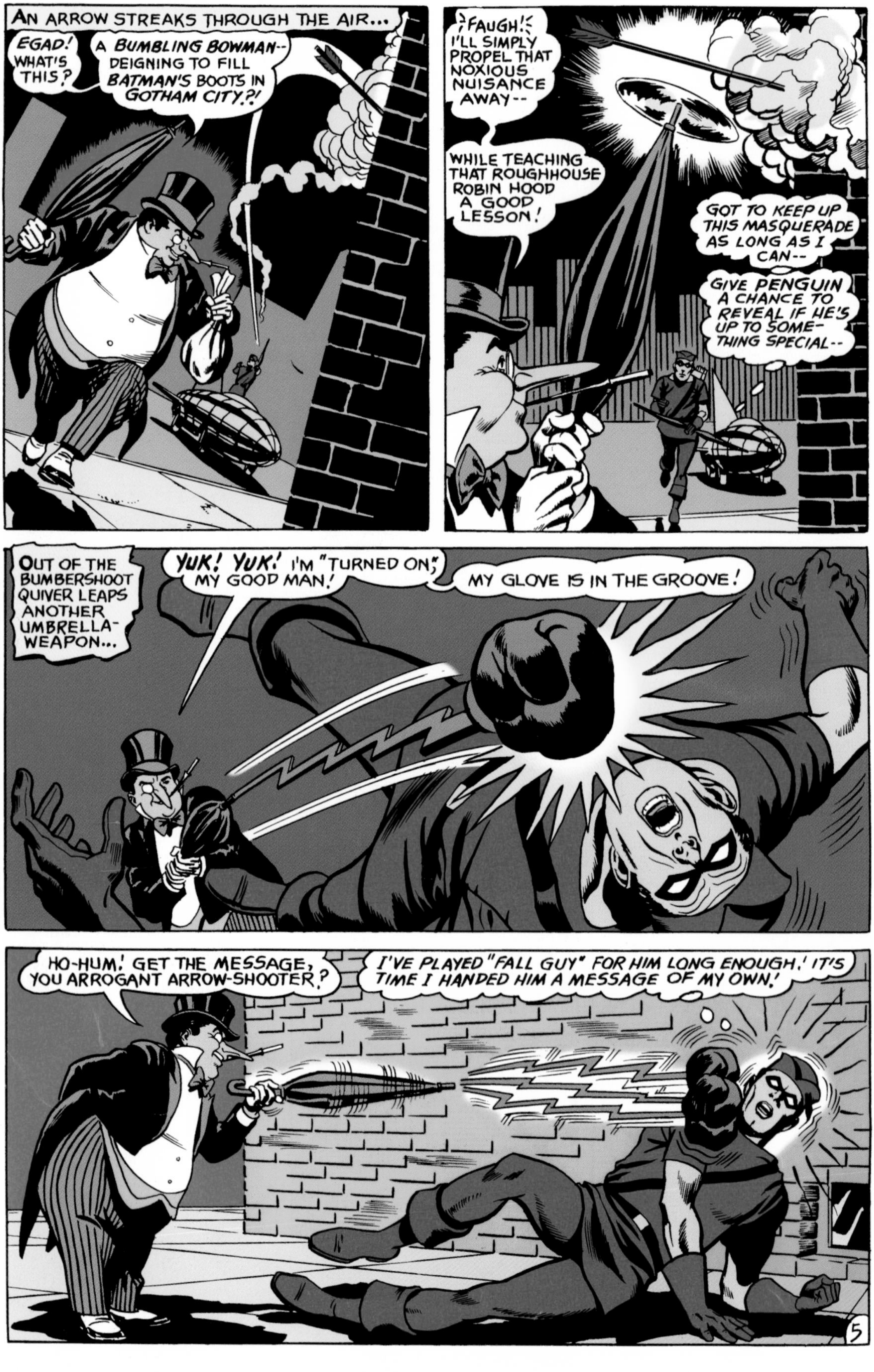
AN ARROW STREAKS THROUGH THE AIR...
EGAD! WHAT'S THIS?
A BUMBLING BOWMAN-- DEIGNING TO FILL BATMAN'S BOOTS IN GOTHAM CITY?!
¡FAUGH!¡ I'LL SIMPLY PROPEL THAT NOXIOUS NUISANCE AWAY--
WHILE TEACHING THAT ROUGHHOUSE ROBIN HOOD A GOOD LESSON!
GOT TO KEEP UP THIS MASQUERADE AS LONG AS I CAN--
GIVE PENGUIN A CHANCE TO REVEAL IF HE'S UP TO SOMETHING SPECIAL--
OUT OF THE BUMBERSHOOT QUIVER LEAPS ANOTHER UMBRELLA-WEAPON...
YUK! YUK! I'M "TURNED ON," MY GOOD MAN!
MY GLOVE IS IN THE GROOVE!
HO-HUM! GET THE MESSAGE, YOU ARROGANT ARROW-SHOOTER?
I'VE PLAYED "FALL GUY" FOR HIM LONG ENOUGH! IT'S TIME I HANDED HIM A MESSAGE OF MY OWN!
5

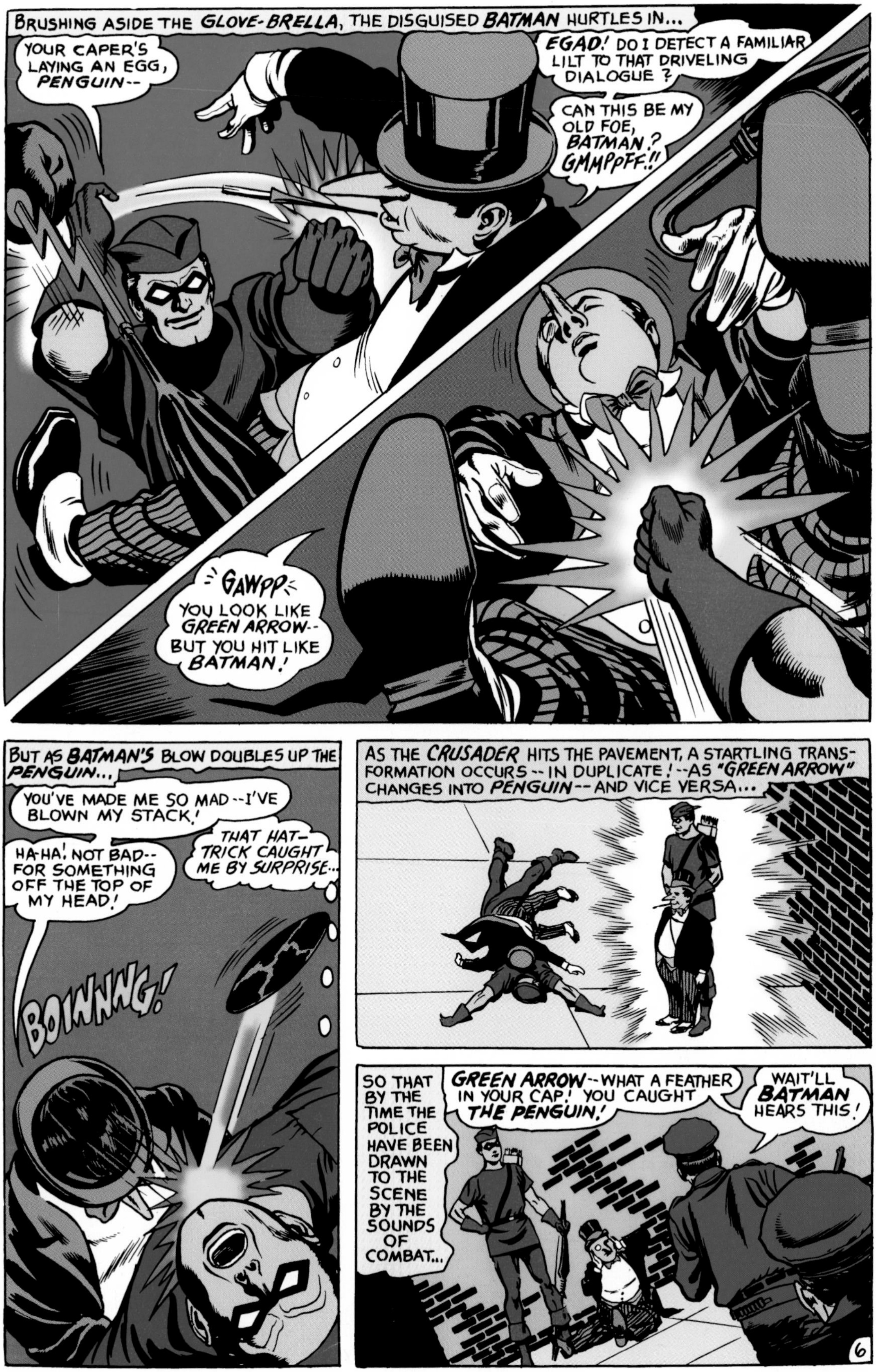
BRUSHING ASIDE THE GLOVE-BRELLA, THE DISGUISED BATMAN HURTLES IN...
YOUR CAPER'S LAYING AN EGG, PENGUIN--
EGAD! DO I DETECT A FAMILIAR LILT TO THAT DRIVELING DIALOGUE ?
CAN THIS BE MY OLD FOE, BATMAN ? GMMPPFF !!
GAWPP
YOU LOOK LIKE GREEN ARROW-- BUT YOU HIT LIKE BATMAN!
BUT AS BATMAN'S BLOW DOUBLES UP THE PENGUIN...
YOU'VE MADE ME SO MAD--I'VE BLOWN MY STACK!
HA-HA! NOT BAD-- FOR SOMETHING OFF THE TOP OF MY HEAD!
THAT HAT-TRICK CAUGHT ME BY SURPRISE...
BOINNNG!
AS THE CRUSADER HITS THE PAVEMENT, A STARTLING TRANSFORMATION OCCURS -- IN DUPLICATE! --AS "GREEN ARROW" CHANGES INTO PENGUIN-- AND VICE VERSA...
SO THAT BY THE TIME THE POLICE HAVE BEEN DRAWN TO THE SCENE BY THE SOUNDS OF COMBAT...
GREEN ARROW--WHAT A FEATHER IN YOUR CAP! YOU CAUGHT THE PENGUIN!
WAIT'LL BATMAN HEARS THIS!
6

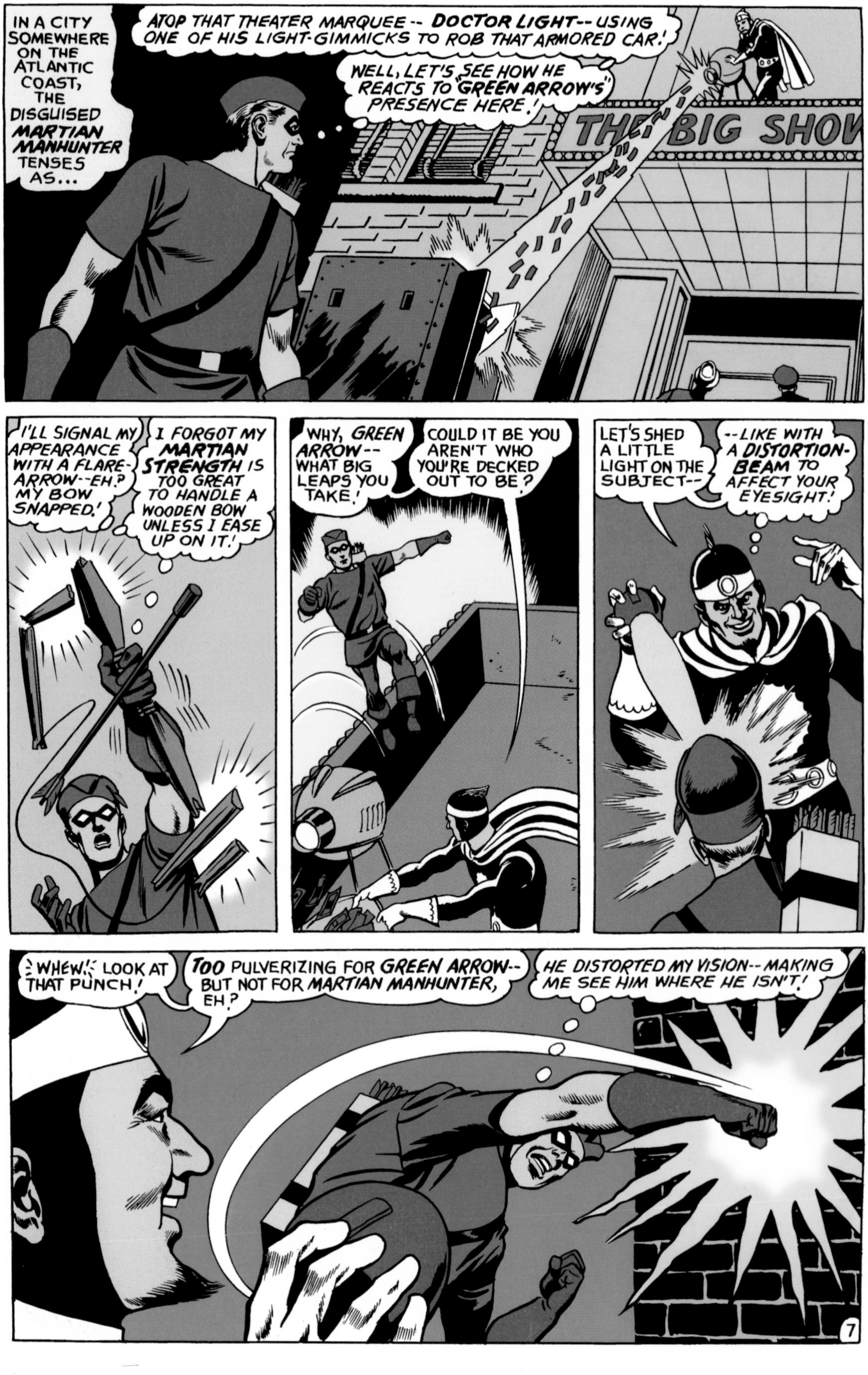
IN A CITY SOMEWHERE ON THE ATLANTIC COAST, THE DISGUISED MARTIAN MANHUNTER TENSES AS...
ATOP THAT THEATER MARQUEE -- DOCTOR LIGHT -- USING ONE OF HIS LIGHT-GIMMICKS TO ROB THAT ARMORED CAR!
WELL, LET'S SEE HOW HE REACTS TO "GREEN ARROW'S" PRESENCE HERE!
THE BIG SHOW
I'LL SIGNAL MY APPEARANCE WITH A FLARE-ARROW--EH? MY BOW SNAPPED!
I FORGOT MY MARTIAN STRENGTH IS TOO GREAT TO HANDLE A WOODEN BOW UNLESS I EASE UP ON IT!
WHY, GREEN ARROW -- WHAT BIG LEAPS YOU TAKE!
COULD IT BE YOU AREN'T WHO YOU'RE DECKED OUT TO BE?
LET'S SHED A LITTLE LIGHT ON THE SUBJECT--
--LIKE WITH A DISTORTION-BEAM TO AFFECT YOUR EYESIGHT!
WHEW! LOOK AT THAT PUNCH!
TOO PULVERIZING FOR GREEN ARROW-- BUT NOT FOR MARTIAN MANHUNTER, EH?
HE DISTORTED MY VISION--MAKING ME SEE HIM WHERE HE ISN'T!
7

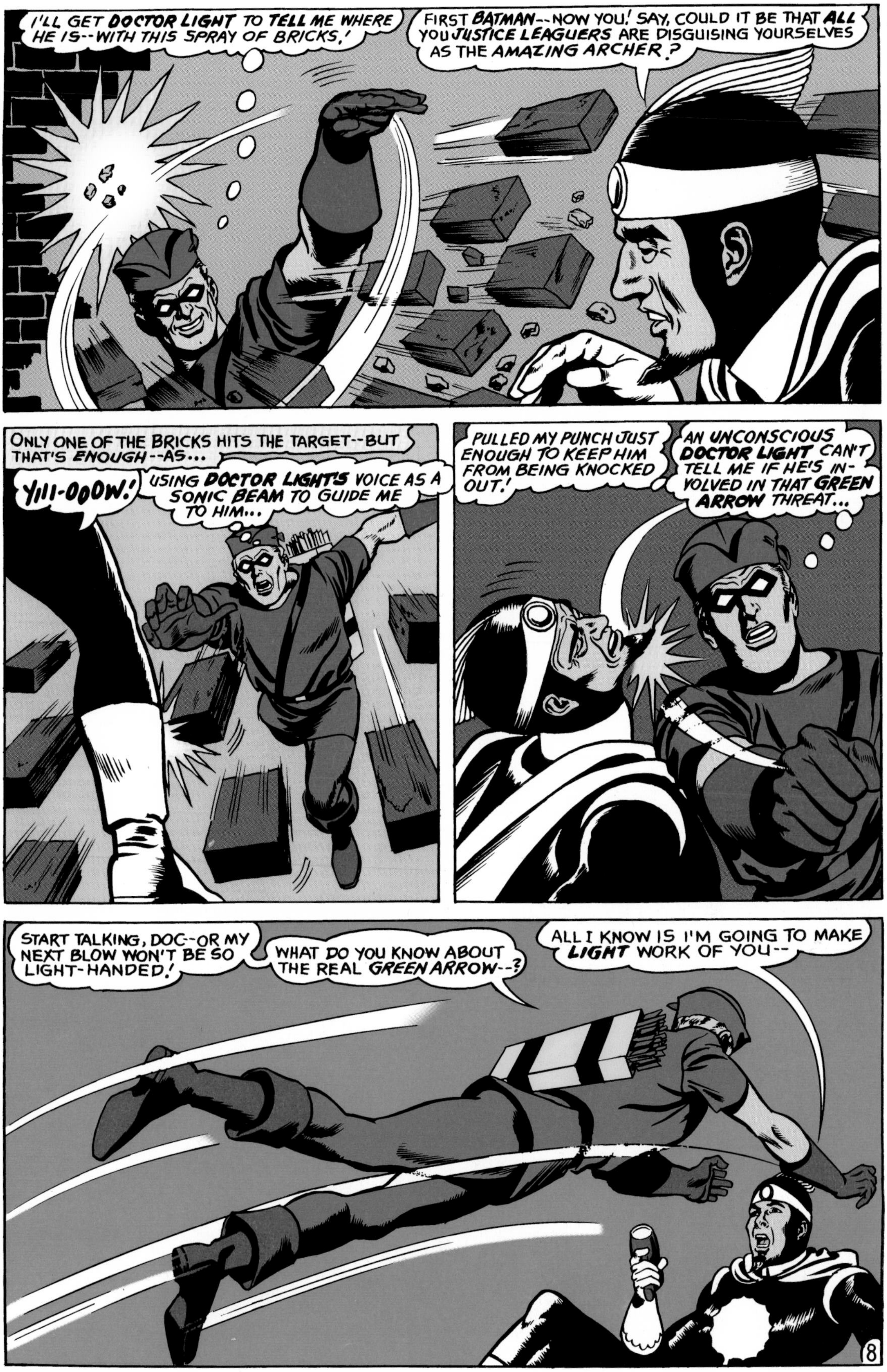
I'LL GET DOCTOR LIGHT TO TELL ME WHERE HE IS--WITH THIS SPRAY OF BRICKS!
FIRST BATMAN--NOW YOU! SAY, COULD IT BE THAT ALL YOU JUSTICE LEAGUERS ARE DISGUISING YOURSELVES AS THE AMAZING ARCHER?
ONLY ONE OF THE BRICKS HITS THE TARGET--BUT THAT'S ENOUGH--AS...
YIII-OOOW!
USING DOCTOR LIGHT'S VOICE AS A SONIC BEAM TO GUIDE ME TO HIM...
PULLED MY PUNCH JUST ENOUGH TO KEEP HIM FROM BEING KNOCKED OUT!
AN UNCONSCIOUS DOCTOR LIGHT CAN'T TELL ME IF HE'S INVOLVED IN THAT GREEN ARROW THREAT...
START TALKING, DOC--OR MY NEXT BLOW WON'T BE SO LIGHT-HANDED!
WHAT DO YOU KNOW ABOUT THE REAL GREEN ARROW--?
ALL I KNOW IS I'M GOING TO MAKE LIGHT WORK OF YOU--
8

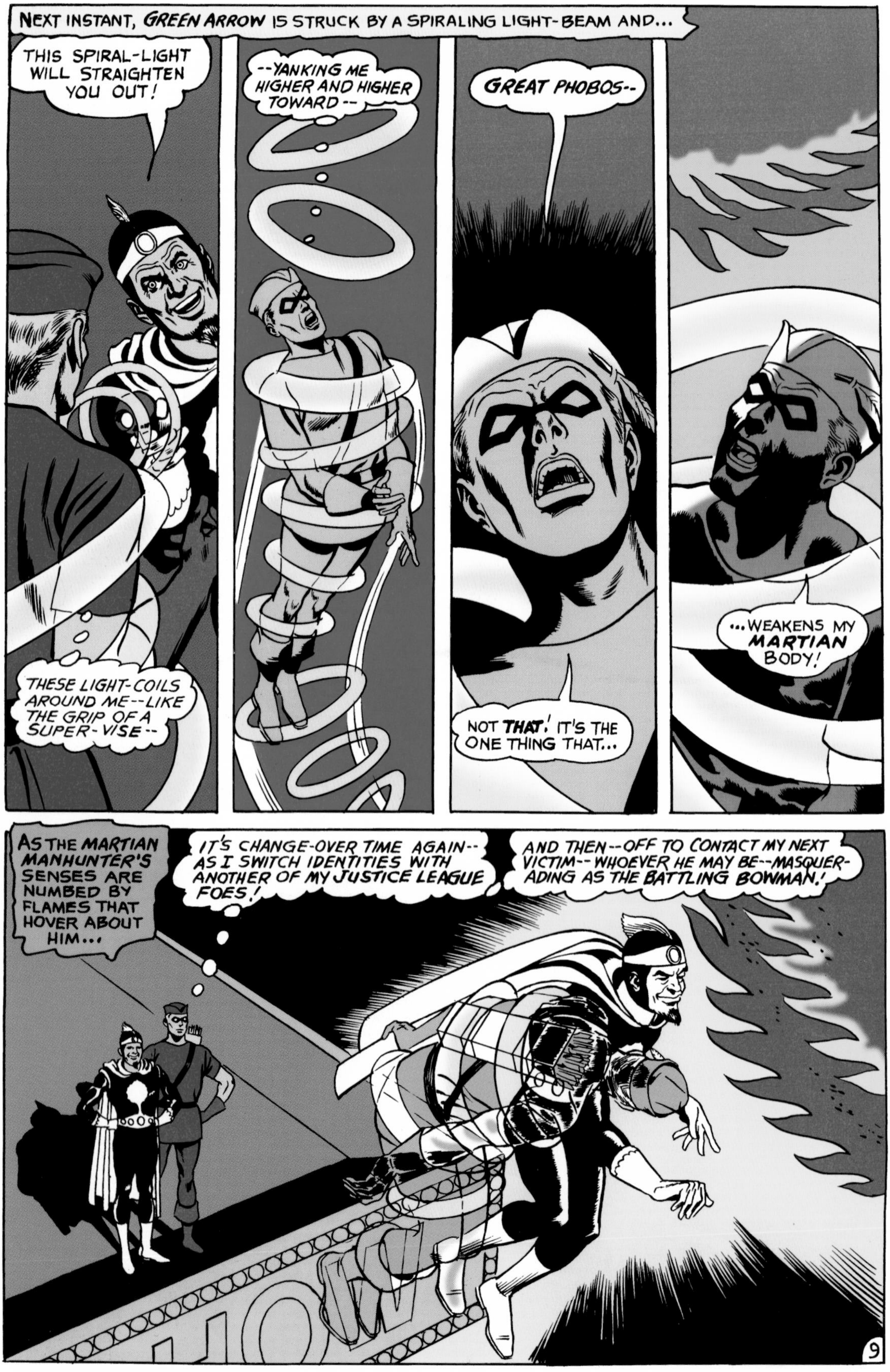
NEXT INSTANT, GREEN ARROW IS STRUCK BY A SPIRALING LIGHT-BEAM AND...
THIS SPIRAL-LIGHT WILL STRAIGHTEN YOU OUT!
THESE LIGHT-COILS AROUND ME--LIKE THE GRIP OF A SUPER-VISE--
--YANKING ME HIGHER AND HIGHER TOWARD--
GREAT PHOBOS--
NOT THAT! IT'S THE ONE THING THAT...
...WEAKENS MY MARTIAN BODY!
AS THE MARTIAN MANHUNTER'S SENSES ARE NUMBED BY FLAMES THAT HOVER ABOUT HIM...
IT'S CHANGE-OVER TIME AGAIN--AS I SWITCH IDENTITIES WITH ANOTHER OF MY JUSTICE LEAGUE FOES!
AND THEN--OFF TO CONTACT MY NEXT VICTIM--WHOEVER HE MAY BE--MASQUERADING AS THE BATTLING BOWMAN!
9

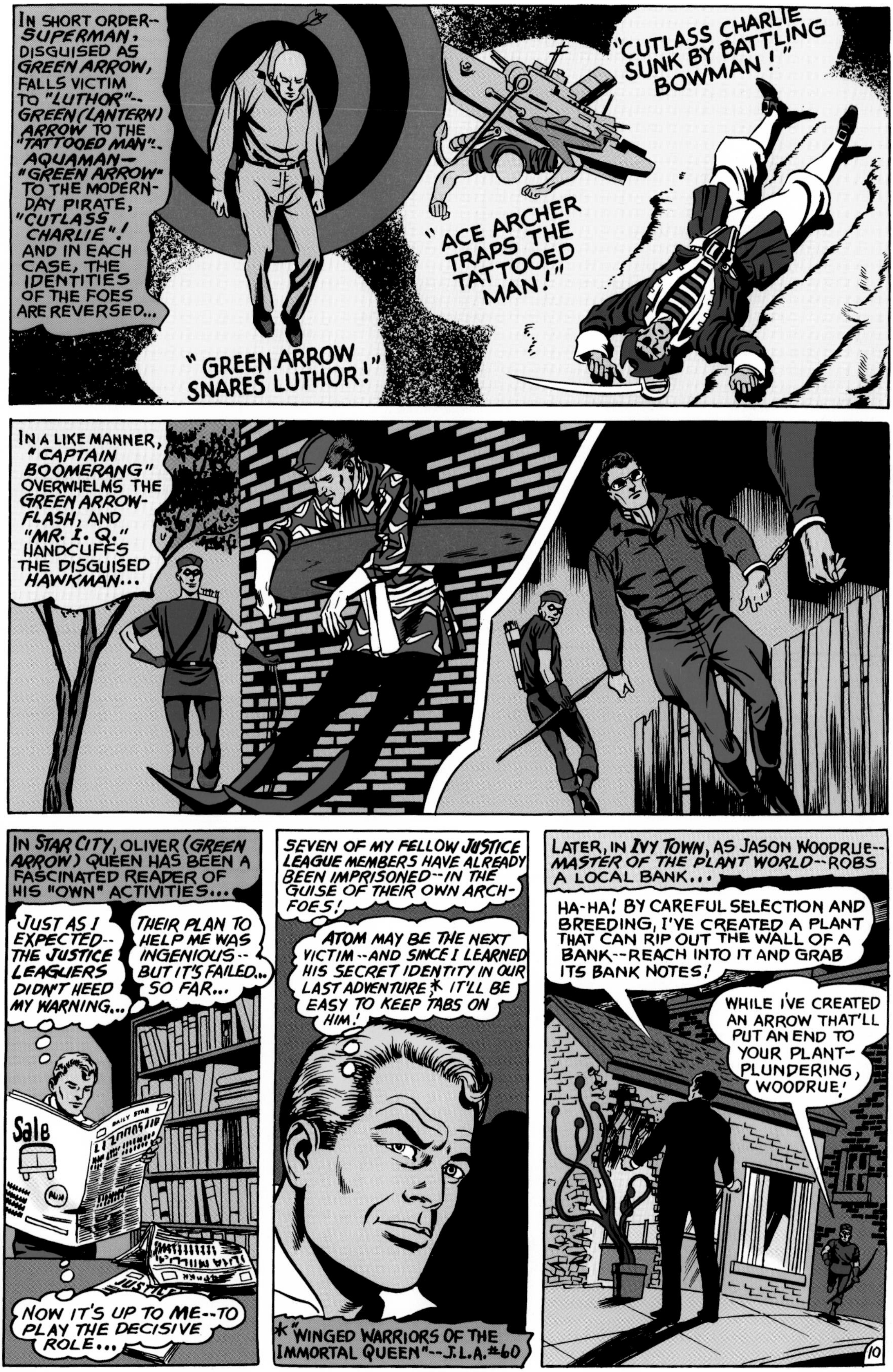

IN SHORT ORDER-- SUPERMAN, DISGUISED AS GREEN ARROW, FALLS VICTIM TO "LUTHOR"-- GREEN (LANTERN) ARROW TO THE "TATTOOED MAN"-- AQUAMAN-- "GREEN ARROW" TO THE MODERN-DAY PIRATE, "CUTLASS CHARLIE"! AND IN EACH CASE, THE IDENTITIES OF THE FOES ARE REVERSED...
"CUTLASS CHARLIE SUNK BY BATTLING BOWMAN!"
"ACE ARCHER TRAPS THE TATTOOED MAN!"
"GREEN ARROW SNARES LUTHOR!"
IN A LIKE MANNER, "CAPTAIN BOOMERANG" OVERWHELMS THE GREEN ARROW-FLASH, AND "MR. I. Q." HANDCUFFS THE DISGUISED HAWKMAN...
IN STAR CITY, OLIVER (GREEN ARROW) QUEEN HAS BEEN A FASCINATED READER OF HIS "OWN" ACTIVITIES...
JUST AS I EXPECTED-- THE JUSTICE LEAGUERS DIDN'T HEED MY WARNING...
THEIR PLAN TO HELP ME WAS INGENIOUS-- BUT IT'S FAILED... SO FAR...
Sale
DAILY STAR
NOW IT'S UP TO ME--TO PLAY THE DECISIVE ROLE...
SEVEN OF MY FELLOW JUSTICE LEAGUE MEMBERS HAVE ALREADY BEEN IMPRISONED--IN THE GUISE OF THEIR OWN ARCH-FOES!
ATOM MAY BE THE NEXT VICTIM--AND SINCE I LEARNED HIS SECRET IDENTITY IN OUR LAST ADVENTURE,* IT'LL BE EASY TO KEEP TABS ON HIM!
*"WINGED WARRIORS OF THE IMMORTAL QUEEN"--J.L.A. #60
LATER, IN IVY TOWN, AS JASON WOODRUE-- MASTER OF THE PLANT WORLD--ROBS A LOCAL BANK...
HA-HA! BY CAREFUL SELECTION AND BREEDING, I'VE CREATED A PLANT THAT CAN RIP OUT THE WALL OF A BANK--REACH INTO IT AND GRAB ITS BANK NOTES!
WHILE I'VE CREATED AN ARROW THAT'LL PUT AN END TO YOUR PLANT-PLUNDERING, WOODRUE!
10

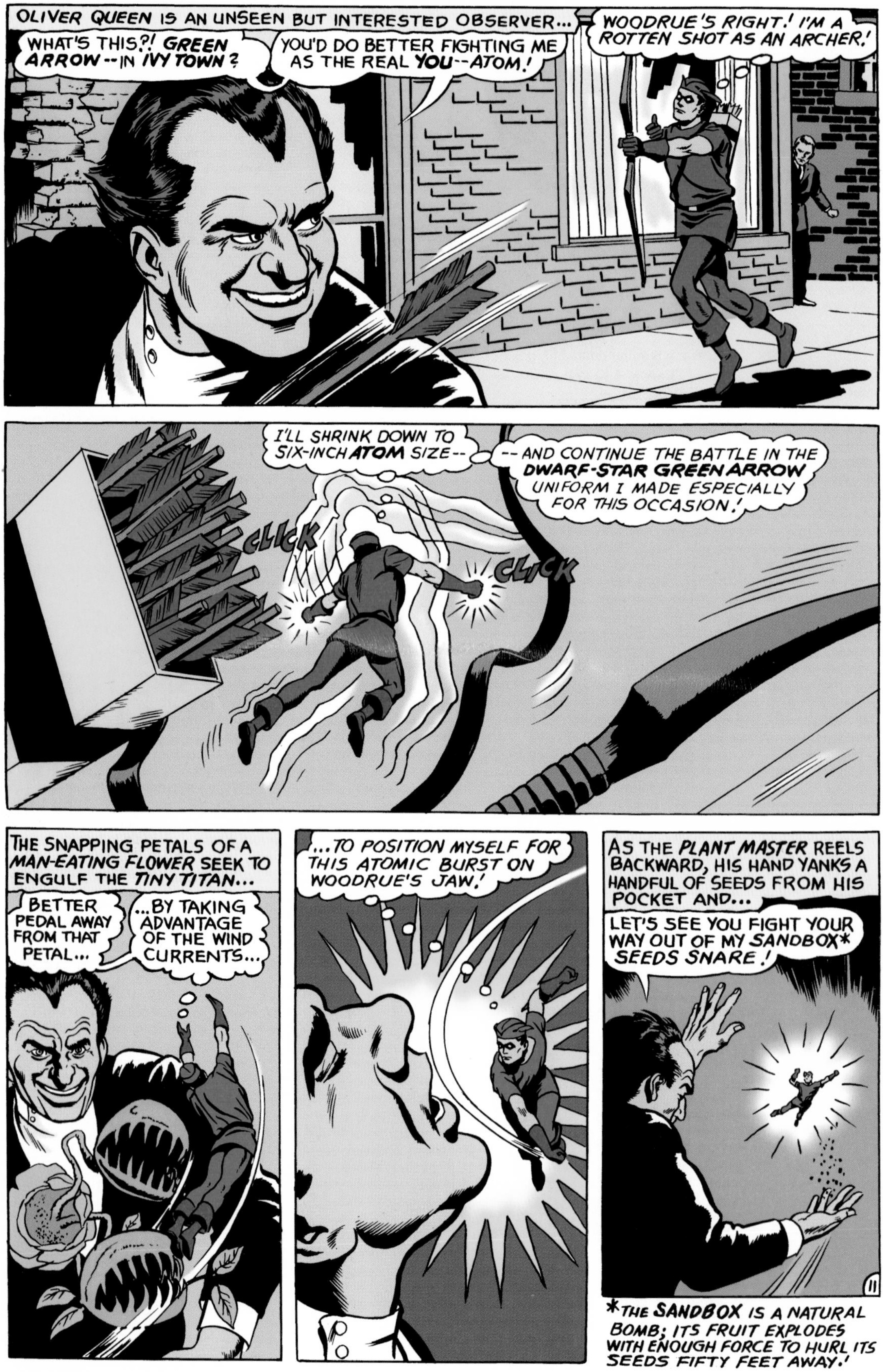
OLIVER QUEEN IS AN UNSEEN BUT INTERESTED OBSERVER...
WHAT'S THIS?! GREEN ARROW--IN IVY TOWN?
YOU'D DO BETTER FIGHTING ME AS THE REAL YOU--ATOM!
WOODRUE'S RIGHT! I'M A ROTTEN SHOT AS AN ARCHER!
I'LL SHRINK DOWN TO SIX-INCH ATOM SIZE--
--AND CONTINUE THE BATTLE IN THE DWARF-STAR GREEN ARROW UNIFORM I MADE ESPECIALLY FOR THIS OCCASION!
CLICK
CLICK
THE SNAPPING PETALS OF A MAN-EATING FLOWER SEEK TO ENGULF THE TINY TITAN...
BETTER PEDAL AWAY FROM THAT PETAL...
...BY TAKING ADVANTAGE OF THE WIND CURRENTS...
...TO POSITION MYSELF FOR THIS ATOMIC BURST ON WOODRUE'S JAW!
AS THE PLANT MASTER REELS BACKWARD, HIS HAND YANKS A HANDFUL OF SEEDS FROM HIS POCKET AND...
LET'S SEE YOU FIGHT YOUR WAY OUT OF MY SANDBOX* SEEDS SNARE!
11

*THE SANDBOX IS A NATURAL BOMB; ITS FRUIT EXPLODES WITH ENOUGH FORCE TO HURL ITS SEEDS FIFTY FEET AWAY!

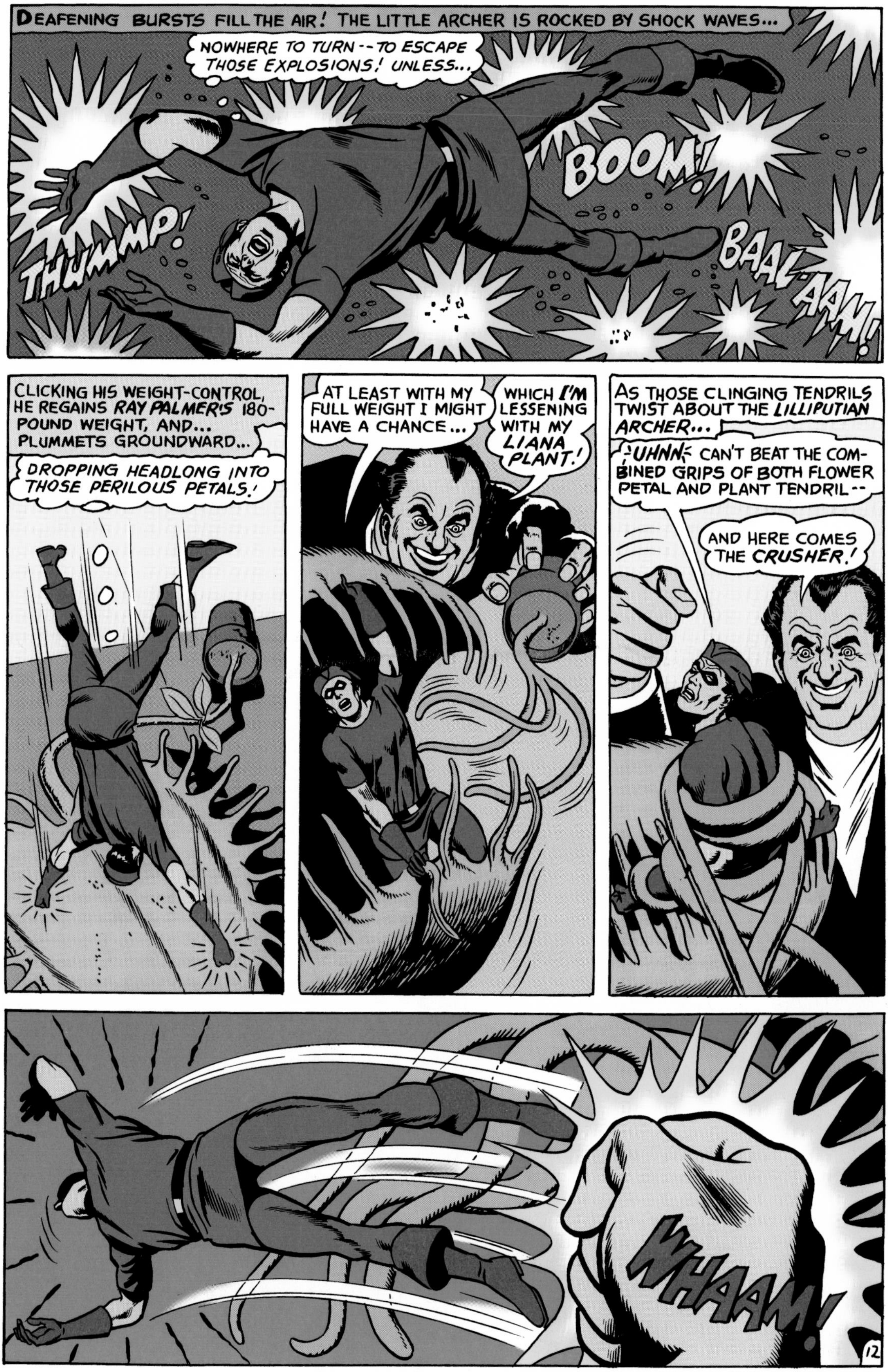
DEAFENING BURSTS FILL THE AIR! THE LITTLE ARCHER IS ROCKED BY SHOCK WAVES...
NOWHERE TO TURN--TO ESCAPE THOSE EXPLOSIONS! UNLESS...
BOOM!
THUMMP!
BAAL-AAM!
CLICKING HIS WEIGHT-CONTROL, HE REGAINS RAY PALMER'S 180-POUND WEIGHT, AND... PLUMMETS GROUNDWARD...
DROPPING HEADLONG INTO THOSE PERILOUS PETALS!
AT LEAST WITH MY FULL WEIGHT I MIGHT HAVE A CHANCE...
WHICH I'M LESSENING WITH MY LIANA PLANT!
AS THOSE CLINGING TENDRILS TWIST ABOUT THE LILLIPUTIAN ARCHER...
-UHNN- CAN'T BEAT THE COMBINED GRIPS OF BOTH FLOWER PETAL AND PLANT TENDRIL--
AND HERE COMES THE CRUSHER!
WHAAM!
12

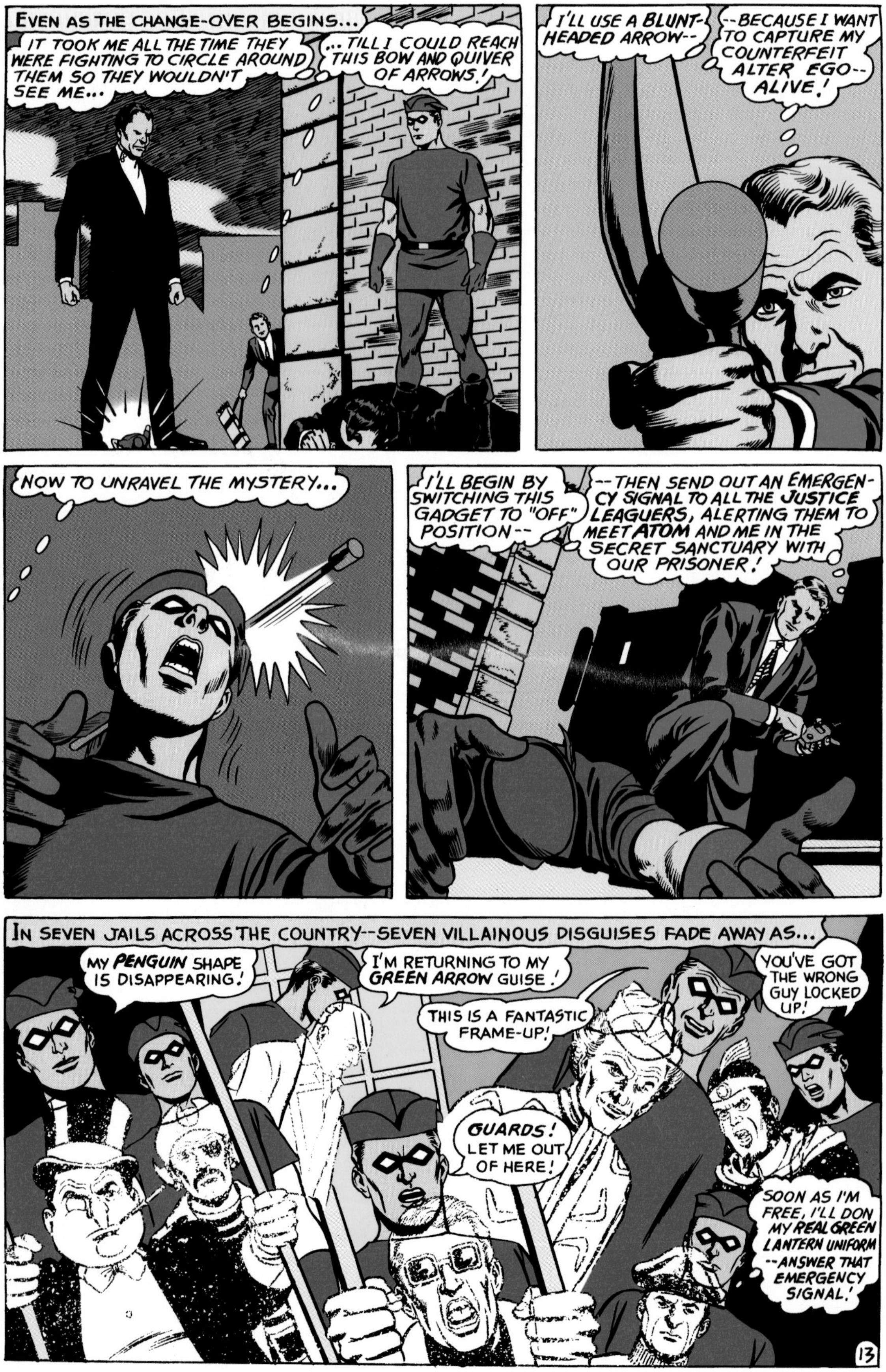
EVEN AS THE CHANGE-OVER BEGINS...
IT TOOK ME ALL THE TIME THEY WERE FIGHTING TO CIRCLE AROUND THEM SO THEY WOULDN'T SEE ME...
...TILL I COULD REACH THIS BOW AND QUIVER OF ARROWS!
I'LL USE A BLUNT-HEADED ARROW--
--BECAUSE I WANT TO CAPTURE MY COUNTERFEIT ALTER EGO--ALIVE!
NOW TO UNRAVEL THE MYSTERY...
I'LL BEGIN BY SWITCHING THIS GADGET TO "OFF" POSITION--
--THEN SEND OUT AN EMERGENCY SIGNAL TO ALL THE JUSTICE LEAGUERS, ALERTING THEM TO MEET ATOM AND ME IN THE SECRET SANCTUARY WITH OUR PRISONER!
IN SEVEN JAILS ACROSS THE COUNTRY--SEVEN VILLAINOUS DISGUISES FADE AWAY AS...
MY PENGUIN SHAPE IS DISAPPEARING!
I'M RETURNING TO MY GREEN ARROW GUISE!
THIS IS A FANTASTIC FRAME-UP!
YOU'VE GOT THE WRONG GUY LOCKED UP!
GUARDS! LET ME OUT OF HERE!
SOON AS I'M FREE, I'LL DON MY REAL GREEN LANTERN UNIFORM --ANSWER THAT EMERGENCY SIGNAL!
13

ON PARADISE ISLAND, AS THE SIGNAL REACHES WONDER WOMAN...
GREAT HERA! BEFORE I COULD DO ANYTHING TO SOLVE THIS MYSTERY, IT'S BEEN SOLVED!
OR HAS IT?
IN HAPPY HARBOR...
"SNAPPER" CARR MISSED OUT ON THE REGULAR MEETING...
BUT AN EMERGENCY CAN'T BE BRUSHED OFF!
14

JUSTICE LEAGUE of AMERICA

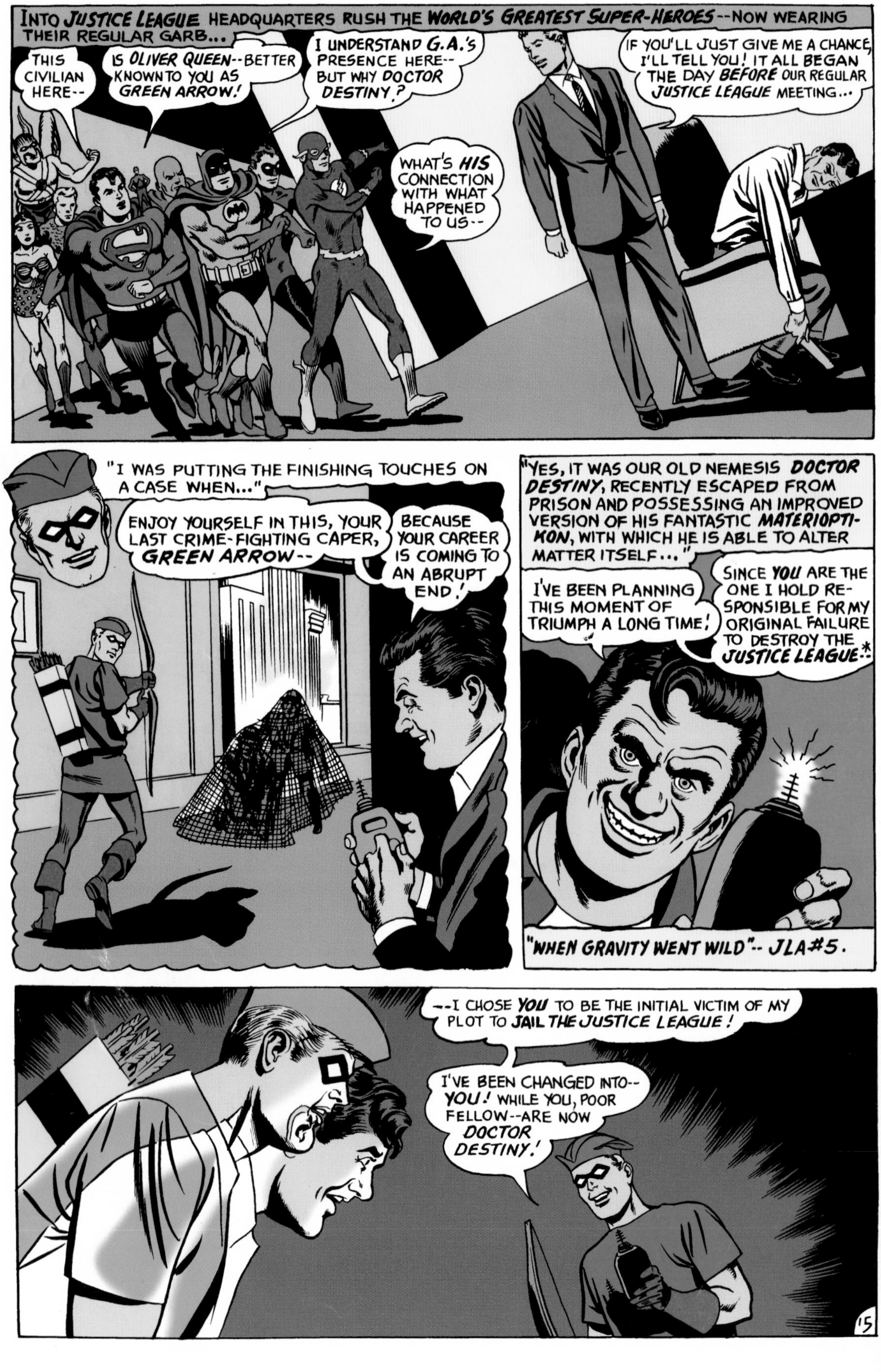
INTO JUSTICE LEAGUE HEADQUARTERS RUSH THE WORLD'S GREATEST SUPER-HEROES--NOW WEARING THEIR REGULAR GARB...
THIS CIVILIAN HERE--
IS OLIVER QUEEN--BETTER KNOWN TO YOU AS GREEN ARROW!
I UNDERSTAND G.A.'S PRESENCE HERE--BUT WHY DOCTOR DESTINY?
WHAT'S HIS CONNECTION WITH WHAT HAPPENED TO US--
IF YOU'LL JUST GIVE ME A CHANCE, I'LL TELL YOU! IT ALL BEGAN THE DAY BEFORE OUR REGULAR JUSTICE LEAGUE MEETING...
"I WAS PUTTING THE FINISHING TOUCHES ON A CASE WHEN..."
ENJOY YOURSELF IN THIS, YOUR LAST CRIME-FIGHTING CAPER, GREEN ARROW--
BECAUSE YOUR CAREER IS COMING TO AN ABRUPT END!
"YES, IT WAS OUR OLD NEMESIS DOCTOR DESTINY, RECENTLY ESCAPED FROM PRISON AND POSSESSING AN IMPROVED VERSION OF HIS FANTASTIC MATERIOPTIKON, WITH WHICH HE IS ABLE TO ALTER MATTER ITSELF..."
I'VE BEEN PLANNING THIS MOMENT OF TRIUMPH A LONG TIME!
SINCE YOU ARE THE ONE I HOLD RESPONSIBLE FOR MY ORIGINAL FAILURE TO DESTROY THE JUSTICE LEAGUE.*
*"WHEN GRAVITY WENT WILD"-- JLA#5.
--I CHOSE YOU TO BE THE INITIAL VICTIM OF MY PLOT TO JAIL THE JUSTICE LEAGUE!
I'VE BEEN CHANGED INTO--YOU! WHILE YOU, POOR FELLOW--ARE NOW DOCTOR DESTINY!

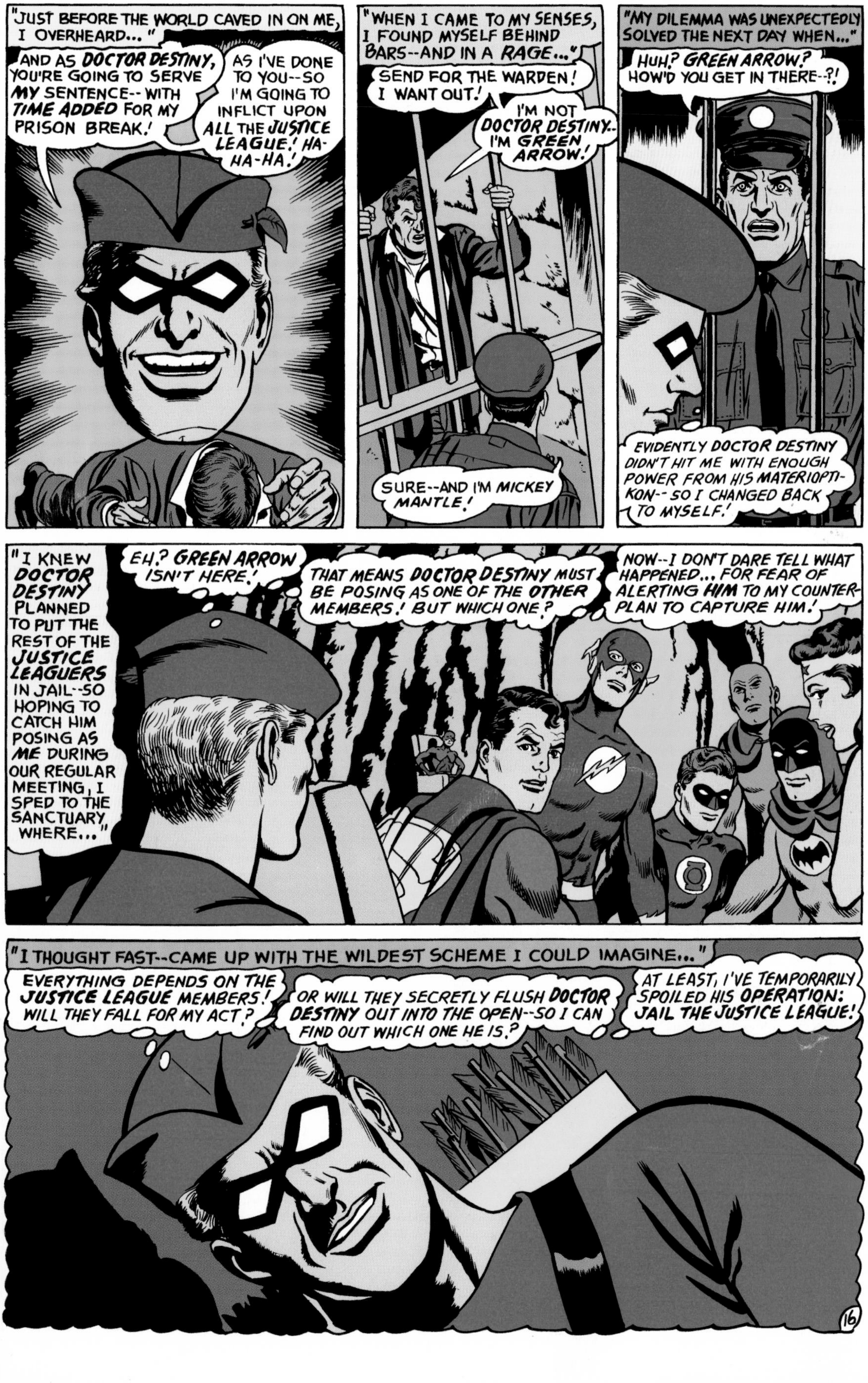
"JUST BEFORE THE WORLD CAVED IN ON ME, I OVERHEARD..."
AND AS DOCTOR DESTINY, YOU'RE GOING TO SERVE MY SENTENCE-- WITH TIME ADDED FOR MY PRISON BREAK!
AS I'VE DONE TO YOU--SO I'M GOING TO INFLICT UPON ALL THE JUSTICE LEAGUE! HA-HA-HA!
"WHEN I CAME TO MY SENSES, I FOUND MYSELF BEHIND BARS--AND IN A RAGE..."
SEND FOR THE WARDEN! I WANT OUT!
I'M NOT DOCTOR DESTINY.. I'M GREEN ARROW!
SURE--AND I'M MICKEY MANTLE!
"MY DILEMMA WAS UNEXPECTEDLY SOLVED THE NEXT DAY WHEN..."
HUH? GREEN ARROW? HOW'D YOU GET IN THERE--?!
EVIDENTLY DOCTOR DESTINY DIDN'T HIT ME WITH ENOUGH POWER FROM HIS MATERIOPTIKON-- SO I CHANGED BACK TO MYSELF!
"I KNEW DOCTOR DESTINY PLANNED TO PUT THE REST OF THE JUSTICE LEAGUERS IN JAIL--SO HOPING TO CATCH HIM POSING AS ME DURING OUR REGULAR MEETING, I SPED TO THE SANCTUARY, WHERE..."
EH? GREEN ARROW ISN'T HERE!
THAT MEANS DOCTOR DESTINY MUST BE POSING AS ONE OF THE OTHER MEMBERS! BUT WHICH ONE?
NOW--I DON'T DARE TELL WHAT HAPPENED... FOR FEAR OF ALERTING HIM TO MY COUNTER-PLAN TO CAPTURE HIM!
"I THOUGHT FAST--CAME UP WITH THE WILDEST SCHEME I COULD IMAGINE..."
EVERYTHING DEPENDS ON THE JUSTICE LEAGUE MEMBERS! WILL THEY FALL FOR MY ACT?
OR WILL THEY SECRETLY FLUSH DOCTOR DESTINY OUT INTO THE OPEN--SO I CAN FIND OUT WHICH ONE HE IS?
AT LEAST, I'VE TEMPORARILY SPOILED HIS OPERATION: JAIL THE JUSTICE LEAGUE!
16

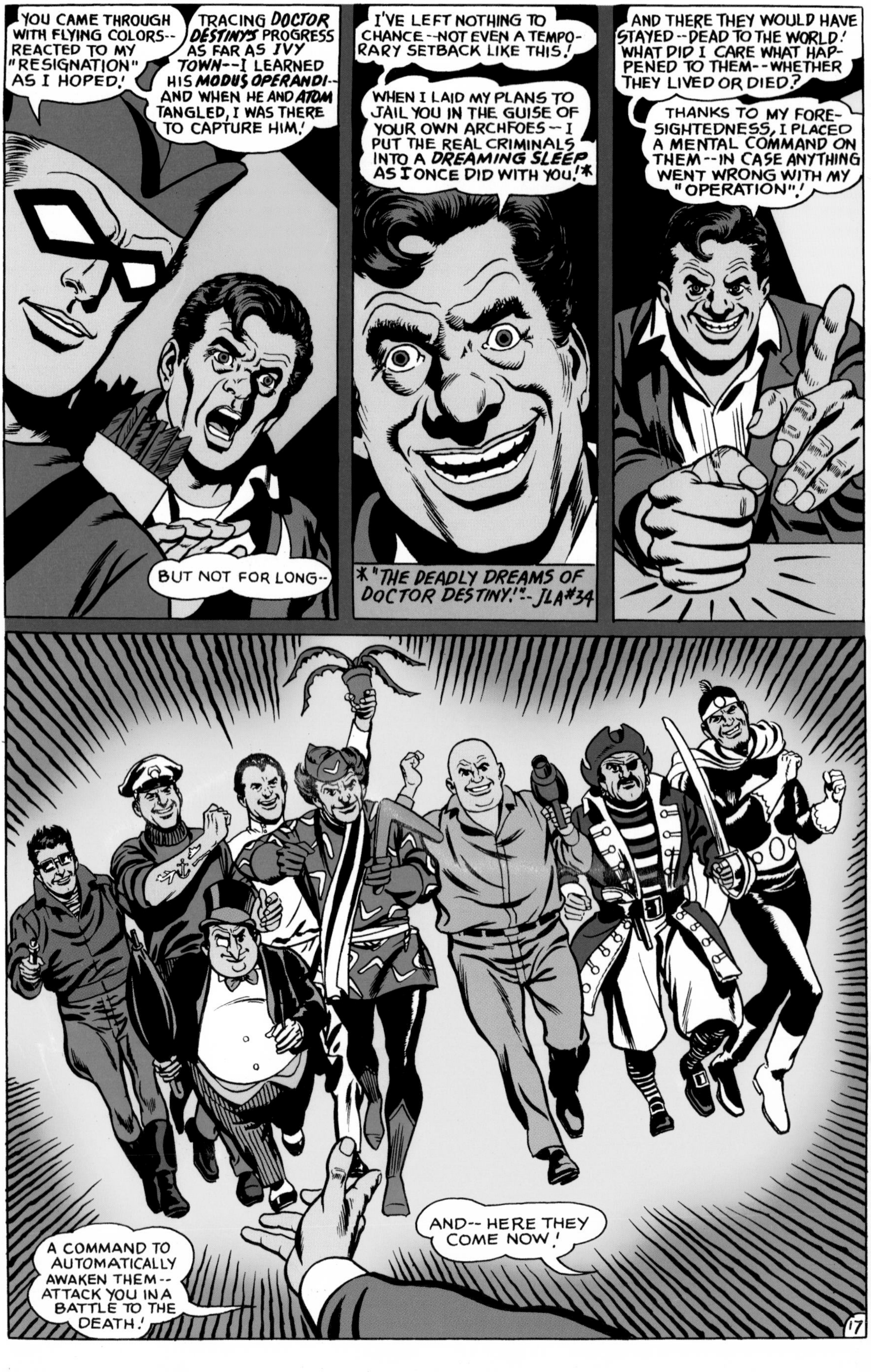

YOU CAME THROUGH WITH FLYING COLORS-- REACTED TO MY "RESIGNATION" AS I HOPED!
TRACING DOCTOR DESTINY'S PROGRESS AS FAR AS IVY TOWN--I LEARNED HIS MODUS OPERANDI-- AND WHEN HE AND ATOM TANGLED, I WAS THERE TO CAPTURE HIM!
BUT NOT FOR LONG--
I'VE LEFT NOTHING TO CHANCE--NOT EVEN A TEMPORARY SETBACK LIKE THIS!
WHEN I LAID MY PLANS TO JAIL YOU IN THE GUISE OF YOUR OWN ARCHFOES--I PUT THE REAL CRIMINALS INTO A DREAMING SLEEP AS I ONCE DID WITH YOU!*
*"THE DEADLY DREAMS OF DOCTOR DESTINY!"--JLA #34
AND THERE THEY WOULD HAVE STAYED--DEAD TO THE WORLD! WHAT DID I CARE WHAT HAPPENED TO THEM--WHETHER THEY LIVED OR DIED?
THANKS TO MY FORESIGHTEDNESS, I PLACED A MENTAL COMMAND ON THEM--IN CASE ANYTHING WENT WRONG WITH MY "OPERATION"!
A COMMAND TO AUTOMATICALLY AWAKEN THEM-- ATTACK YOU IN A BATTLE TO THE DEATH!
AND--HERE THEY COME NOW!
17

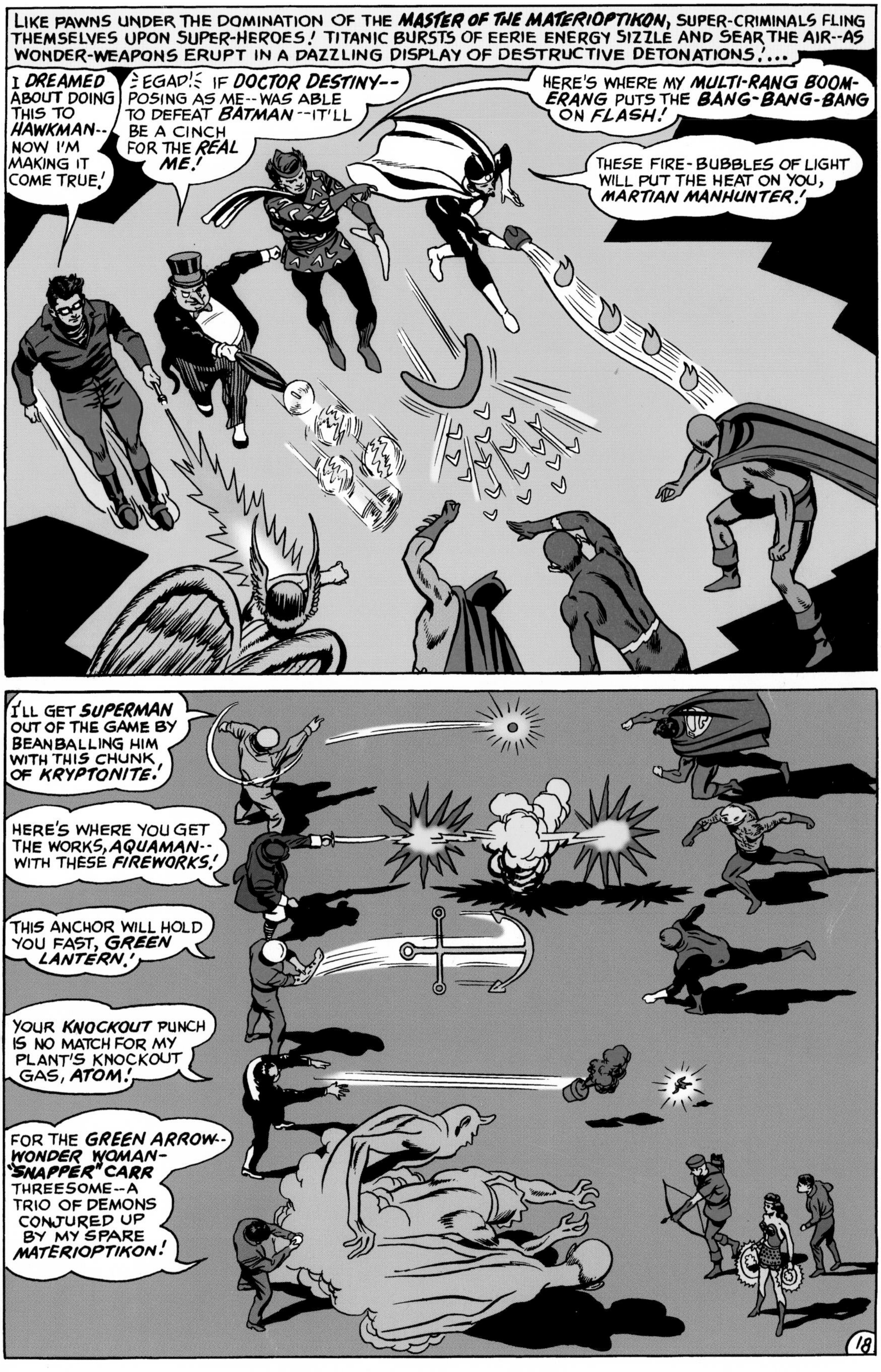
LIKE PAWNS UNDER THE DOMINATION OF THE MASTER OF THE MATERIOPTIKON, SUPER-CRIMINALS FLING THEMSELVES UPON SUPER-HEROES! TITANIC BURSTS OF EERIE ENERGY SIZZLE AND SEAR THE AIR--AS WONDER-WEAPONS ERUPT IN A DAZZLING DISPLAY OF DESTRUCTIVE DETONATIONS!...
I DREAMED ABOUT DOING THIS TO HAWKMAN--NOW I'M MAKING IT COME TRUE!
EGAD! IF DOCTOR DESTINY--POSING AS ME--WAS ABLE TO DEFEAT BATMAN--IT'LL BE A CINCH FOR THE REAL ME!
HERE'S WHERE MY MULTI-RANG BOOM-ERANG PUTS THE BANG-BANG-BANG ON FLASH!
THESE FIRE-BUBBLES OF LIGHT WILL PUT THE HEAT ON YOU, MARTIAN MANHUNTER!
I'LL GET SUPERMAN OUT OF THE GAME BY BEANBALLING HIM WITH THIS CHUNK OF KRYPTONITE!
HERE'S WHERE YOU GET THE WORKS, AQUAMAN--WITH THESE FIREWORKS!
THIS ANCHOR WILL HOLD YOU FAST, GREEN LANTERN!
YOUR KNOCKOUT PUNCH IS NO MATCH FOR MY PLANT'S KNOCKOUT GAS, ATOM!
FOR THE GREEN ARROW--WONDER WOMAN--"SNAPPER" CARR THREESOME--A TRIO OF DEMONS CONJURED UP BY MY SPARE MATERIOPTIKON!
18

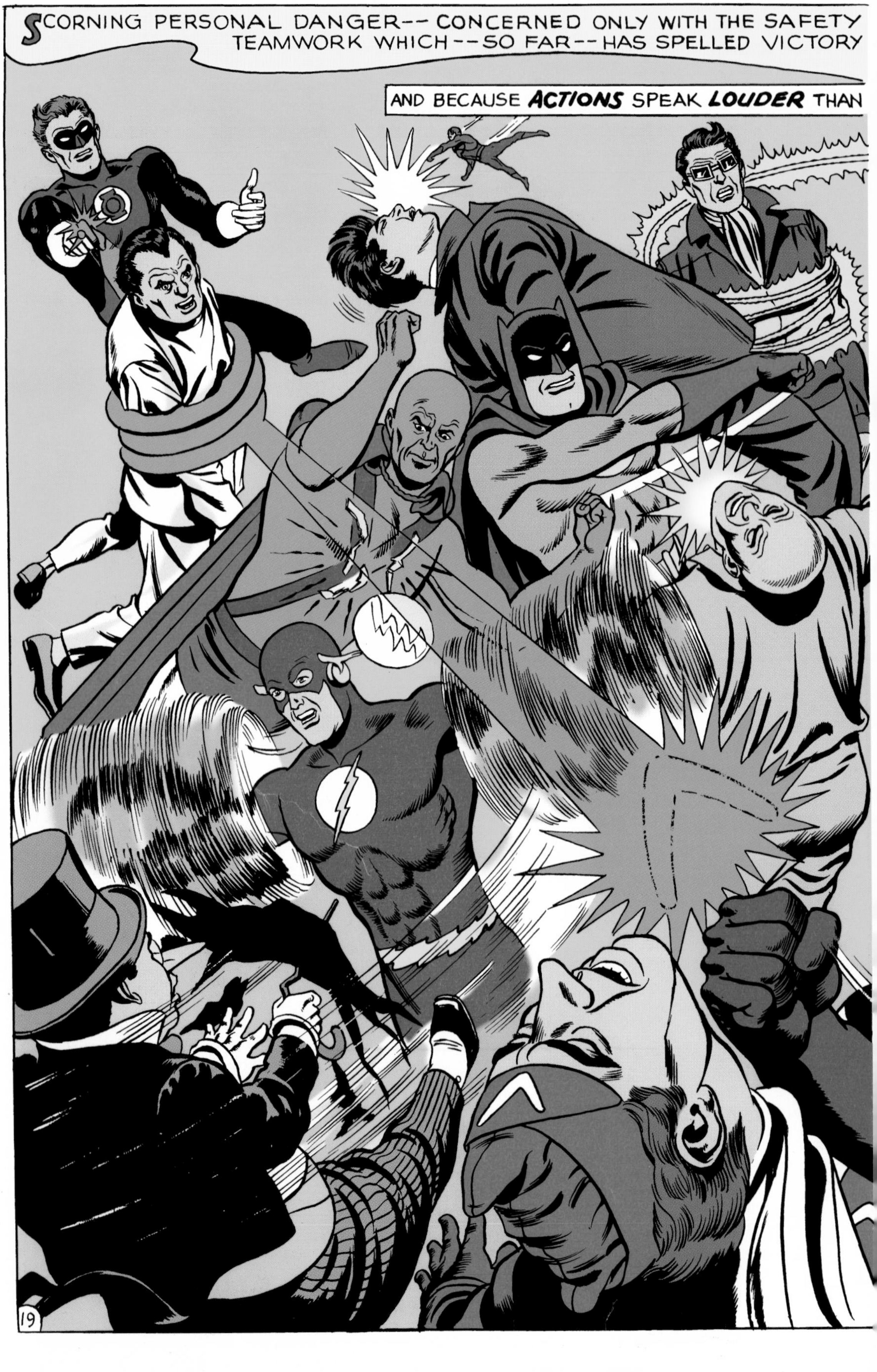
SCORNING PERSONAL DANGER-- CONCERNED ONLY WITH THE SAFETY
TEAMWORK WHICH--SO FAR--HAS SPELLED VICTORY
AND BECAUSE ACTIONS SPEAK LOUDER THAN
19

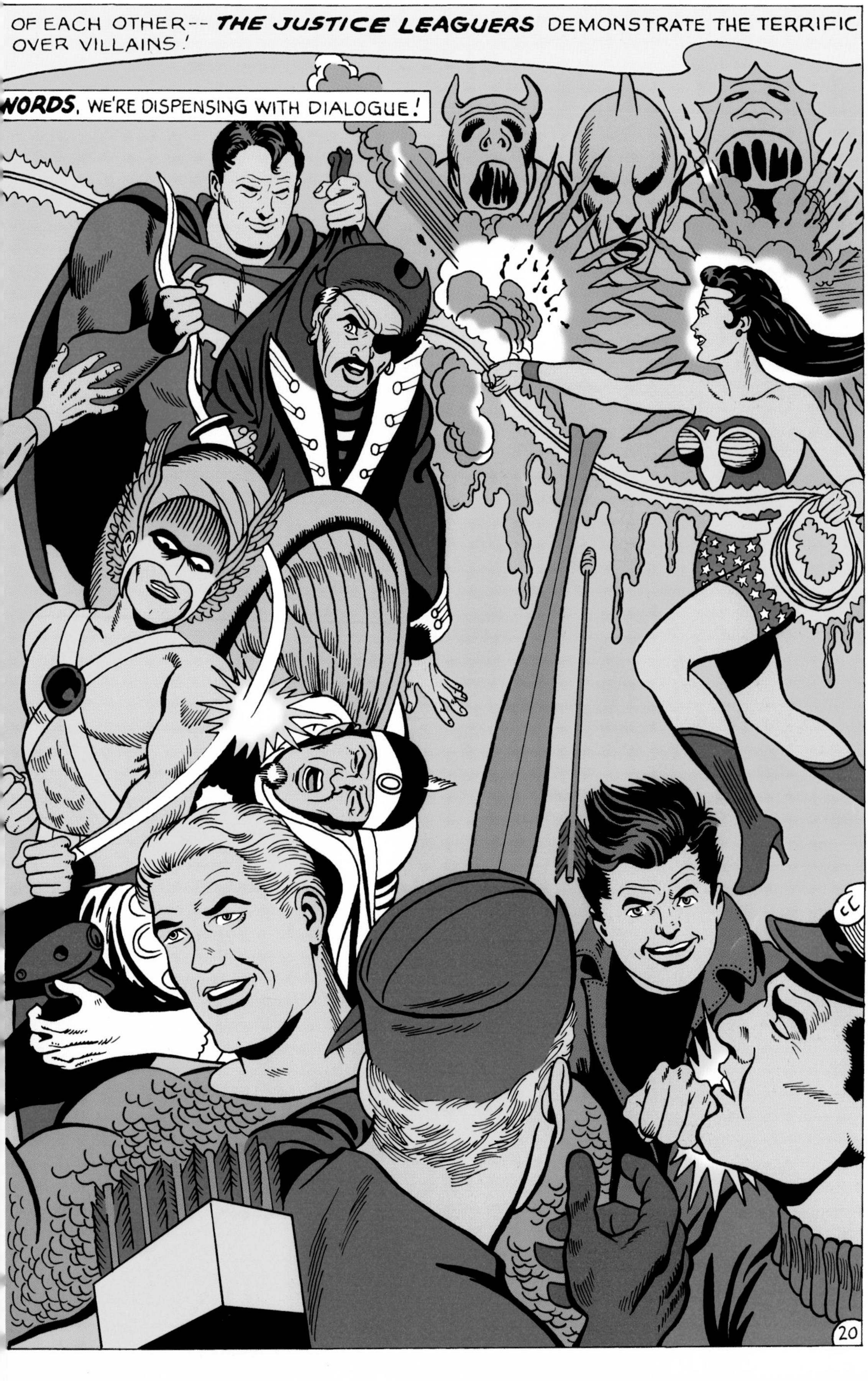
OF EACH OTHER-- THE JUSTICE LEAGUERS DEMONSTRATE THE TERRIFIC
OVER VILLAINS!
WORDS, WE'RE DISPENSING WITH DIALOGUE!
20

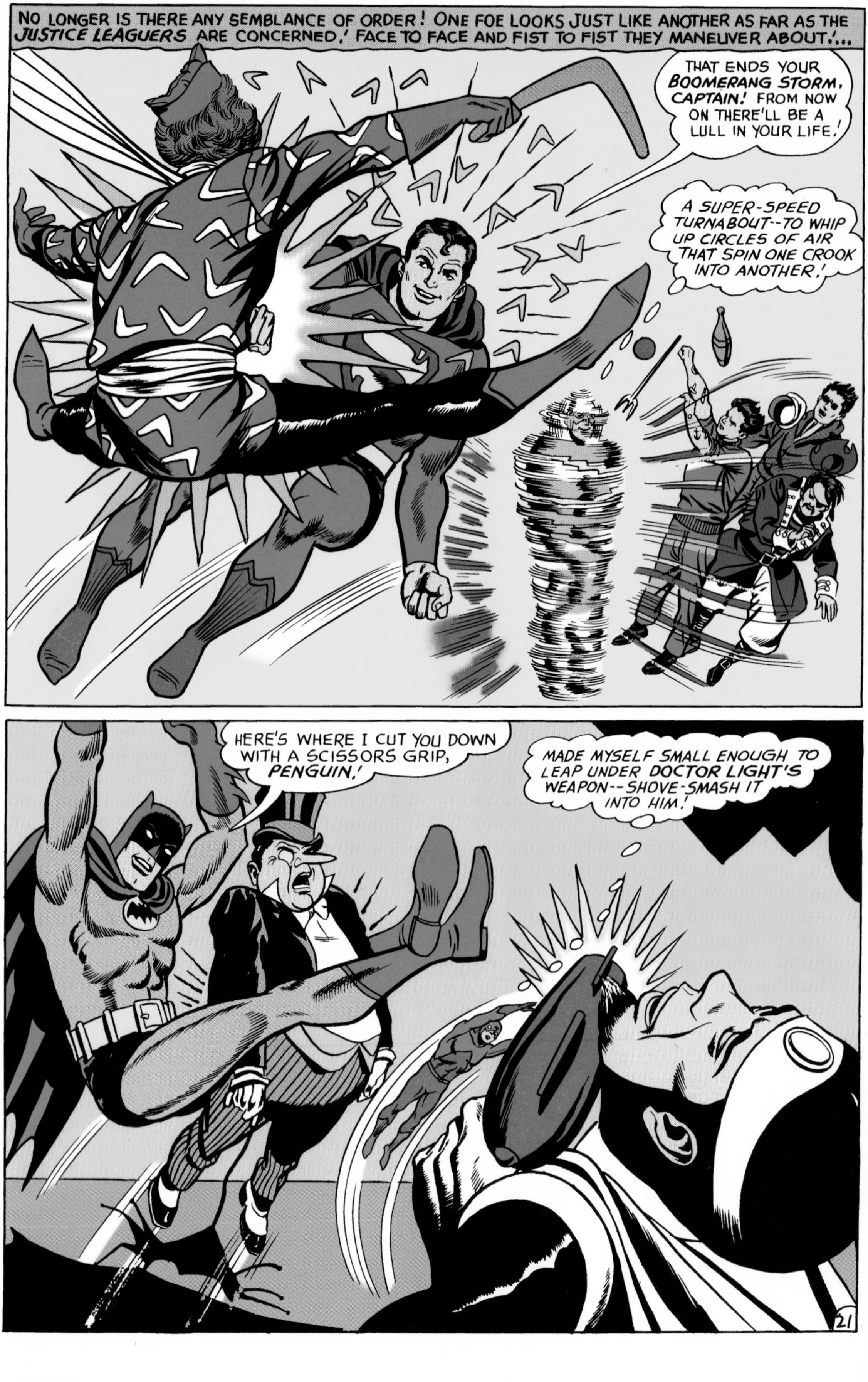
NO LONGER IS THERE ANY SEMBLANCE OF ORDER! ONE FOE LOOKS JUST LIKE ANOTHER AS FAR AS THE JUSTICE LEAGUERS ARE CONCERNED! FACE TO FACE AND FIST TO FIST THEY MANEUVER ABOUT!...
THAT ENDS YOUR BOOMERANG STORM, CAPTAIN! FROM NOW ON THERE'LL BE A LULL IN YOUR LIFE!
A SUPER-SPEED TURNABOUT--TO WHIP UP CIRCLES OF AIR THAT SPIN ONE CROOK INTO ANOTHER!
HERE'S WHERE I CUT YOU DOWN WITH A SCISSORS GRIP, PENGUIN!
MADE MYSELF SMALL ENOUGH TO LEAP UNDER DOCTOR LIGHT'S WEAPON--SHOVE-SMASH IT INTO HIM!
21

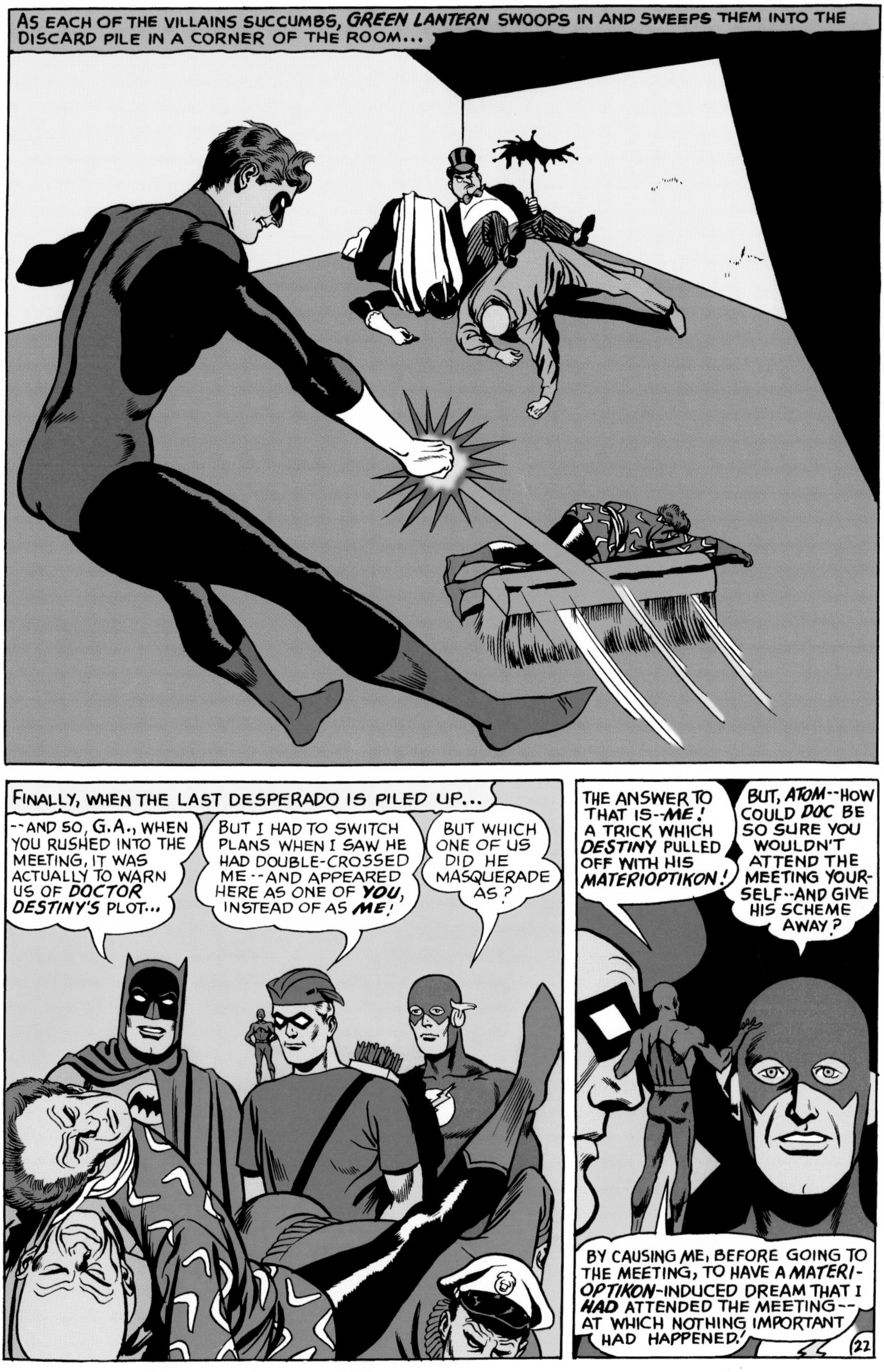
AS EACH OF THE VILLAINS SUCCUMBS, GREEN LANTERN SWOOPS IN AND SWEEPS THEM INTO THE DISCARD PILE IN A CORNER OF THE ROOM...
FINALLY, WHEN THE LAST DESPERADO IS PILED UP...
--AND SO, G.A., WHEN YOU RUSHED INTO THE MEETING, IT WAS ACTUALLY TO WARN US OF DOCTOR DESTINY'S PLOT...
BUT I HAD TO SWITCH PLANS WHEN I SAW HE HAD DOUBLE-CROSSED ME--AND APPEARED HERE AS ONE OF YOU, INSTEAD OF AS ME!
BUT WHICH ONE OF US DID HE MASQUERADE AS?
THE ANSWER TO THAT IS--ME! A TRICK WHICH DESTINY PULLED OFF WITH HIS MATERIOPTIKON!
BUT, ATOM--HOW COULD DOC BE SO SURE YOU WOULDN'T ATTEND THE MEETING YOURSELF--AND GIVE HIS SCHEME AWAY?
BY CAUSING ME, BEFORE GOING TO THE MEETING, TO HAVE A MATERIOPTIKON-INDUCED DREAM THAT I HAD ATTENDED THE MEETING--AT WHICH NOTHING IMPORTANT HAD HAPPENED!
22

WHEN I PHONED ATOM IN HIS CIVILIAN IDENTITY TO ASK HIM WHAT HE THOUGHT OF GREEN ARROW'S STRANGE ACTIONS, WE BOTH SUDDENLY REALIZED ATOM HAD BEEN IMPERSONATED BY SOMEONE--
WHEREUPON I ALSO DECIDED TO BAIT A TRAP FOR HIM BY MASQUERADING AS GREEN ARROW...
HOLD IT! JUST WHAT WAS IT THAT REVEALED THE REAL ATOM WASN'T AT THE MEETING?
WHEN I ARRIVED AT HEADQUARTERS, "ATOM" WAS ALREADY THERE! BUT I WAS THE SECOND MEMBER TO SHOW UP--AND YOU ALL KNOW ATOM GOES TO OUR MEETINGS BY TELEPHONE...
AND IF "I" WAS THE FIRST ONE THERE-- WHO LIFTED THE TELEPHONE RECEIVER TO LET "ME" IN?
IT MADE ME SUSPICIOUS, SO I PHONED ATOM TO CHECK IT OUT--AND YOU KNOW THE REST!
AND IN A PRISON CELL THAT HAD BEEN "RE-SERVED" FOR A JUSTICE LEAGUER...
I CAN REMEMBER WAKING OUT OF A SOUND SLEEP-- AND FIGHTING BATMAN AND THE JUSTICE LEAGUE IN THEIR SECRET HEADQUARTERS...
BUT I CAN'T REMEMBER HOW I GOT THERE... OR WHERE IT IS!
EGAD! WHY CAN'T I REMEMBER?
23
The End

JUSTICE LEAGUE of AMERICA

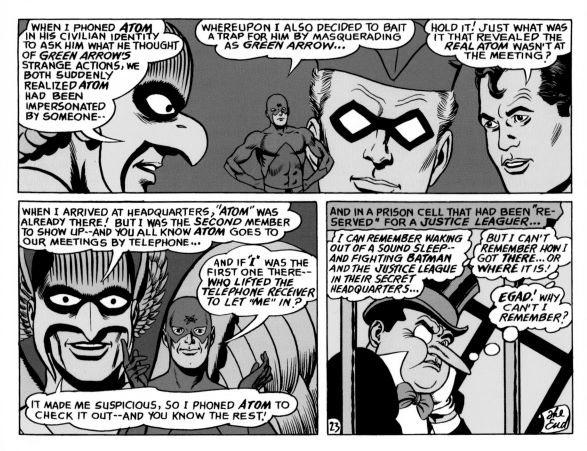

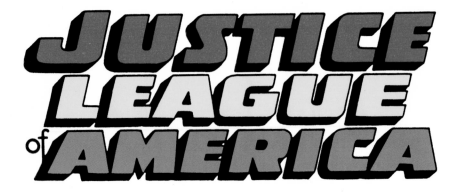

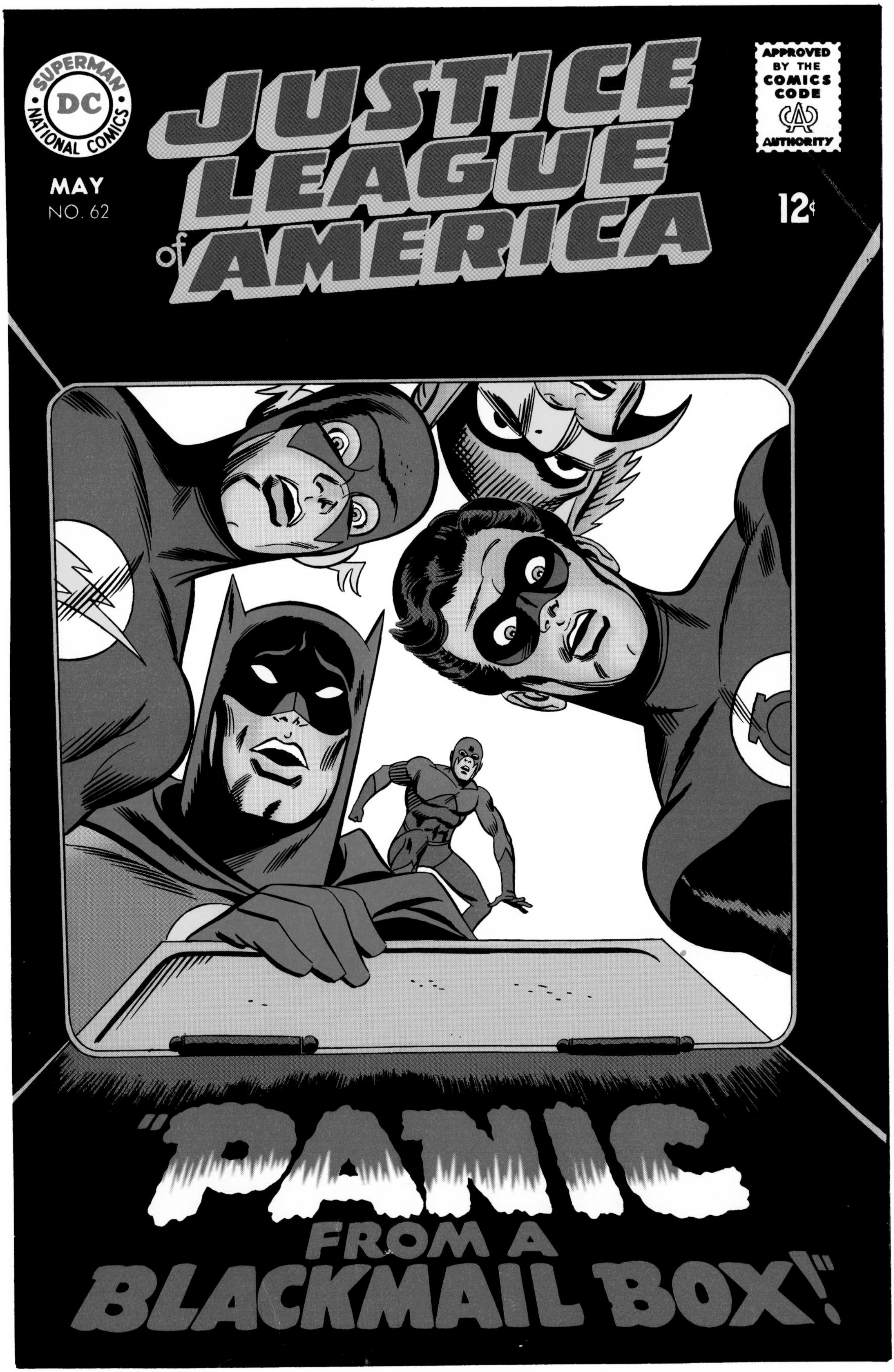
SUPERMAN DC NATIONAL COMICS
MAY
NO. 62
JUSTICE LEAGUE of AMERICA
APPROVED BY THE COMICS CODE AUTHORITY
12¢
"PANIC FROM A BLACKMAIL BOX!"

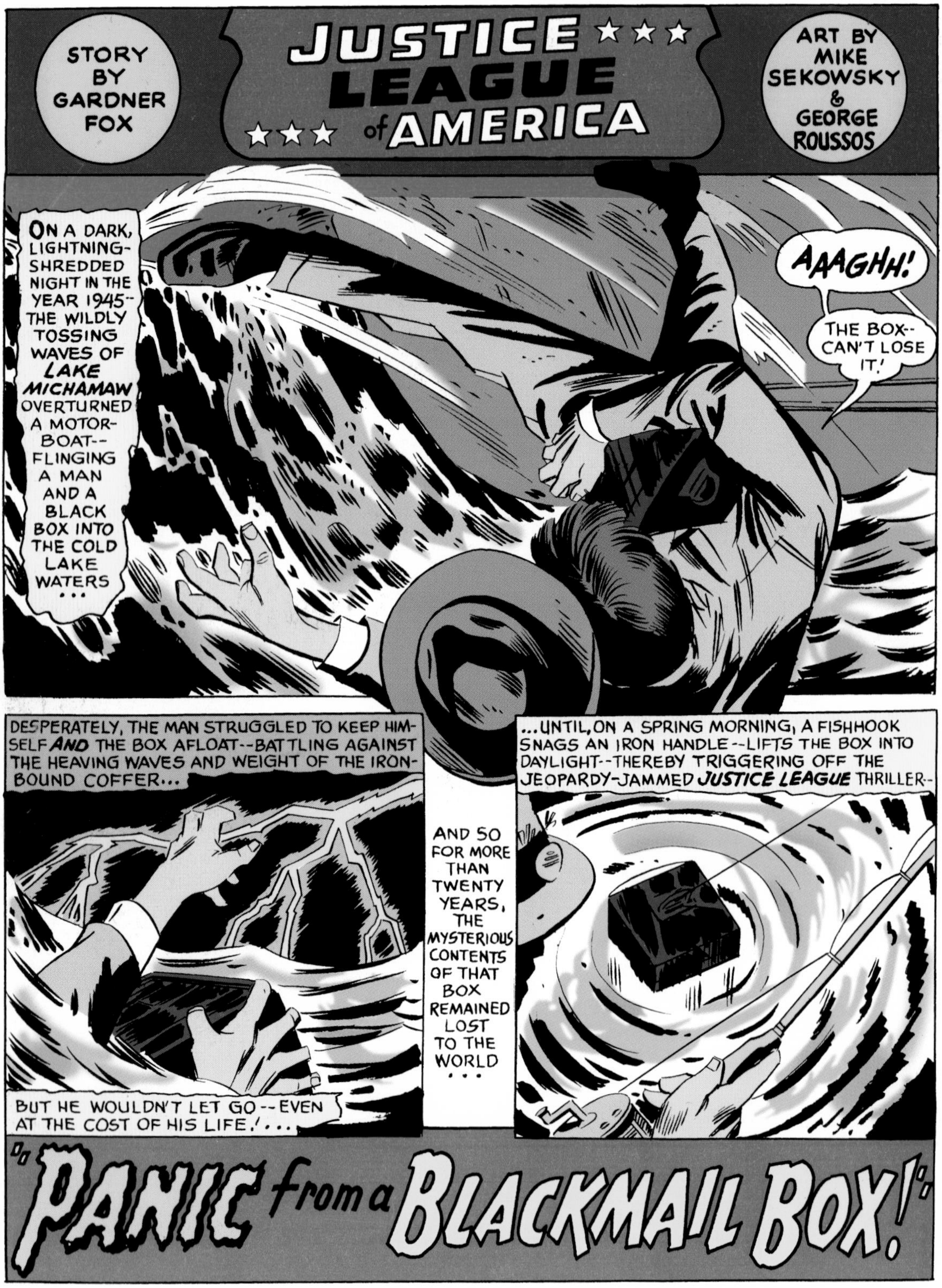
STORY BY GARDNER FOX
JUSTICE LEAGUE of AMERICA
ART BY MIKE SEKOWSKY & GEORGE ROUSSOS
ON A DARK, LIGHTNING-SHREDDED NIGHT IN THE YEAR 1945-- THE WILDLY TOSSING WAVES OF LAKE MICHAMAW OVERTURNED A MOTOR-BOAT--FLINGING A MAN AND A BLACK BOX INTO THE COLD LAKE WATERS ...
AAAGHH!
THE BOX--CAN'T LOSE IT!
DESPERATELY, THE MAN STRUGGLED TO KEEP HIMSELF AND THE BOX AFLOAT--BATTLING AGAINST THE HEAVING WAVES AND WEIGHT OF THE IRON-BOUND COFFER...
BUT HE WOULDN'T LET GO--EVEN AT THE COST OF HIS LIFE!...
AND SO FOR MORE THAN TWENTY YEARS, THE MYSTERIOUS CONTENTS OF THAT BOX REMAINED LOST TO THE WORLD ...
...UNTIL, ON A SPRING MORNING, A FISHHOOK SNAGS AN IRON HANDLE--LIFTS THE BOX INTO DAYLIGHT--THEREBY TRIGGERING OFF THE JEOPARDY-JAMMED JUSTICE LEAGUE THRILLER--
"PANIC from a BLACKMAIL BOX!"

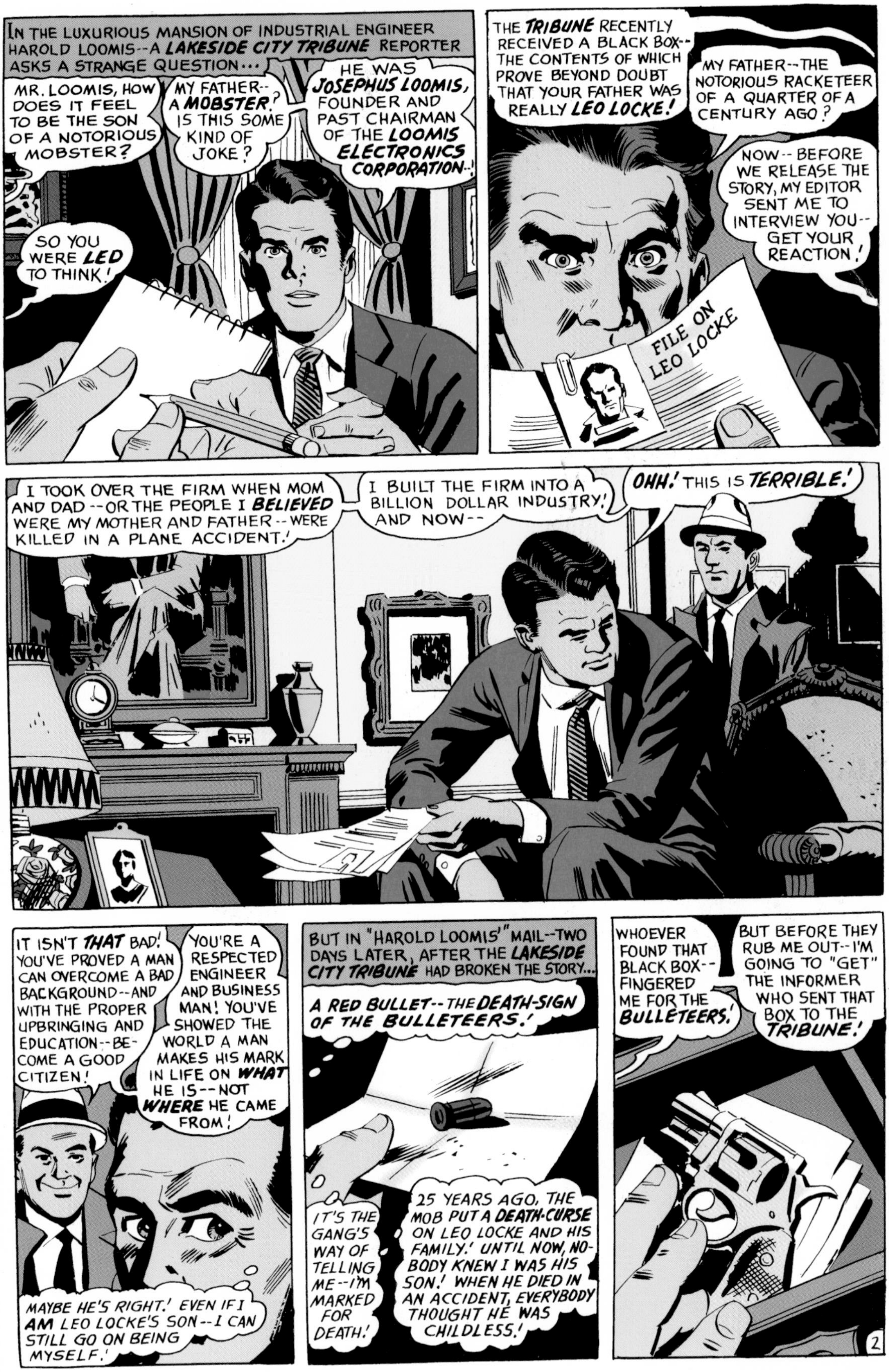
IN THE LUXURIOUS MANSION OF INDUSTRIAL ENGINEER HAROLD LOOMIS--A LAKESIDE CITY TRIBUNE REPORTER ASKS A STRANGE QUESTION...
MR. LOOMIS, HOW DOES IT FEEL TO BE THE SON OF A NOTORIOUS MOBSTER?
MY FATHER-- A MOBSTER? IS THIS SOME KIND OF JOKE?
HE WAS JOSEPHUS LOOMIS, FOUNDER AND PAST CHAIRMAN OF THE LOOMIS ELECTRONICS CORPORATION--!
SO YOU WERE LED TO THINK!
THE TRIBUNE RECENTLY RECEIVED A BLACK BOX-- THE CONTENTS OF WHICH PROVE BEYOND DOUBT THAT YOUR FATHER WAS REALLY LEO LOCKE!
MY FATHER--THE NOTORIOUS RACKETEER OF A QUARTER OF A CENTURY AGO?
NOW-- BEFORE WE RELEASE THE STORY, MY EDITOR SENT ME TO INTERVIEW YOU-- GET YOUR REACTION!
FILE ON LEO LOCKE
I TOOK OVER THE FIRM WHEN MOM AND DAD --OR THE PEOPLE I BELIEVED WERE MY MOTHER AND FATHER --WERE KILLED IN A PLANE ACCIDENT!
I BUILT THE FIRM INTO A BILLION DOLLAR INDUSTRY! AND NOW--
OHH! THIS IS TERRIBLE!
IT ISN'T THAT BAD! YOU'VE PROVED A MAN CAN OVERCOME A BAD BACKGROUND--AND WITH THE PROPER UPBRINGING AND EDUCATION--BE-COME A GOOD CITIZEN!
YOU'RE A RESPECTED ENGINEER AND BUSINESS MAN! YOU'VE SHOWED THE WORLD A MAN MAKES HIS MARK IN LIFE ON WHAT HE IS--NOT WHERE HE CAME FROM!
MAYBE HE'S RIGHT! EVEN IF I AM LEO LOCKE'S SON--I CAN STILL GO ON BEING MYSELF!
BUT IN "HAROLD LOOMIS'" MAIL--TWO DAYS LATER, AFTER THE LAKESIDE CITY TRIBUNE HAD BROKEN THE STORY...
A RED BULLET--THE DEATH-SIGN OF THE BULLETEERS!
IT'S THE GANG'S WAY OF TELLING ME--I'M MARKED FOR DEATH!
25 YEARS AGO, THE MOB PUT A DEATH-CURSE ON LEO LOCKE AND HIS FAMILY! UNTIL NOW, NO-BODY KNEW I WAS HIS SON! WHEN HE DIED IN AN ACCIDENT, EVERYBODY THOUGHT HE WAS CHILDLESS!
WHOEVER FOUND THAT BLACK BOX-- FINGERED ME FOR THE BULLETEERS!
BUT BEFORE THEY RUB ME OUT--I'M GOING TO "GET" THE INFORMER WHO SENT THAT BOX TO THE TRIBUNE!
2

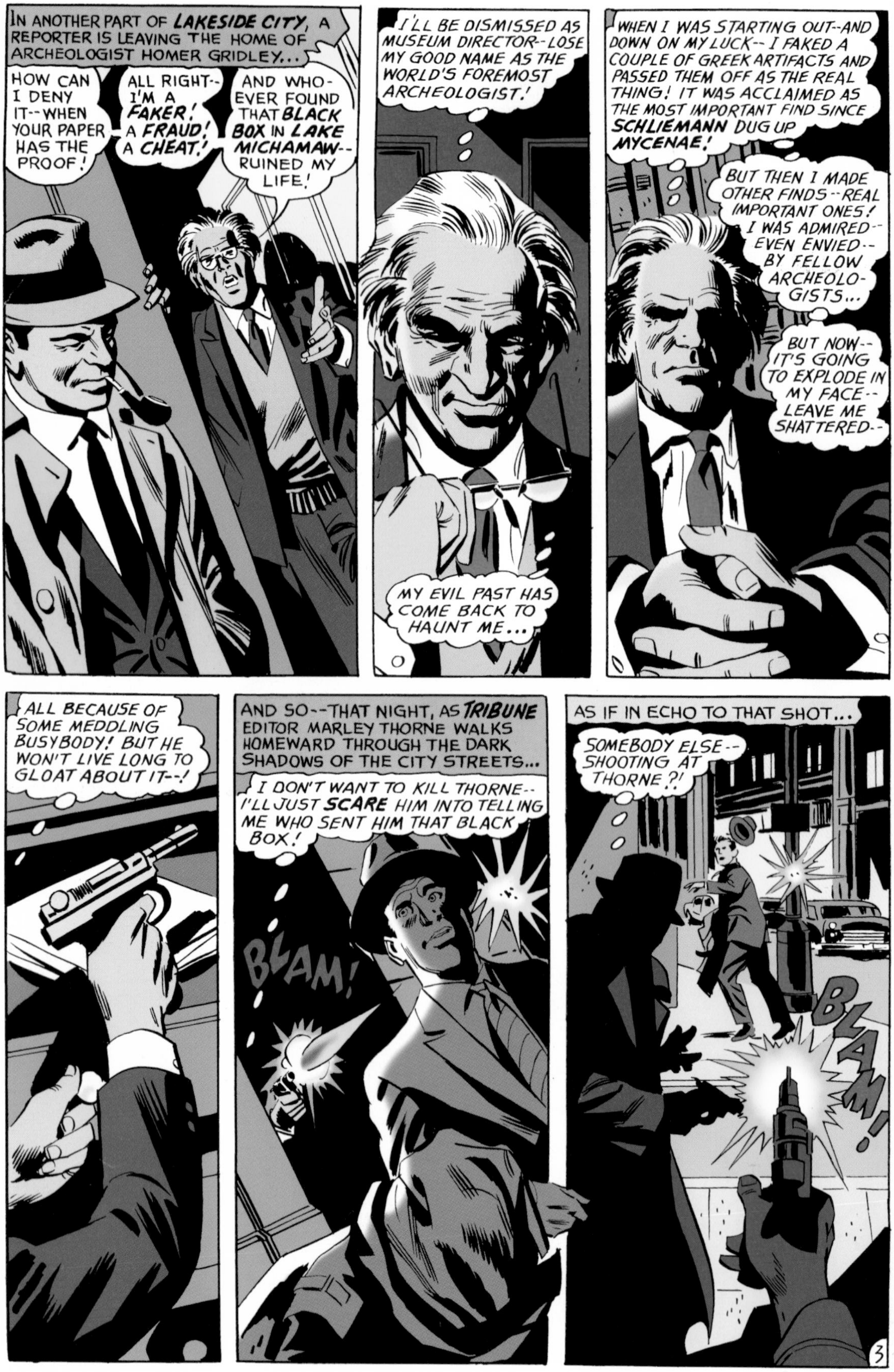
IN ANOTHER PART OF LAKESIDE CITY, A REPORTER IS LEAVING THE HOME OF ARCHEOLOGIST HOMER GRIDLEY...
HOW CAN I DENY IT--WHEN YOUR PAPER HAS THE PROOF!
ALL RIGHT--I'M A FAKER! A FRAUD! A CHEAT!
AND WHO-EVER FOUND THAT BLACK BOX IN LAKE MICHAMAW--RUINED MY LIFE!
I'LL BE DISMISSED AS MUSEUM DIRECTOR--LOSE MY GOOD NAME AS THE WORLD'S FOREMOST ARCHEOLOGIST!
MY EVIL PAST HAS COME BACK TO HAUNT ME...
WHEN I WAS STARTING OUT--AND DOWN ON MY LUCK--I FAKED A COUPLE OF GREEK ARTIFACTS AND PASSED THEM OFF AS THE REAL THING! IT WAS ACCLAIMED AS THE MOST IMPORTANT FIND SINCE SCHLIEMANN DUG UP MYCENAE!
BUT THEN I MADE OTHER FINDS--REAL IMPORTANT ONES! I WAS ADMIRED--EVEN ENVIED--BY FELLOW ARCHEOLO-GISTS...
BUT NOW--IT'S GOING TO EXPLODE IN MY FACE--LEAVE ME SHATTERED--
ALL BECAUSE OF SOME MEDDLING BUSYBODY! BUT HE WON'T LIVE LONG TO GLOAT ABOUT IT--!
AND SO--THAT NIGHT, AS TRIBUNE EDITOR MARLEY THORNE WALKS HOMEWARD THROUGH THE DARK SHADOWS OF THE CITY STREETS...
I DON'T WANT TO KILL THORNE--I'LL JUST SCARE HIM INTO TELLING ME WHO SENT HIM THAT BLACK BOX!
BLAM!
AS IF IN ECHO TO THAT SHOT...
SOMEBODY ELSE--SHOOTING AT THORNE?!
BLAM!
3

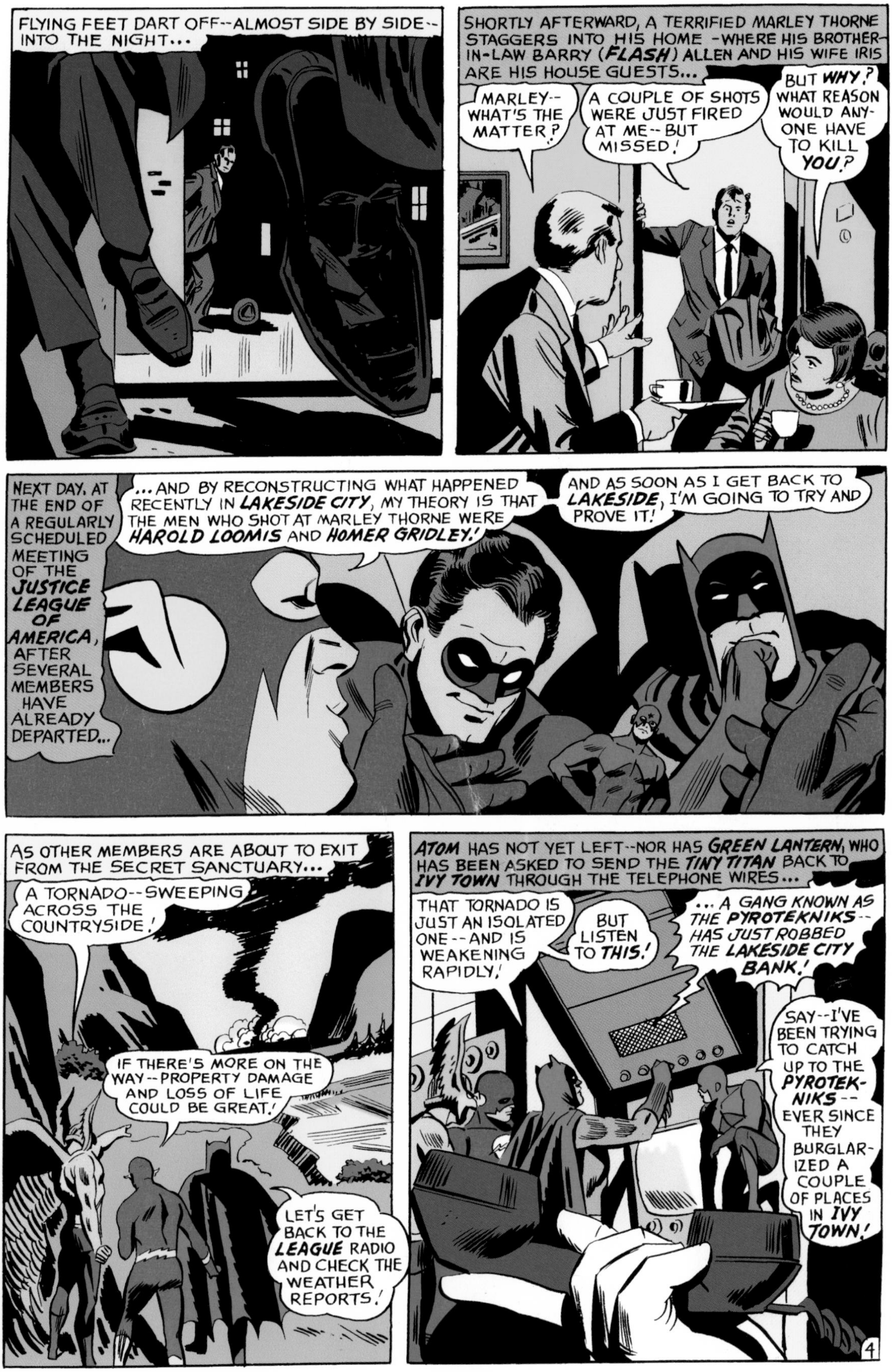
FLYING FEET DART OFF--ALMOST SIDE BY SIDE--INTO THE NIGHT...
SHORTLY AFTERWARD, A TERRIFIED MARLEY THORNE STAGGERS INTO HIS HOME -WHERE HIS BROTHER-IN-LAW BARRY (FLASH) ALLEN AND HIS WIFE IRIS ARE HIS HOUSE GUESTS...
MARLEY--WHAT'S THE MATTER?
A COUPLE OF SHOTS WERE JUST FIRED AT ME--BUT MISSED!
BUT WHY? WHAT REASON WOULD ANYONE HAVE TO KILL YOU?
NEXT DAY, AT THE END OF A REGULARLY SCHEDULED MEETING OF THE JUSTICE LEAGUE OF AMERICA, AFTER SEVERAL MEMBERS HAVE ALREADY DEPARTED...
...AND BY RECONSTRUCTING WHAT HAPPENED RECENTLY IN LAKESIDE CITY, MY THEORY IS THAT THE MEN WHO SHOT AT MARLEY THORNE WERE HAROLD LOOMIS AND HOMER GRIDLEY!
AND AS SOON AS I GET BACK TO LAKESIDE, I'M GOING TO TRY AND PROVE IT!
AS OTHER MEMBERS ARE ABOUT TO EXIT FROM THE SECRET SANCTUARY...
A TORNADO--SWEEPING ACROSS THE COUNTRYSIDE!
IF THERE'S MORE ON THE WAY--PROPERTY DAMAGE AND LOSS OF LIFE COULD BE GREAT!
LET'S GET BACK TO THE LEAGUE RADIO AND CHECK THE WEATHER REPORTS!
ATOM HAS NOT YET LEFT--NOR HAS GREEN LANTERN, WHO HAS BEEN ASKED TO SEND THE TINY TITAN BACK TO IVY TOWN THROUGH THE TELEPHONE WIRES...
THAT TORNADO IS JUST AN ISOLATED ONE--AND IS WEAKENING RAPIDLY!
BUT LISTEN TO THIS!
...A GANG KNOWN AS THE PYROTEKNIKS--HAS JUST ROBBED THE LAKESIDE CITY BANK!
SAY--I'VE BEEN TRYING TO CATCH UP TO THE PYROTEKNIKS--EVER SINCE THEY BURGLARIZED A COUPLE OF PLACES IN IVY TOWN!
4

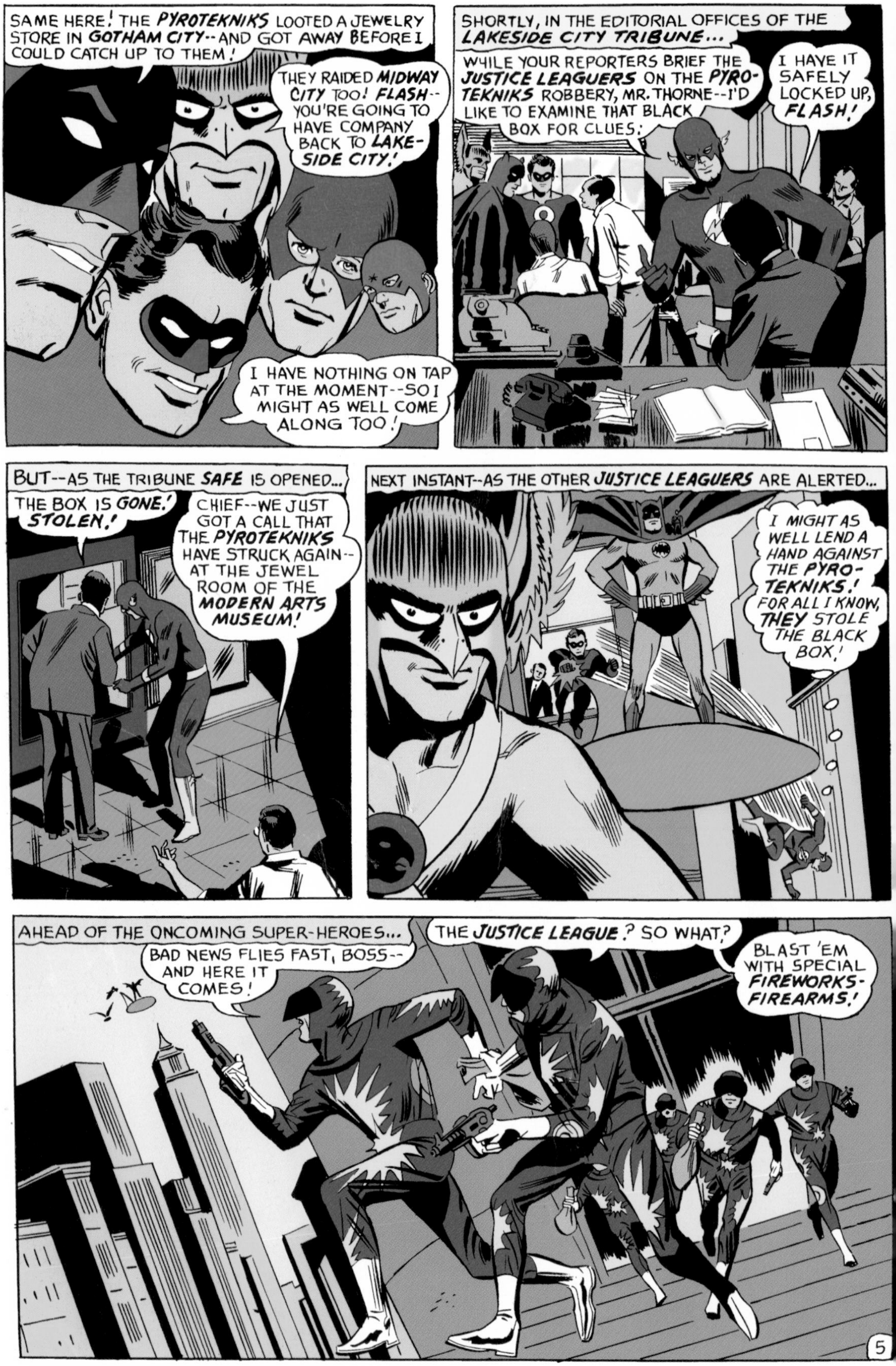
SAME HERE! THE PYROTEKNIKS LOOTED A JEWELRY STORE IN GOTHAM CITY--AND GOT AWAY BEFORE I COULD CATCH UP TO THEM!
THEY RAIDED MIDWAY CITY TOO! FLASH--YOU'RE GOING TO HAVE COMPANY BACK TO LAKESIDE CITY!
I HAVE NOTHING ON TAP AT THE MOMENT--SO I MIGHT AS WELL COME ALONG TOO!
SHORTLY, IN THE EDITORIAL OFFICES OF THE LAKESIDE CITY TRIBUNE...
WHILE YOUR REPORTERS BRIEF THE JUSTICE LEAGUERS ON THE PYROTEKNIKS ROBBERY, MR. THORNE--I'D LIKE TO EXAMINE THAT BLACK BOX FOR CLUES!
I HAVE IT SAFELY LOCKED UP, FLASH!
BUT--AS THE TRIBUNE SAFE IS OPENED...
THE BOX IS GONE! STOLEN!
CHIEF--WE JUST GOT A CALL THAT THE PYROTEKNIKS HAVE STRUCK AGAIN--AT THE JEWEL ROOM OF THE MODERN ARTS MUSEUM!
NEXT INSTANT--AS THE OTHER JUSTICE LEAGUERS ARE ALERTED...
I MIGHT AS WELL LEND A HAND AGAINST THE PYROTEKNIKS! FOR ALL I KNOW, THEY STOLE THE BLACK BOX!
AHEAD OF THE ONCOMING SUPER-HEROES...
BAD NEWS FLIES FAST, BOSS--AND HERE IT COMES!
THE JUSTICE LEAGUE? SO WHAT?
BLAST 'EM WITH SPECIAL FIREWORKS-FIREARMS!
5

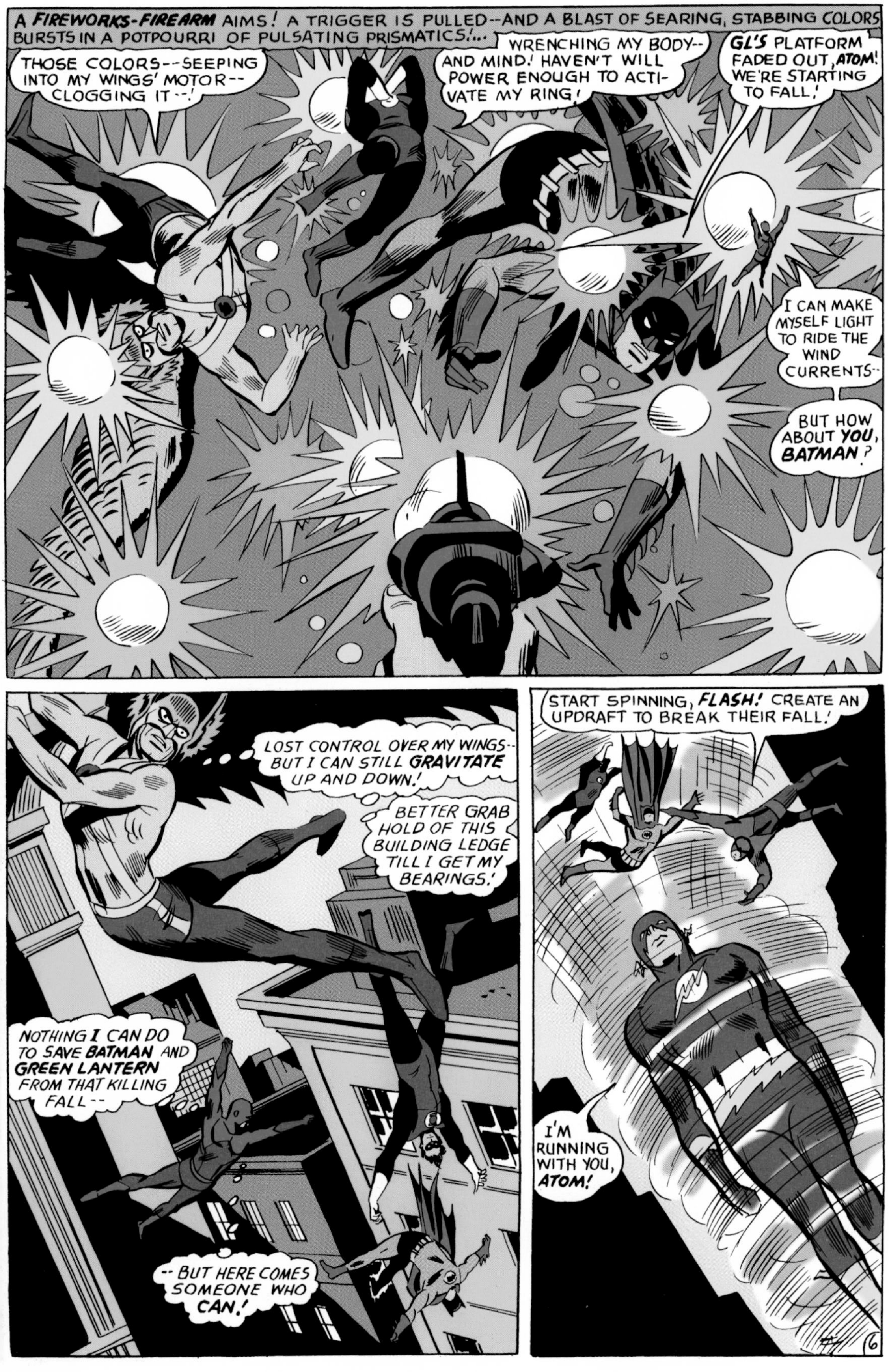
A FIREWORKS-FIREARM AIMS! A TRIGGER IS PULLED--AND A BLAST OF SEARING, STABBING COLORS BURSTS IN A POTPOURRI OF PULSATING PRISMATICS!...
THOSE COLORS--SEEPING INTO MY WINGS' MOTOR--CLOGGING IT--!
WRENCHING MY BODY--AND MIND! HAVEN'T WILL POWER ENOUGH TO ACTIVATE MY RING!
GL'S PLATFORM FADED OUT, ATOM! WE'RE STARTING TO FALL!
I CAN MAKE MYSELF LIGHT TO RIDE THE WIND CURRENTS--
BUT HOW ABOUT YOU, BATMAN?
LOST CONTROL OVER MY WINGS--BUT I CAN STILL GRAVITATE UP AND DOWN!
BETTER GRAB HOLD OF THIS BUILDING LEDGE TILL I GET MY BEARINGS!
NOTHING I CAN DO TO SAVE BATMAN AND GREEN LANTERN FROM THAT KILLING FALL--
--BUT HERE COMES SOMEONE WHO CAN!
START SPINNING, FLASH! CREATE AN UPDRAFT TO BREAK THEIR FALL!
I'M RUNNING WITH YOU, ATOM!
6

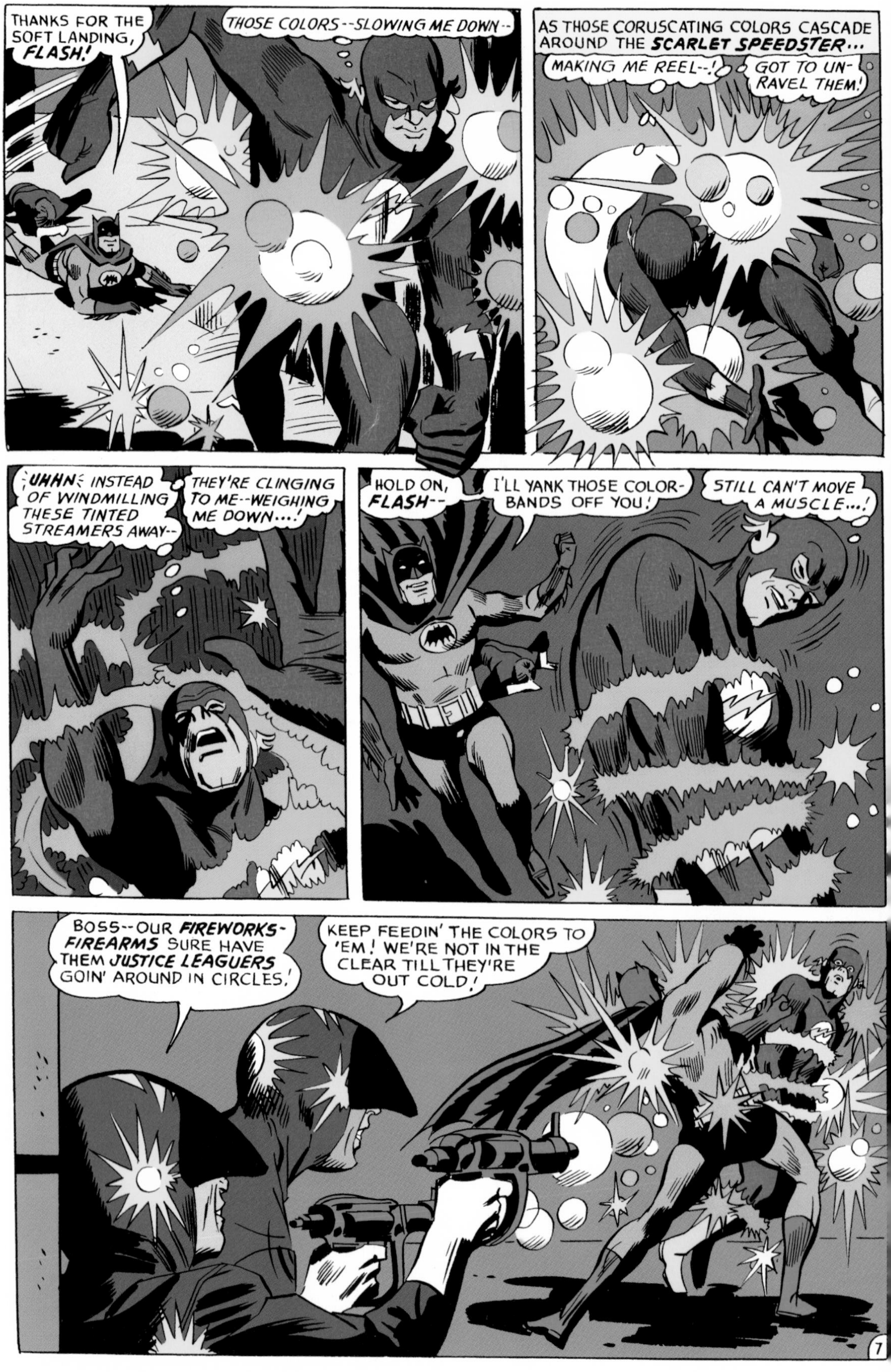
THANKS FOR THE SOFT LANDING, FLASH!
THOSE COLORS--SLOWING ME DOWN--
AS THOSE CORUSCATING COLORS CASCADE AROUND THE SCARLET SPEEDSTER...
MAKING ME REEL--!
GOT TO UN-RAVEL THEM!
UHHN INSTEAD OF WINDMILLING THESE TINTED STREAMERS AWAY--
THEY'RE CLINGING TO ME--WEIGHING ME DOWN...!
HOLD ON, FLASH--
I'LL YANK THOSE COLOR-BANDS OFF YOU!
STILL CAN'T MOVE A MUSCLE...!
BOSS--OUR FIREWORKS-FIREARMS SURE HAVE THEM JUSTICE LEAGUERS GOIN' AROUND IN CIRCLES!
KEEP FEEDIN' THE COLORS TO 'EM! WE'RE NOT IN THE CLEAR TILL THEY'RE OUT COLD!
7

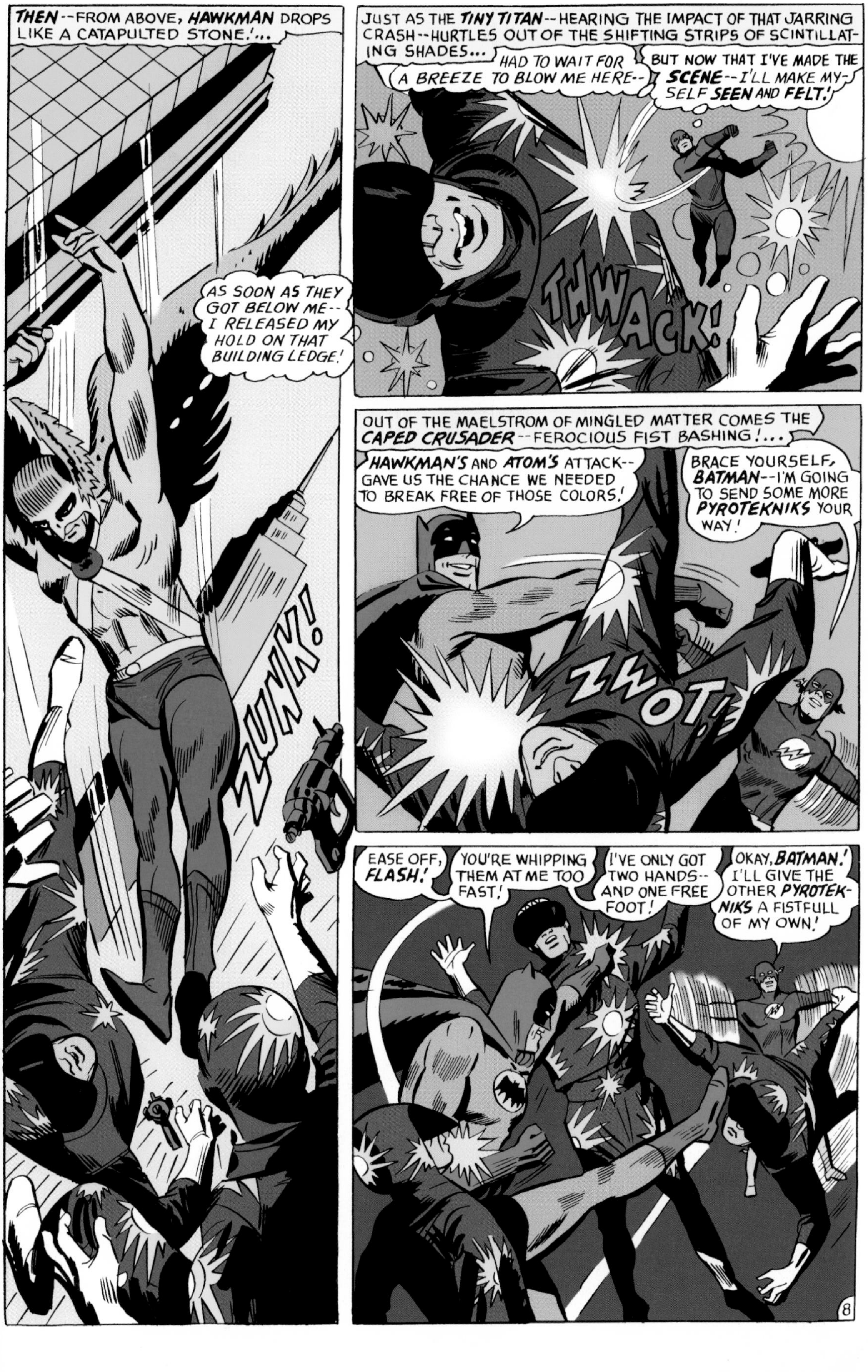
THEN--FROM ABOVE, HAWKMAN DROPS LIKE A CATAPULTED STONE!...
AS SOON AS THEY GOT BELOW ME--I RELEASED MY HOLD ON THAT BUILDING LEDGE!
ZUNK!
JUST AS THE TINY TITAN--HEARING THE IMPACT OF THAT JARRING CRASH--HURTLES OUT OF THE SHIFTING STRIPS OF SCINTILLATING SHADES...
HAD TO WAIT FOR A BREEZE TO BLOW ME HERE--
BUT NOW THAT I'VE MADE THE SCENE--I'LL MAKE MYSELF SEEN AND FELT!
THWACK!
OUT OF THE MAELSTROM OF MINGLED MATTER COMES THE CAPED CRUSADER--FEROCIOUS FIST BASHING!...
HAWKMAN'S AND ATOM'S ATTACK--GAVE US THE CHANCE WE NEEDED TO BREAK FREE OF THOSE COLORS!
BRACE YOURSELF, BATMAN--I'M GOING TO SEND SOME MORE PYROTEKNIKS YOUR WAY!
ZWOT!
EASE OFF, FLASH!
YOU'RE WHIPPING THEM AT ME TOO FAST!
I'VE ONLY GOT TWO HANDS--AND ONE FREE FOOT!
OKAY, BATMAN! I'LL GIVE THE OTHER PYROTEKNIKS A FISTFULL OF MY OWN!
8

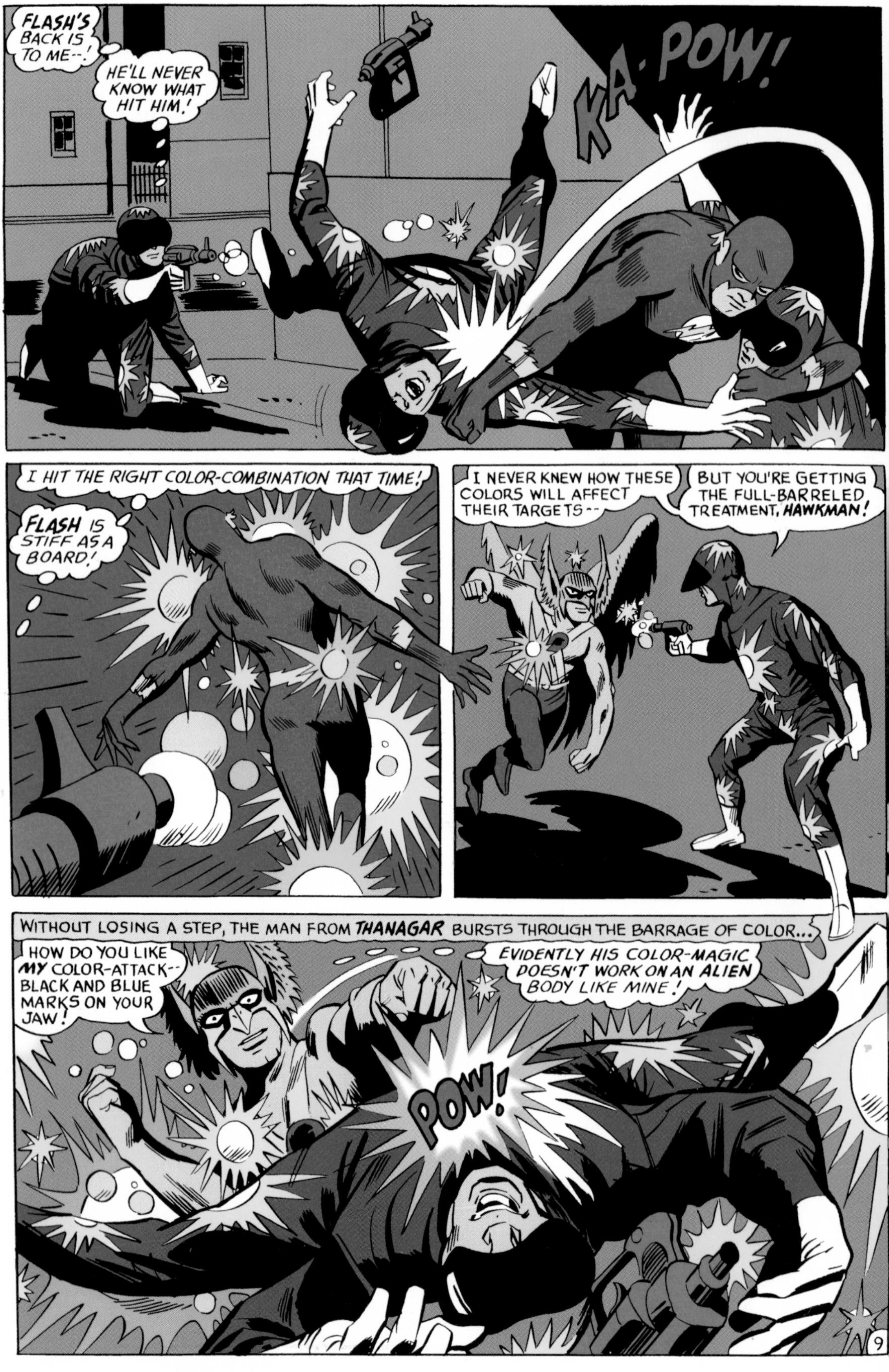
FLASH'S BACK IS TO ME--!
HE'LL NEVER KNOW WHAT HIT HIM!
KA-POW!
I HIT THE RIGHT COLOR-COMBINATION THAT TIME!
FLASH IS STIFF AS A BOARD!
I NEVER KNEW HOW THESE COLORS WILL AFFECT THEIR TARGETS--
BUT YOU'RE GETTING THE FULL-BARRELED TREATMENT, HAWKMAN!
WITHOUT LOSING A STEP, THE MAN FROM THANAGAR BURSTS THROUGH THE BARRAGE OF COLOR...
HOW DO YOU LIKE MY COLOR-ATTACK-- BLACK AND BLUE MARKS ON YOUR JAW!
EVIDENTLY HIS COLOR-MAGIC DOESN'T WORK ON AN ALIEN BODY LIKE MINE!
POW!
9

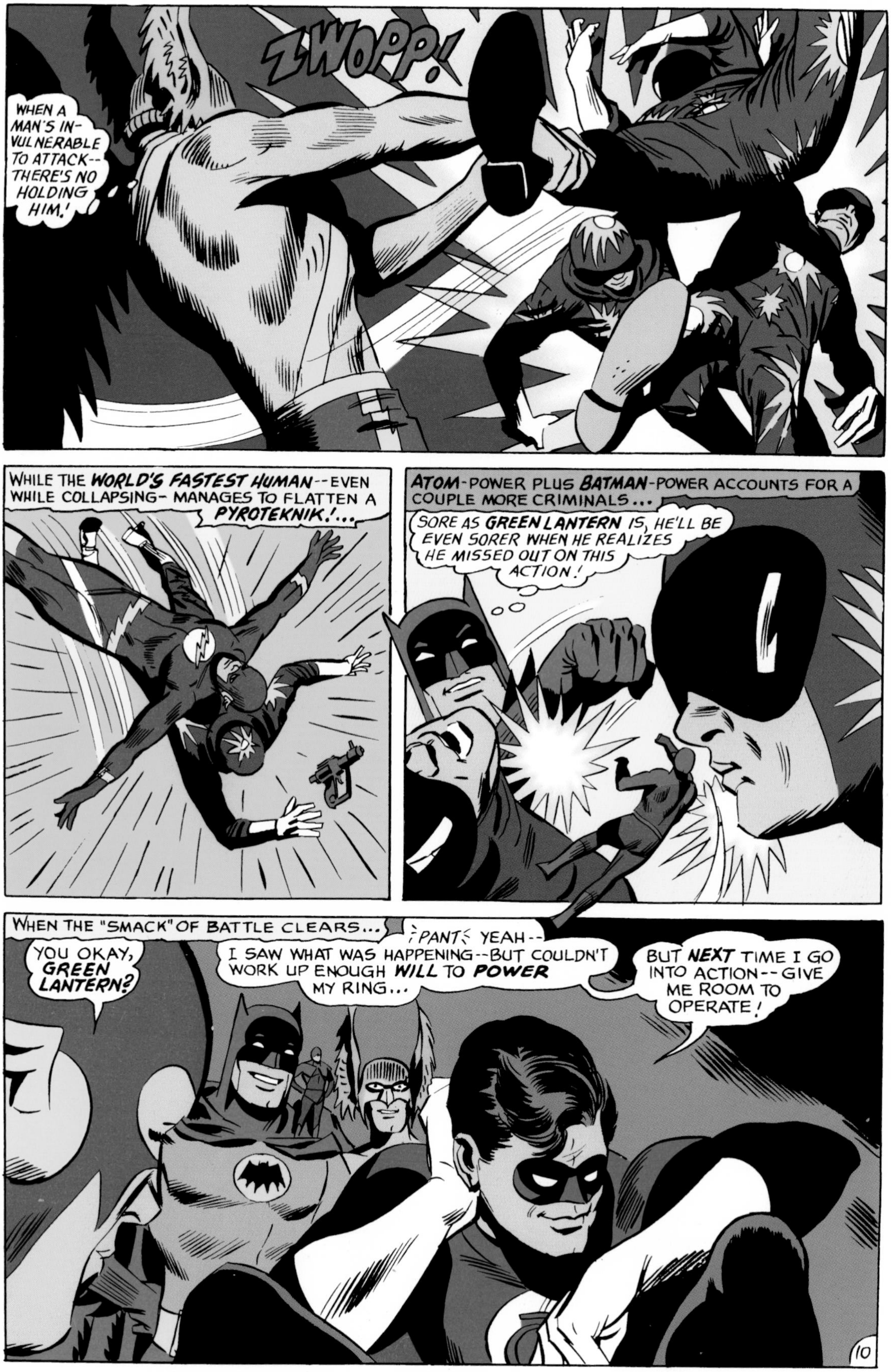
ZWOPP!
WHEN A MAN'S INVULNERABLE TO ATTACK--THERE'S NO HOLDING HIM!
WHILE THE WORLD'S FASTEST HUMAN--EVEN WHILE COLLAPSING- MANAGES TO FLATTEN A PYROTEKNIK!...
ATOM-POWER PLUS BATMAN-POWER ACCOUNTS FOR A COUPLE MORE CRIMINALS...
SORE AS GREEN LANTERN IS, HE'LL BE EVEN SORER WHEN HE REALIZES HE MISSED OUT ON THIS ACTION!
WHEN THE "SMACK" OF BATTLE CLEARS...
YOU OKAY, GREEN LANTERN?
PANT YEAH--
I SAW WHAT WAS HAPPENING--BUT COULDN'T WORK UP ENOUGH WILL TO POWER MY RING...
BUT NEXT TIME I GO INTO ACTION--GIVE ME ROOM TO OPERATE!
10

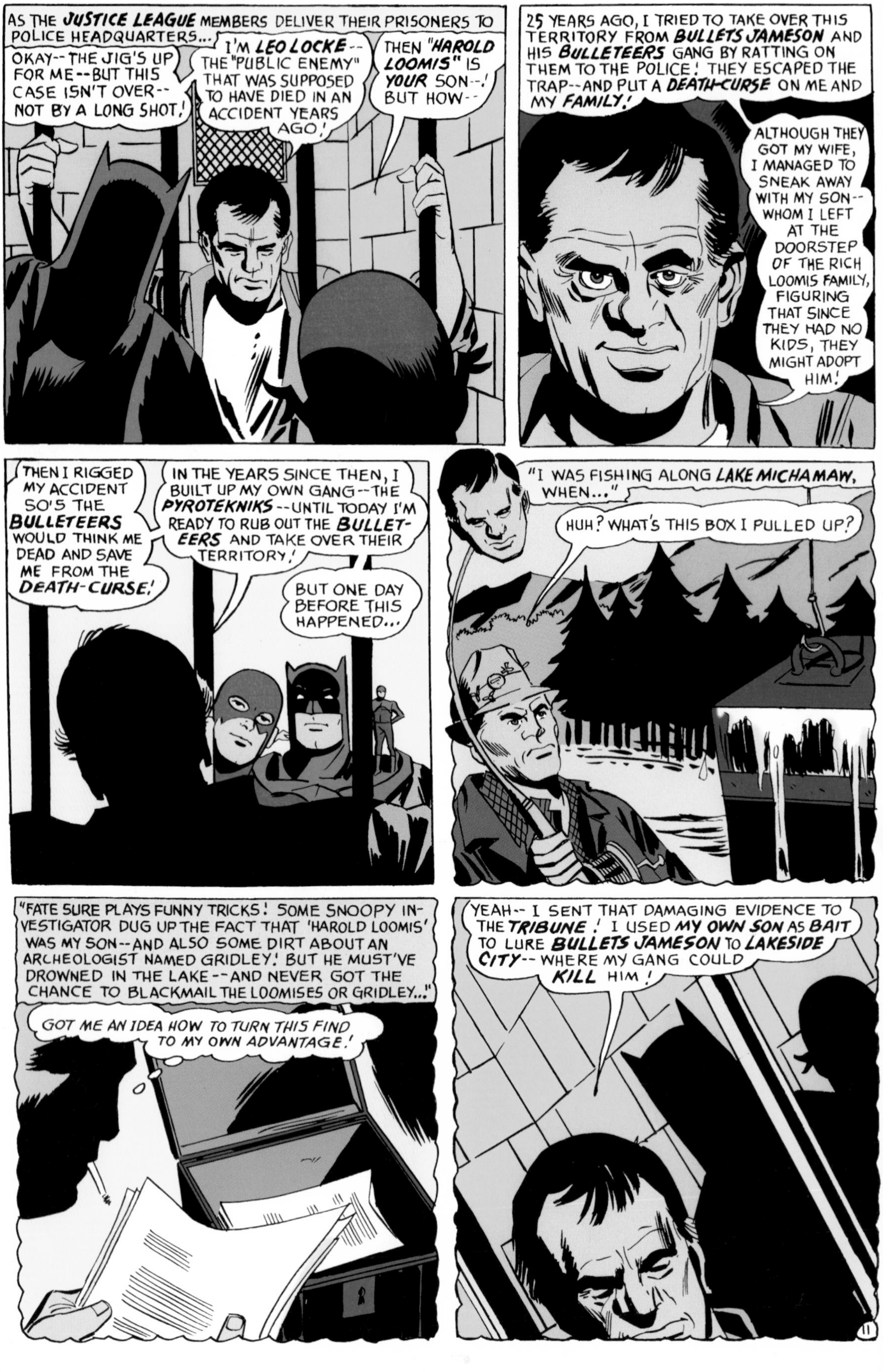
AS THE JUSTICE LEAGUE MEMBERS DELIVER THEIR PRISONERS TO POLICE HEADQUARTERS...
OKAY-- THE JIG'S UP FOR ME--BUT THIS CASE ISN'T OVER-- NOT BY A LONG SHOT!
I'M LEO LOCKE-- THE "PUBLIC ENEMY" THAT WAS SUPPOSED TO HAVE DIED IN AN ACCIDENT YEARS AGO!
THEN "HAROLD LOOMIS" IS YOUR SON--! BUT HOW--
25 YEARS AGO, I TRIED TO TAKE OVER THIS TERRITORY FROM BULLETS JAMESON AND HIS BULLETEERS GANG BY RATTING ON THEM TO THE POLICE! THEY ESCAPED THE TRAP--AND PUT A DEATH-CURSE ON ME AND MY FAMILY!
ALTHOUGH THEY GOT MY WIFE, I MANAGED TO SNEAK AWAY WITH MY SON-- WHOM I LEFT AT THE DOORSTEP OF THE RICH LOOMIS FAMILY, FIGURING THAT SINCE THEY HAD NO KIDS, THEY MIGHT ADOPT HIM!
THEN I RIGGED MY ACCIDENT SO'S THE BULLETEERS WOULD THINK ME DEAD AND SAVE ME FROM THE DEATH-CURSE!
IN THE YEARS SINCE THEN, I BUILT UP MY OWN GANG--THE PYROTEKNIKS--UNTIL TODAY I'M READY TO RUB OUT THE BULLETEERS AND TAKE OVER THEIR TERRITORY!
BUT ONE DAY BEFORE THIS HAPPENED...
"I WAS FISHING ALONG LAKE MICHAMAW, WHEN..."
HUH? WHAT'S THIS BOX I PULLED UP?
"FATE SURE PLAYS FUNNY TRICKS! SOME SNOOPY INVESTIGATOR DUG UP THE FACT THAT 'HAROLD LOOMIS' WAS MY SON--AND ALSO SOME DIRT ABOUT AN ARCHEOLOGIST NAMED GRIDLEY! BUT HE MUST'VE DROWNED IN THE LAKE--AND NEVER GOT THE CHANCE TO BLACKMAIL THE LOOMISES OR GRIDLEY..."
GOT ME AN IDEA HOW TO TURN THIS FIND TO MY OWN ADVANTAGE!
YEAH-- I SENT THAT DAMAGING EVIDENCE TO THE TRIBUNE! I USED MY OWN SON AS BAIT TO LURE BULLETS JAMESON TO LAKESIDE CITY-- WHERE MY GANG COULD KILL HIM!
11

A BROKEN MAN PLEADS HARSHLY--HIS VOICE RACKED BY SOBS--FOR THE LIFE OF THE SON HE ABANDONED...
PLEASE--YOU GOTTA SAVE HIM FROM THE BULLETEERS!
YOU ARRESTED ME AND MY GANG--SO I CAN'T PROTECT HIM THE WAY I INTENDED!
YOU CAN'T LET HIM DIE FOR SOMETHING I DID!
TO KEEP MY GANG IN LINE, WE PULLED OFF ROBBERIES IN LAKESIDE CITY--BUT HOW'D I KNOW YOU GUYS WOULD SHOW UP HERE TO STOP ME?
PLEASE--YOU GOTTA SAVE MY BOY!
OR ELSE I'LL BE THE MAN WHO MURDERED HIS OWN SON!
CAN THE JUSTICE LEAGUE OF AMERICA TURN DOWN SUCH A PLEA--STRAIGHT FROM THE HEART OF A SOBBING FATHER? EVEN THOUGH THE MAN WHO MAKES THAT PLEA IS A HARDENED CRIMINAL? STORY CONTINUES ON NEXT PAGE FOLLOWING!
12

JUSTICE LEAGUE of AMERICA

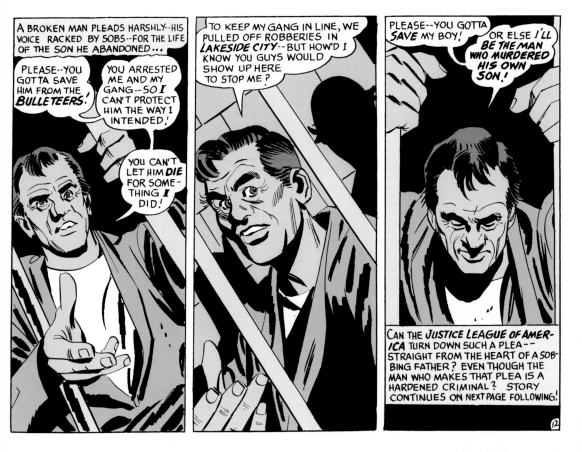

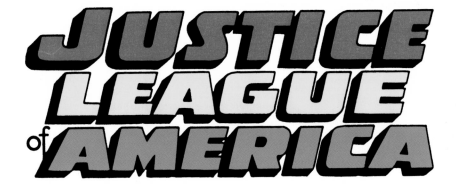

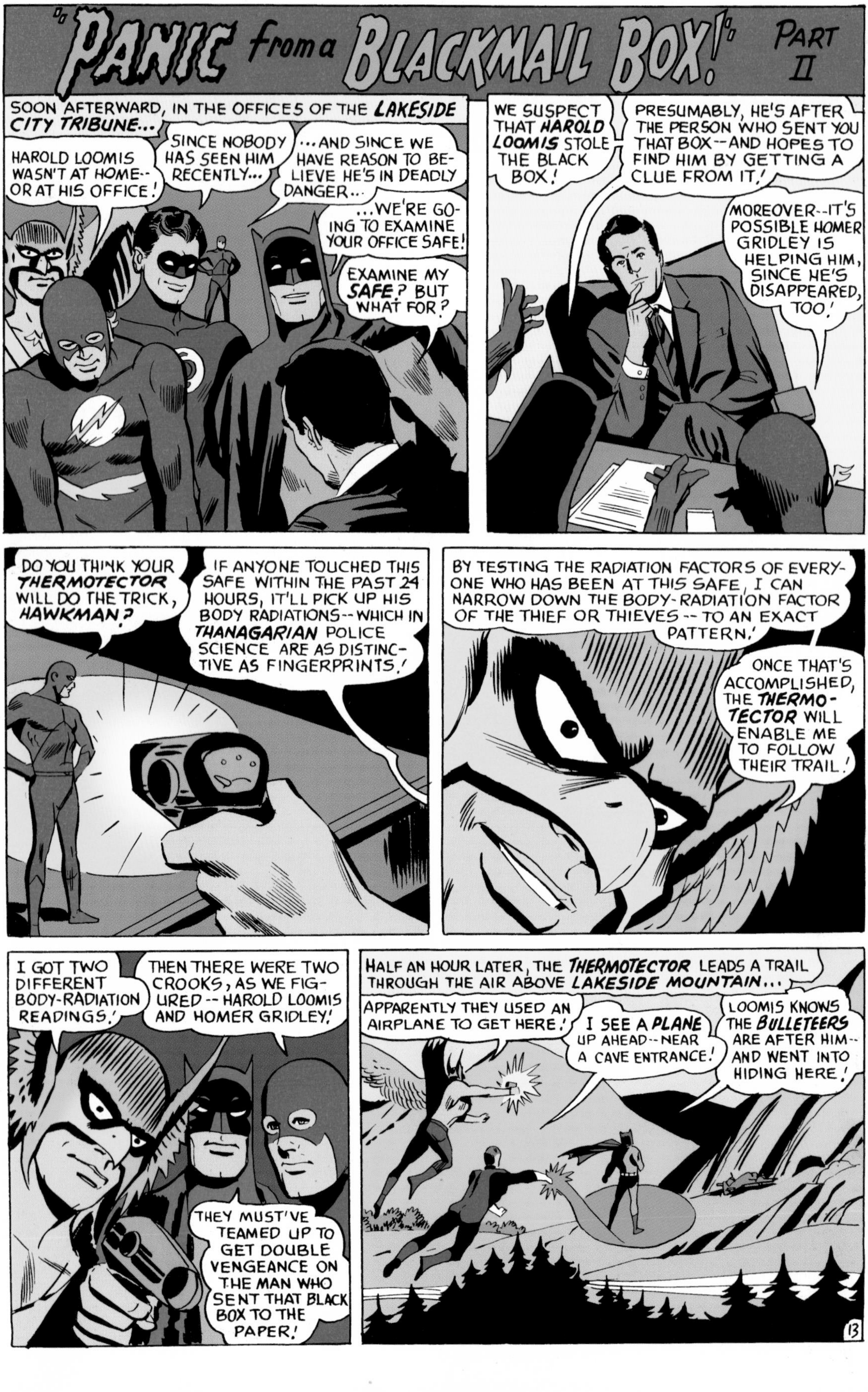
"PANIC from a BLACKMAIL BOX!" PART II
SOON AFTERWARD, IN THE OFFICES OF THE LAKESIDE CITY TRIBUNE...
HAROLD LOOMIS WASN'T AT HOME-- OR AT HIS OFFICE!
SINCE NOBODY HAS SEEN HIM RECENTLY...
...AND SINCE WE HAVE REASON TO BELIEVE HE'S IN DEADLY DANGER...
...WE'RE GOING TO EXAMINE YOUR OFFICE SAFE!
EXAMINE MY SAFE? BUT WHAT FOR?
WE SUSPECT THAT HAROLD LOOMIS STOLE THE BLACK BOX!
PRESUMABLY, HE'S AFTER THE PERSON WHO SENT YOU THAT BOX--AND HOPES TO FIND HIM BY GETTING A CLUE FROM IT!
MOREOVER--IT'S POSSIBLE HOMER GRIDLEY IS HELPING HIM, SINCE HE'S DISAPPEARED, TOO!
DO YOU THINK YOUR THERMOTECTOR WILL DO THE TRICK, HAWKMAN?
IF ANYONE TOUCHED THIS SAFE WITHIN THE PAST 24 HOURS, IT'LL PICK UP HIS BODY RADIATIONS--WHICH IN THANAGARIAN POLICE SCIENCE ARE AS DISTINCTIVE AS FINGERPRINTS!
BY TESTING THE RADIATION FACTORS OF EVERYONE WHO HAS BEEN AT THIS SAFE, I CAN NARROW DOWN THE BODY-RADIATION FACTOR OF THE THIEF OR THIEVES -- TO AN EXACT PATTERN!
ONCE THAT'S ACCOMPLISHED, THE THERMOTECTOR WILL ENABLE ME TO FOLLOW THEIR TRAIL!
I GOT TWO DIFFERENT BODY-RADIATION READINGS!
THEN THERE WERE TWO CROOKS, AS WE FIGURED -- HAROLD LOOMIS AND HOMER GRIDLEY!
THEY MUST'VE TEAMED UP TO GET DOUBLE VENGEANCE ON THE MAN WHO SENT THAT BLACK BOX TO THE PAPER!
HALF AN HOUR LATER, THE THERMOTECTOR LEADS A TRAIL THROUGH THE AIR ABOVE LAKESIDE MOUNTAIN...
APPARENTLY THEY USED AN AIRPLANE TO GET HERE!
I SEE A PLANE UP AHEAD--NEAR A CAVE ENTRANCE!
LOOMIS KNOWS THE BULLETEERS ARE AFTER HIM--AND WENT INTO HIDING HERE!
13

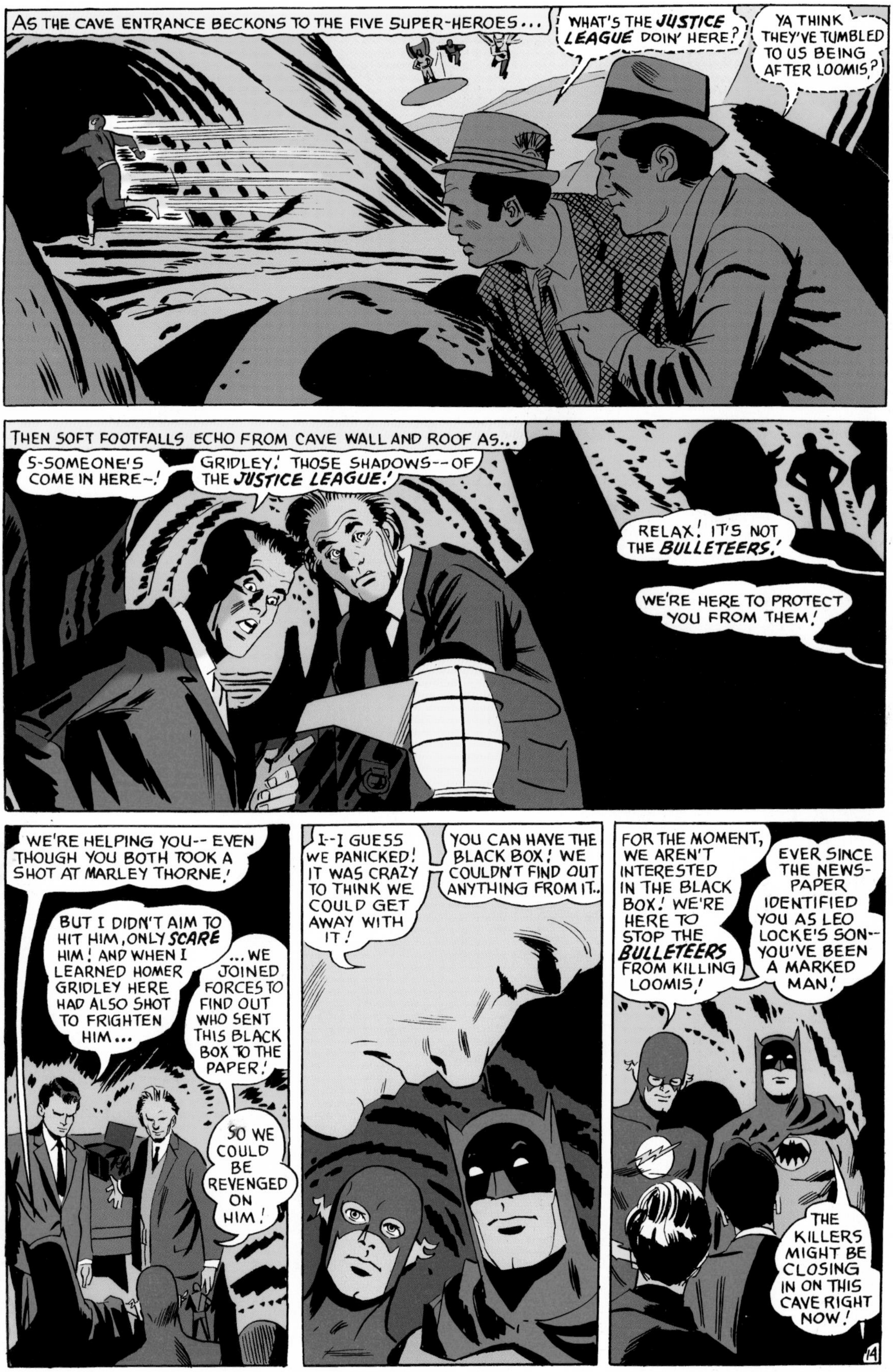
AS THE CAVE ENTRANCE BECKONS TO THE FIVE SUPER-HEROES...
WHAT'S THE JUSTICE LEAGUE DOIN' HERE?
YA THINK THEY'VE TUMBLED TO US BEING AFTER LOOMIS?
THEN SOFT FOOTFALLS ECHO FROM CAVE WALL AND ROOF AS...
S-SOMEONE'S COME IN HERE--!
GRIDLEY! THOSE SHADOWS--OF THE JUSTICE LEAGUE!
RELAX! IT'S NOT THE BULLETEERS!
WE'RE HERE TO PROTECT YOU FROM THEM!
WE'RE HELPING YOU-- EVEN THOUGH YOU BOTH TOOK A SHOT AT MARLEY THORNE!
BUT I DIDN'T AIM TO HIT HIM, ONLY SCARE HIM! AND WHEN I LEARNED HOMER GRIDLEY HERE HAD ALSO SHOT TO FRIGHTEN HIM...
...WE JOINED FORCES TO FIND OUT WHO SENT THIS BLACK BOX TO THE PAPER!
SO WE COULD BE REVENGED ON HIM!
I--I GUESS WE PANICKED! IT WAS CRAZY TO THINK WE COULD GET AWAY WITH IT!
YOU CAN HAVE THE BLACK BOX! WE COULDN'T FIND OUT ANYTHING FROM IT..
FOR THE MOMENT, WE AREN'T INTERESTED IN THE BLACK BOX! WE'RE HERE TO STOP THE BULLETEERS FROM KILLING LOOMIS!
EVER SINCE THE NEWS-PAPER IDENTIFIED YOU AS LEO LOCKE'S SON--YOU'VE BEEN A MARKED MAN!
THE KILLERS MIGHT BE CLOSING IN ON THIS CAVE RIGHT NOW!
14

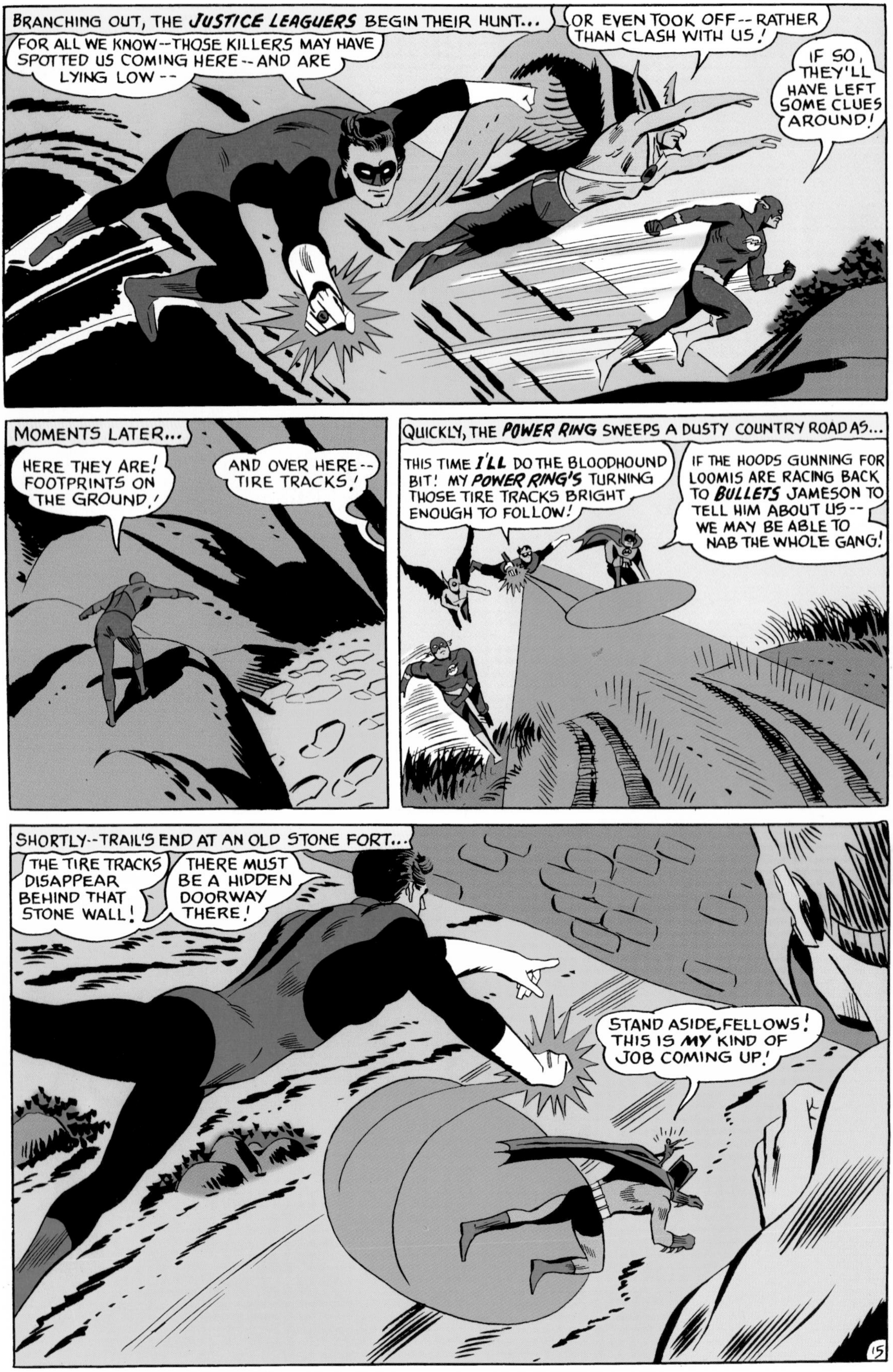
BRANCHING OUT, THE JUSTICE LEAGUERS BEGIN THEIR HUNT...
FOR ALL WE KNOW--THOSE KILLERS MAY HAVE SPOTTED US COMING HERE--AND ARE LYING LOW--
OR EVEN TOOK OFF--RATHER THAN CLASH WITH US!
IF SO, THEY'LL HAVE LEFT SOME CLUES AROUND!
MOMENTS LATER...
HERE THEY ARE! FOOTPRINTS ON THE GROUND!
AND OVER HERE--TIRE TRACKS!
QUICKLY, THE POWER RING SWEEPS A DUSTY COUNTRY ROAD AS...
THIS TIME I'LL DO THE BLOODHOUND BIT! MY POWER RING'S TURNING THOSE TIRE TRACKS BRIGHT ENOUGH TO FOLLOW!
IF THE HOODS GUNNING FOR LOOMIS ARE RACING BACK TO BULLETS JAMESON TO TELL HIM ABOUT US--WE MAY BE ABLE TO NAB THE WHOLE GANG!
SHORTLY--TRAIL'S END AT AN OLD STONE FORT...
THE TIRE TRACKS DISAPPEAR BEHIND THAT STONE WALL!
THERE MUST BE A HIDDEN DOORWAY THERE!
STAND ASIDE, FELLOWS! THIS IS MY KIND OF JOB COMING UP!
15

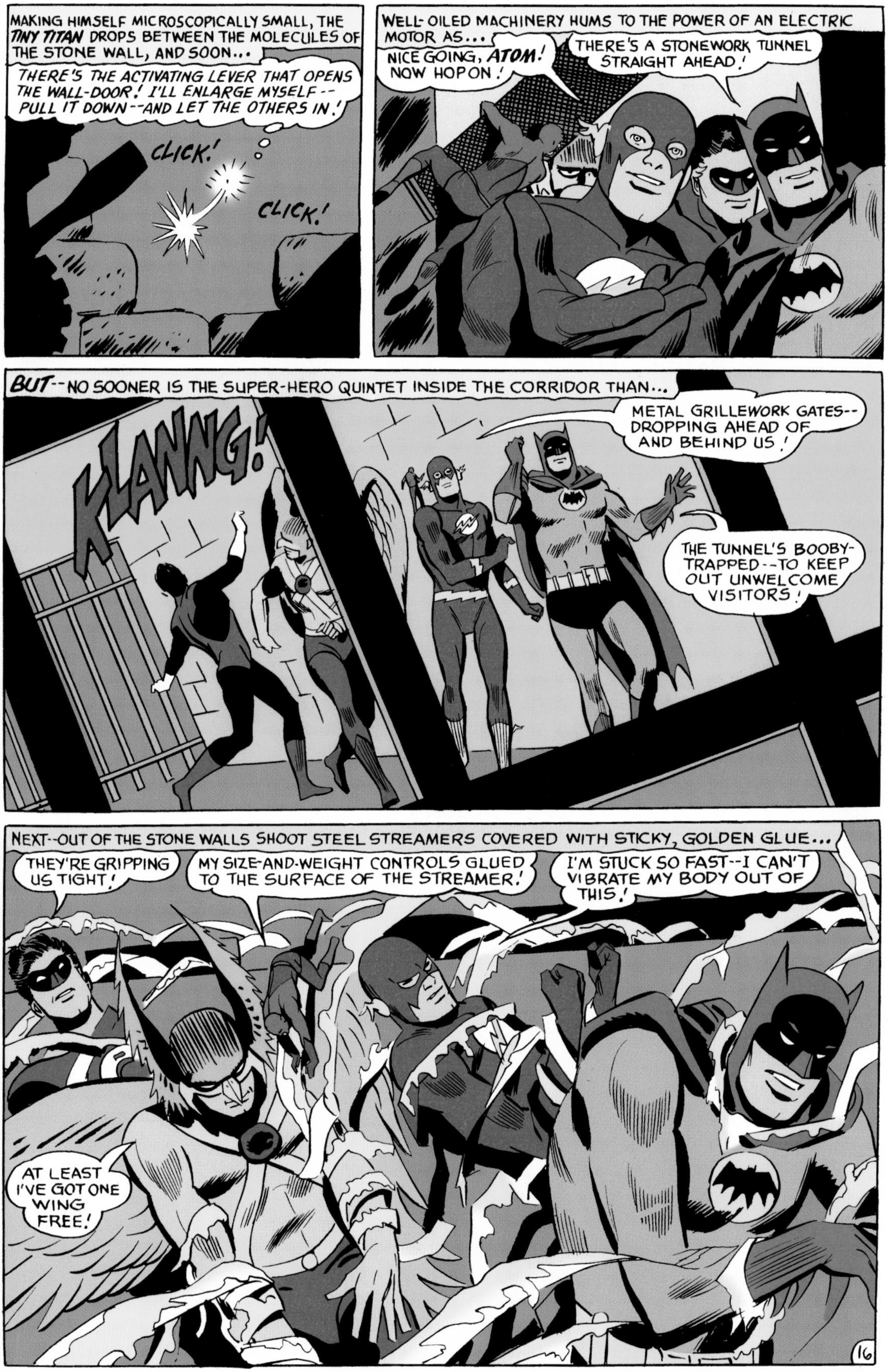
MAKING HIMSELF MICROSCOPICALLY SMALL, THE TINY TITAN DROPS BETWEEN THE MOLECULES OF THE STONE WALL, AND SOON...
THERE'S THE ACTIVATING LEVER THAT OPENS THE WALL-DOOR! I'LL ENLARGE MYSELF -- PULL IT DOWN -- AND LET THE OTHERS IN!
CLICK!
CLICK!
WELL-OILED MACHINERY HUMS TO THE POWER OF AN ELECTRIC MOTOR AS...
NICE GOING, ATOM! NOW HOP ON!
THERE'S A STONEWORK TUNNEL STRAIGHT AHEAD!
BUT -- NO SOONER IS THE SUPER-HERO QUINTET INSIDE THE CORRIDOR THAN...
KLANNG!
METAL GRILLEWORK GATES -- DROPPING AHEAD OF AND BEHIND US!
THE TUNNEL'S BOOBY-TRAPPED -- TO KEEP OUT UNWELCOME VISITORS!
NEXT -- OUT OF THE STONE WALLS SHOOT STEEL STREAMERS COVERED WITH STICKY, GOLDEN GLUE...
THEY'RE GRIPPING US TIGHT!
MY SIZE-AND-WEIGHT CONTROLS GLUED TO THE SURFACE OF THE STREAMER!
I'M STUCK SO FAST -- I CAN'T VIBRATE MY BODY OUT OF THIS!
AT LEAST I'VE GOT ONE WING FREE!
16

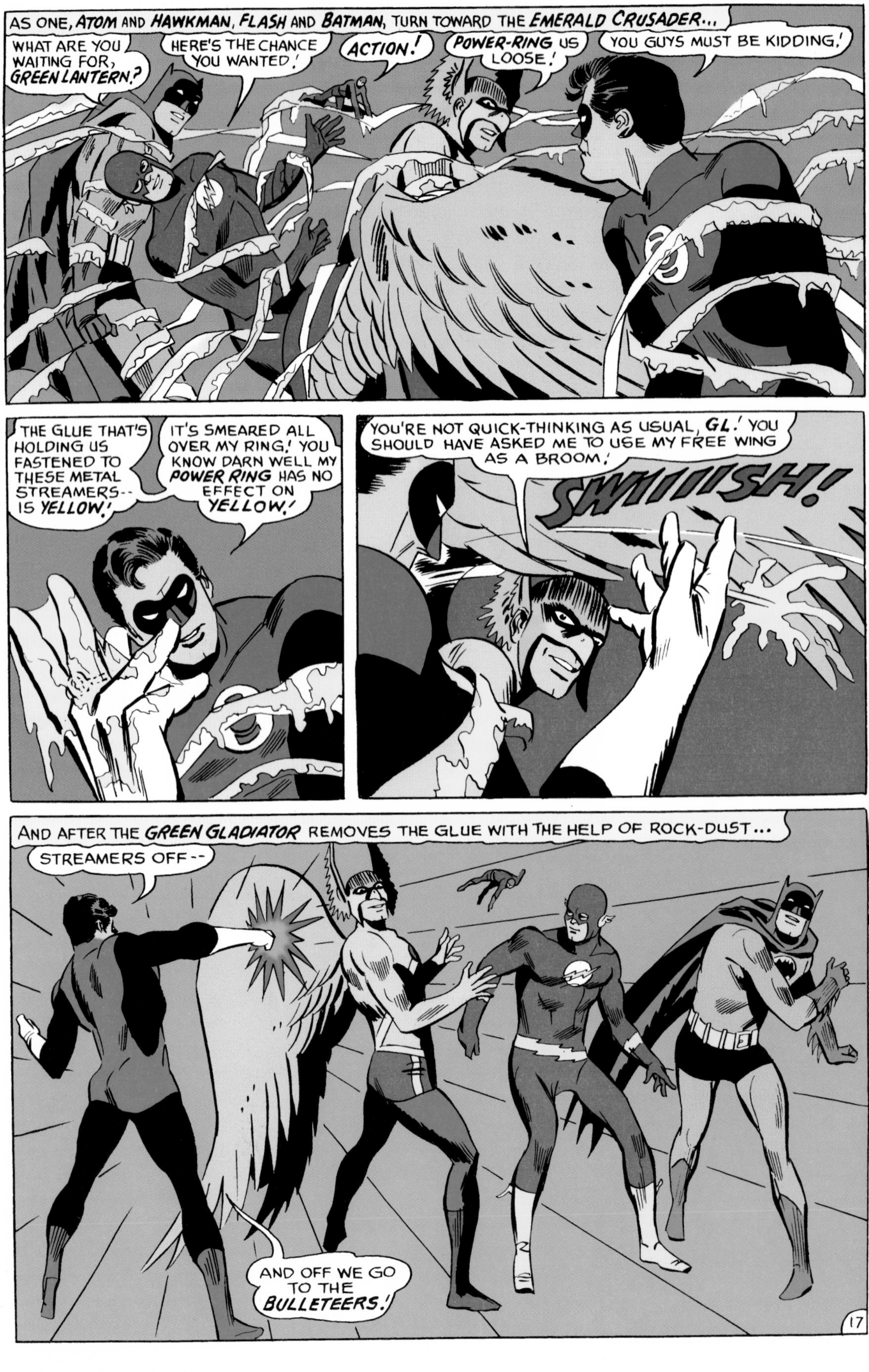
AS ONE, ATOM AND HAWKMAN, FLASH AND BATMAN, TURN TOWARD THE EMERALD CRUSADER...
WHAT ARE YOU WAITING FOR, GREEN LANTERN?
HERE'S THE CHANCE YOU WANTED!
ACTION!
POWER-RING US LOOSE!
YOU GUYS MUST BE KIDDING!
THE GLUE THAT'S HOLDING US FASTENED TO THESE METAL STREAMERS-- IS YELLOW!
IT'S SMEARED ALL OVER MY RING! YOU KNOW DARN WELL MY POWER RING HAS NO EFFECT ON YELLOW!
YOU'RE NOT QUICK-THINKING AS USUAL, GL! YOU SHOULD HAVE ASKED ME TO USE MY FREE WING AS A BROOM!
SWIIIISH!
AND AFTER THE GREEN GLADIATOR REMOVES THE GLUE WITH THE HELP OF ROCK-DUST...
STREAMERS OFF--
AND OFF WE GO TO THE BULLETEERS!
17

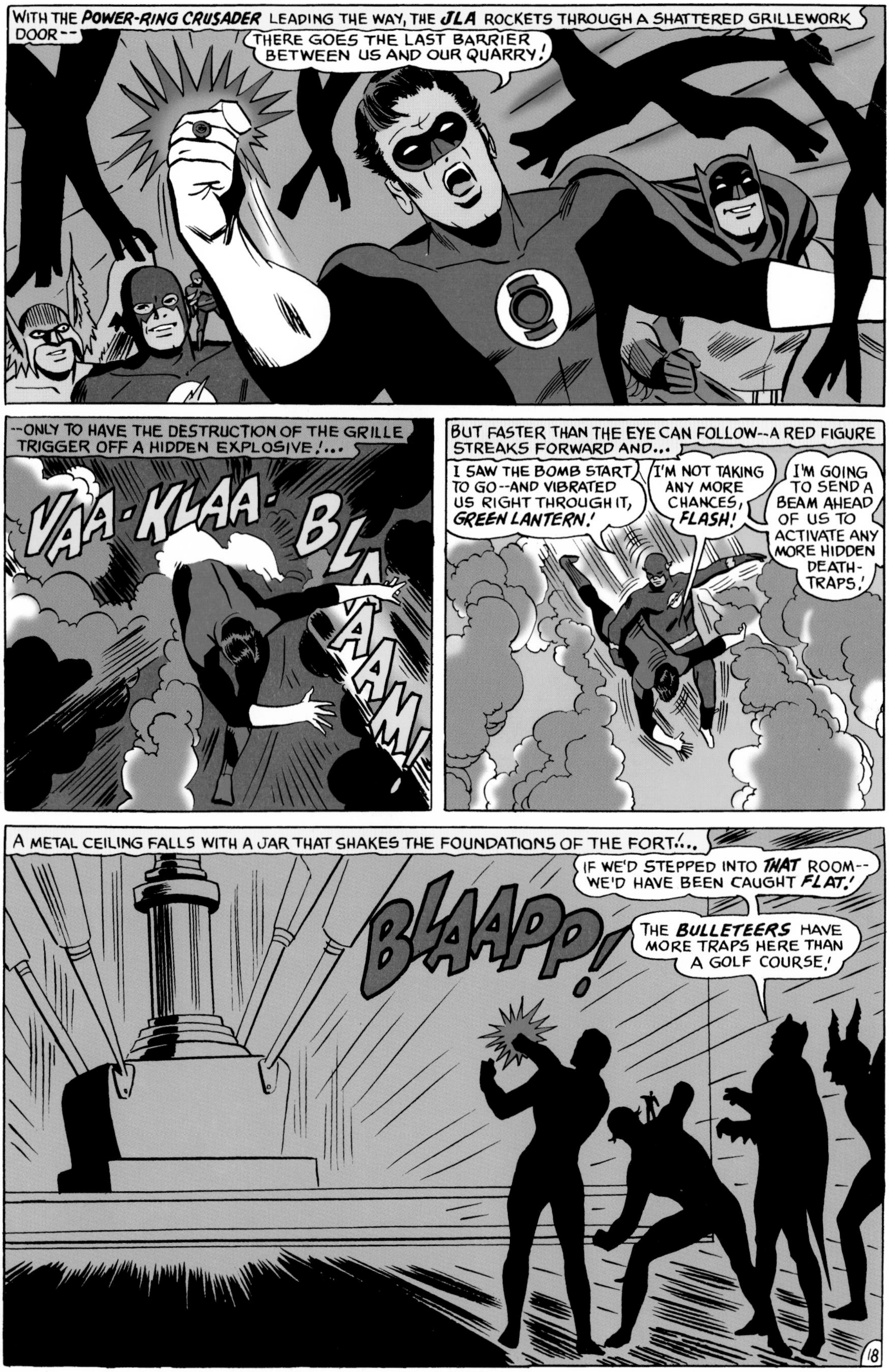
WITH THE POWER-RING CRUSADER LEADING THE WAY, THE JLA ROCKETS THROUGH A SHATTERED GRILLEWORK DOOR--
THERE GOES THE LAST BARRIER BETWEEN US AND OUR QUARRY!
--ONLY TO HAVE THE DESTRUCTION OF THE GRILLE TRIGGER OFF A HIDDEN EXPLOSIVE!...
VAA-KLAA-BLAAAM!
BUT FASTER THAN THE EYE CAN FOLLOW--A RED FIGURE STREAKS FORWARD AND...
I SAW THE BOMB START TO GO--AND VIBRATED US RIGHT THROUGH IT, GREEN LANTERN!
I'M NOT TAKING ANY MORE CHANCES, FLASH!
I'M GOING TO SEND A BEAM AHEAD OF US TO ACTIVATE ANY MORE HIDDEN DEATH-TRAPS!
A METAL CEILING FALLS WITH A JAR THAT SHAKES THE FOUNDATIONS OF THE FORT!...
BLAAPP!
IF WE'D STEPPED INTO THAT ROOM--WE'D HAVE BEEN CAUGHT FLAT!
THE BULLETEERS HAVE MORE TRAPS HERE THAN A GOLF COURSE!
18

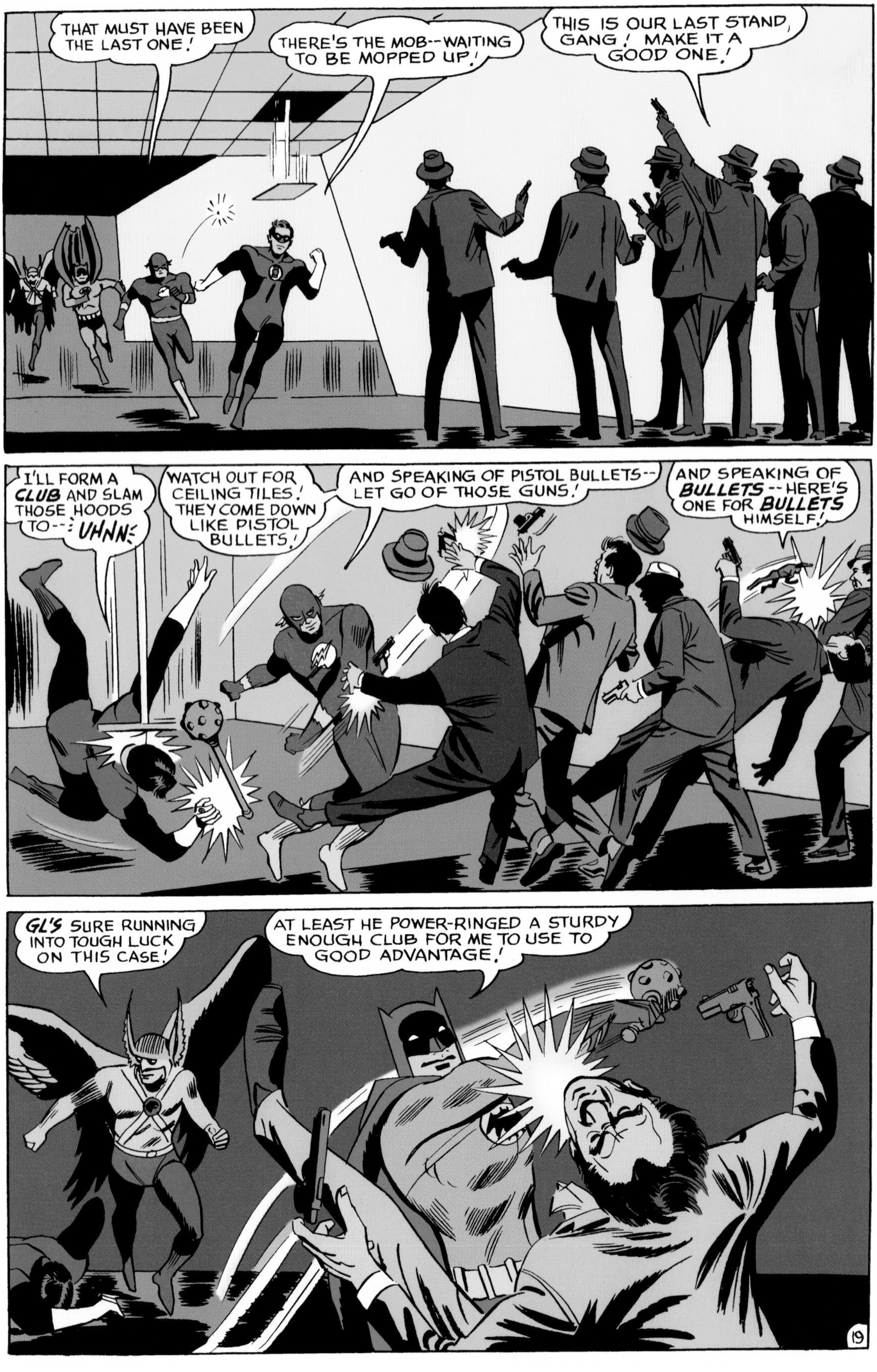
THAT MUST HAVE BEEN THE LAST ONE!
THERE'S THE MOB--WAITING TO BE MOPPED UP!
THIS IS OUR LAST STAND, GANG! MAKE IT A GOOD ONE!
I'LL FORM A CLUB AND SLAM THOSE HOODS TO-- UHNN
WATCH OUT FOR CEILING TILES! THEY COME DOWN LIKE PISTOL BULLETS!
AND SPEAKING OF PISTOL BULLETS-- LET GO OF THOSE GUNS!
AND SPEAKING OF BULLETS--HERE'S ONE FOR BULLETS HIMSELF!
GL'S SURE RUNNING INTO TOUGH LUCK ON THIS CASE!
AT LEAST HE POWER-RINGED A STURDY ENOUGH CLUB FOR ME TO USE TO GOOD ADVANTAGE!
19

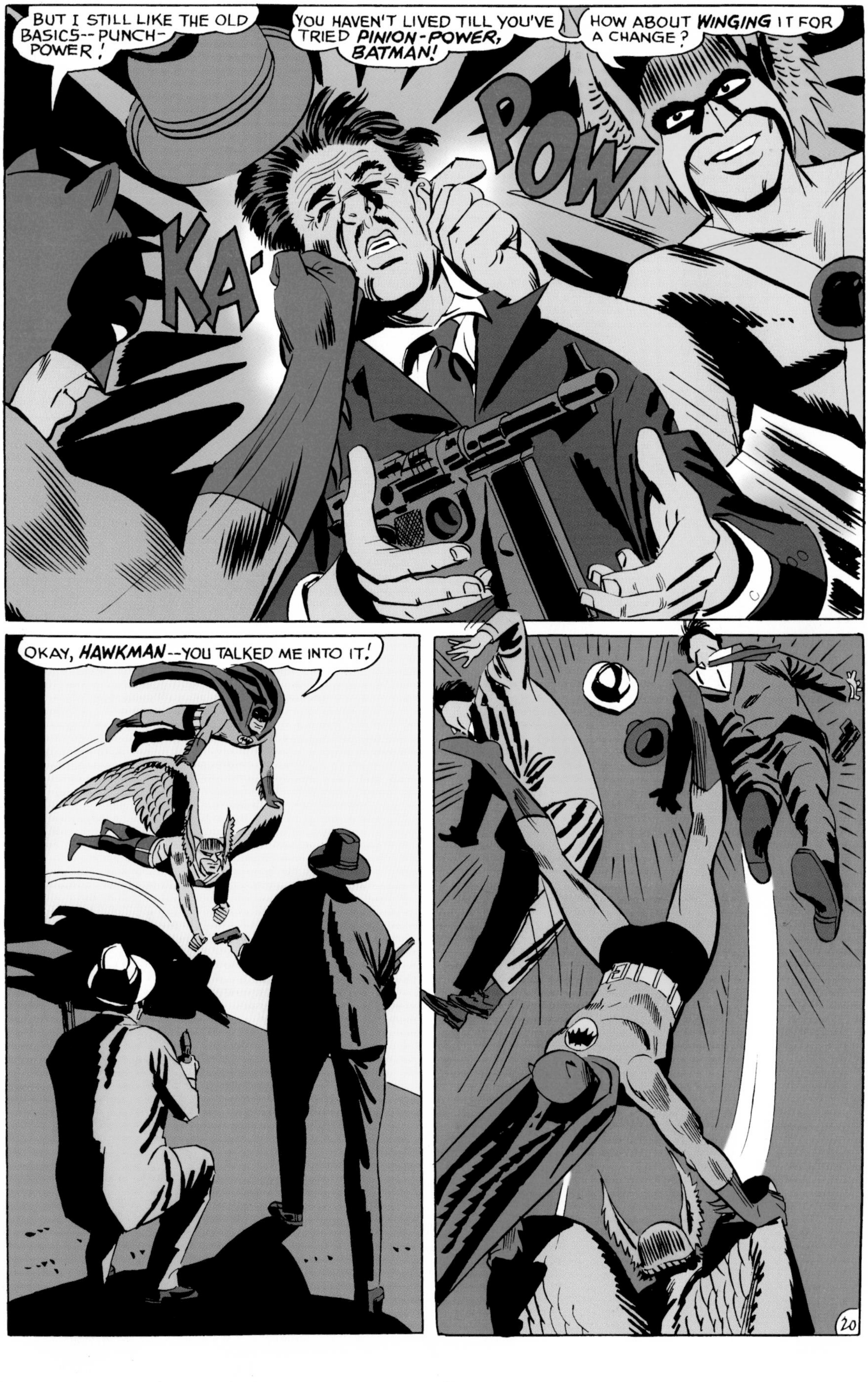
BUT I STILL LIKE THE OLD BASICS--PUNCH-POWER!
YOU HAVEN'T LIVED TILL YOU'VE TRIED PINION-POWER, BATMAN!
HOW ABOUT WINGING IT FOR A CHANGE?
KA-
POW
OKAY, HAWKMAN--YOU TALKED ME INTO IT!
20

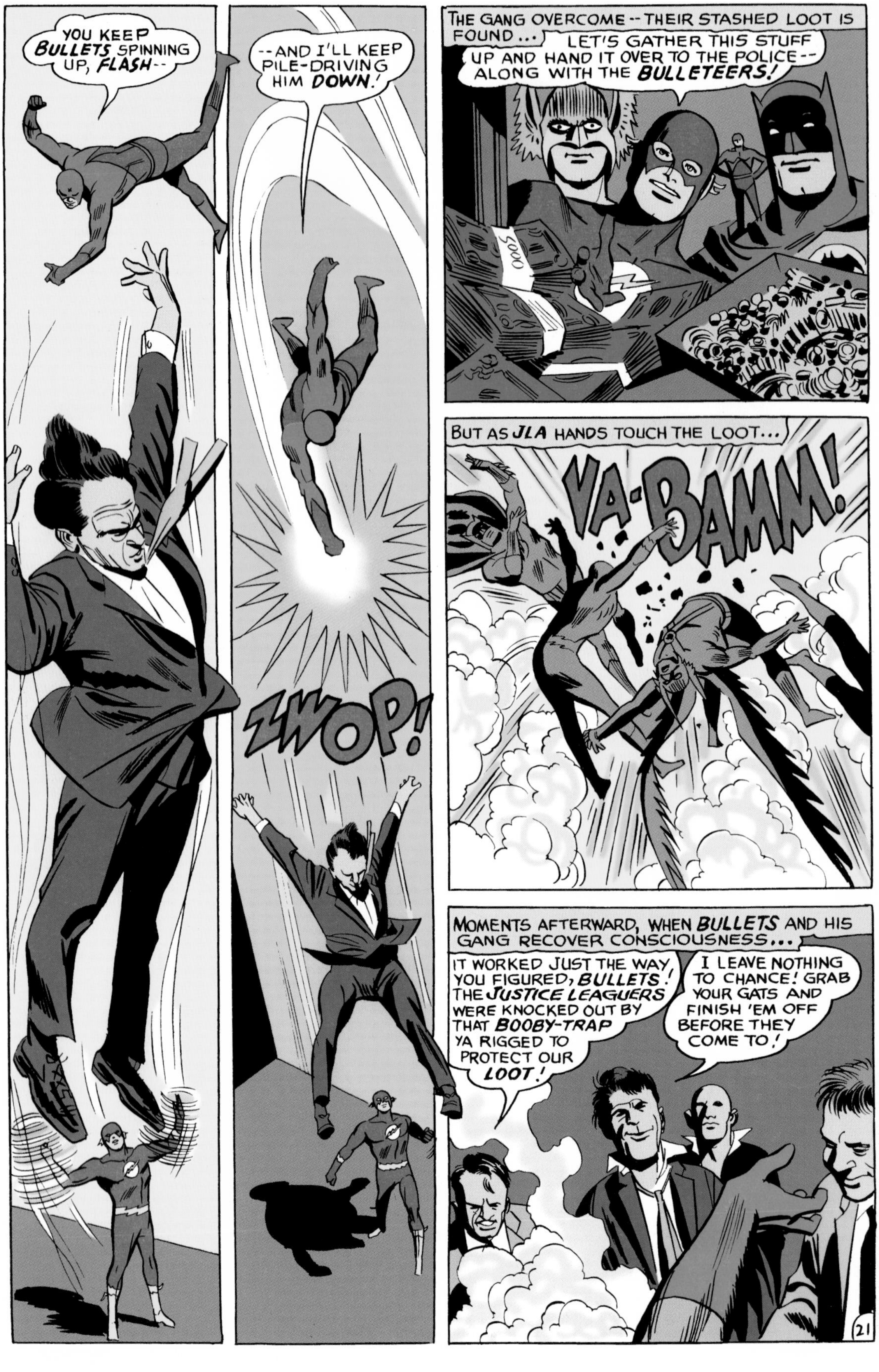
YOU KEEP BULLETS SPINNING UP, FLASH--
--AND I'LL KEEP PILE-DRIVING HIM DOWN!
ZWOP!
THE GANG OVERCOME -- THEIR STASHED LOOT IS FOUND...
LET'S GATHER THIS STUFF UP AND HAND IT OVER TO THE POLICE -- ALONG WITH THE BULLETEERS!
5000
BUT AS JLA HANDS TOUCH THE LOOT...
VA-BAMM!
MOMENTS AFTERWARD, WHEN BULLETS AND HIS GANG RECOVER CONSCIOUSNESS...
IT WORKED JUST THE WAY YOU FIGURED, BULLETS! THE JUSTICE LEAGUERS WERE KNOCKED OUT BY THAT BOOBY-TRAP YA RIGGED TO PROTECT OUR LOOT!
I LEAVE NOTHING TO CHANCE! GRAB YOUR GATS AND FINISH 'EM OFF BEFORE THEY COME TO!
21

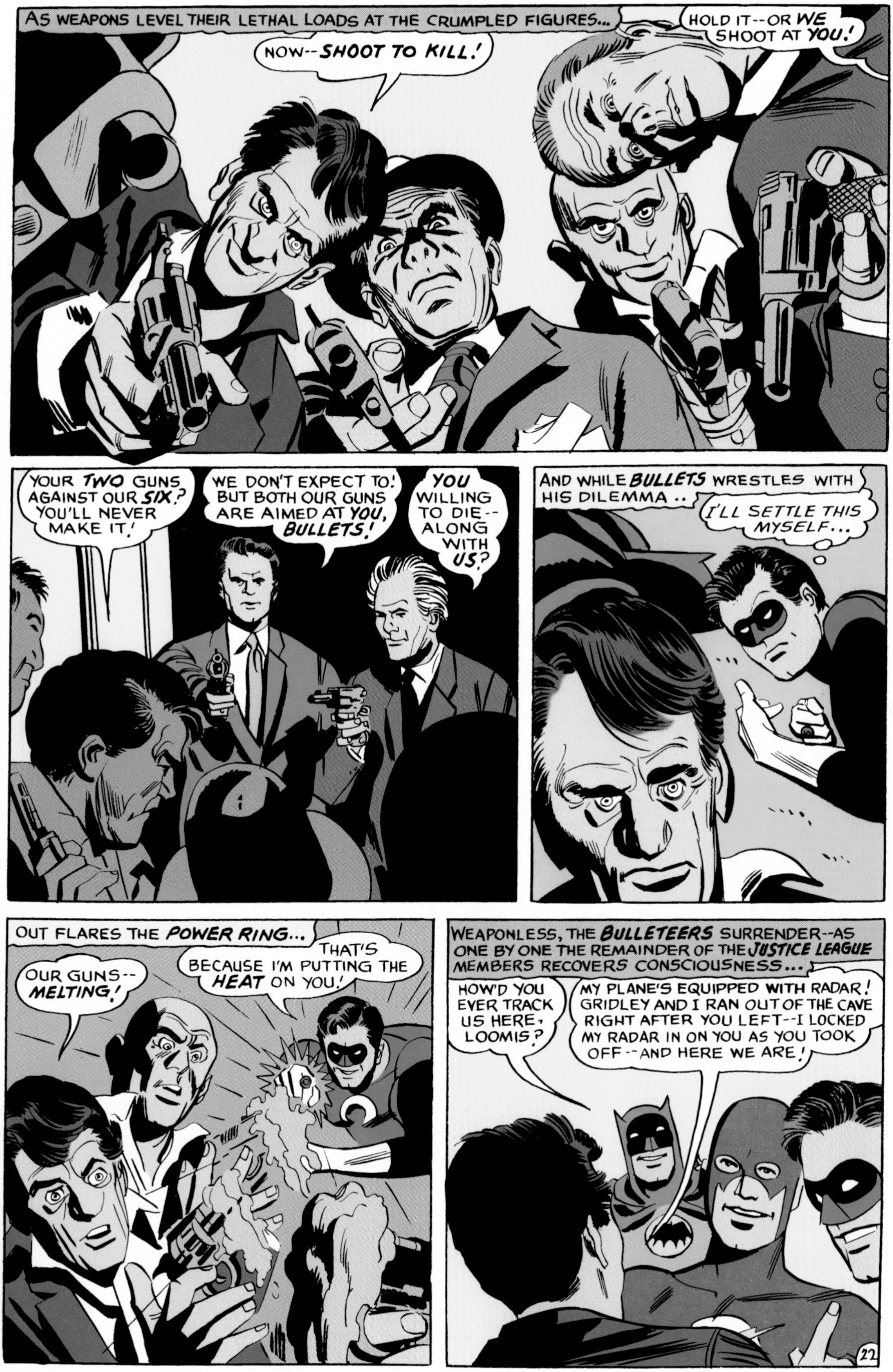
AS WEAPONS LEVEL THEIR LETHAL LOADS AT THE CRUMPLED FIGURES...
NOW--SHOOT TO KILL!
HOLD IT--OR WE SHOOT AT YOU!
YOUR TWO GUNS AGAINST OUR SIX? YOU'LL NEVER MAKE IT!
WE DON'T EXPECT TO! BUT BOTH OUR GUNS ARE AIMED AT YOU, BULLETS!
YOU WILLING TO DIE--ALONG WITH US?
AND WHILE BULLETS WRESTLES WITH HIS DILEMMA..
I'LL SETTLE THIS MYSELF...
OUT FLARES THE POWER RING...
OUR GUNS--MELTING!
THAT'S BECAUSE I'M PUTTING THE HEAT ON YOU!
WEAPONLESS, THE BULLETEERS SURRENDER--AS ONE BY ONE THE REMAINDER OF THE JUSTICE LEAGUE MEMBERS RECOVERS CONSCIOUSNESS...
HOW'D YOU EVER TRACK US HERE, LOOMIS?
MY PLANE'S EQUIPPED WITH RADAR! GRIDLEY AND I RAN OUT OF THE CAVE RIGHT AFTER YOU LEFT--I LOCKED MY RADAR IN ON YOU AS YOU TOOK OFF--AND HERE WE ARE!
22

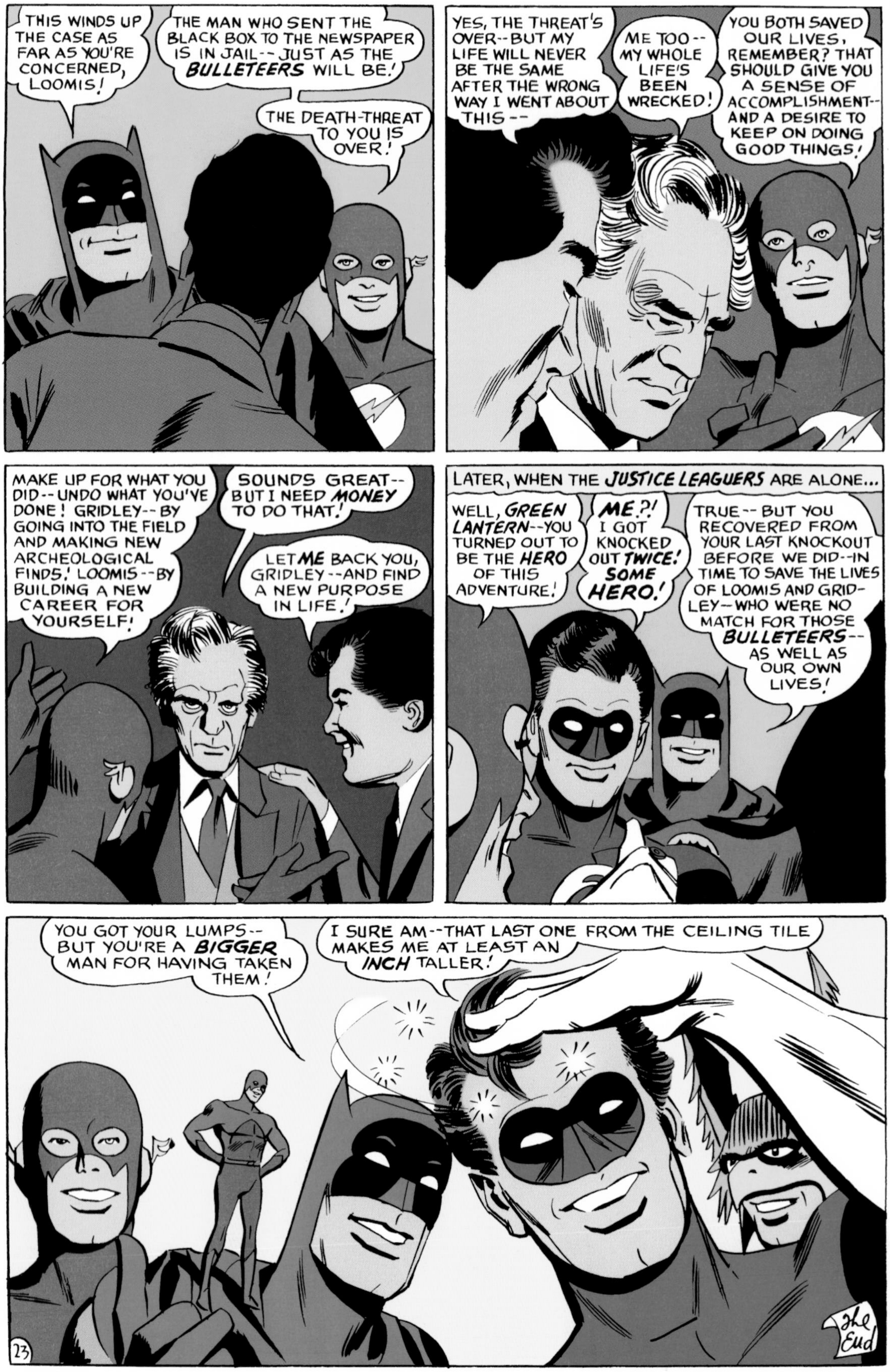
THIS WINDS UP THE CASE AS FAR AS YOU'RE CONCERNED, LOOMIS!
THE MAN WHO SENT THE BLACK BOX TO THE NEWSPAPER IS IN JAIL--JUST AS THE BULLETEERS WILL BE!
THE DEATH-THREAT TO YOU IS OVER!
YES, THE THREAT'S OVER--BUT MY LIFE WILL NEVER BE THE SAME AFTER THE WRONG WAY I WENT ABOUT THIS--
ME TOO--MY WHOLE LIFE'S BEEN WRECKED!
YOU BOTH SAVED OUR LIVES, REMEMBER? THAT SHOULD GIVE YOU A SENSE OF ACCOMPLISHMENT--AND A DESIRE TO KEEP ON DOING GOOD THINGS!
MAKE UP FOR WHAT YOU DID--UNDO WHAT YOU'VE DONE! GRIDLEY--BY GOING INTO THE FIELD AND MAKING NEW ARCHEOLOGICAL FINDS! LOOMIS--BY BUILDING A NEW CAREER FOR YOURSELF!
SOUNDS GREAT--BUT I NEED MONEY TO DO THAT!
LET ME BACK YOU, GRIDLEY--AND FIND A NEW PURPOSE IN LIFE!
LATER, WHEN THE JUSTICE LEAGUERS ARE ALONE...
WELL, GREEN LANTERN--YOU TURNED OUT TO BE THE HERO OF THIS ADVENTURE!
ME?! I GOT KNOCKED OUT TWICE! SOME HERO!
TRUE--BUT YOU RECOVERED FROM YOUR LAST KNOCKOUT BEFORE WE DID--IN TIME TO SAVE THE LIVES OF LOOMIS AND GRIDLEY--WHO WERE NO MATCH FOR THOSE BULLETEERS--AS WELL AS OUR OWN LIVES!
YOU GOT YOUR LUMPS--BUT YOU'RE A BIGGER MAN FOR HAVING TAKEN THEM!
I SURE AM--THAT LAST ONE FROM THE CEILING TILE MAKES ME AT LEAST AN INCH TALLER!
23
The End

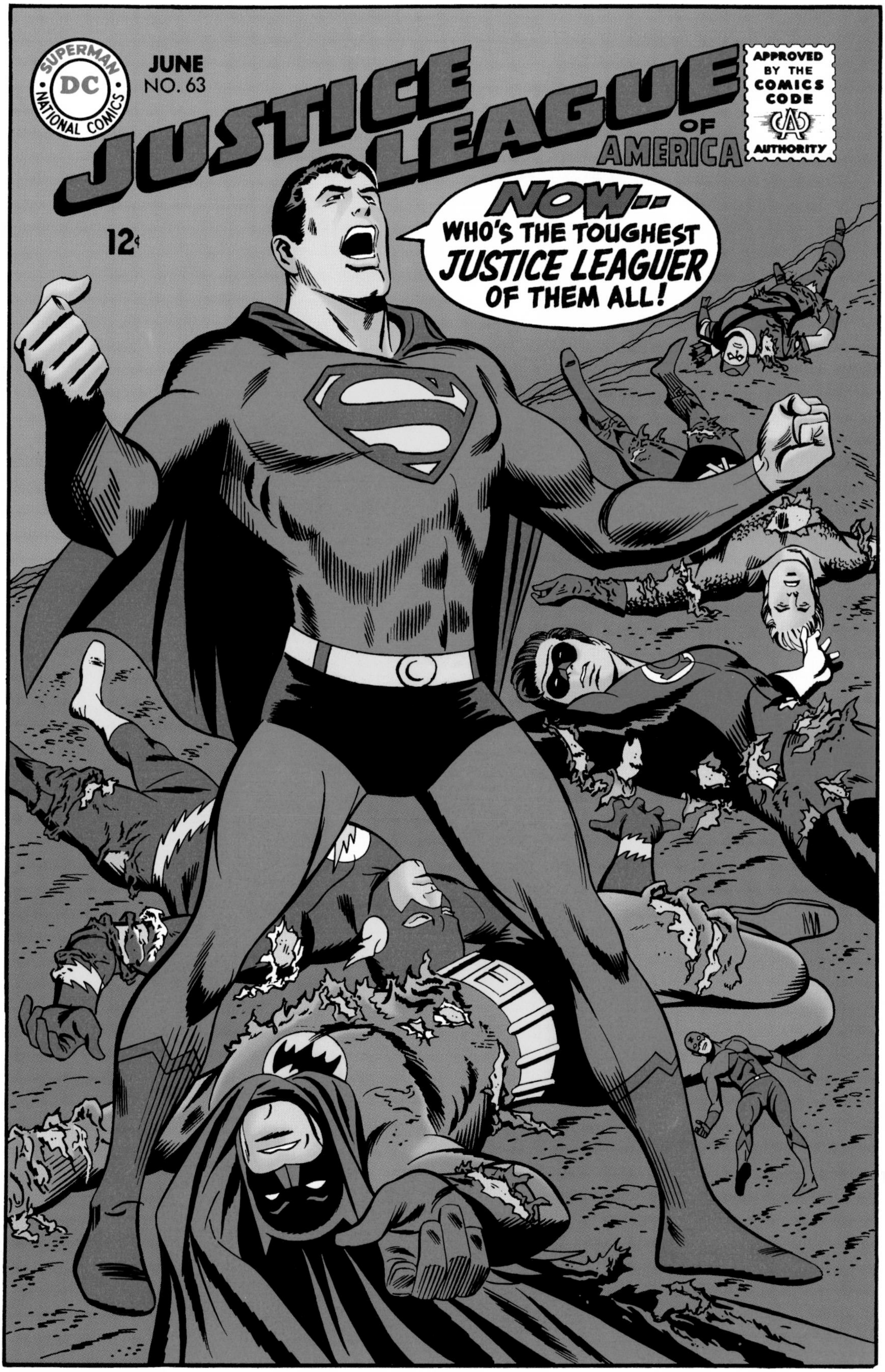
SUPERMAN DC NATIONAL COMICS
JUNE
NO. 63
JUSTICE LEAGUE OF AMERICA
APPROVED BY THE COMICS CODE AUTHORITY
12¢
NOW--
WHO'S THE TOUGHEST JUSTICE LEAGUER OF THEM ALL!

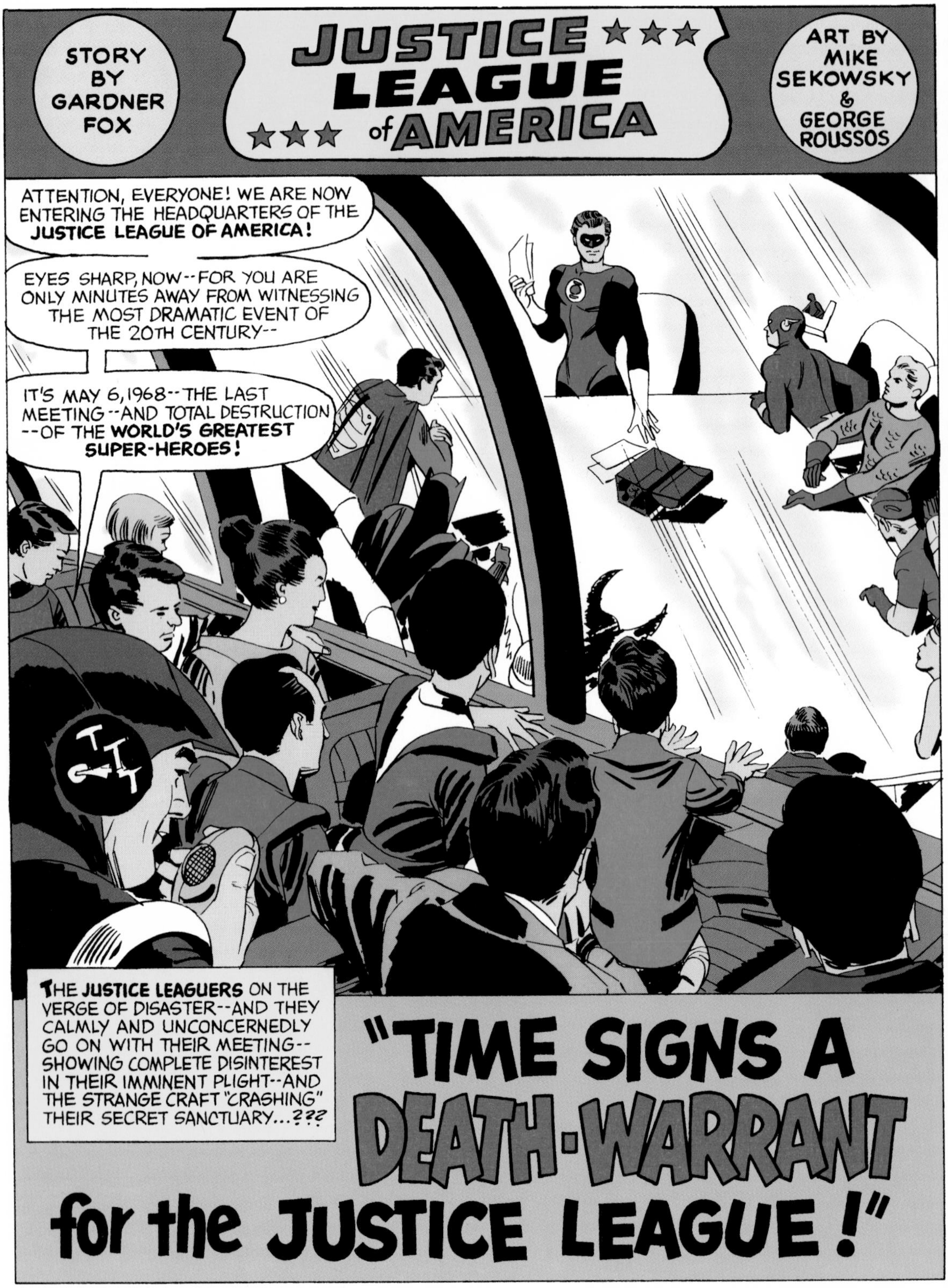
STORY BY GARDNER FOX
JUSTICE LEAGUE of AMERICA
ART BY MIKE SEKOWSKY & GEORGE ROUSSOS
ATTENTION, EVERYONE! WE ARE NOW ENTERING THE HEADQUARTERS OF THE JUSTICE LEAGUE OF AMERICA!
EYES SHARP, NOW--FOR YOU ARE ONLY MINUTES AWAY FROM WITNESSING THE MOST DRAMATIC EVENT OF THE 20TH CENTURY--
IT'S MAY 6, 1968--THE LAST MEETING--AND TOTAL DESTRUCTION--OF THE WORLD'S GREATEST SUPER-HEROES!
THE JUSTICE LEAGUERS ON THE VERGE OF DISASTER--AND THEY CALMLY AND UNCONCERNEDLY GO ON WITH THEIR MEETING--SHOWING COMPLETE DISINTEREST IN THEIR IMMINENT PLIGHT--AND THE STRANGE CRAFT "CRASHING" THEIR SECRET SANCTUARY...???
"TIME SIGNS A DEATH-WARRANT for the JUSTICE LEAGUE!"

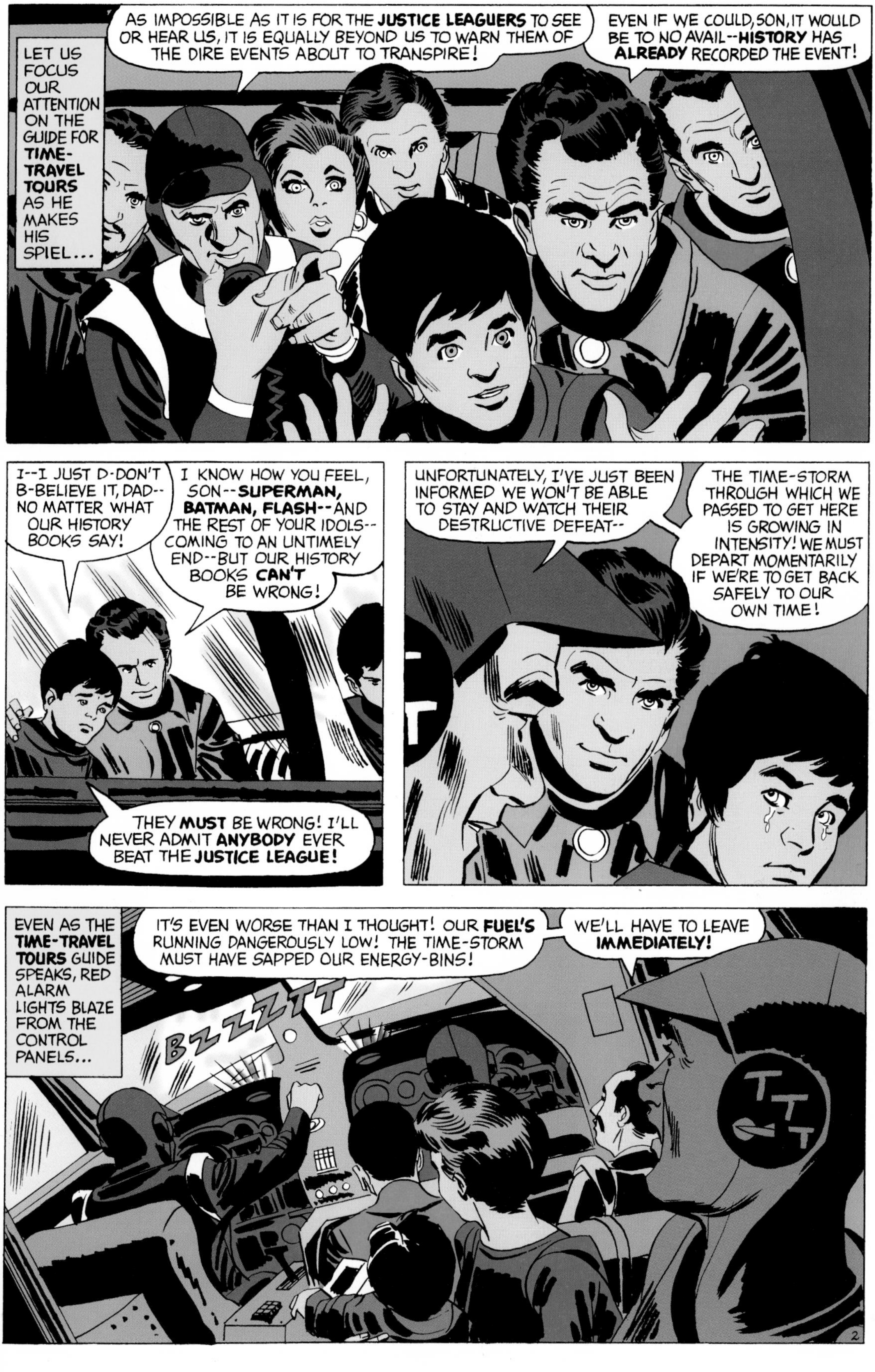
LET US FOCUS OUR ATTENTION ON THE GUIDE FOR TIME-TRAVEL TOURS AS HE MAKES HIS SPIEL...
AS IMPOSSIBLE AS IT IS FOR THE JUSTICE LEAGUERS TO SEE OR HEAR US, IT IS EQUALLY BEYOND US TO WARN THEM OF THE DIRE EVENTS ABOUT TO TRANSPIRE!
EVEN IF WE COULD, SON, IT WOULD BE TO NO AVAIL--HISTORY HAS ALREADY RECORDED THE EVENT!
I--I JUST D-DON'T B-BELIEVE IT, DAD--NO MATTER WHAT OUR HISTORY BOOKS SAY!
I KNOW HOW YOU FEEL, SON--SUPERMAN, BATMAN, FLASH--AND THE REST OF YOUR IDOLS--COMING TO AN UNTIMELY END--BUT OUR HISTORY BOOKS CAN'T BE WRONG!
THEY MUST BE WRONG! I'LL NEVER ADMIT ANYBODY EVER BEAT THE JUSTICE LEAGUE!
UNFORTUNATELY, I'VE JUST BEEN INFORMED WE WON'T BE ABLE TO STAY AND WATCH THEIR DESTRUCTIVE DEFEAT--
THE TIME-STORM THROUGH WHICH WE PASSED TO GET HERE IS GROWING IN INTENSITY! WE MUST DEPART MOMENTARILY IF WE'RE TO GET BACK SAFELY TO OUR OWN TIME!
EVEN AS THE TIME-TRAVEL TOURS GUIDE SPEAKS, RED ALARM LIGHTS BLAZE FROM THE CONTROL PANELS...
IT'S EVEN WORSE THAN I THOUGHT! OUR FUEL'S RUNNING DANGEROUSLY LOW! THE TIME-STORM MUST HAVE SAPPED OUR ENERGY-BINS!
WE'LL HAVE TO LEAVE IMMEDIATELY!
BZZZZTT
2

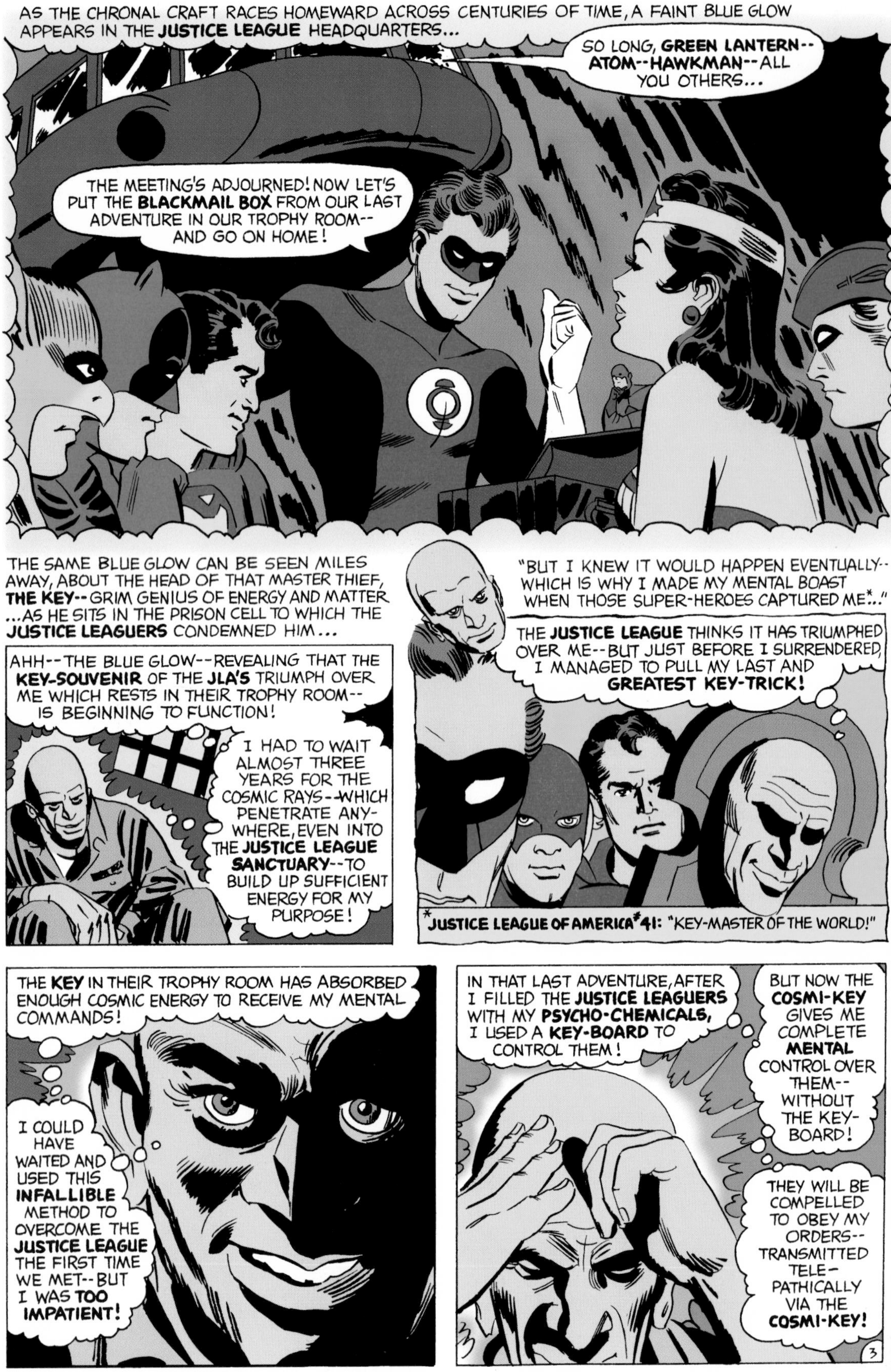
AS THE CHRONAL CRAFT RACES HOMEWARD ACROSS CENTURIES OF TIME, A FAINT BLUE GLOW APPEARS IN THE JUSTICE LEAGUE HEADQUARTERS...
SO LONG, GREEN LANTERN--ATOM--HAWKMAN--ALL YOU OTHERS...
THE MEETING'S ADJOURNED! NOW LET'S PUT THE BLACKMAIL BOX FROM OUR LAST ADVENTURE IN OUR TROPHY ROOM--AND GO ON HOME!
THE SAME BLUE GLOW CAN BE SEEN MILES AWAY, ABOUT THE HEAD OF THAT MASTER THIEF, THE KEY--GRIM GENIUS OF ENERGY AND MATTER ...AS HE SITS IN THE PRISON CELL TO WHICH THE JUSTICE LEAGUERS CONDEMNED HIM...
AHH--THE BLUE GLOW--REVEALING THAT THE KEY-SOUVENIR OF THE JLA'S TRIUMPH OVER ME WHICH RESTS IN THEIR TROPHY ROOM--IS BEGINNING TO FUNCTION!
I HAD TO WAIT ALMOST THREE YEARS FOR THE COSMIC RAYS--WHICH PENETRATE ANYWHERE, EVEN INTO THE JUSTICE LEAGUE SANCTUARY--TO BUILD UP SUFFICIENT ENERGY FOR MY PURPOSE!
"BUT I KNEW IT WOULD HAPPEN EVENTUALLY--WHICH IS WHY I MADE MY MENTAL BOAST WHEN THOSE SUPER-HEROES CAPTURED ME*..."
THE JUSTICE LEAGUE THINKS IT HAS TRIUMPHED OVER ME--BUT JUST BEFORE I SURRENDERED, I MANAGED TO PULL MY LAST AND GREATEST KEY-TRICK!
*JUSTICE LEAGUE OF AMERICA #41: "KEY-MASTER OF THE WORLD!"
THE KEY IN THEIR TROPHY ROOM HAS ABSORBED ENOUGH COSMIC ENERGY TO RECEIVE MY MENTAL COMMANDS!
I COULD HAVE WAITED AND USED THIS INFALLIBLE METHOD TO OVERCOME THE JUSTICE LEAGUE THE FIRST TIME WE MET--BUT I WAS TOO IMPATIENT!
IN THAT LAST ADVENTURE, AFTER I FILLED THE JUSTICE LEAGUERS WITH MY PSYCHO-CHEMICALS, I USED A KEY-BOARD TO CONTROL THEM!
BUT NOW THE COSMI-KEY GIVES ME COMPLETE MENTAL CONTROL OVER THEM--WITHOUT THE KEY-BOARD!
THEY WILL BE COMPELLED TO OBEY MY ORDERS--TRANSMITTED TELE-PATHICALLY VIA THE COSMI-KEY!
3

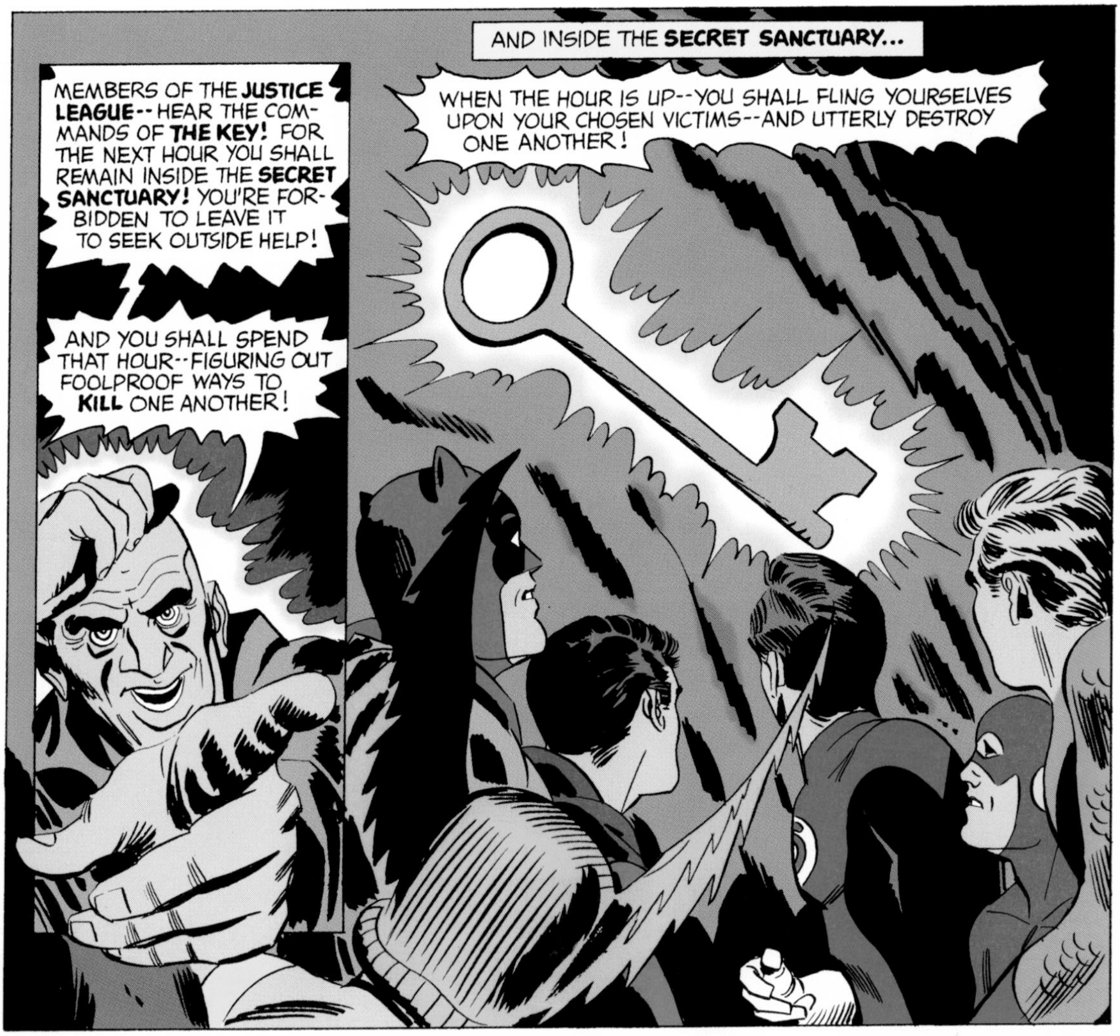
AND INSIDE THE SECRET SANCTUARY...
MEMBERS OF THE JUSTICE LEAGUE--HEAR THE COMMANDS OF THE KEY! FOR THE NEXT HOUR YOU SHALL REMAIN INSIDE THE SECRET SANCTUARY! YOU'RE FORBIDDEN TO LEAVE IT TO SEEK OUTSIDE HELP!
WHEN THE HOUR IS UP--YOU SHALL FLING YOURSELVES UPON YOUR CHOSEN VICTIMS--AND UTTERLY DESTROY ONE ANOTHER!
AND YOU SHALL SPEND THAT HOUR--FIGURING OUT FOOLPROOF WAYS TO KILL ONE ANOTHER!

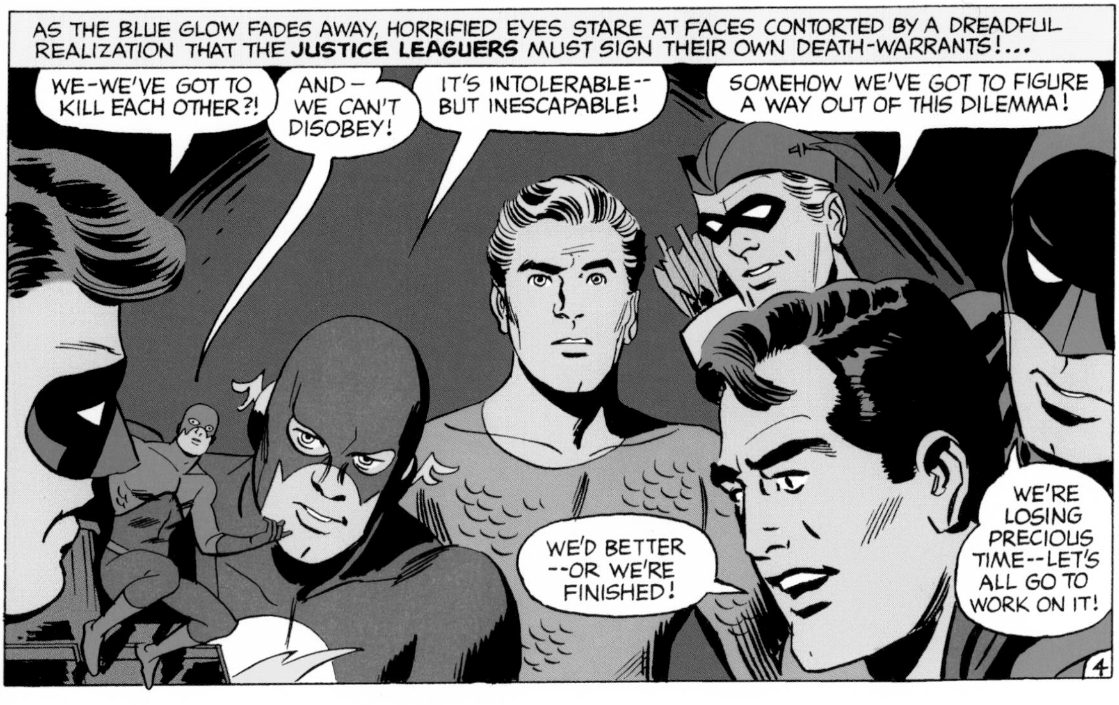
AS THE BLUE GLOW FADES AWAY, HORRIFIED EYES STARE AT FACES CONTORTED BY A DREADFUL REALIZATION THAT THE JUSTICE LEAGUERS MUST SIGN THEIR OWN DEATH-WARRANTS!...
WE-WE'VE GOT TO KILL EACH OTHER?!
AND-- WE CAN'T DISOBEY!
IT'S INTOLERABLE--BUT INESCAPABLE!
SOMEHOW WE'VE GOT TO FIGURE A WAY OUT OF THIS DILEMMA!
WE'D BETTER--OR WE'RE FINISHED!
WE'RE LOSING PRECIOUS TIME--LET'S ALL GO TO WORK ON IT!
4

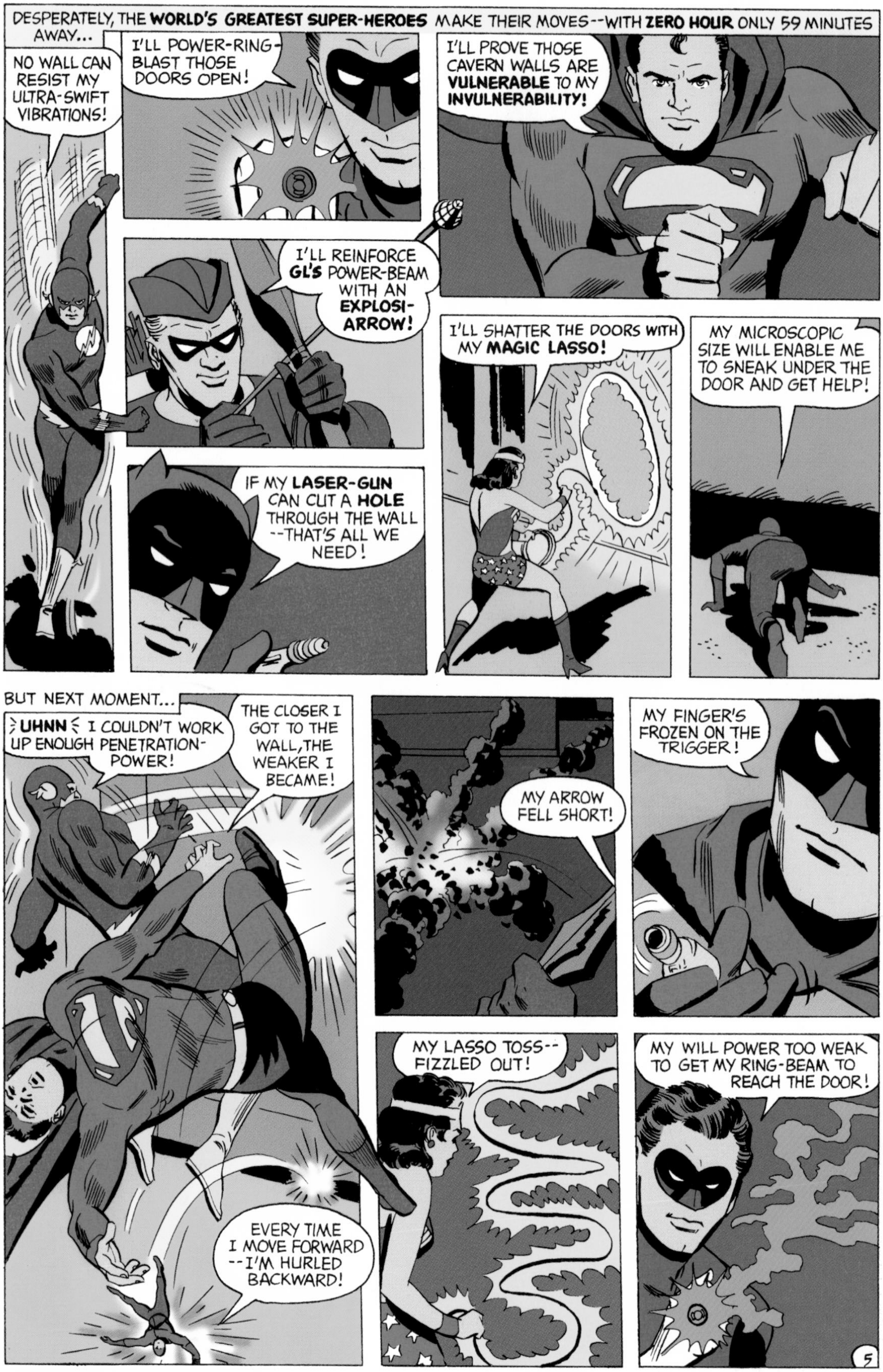
DESPERATELY, THE WORLD'S GREATEST SUPER-HEROES MAKE THEIR MOVES--WITH ZERO HOUR ONLY 59 MINUTES AWAY...
NO WALL CAN RESIST MY ULTRA-SWIFT VIBRATIONS!
I'LL POWER-RING-BLAST THOSE DOORS OPEN!
I'LL PROVE THOSE CAVERN WALLS ARE VULNERABLE TO MY INVULNERABILITY!
I'LL REINFORCE GL'S POWER-BEAM WITH AN EXPLOSI-ARROW!
IF MY LASER-GUN CAN CUT A HOLE THROUGH THE WALL --THAT'S ALL WE NEED!
I'LL SHATTER THE DOORS WITH MY MAGIC LASSO!
MY MICROSCOPIC SIZE WILL ENABLE ME TO SNEAK UNDER THE DOOR AND GET HELP!
BUT NEXT MOMENT...
UHNN I COULDN'T WORK UP ENOUGH PENETRATION-POWER!
THE CLOSER I GOT TO THE WALL, THE WEAKER I BECAME!
EVERY TIME I MOVE FORWARD --I'M HURLED BACKWARD!
MY ARROW FELL SHORT!
MY FINGER'S FROZEN ON THE TRIGGER!
MY LASSO TOSS--FIZZLED OUT!
MY WILL POWER TOO WEAK TO GET MY RING-BEAM TO REACH THE DOOR!
5

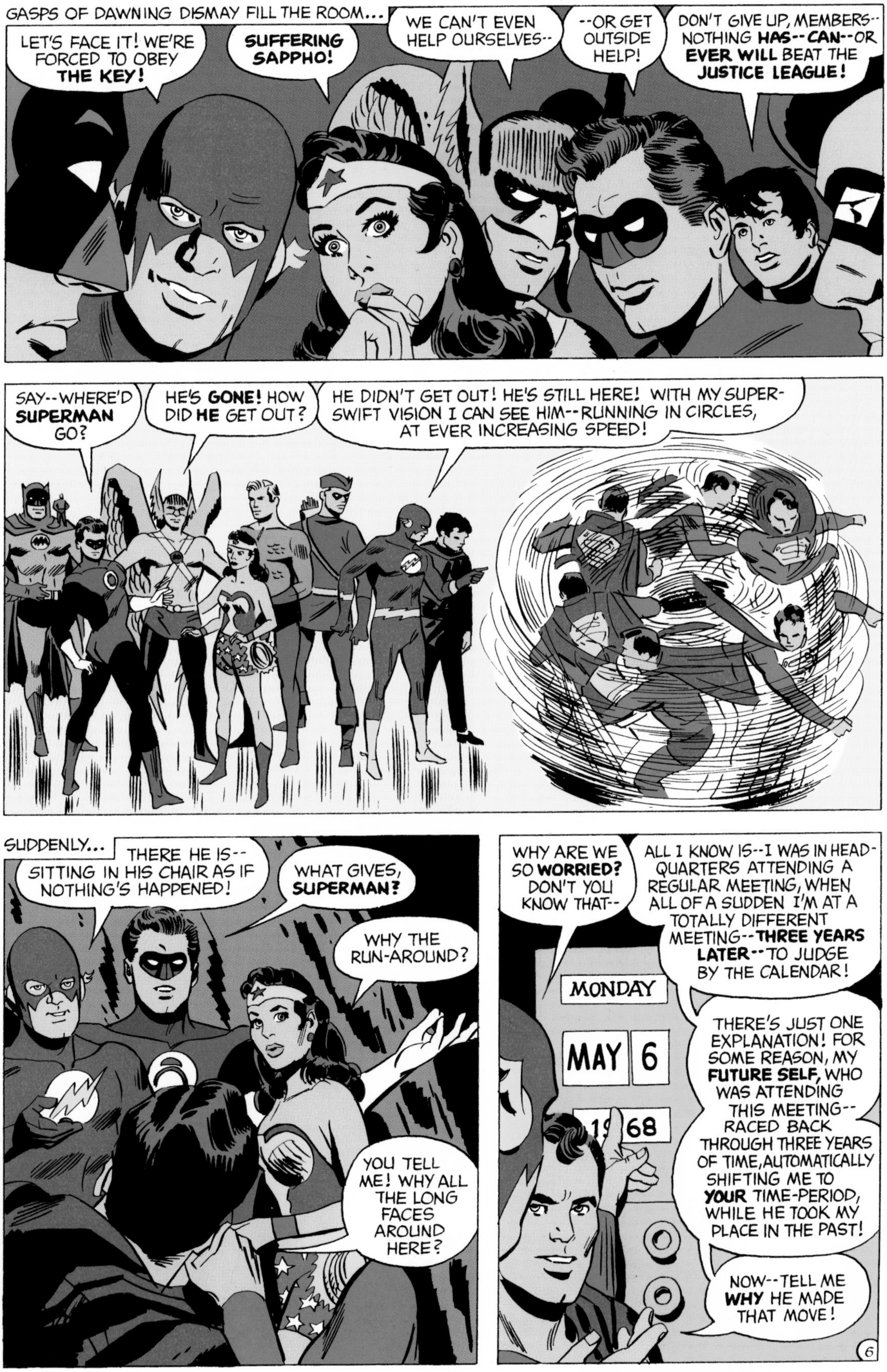
GASPS OF DAWNING DISMAY FILL THE ROOM...
LET'S FACE IT! WE'RE FORCED TO OBEY THE KEY!
SUFFERING SAPPHO!
WE CAN'T EVEN HELP OURSELVES--
--OR GET OUTSIDE HELP!
DON'T GIVE UP, MEMBERS--NOTHING HAS--CAN--OR EVER WILL BEAT THE JUSTICE LEAGUE!
SAY--WHERE'D SUPERMAN GO?
HE'S GONE! HOW DID HE GET OUT?
HE DIDN'T GET OUT! HE'S STILL HERE! WITH MY SUPER-SWIFT VISION I CAN SEE HIM--RUNNING IN CIRCLES, AT EVER INCREASING SPEED!
SUDDENLY...
THERE HE IS--SITTING IN HIS CHAIR AS IF NOTHING'S HAPPENED!
WHAT GIVES, SUPERMAN?
WHY THE RUN-AROUND?
YOU TELL ME! WHY ALL THE LONG FACES AROUND HERE?
WHY ARE WE SO WORRIED? DON'T YOU KNOW THAT--
ALL I KNOW IS--I WAS IN HEAD-QUARTERS ATTENDING A REGULAR MEETING, WHEN ALL OF A SUDDEN I'M AT A TOTALLY DIFFERENT MEETING--THREE YEARS LATER--TO JUDGE BY THE CALENDAR!
MONDAY
MAY 6
68
THERE'S JUST ONE EXPLANATION! FOR SOME REASON, MY FUTURE SELF, WHO WAS ATTENDING THIS MEETING--RACED BACK THROUGH THREE YEARS OF TIME, AUTOMATICALLY SHIFTING ME TO YOUR TIME-PERIOD, WHILE HE TOOK MY PLACE IN THE PAST!
NOW--TELL ME WHY HE MADE THAT MOVE!
6

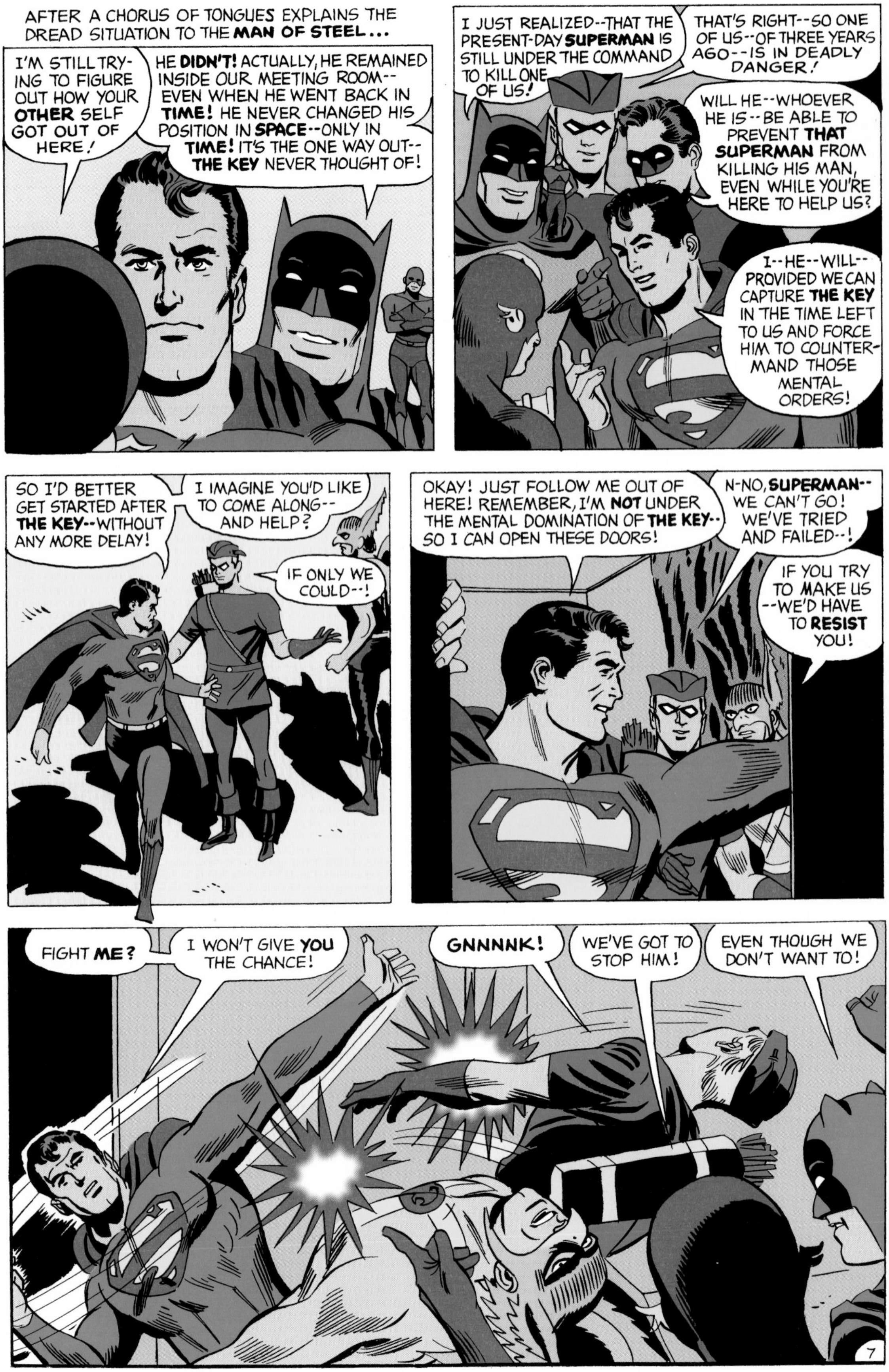
AFTER A CHORUS OF TONGUES EXPLAINS THE DREAD SITUATION TO THE MAN OF STEEL...
I'M STILL TRYING TO FIGURE OUT HOW YOUR OTHER SELF GOT OUT OF HERE!
HE DIDN'T! ACTUALLY, HE REMAINED INSIDE OUR MEETING ROOM-- EVEN WHEN HE WENT BACK IN TIME! HE NEVER CHANGED HIS POSITION IN SPACE--ONLY IN TIME! IT'S THE ONE WAY OUT-- THE KEY NEVER THOUGHT OF!
I JUST REALIZED--THAT THE PRESENT-DAY SUPERMAN IS STILL UNDER THE COMMAND TO KILL ONE OF US!
THAT'S RIGHT--SO ONE OF US--OF THREE YEARS AGO--IS IN DEADLY DANGER!
WILL HE--WHOEVER HE IS--BE ABLE TO PREVENT THAT SUPERMAN FROM KILLING HIS MAN, EVEN WHILE YOU'RE HERE TO HELP US?
I--HE--WILL--PROVIDED WE CAN CAPTURE THE KEY IN THE TIME LEFT TO US AND FORCE HIM TO COUNTERMAND THOSE MENTAL ORDERS!
SO I'D BETTER GET STARTED AFTER THE KEY--WITHOUT ANY MORE DELAY!
I IMAGINE YOU'D LIKE TO COME ALONG-- AND HELP?
IF ONLY WE COULD--!
OKAY! JUST FOLLOW ME OUT OF HERE! REMEMBER, I'M NOT UNDER THE MENTAL DOMINATION OF THE KEY-- SO I CAN OPEN THESE DOORS!
N-NO, SUPERMAN-- WE CAN'T GO! WE'VE TRIED AND FAILED--!
IF YOU TRY TO MAKE US --WE'D HAVE TO RESIST YOU!
FIGHT ME?
I WON'T GIVE YOU THE CHANCE!
GNNNNK!
WE'VE GOT TO STOP HIM!
EVEN THOUGH WE DON'T WANT TO!
7

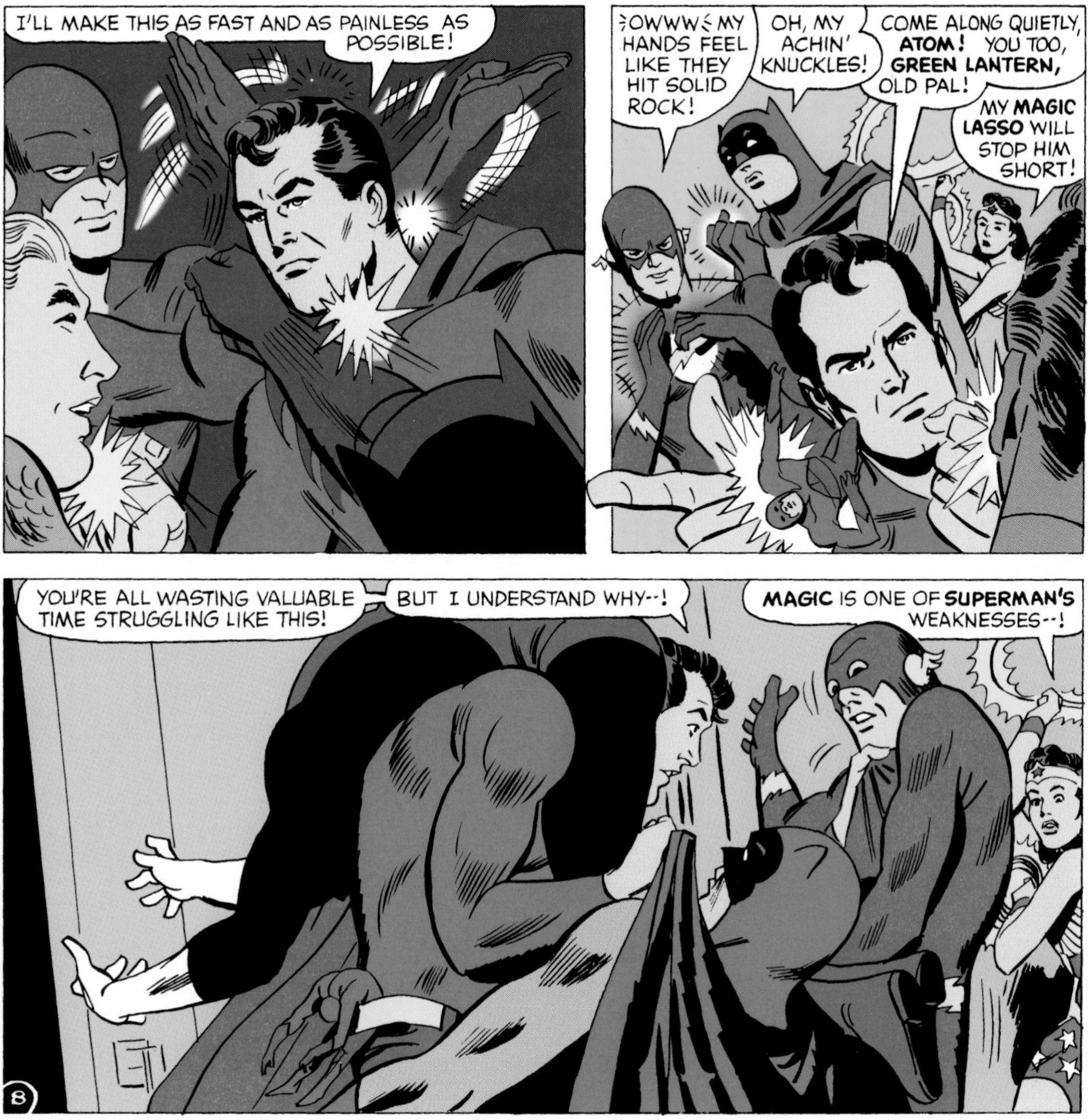
I'LL MAKE THIS AS FAST AND AS PAINLESS AS POSSIBLE!
OWWW MY HANDS FEEL LIKE THEY HIT SOLID ROCK!
OH, MY ACHIN' KNUCKLES!
COME ALONG QUIETLY, **ATOM!** YOU TOO, **GREEN LANTERN,** OLD PAL!
MY **MAGIC LASSO** WILL STOP HIM SHORT!
YOU'RE ALL WASTING VALUABLE TIME STRUGGLING LIKE THIS!
BUT I UNDERSTAND WHY--!
MAGIC IS ONE OF **SUPERMAN'S** WEAKNESSES--!
8

JUSTICE LEAGUE of AMERICA

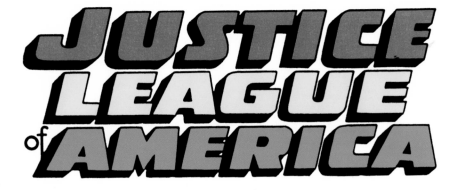

BEFORE **WONDER WOMAN** CAN COMPLETE HER CAST, THE **MAN OF STEEL** BLOWS HIS SUPER-BREATH AT HER...

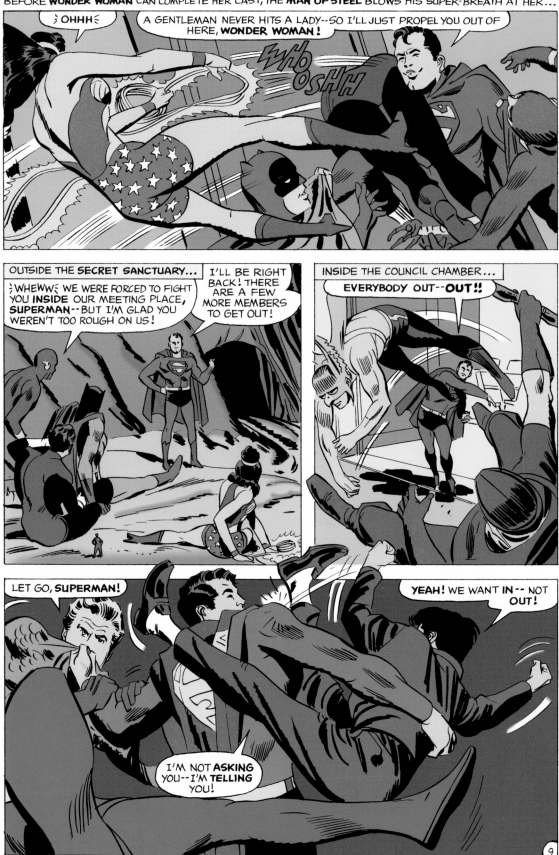

OHHH

A GENTLEMAN NEVER HITS A LADY--SO I'LL JUST PROPEL YOU OUT OF HERE, **WONDER WOMAN!**

WHOOSHH

OUTSIDE THE **SECRET SANCTUARY**...

WHEWW WE WERE FORCED TO FIGHT YOU **INSIDE** OUR MEETING PLACE, **SUPERMAN**--BUT I'M GLAD YOU WEREN'T TOO ROUGH ON US!

I'LL BE RIGHT BACK! THERE ARE A FEW MORE MEMBERS TO GET OUT!

INSIDE THE COUNCIL CHAMBER...

EVERYBODY OUT--**OUT!!**

LET GO, **SUPERMAN!**

YEAH! WE WANT **IN** -- NOT OUT!

I'M NOT **ASKING** YOU--I'M **TELLING** YOU!

9

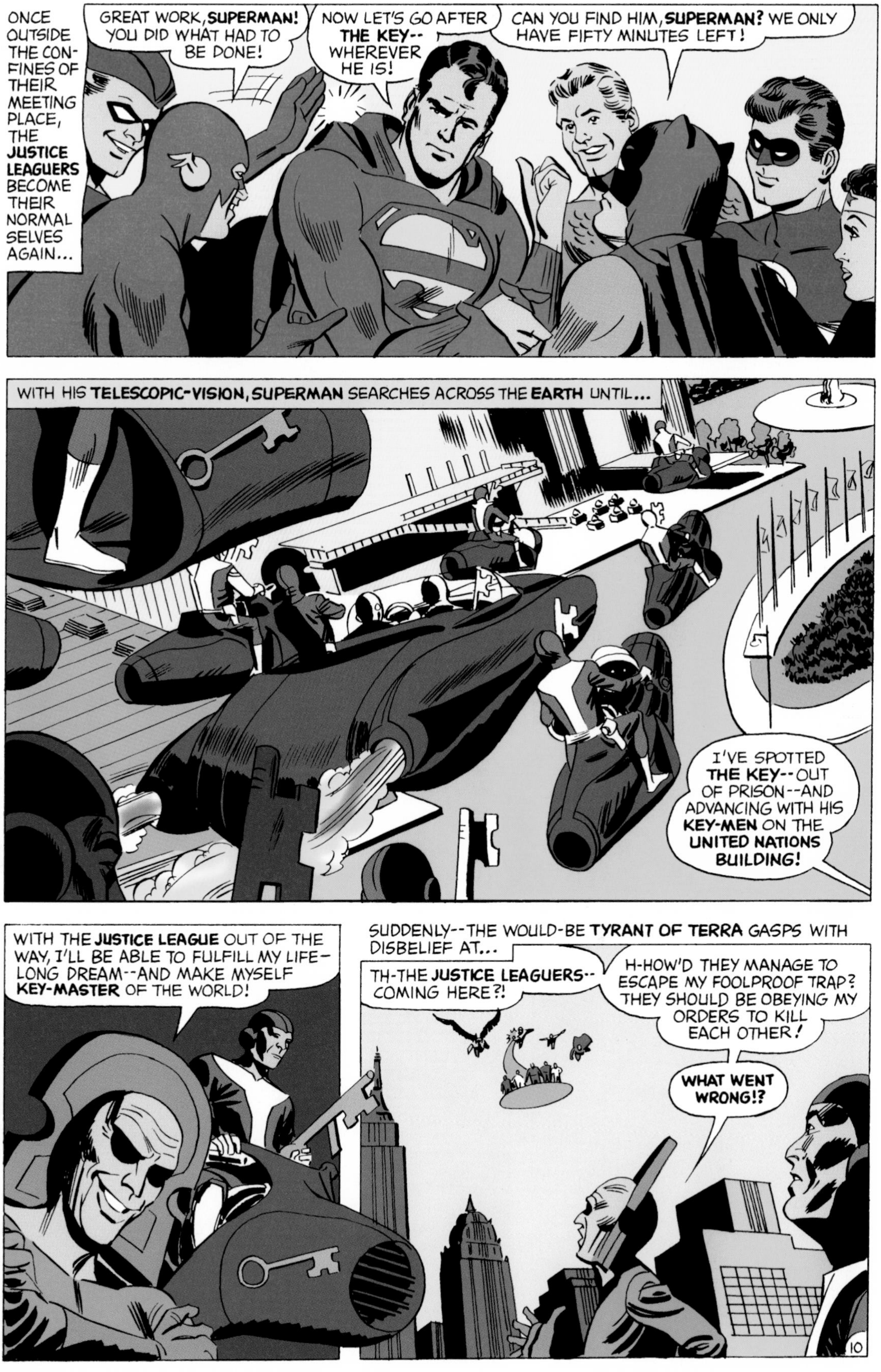
ONCE OUTSIDE THE CONFINES OF THEIR MEETING PLACE, THE JUSTICE LEAGUERS BECOME THEIR NORMAL SELVES AGAIN...
GREAT WORK, SUPERMAN! YOU DID WHAT HAD TO BE DONE!
NOW LET'S GO AFTER THE KEY-- WHEREVER HE IS!
CAN YOU FIND HIM, SUPERMAN? WE ONLY HAVE FIFTY MINUTES LEFT!
WITH HIS TELESCOPIC-VISION, SUPERMAN SEARCHES ACROSS THE EARTH UNTIL...
I'VE SPOTTED THE KEY--OUT OF PRISON--AND ADVANCING WITH HIS KEY-MEN ON THE UNITED NATIONS BUILDING!
WITH THE JUSTICE LEAGUE OUT OF THE WAY, I'LL BE ABLE TO FULFILL MY LIFE-LONG DREAM--AND MAKE MYSELF KEY-MASTER OF THE WORLD!
SUDDENLY--THE WOULD-BE TYRANT OF TERRA GASPS WITH DISBELIEF AT...
TH-THE JUSTICE LEAGUERS-- COMING HERE?!
H-HOW'D THEY MANAGE TO ESCAPE MY FOOLPROOF TRAP? THEY SHOULD BE OBEYING MY ORDERS TO KILL EACH OTHER!
WHAT WENT WRONG!?
10

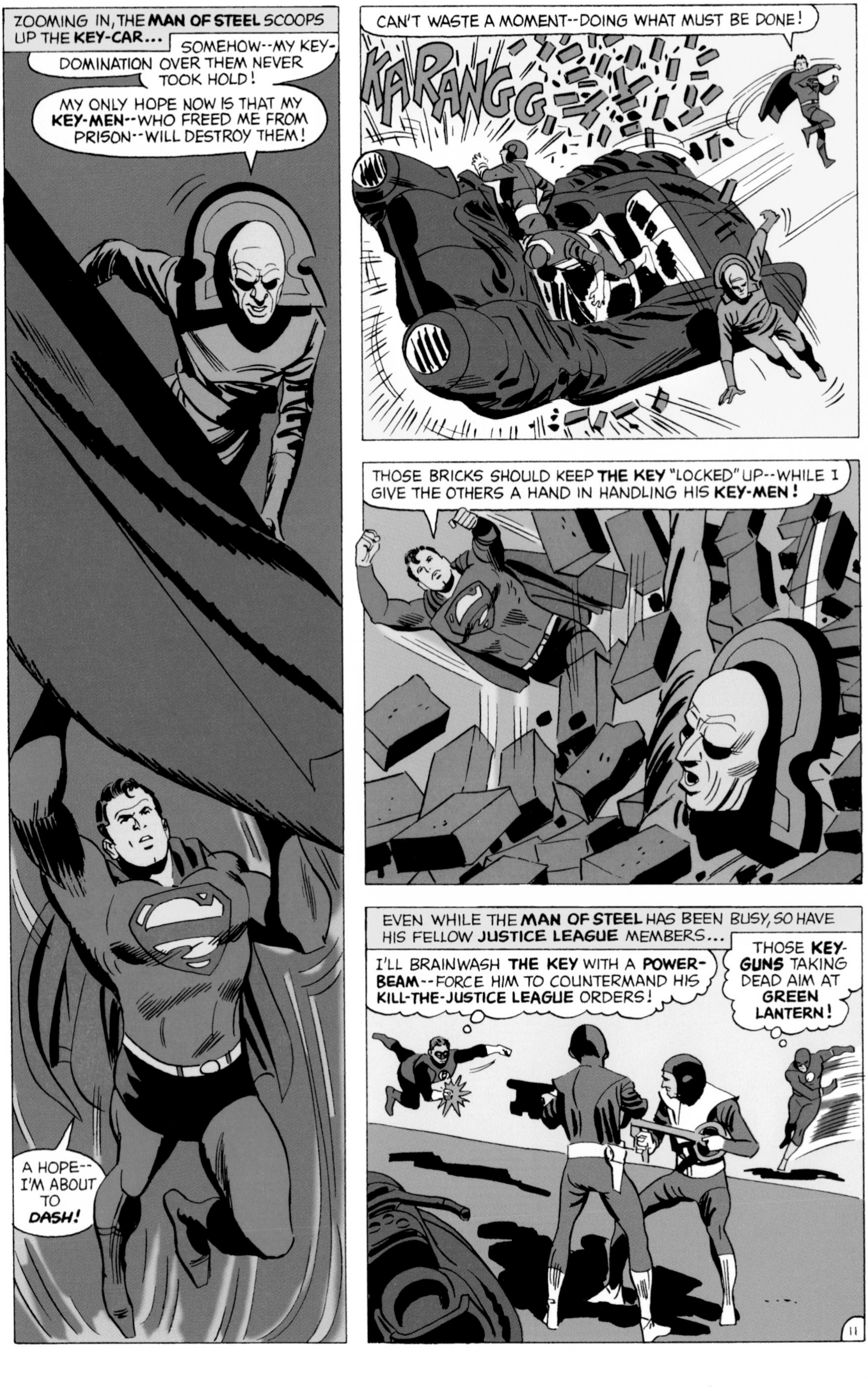
ZOOMING IN, THE MAN OF STEEL SCOOPS UP THE KEY-CAR...
SOMEHOW--MY KEY-DOMINATION OVER THEM NEVER TOOK HOLD!
MY ONLY HOPE NOW IS THAT MY KEY-MEN--WHO FREED ME FROM PRISON--WILL DESTROY THEM!
A HOPE--I'M ABOUT TO DASH!
CAN'T WASTE A MOMENT--DOING WHAT MUST BE DONE!
KARANGG
THOSE BRICKS SHOULD KEEP THE KEY "LOCKED" UP--WHILE I GIVE THE OTHERS A HAND IN HANDLING HIS KEY-MEN!
EVEN WHILE THE MAN OF STEEL HAS BEEN BUSY, SO HAVE HIS FELLOW JUSTICE LEAGUE MEMBERS...
I'LL BRAINWASH THE KEY WITH A POWER-BEAM--FORCE HIM TO COUNTERMAND HIS KILL-THE-JUSTICE LEAGUE ORDERS!
THOSE KEY-GUNS TAKING DEAD AIM AT GREEN LANTERN!
11

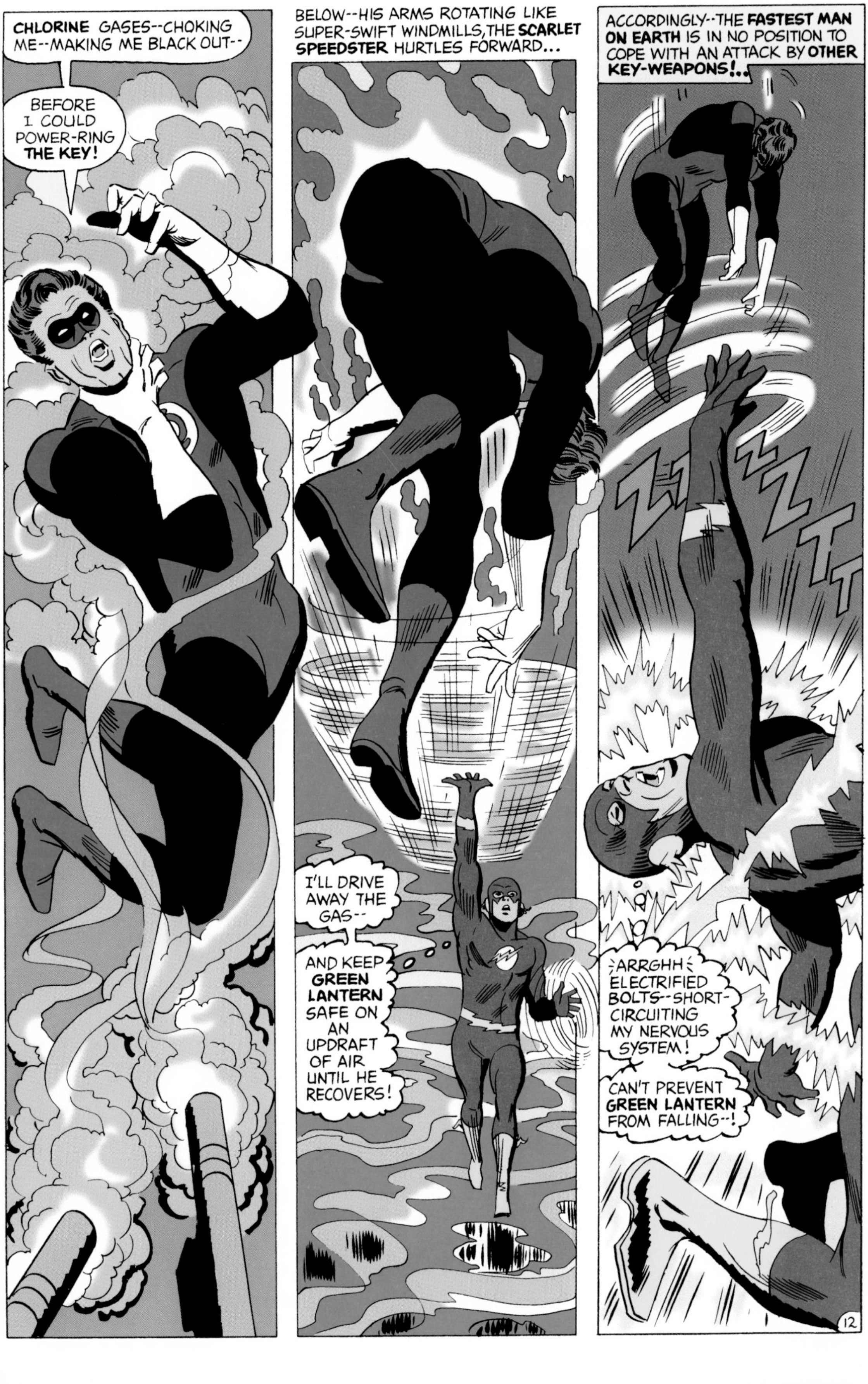
CHLORINE GASES--CHOKING ME--MAKING ME BLACK OUT--
BEFORE I COULD POWER-RING THE KEY!
BELOW--HIS ARMS ROTATING LIKE SUPER-SWIFT WINDMILLS, THE SCARLET SPEEDSTER HURTLES FORWARD...
I'LL DRIVE AWAY THE GAS--
AND KEEP GREEN LANTERN SAFE ON AN UPDRAFT OF AIR UNTIL HE RECOVERS!
ACCORDINGLY--THE FASTEST MAN ON EARTH IS IN NO POSITION TO COPE WITH AN ATTACK BY OTHER KEY-WEAPONS!..
ZZZTTT
ARRGHH ELECTRIFIED BOLTS--SHORT-CIRCUITING MY NERVOUS SYSTEM!
CAN'T PREVENT GREEN LANTERN FROM FALLING--!
12

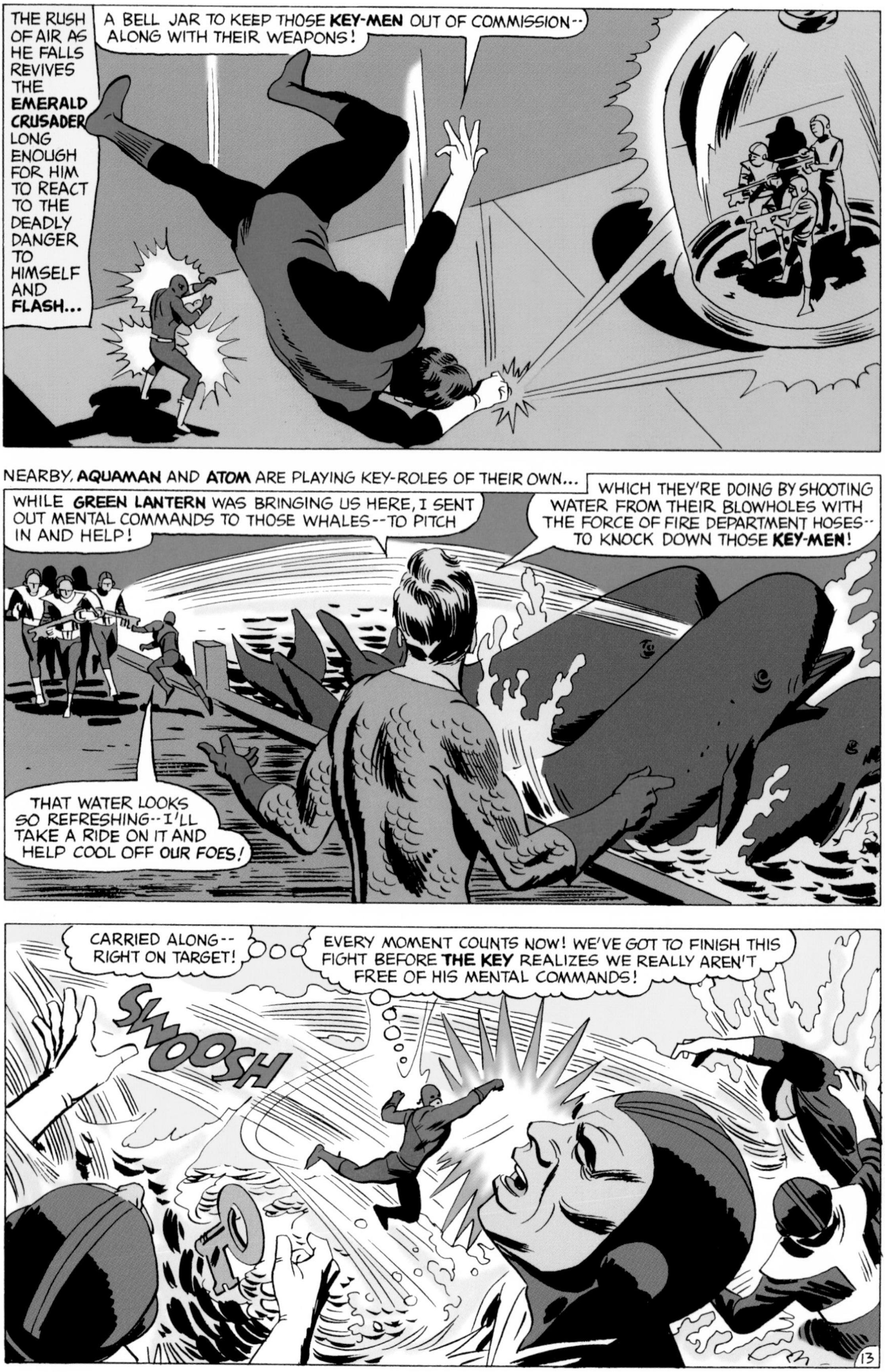
THE RUSH OF AIR AS HE FALLS REVIVES THE EMERALD CRUSADER LONG ENOUGH FOR HIM TO REACT TO THE DEADLY DANGER TO HIMSELF AND FLASH...
A BELL JAR TO KEEP THOSE KEY-MEN OUT OF COMMISSION-- ALONG WITH THEIR WEAPONS!
NEARBY, AQUAMAN AND ATOM ARE PLAYING KEY-ROLES OF THEIR OWN...
WHILE GREEN LANTERN WAS BRINGING US HERE, I SENT OUT MENTAL COMMANDS TO THOSE WHALES--TO PITCH IN AND HELP!
WHICH THEY'RE DOING BY SHOOTING WATER FROM THEIR BLOWHOLES WITH THE FORCE OF FIRE DEPARTMENT HOSES-- TO KNOCK DOWN THOSE KEY-MEN!
THAT WATER LOOKS SO REFRESHING--I'LL TAKE A RIDE ON IT AND HELP COOL OFF OUR FOES!
CARRIED ALONG-- RIGHT ON TARGET!
EVERY MOMENT COUNTS NOW! WE'VE GOT TO FINISH THIS FIGHT BEFORE THE KEY REALIZES WE REALLY AREN'T FREE OF HIS MENTAL COMMANDS!
SWOOSH
13

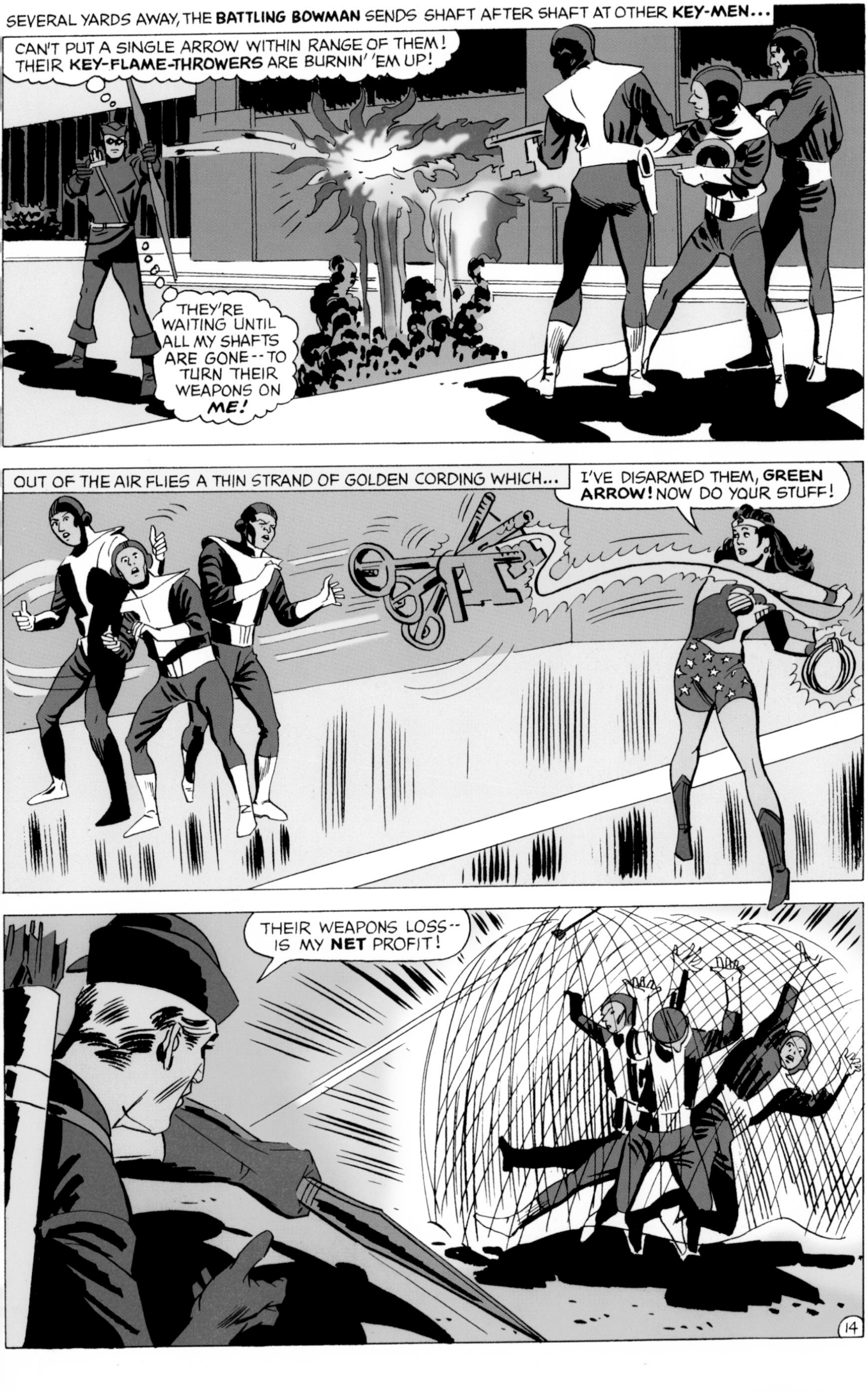
SEVERAL YARDS AWAY, THE BATTLING BOWMAN SENDS SHAFT AFTER SHAFT AT OTHER KEY-MEN...
CAN'T PUT A SINGLE ARROW WITHIN RANGE OF THEM! THEIR KEY-FLAME-THROWERS ARE BURNIN' 'EM UP!
THEY'RE WAITING UNTIL ALL MY SHAFTS ARE GONE--TO TURN THEIR WEAPONS ON ME!
OUT OF THE AIR FLIES A THIN STRAND OF GOLDEN CORDING WHICH...
I'VE DISARMED THEM, GREEN ARROW! NOW DO YOUR STUFF!
THEIR WEAPONS LOSS--IS MY NET PROFIT!
14

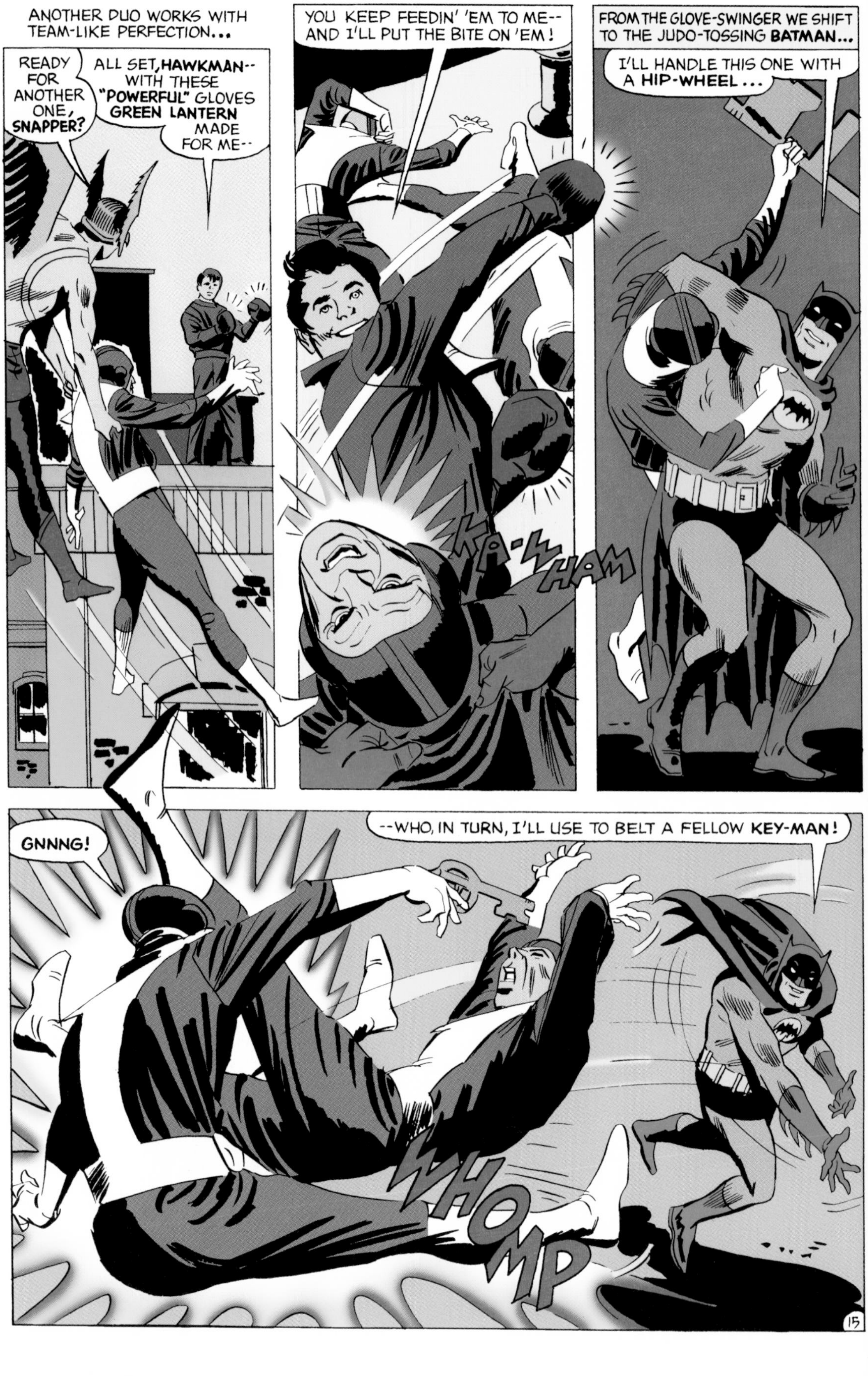
ANOTHER DUO WORKS WITH TEAM-LIKE PERFECTION...
READY FOR ANOTHER ONE, SNAPPER?
ALL SET, HAWKMAN-- WITH THESE "POWERFUL" GLOVES GREEN LANTERN MADE FOR ME--
YOU KEEP FEEDIN' 'EM TO ME-- AND I'LL PUT THE BITE ON 'EM!
KA-WHAM
FROM THE GLOVE-SWINGER WE SHIFT TO THE JUDO-TOSSING BATMAN...
I'LL HANDLE THIS ONE WITH A HIP-WHEEL...
GNNNG!
--WHO, IN TURN, I'LL USE TO BELT A FELLOW KEY-MAN!
WHOMP
15

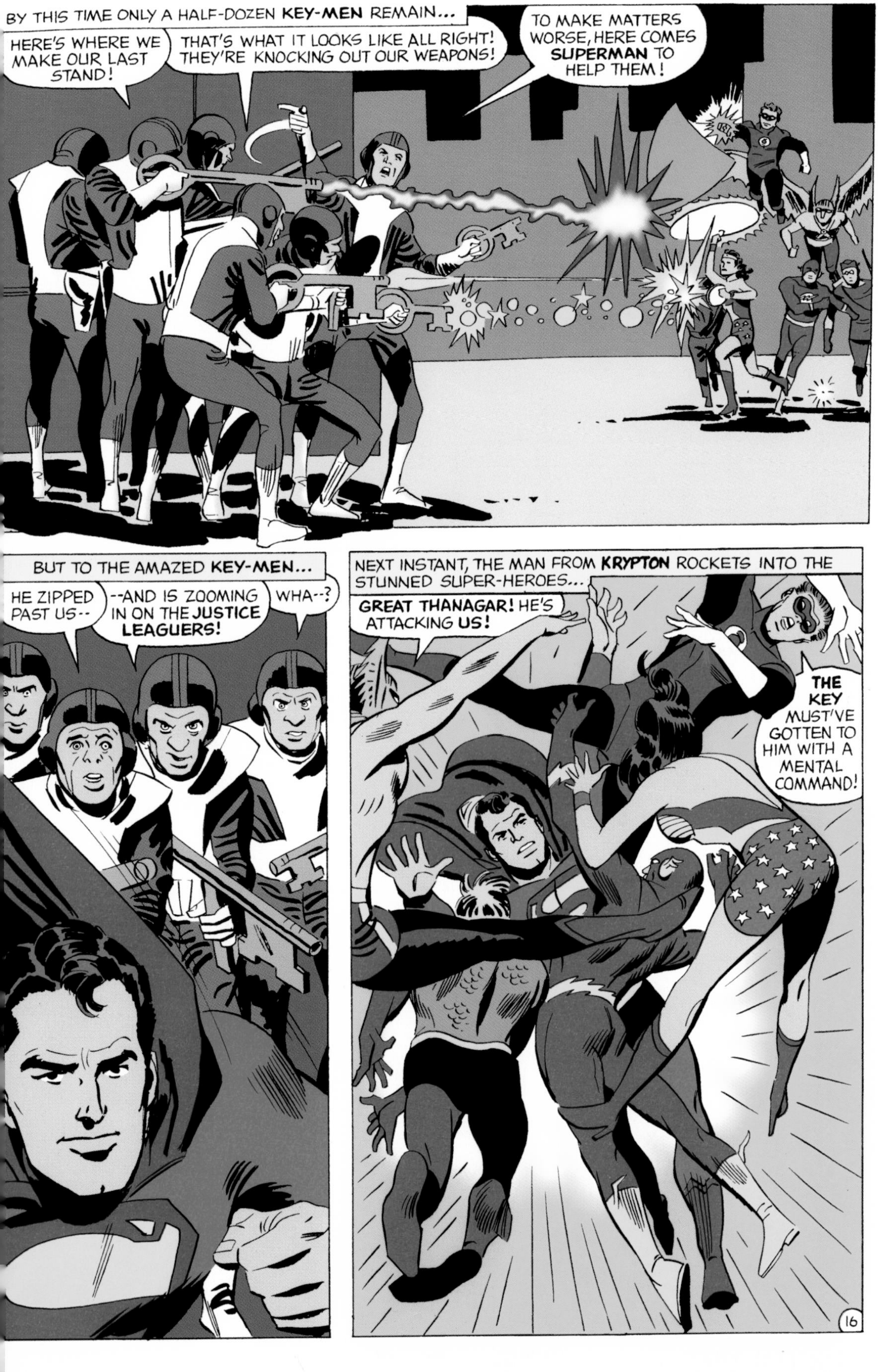

BY THIS TIME ONLY A HALF-DOZEN **KEY-MEN** REMAIN...
HERE'S WHERE WE MAKE OUR LAST STAND!
THAT'S WHAT IT LOOKS LIKE ALL RIGHT! THEY'RE KNOCKING OUT OUR WEAPONS!
TO MAKE MATTERS WORSE, HERE COMES **SUPERMAN** TO HELP THEM!
BUT TO THE AMAZED **KEY-MEN**...
HE ZIPPED PAST US--
--AND IS ZOOMING IN ON THE **JUSTICE LEAGUERS!**
WHA--?
NEXT INSTANT, THE MAN FROM **KRYPTON** ROCKETS INTO THE STUNNED SUPER-HEROES...
GREAT THANAGAR! HE'S ATTACKING **US!**
THE KEY MUST'VE GOTTEN TO HIM WITH A MENTAL COMMAND!
16

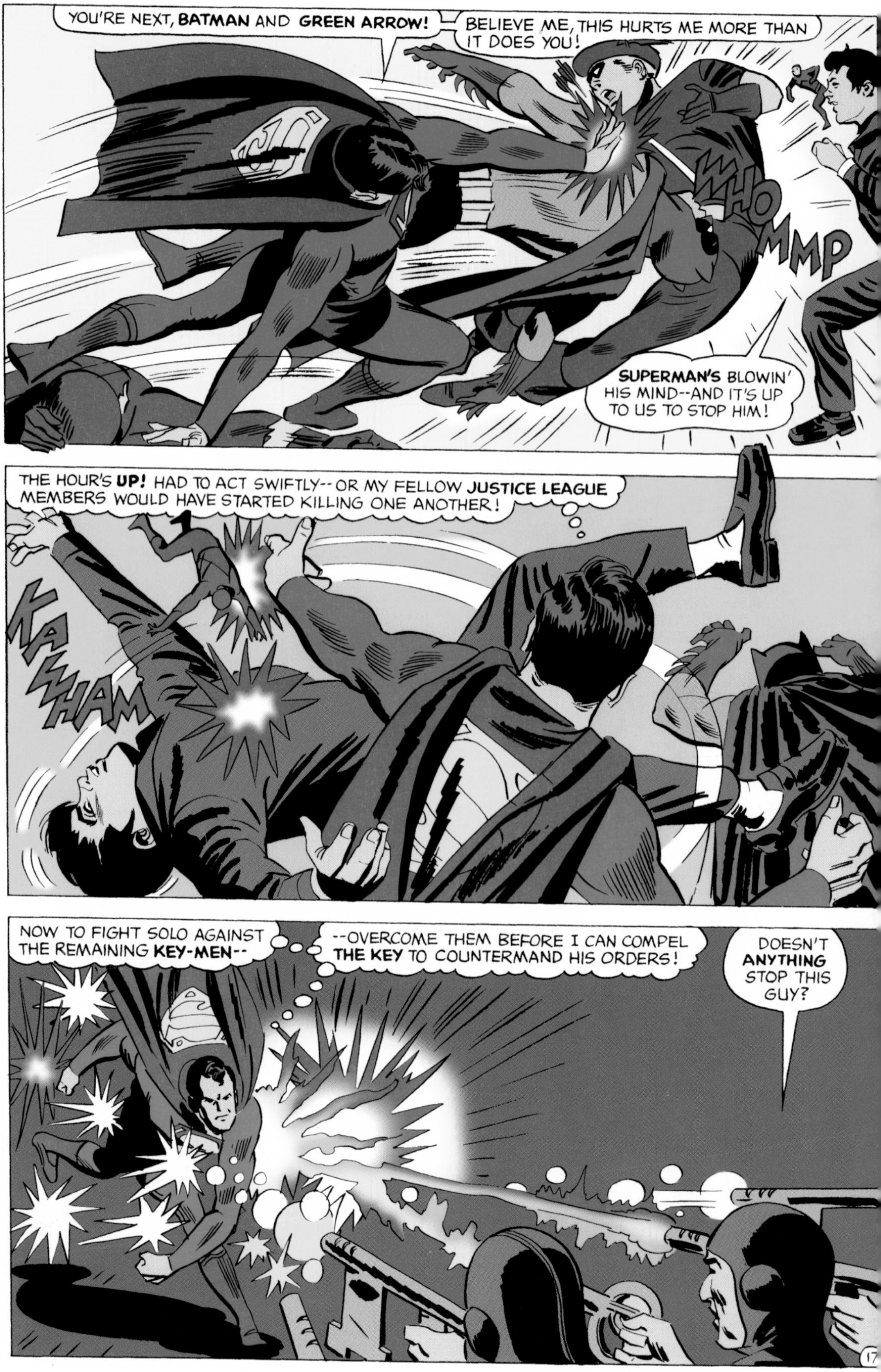
YOU'RE NEXT, BATMAN AND GREEN ARROW!
BELIEVE ME, THIS HURTS ME MORE THAN IT DOES YOU!
WHOMMP
SUPERMAN'S BLOWIN' HIS MIND--AND IT'S UP TO US TO STOP HIM!
THE HOUR'S UP! HAD TO ACT SWIFTLY--OR MY FELLOW JUSTICE LEAGUE MEMBERS WOULD HAVE STARTED KILLING ONE ANOTHER!
KAWHAM
NOW TO FIGHT SOLO AGAINST THE REMAINING KEY-MEN--
--OVERCOME THEM BEFORE I CAN COMPEL THE KEY TO COUNTERMAND HIS ORDERS!
DOESN'T ANYTHING STOP THIS GUY?
17

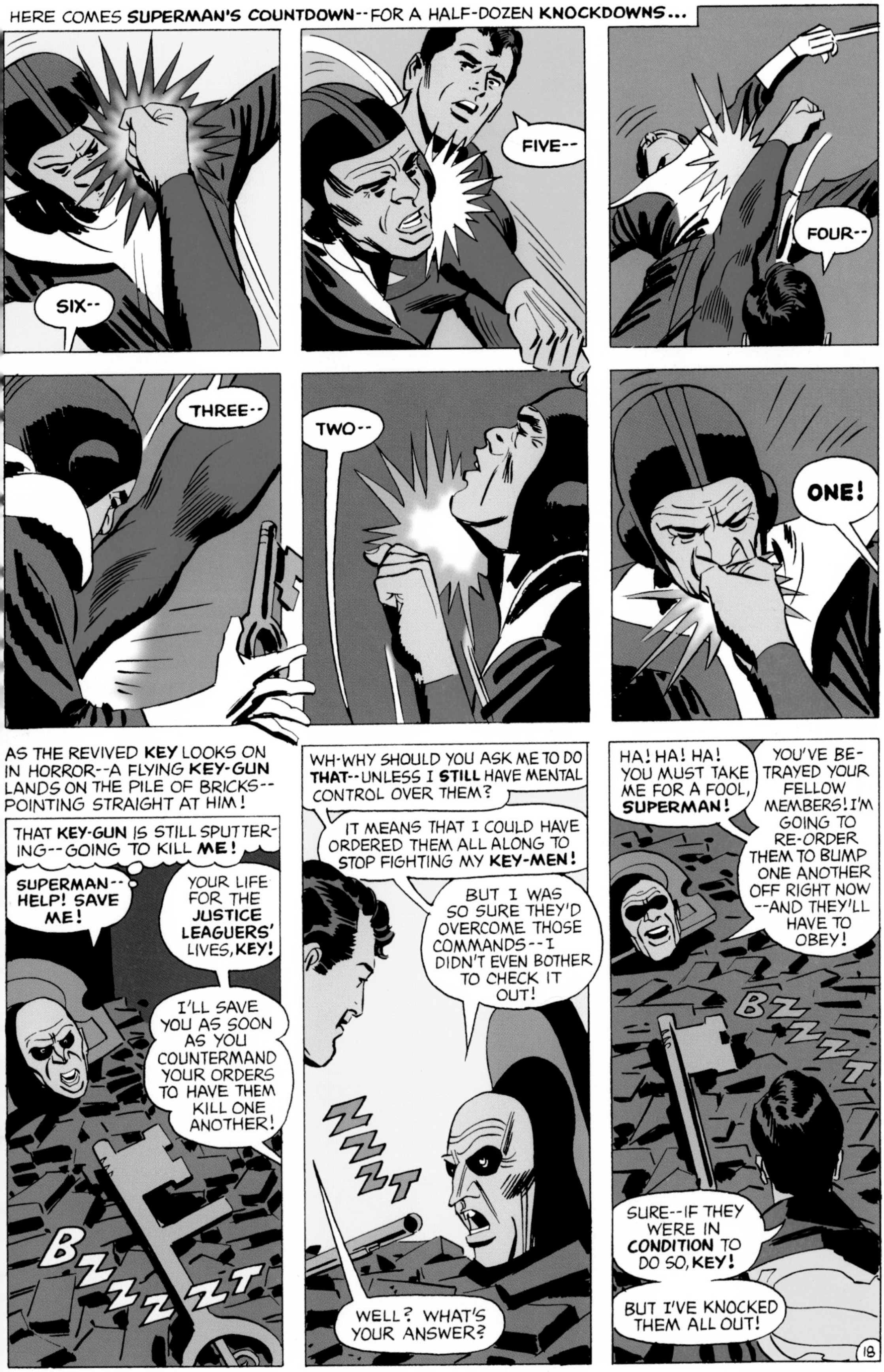
HERE COMES SUPERMAN'S COUNTDOWN--FOR A HALF-DOZEN KNOCKDOWNS...
SIX--
FIVE--
FOUR--
THREE--
TWO--
ONE!
AS THE REVIVED KEY LOOKS ON IN HORROR--A FLYING KEY-GUN LANDS ON THE PILE OF BRICKS--POINTING STRAIGHT AT HIM!
THAT KEY-GUN IS STILL SPUTTERING--GOING TO KILL ME!
SUPERMAN--HELP! SAVE ME!
YOUR LIFE FOR THE JUSTICE LEAGUERS' LIVES, KEY!
I'LL SAVE YOU AS SOON AS YOU COUNTERMAND YOUR ORDERS TO HAVE THEM KILL ONE ANOTHER!
BZZZZZT
WH-WHY SHOULD YOU ASK ME TO DO THAT--UNLESS I STILL HAVE MENTAL CONTROL OVER THEM?
IT MEANS THAT I COULD HAVE ORDERED THEM ALL ALONG TO STOP FIGHTING MY KEY-MEN!
BUT I WAS SO SURE THEY'D OVERCOME THOSE COMMANDS--I DIDN'T EVEN BOTHER TO CHECK IT OUT!
ZZZZT
WELL? WHAT'S YOUR ANSWER?
HA! HA! HA! YOU MUST TAKE ME FOR A FOOL, SUPERMAN!
YOU'VE BETRAYED YOUR FELLOW MEMBERS! I'M GOING TO RE-ORDER THEM TO BUMP ONE ANOTHER OFF RIGHT NOW--AND THEY'LL HAVE TO OBEY!
BZZZZT
SURE--IF THEY WERE IN CONDITION TO DO SO, KEY!
BUT I'VE KNOCKED THEM ALL OUT!
18

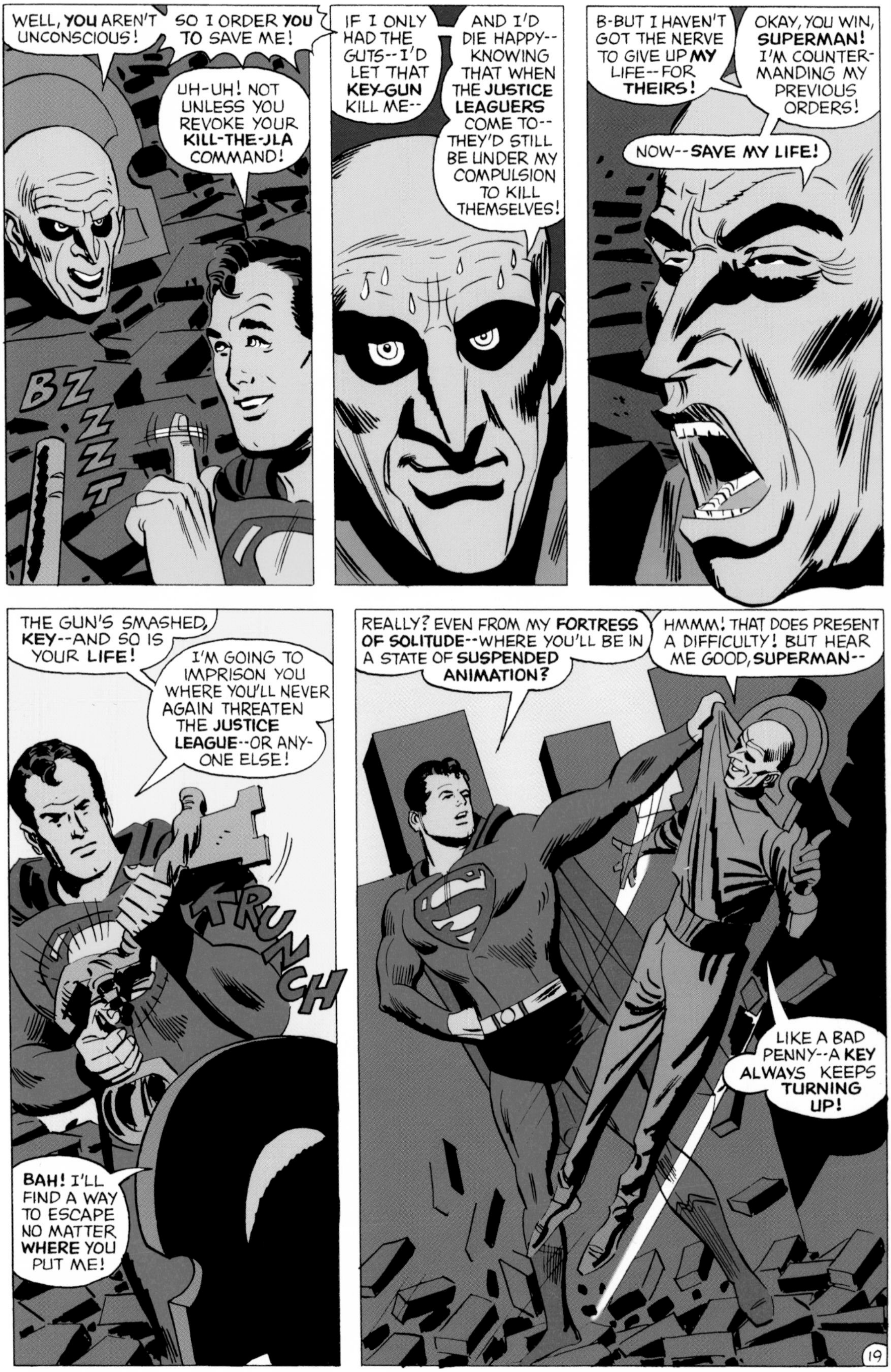
WELL, YOU AREN'T UNCONSCIOUS!
SO I ORDER YOU TO SAVE ME!
UH-UH! NOT UNLESS YOU REVOKE YOUR KILL-THE-JLA COMMAND!
BZZZT
IF I ONLY HAD THE GUTS--I'D LET THAT KEY-GUN KILL ME--
AND I'D DIE HAPPY--KNOWING THAT WHEN THE JUSTICE LEAGUERS COME TO--THEY'D STILL BE UNDER MY COMPULSION TO KILL THEMSELVES!
B-BUT I HAVEN'T GOT THE NERVE TO GIVE UP MY LIFE--FOR THEIRS!
OKAY, YOU WIN, SUPERMAN! I'M COUNTER-MANDING MY PREVIOUS ORDERS!
NOW--SAVE MY LIFE!
THE GUN'S SMASHED, KEY--AND SO IS YOUR LIFE!
I'M GOING TO IMPRISON YOU WHERE YOU'LL NEVER AGAIN THREATEN THE JUSTICE LEAGUE--OR ANY-ONE ELSE!
KRUNCH
BAH! I'LL FIND A WAY TO ESCAPE NO MATTER WHERE YOU PUT ME!
REALLY? EVEN FROM MY FORTRESS OF SOLITUDE--WHERE YOU'LL BE IN A STATE OF SUSPENDED ANIMATION?
HMMM! THAT DOES PRESENT A DIFFICULTY! BUT HEAR ME GOOD, SUPERMAN--
LIKE A BAD PENNY--A KEY ALWAYS KEEPS TURNING UP!
19

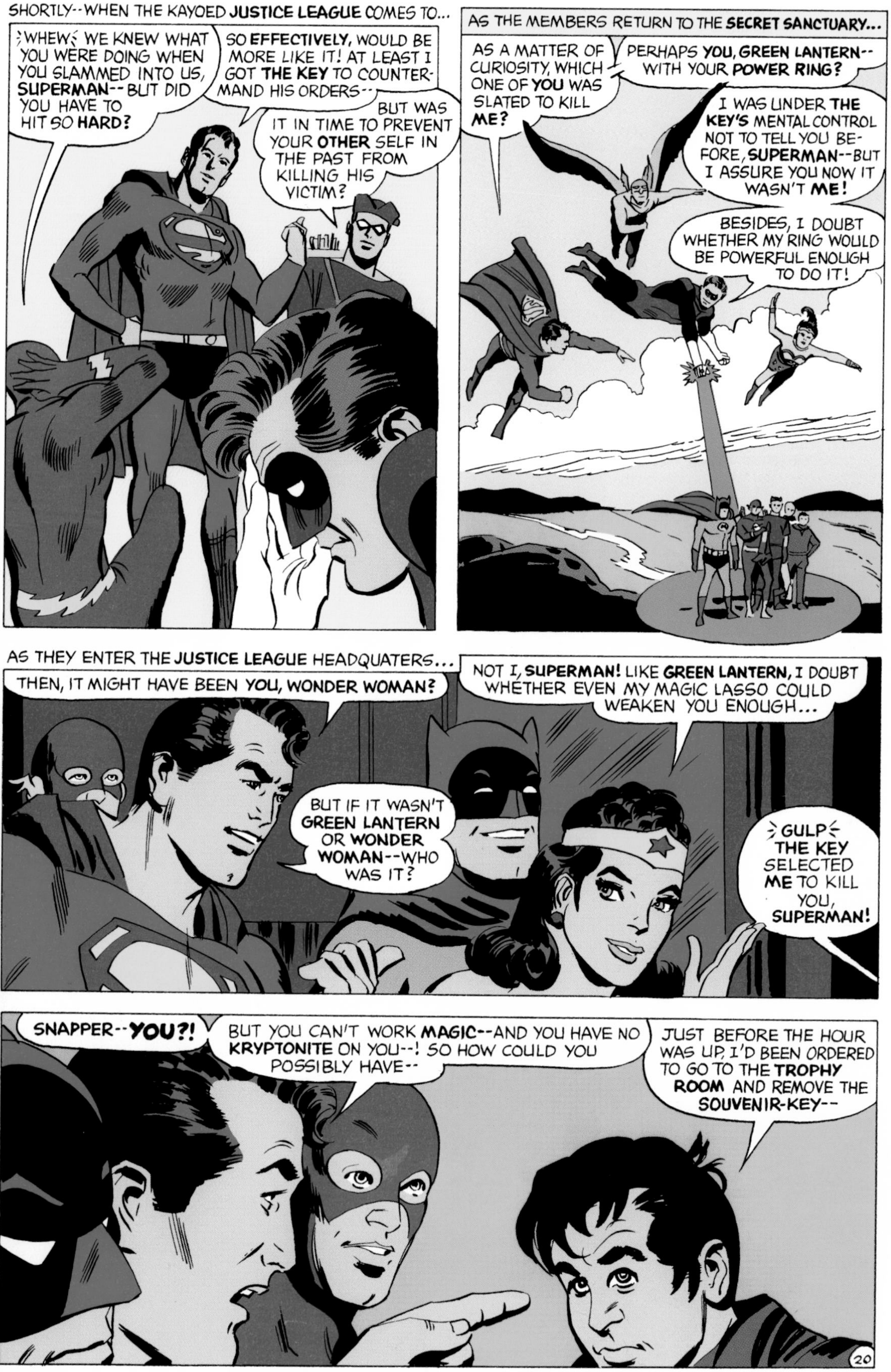
SHORTLY--WHEN THE KAYOED JUSTICE LEAGUE COMES TO...
WHEW! WE KNEW WHAT YOU WERE DOING WHEN YOU SLAMMED INTO US, SUPERMAN--BUT DID YOU HAVE TO HIT SO HARD?
SO EFFECTIVELY, WOULD BE MORE LIKE IT! AT LEAST I GOT THE KEY TO COUNTERMAND HIS ORDERS--
BUT WAS IT IN TIME TO PREVENT YOUR OTHER SELF IN THE PAST FROM KILLING HIS VICTIM?
AS THE MEMBERS RETURN TO THE SECRET SANCTUARY...
AS A MATTER OF CURIOSITY, WHICH ONE OF YOU WAS SLATED TO KILL ME?
PERHAPS YOU, GREEN LANTERN--WITH YOUR POWER RING?
I WAS UNDER THE KEY'S MENTAL CONTROL NOT TO TELL YOU BEFORE, SUPERMAN--BUT I ASSURE YOU NOW IT WASN'T ME!
BESIDES, I DOUBT WHETHER MY RING WOULD BE POWERFUL ENOUGH TO DO IT!
AS THEY ENTER THE JUSTICE LEAGUE HEADQUATERS...
THEN, IT MIGHT HAVE BEEN YOU, WONDER WOMAN?
NOT I, SUPERMAN! LIKE GREEN LANTERN, I DOUBT WHETHER EVEN MY MAGIC LASSO COULD WEAKEN YOU ENOUGH...
BUT IF IT WASN'T GREEN LANTERN OR WONDER WOMAN--WHO WAS IT?
GULP! THE KEY SELECTED ME TO KILL YOU, SUPERMAN!
SNAPPER--YOU?!
BUT YOU CAN'T WORK MAGIC--AND YOU HAVE NO KRYPTONITE ON YOU--! SO HOW COULD YOU POSSIBLY HAVE--
JUST BEFORE THE HOUR WAS UP, I'D BEEN ORDERED TO GO TO THE TROPHY ROOM AND REMOVE THE SOUVENIR-KEY--
20

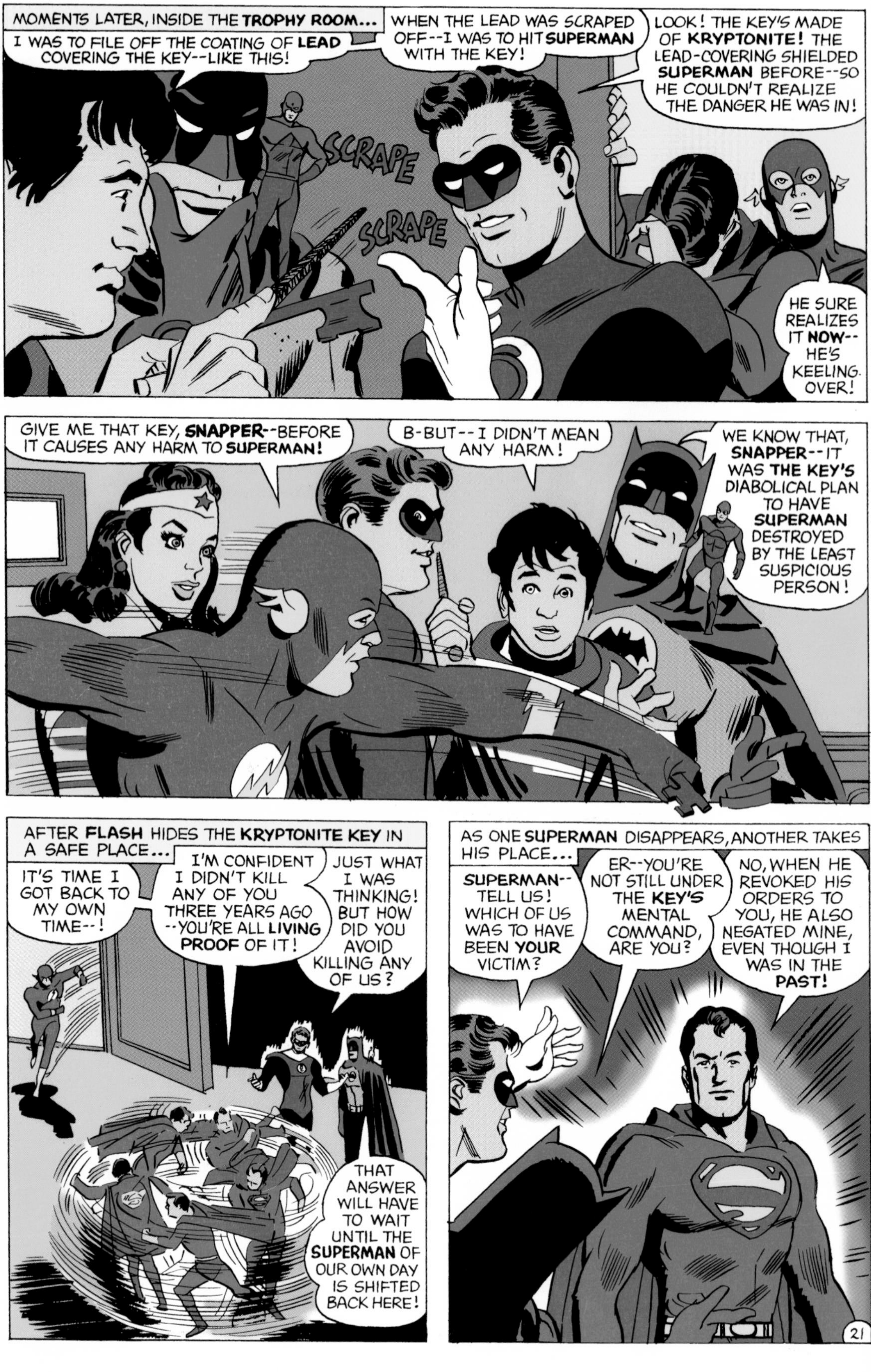
MOMENTS LATER, INSIDE THE TROPHY ROOM...
I WAS TO FILE OFF THE COATING OF LEAD COVERING THE KEY--LIKE THIS!
WHEN THE LEAD WAS SCRAPED OFF--I WAS TO HIT SUPERMAN WITH THE KEY!
LOOK! THE KEY'S MADE OF KRYPTONITE! THE LEAD-COVERING SHIELDED SUPERMAN BEFORE--SO HE COULDN'T REALIZE THE DANGER HE WAS IN!
SCRAPE
SCRAPE
HE SURE REALIZES IT NOW--HE'S KEELING OVER!
GIVE ME THAT KEY, SNAPPER--BEFORE IT CAUSES ANY HARM TO SUPERMAN!
B-BUT--I DIDN'T MEAN ANY HARM!
WE KNOW THAT, SNAPPER--IT WAS THE KEY'S DIABOLICAL PLAN TO HAVE SUPERMAN DESTROYED BY THE LEAST SUSPICIOUS PERSON!
AFTER FLASH HIDES THE KRYPTONITE KEY IN A SAFE PLACE...
IT'S TIME I GOT BACK TO MY OWN TIME--!
I'M CONFIDENT I DIDN'T KILL ANY OF YOU THREE YEARS AGO--YOU'RE ALL LIVING PROOF OF IT!
JUST WHAT I WAS THINKING! BUT HOW DID YOU AVOID KILLING ANY OF US?
THAT ANSWER WILL HAVE TO WAIT UNTIL THE SUPERMAN OF OUR OWN DAY IS SHIFTED BACK HERE!
AS ONE SUPERMAN DISAPPEARS, ANOTHER TAKES HIS PLACE...
SUPERMAN--TELL US! WHICH OF US WAS TO HAVE BEEN YOUR VICTIM?
ER--YOU'RE NOT STILL UNDER THE KEY'S MENTAL COMMAND, ARE YOU?
NO, WHEN HE REVOKED HIS ORDERS TO YOU, HE ALSO NEGATED MINE, EVEN THOUGH I WAS IN THE PAST!
21

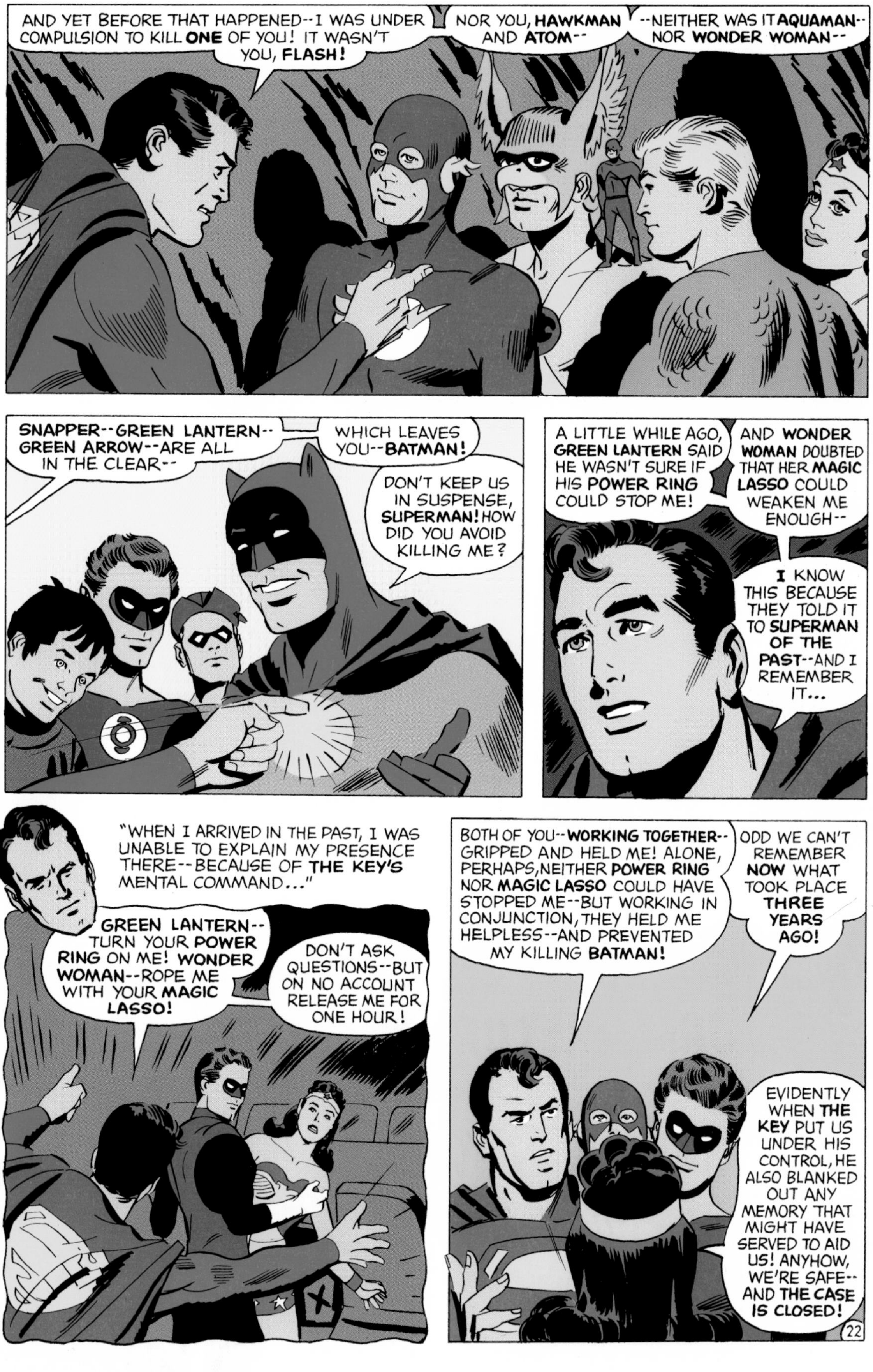
AND YET BEFORE THAT HAPPENED--I WAS UNDER COMPULSION TO KILL ONE OF YOU! IT WASN'T YOU, FLASH!
NOR YOU, HAWKMAN AND ATOM--
--NEITHER WAS IT AQUAMAN--NOR WONDER WOMAN--
SNAPPER--GREEN LANTERN--GREEN ARROW--ARE ALL IN THE CLEAR--
WHICH LEAVES YOU--BATMAN!
DON'T KEEP US IN SUSPENSE, SUPERMAN! HOW DID YOU AVOID KILLING ME?
A LITTLE WHILE AGO, GREEN LANTERN SAID HE WASN'T SURE IF HIS POWER RING COULD STOP ME!
AND WONDER WOMAN DOUBTED THAT HER MAGIC LASSO COULD WEAKEN ME ENOUGH--
I KNOW THIS BECAUSE THEY TOLD IT TO SUPERMAN OF THE PAST--AND I REMEMBER IT...
"WHEN I ARRIVED IN THE PAST, I WAS UNABLE TO EXPLAIN MY PRESENCE THERE--BECAUSE OF THE KEY'S MENTAL COMMAND..."
GREEN LANTERN--TURN YOUR POWER RING ON ME! WONDER WOMAN--ROPE ME WITH YOUR MAGIC LASSO!
DON'T ASK QUESTIONS--BUT ON NO ACCOUNT RELEASE ME FOR ONE HOUR!
BOTH OF YOU--WORKING TOGETHER--GRIPPED AND HELD ME! ALONE, PERHAPS, NEITHER POWER RING NOR MAGIC LASSO COULD HAVE STOPPED ME--BUT WORKING IN CONJUNCTION, THEY HELD ME HELPLESS--AND PREVENTED MY KILLING BATMAN!
ODD WE CAN'T REMEMBER NOW WHAT TOOK PLACE THREE YEARS AGO!
EVIDENTLY WHEN THE KEY PUT US UNDER HIS CONTROL, HE ALSO BLANKED OUT ANY MEMORY THAT MIGHT HAVE SERVED TO AID US! ANYHOW, WE'RE SAFE--AND THE CASE IS CLOSED!
22

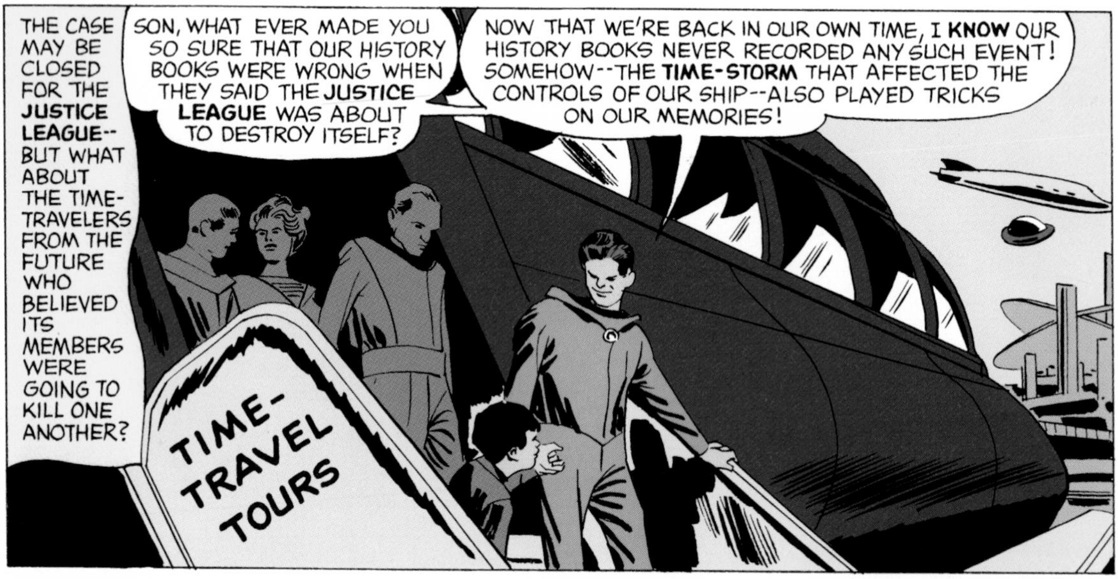
THE CASE MAY BE CLOSED FOR THE JUSTICE LEAGUE-- BUT WHAT ABOUT THE TIME-TRAVELERS FROM THE FUTURE WHO BELIEVED ITS MEMBERS WERE GOING TO KILL ONE ANOTHER?
SON, WHAT EVER MADE YOU SO SURE THAT OUR HISTORY BOOKS WERE WRONG WHEN THEY SAID THE JUSTICE LEAGUE WAS ABOUT TO DESTROY ITSELF?
NOW THAT WE'RE BACK IN OUR OWN TIME, I KNOW OUR HISTORY BOOKS NEVER RECORDED ANY SUCH EVENT! SOMEHOW--THE TIME-STORM THAT AFFECTED THE CONTROLS OF OUR SHIP--ALSO PLAYED TRICKS ON OUR MEMORIES!
TIME-TRAVEL TOURS

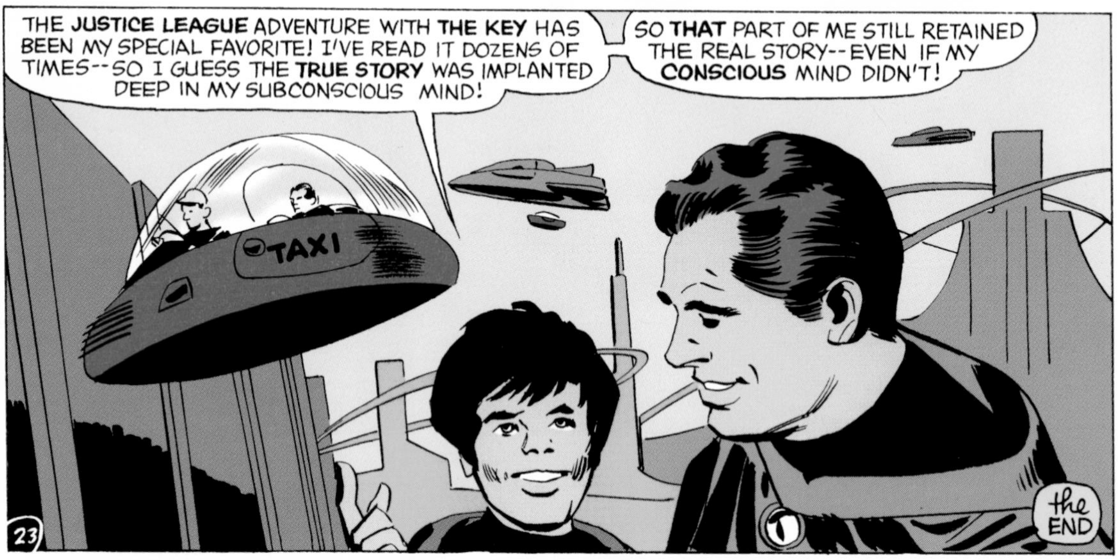
THE JUSTICE LEAGUE ADVENTURE WITH THE KEY HAS BEEN MY SPECIAL FAVORITE! I'VE READ IT DOZENS OF TIMES--SO I GUESS THE TRUE STORY WAS IMPLANTED DEEP IN MY SUBCONSCIOUS MIND!
SO THAT PART OF ME STILL RETAINED THE REAL STORY--EVEN IF MY CONSCIOUS MIND DIDN'T!
TAXI
23
the END

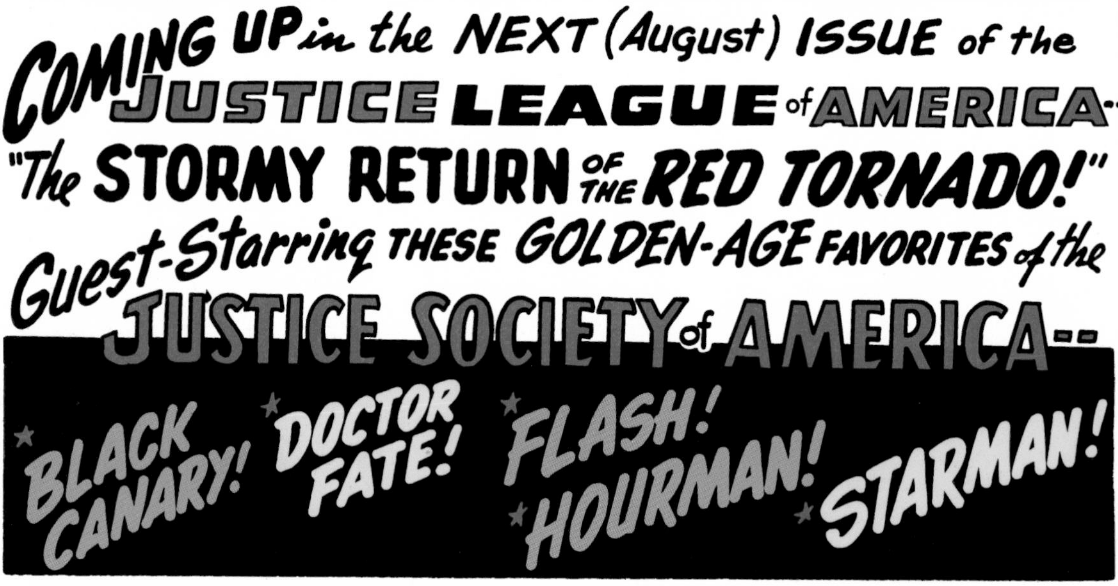
COMING UP in the NEXT (August) ISSUE of the
JUSTICE LEAGUE of AMERICA--
"The STORMY RETURN OF THE RED TORNADO!"
Guest-Starring THESE GOLDEN-AGE FAVORITES of the
JUSTICE SOCIETY of AMERICA--
BLACK CANARY!
DOCTOR FATE!
FLASH!
HOURMAN!
STARMAN!

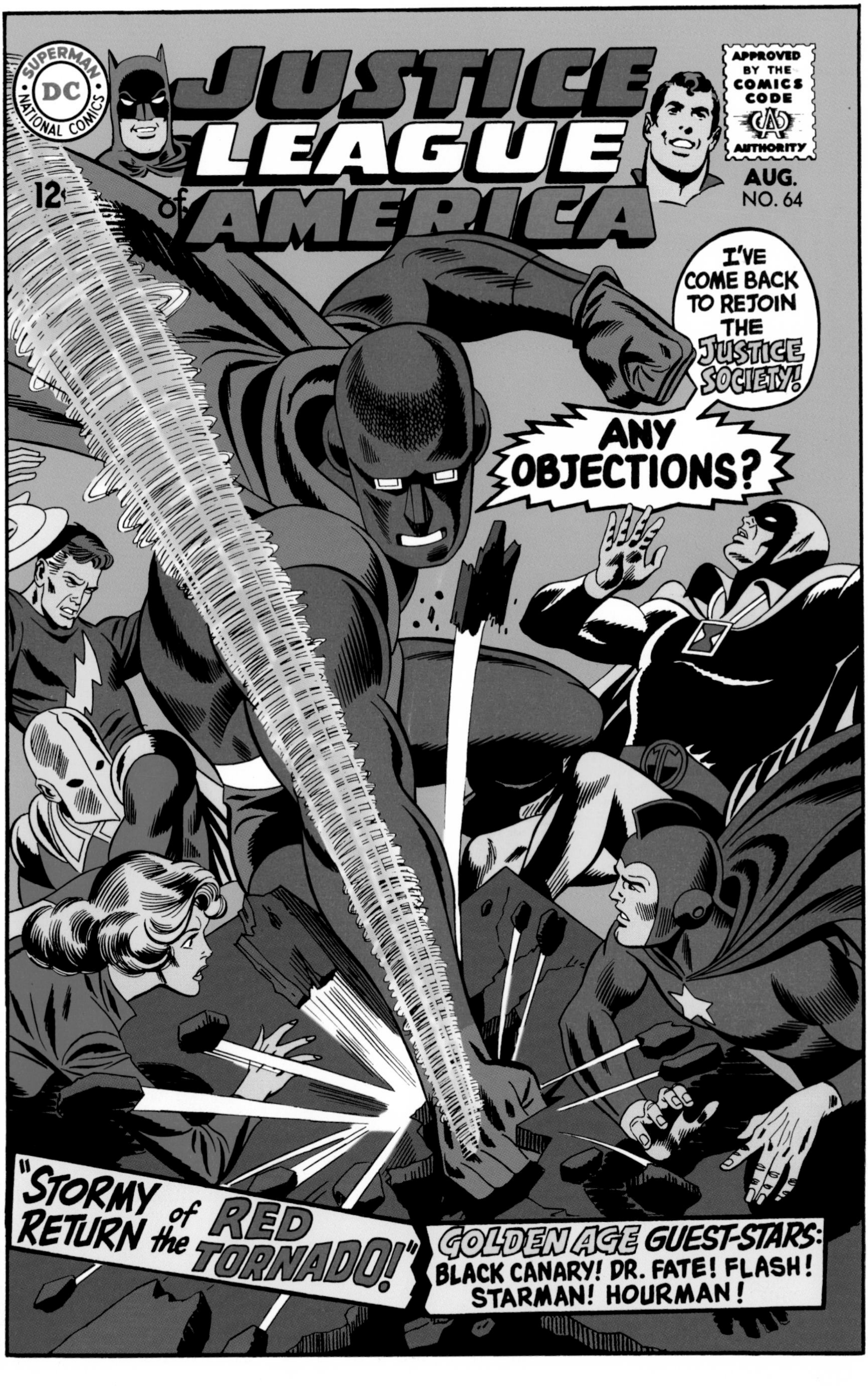

SUPERMAN DC NATIONAL COMICS
JUSTICE LEAGUE of AMERICA
12¢
APPROVED BY THE COMICS CODE AUTHORITY
AUG. NO. 64
I'VE COME BACK TO REJOIN THE JUSTICE SOCIETY!
ANY OBJECTIONS?
"STORMY RETURN of the RED TORNADO!"
GOLDEN AGE GUEST-STARS: BLACK CANARY! DR. FATE! FLASH! STARMAN! HOURMAN!

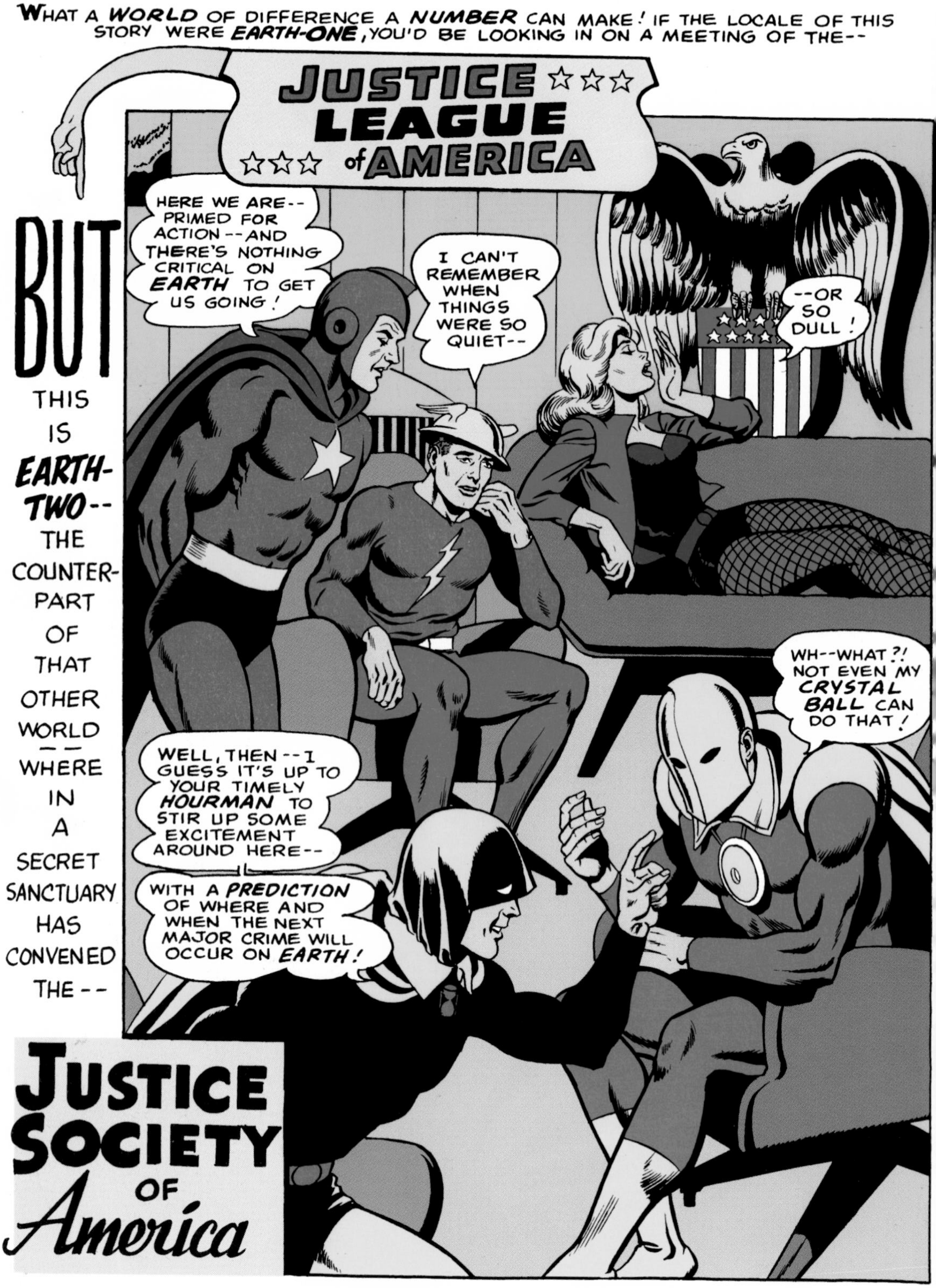
WHAT A WORLD OF DIFFERENCE A NUMBER CAN MAKE! IF THE LOCALE OF THIS STORY WERE EARTH-ONE, YOU'D BE LOOKING IN ON A MEETING OF THE--
JUSTICE LEAGUE of AMERICA
BUT THIS IS EARTH-TWO-- THE COUNTERPART OF THAT OTHER WORLD -- WHERE IN A SECRET SANCTUARY HAS CONVENED THE --
HERE WE ARE-- PRIMED FOR ACTION -- AND THERE'S NOTHING CRITICAL ON EARTH TO GET US GOING!
I CAN'T REMEMBER WHEN THINGS WERE SO QUIET--
--OR SO DULL!
WELL, THEN -- I GUESS IT'S UP TO YOUR TIMELY HOURMAN TO STIR UP SOME EXCITEMENT AROUND HERE--
WITH A PREDICTION OF WHERE AND WHEN THE NEXT MAJOR CRIME WILL OCCUR ON EARTH!
WH--WHAT?! NOT EVEN MY CRYSTAL BALL CAN DO THAT!
JUSTICE SOCIETY OF America

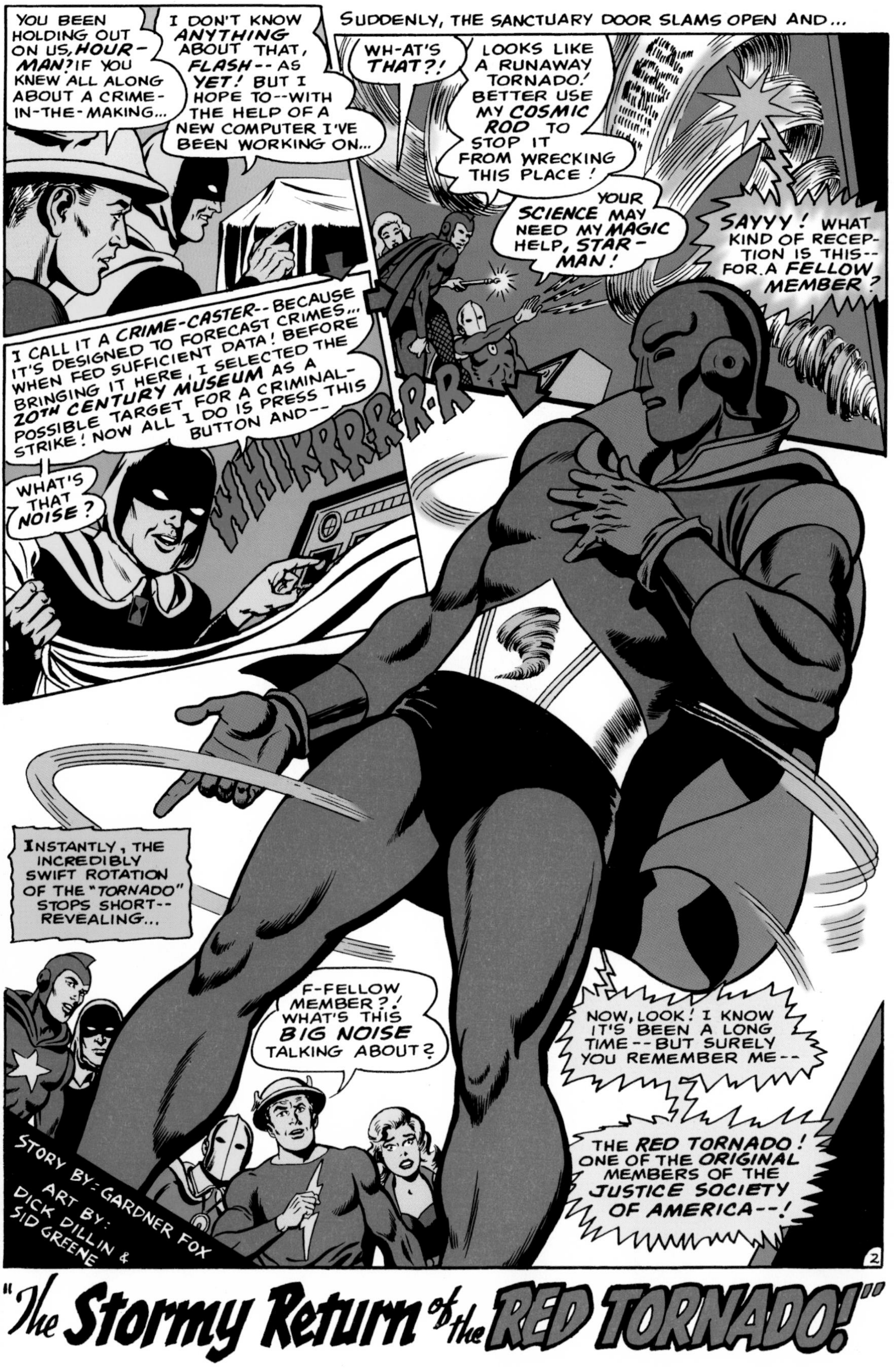
YOU BEEN HOLDING OUT ON US, HOUR-MAN? IF YOU KNEW ALL ALONG ABOUT A CRIME-IN-THE-MAKING...
I DON'T KNOW ANYTHING ABOUT THAT, FLASH-- AS YET! BUT I HOPE TO--WITH THE HELP OF A NEW COMPUTER I'VE BEEN WORKING ON...
I CALL IT A CRIME-CASTER-- BECAUSE IT'S DESIGNED TO FORECAST CRIMES... WHEN FED SUFFICIENT DATA! BEFORE BRINGING IT HERE, I SELECTED THE 20TH CENTURY MUSEUM AS A POSSIBLE TARGET FOR A CRIMINAL-STRIKE! NOW ALL I DO IS PRESS THIS BUTTON AND--
WHAT'S THAT NOISE?
WHIRRR-R-R-R
SUDDENLY, THE SANCTUARY DOOR SLAMS OPEN AND...
WH-AT'S THAT?!
LOOKS LIKE A RUNAWAY TORNADO! BETTER USE MY COSMIC ROD TO STOP IT FROM WRECKING THIS PLACE!
YOUR SCIENCE MAY NEED MY MAGIC HELP, STAR-MAN!
SAYYY! WHAT KIND OF RECEP-TION IS THIS-- FOR A FELLOW MEMBER?
INSTANTLY, THE INCREDIBLY SWIFT ROTATION OF THE "TORNADO" STOPS SHORT-- REVEALING...
F-FELLOW MEMBER?! WHAT'S THIS BIG NOISE TALKING ABOUT?
NOW, LOOK! I KNOW IT'S BEEN A LONG TIME -- BUT SURELY YOU REMEMBER ME--
THE RED TORNADO! ONE OF THE ORIGINAL MEMBERS OF THE JUSTICE SOCIETY OF AMERICA--!
STORY BY: GARDNER FOX
ART BY: DICK DILLIN & SID GREENE
2
"The Stormy Return of the RED TORNADO!"

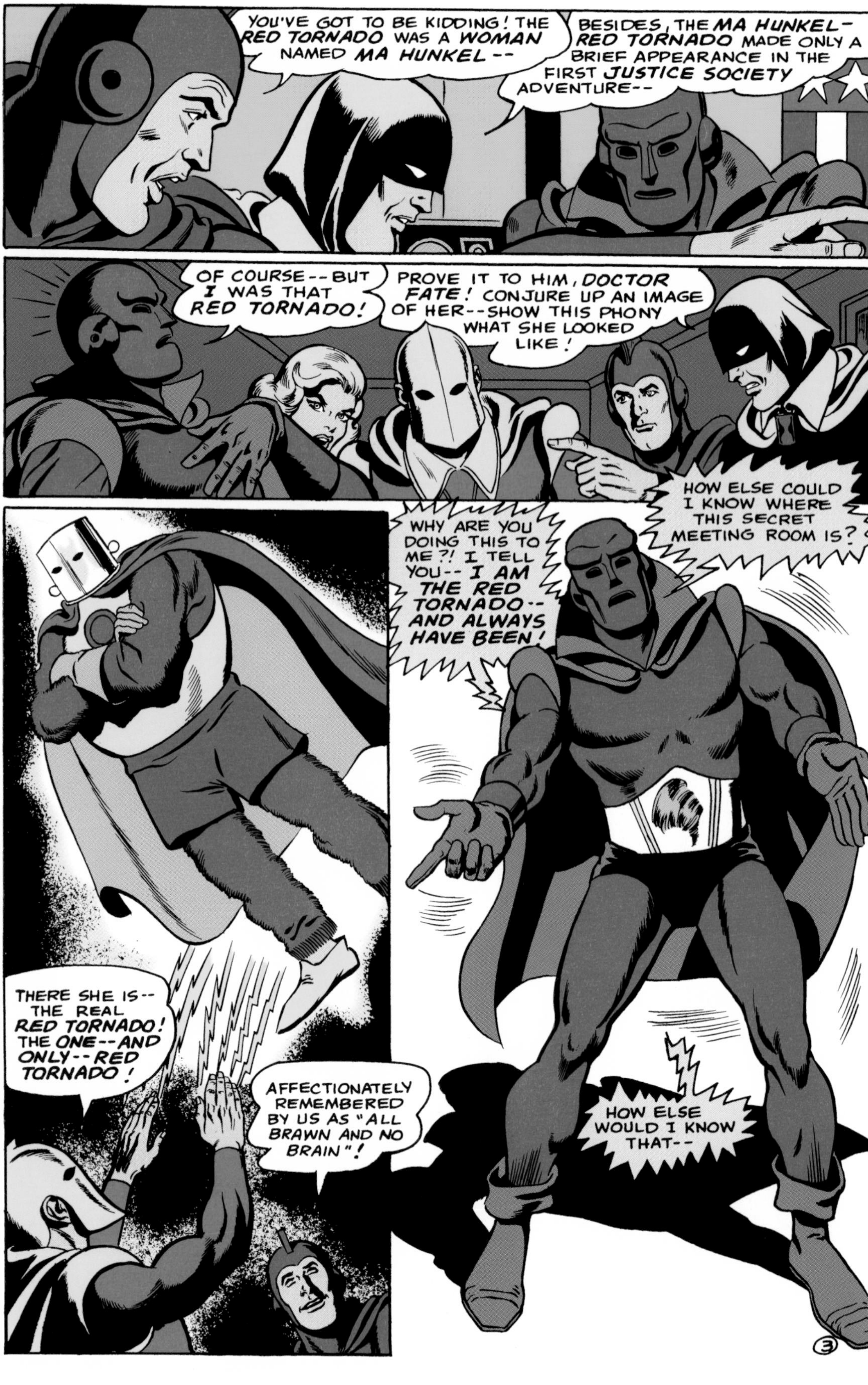
YOU'VE GOT TO BE KIDDING! THE RED TORNADO WAS A WOMAN NAMED MA HUNKEL--
BESIDES, THE MA HUNKEL-RED TORNADO MADE ONLY A BRIEF APPEARANCE IN THE FIRST JUSTICE SOCIETY ADVENTURE--
OF COURSE--BUT I WAS THAT RED TORNADO!
PROVE IT TO HIM, DOCTOR FATE! CONJURE UP AN IMAGE OF HER--SHOW THIS PHONY WHAT SHE LOOKED LIKE!
THERE SHE IS-- THE REAL RED TORNADO! THE ONE--AND ONLY--RED TORNADO!
AFFECTIONATELY REMEMBERED BY US AS "ALL BRAWN AND NO BRAIN"!
WHY ARE YOU DOING THIS TO ME?! I TELL YOU-- I AM THE RED TORNADO-- AND ALWAYS HAVE BEEN!
HOW ELSE COULD I KNOW WHERE THIS SECRET MEETING ROOM IS?
HOW ELSE WOULD I KNOW THAT--
3

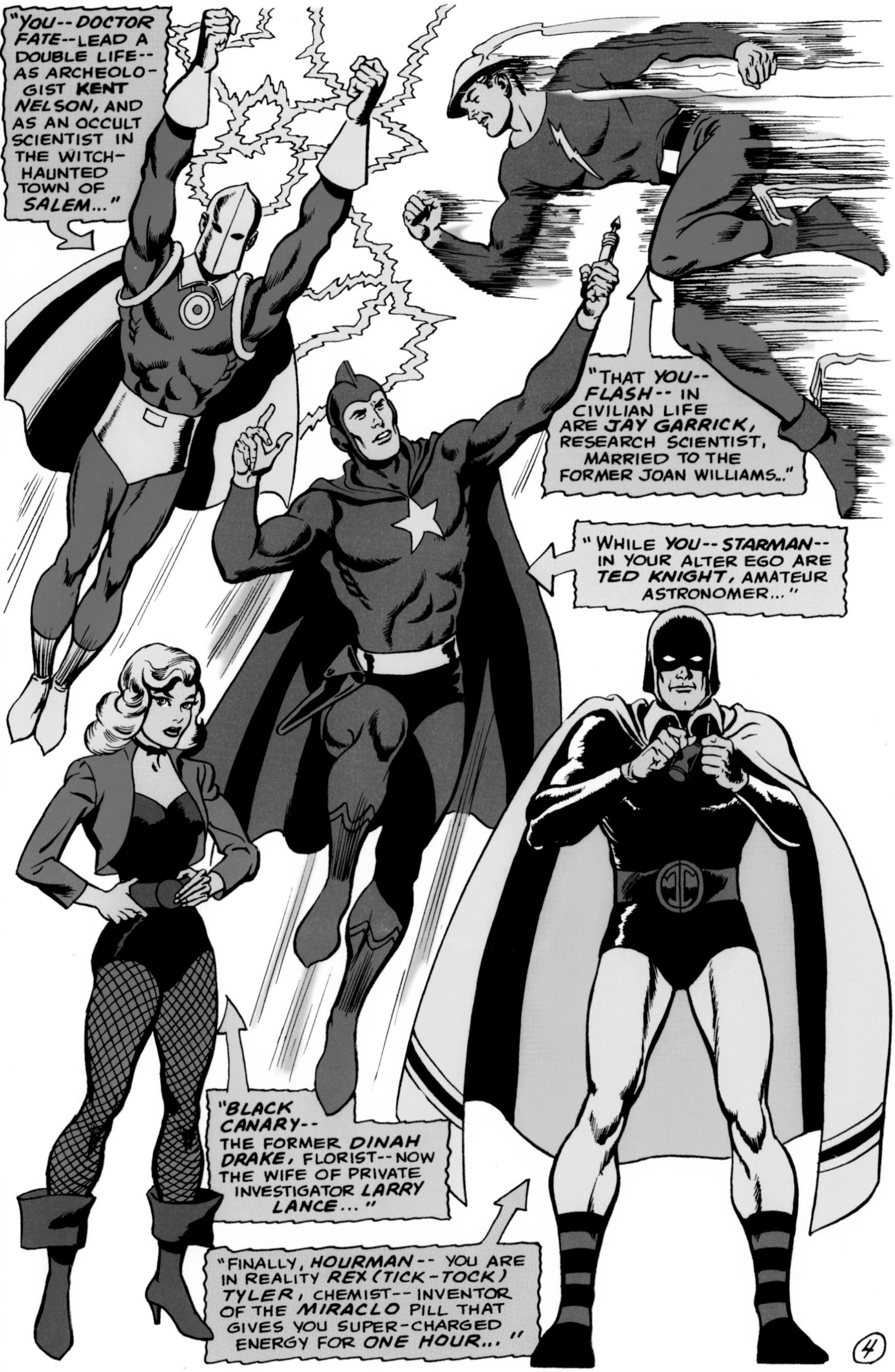
"YOU--DOCTOR FATE--LEAD A DOUBLE LIFE--AS ARCHEOLOGIST KENT NELSON, AND AS AN OCCULT SCIENTIST IN THE WITCH-HAUNTED TOWN OF SALEM..."
"THAT YOU--FLASH--IN CIVILIAN LIFE ARE JAY GARRICK, RESEARCH SCIENTIST, MARRIED TO THE FORMER JOAN WILLIAMS..."
"WHILE YOU--STARMAN--IN YOUR ALTER EGO ARE TED KNIGHT, AMATEUR ASTRONOMER..."
"BLACK CANARY--THE FORMER DINAH DRAKE, FLORIST--NOW THE WIFE OF PRIVATE INVESTIGATOR LARRY LANCE..."
"FINALLY, HOURMAN--YOU ARE IN REALITY REX (TICK-TOCK) TYLER, CHEMIST--INVENTOR OF THE MIRACLO PILL THAT GIVES YOU SUPER-CHARGED ENERGY FOR ONE HOUR..."
4

WELL, THEN--SINCE YOU KNOW ALL ABOUT *OUR* SECRET IDENTITIES-- *WHO ARE YOU IN REAL LIFE?*

WHY--I, ER-- I D-DON'T KNOW...!

THERE'S ONE WAY TO FIND OUT! REMOVE YOUR FACE-MASK!

MAYBE ONE OF US WILL KNOW YOU!

I--HOPE SO...

AS THE MASK IS RIPPED OFF, THERE IS A LONG MOMENT OF STUNNED SILENCE--BROKEN AT LAST BY...

HE--HAS-- NO--FACE!

HE'S BEEN COMMUNICATING WITH US BY *TELEPATHY!*

THEN HOW CAN HE TALK-- SEE--??

HE MUST *SEE* BY SOME FORM OF *EXTRA-SENSORY PERCEPTION!*

MY *CRIME-CASTER'S* COMPLETED ITS CRIME-PREDICTION!

NOW--YOU MUST UNDER-STAND THAT IT'S STILL IN A VERY ELE-MENTARY STAGE --AND MAY NOT PIN-POINT THE EXACT TIME--

NEVER MIND THE EXPLA-NATIONS, *HOURMAN!* WHAT DID THE 'CASTER COME UP WITH?

KLIDNNGG

IT FORECASTS A ROBBERY OF THE *20TH CENTURY MUSEUM*-- SOME-TIME TODAY!

IF THIS WORKS OUT, *HOURMAN,* YOU'LL HAVE MADE A TRE-MENDOUS CRIME-FIGHTING BREAK-THROUGH!

AS LONG AS THE TIME-CRIME COULD BE *NOW*-- WE'D BETTER RUSH OVER TO THE MUSEUM!

I'M GOING WITH YOU! PROVE MY-SELF TO YOU--!

OKAY! BUT THE MYSTERY ABOUT YOU ISN'T SOLVED YET, *RED TORNADO*-- NOT BY A LONG SHOT!

⑤

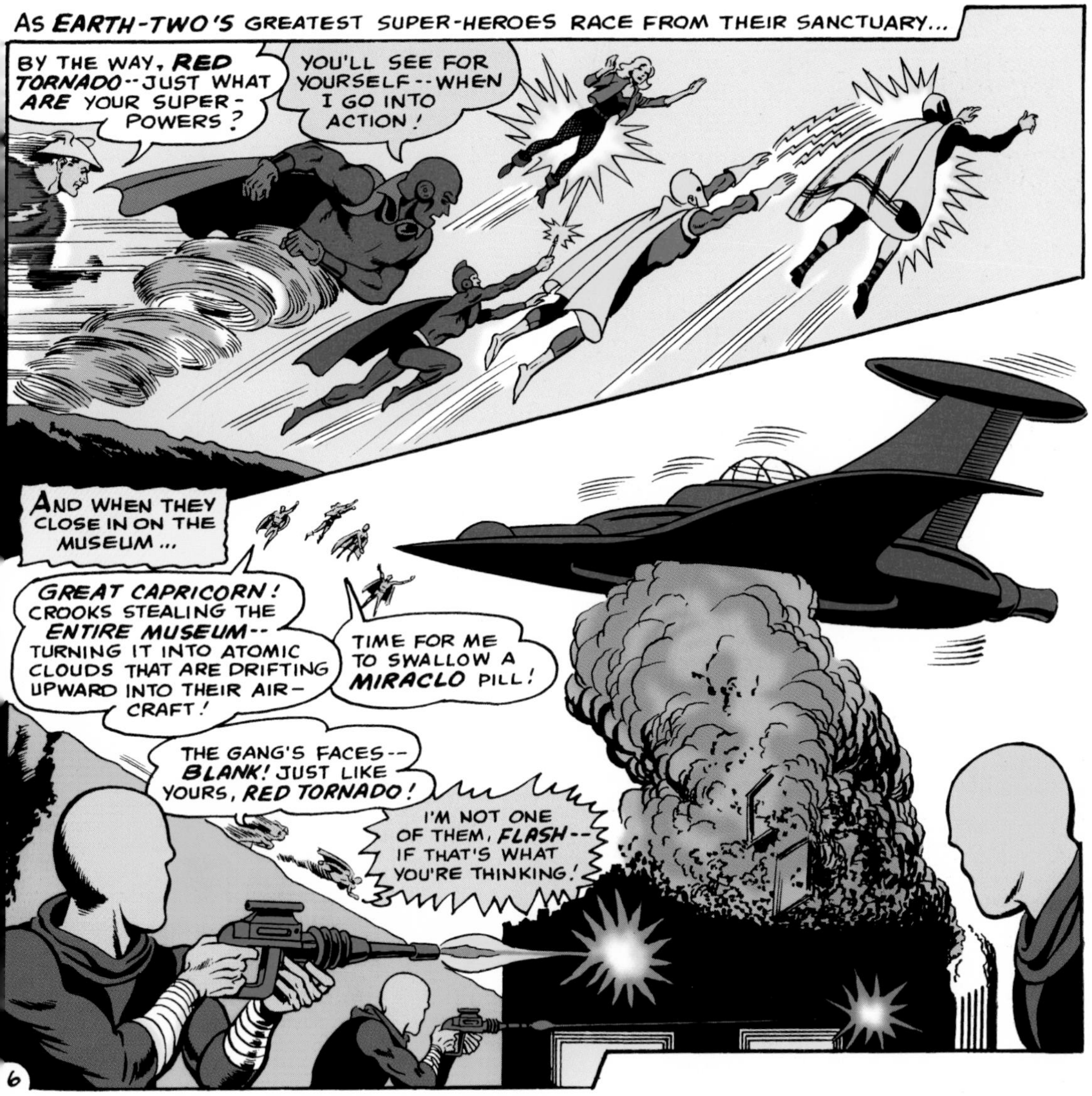
AS EARTH-TWO'S GREATEST SUPER-HEROES RACE FROM THEIR SANCTUARY...
BY THE WAY, RED TORNADO-- JUST WHAT ARE YOUR SUPER-POWERS?
YOU'LL SEE FOR YOURSELF--WHEN I GO INTO ACTION!
AND WHEN THEY CLOSE IN ON THE MUSEUM...
GREAT CAPRICORN! CROOKS STEALING THE ENTIRE MUSEUM-- TURNING IT INTO ATOMIC CLOUDS THAT ARE DRIFTING UPWARD INTO THEIR AIR-CRAFT!
TIME FOR ME TO SWALLOW A MIRACLO PILL!
THE GANG'S FACES-- BLANK! JUST LIKE YOURS, RED TORNADO!
I'M NOT ONE OF THEM, FLASH-- IF THAT'S WHAT YOU'RE THINKING!
6

JUSTICE LEAGUE of AMERICA

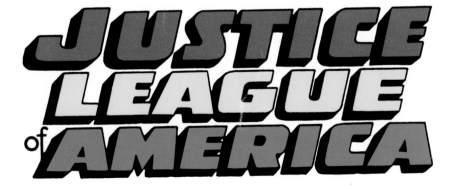

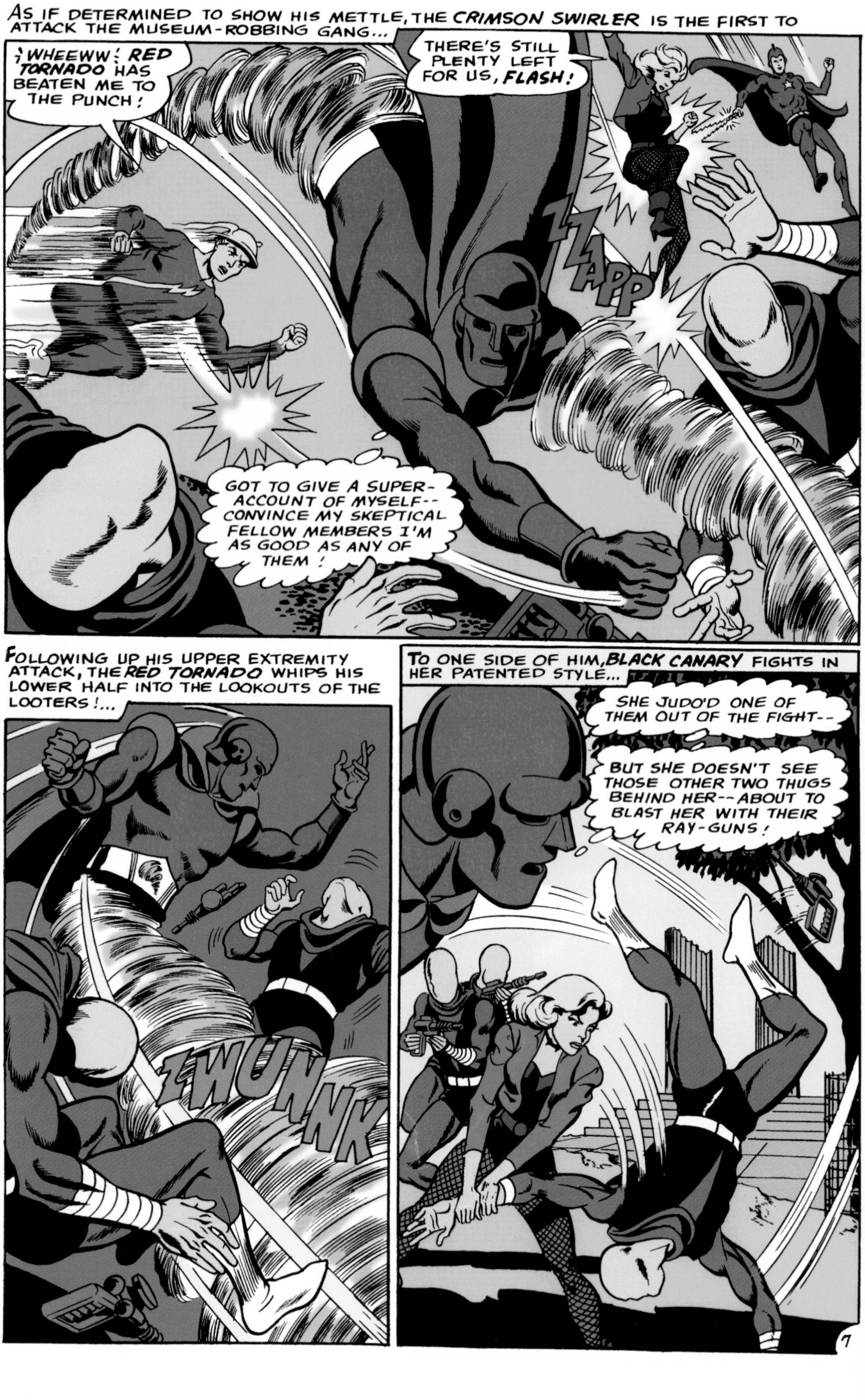
AS IF DETERMINED TO SHOW HIS METTLE, THE CRIMSON SWIRLER IS THE FIRST TO ATTACK THE MUSEUM-ROBBING GANG...
¡WHEEWW! RED TORNADO HAS BEATEN ME TO THE PUNCH!
THERE'S STILL PLENTY LEFT FOR US, FLASH!
ZZAPP
GOT TO GIVE A SUPER-ACCOUNT OF MYSELF-- CONVINCE MY SKEPTICAL FELLOW MEMBERS I'M AS GOOD AS ANY OF THEM!
FOLLOWING UP HIS UPPER EXTREMITY ATTACK, THE RED TORNADO WHIPS HIS LOWER HALF INTO THE LOOKOUTS OF THE LOOTERS!...
TWUNNNK
TO ONE SIDE OF HIM, BLACK CANARY FIGHTS IN HER PATENTED STYLE...
SHE JUDO'D ONE OF THEM OUT OF THE FIGHT--
BUT SHE DOESN'T SEE THOSE OTHER TWO THUGS BEHIND HER--ABOUT TO BLAST HER WITH THEIR RAY-GUNS!
7

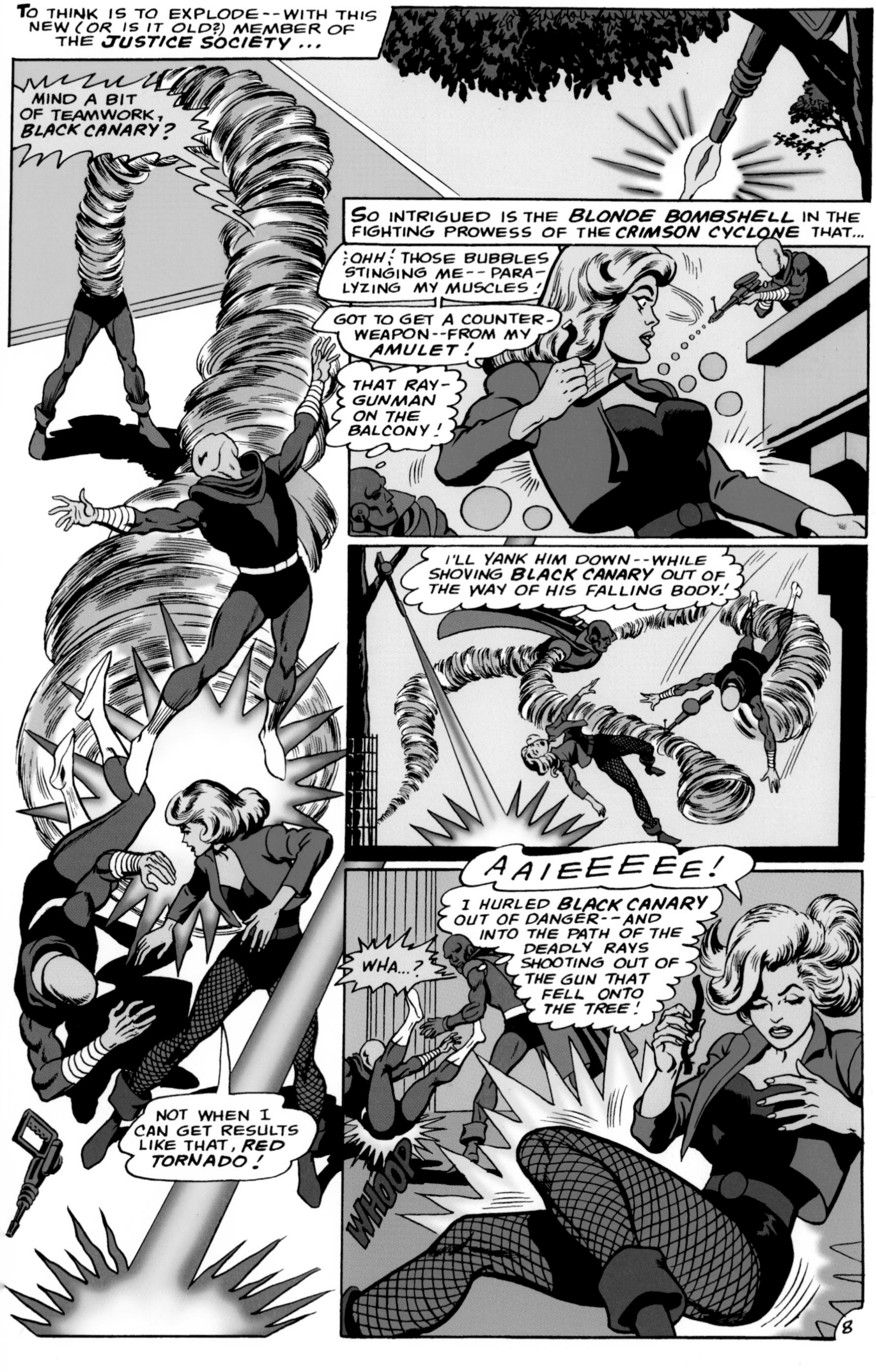
TO THINK IS TO EXPLODE--WITH THIS NEW (OR IS IT OLD?) MEMBER OF THE JUSTICE SOCIETY ...
MIND A BIT OF TEAMWORK, BLACK CANARY?
NOT WHEN I CAN GET RESULTS LIKE THAT, RED TORNADO!
SO INTRIGUED IS THE BLONDE BOMBSHELL IN THE FIGHTING PROWESS OF THE CRIMSON CYCLONE THAT...
¡OHH! THOSE BUBBLES STINGING ME--PARALYZING MY MUSCLES!
GOT TO GET A COUNTER-WEAPON--FROM MY AMULET!
THAT RAY-GUNMAN ON THE BALCONY!
I'LL YANK HIM DOWN--WHILE SHOVING BLACK CANARY OUT OF THE WAY OF HIS FALLING BODY!
AAIEEEEEE!
I HURLED BLACK CANARY OUT OF DANGER--AND INTO THE PATH OF THE DEADLY RAYS SHOOTING OUT OF THE GUN THAT FELL ONTO THE TREE!
WHA...?
WHOOP
8

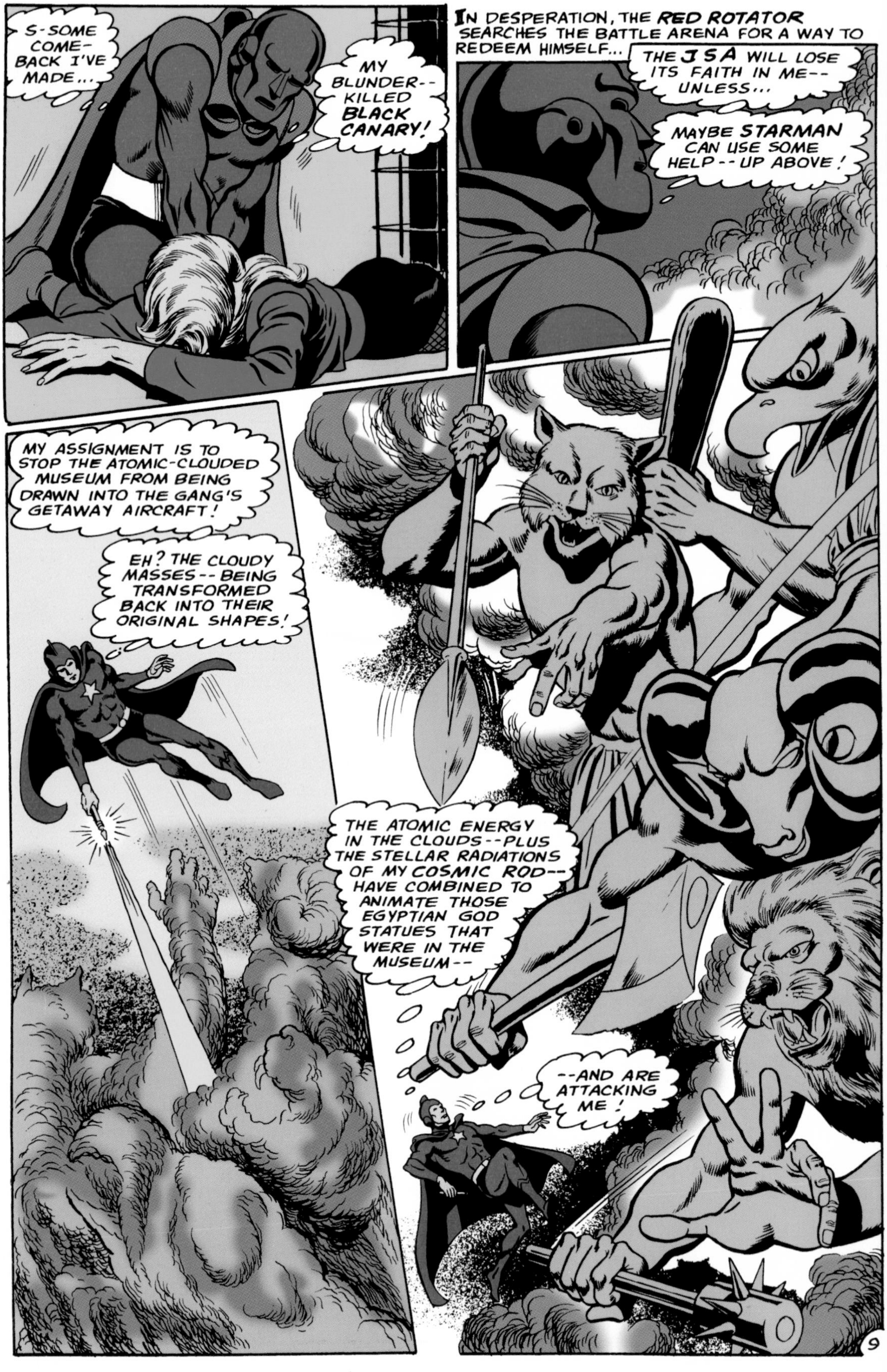
S-SOME COME-BACK I'VE MADE...
MY BLUNDER--KILLED BLACK CANARY!
IN DESPERATION, THE RED ROTATOR SEARCHES THE BATTLE ARENA FOR A WAY TO REDEEM HIMSELF...
THE JSA WILL LOSE ITS FAITH IN ME--UNLESS...
MAYBE STARMAN CAN USE SOME HELP--UP ABOVE!
MY ASSIGNMENT IS TO STOP THE ATOMIC-CLOUDED MUSEUM FROM BEING DRAWN INTO THE GANG'S GETAWAY AIRCRAFT!
EH? THE CLOUDY MASSES--BEING TRANSFORMED BACK INTO THEIR ORIGINAL SHAPES!
THE ATOMIC ENERGY IN THE CLOUDS--PLUS THE STELLAR RADIATIONS OF MY COSMIC ROD--HAVE COMBINED TO ANIMATE THOSE EGYPTIAN GOD STATUES THAT WERE IN THE MUSEUM--
--AND ARE ATTACKING ME!
9

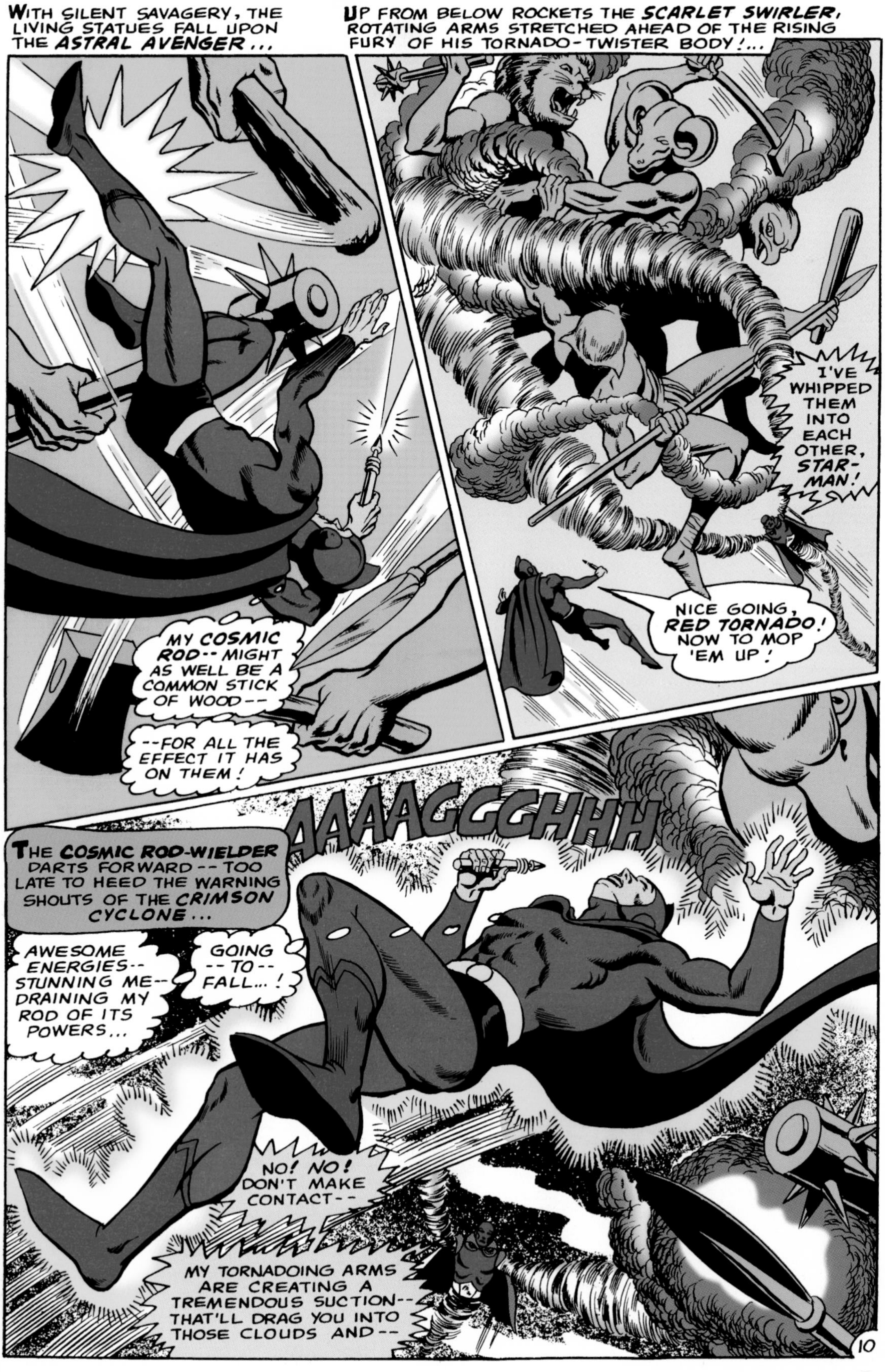
WITH SILENT SAVAGERY, THE LIVING STATUES FALL UPON THE ASTRAL AVENGER...
MY COSMIC ROD-- MIGHT AS WELL BE A COMMON STICK OF WOOD--
--FOR ALL THE EFFECT IT HAS ON THEM!
UP FROM BELOW ROCKETS THE SCARLET SWIRLER, ROTATING ARMS STRETCHED AHEAD OF THE RISING FURY OF HIS TORNADO-TWISTER BODY!...
I'VE WHIPPED THEM INTO EACH OTHER, STAR-MAN!
NICE GOING, RED TORNADO! NOW TO MOP 'EM UP!
AAAAGGGHHH
THE COSMIC ROD-WIELDER DARTS FORWARD -- TOO LATE TO HEED THE WARNING SHOUTS OF THE CRIMSON CYCLONE...
AWESOME ENERGIES-- STUNNING ME-- DRAINING MY ROD OF ITS POWERS...
GOING --TO-- FALL...!
NO! NO! DON'T MAKE CONTACT--
MY TORNADOING ARMS ARE CREATING A TREMENDOUS SUCTION-- THAT'LL DRAG YOU INTO THOSE CLOUDS AND--
10

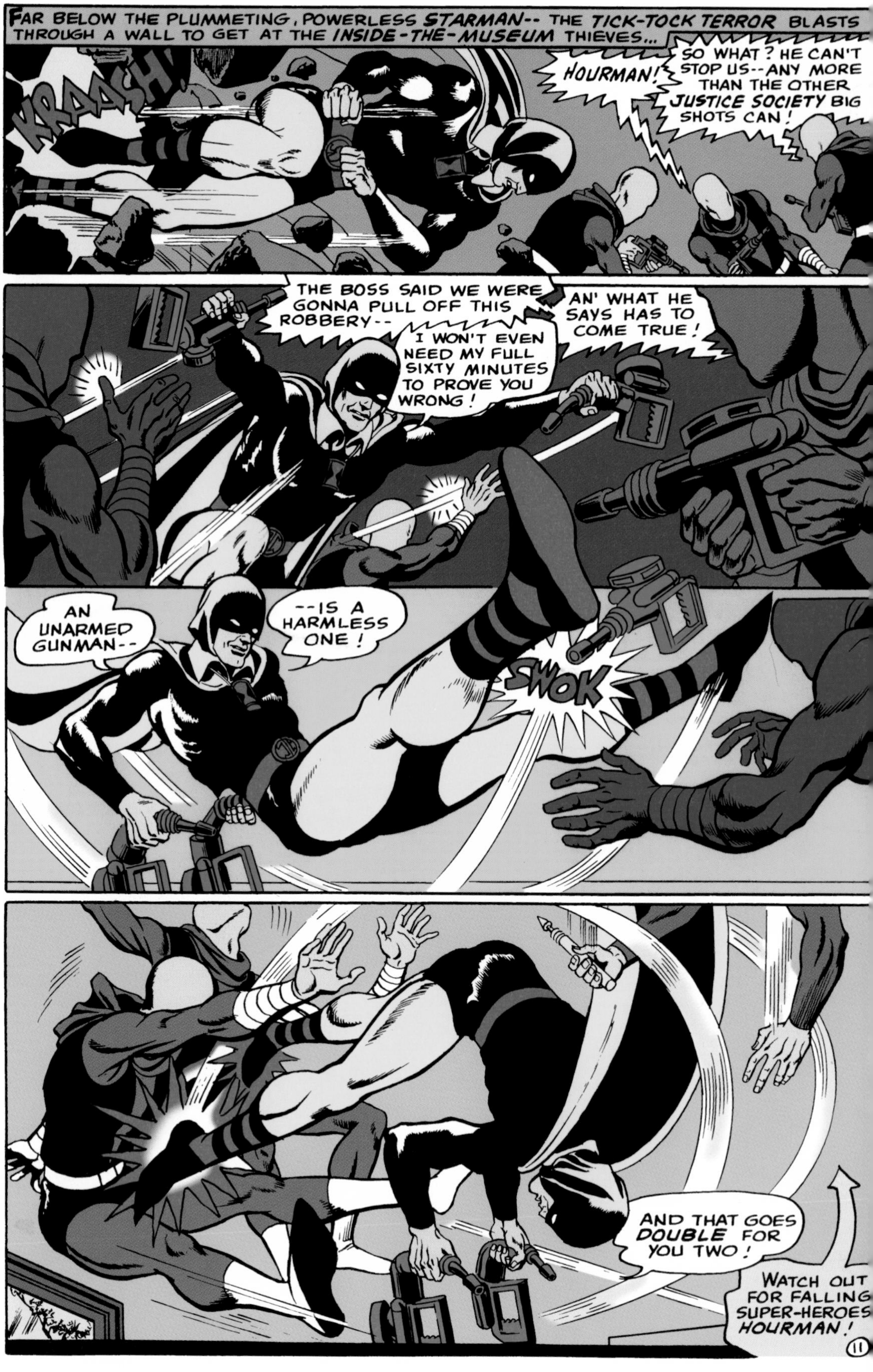
FAR BELOW THE PLUMMETING, POWERLESS STARMAN-- THE TICK-TOCK TERROR BLASTS THROUGH A WALL TO GET AT THE INSIDE-THE-MUSEUM THIEVES...
KRAASH!
HOURMAN!
SO WHAT? HE CAN'T STOP US--ANY MORE THAN THE OTHER JUSTICE SOCIETY BIG SHOTS CAN!
THE BOSS SAID WE WERE GONNA PULL OFF THIS ROBBERY--
AN' WHAT HE SAYS HAS TO COME TRUE!
I WON'T EVEN NEED MY FULL SIXTY MINUTES TO PROVE YOU WRONG!
AN UNARMED GUNMAN--
--IS A HARMLESS ONE!
SWOK
AND THAT GOES DOUBLE FOR YOU TWO!
WATCH OUT FOR FALLING SUPER-HEROES HOURMAN!
11

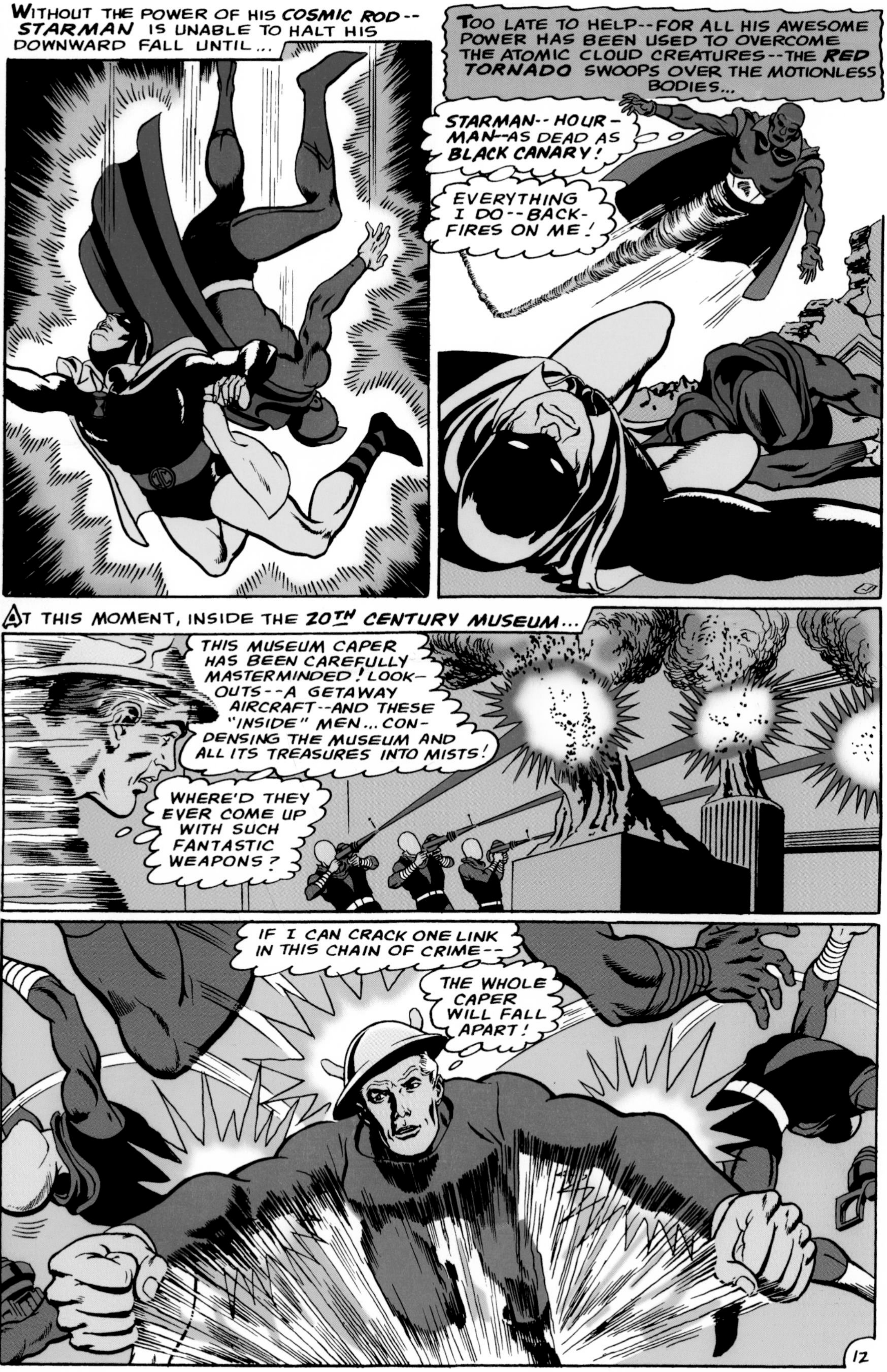
WITHOUT THE POWER OF HIS COSMIC ROD-- STARMAN IS UNABLE TO HALT HIS DOWNWARD FALL UNTIL...
TOO LATE TO HELP--FOR ALL HIS AWESOME POWER HAS BEEN USED TO OVERCOME THE ATOMIC CLOUD CREATURES--THE RED TORNADO SWOOPS OVER THE MOTIONLESS BODIES...
STARMAN-- HOUR-MAN--AS DEAD AS BLACK CANARY!
EVERYTHING I DO--BACK-FIRES ON ME!
AT THIS MOMENT, INSIDE THE 20TH CENTURY MUSEUM...
THIS MUSEUM CAPER HAS BEEN CAREFULLY MASTERMINDED! LOOK-OUTS--A GETAWAY AIRCRAFT--AND THESE "INSIDE" MEN... CON-DENSING THE MUSEUM AND ALL ITS TREASURES INTO MISTS!
WHERE'D THEY EVER COME UP WITH SUCH FANTASTIC WEAPONS?
IF I CAN CRACK ONE LINK IN THIS CHAIN OF CRIME--
THE WHOLE CAPER WILL FALL APART!
12

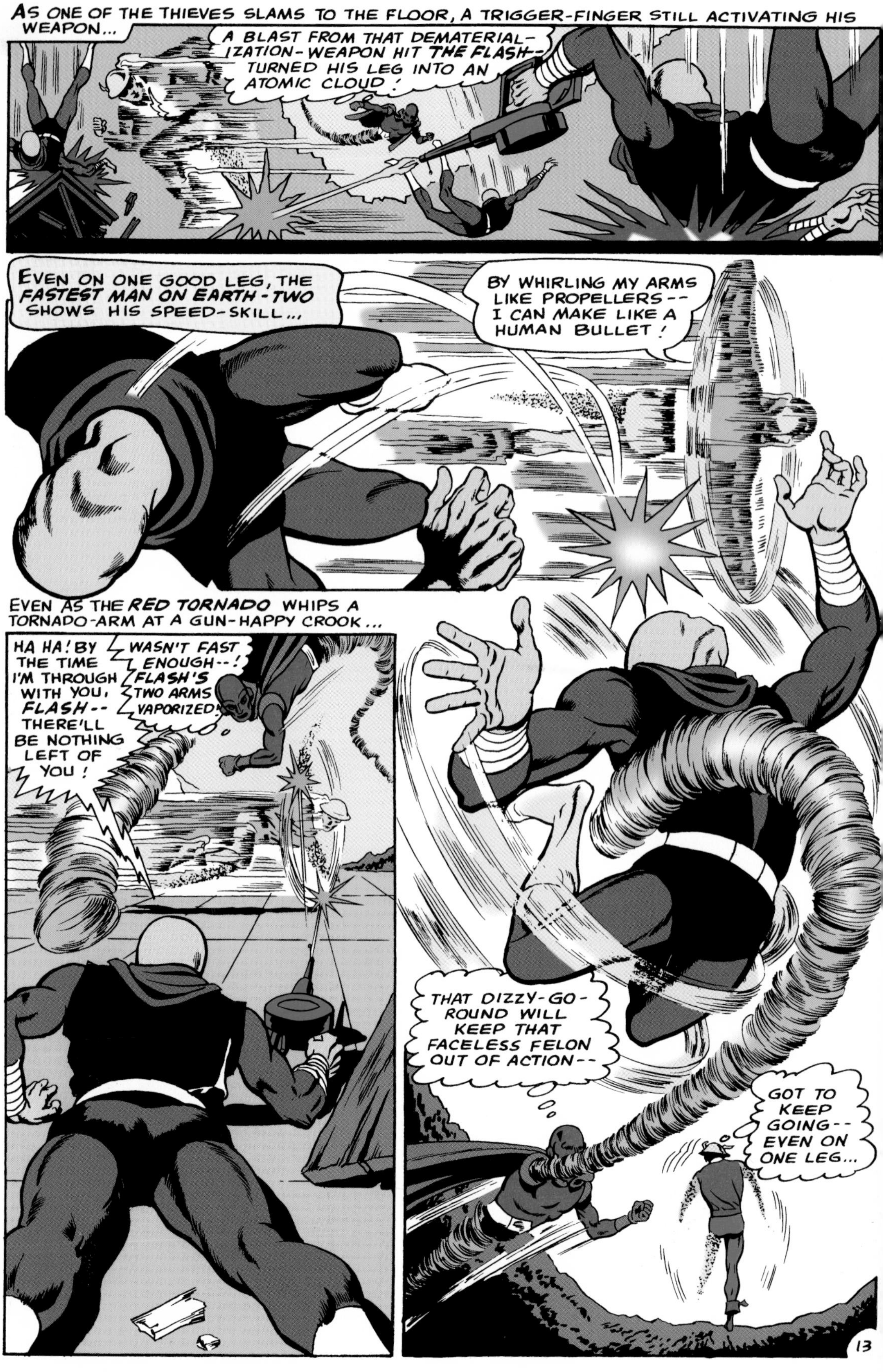
AS ONE OF THE THIEVES SLAMS TO THE FLOOR, A TRIGGER-FINGER STILL ACTIVATING HIS WEAPON...
A BLAST FROM THAT DEMATERIALIZATION-WEAPON HIT THE FLASH--TURNED HIS LEG INTO AN ATOMIC CLOUD!
EVEN ON ONE GOOD LEG, THE FASTEST MAN ON EARTH-TWO SHOWS HIS SPEED-SKILL...
BY WHIRLING MY ARMS LIKE PROPELLERS--I CAN MAKE LIKE A HUMAN BULLET!
EVEN AS THE RED TORNADO WHIPS A TORNADO-ARM AT A GUN-HAPPY CROOK...
HA HA! BY THE TIME I'M THROUGH WITH YOU, FLASH--THERE'LL BE NOTHING LEFT OF YOU!
WASN'T FAST ENOUGH--! FLASH'S TWO ARMS VAPORIZED!
THAT DIZZY-GO-ROUND WILL KEEP THAT FACELESS FELON OUT OF ACTION--
GOT TO KEEP GOING--EVEN ON ONE LEG...
13

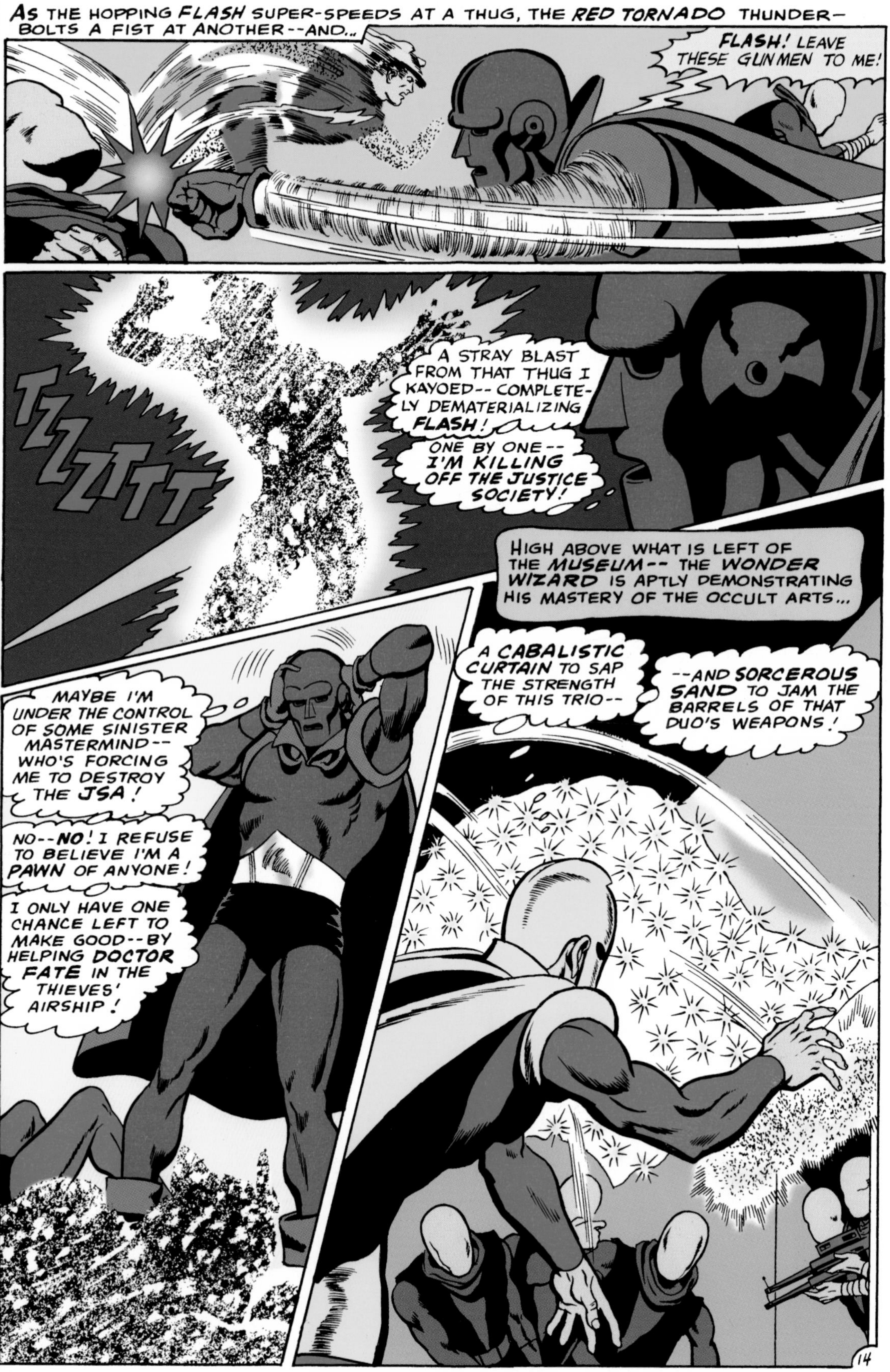
AS THE HOPPING FLASH SUPER-SPEEDS AT A THUG, THE RED TORNADO THUNDER-BOLTS A FIST AT ANOTHER--AND..
FLASH! LEAVE THESE GUNMEN TO ME!
TZZZTTTT
A STRAY BLAST FROM THAT THUG I KAYOED-- COMPLETELY DEMATERIALIZING FLASH!
ONE BY ONE-- I'M KILLING OFF THE JUSTICE SOCIETY!
HIGH ABOVE WHAT IS LEFT OF THE MUSEUM-- THE WONDER WIZARD IS APTLY DEMONSTRATING HIS MASTERY OF THE OCCULT ARTS...
A CABALISTIC CURTAIN TO SAP THE STRENGTH OF THIS TRIO--
--AND SORCEROUS SAND TO JAM THE BARRELS OF THAT DUO'S WEAPONS!
MAYBE I'M UNDER THE CONTROL OF SOME SINISTER MASTERMIND-- WHO'S FORCING ME TO DESTROY THE JSA!
NO--NO! I REFUSE TO BELIEVE I'M A PAWN OF ANYONE!
I ONLY HAVE ONE CHANCE LEFT TO MAKE GOOD--BY HELPING DOCTOR FATE IN THE THIEVES' AIRSHIP!
14

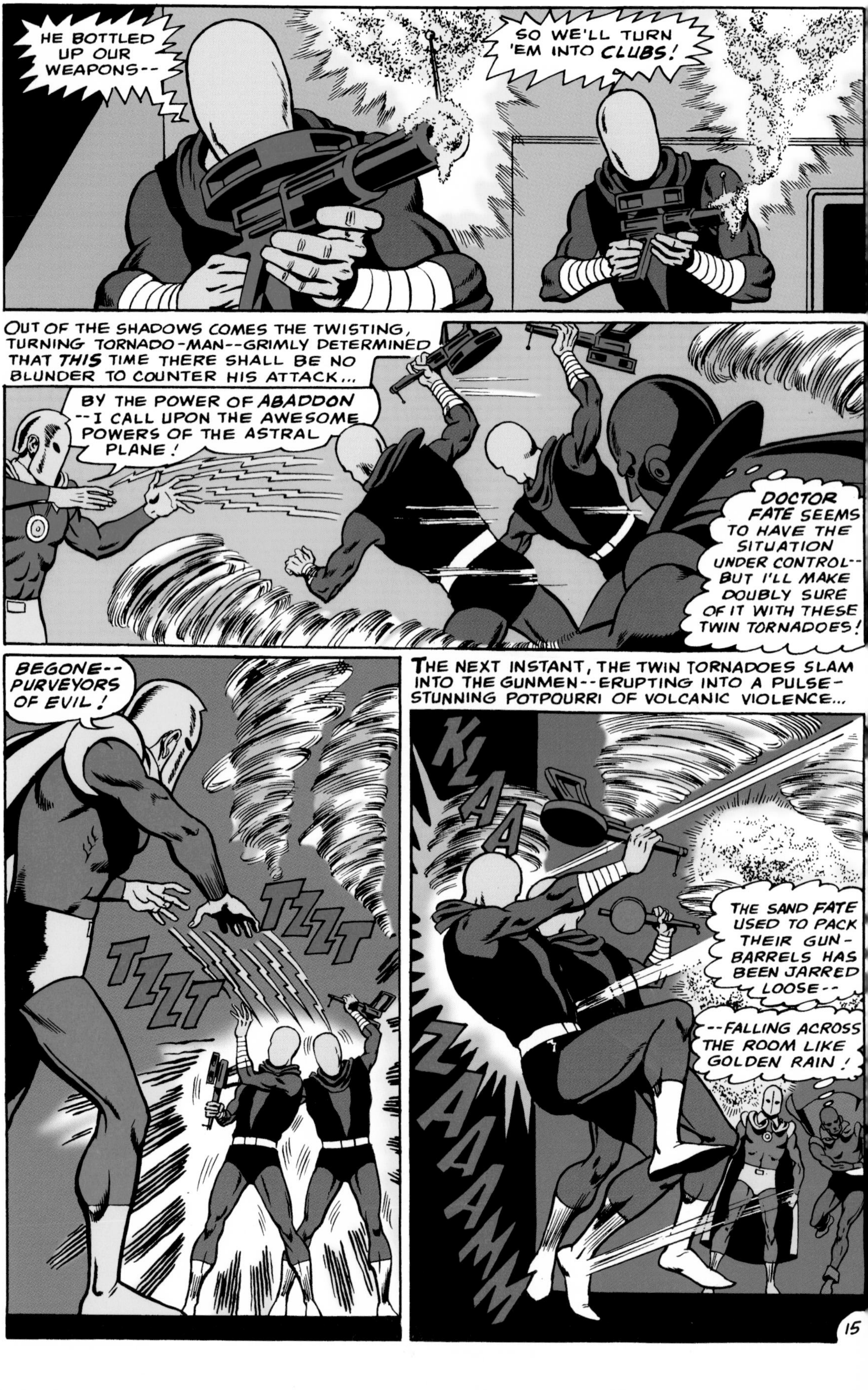
HE BOTTLED UP OUR WEAPONS--
SO WE'LL TURN 'EM INTO CLUBS!
OUT OF THE SHADOWS COMES THE TWISTING, TURNING TORNADO-MAN--GRIMLY DETERMINED THAT THIS TIME THERE SHALL BE NO BLUNDER TO COUNTER HIS ATTACK...
BY THE POWER OF ABADDON --I CALL UPON THE AWESOME POWERS OF THE ASTRAL PLANE!
DOCTOR FATE SEEMS TO HAVE THE SITUATION UNDER CONTROL--BUT I'LL MAKE DOUBLY SURE OF IT WITH THESE TWIN TORNADOES!
BEGONE--PURVEYORS OF EVIL!
TZZT
TZZT
THE NEXT INSTANT, THE TWIN TORNADOES SLAM INTO THE GUNMEN--ERUPTING INTO A PULSE-STUNNING POTPOURRI OF VOLCANIC VIOLENCE...
KLAAA
THE SAND FATE USED TO PACK THEIR GUN-BARRELS HAS BEEN JARRED LOOSE--
--FALLING ACROSS THE ROOM LIKE GOLDEN RAIN!
ZAAAAMM

AS THE GOLDEN SAND-RAIN DROPS WITH ELECTRIFYING FORCE UPON THE SCARLET SWIRLER AND MAGIC MASTER...
SAND--SHOOTING BOLTS OF EERIE ENERGY INTO ME... NULLIFYING MY MAGIC POWERS... NUMBING ME...
P-PARALYZING ME TOO...
THIS TIME I NOT ONLY DOOMED DOCTOR FATE-- BUT MY-SELF, TOO!
16
DUMP THEIR BODIES OUT THE EJECTION HATCH!
THEN LOWER THE SHIP TO THE GROUND--PICK UP THE REST OF THE GANG --AND LET'S CLEAR OUT OF HERE WITH OUR LOOT!
THANKS TO THE INTERVENTION OF THE RED TORNADO, THESE JUSTICE SOCIETY MEMBERS HAVE BEEN UTTERLY DESTROYED! HA, HA, HA!
STORY CONTINUES ON THE NEXT PAGE FOLLOWING!

JUSTICE LEAGUE of AMERICA

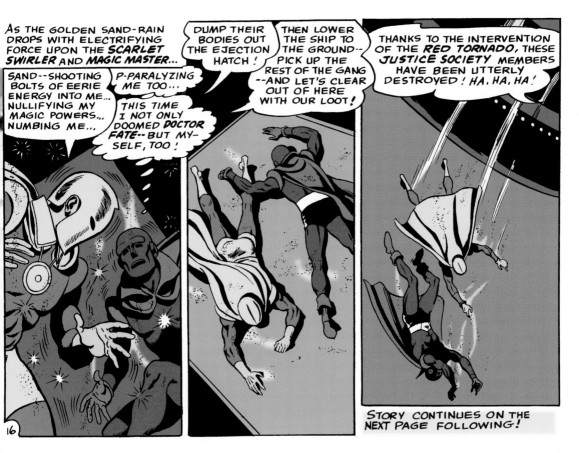

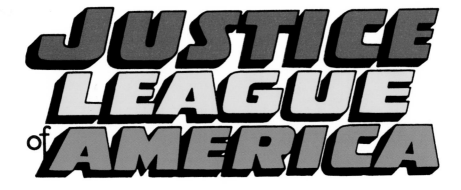

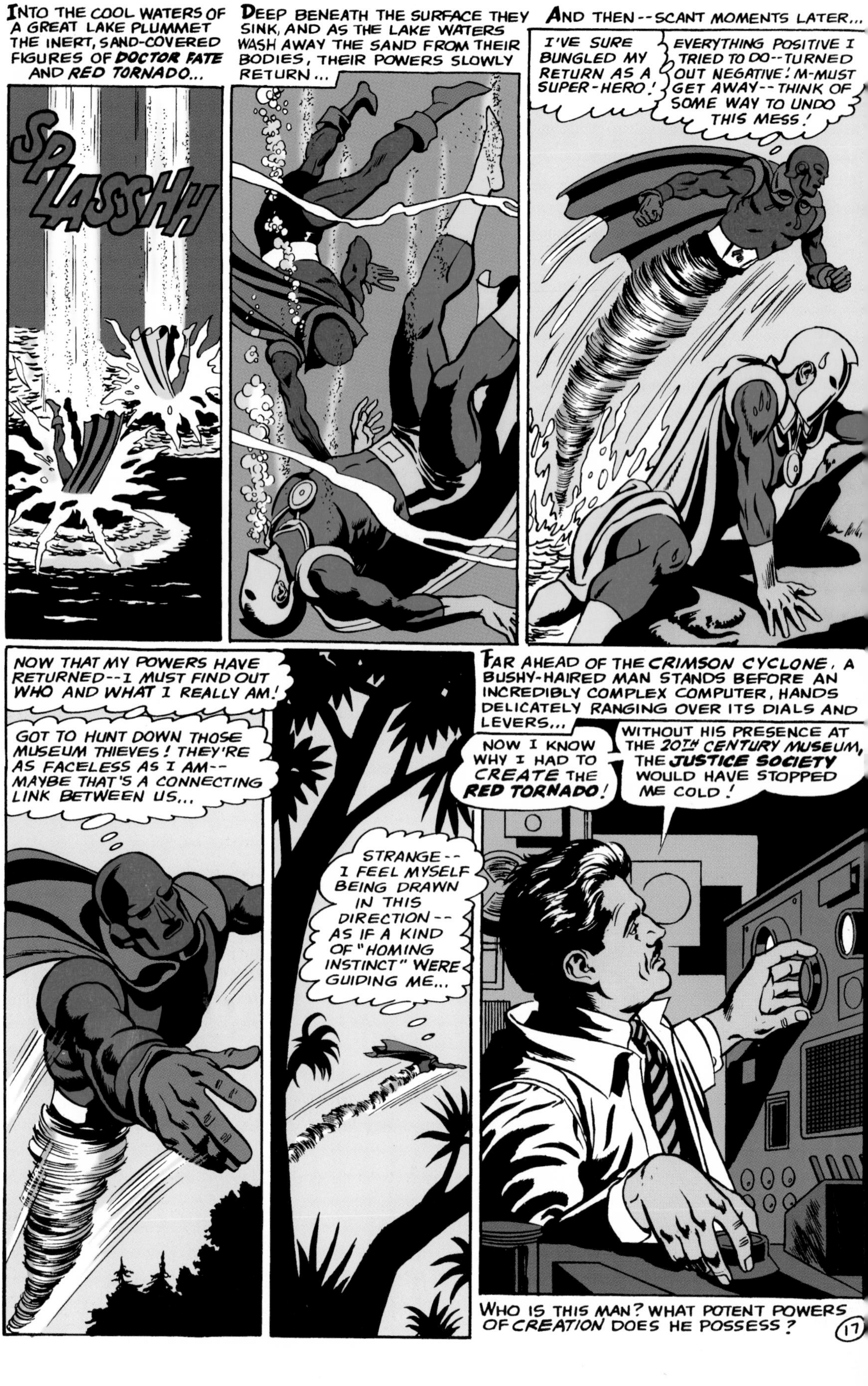
INTO THE COOL WATERS OF A GREAT LAKE PLUMMET THE INERT, SAND-COVERED FIGURES OF DOCTOR FATE AND RED TORNADO...
SPLASSHH
DEEP BENEATH THE SURFACE THEY SINK, AND AS THE LAKE WATERS WASH AWAY THE SAND FROM THEIR BODIES, THEIR POWERS SLOWLY RETURN...
AND THEN--SCANT MOMENTS LATER...
I'VE SURE BUNGLED MY RETURN AS A SUPER-HERO!
EVERYTHING POSITIVE I TRIED TO DO--TURNED OUT NEGATIVE! M-MUST GET AWAY--THINK OF SOME WAY TO UNDO THIS MESS!
NOW THAT MY POWERS HAVE RETURNED--I MUST FIND OUT WHO AND WHAT I REALLY AM!
GOT TO HUNT DOWN THOSE MUSEUM THIEVES! THEY'RE AS FACELESS AS I AM--MAYBE THAT'S A CONNECTING LINK BETWEEN US...
STRANGE--I FEEL MYSELF BEING DRAWN IN THIS DIRECTION--AS IF A KIND OF "HOMING INSTINCT" WERE GUIDING ME...
FAR AHEAD OF THE CRIMSON CYCLONE, A BUSHY-HAIRED MAN STANDS BEFORE AN INCREDIBLY COMPLEX COMPUTER, HANDS DELICATELY RANGING OVER ITS DIALS AND LEVERS...
NOW I KNOW WHY I HAD TO CREATE THE RED TORNADO!
WITHOUT HIS PRESENCE AT THE 20TH CENTURY MUSEUM, THE JUSTICE SOCIETY WOULD HAVE STOPPED ME COLD!
WHO IS THIS MAN? WHAT POTENT POWERS OF CREATION DOES HE POSSESS?
17

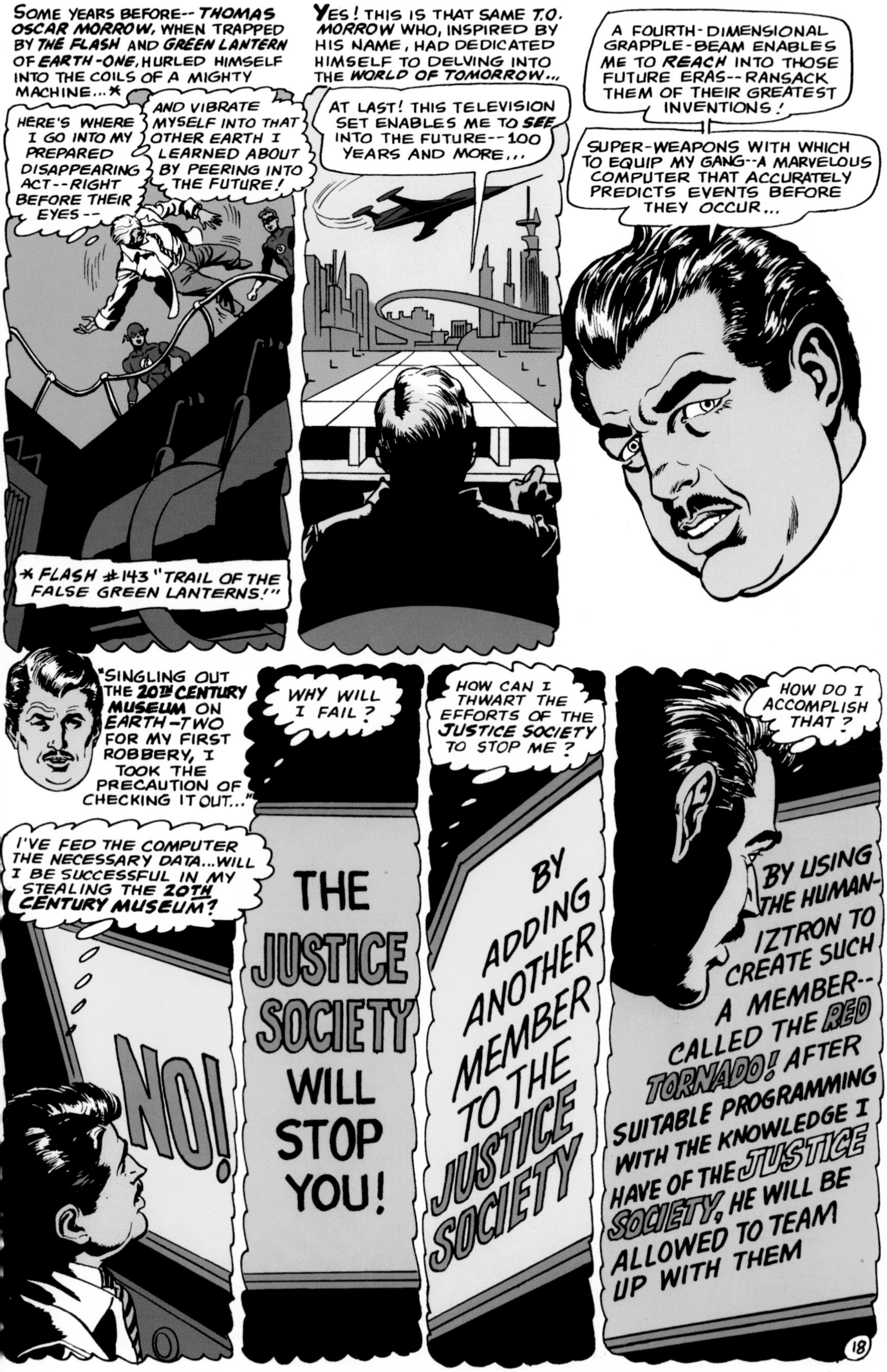
SOME YEARS BEFORE-- THOMAS OSCAR MORROW, WHEN TRAPPED BY THE FLASH AND GREEN LANTERN OF EARTH-ONE, HURLED HIMSELF INTO THE COILS OF A MIGHTY MACHINE...*
HERE'S WHERE I GO INTO MY PREPARED DISAPPEARING ACT--RIGHT BEFORE THEIR EYES--
AND VIBRATE MYSELF INTO THAT OTHER EARTH I LEARNED ABOUT BY PEERING INTO THE FUTURE!
* FLASH #143 "TRAIL OF THE FALSE GREEN LANTERNS!"
YES! THIS IS THAT SAME T.O. MORROW WHO, INSPIRED BY HIS NAME, HAD DEDICATED HIMSELF TO DELVING INTO THE WORLD OF TOMORROW...
AT LAST! THIS TELEVISION SET ENABLES ME TO SEE INTO THE FUTURE--100 YEARS AND MORE...
A FOURTH-DIMENSIONAL GRAPPLE-BEAM ENABLES ME TO REACH INTO THOSE FUTURE ERAS--RANSACK THEM OF THEIR GREATEST INVENTIONS!
SUPER-WEAPONS WITH WHICH TO EQUIP MY GANG--A MARVELOUS COMPUTER THAT ACCURATELY PREDICTS EVENTS BEFORE THEY OCCUR...
"SINGLING OUT THE 20TH CENTURY MUSEUM ON EARTH-TWO FOR MY FIRST ROBBERY, I TOOK THE PRECAUTION OF CHECKING IT OUT..."
I'VE FED THE COMPUTER THE NECESSARY DATA...WILL I BE SUCCESSFUL IN MY STEALING THE 20TH CENTURY MUSEUM?
NO!
WHY WILL I FAIL?
THE JUSTICE SOCIETY WILL STOP YOU!
HOW CAN I THWART THE EFFORTS OF THE JUSTICE SOCIETY TO STOP ME?
BY ADDING ANOTHER MEMBER TO THE JUSTICE SOCIETY
HOW DO I ACCOMPLISH THAT?
BY USING THE HUMAN-IZTRON TO CREATE SUCH A MEMBER--CALLED THE RED TORNADO! AFTER SUITABLE PROGRAMMING WITH THE KNOWLEDGE I HAVE OF THE JUSTICE SOCIETY, HE WILL BE ALLOWED TO TEAM UP WITH THEM
18

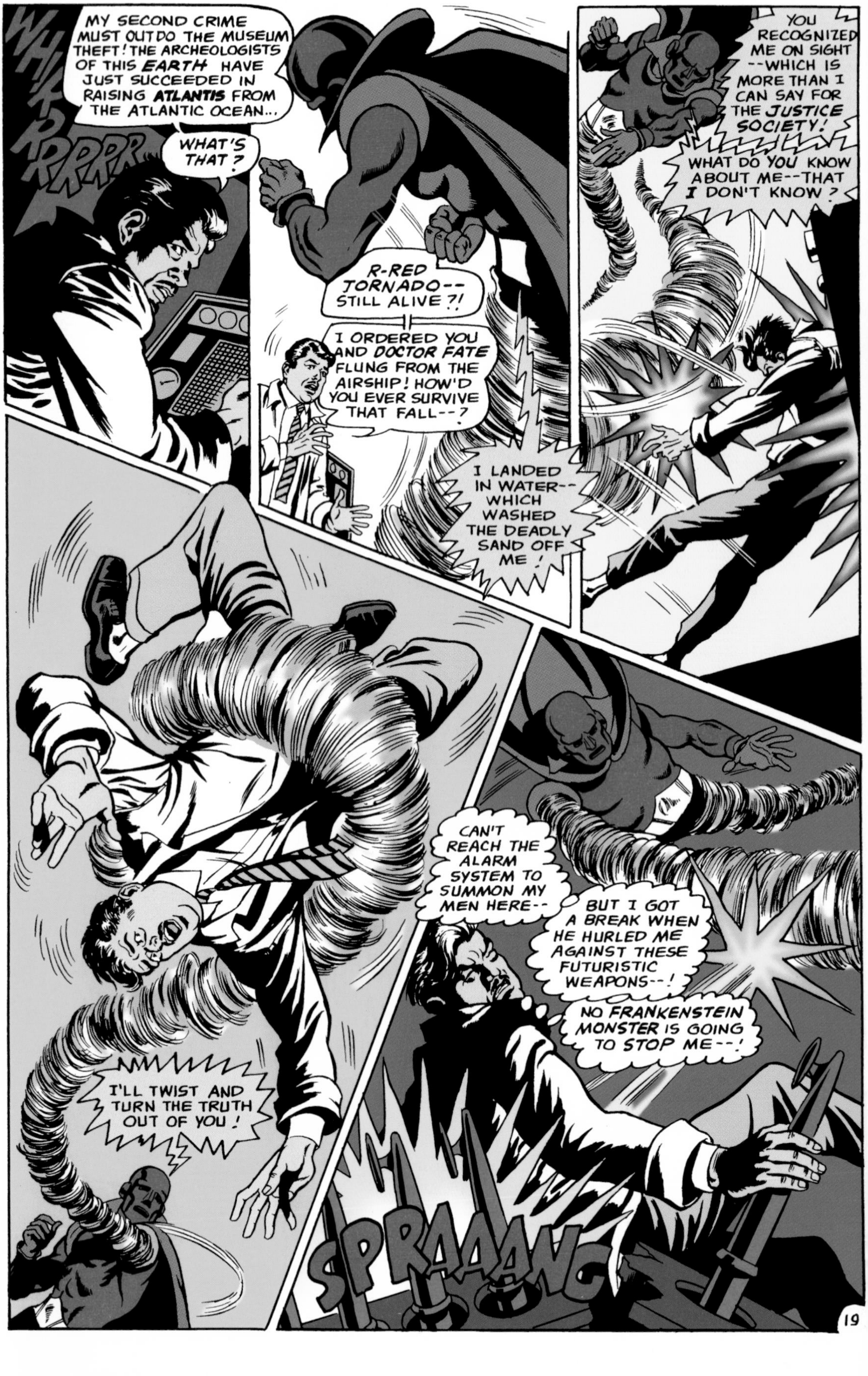
WHIRRRRRR
MY SECOND CRIME MUST OUTDO THE MUSEUM THEFT! THE ARCHEOLOGISTS OF THIS EARTH HAVE JUST SUCCEEDED IN RAISING ATLANTIS FROM THE ATLANTIC OCEAN...
WHAT'S THAT?
R-RED TORNADO-- STILL ALIVE?!
I ORDERED YOU AND DOCTOR FATE FLUNG FROM THE AIRSHIP! HOW'D YOU EVER SURVIVE THAT FALL--?
I LANDED IN WATER-- WHICH WASHED THE DEADLY SAND OFF ME!
YOU RECOGNIZED ME ON SIGHT --WHICH IS MORE THAN I CAN SAY FOR THE JUSTICE SOCIETY!
WHAT DO YOU KNOW ABOUT ME--THAT I DON'T KNOW?
I'LL TWIST AND TURN THE TRUTH OUT OF YOU!
CAN'T REACH THE ALARM SYSTEM TO SUMMON MY MEN HERE--
BUT I GOT A BREAK WHEN HE HURLED ME AGAINST THESE FUTURISTIC WEAPONS--!
NO FRANKENSTEIN MONSTER IS GOING TO STOP ME--!
SPRAAAANG
19

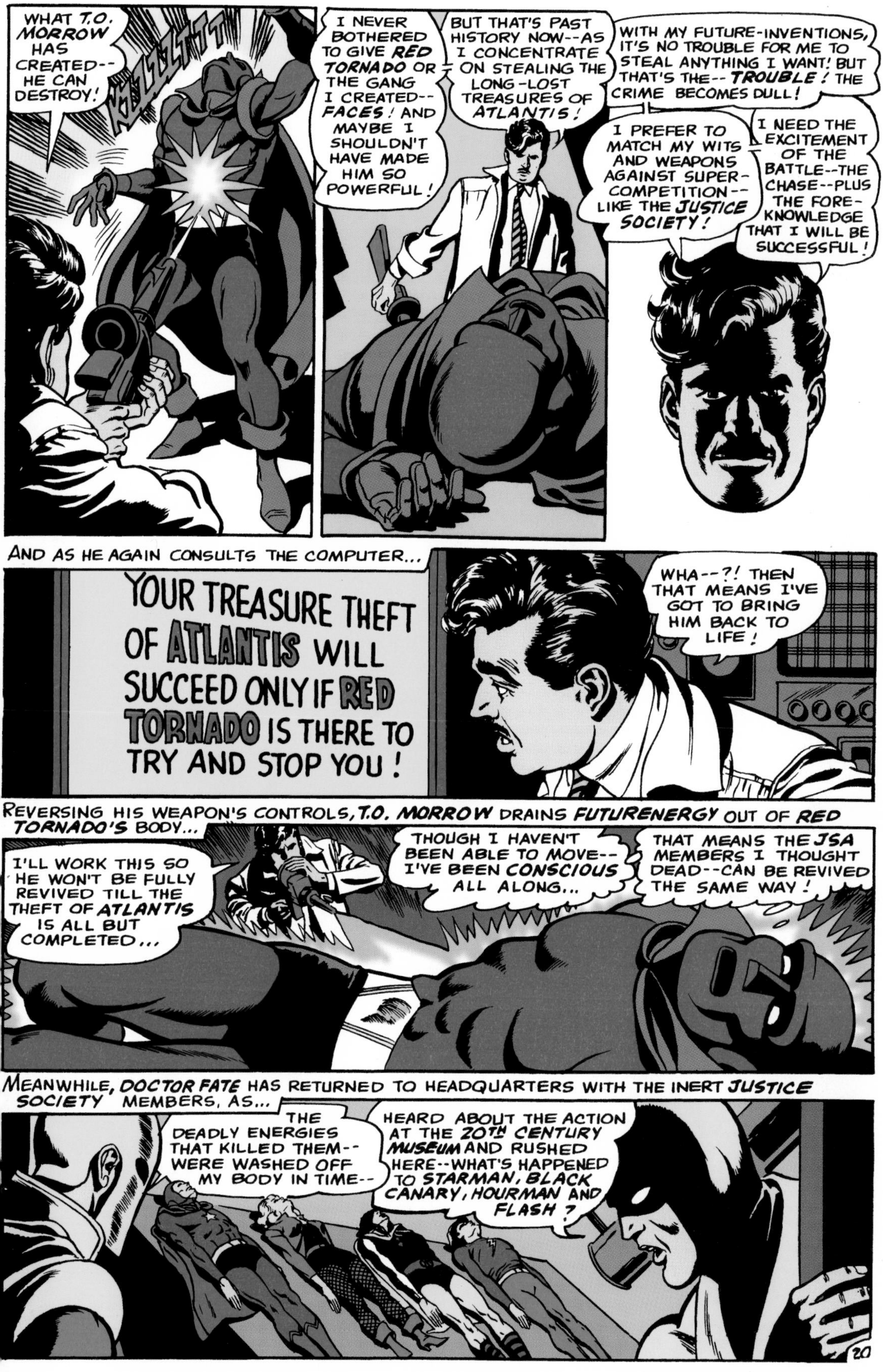
WHAT T.O. MORROW HAS CREATED-- HE CAN DESTROY!
KZZZTTTT
I NEVER BOTHERED TO GIVE RED TORNADO OR THE GANG I CREATED-- FACES! AND MAYBE I SHOULDN'T HAVE MADE HIM SO POWERFUL!
BUT THAT'S PAST HISTORY NOW--AS I CONCENTRATE ON STEALING THE LONG-LOST TREASURES OF ATLANTIS!
WITH MY FUTURE-INVENTIONS, IT'S NO TROUBLE FOR ME TO STEAL ANYTHING I WANT! BUT THAT'S THE-- TROUBLE! THE CRIME BECOMES DULL!
I PREFER TO MATCH MY WITS AND WEAPONS AGAINST SUPER-COMPETITION-- LIKE THE JUSTICE SOCIETY!
I NEED THE EXCITEMENT OF THE BATTLE--THE CHASE--PLUS THE FORE-KNOWLEDGE THAT I WILL BE SUCCESSFUL!
AND AS HE AGAIN CONSULTS THE COMPUTER...
YOUR TREASURE THEFT OF ATLANTIS WILL SUCCEED ONLY IF RED TORNADO IS THERE TO TRY AND STOP YOU!
WHA--?! THEN THAT MEANS I'VE GOT TO BRING HIM BACK TO LIFE!
REVERSING HIS WEAPON'S CONTROLS, T.O. MORROW DRAINS FUTURENERGY OUT OF RED TORNADO'S BODY...
I'LL WORK THIS SO HE WON'T BE FULLY REVIVED TILL THE THEFT OF ATLANTIS IS ALL BUT COMPLETED...
THOUGH I HAVEN'T BEEN ABLE TO MOVE-- I'VE BEEN CONSCIOUS ALL ALONG...
THAT MEANS THE JSA MEMBERS I THOUGHT DEAD--CAN BE REVIVED THE SAME WAY!
MEANWHILE, DOCTOR FATE HAS RETURNED TO HEADQUARTERS WITH THE INERT JUSTICE SOCIETY MEMBERS, AS...
THE DEADLY ENERGIES THAT KILLED THEM--WERE WASHED OFF MY BODY IN TIME--
HEARD ABOUT THE ACTION AT THE 20TH CENTURY MUSEUM AND RUSHED HERE--WHAT'S HAPPENED TO STARMAN, BLACK CANARY, HOURMAN AND FLASH?
20

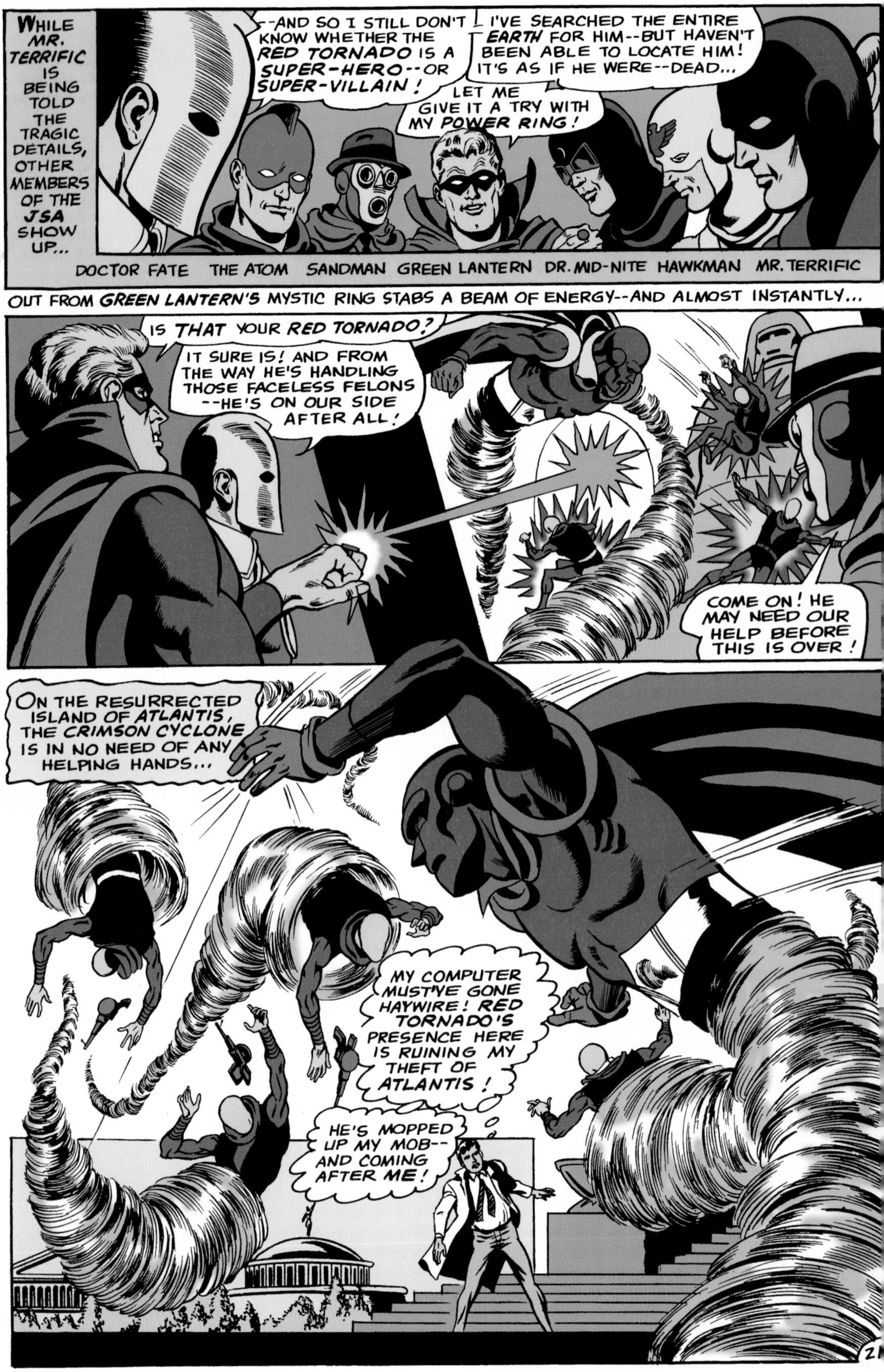
WHILE MR. TERRIFIC IS BEING TOLD THE TRAGIC DETAILS, OTHER MEMBERS OF THE JSA SHOW UP...
--AND SO I STILL DON'T KNOW WHETHER THE RED TORNADO IS A SUPER-HERO--OR SUPER-VILLAIN!
I'VE SEARCHED THE ENTIRE EARTH FOR HIM--BUT HAVEN'T BEEN ABLE TO LOCATE HIM! IT'S AS IF HE WERE--DEAD...
LET ME GIVE IT A TRY WITH MY POWER RING!
DOCTOR FATE THE ATOM SANDMAN GREEN LANTERN DR. MID-NITE HAWKMAN MR. TERRIFIC
OUT FROM GREEN LANTERN'S MYSTIC RING STABS A BEAM OF ENERGY--AND ALMOST INSTANTLY...
IS THAT YOUR RED TORNADO?
IT SURE IS! AND FROM THE WAY HE'S HANDLING THOSE FACELESS FELONS --HE'S ON OUR SIDE AFTER ALL!
COME ON! HE MAY NEED OUR HELP BEFORE THIS IS OVER!
ON THE RESURRECTED ISLAND OF ATLANTIS, THE CRIMSON CYCLONE IS IN NO NEED OF ANY HELPING HANDS...
MY COMPUTER MUST'VE GONE HAYWIRE! RED TORNADO'S PRESENCE HERE IS RUINING MY THEFT OF ATLANTIS!
HE'S MOPPED UP MY MOB--AND COMING AFTER ME!

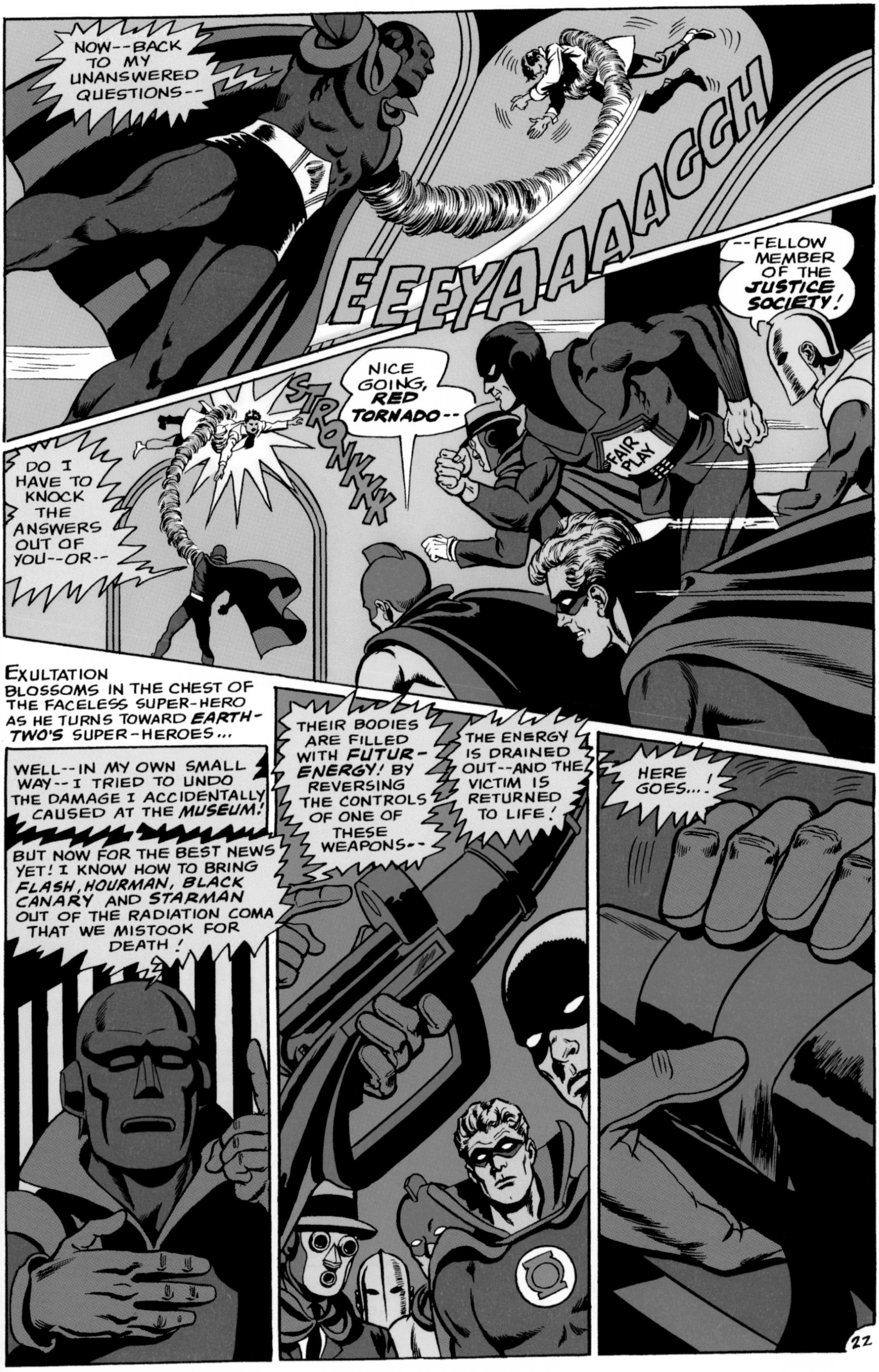
NOW--BACK TO MY UNANSWERED QUESTIONS--
EEEYAAAAAACGH
--FELLOW MEMBER OF THE JUSTICE SOCIETY!
NICE GOING, RED TORNADO--
STRONKKK
DO I HAVE TO KNOCK THE ANSWERS OUT OF YOU--OR--
FAIR PLAY
EXULTATION BLOSSOMS IN THE CHEST OF THE FACELESS SUPER-HERO AS HE TURNS TOWARD EARTH-TWO'S SUPER-HEROES...
WELL--IN MY OWN SMALL WAY--I TRIED TO UNDO THE DAMAGE I ACCIDENTALLY CAUSED AT THE MUSEUM!
BUT NOW FOR THE BEST NEWS YET! I KNOW HOW TO BRING FLASH, HOURMAN, BLACK CANARY AND STARMAN OUT OF THE RADIATION COMA THAT WE MISTOOK FOR DEATH!
THEIR BODIES ARE FILLED WITH FUTUR-ENERGY! BY REVERSING THE CONTROLS OF ONE OF THESE WEAPONS--
THE ENERGY IS DRAINED OUT--AND THE VICTIM IS RETURNED TO LIFE!
HERE GOES...!
22

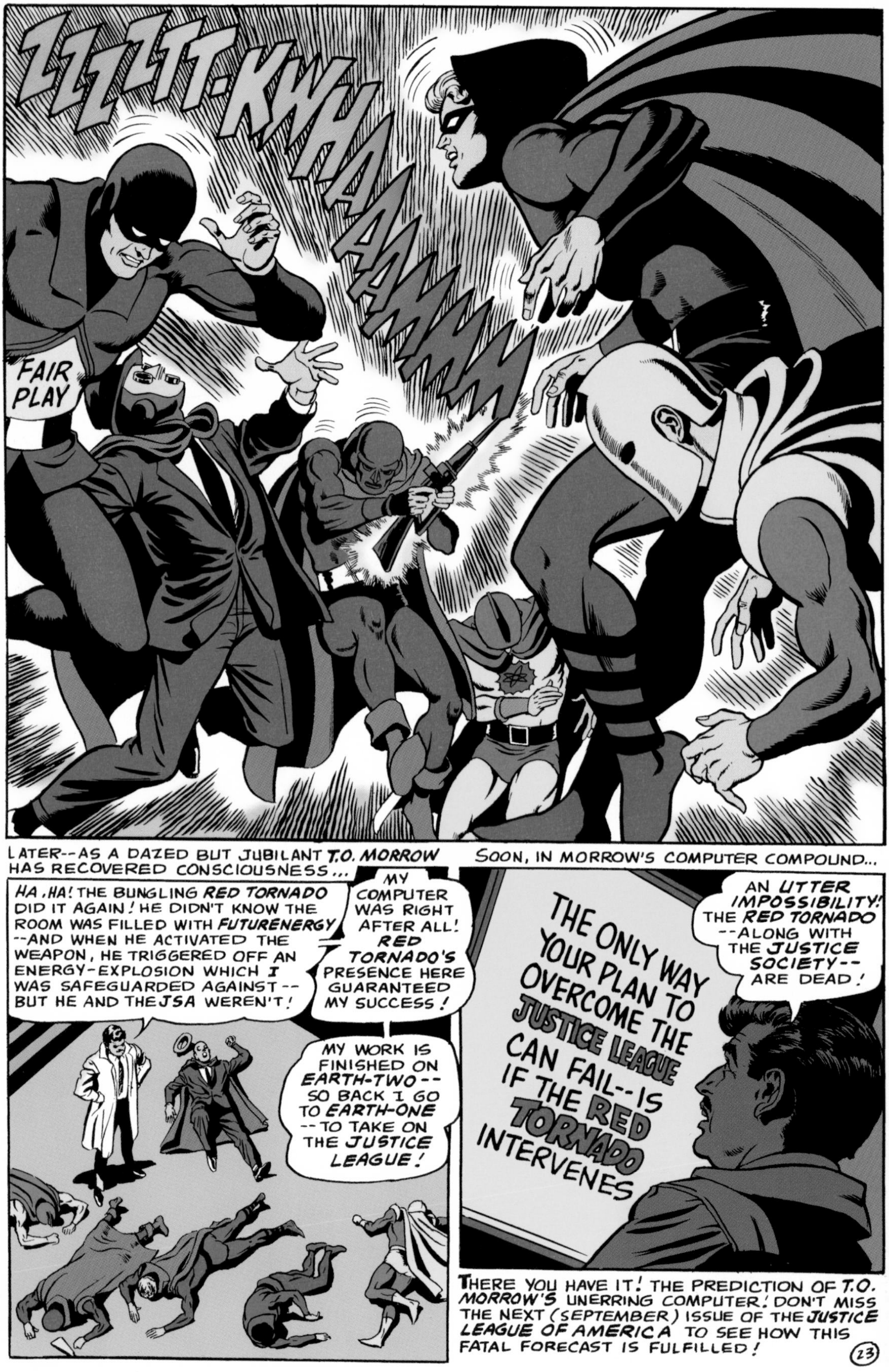
ZZZZZT-KWHAAAMMM
FAIR PLAY
LATER--AS A DAZED BUT JUBILANT T.O. MORROW HAS RECOVERED CONSCIOUSNESS...
HA, HA! THE BUNGLING RED TORNADO DID IT AGAIN! HE DIDN'T KNOW THE ROOM WAS FILLED WITH FUTURENERGY --AND WHEN HE ACTIVATED THE WEAPON, HE TRIGGERED OFF AN ENERGY-EXPLOSION WHICH I WAS SAFEGUARDED AGAINST -- BUT HE AND THE JSA WEREN'T!
MY COMPUTER WAS RIGHT AFTER ALL! RED TORNADO'S PRESENCE HERE GUARANTEED MY SUCCESS!
MY WORK IS FINISHED ON EARTH-TWO -- SO BACK I GO TO EARTH-ONE -- TO TAKE ON THE JUSTICE LEAGUE!
SOON, IN MORROW'S COMPUTER COMPOUND...
THE ONLY WAY YOUR PLAN TO OVERCOME THE JUSTICE LEAGUE CAN FAIL--IS IF THE RED TORNADO INTERVENES
AN UTTER IMPOSSIBILITY! THE RED TORNADO --ALONG WITH THE JUSTICE SOCIETY-- ARE DEAD!
THERE YOU HAVE IT! THE PREDICTION OF T.O. MORROW'S UNERRING COMPUTER! DON'T MISS THE NEXT (SEPTEMBER) ISSUE OF THE JUSTICE LEAGUE OF AMERICA TO SEE HOW THIS FATAL FORECAST IS FULFILLED!
23

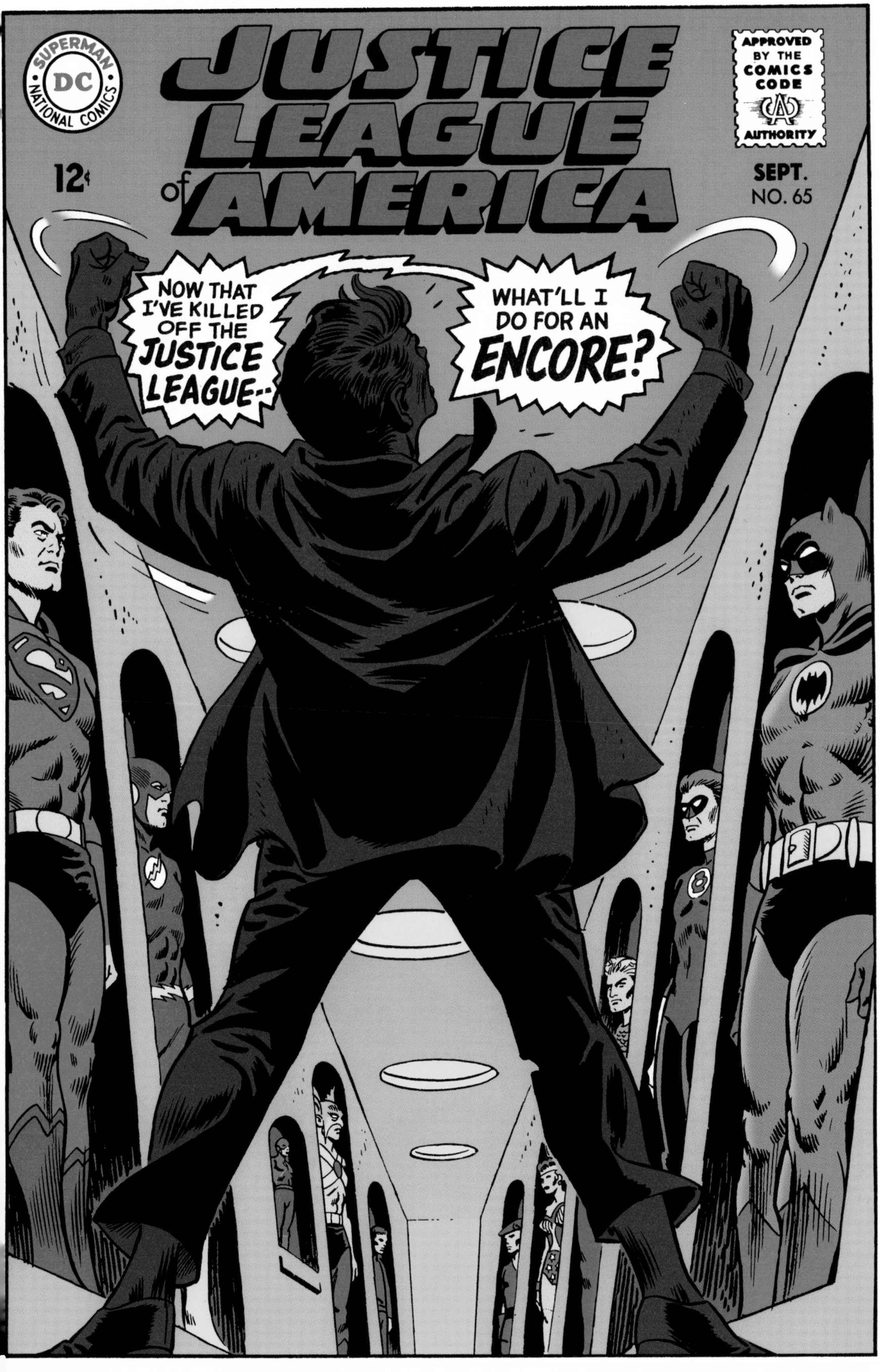
SUPERMAN
DC
NATIONAL COMICS
JUSTICE LEAGUE of AMERICA
APPROVED BY THE COMICS CODE AUTHORITY
12¢
SEPT.
NO. 65
NOW THAT I'VE KILLED OFF THE JUSTICE LEAGUE--
WHAT'LL I DO FOR AN ENCORE?

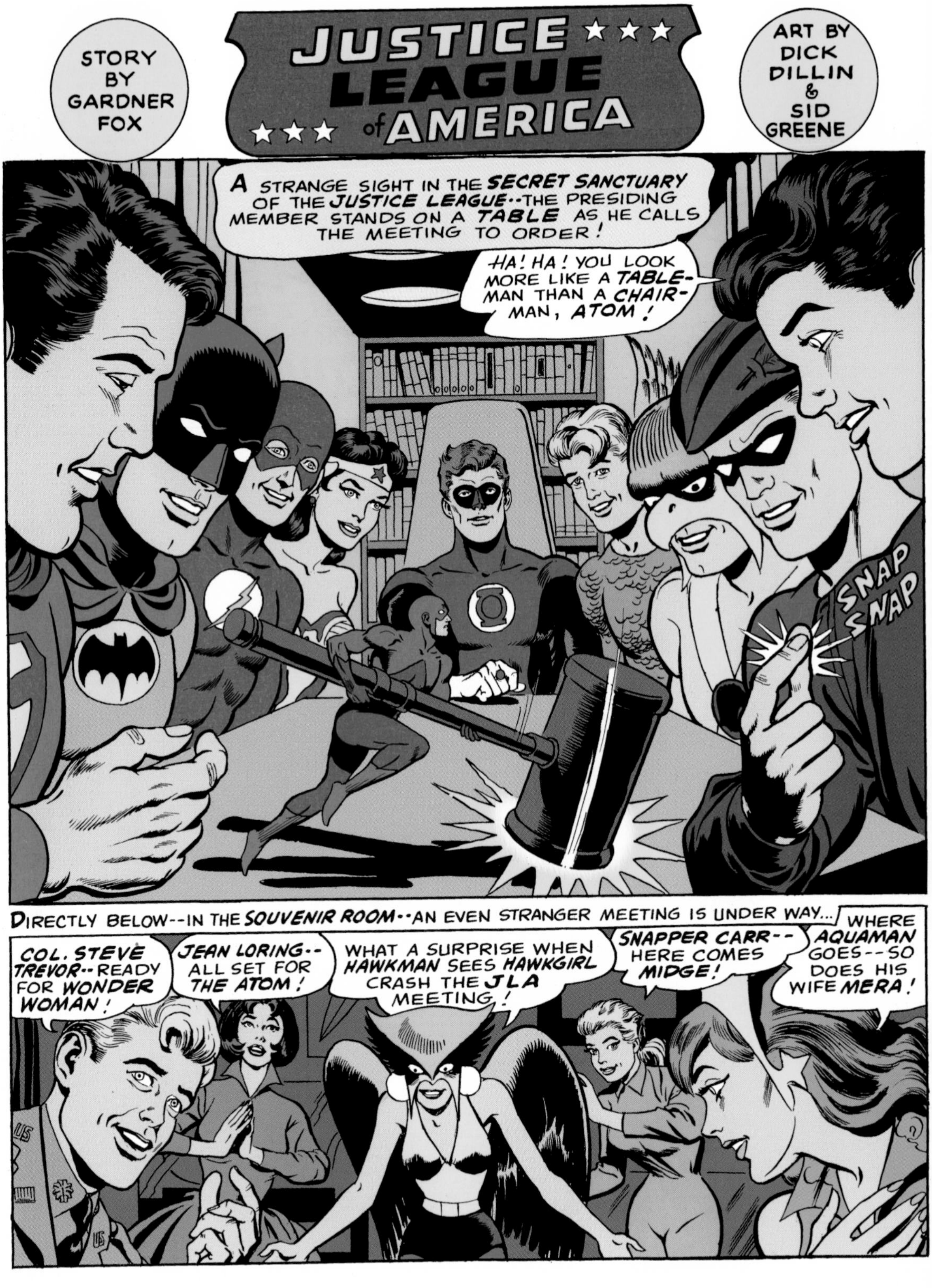
STORY BY GARDNER FOX
JUSTICE LEAGUE of AMERICA
ART BY DICK DILLIN & SID GREENE
A STRANGE SIGHT IN THE SECRET SANCTUARY OF THE JUSTICE LEAGUE--THE PRESIDING MEMBER STANDS ON A TABLE AS HE CALLS THE MEETING TO ORDER!
HA! HA! YOU LOOK MORE LIKE A TABLE-MAN THAN A CHAIR-MAN, ATOM!
SNAP SNAP
DIRECTLY BELOW--IN THE SOUVENIR ROOM--AN EVEN STRANGER MEETING IS UNDER WAY...
COL. STEVE TREVOR--READY FOR WONDER WOMAN!
JEAN LORING--ALL SET FOR THE ATOM!
WHAT A SURPRISE WHEN HAWKMAN SEES HAWKGIRL CRASH THE JLA MEETING!
SNAPPER CARR--HERE COMES MIDGE!
WHERE AQUAMAN GOES--SO DOES HIS WIFE MERA!

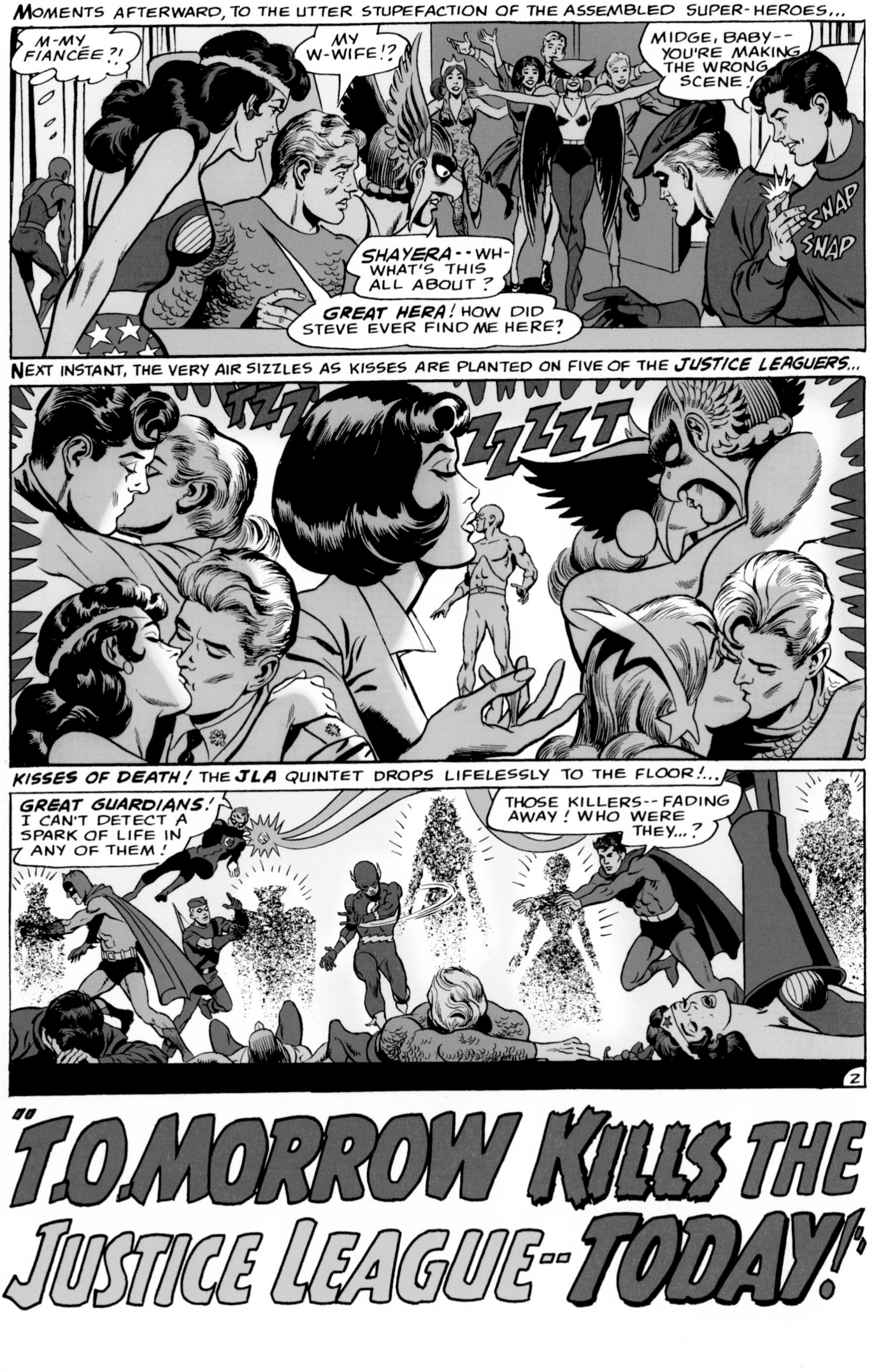
MOMENTS AFTERWARD, TO THE UTTER STUPEFACTION OF THE ASSEMBLED SUPER-HEROES...
M-MY FIANCÉE?!
MY W-WIFE!?
MIDGE, BABY-- YOU'RE MAKING THE WRONG SCENE!
SNAP SNAP
SHAYERA--WH- WHAT'S THIS ALL ABOUT?
GREAT HERA! HOW DID STEVE EVER FIND ME HERE?
NEXT INSTANT, THE VERY AIR SIZZLES AS KISSES ARE PLANTED ON FIVE OF THE JUSTICE LEAGUERS...
TZZT
ZZZZT
KISSES OF DEATH! THE JLA QUINTET DROPS LIFELESSLY TO THE FLOOR!...
GREAT GUARDIANS! I CAN'T DETECT A SPARK OF LIFE IN ANY OF THEM!
THOSE KILLERS--FADING AWAY! WHO WERE THEY...?
2
"T.O.MORROW KILLS THE JUSTICE LEAGUE--TODAY!"

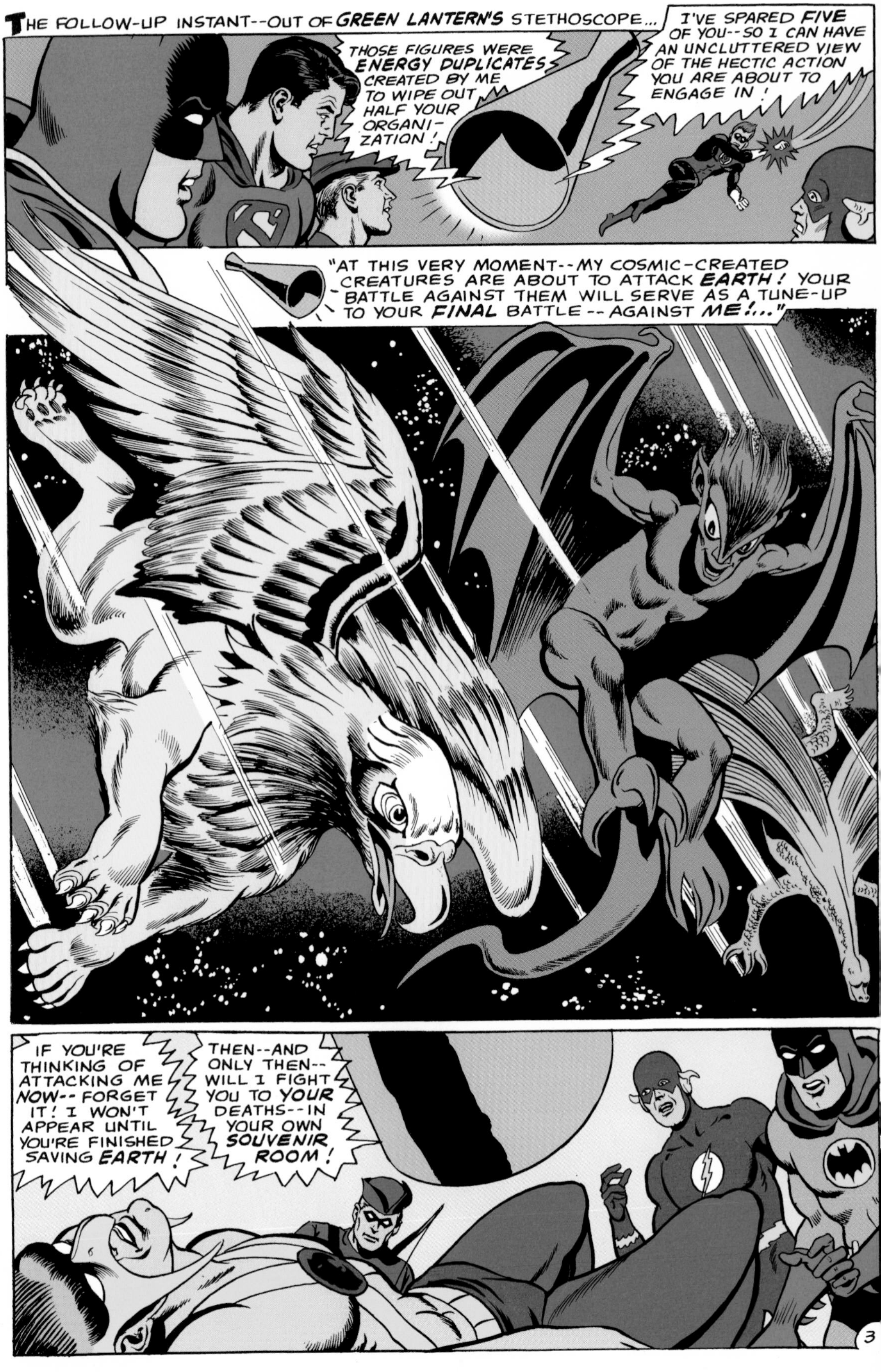
THE FOLLOW-UP INSTANT--OUT OF GREEN LANTERN'S STETHOSCOPE...
THOSE FIGURES WERE ENERGY DUPLICATES CREATED BY ME TO WIPE OUT HALF YOUR ORGANI-ZATION!
I'VE SPARED FIVE OF YOU--SO I CAN HAVE AN UNCLUTTERED VIEW OF THE HECTIC ACTION YOU ARE ABOUT TO ENGAGE IN!
"AT THIS VERY MOMENT--MY COSMIC-CREATED CREATURES ARE ABOUT TO ATTACK EARTH! YOUR BATTLE AGAINST THEM WILL SERVE AS A TUNE-UP TO YOUR FINAL BATTLE--AGAINST ME!..."
IF YOU'RE THINKING OF ATTACKING ME NOW--FORGET IT! I WON'T APPEAR UNTIL YOU'RE FINISHED SAVING EARTH!
THEN--AND ONLY THEN--WILL I FIGHT YOU TO YOUR DEATHS--IN YOUR OWN SOUVENIR ROOM!
3

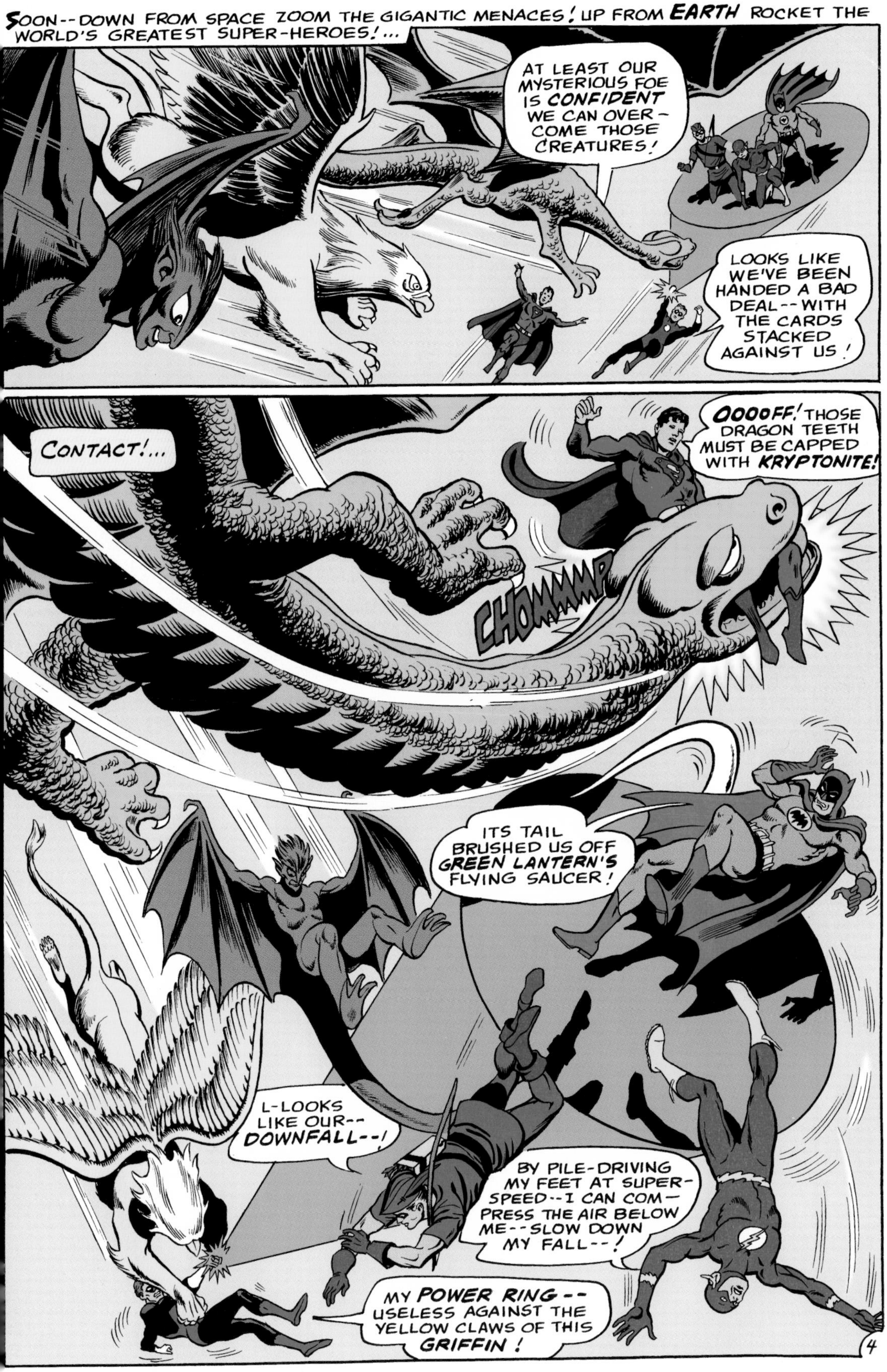
SOON--DOWN FROM SPACE ZOOM THE GIGANTIC MENACES! UP FROM EARTH ROCKET THE WORLD'S GREATEST SUPER-HEROES!...
AT LEAST OUR MYSTERIOUS FOE IS CONFIDENT WE CAN OVER-COME THOSE CREATURES!
LOOKS LIKE WE'VE BEEN HANDED A BAD DEAL--WITH THE CARDS STACKED AGAINST US!
CONTACT!...
OOOOFF! THOSE DRAGON TEETH MUST BE CAPPED WITH KRYPTONITE!
CHOMMMP
ITS TAIL BRUSHED US OFF GREEN LANTERN'S FLYING SAUCER!
L-LOOKS LIKE OUR--DOWNFALL--!
BY PILE-DRIVING MY FEET AT SUPER-SPEED--I CAN COM-PRESS THE AIR BELOW ME--SLOW DOWN MY FALL--!
MY POWER RING--USELESS AGAINST THE YELLOW CLAWS OF THIS GRIFFIN!
4

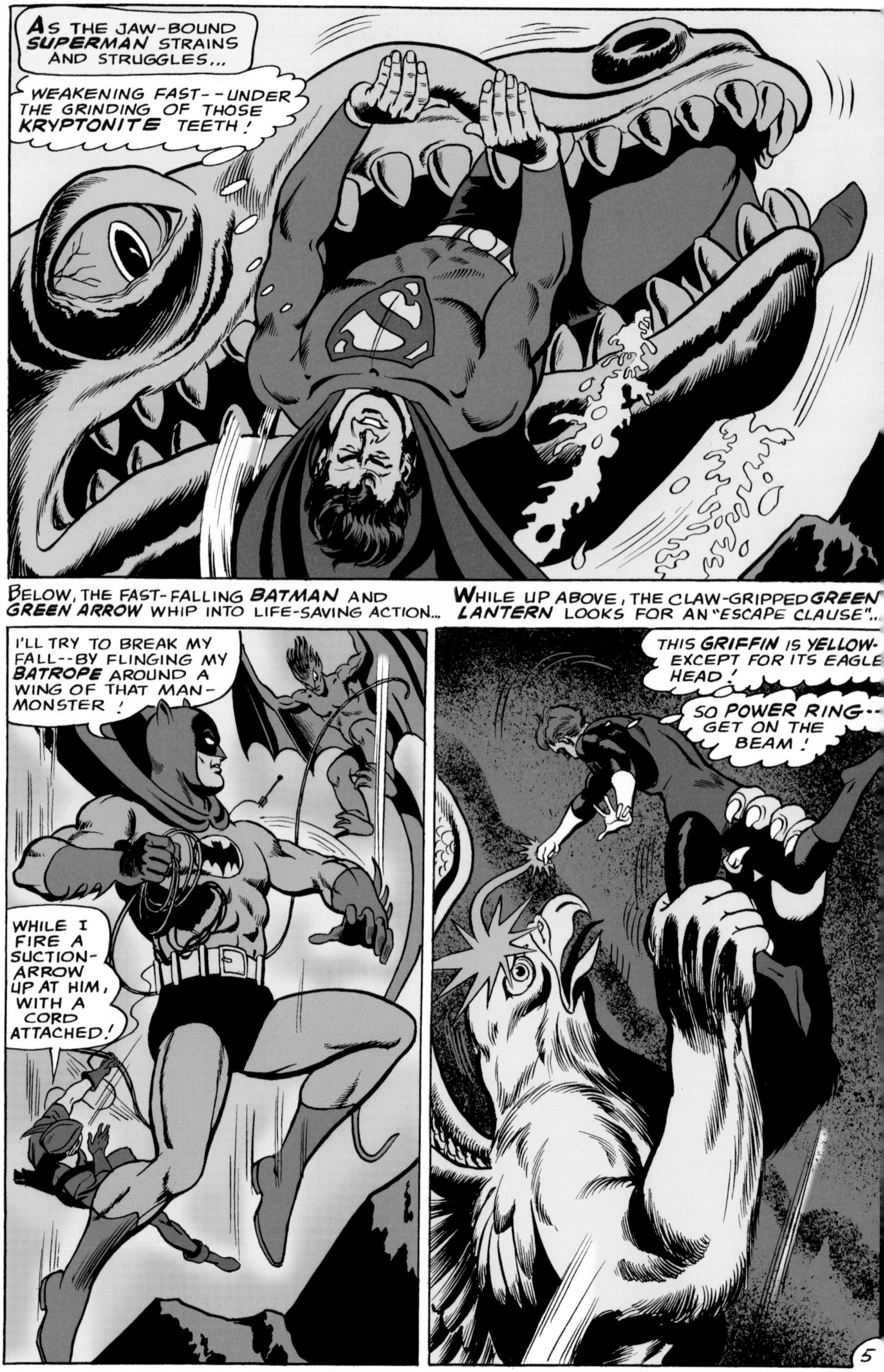
AS THE JAW-BOUND SUPERMAN STRAINS AND STRUGGLES...
WEAKENING FAST--UNDER THE GRINDING OF THOSE KRYPTONITE TEETH!
BELOW, THE FAST-FALLING BATMAN AND GREEN ARROW WHIP INTO LIFE-SAVING ACTION...
I'LL TRY TO BREAK MY FALL--BY FLINGING MY BATROPE AROUND A WING OF THAT MAN-MONSTER!
WHILE I FIRE A SUCTION-ARROW UP AT HIM, WITH A CORD ATTACHED!
WHILE UP ABOVE, THE CLAW-GRIPPED GREEN LANTERN LOOKS FOR AN "ESCAPE CLAUSE"...
THIS GRIFFIN IS YELLOW-EXCEPT FOR ITS EAGLE HEAD!
SO POWER RING--GET ON THE BEAM!
5

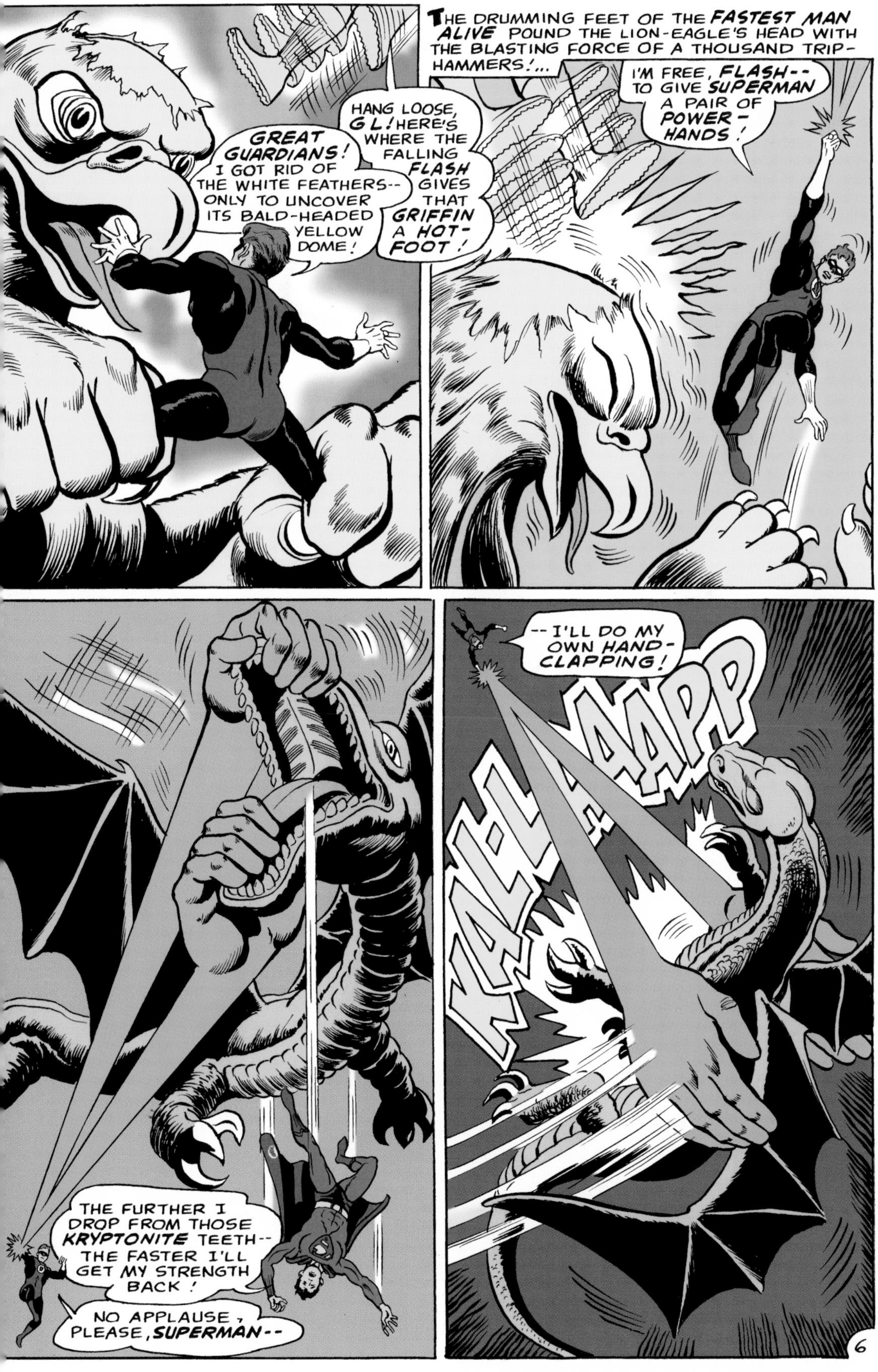
GREAT GUARDIANS! I GOT RID OF THE WHITE FEATHERS-- ONLY TO UNCOVER ITS BALD-HEADED YELLOW DOME!
HANG LOOSE, G L! HERE'S WHERE THE FALLING FLASH GIVES THAT GRIFFIN A HOT-FOOT!
THE DRUMMING FEET OF THE FASTEST MAN ALIVE POUND THE LION-EAGLE'S HEAD WITH THE BLASTING FORCE OF A THOUSAND TRIP-HAMMERS!...
I'M FREE, FLASH-- TO GIVE SUPERMAN A PAIR OF POWER-HANDS!
THE FURTHER I DROP FROM THOSE KRYPTONITE TEETH-- THE FASTER I'LL GET MY STRENGTH BACK!
NO APPLAUSE, PLEASE, SUPERMAN--
--I'LL DO MY OWN HAND-CLAPPING!
KAH-LAAAPP
6

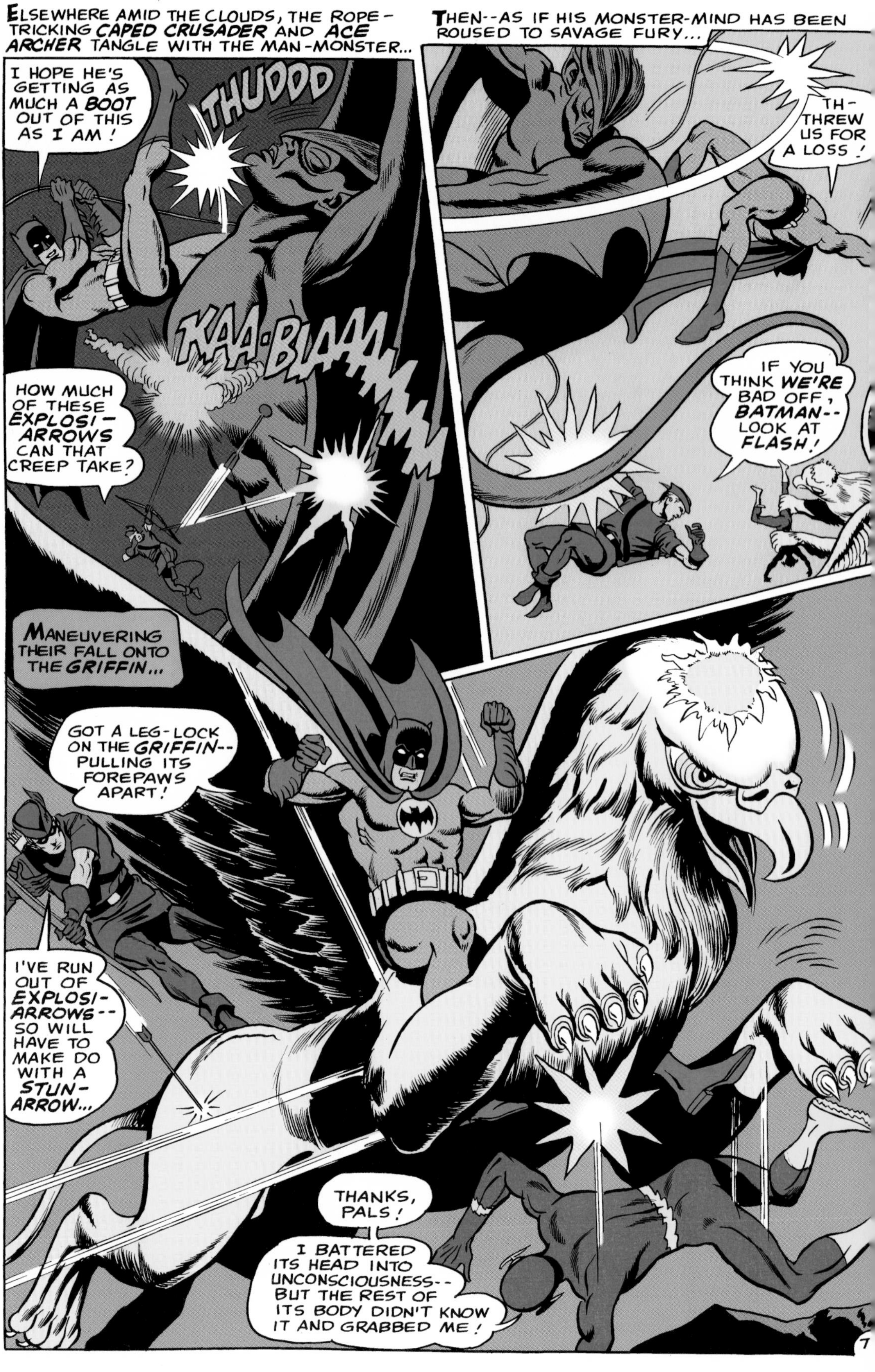
ELSEWHERE AMID THE CLOUDS, THE ROPE-TRICKING CAPED CRUSADER AND ACE ARCHER TANGLE WITH THE MAN-MONSTER...
I HOPE HE'S GETTING AS MUCH A BOOT OUT OF THIS AS I AM!
THUDDD
KAA-BLAAAMM
HOW MUCH OF THESE EXPLOSI-ARROWS CAN THAT CREEP TAKE?
THEN--AS IF HIS MONSTER-MIND HAS BEEN ROUSED TO SAVAGE FURY...
TH-THREW US FOR A LOSS!
IF YOU THINK WE'RE BAD OFF, BATMAN--LOOK AT FLASH!
MANEUVERING THEIR FALL ONTO THE GRIFFIN...
GOT A LEG-LOCK ON THE GRIFFIN--PULLING ITS FOREPAWS APART!
I'VE RUN OUT OF EXPLOSI-ARROWS--SO WILL HAVE TO MAKE DO WITH A STUN-ARROW...
THANKS, PALS!
I BATTERED ITS HEAD INTO UNCONSCIOUSNESS--BUT THE REST OF ITS BODY DIDN'T KNOW IT AND GRABBED ME!
7

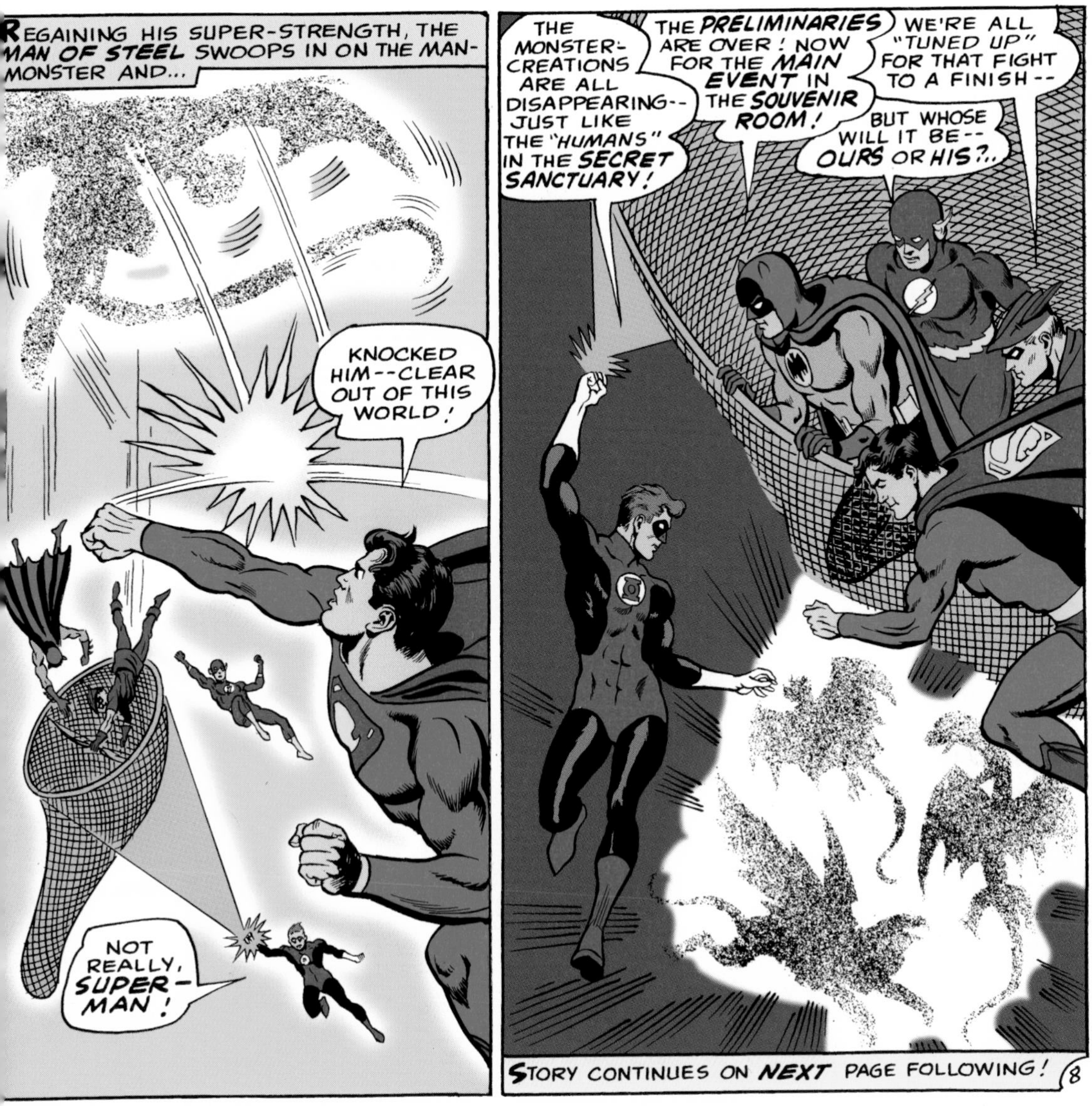
REGAINING HIS SUPER-STRENGTH, THE MAN OF STEEL SWOOPS IN ON THE MAN-MONSTER AND...
KNOCKED HIM--CLEAR OUT OF THIS WORLD!
NOT REALLY, SUPER-MAN!
THE MONSTER-CREATIONS ARE ALL DISAPPEARING--JUST LIKE THE "HUMANS" IN THE SECRET SANCTUARY!
THE PRELIMINARIES ARE OVER! NOW FOR THE MAIN EVENT IN THE SOUVENIR ROOM!
WE'RE ALL "TUNED UP" FOR THAT FIGHT TO A FINISH--
BUT WHOSE WILL IT BE--OURS OR HIS?..
STORY CONTINUES ON NEXT PAGE FOLLOWING!
8

JUSTICE LEAGUE of AMERICA

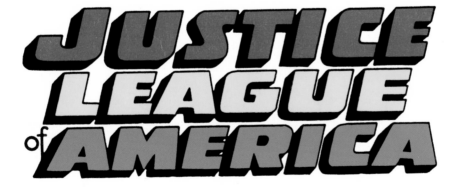

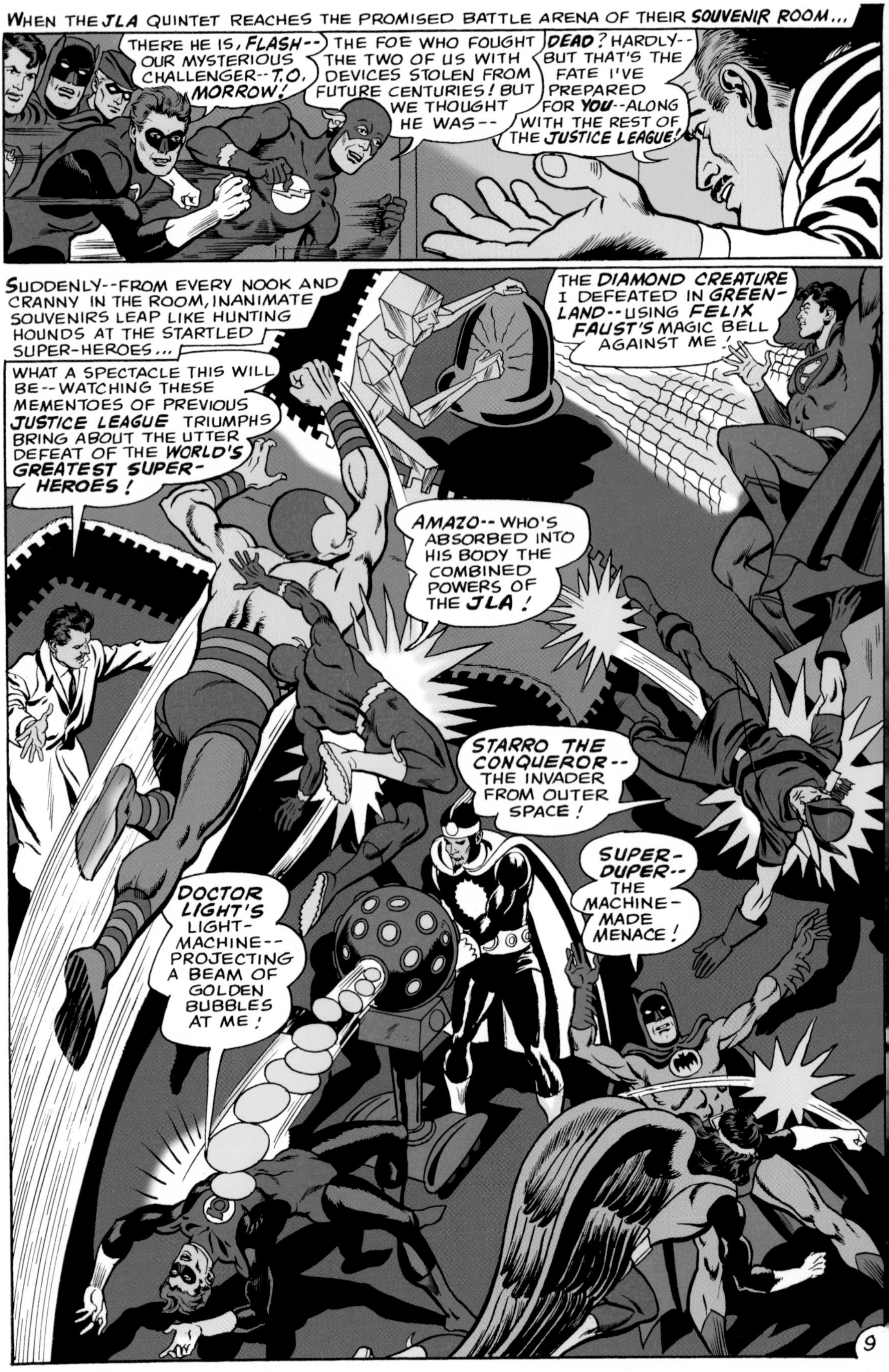
WHEN THE JLA QUINTET REACHES THE PROMISED BATTLE ARENA OF THEIR SOUVENIR ROOM...
THERE HE IS, FLASH-- OUR MYSTERIOUS CHALLENGER--T.O. MORROW!
THE FOE WHO FOUGHT THE TWO OF US WITH DEVICES STOLEN FROM FUTURE CENTURIES! BUT WE THOUGHT HE WAS--
DEAD? HARDLY-- BUT THAT'S THE FATE I'VE PREPARED FOR YOU--ALONG WITH THE REST OF THE JUSTICE LEAGUE!
SUDDENLY--FROM EVERY NOOK AND CRANNY IN THE ROOM, INANIMATE SOUVENIRS LEAP LIKE HUNTING HOUNDS AT THE STARTLED SUPER-HEROES...
WHAT A SPECTACLE THIS WILL BE--WATCHING THESE MEMENTOES OF PREVIOUS JUSTICE LEAGUE TRIUMPHS BRING ABOUT THE UTTER DEFEAT OF THE WORLD'S GREATEST SUPER-HEROES!
THE DIAMOND CREATURE I DEFEATED IN GREEN-LAND--USING FELIX FAUST'S MAGIC BELL AGAINST ME!
AMAZO-- WHO'S ABSORBED INTO HIS BODY THE COMBINED POWERS OF THE JLA!
STARRO THE CONQUEROR-- THE INVADER FROM OUTER SPACE!
SUPER-DUPER-- THE MACHINE-MADE MENACE!
DOCTOR LIGHT'S LIGHT-MACHINE-- PROJECTING A BEAM OF GOLDEN BUBBLES AT ME!
9

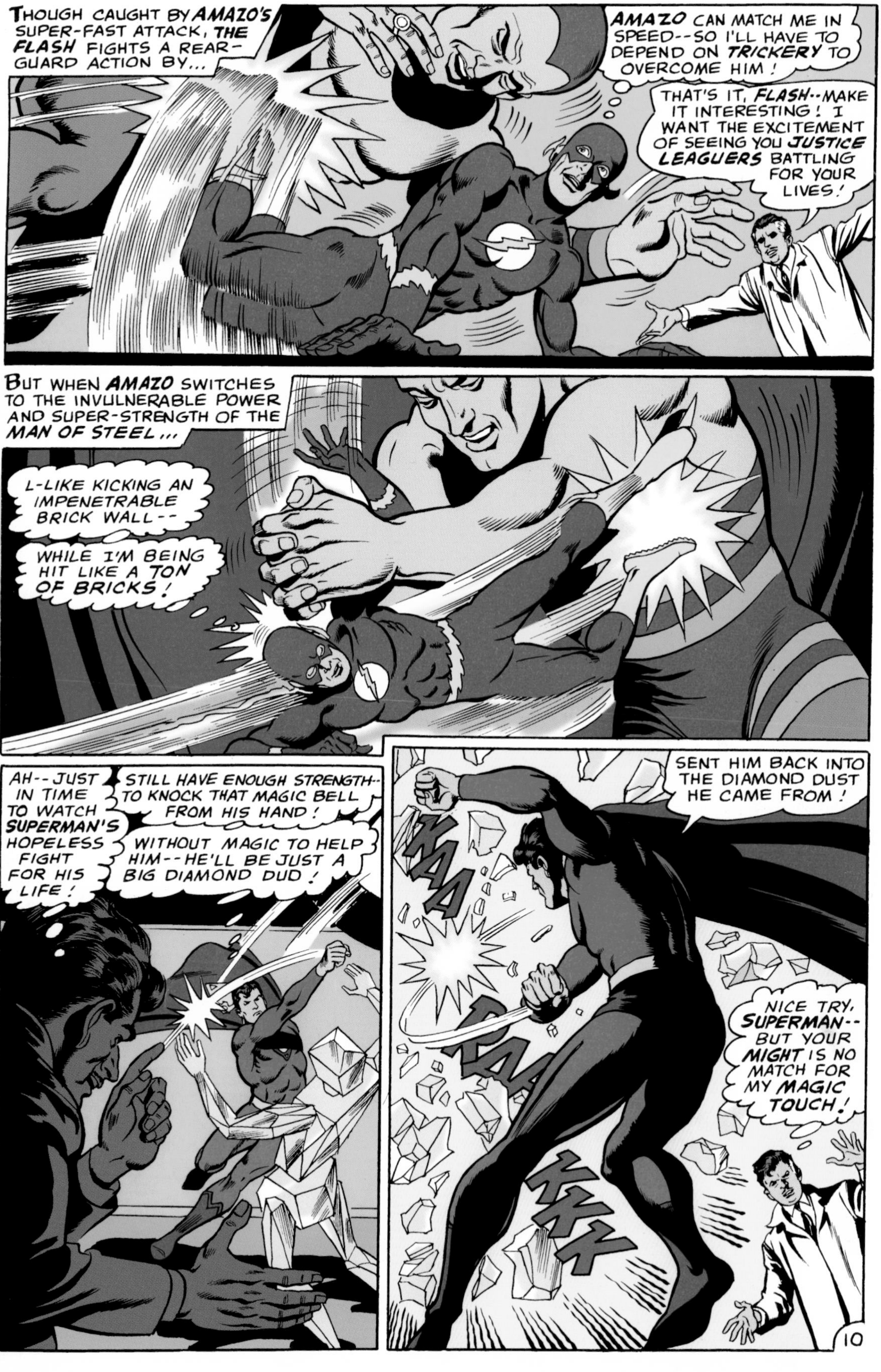
THOUGH CAUGHT BY AMAZO'S SUPER-FAST ATTACK, THE FLASH FIGHTS A REAR-GUARD ACTION BY...
AMAZO CAN MATCH ME IN SPEED--SO I'LL HAVE TO DEPEND ON TRICKERY TO OVERCOME HIM!
THAT'S IT, FLASH--MAKE IT INTERESTING! I WANT THE EXCITEMENT OF SEEING YOU JUSTICE LEAGUERS BATTLING FOR YOUR LIVES!
BUT WHEN AMAZO SWITCHES TO THE INVULNERABLE POWER AND SUPER-STRENGTH OF THE MAN OF STEEL...
L-LIKE KICKING AN IMPENETRABLE BRICK WALL--
WHILE I'M BEING HIT LIKE A TON OF BRICKS!
AH--JUST IN TIME TO WATCH SUPERMAN'S HOPELESS FIGHT FOR HIS LIFE!
STILL HAVE ENOUGH STRENGTH--TO KNOCK THAT MAGIC BELL FROM HIS HAND!
WITHOUT MAGIC TO HELP HIM--HE'LL BE JUST A BIG DIAMOND DUD!
SENT HIM BACK INTO THE DIAMOND DUST HE CAME FROM!
KAA
BRAA
KKK
NICE TRY, SUPERMAN--BUT YOUR MIGHT IS NO MATCH FOR MY MAGIC TOUCH!
10

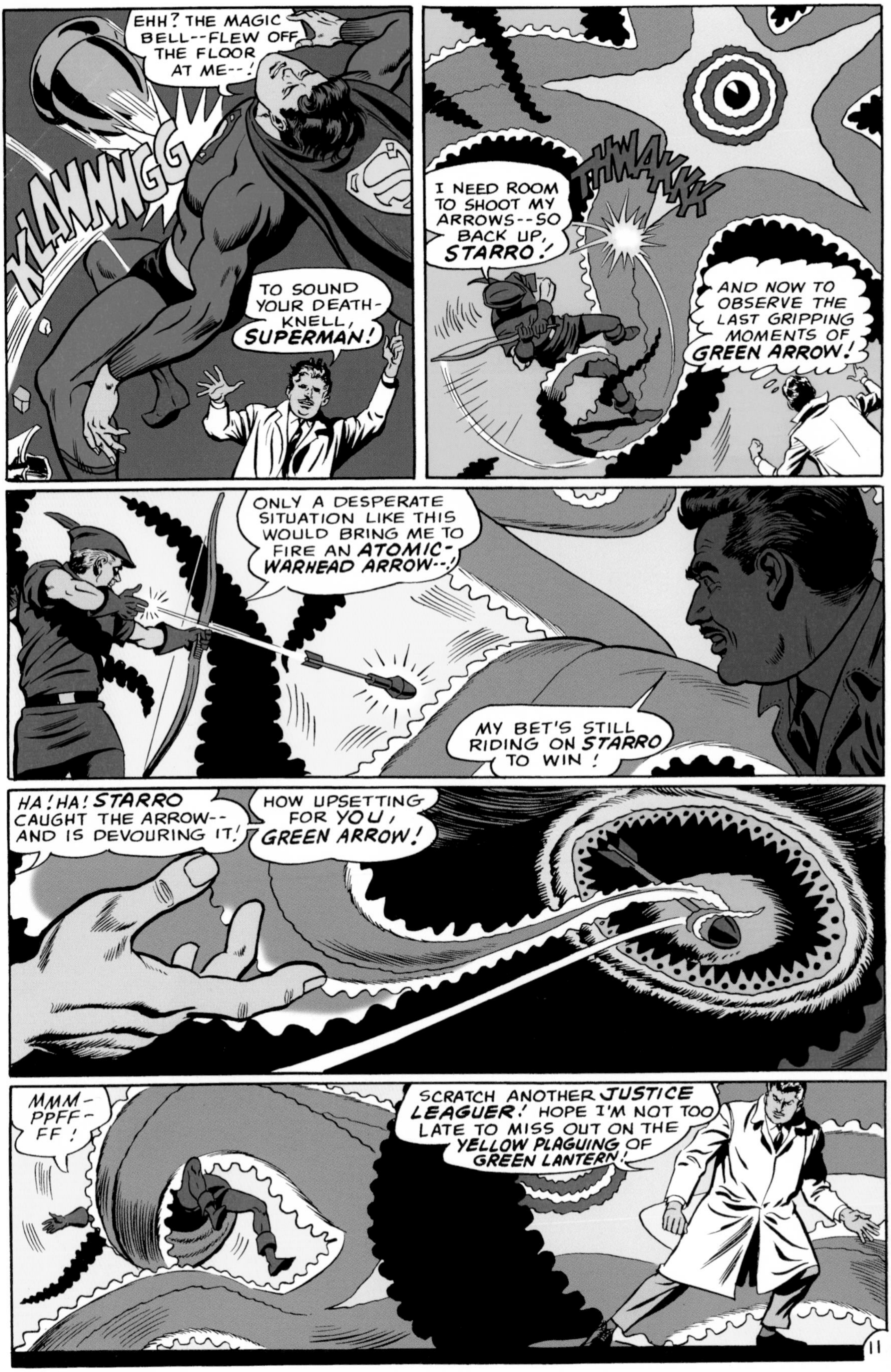
EHH? THE MAGIC BELL--FLEW OFF THE FLOOR AT ME--!
KLANNNGG
TO SOUND YOUR DEATH-KNELL, SUPERMAN!
THWAKKK
I NEED ROOM TO SHOOT MY ARROWS--SO BACK UP, STARRO!
AND NOW TO OBSERVE THE LAST GRIPPING MOMENTS OF GREEN ARROW!
ONLY A DESPERATE SITUATION LIKE THIS WOULD BRING ME TO FIRE AN ATOMIC-WARHEAD ARROW--!
MY BET'S STILL RIDING ON STARRO TO WIN!
HA! HA! STARRO CAUGHT THE ARROW--AND IS DEVOURING IT!
HOW UPSETTING FOR YOU, GREEN ARROW!
MMM-PPFF-FF!
SCRATCH ANOTHER JUSTICE LEAGUER! HOPE I'M NOT TOO LATE TO MISS OUT ON THE YELLOW PLAGUING OF GREEN LANTERN!
11

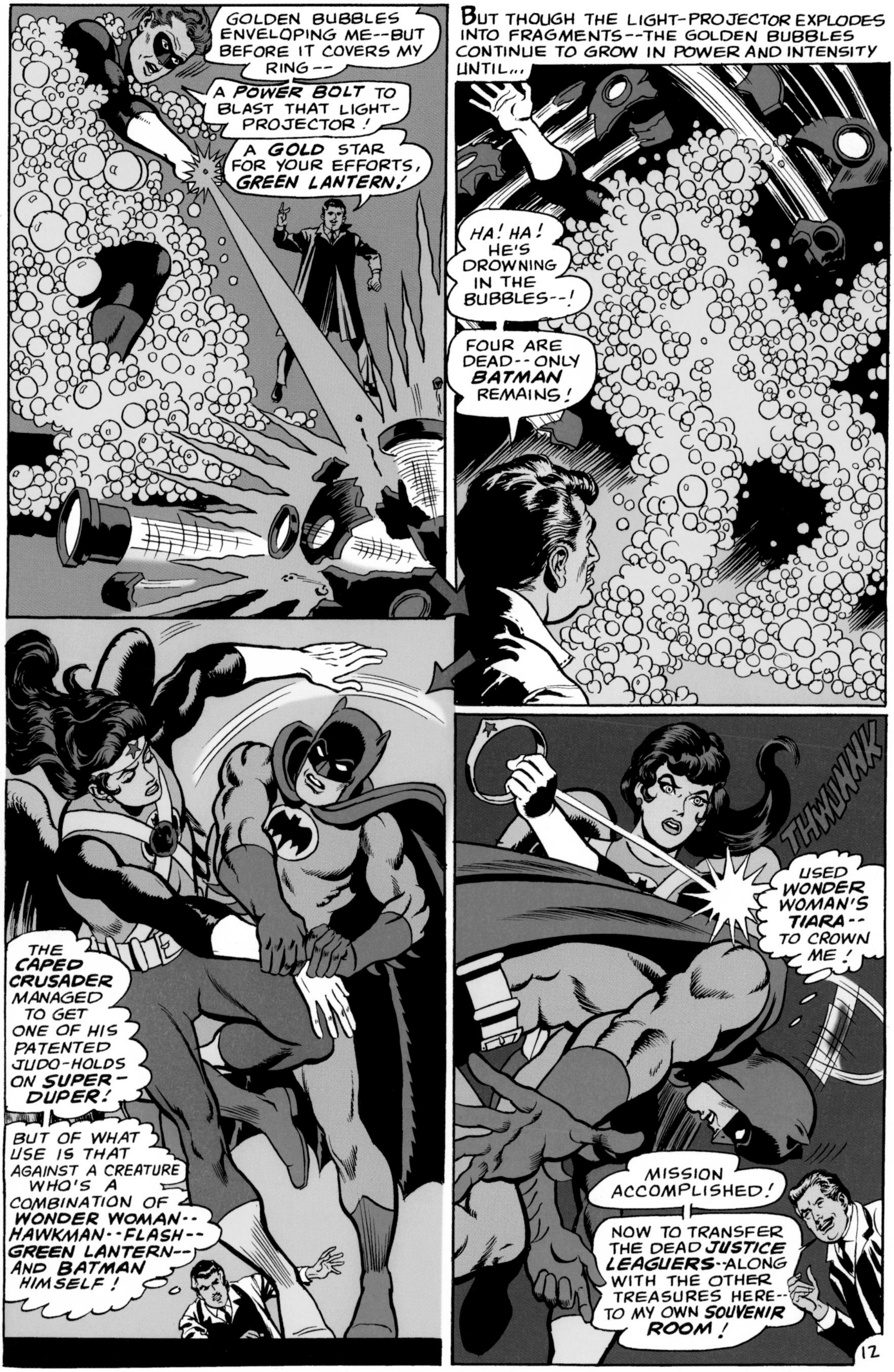
GOLDEN BUBBLES ENVELOPING ME--BUT BEFORE IT COVERS MY RING--
A POWER BOLT TO BLAST THAT LIGHT-PROJECTOR!
A GOLD STAR FOR YOUR EFFORTS, GREEN LANTERN!
BUT THOUGH THE LIGHT-PROJECTOR EXPLODES INTO FRAGMENTS--THE GOLDEN BUBBLES CONTINUE TO GROW IN POWER AND INTENSITY UNTIL...
HA! HA! HE'S DROWNING IN THE BUBBLES--!
FOUR ARE DEAD--ONLY BATMAN REMAINS!
THE CAPED CRUSADER MANAGED TO GET ONE OF HIS PATENTED JUDO-HOLDS ON SUPER-DUPER!
BUT OF WHAT USE IS THAT AGAINST A CREATURE WHO'S A COMBINATION OF WONDER WOMAN--HAWKMAN--FLASH--GREEN LANTERN--AND BATMAN HIMSELF!
THWUNNK
USED WONDER WOMAN'S TIARA--TO CROWN ME!
MISSION ACCOMPLISHED!
NOW TO TRANSFER THE DEAD JUSTICE LEAGUERS--ALONG WITH THE OTHER TREASURES HERE--TO MY OWN SOUVENIR ROOM!
12

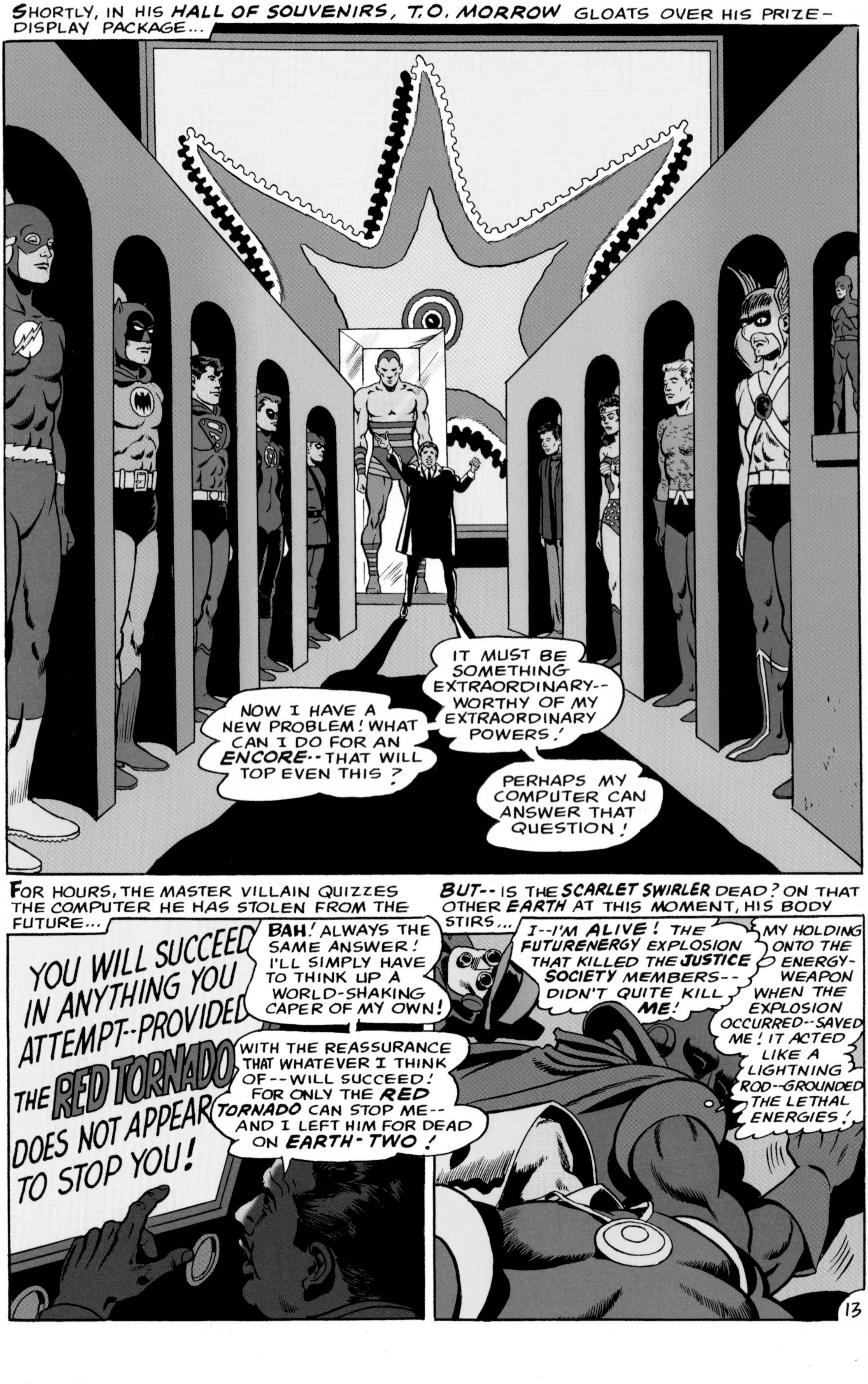
SHORTLY, IN HIS HALL OF SOUVENIRS, T.O. MORROW GLOATS OVER HIS PRIZE-DISPLAY PACKAGE...
NOW I HAVE A NEW PROBLEM! WHAT CAN I DO FOR AN ENCORE--THAT WILL TOP EVEN THIS?
IT MUST BE SOMETHING EXTRAORDINARY--WORTHY OF MY EXTRAORDINARY POWERS!
PERHAPS MY COMPUTER CAN ANSWER THAT QUESTION!
FOR HOURS, THE MASTER VILLAIN QUIZZES THE COMPUTER HE HAS STOLEN FROM THE FUTURE...
YOU WILL SUCCEED IN ANYTHING YOU ATTEMPT--PROVIDED THE RED TORNADO DOES NOT APPEAR TO STOP YOU!
BAH! ALWAYS THE SAME ANSWER! I'LL SIMPLY HAVE TO THINK UP A WORLD-SHAKING CAPER OF MY OWN!
WITH THE REASSURANCE THAT WHATEVER I THINK OF--WILL SUCCEED! FOR ONLY THE RED TORNADO CAN STOP ME--AND I LEFT HIM FOR DEAD ON EARTH-TWO!
BUT--IS THE SCARLET SWIRLER DEAD? ON THAT OTHER EARTH AT THIS MOMENT, HIS BODY STIRS...
I--I'M ALIVE! THE FUTURENERGY EXPLOSION THAT KILLED THE JUSTICE SOCIETY MEMBERS--DIDN'T QUITE KILL ME!
MY HOLDING ONTO THE ENERGY-WEAPON WHEN THE EXPLOSION OCCURRED--SAVED ME! IT ACTED LIKE A LIGHTNING ROD--GROUNDED THE LETHAL ENERGIES!
13

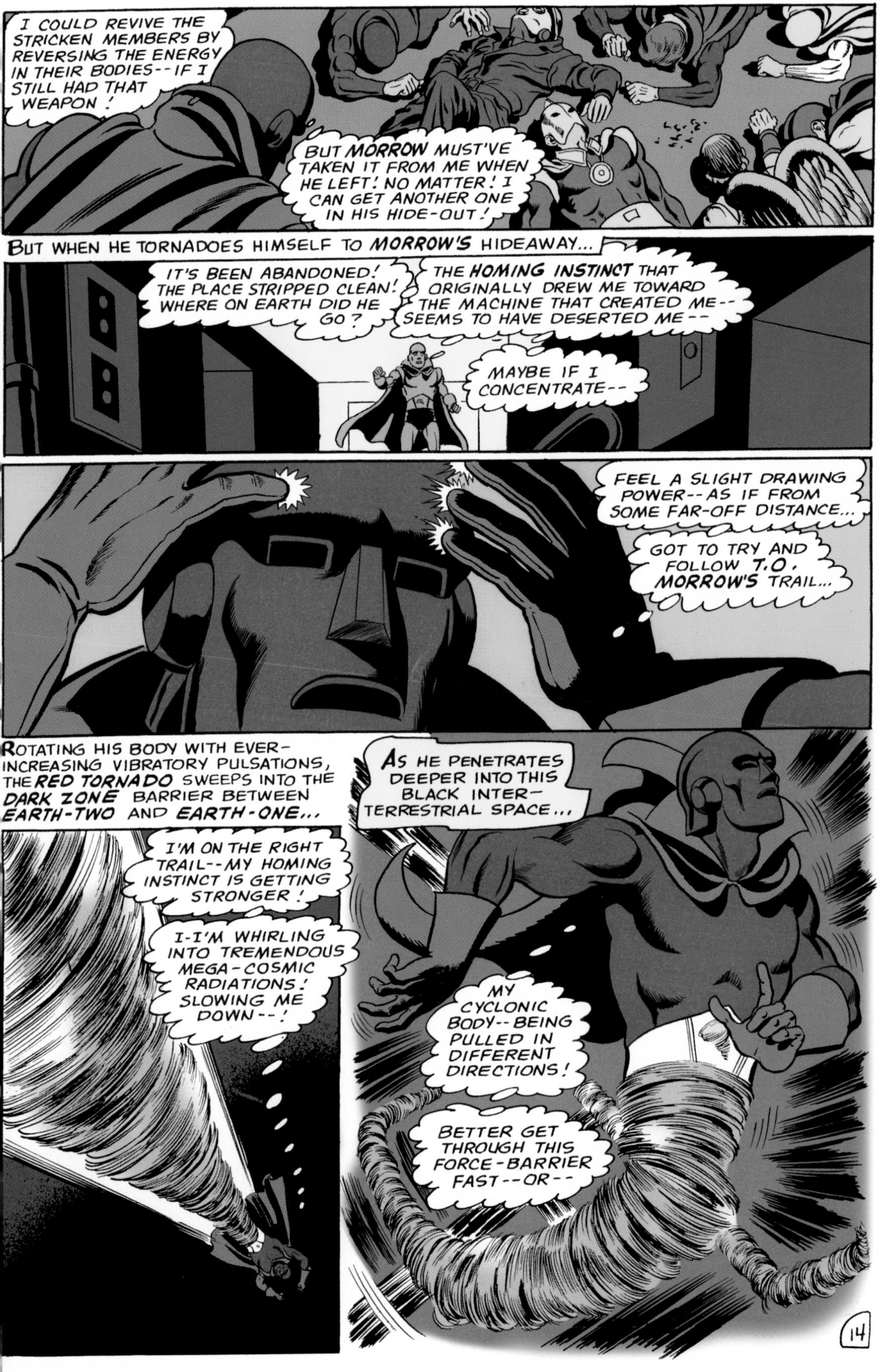
I COULD REVIVE THE STRICKEN MEMBERS BY REVERSING THE ENERGY IN THEIR BODIES--IF I STILL HAD THAT WEAPON!
BUT MORROW MUST'VE TAKEN IT FROM ME WHEN HE LEFT! NO MATTER! I CAN GET ANOTHER ONE IN HIS HIDE-OUT!
BUT WHEN HE TORNADOES HIMSELF TO MORROW'S HIDEAWAY...
IT'S BEEN ABANDONED! THE PLACE STRIPPED CLEAN! WHERE ON EARTH DID HE GO?
THE HOMING INSTINCT THAT ORIGINALLY DREW ME TOWARD THE MACHINE THAT CREATED ME--SEEMS TO HAVE DESERTED ME--
MAYBE IF I CONCENTRATE--
FEEL A SLIGHT DRAWING POWER--AS IF FROM SOME FAR-OFF DISTANCE...
GOT TO TRY AND FOLLOW T.O. MORROW'S TRAIL...
ROTATING HIS BODY WITH EVER-INCREASING VIBRATORY PULSATIONS, THE RED TORNADO SWEEPS INTO THE DARK ZONE BARRIER BETWEEN EARTH-TWO AND EARTH-ONE...
I'M ON THE RIGHT TRAIL--MY HOMING INSTINCT IS GETTING STRONGER!
I-I'M WHIRLING INTO TREMENDOUS MEGA-COSMIC RADIATIONS! SLOWING ME DOWN--!
AS HE PENETRATES DEEPER INTO THIS BLACK INTER-TERRESTRIAL SPACE...
MY CYCLONIC BODY--BEING PULLED IN DIFFERENT DIRECTIONS!
BETTER GET THROUGH THIS FORCE-BARRIER FAST--OR--
14

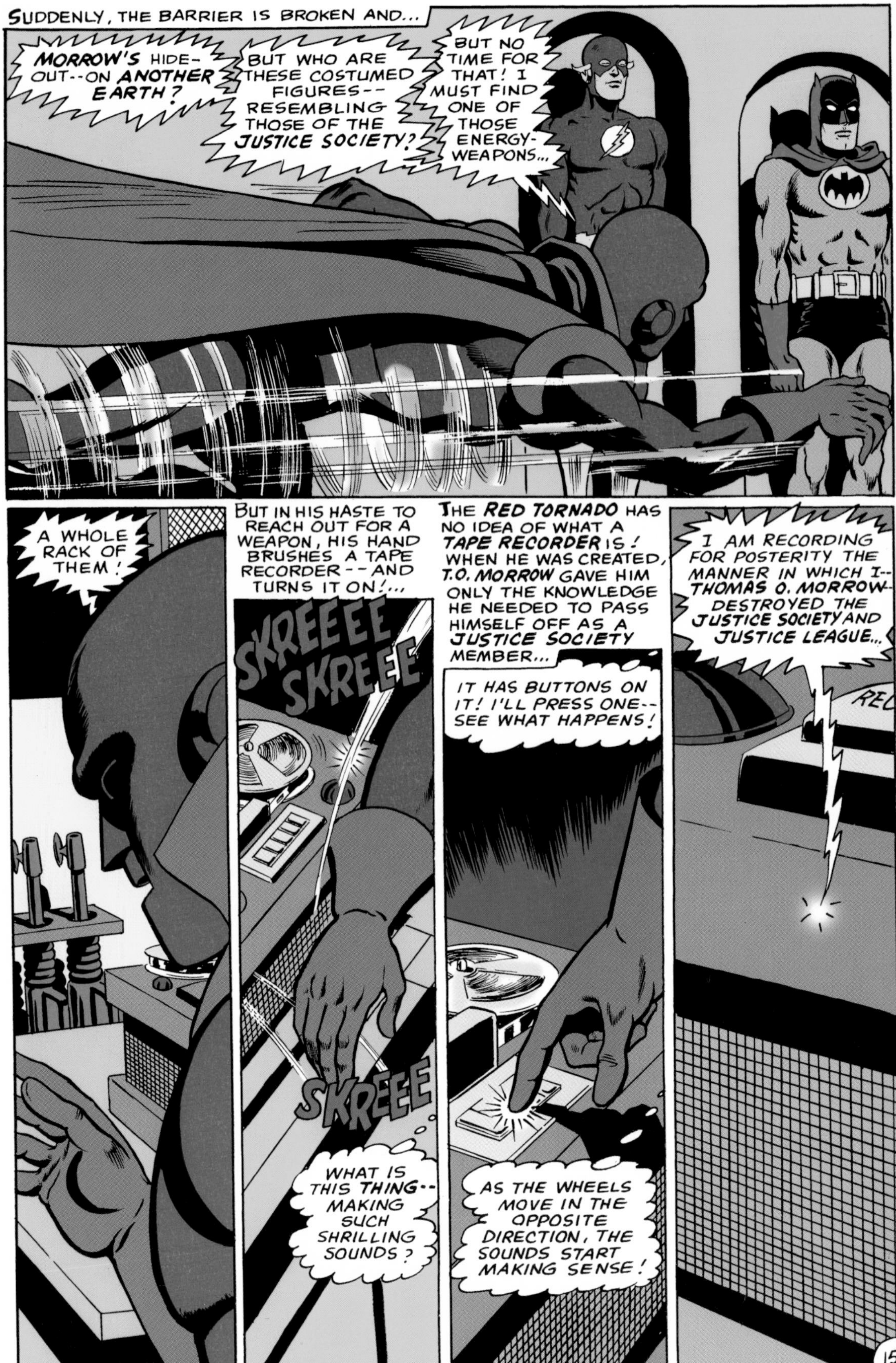
SUDDENLY, THE BARRIER IS BROKEN AND...
MORROW'S HIDE-OUT--ON ANOTHER EARTH?
BUT WHO ARE THESE COSTUMED FIGURES-- RESEMBLING THOSE OF THE JUSTICE SOCIETY?
BUT NO TIME FOR THAT! I MUST FIND ONE OF THOSE ENERGY-WEAPONS...
A WHOLE RACK OF THEM!
BUT IN HIS HASTE TO REACH OUT FOR A WEAPON, HIS HAND BRUSHES A TAPE RECORDER--AND TURNS IT ON!...
SKREEEE SKREEE
SKREEE
WHAT IS THIS THING--MAKING SUCH SHRILLING SOUNDS?
THE RED TORNADO HAS NO IDEA OF WHAT A TAPE RECORDER IS! WHEN HE WAS CREATED, T.O. MORROW GAVE HIM ONLY THE KNOWLEDGE HE NEEDED TO PASS HIMSELF OFF AS A JUSTICE SOCIETY MEMBER...
IT HAS BUTTONS ON IT! I'LL PRESS ONE--SEE WHAT HAPPENS!
AS THE WHEELS MOVE IN THE OPPOSITE DIRECTION, THE SOUNDS START MAKING SENSE!
I AM RECORDING FOR POSTERITY THE MANNER IN WHICH I--THOMAS O. MORROW--DESTROYED THE JUSTICE SOCIETY AND JUSTICE LEAGUE...
15

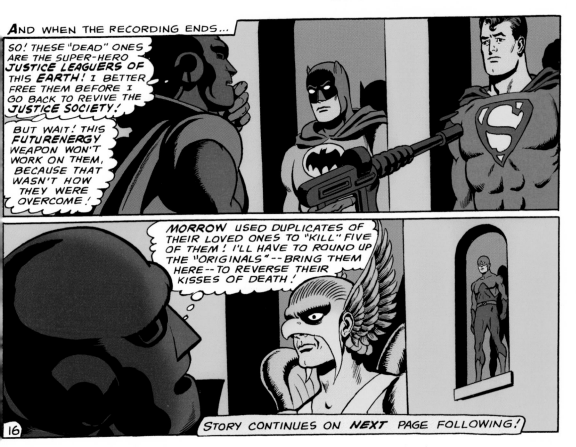

AND WHEN THE RECORDING ENDS...

SO! THESE "DEAD" ONES ARE THE SUPER-HERO *JUSTICE LEAGUERS* OF THIS *EARTH*! I BETTER FREE THEM BEFORE I GO BACK TO REVIVE THE *JUSTICE SOCIETY!*

BUT WAIT! THIS *FUTURENERGY* WEAPON WON'T WORK ON THEM, BECAUSE THAT WASN'T HOW THEY WERE OVERCOME!

MORROW USED DUPLICATES OF THEIR LOVED ONES TO "KILL" FIVE OF THEM! I'LL HAVE TO ROUND UP THE "ORIGINALS" -- BRING THEM HERE -- TO REVERSE THEIR KISSES OF DEATH!

16

STORY CONTINUES ON *NEXT* PAGE FOLLOWING!

JUSTICE LEAGUE of AMERICA

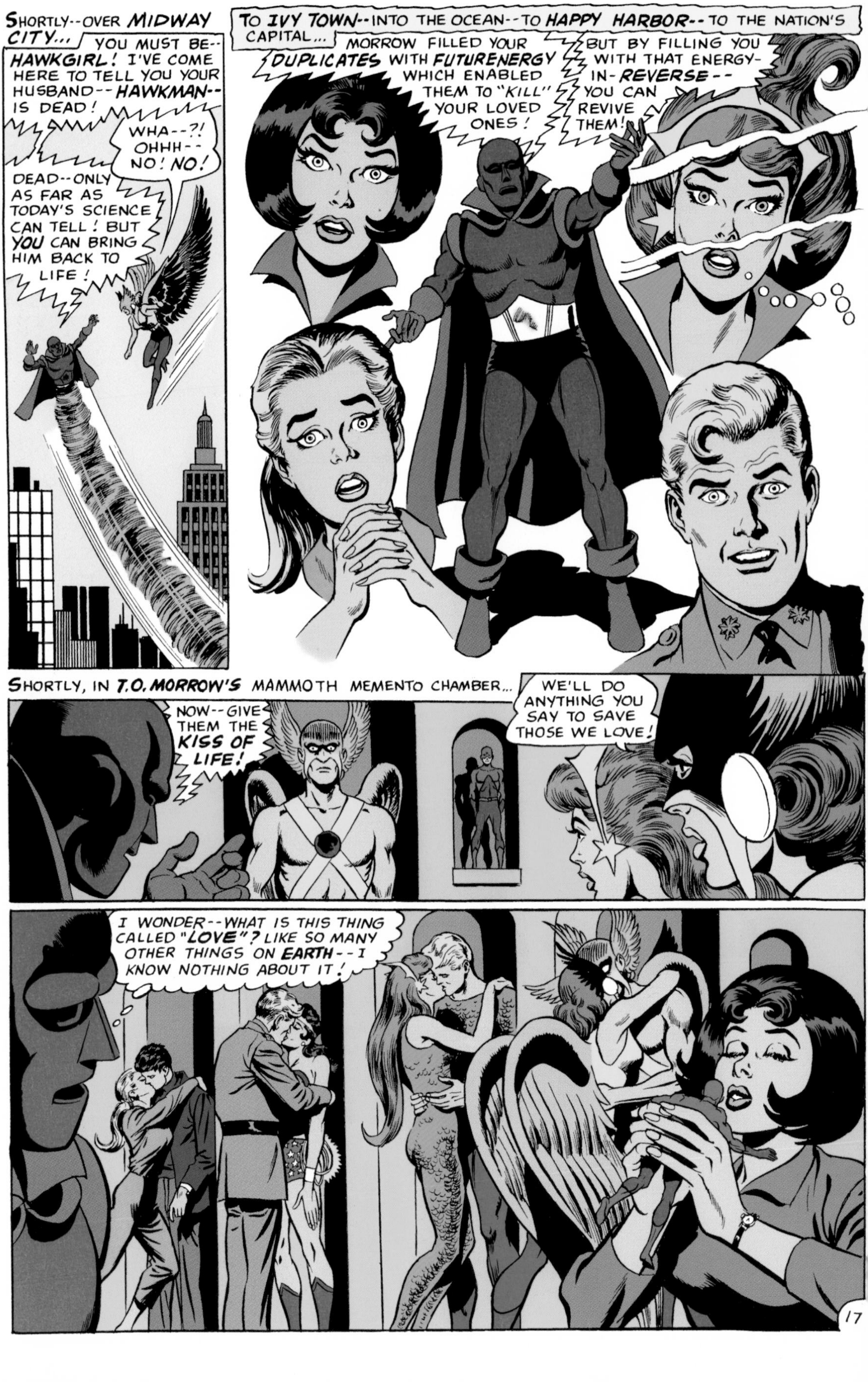
SHORTLY--OVER MIDWAY CITY...
YOU MUST BE--HAWKGIRL! I'VE COME HERE TO TELL YOU YOUR HUSBAND--HAWKMAN--IS DEAD!
WHA--?! OHHH--NO! NO!
DEAD--ONLY AS FAR AS TODAY'S SCIENCE CAN TELL! BUT YOU CAN BRING HIM BACK TO LIFE!
TO IVY TOWN--INTO THE OCEAN--TO HAPPY HARBOR--TO THE NATION'S CAPITAL...
MORROW FILLED YOUR DUPLICATES WITH FUTURENERGY WHICH ENABLED THEM TO "KILL" YOUR LOVED ONES!
BUT BY FILLING YOU WITH THAT ENERGY-IN-REVERSE--YOU CAN REVIVE THEM!
SHORTLY, IN T.O. MORROW'S MAMMOTH MEMENTO CHAMBER...
NOW--GIVE THEM THE KISS OF LIFE!
WE'LL DO ANYTHING YOU SAY TO SAVE THOSE WE LOVE!
I WONDER--WHAT IS THIS THING CALLED "LOVE"? LIKE SO MANY OTHER THINGS ON EARTH--I KNOW NOTHING ABOUT IT!
17

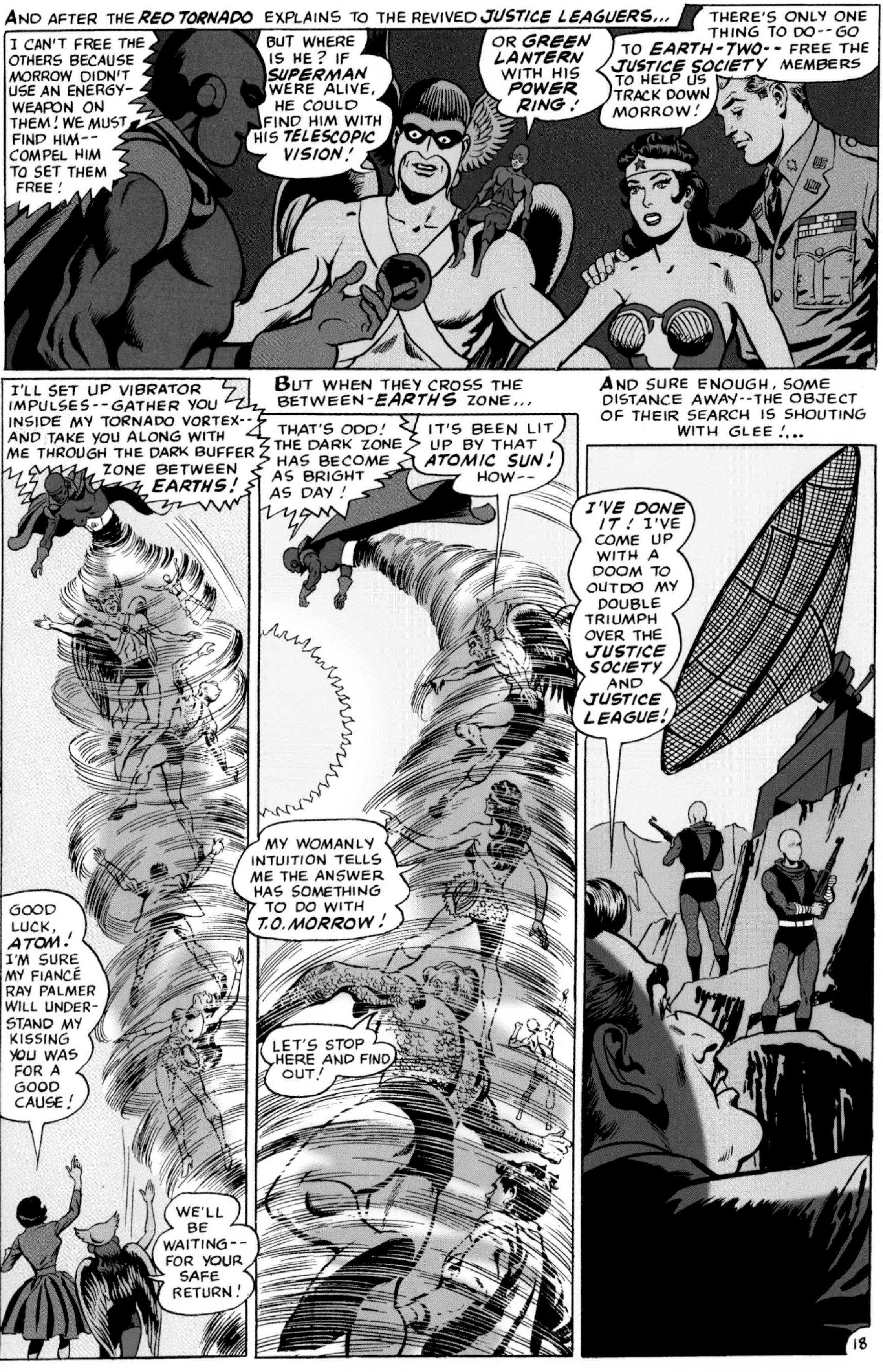
AND AFTER THE RED TORNADO EXPLAINS TO THE REVIVED JUSTICE LEAGUERS...
I CAN'T FREE THE OTHERS BECAUSE MORROW DIDN'T USE AN ENERGY-WEAPON ON THEM! WE MUST FIND HIM-- COMPEL HIM TO SET THEM FREE!
BUT WHERE IS HE? IF SUPERMAN WERE ALIVE, HE COULD FIND HIM WITH HIS TELESCOPIC VISION!
OR GREEN LANTERN WITH HIS POWER RING!
THERE'S ONLY ONE THING TO DO--GO TO EARTH-TWO-- FREE THE JUSTICE SOCIETY MEMBERS TO HELP US TRACK DOWN MORROW!
I'LL SET UP VIBRATOR IMPULSES--GATHER YOU INSIDE MY TORNADO VORTEX-- AND TAKE YOU ALONG WITH ME THROUGH THE DARK BUFFER ZONE BETWEEN EARTHS!
GOOD LUCK, ATOM! I'M SURE MY FIANCÉ RAY PALMER WILL UNDERSTAND MY KISSING YOU WAS FOR A GOOD CAUSE!
WE'LL BE WAITING-- FOR YOUR SAFE RETURN!
BUT WHEN THEY CROSS THE BETWEEN-EARTHS ZONE...
THAT'S ODD! THE DARK ZONE HAS BECOME AS BRIGHT AS DAY!
IT'S BEEN LIT UP BY THAT ATOMIC SUN! HOW--
MY WOMANLY INTUITION TELLS ME THE ANSWER HAS SOMETHING TO DO WITH T.O. MORROW!
LET'S STOP HERE AND FIND OUT!
AND SURE ENOUGH, SOME DISTANCE AWAY--THE OBJECT OF THEIR SEARCH IS SHOUTING WITH GLEE!...
I'VE DONE IT! I'VE COME UP WITH A DOOM TO OUTDO MY DOUBLE TRIUMPH OVER THE JUSTICE SOCIETY AND JUSTICE LEAGUE!
18

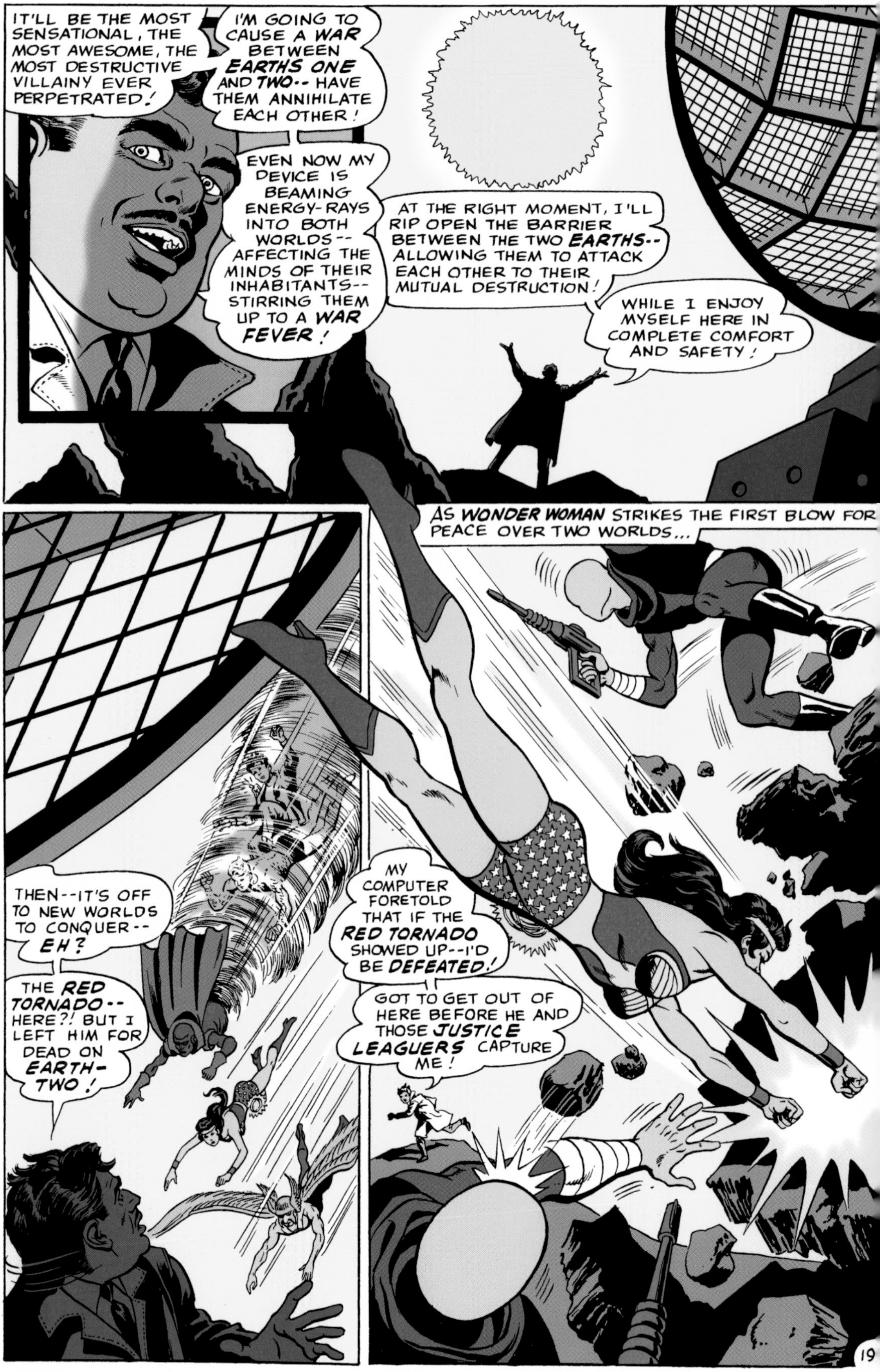
IT'LL BE THE MOST SENSATIONAL, THE MOST AWESOME, THE MOST DESTRUCTIVE VILLAINY EVER PERPETRATED!
I'M GOING TO CAUSE A WAR BETWEEN EARTHS ONE AND TWO-- HAVE THEM ANNIHILATE EACH OTHER!
EVEN NOW MY DEVICE IS BEAMING ENERGY-RAYS INTO BOTH WORLDS-- AFFECTING THE MINDS OF THEIR INHABITANTS-- STIRRING THEM UP TO A WAR FEVER!
AT THE RIGHT MOMENT, I'LL RIP OPEN THE BARRIER BETWEEN THE TWO EARTHS-- ALLOWING THEM TO ATTACK EACH OTHER TO THEIR MUTUAL DESTRUCTION!
WHILE I ENJOY MYSELF HERE IN COMPLETE COMFORT AND SAFETY!
THEN--IT'S OFF TO NEW WORLDS TO CONQUER-- EH?
THE RED TORNADO-- HERE?! BUT I LEFT HIM FOR DEAD ON EARTH-TWO!
AS WONDER WOMAN STRIKES THE FIRST BLOW FOR PEACE OVER TWO WORLDS...
MY COMPUTER FORETOLD THAT IF THE RED TORNADO SHOWED UP--I'D BE DEFEATED!
GOT TO GET OUT OF HERE BEFORE HE AND THOSE JUSTICE LEAGUERS CAPTURE ME!
19

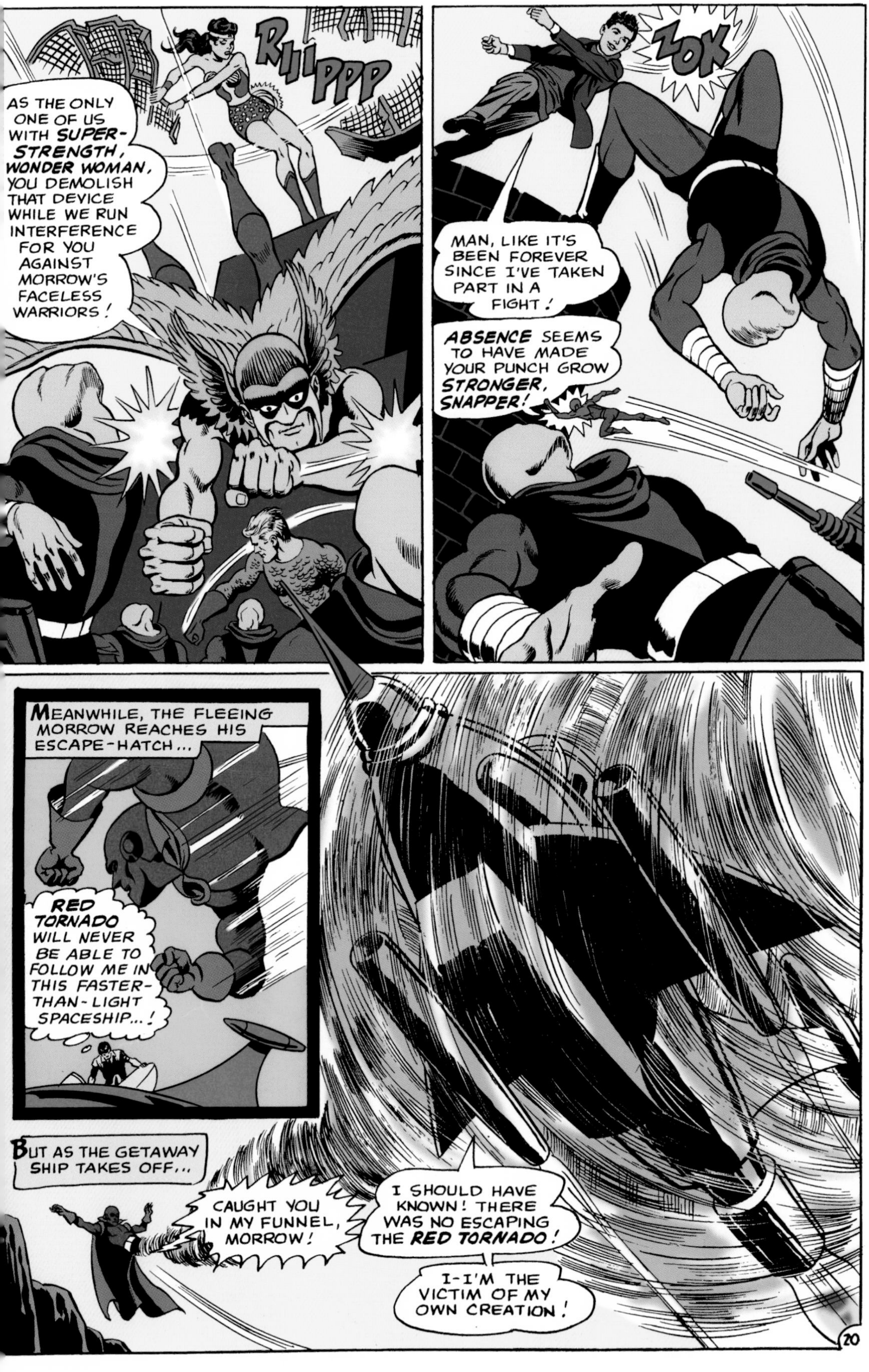
RIIIPPP
AS THE ONLY ONE OF US WITH SUPER-STRENGTH, WONDER WOMAN, YOU DEMOLISH THAT DEVICE WHILE WE RUN INTERFERENCE FOR YOU AGAINST MORROW'S FACELESS WARRIORS!
ZOK
MAN, LIKE IT'S BEEN FOREVER SINCE I'VE TAKEN PART IN A FIGHT!
ABSENCE SEEMS TO HAVE MADE YOUR PUNCH GROW STRONGER, SNAPPER!
MEANWHILE, THE FLEEING MORROW REACHES HIS ESCAPE-HATCH...
RED TORNADO WILL NEVER BE ABLE TO FOLLOW ME IN THIS FASTER-THAN-LIGHT SPACESHIP...!
BUT AS THE GETAWAY SHIP TAKES OFF...
CAUGHT YOU IN MY FUNNEL, MORROW!
I SHOULD HAVE KNOWN! THERE WAS NO ESCAPING THE RED TORNADO!
I-I'M THE VICTIM OF MY OWN CREATION!
20

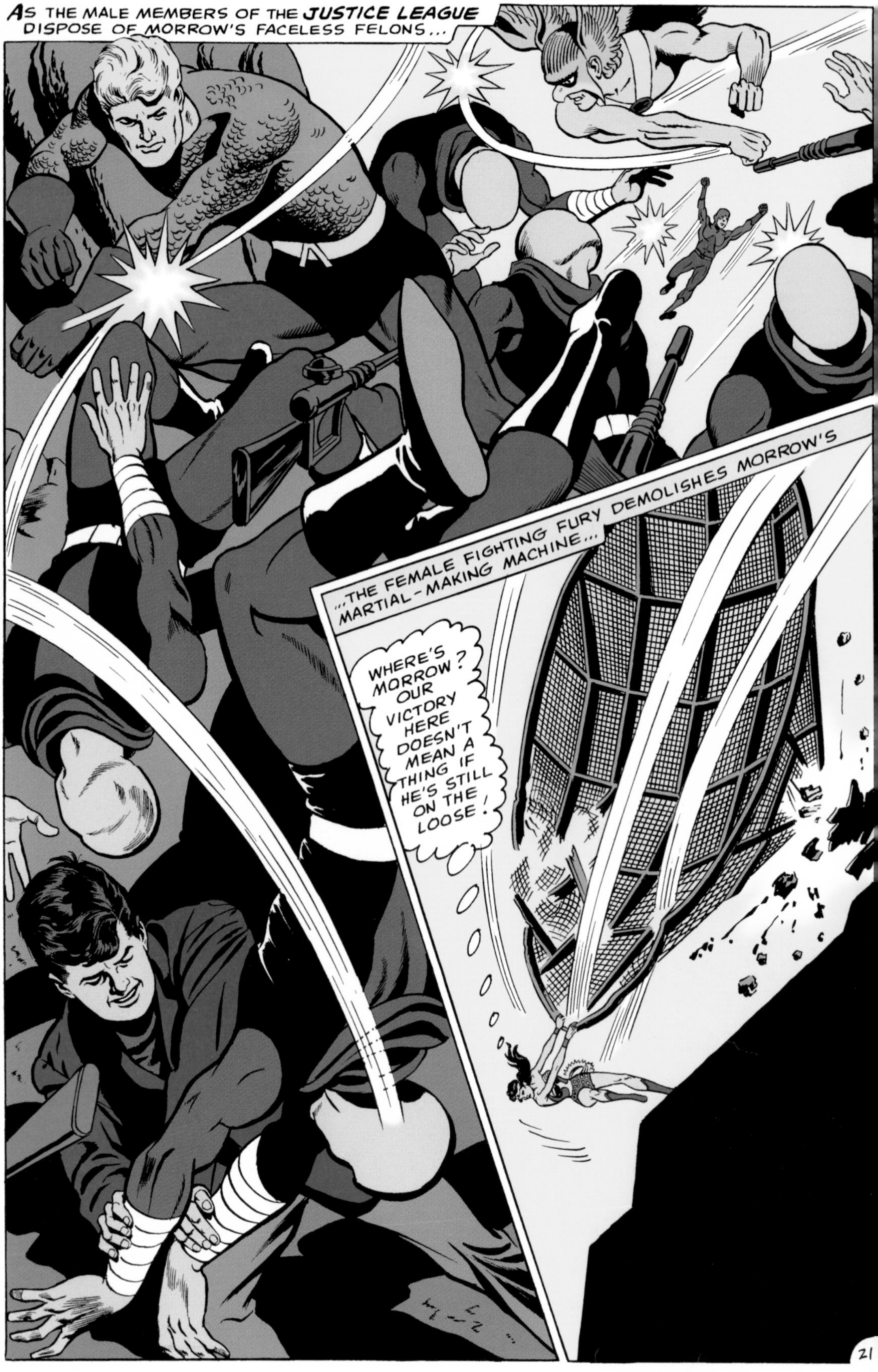
AS THE MALE MEMBERS OF THE JUSTICE LEAGUE DISPOSE OF MORROW'S FACELESS FELONS...
...THE FEMALE FIGHTING FURY DEMOLISHES MORROW'S MARTIAL-MAKING MACHINE...
WHERE'S MORROW? OUR VICTORY HERE DOESN'T MEAN A THING IF HE'S STILL ON THE LOOSE!
21

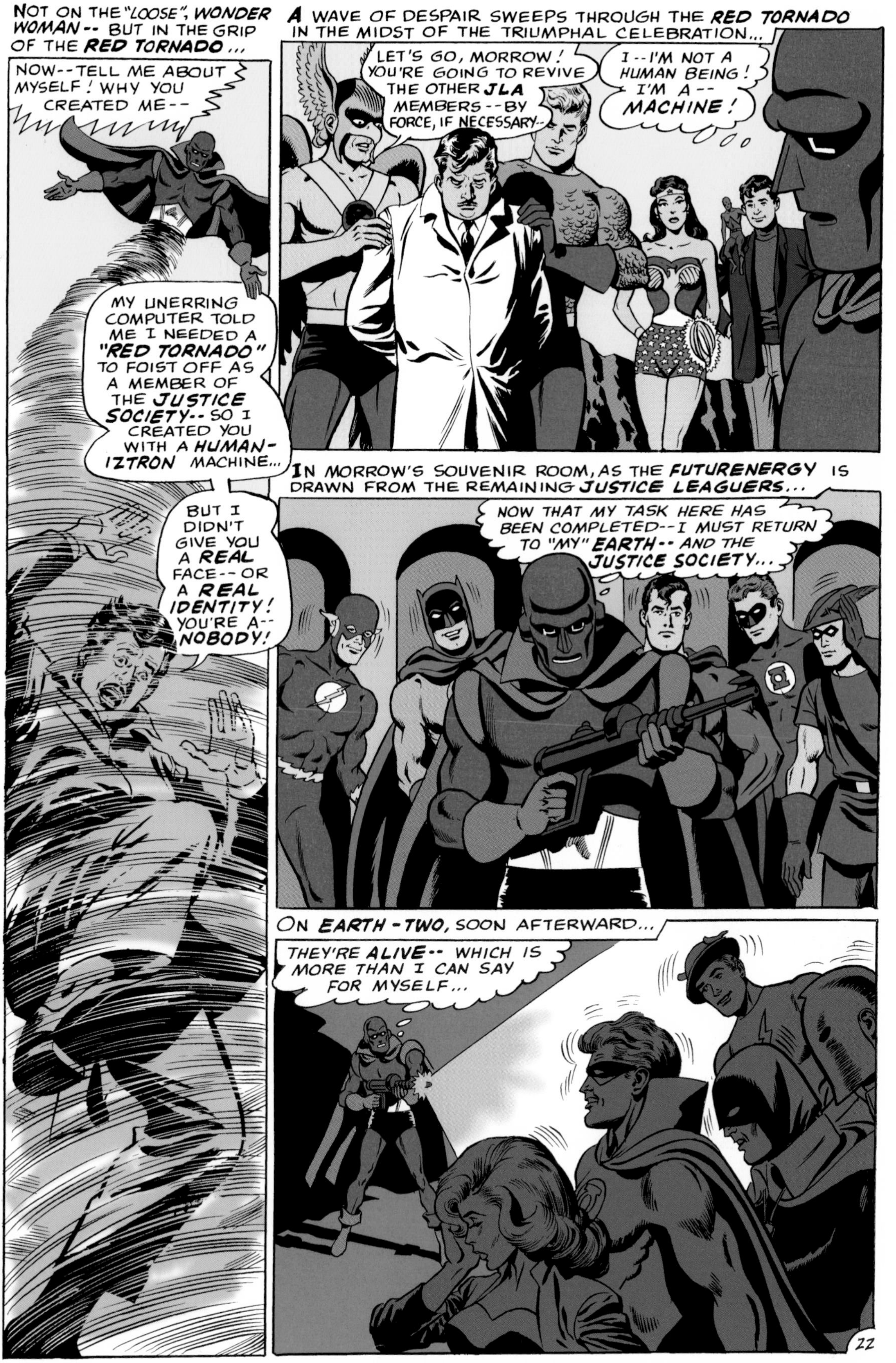
NOT ON THE "LOOSE", WONDER WOMAN-- BUT IN THE GRIP OF THE RED TORNADO...
NOW--TELL ME ABOUT MYSELF! WHY YOU CREATED ME--
MY UNERRING COMPUTER TOLD ME I NEEDED A "RED TORNADO" TO FOIST OFF AS A MEMBER OF THE JUSTICE SOCIETY-- SO I CREATED YOU WITH A HUMAN-IZTRON MACHINE...
BUT I DIDN'T GIVE YOU A REAL FACE-- OR A REAL IDENTITY! YOU'RE A-- NOBODY!
A WAVE OF DESPAIR SWEEPS THROUGH THE RED TORNADO IN THE MIDST OF THE TRIUMPHAL CELEBRATION...
LET'S GO, MORROW! YOU'RE GOING TO REVIVE THE OTHER JLA MEMBERS--BY FORCE, IF NECESSARY--
I--I'M NOT A HUMAN BEING! I'M A-- MACHINE!
IN MORROW'S SOUVENIR ROOM, AS THE FUTURENERGY IS DRAWN FROM THE REMAINING JUSTICE LEAGUERS...
NOW THAT MY TASK HERE HAS BEEN COMPLETED--I MUST RETURN TO "MY" EARTH-- AND THE JUSTICE SOCIETY...
ON EARTH-TWO, SOON AFTERWARD...
THEY'RE ALIVE-- WHICH IS MORE THAN I CAN SAY FOR MYSELF...
22

THE QUESTION BEFORE US NOW IS--WHAT ARE WE GOING TO DO ABOUT THE RED TORNADO?
HE CAME THROUGH WITH FLYING COLORS--SO I NOMINATE HIM FOR FULL MEMBERSHIP IN THE JUSTICE SOCIETY!
THANK YOU--I AM HONORED! BUT I WANT SOMETHING MORE OUT OF LIFE THAN THAT!
I WANT TO BE SOMEBODY! I WANT A FACE... AN IDENTITY I CAN CALL MY OWN!
I WANT A PERSONALITY... EMOTIONS... A HOME! I WANT TO PUT DOWN ROOTS... TO BELONG!
SOMEWHERE--IN THIS WIDE, WIDE WORLD--THERE HAS TO BE A PLACE FOR ME!
23
WILL THE RED TORNADO, PRODUCT OF A MACHINE, ACHIEVE HIS GOAL? CAN HE LIVE AS A HUMAN BEING--OR IS HE FATED TO EXIST ONLY AS A SUPER-HUMANOID? IF YOU WOULD LIKE TO SEE FURTHER ADVENTURES OF THE RED TORNADO IN HIS QUEST FOR A PLACE IN THE SUN--PLEASE WRITE AND TELL US SO!

JUSTICE LEAGUE of AMERICA

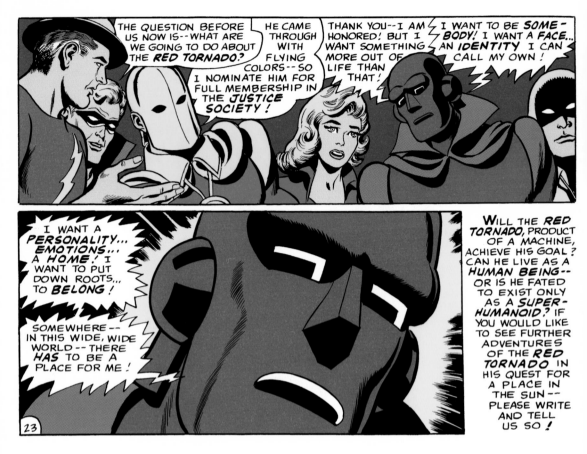

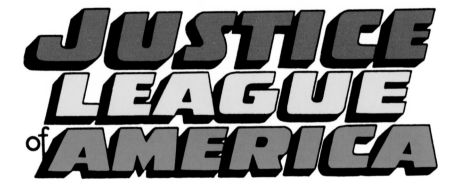

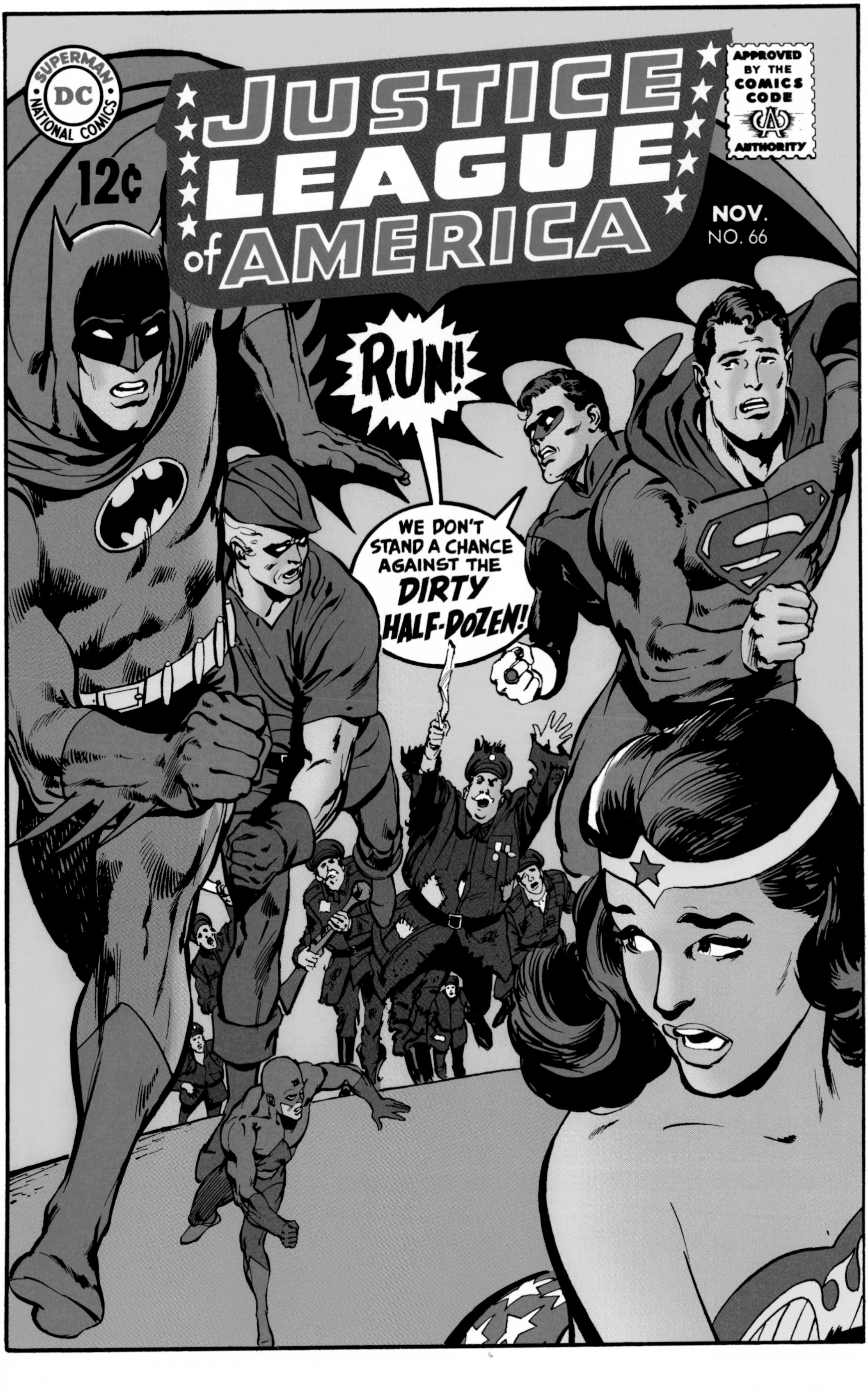
SUPERMAN
DC
NATIONAL COMICS
12¢
JUSTICE LEAGUE of AMERICA
APPROVED BY THE COMICS CODE AUTHORITY
NOV.
NO. 66
RUN!
WE DON'T STAND A CHANCE AGAINST THE DIRTY HALF-DOZEN!

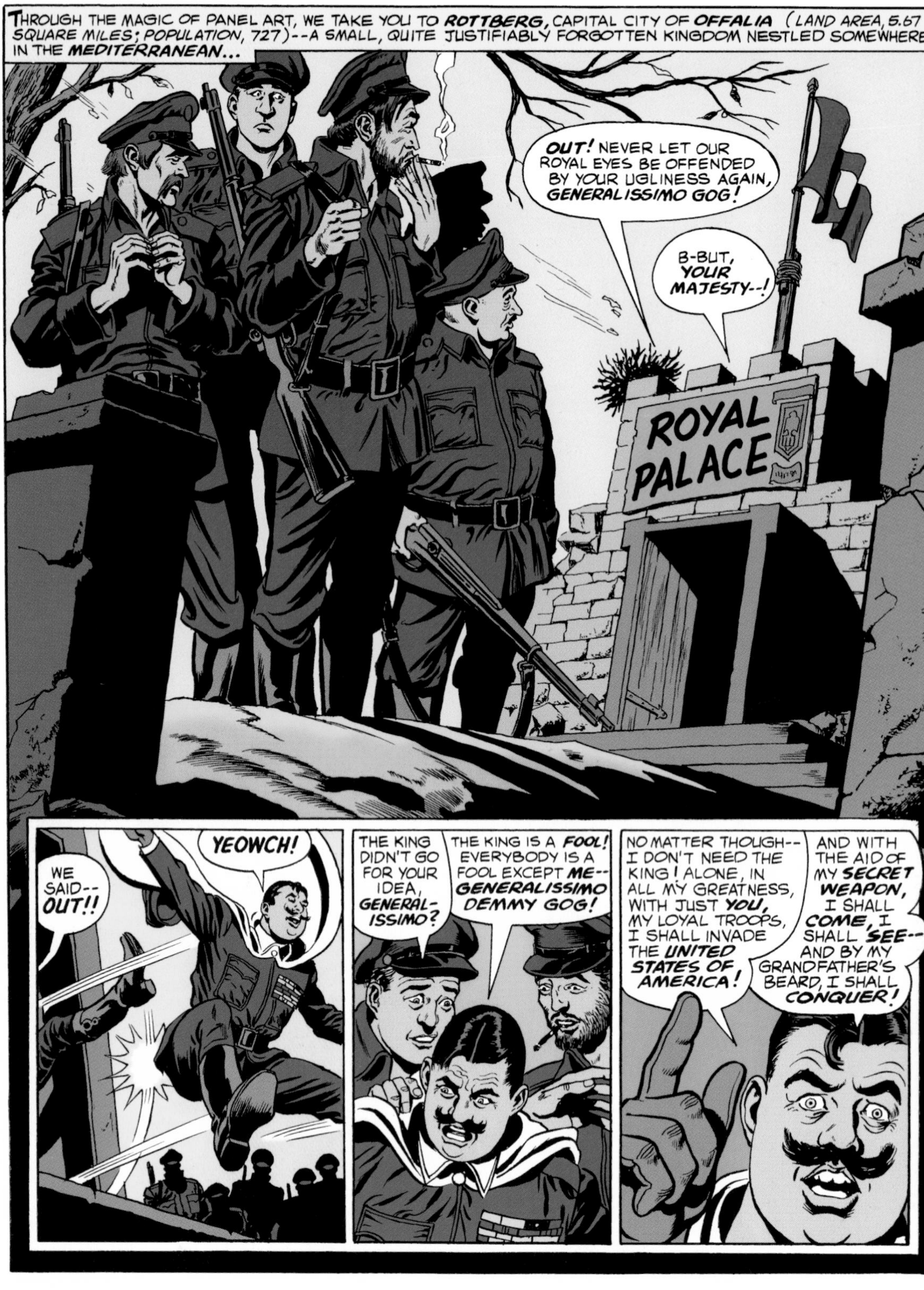
THROUGH THE MAGIC OF PANEL ART, WE TAKE YOU TO ROTTBERG, CAPITAL CITY OF OFFALIA (LAND AREA, 5.67 SQUARE MILES; POPULATION, 727)--A SMALL, QUITE JUSTIFIABLY FORGOTTEN KINGDOM NESTLED SOMEWHERE IN THE MEDITERRANEAN...
OUT! NEVER LET OUR ROYAL EYES BE OFFENDED BY YOUR UGLINESS AGAIN, GENERALISSIMO GOG!
B-BUT, YOUR MAJESTY--!
ROYAL PALACE
WE SAID--OUT!!
YEOWCH!
THE KING DIDN'T GO FOR YOUR IDEA, GENERAL-ISSIMO?
THE KING IS A FOOL! EVERYBODY IS A FOOL EXCEPT ME--GENERALISSIMO DEMMY GOG!
NO MATTER THOUGH--I DON'T NEED THE KING! ALONE, IN ALL MY GREATNESS, WITH JUST YOU, MY LOYAL TROOPS, I SHALL INVADE THE UNITED STATES OF AMERICA!
AND WITH THE AID OF MY SECRET WEAPON, I SHALL COME, I SHALL SEE--AND BY MY GRANDFATHER'S BEARD, I SHALL CONQUER!

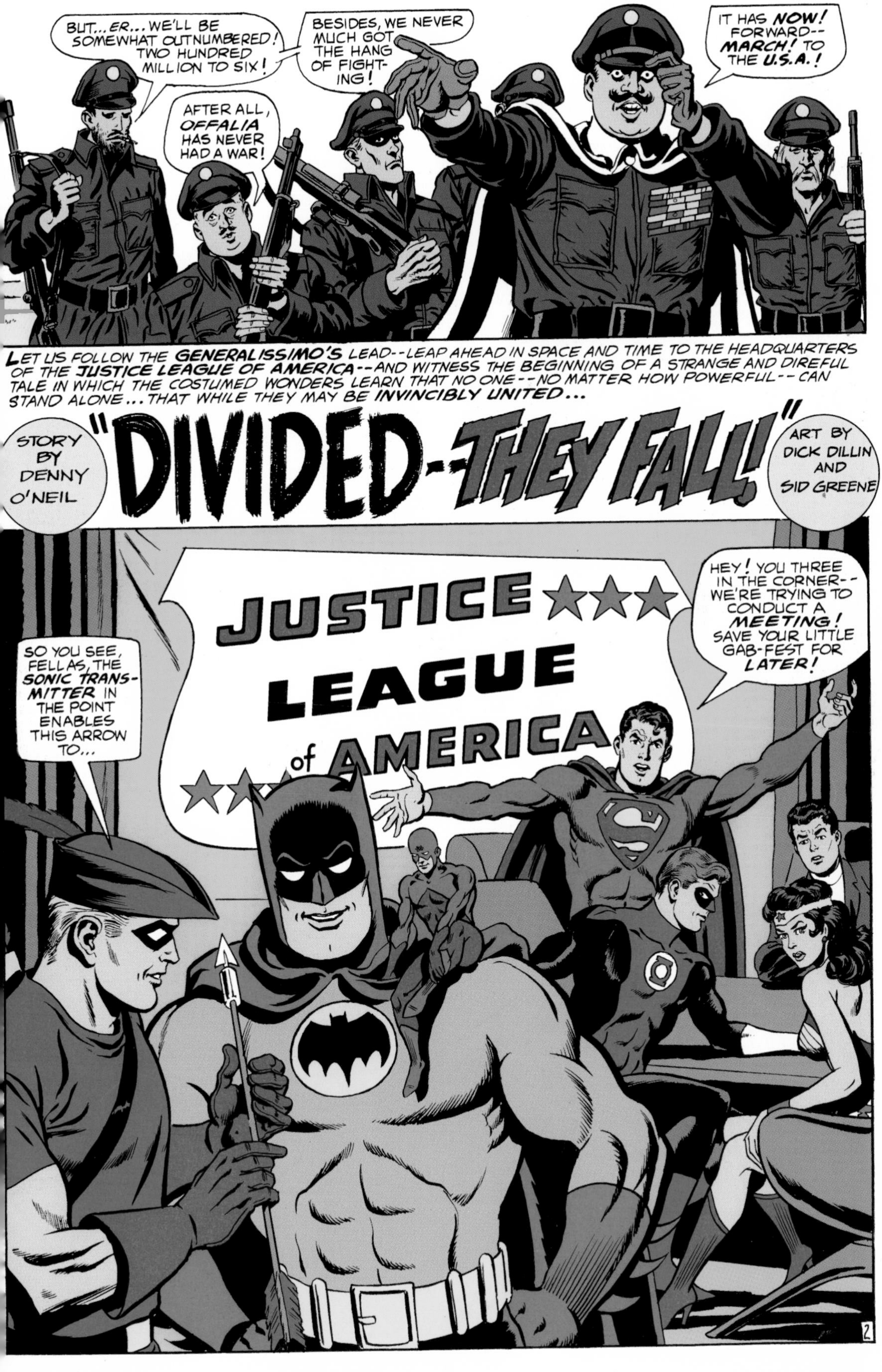
BUT...ER...WE'LL BE SOMEWHAT OUTNUMBERED! TWO HUNDRED MILLION TO SIX!
BESIDES, WE NEVER MUCH GOT THE HANG OF FIGHT-ING!
AFTER ALL, OFFALIA HAS NEVER HAD A WAR!
IT HAS NOW! FORWARD--MARCH! TO THE U.S.A.!
LET US FOLLOW THE GENERALISSIMO'S LEAD--LEAP AHEAD IN SPACE AND TIME TO THE HEADQUARTERS OF THE JUSTICE LEAGUE OF AMERICA--AND WITNESS THE BEGINNING OF A STRANGE AND DIREFUL TALE IN WHICH THE COSTUMED WONDERS LEARN THAT NO ONE--NO MATTER HOW POWERFUL--CAN STAND ALONE...THAT WHILE THEY MAY BE INVINCIBLY UNITED...
STORY BY DENNY O'NEIL
"DIVIDED--THEY FALL!"
ART BY DICK DILLIN AND SID GREENE
JUSTICE LEAGUE of AMERICA
SO YOU SEE, FELLAS, THE SONIC TRANS-MITTER IN THE POINT ENABLES THIS ARROW TO...
HEY! YOU THREE IN THE CORNER--WE'RE TRYING TO CONDUCT A MEETING! SAVE YOUR LITTLE GAB-FEST FOR LATER!
2

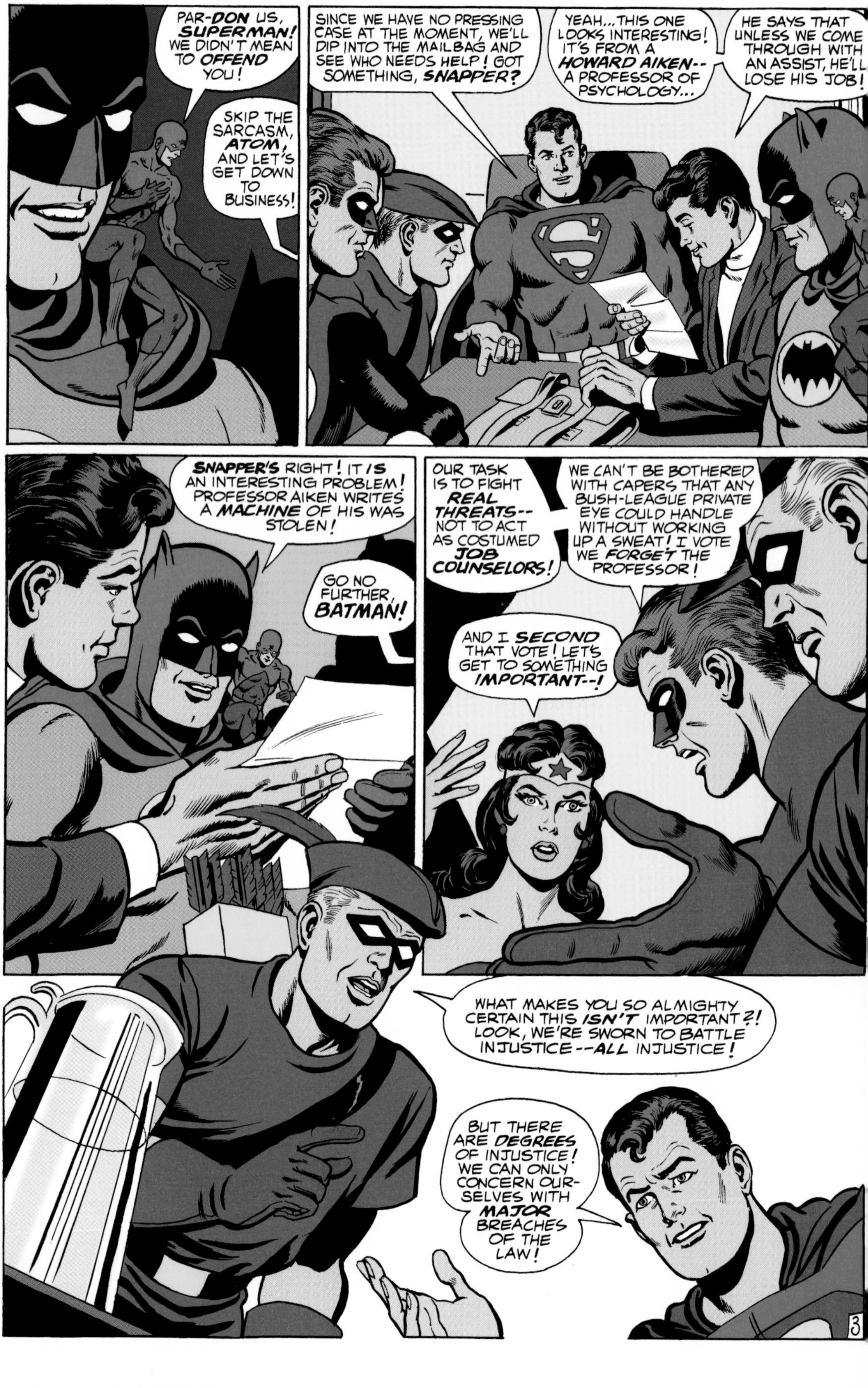

PAR-DON US, SUPERMAN! WE DIDN'T MEAN TO OFFEND YOU!
SKIP THE SARCASM, ATOM, AND LET'S GET DOWN TO BUSINESS!
SINCE WE HAVE NO PRESSING CASE AT THE MOMENT, WE'LL DIP INTO THE MAILBAG AND SEE WHO NEEDS HELP! GOT SOMETHING, SNAPPER?
YEAH... THIS ONE LOOKS INTERESTING! IT'S FROM A HOWARD AIKEN-- A PROFESSOR OF PSYCHOLOGY...
HE SAYS THAT UNLESS WE COME THROUGH WITH AN ASSIST, HE'LL LOSE HIS JOB!
SNAPPER'S RIGHT! IT IS AN INTERESTING PROBLEM! PROFESSOR AIKEN WRITES A MACHINE OF HIS WAS STOLEN!
GO NO FURTHER, BATMAN!
OUR TASK IS TO FIGHT REAL THREATS-- NOT TO ACT AS COSTUMED JOB COUNSELORS!
WE CAN'T BE BOTHERED WITH CAPERS THAT ANY BUSH-LEAGUE PRIVATE EYE COULD HANDLE WITHOUT WORKING UP A SWEAT! I VOTE WE FORGET THE PROFESSOR!
AND I SECOND THAT VOTE! LET'S GET TO SOMETHING IMPORTANT--!
WHAT MAKES YOU SO ALMIGHTY CERTAIN THIS ISN'T IMPORTANT?! LOOK, WE'RE SWORN TO BATTLE INJUSTICE--ALL INJUSTICE!
BUT THERE ARE DEGREES OF INJUSTICE! WE CAN ONLY CONCERN OUR-SELVES WITH MAJOR BREACHES OF THE LAW!
3

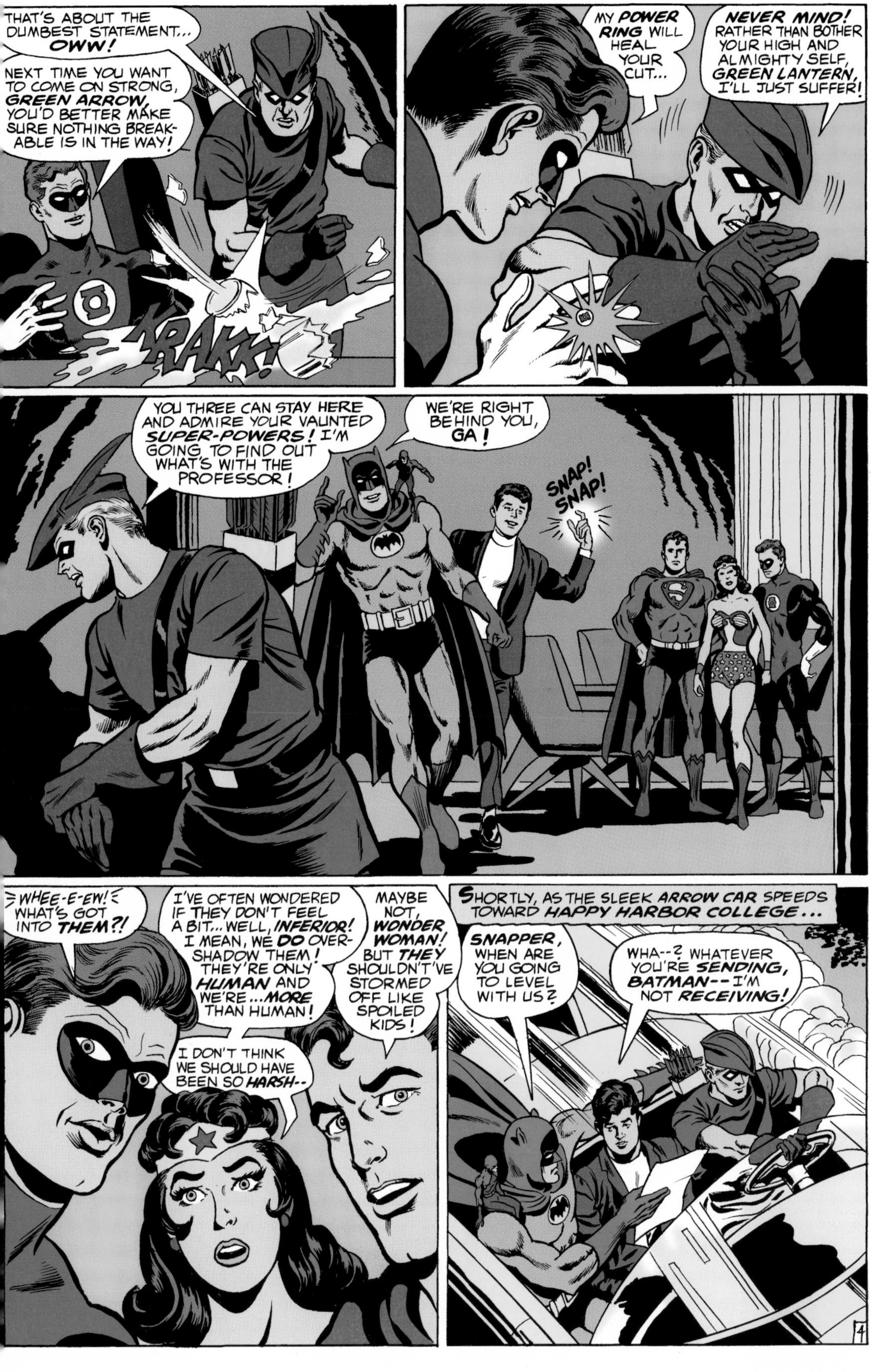
THAT'S ABOUT THE DUMBEST STATEMENT... OWW!
NEXT TIME YOU WANT TO COME ON STRONG, GREEN ARROW, YOU'D BETTER MAKE SURE NOTHING BREAKABLE IS IN THE WAY!
KRAKK!
MY POWER RING WILL HEAL YOUR CUT...
NEVER MIND! RATHER THAN BOTHER YOUR HIGH AND ALMIGHTY SELF, GREEN LANTERN, I'LL JUST SUFFER!
YOU THREE CAN STAY HERE AND ADMIRE YOUR VAUNTED SUPER-POWERS! I'M GOING TO FIND OUT WHAT'S WITH THE PROFESSOR!
WE'RE RIGHT BEHIND YOU, GA!
SNAP! SNAP!
WHEE-E-EW! WHAT'S GOT INTO THEM?!
I'VE OFTEN WONDERED IF THEY DON'T FEEL A BIT... WELL, INFERIOR! I MEAN, WE DO OVERSHADOW THEM! THEY'RE ONLY HUMAN AND WE'RE... MORE THAN HUMAN!
MAYBE NOT, WONDER WOMAN! BUT THEY SHOULDN'T'VE STORMED OFF LIKE SPOILED KIDS!
I DON'T THINK WE SHOULD HAVE BEEN SO HARSH--
SHORTLY, AS THE SLEEK ARROW CAR SPEEDS TOWARD HAPPY HARBOR COLLEGE...
SNAPPER, WHEN ARE YOU GOING TO LEVEL WITH US?
WHA--? WHATEVER YOU'RE SENDING, BATMAN--I'M NOT RECEIVING!
4

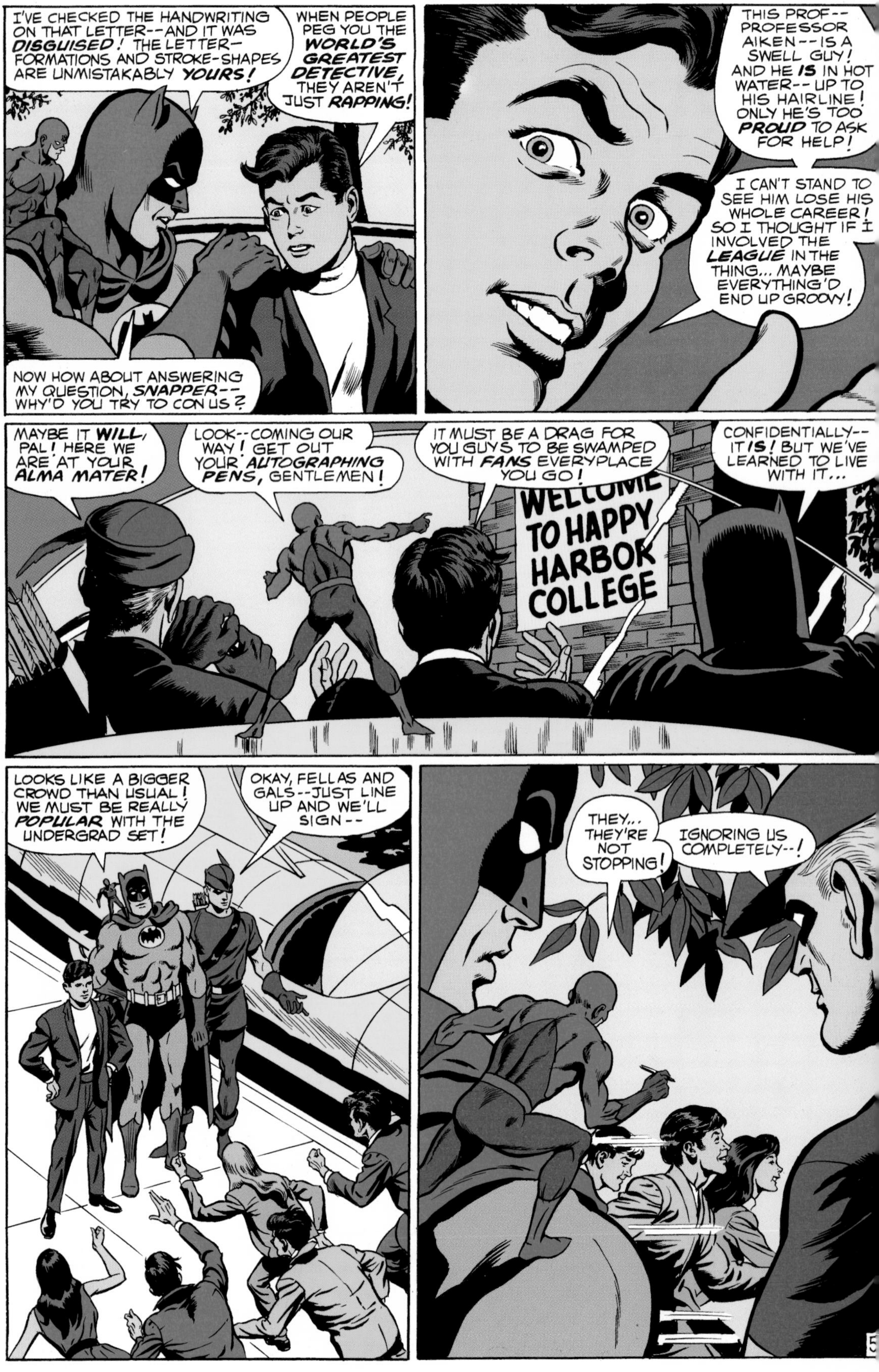
I'VE CHECKED THE HANDWRITING ON THAT LETTER--AND IT WAS DISGUISED! THE LETTER-FORMATIONS AND STROKE-SHAPES ARE UNMISTAKABLY YOURS!
WHEN PEOPLE PEG YOU THE WORLD'S GREATEST DETECTIVE, THEY AREN'T JUST RAPPING!
NOW HOW ABOUT ANSWERING MY QUESTION, SNAPPER-- WHY'D YOU TRY TO CON US?
THIS PROF--PROFESSOR AIKEN--IS A SWELL GUY! AND HE IS IN HOT WATER--UP TO HIS HAIRLINE! ONLY HE'S TOO PROUD TO ASK FOR HELP!
I CAN'T STAND TO SEE HIM LOSE HIS WHOLE CAREER! SO I THOUGHT IF I INVOLVED THE LEAGUE IN THE THING... MAYBE EVERYTHING'D END UP GROOVY!
MAYBE IT WILL, PAL! HERE WE ARE AT YOUR ALMA MATER!
LOOK--COMING OUR WAY! GET OUT YOUR AUTOGRAPHING PENS, GENTLEMEN!
IT MUST BE A DRAG FOR YOU GUYS TO BE SWAMPED WITH FANS EVERYPLACE YOU GO!
CONFIDENTIALLY--IT IS! BUT WE'VE LEARNED TO LIVE WITH IT...
WELCOME TO HAPPY HARBOR COLLEGE
LOOKS LIKE A BIGGER CROWD THAN USUAL! WE MUST BE REALLY POPULAR WITH THE UNDERGRAD SET!
OKAY, FELLAS AND GALS--JUST LINE UP AND WE'LL SIGN--
THEY... THEY'RE NOT STOPPING!
IGNORING US COMPLETELY--!
5

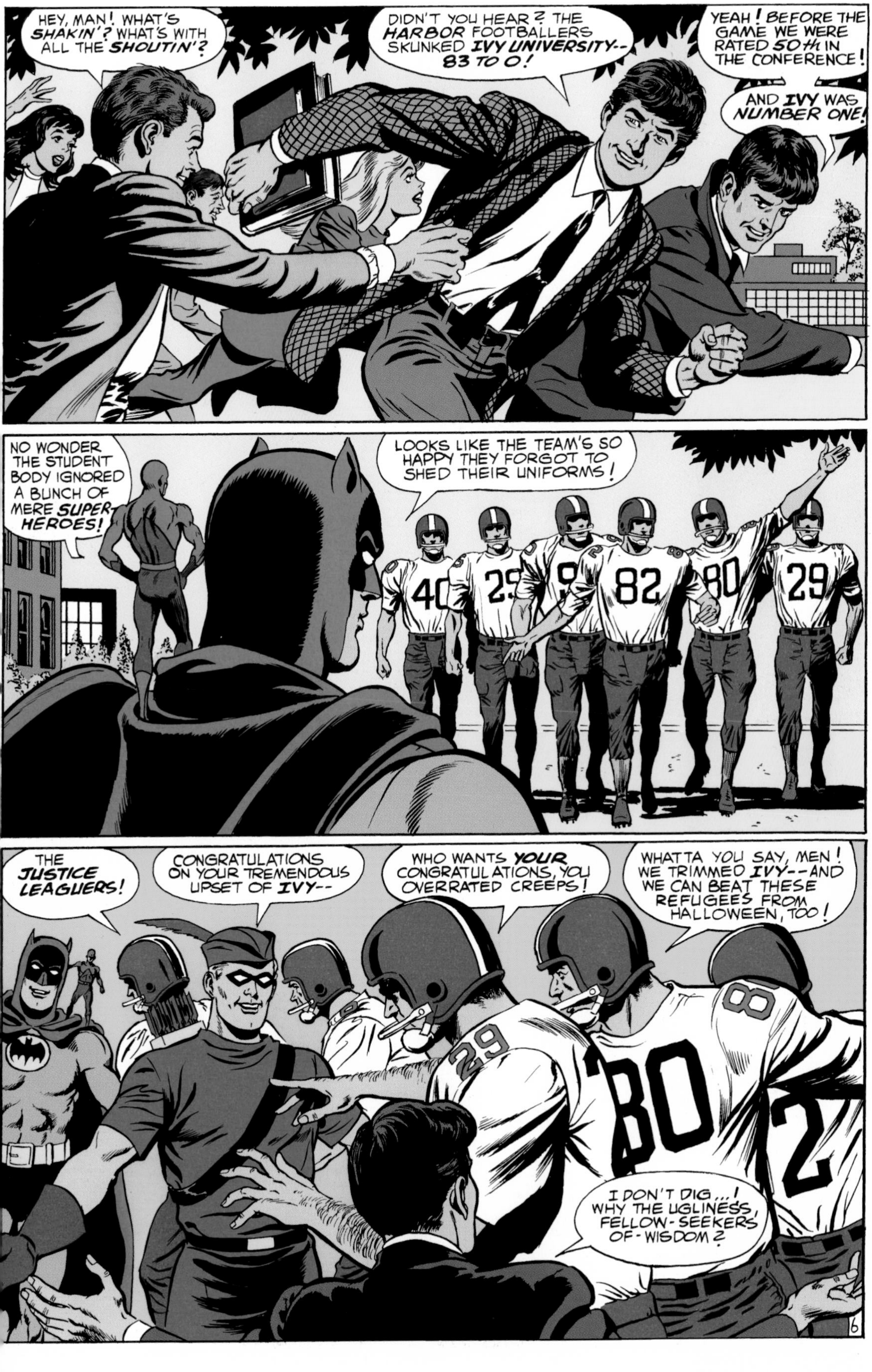
HEY, MAN! WHAT'S SHAKIN'? WHAT'S WITH ALL THE SHOUTIN'?
DIDN'T YOU HEAR? THE HARBOR FOOTBALLERS SKUNKED IVY UNIVERSITY-- 83 TO 0!
YEAH! BEFORE THE GAME WE WERE RATED 50th IN THE CONFERENCE!
AND IVY WAS NUMBER ONE!
NO WONDER THE STUDENT BODY IGNORED A BUNCH OF MERE SUPER-HEROES!
LOOKS LIKE THE TEAM'S SO HAPPY THEY FORGOT TO SHED THEIR UNIFORMS!
THE JUSTICE LEAGUERS!
CONGRATULATIONS ON YOUR TREMENDOUS UPSET OF IVY--
WHO WANTS YOUR CONGRATULATIONS, YOU OVERRATED CREEPS!
WHATTA YOU SAY, MEN! WE TRIMMED IVY--AND WE CAN BEAT THESE REFUGEES FROM HALLOWEEN, TOO!
I DON'T DIG...! WHY THE UGLINESS, FELLOW-SEEKERS OF-WISDOM?
6

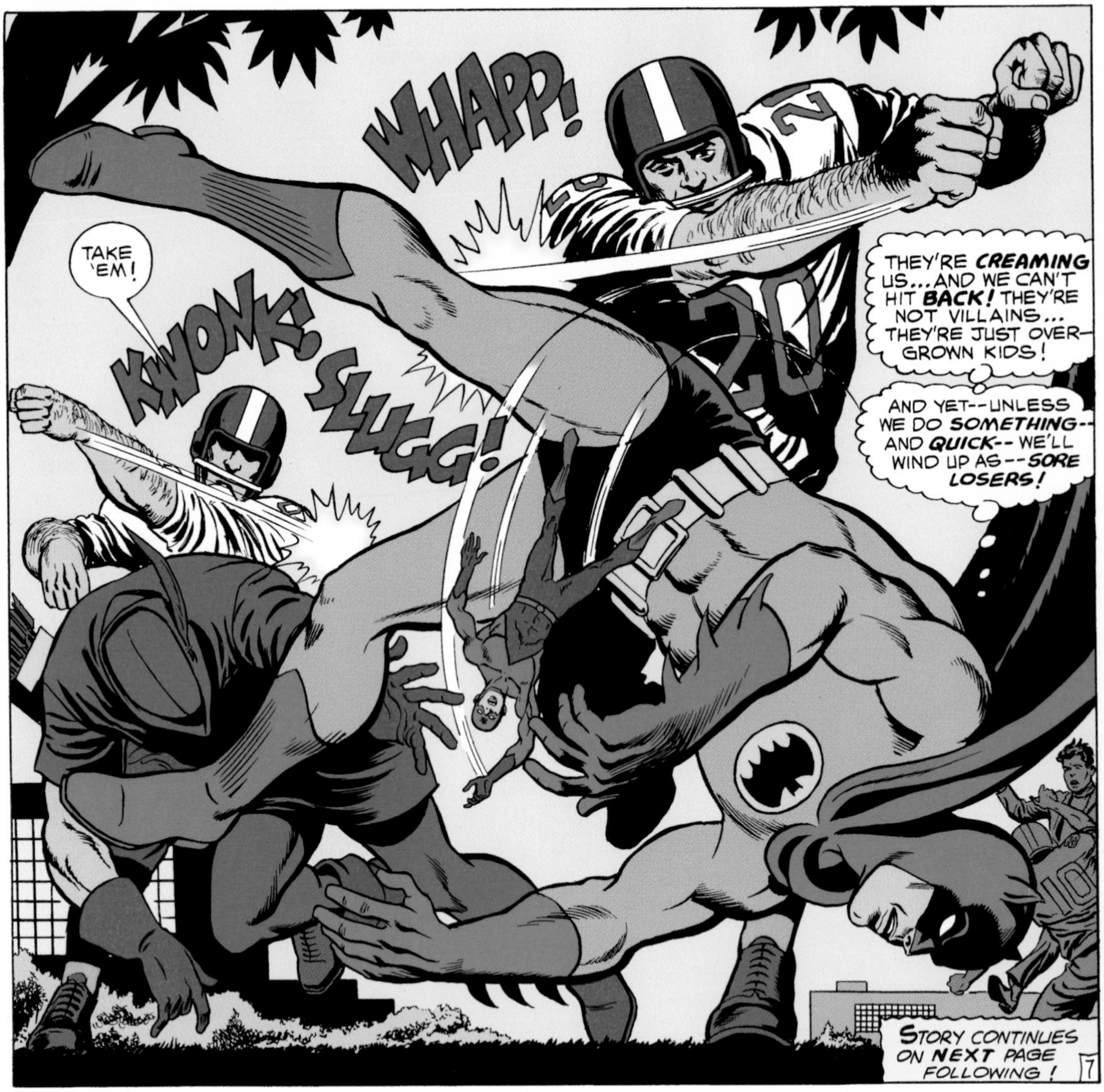
WHAPP!
TAKE 'EM!
KWONK!
SLUGG!
THEY'RE CREAMING US... AND WE CAN'T HIT BACK! THEY'RE NOT VILLAINS... THEY'RE JUST OVER-GROWN KIDS!
AND YET--UNLESS WE DO SOMETHING--AND QUICK--WE'LL WIND UP AS--SORE LOSERS!
STORY CONTINUES ON NEXT PAGE FOLLOWING!
7

JUSTICE LEAGUE of AMERICA

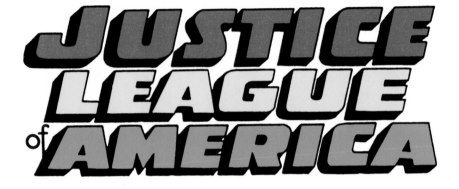

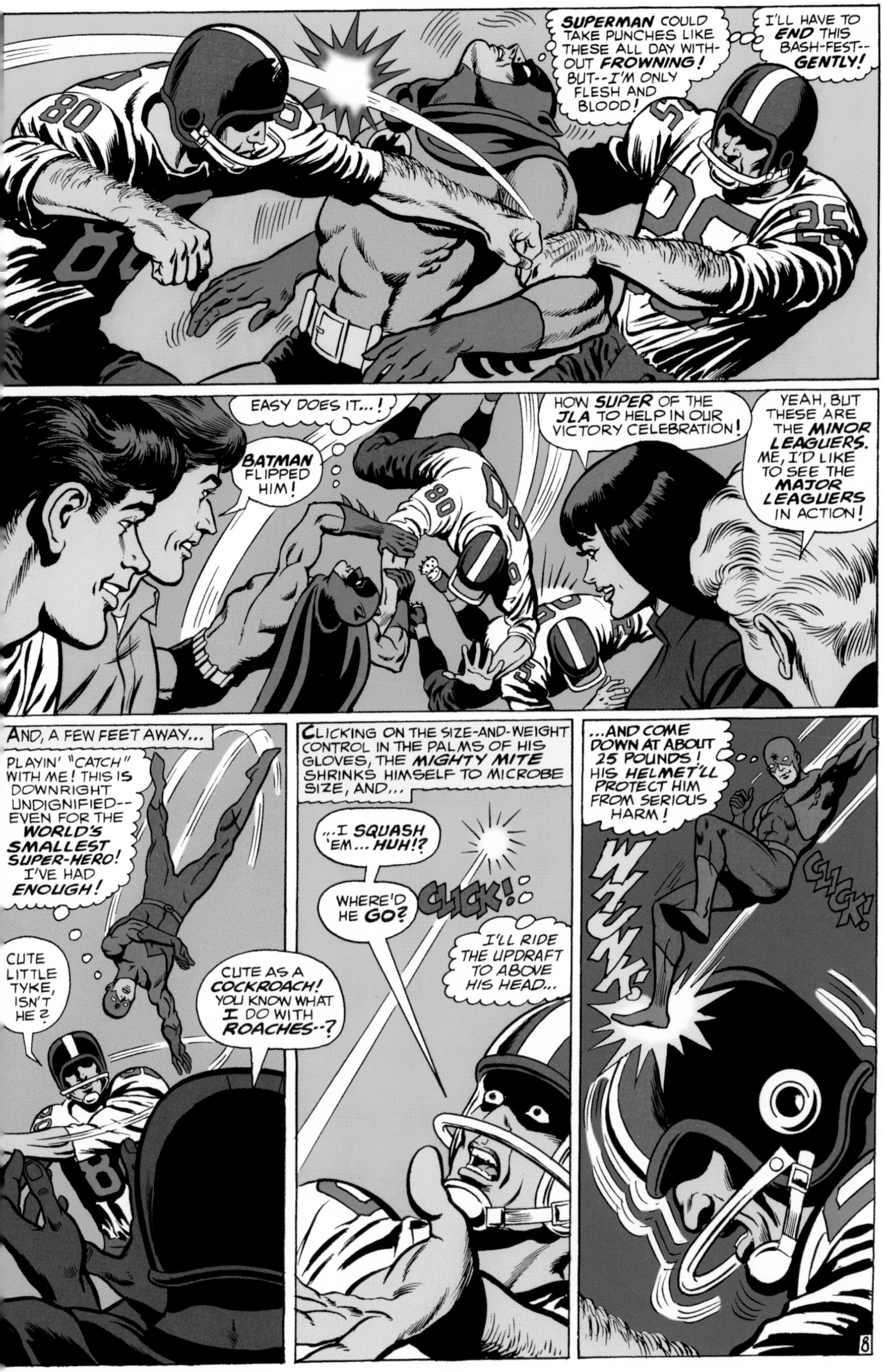
SUPERMAN COULD TAKE PUNCHES LIKE THESE ALL DAY WITHOUT FROWNING! BUT--I'M ONLY FLESH AND BLOOD!
I'LL HAVE TO END THIS BASH-FEST-- GENTLY!
EASY DOES IT...!
BATMAN FLIPPED HIM!
HOW SUPER OF THE JLA TO HELP IN OUR VICTORY CELEBRATION!
YEAH, BUT THESE ARE THE MINOR LEAGUERS. ME, I'D LIKE TO SEE THE MAJOR LEAGUERS IN ACTION!
AND, A FEW FEET AWAY...
PLAYIN' "CATCH" WITH ME! THIS IS DOWNRIGHT UNDIGNIFIED-- EVEN FOR THE WORLD'S SMALLEST SUPER-HERO! I'VE HAD ENOUGH!
CUTE LITTLE TYKE, ISN'T HE?
CUTE AS A COCKROACH! YOU KNOW WHAT I DO WITH ROACHES--?
CLICKING ON THE SIZE-AND-WEIGHT CONTROL IN THE PALMS OF HIS GLOVES, THE MIGHTY MITE SHRINKS HIMSELF TO MICROBE SIZE, AND...
...I SQUASH 'EM... HUH!?
WHERE'D HE GO?
CLICK!
I'LL RIDE THE UPDRAFT TO ABOVE HIS HEAD...
...AND COME DOWN AT ABOUT 25 POUNDS! HIS HELMET'LL PROTECT HIM FROM SERIOUS HARM!
WHUNK!
CLICK!
8

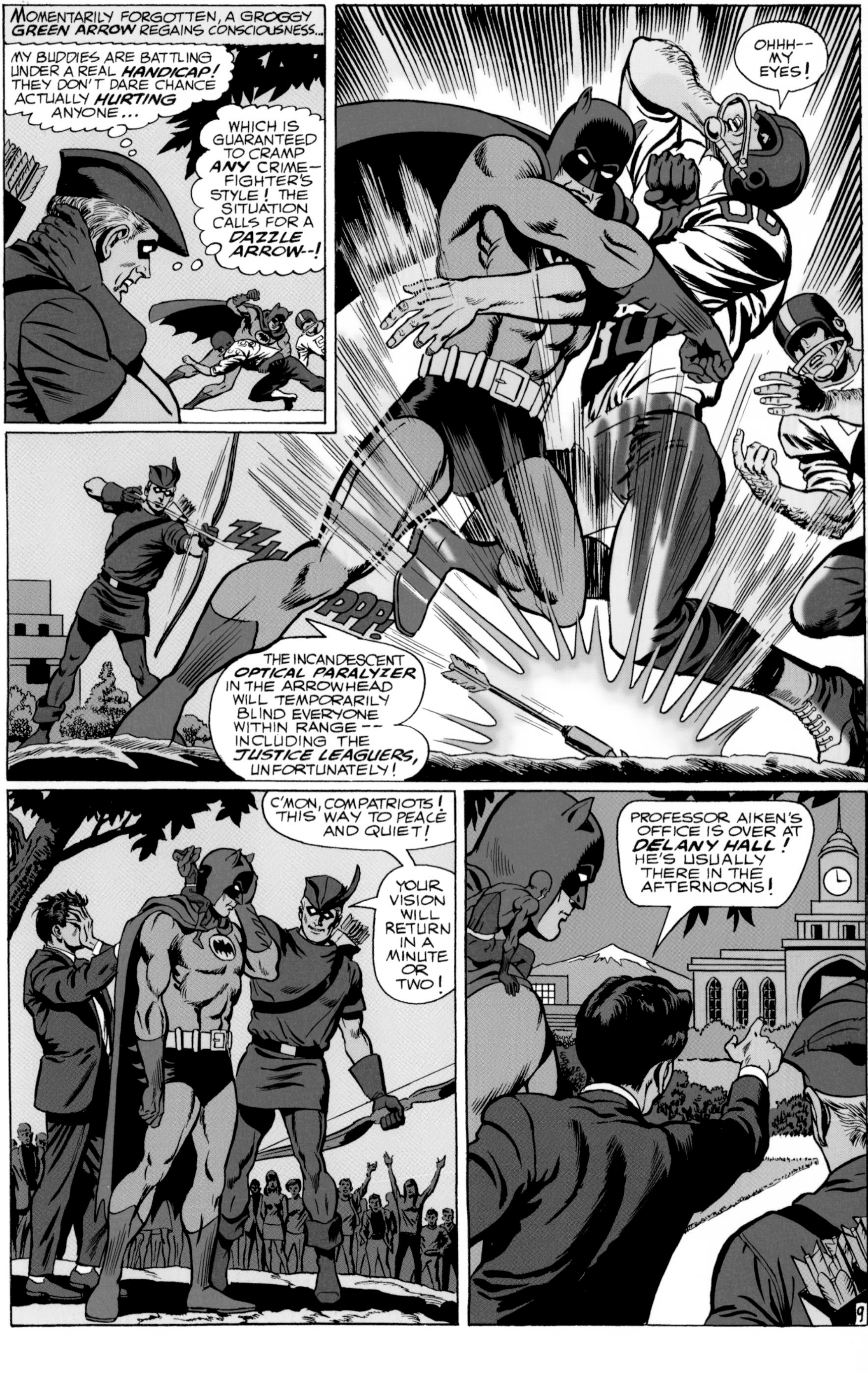
MOMENTARILY FORGOTTEN, A GROGGY GREEN ARROW REGAINS CONSCIOUSNESS...
MY BUDDIES ARE BATTLING UNDER A REAL HANDICAP! THEY DON'T DARE CHANCE ACTUALLY HURTING ANYONE...
WHICH IS GUARANTEED TO CRAMP ANY CRIME-FIGHTER'S STYLE! THE SITUATION CALLS FOR A DAZZLE ARROW--!
OHHH-- MY EYES!
THE INCANDESCENT OPTICAL PARALYZER IN THE ARROWHEAD WILL TEMPORARILY BLIND EVERYONE WITHIN RANGE -- INCLUDING THE JUSTICE LEAGUERS, UNFORTUNATELY!
C'MON, COMPATRIOTS! THIS WAY TO PEACE AND QUIET!
YOUR VISION WILL RETURN IN A MINUTE OR TWO!
PROFESSOR AIKEN'S OFFICE IS OVER AT DELANY HALL! HE'S USUALLY THERE IN THE AFTERNOONS!
9

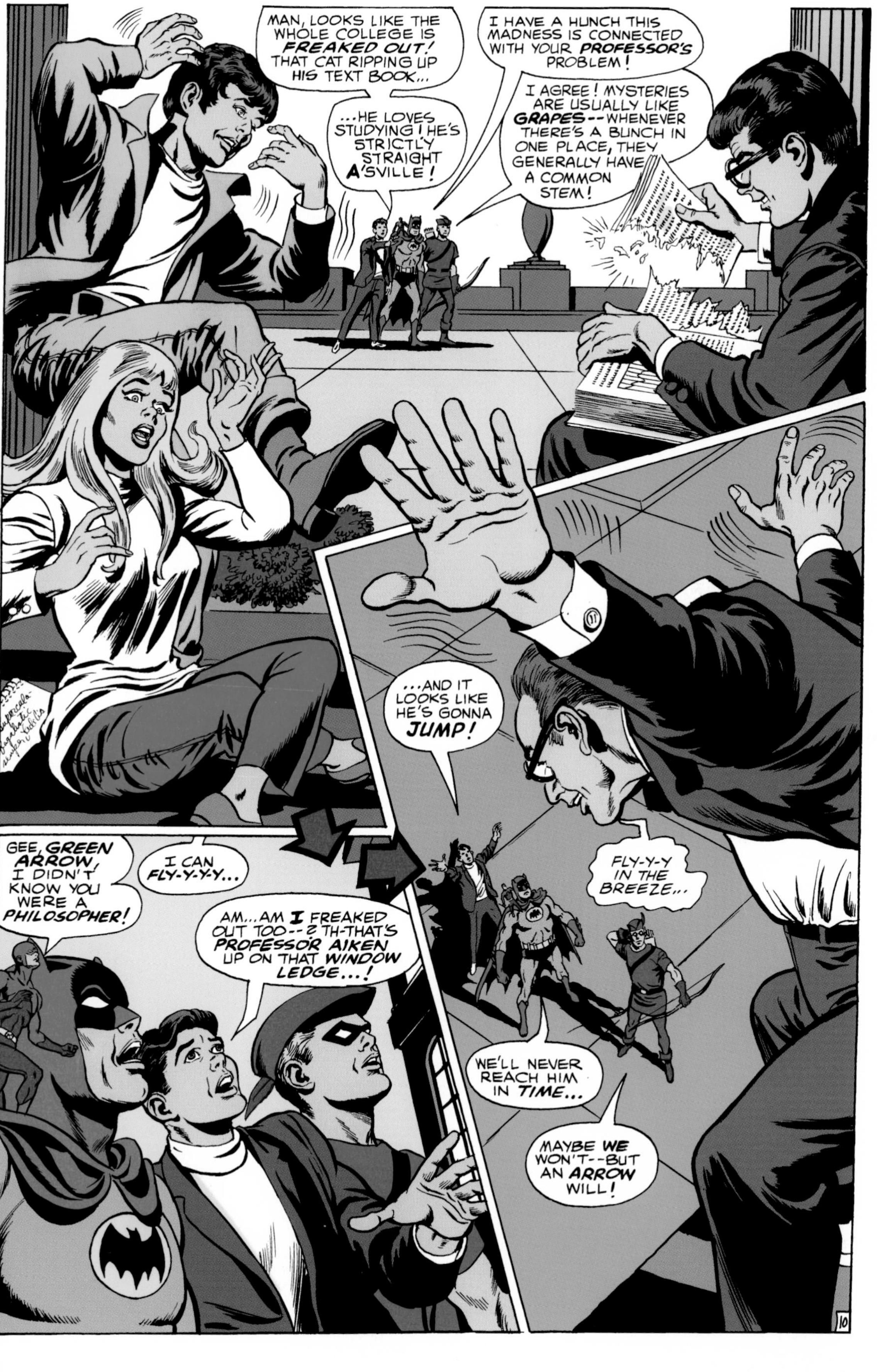
MAN, LOOKS LIKE THE WHOLE COLLEGE IS FREAKED OUT! THAT CAT RIPPING UP HIS TEXT BOOK...
...HE LOVES STUDYING! HE'S STRICTLY STRAIGHT A'SVILLE!
I HAVE A HUNCH THIS MADNESS IS CONNECTED WITH YOUR PROFESSOR'S PROBLEM!
I AGREE! MYSTERIES ARE USUALLY LIKE GRAPES--WHENEVER THERE'S A BUNCH IN ONE PLACE, THEY GENERALLY HAVE A COMMON STEM!
...AND IT LOOKS LIKE HE'S GONNA JUMP!
FLY-Y-Y IN THE BREEZE...
GEE, GREEN ARROW, I DIDN'T KNOW YOU WERE A PHILOSOPHER!
I CAN FLY-Y-Y-Y...
AM...AM I FREAKED OUT TOO--? TH-THAT'S PROFESSOR AIKEN UP ON THAT WINDOW LEDGE...!
WE'LL NEVER REACH HIM IN TIME...
MAYBE WE WON'T--BUT AN ARROW WILL!
10

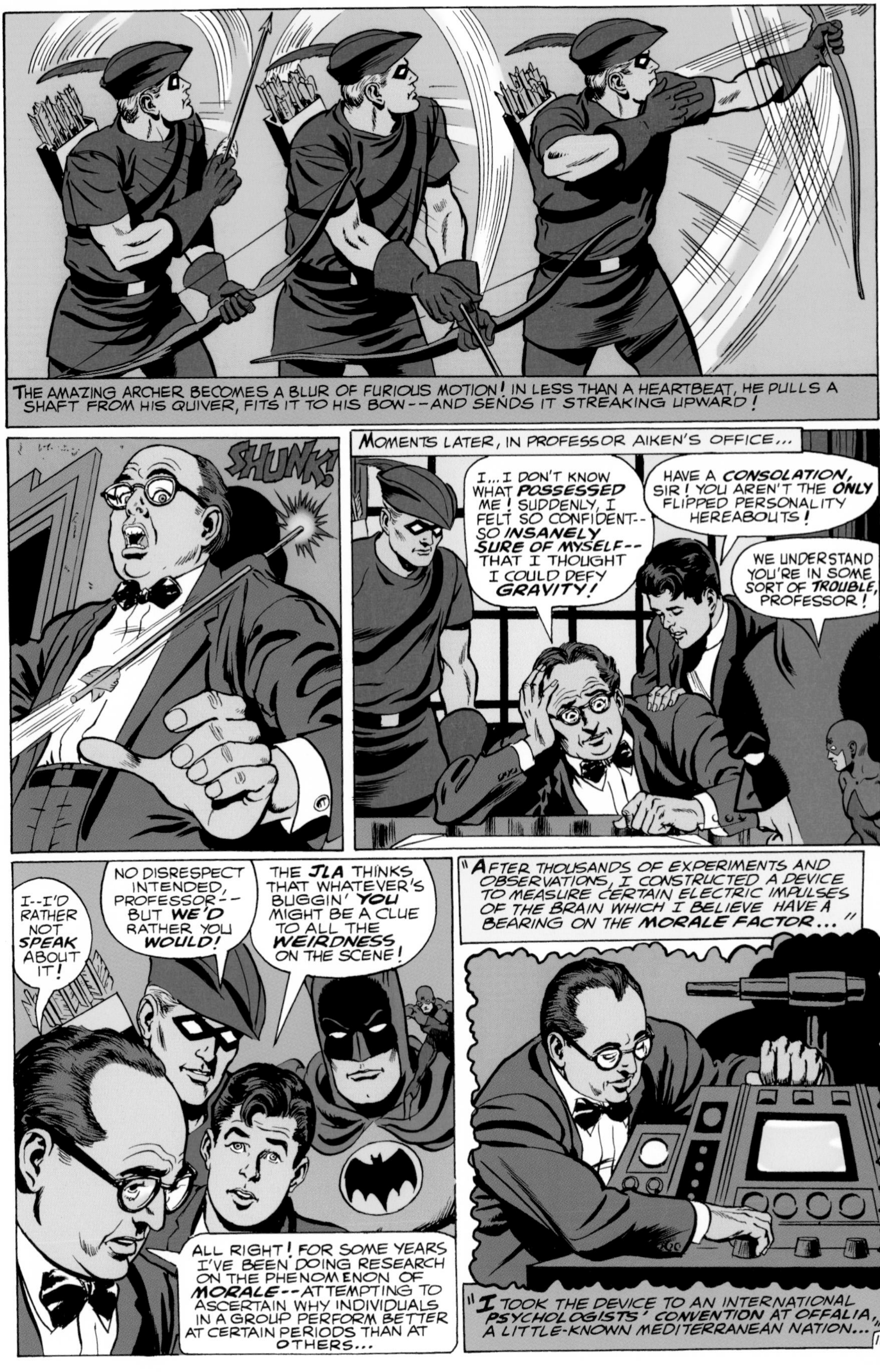
THE AMAZING ARCHER BECOMES A BLUR OF FURIOUS MOTION! IN LESS THAN A HEARTBEAT, HE PULLS A SHAFT FROM HIS QUIVER, FITS IT TO HIS BOW--AND SENDS IT STREAKING UPWARD!
SHUNK!
MOMENTS LATER, IN PROFESSOR AIKEN'S OFFICE...
I...I DON'T KNOW WHAT POSSESSED ME! SUDDENLY, I FELT SO CONFIDENT--SO INSANELY SURE OF MYSELF--THAT I THOUGHT I COULD DEFY GRAVITY!
HAVE A CONSOLATION, SIR! YOU AREN'T THE ONLY FLIPPED PERSONALITY HEREABOUTS!
WE UNDERSTAND YOU'RE IN SOME SORT OF TROUBLE, PROFESSOR!
I--I'D RATHER NOT SPEAK ABOUT IT!
NO DISRESPECT INTENDED, PROFESSOR--BUT WE'D RATHER YOU WOULD!
THE JLA THINKS THAT WHATEVER'S BUGGIN' YOU MIGHT BE A CLUE TO ALL THE WEIRDNESS ON THE SCENE!
ALL RIGHT! FOR SOME YEARS I'VE BEEN DOING RESEARCH ON THE PHENOMENON OF MORALE--ATTEMPTING TO ASCERTAIN WHY INDIVIDUALS IN A GROUP PERFORM BETTER AT CERTAIN PERIODS THAN AT OTHERS...
"AFTER THOUSANDS OF EXPERIMENTS AND OBSERVATIONS, I CONSTRUCTED A DEVICE TO MEASURE CERTAIN ELECTRIC IMPULSES OF THE BRAIN WHICH I BELIEVE HAVE A BEARING ON THE MORALE FACTOR..."
"I TOOK THE DEVICE TO AN INTERNATIONAL PSYCHOLOGISTS' CONVENTION AT OFFALIA, A LITTLE-KNOWN MEDITERRANEAN NATION..."
11

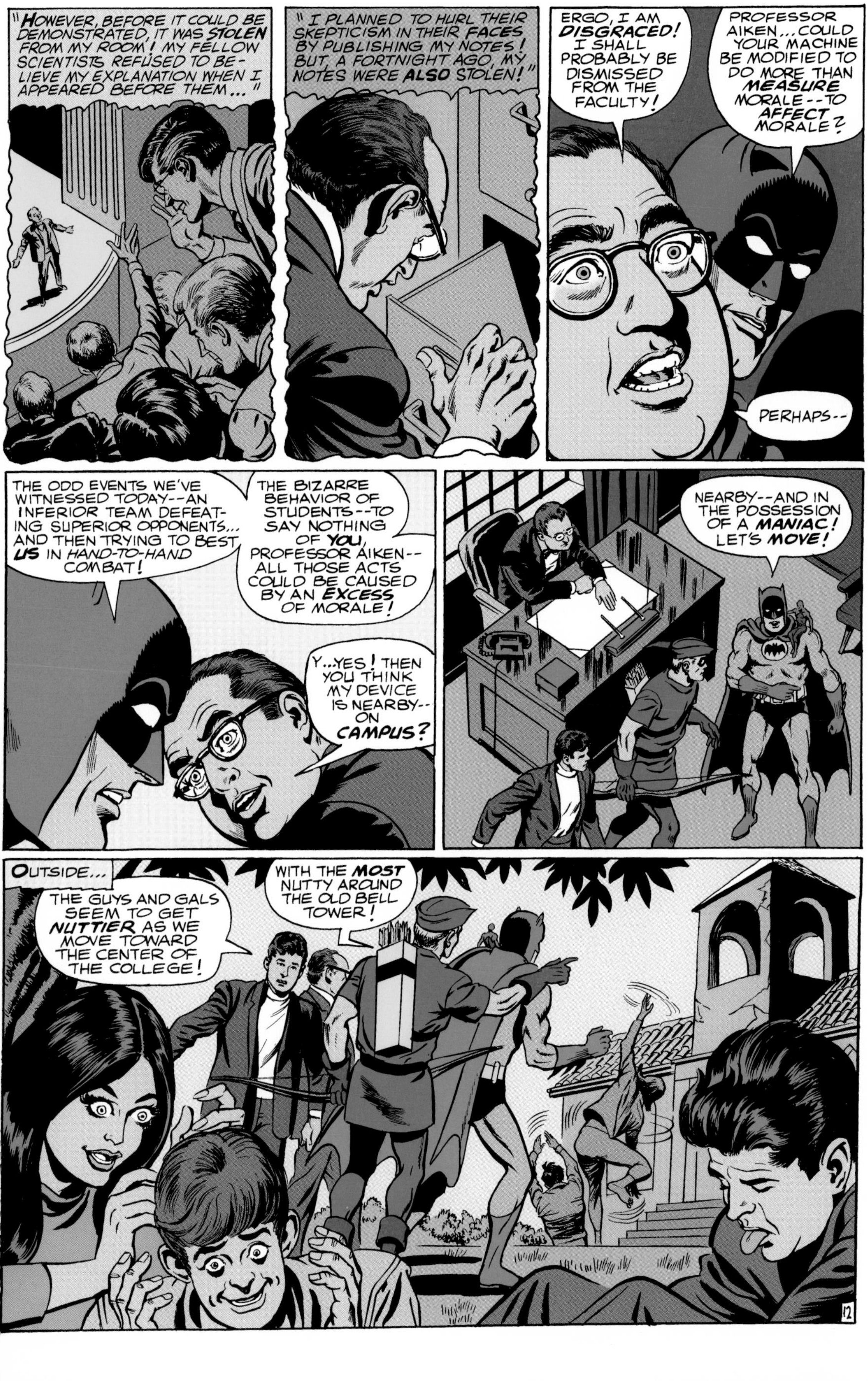
"HOWEVER, BEFORE IT COULD BE DEMONSTRATED, IT WAS STOLEN FROM MY ROOM! MY FELLOW SCIENTISTS REFUSED TO BE-LIEVE MY EXPLANATION WHEN I APPEARED BEFORE THEM..."
"I PLANNED TO HURL THEIR SKEPTICISM IN THEIR FACES BY PUBLISHING MY NOTES! BUT, A FORTNIGHT AGO, MY NOTES WERE ALSO STOLEN!"
ERGO, I AM DISGRACED! I SHALL PROBABLY BE DISMISSED FROM THE FACULTY!
PROFESSOR AIKEN... COULD YOUR MACHINE BE MODIFIED TO DO MORE THAN MEASURE MORALE--TO AFFECT MORALE?
PERHAPS--
THE ODD EVENTS WE'VE WITNESSED TODAY--AN INFERIOR TEAM DEFEATING SUPERIOR OPPONENTS... AND THEN TRYING TO BEST US IN HAND-TO-HAND COMBAT!
THE BIZARRE BEHAVIOR OF STUDENTS--TO SAY NOTHING OF YOU, PROFESSOR AIKEN--ALL THOSE ACTS COULD BE CAUSED BY AN EXCESS OF MORALE!
Y...YES! THEN YOU THINK MY DEVICE IS NEARBY--ON CAMPUS?
NEARBY--AND IN THE POSSESSION OF A MANIAC! LET'S MOVE!
OUTSIDE...
THE GUYS AND GALS SEEM TO GET NUTTIER AS WE MOVE TOWARD THE CENTER OF THE COLLEGE!
WITH THE MOST NUTTY AROUND THE OLD BELL TOWER!
12

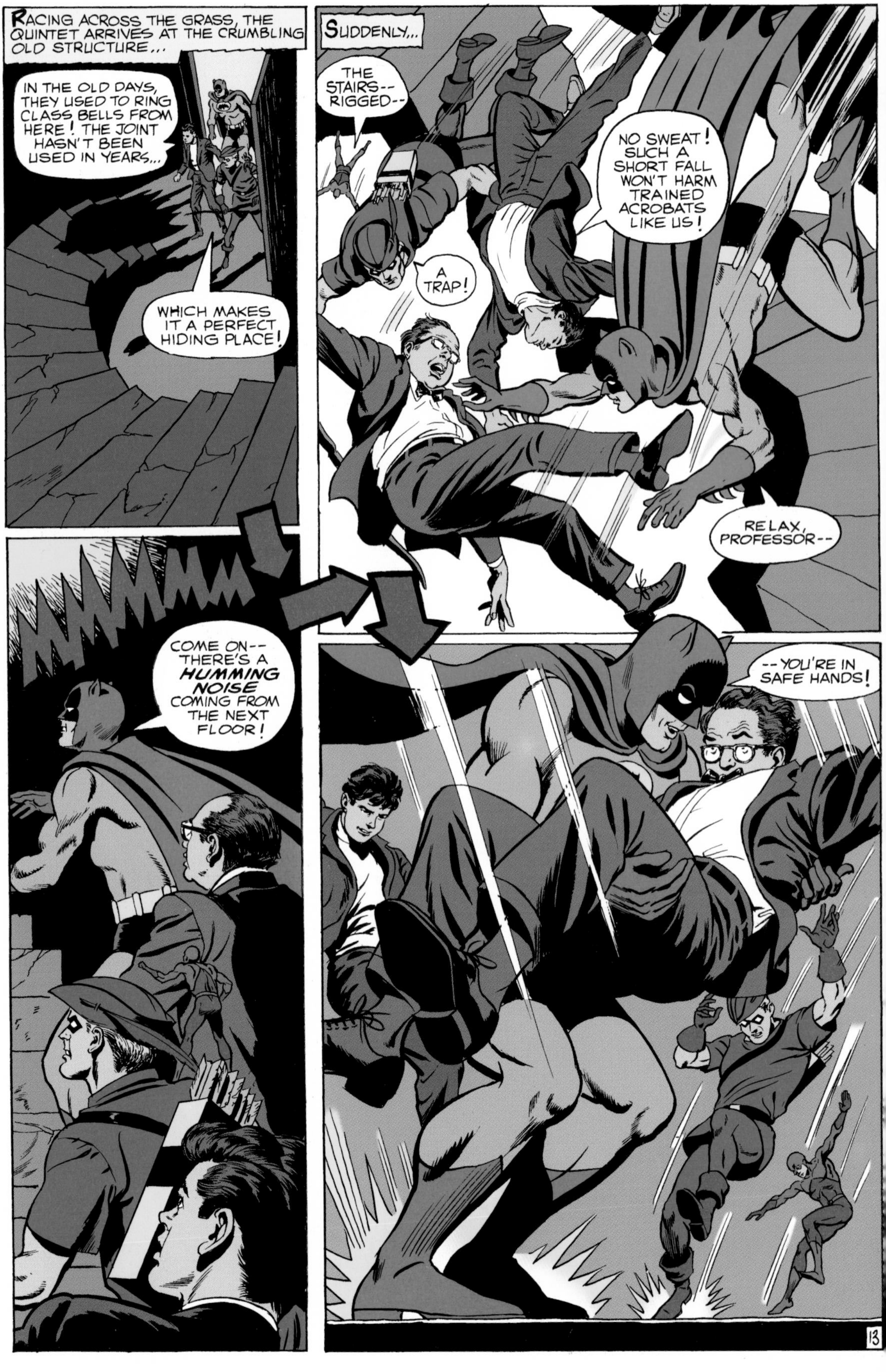
RACING ACROSS THE GRASS, THE QUINTET ARRIVES AT THE CRUMBLING OLD STRUCTURE...
IN THE OLD DAYS, THEY USED TO RING CLASS BELLS FROM HERE! THE JOINT HASN'T BEEN USED IN YEARS...
WHICH MAKES IT A PERFECT HIDING PLACE!
SUDDENLY...
THE STAIRS-- RIGGED--
A TRAP!
NO SWEAT! SUCH A SHORT FALL WON'T HARM TRAINED ACROBATS LIKE US!
RELAX, PROFESSOR--
COME ON-- THERE'S A HUMMING NOISE COMING FROM THE NEXT FLOOR!
--YOU'RE IN SAFE HANDS!
13

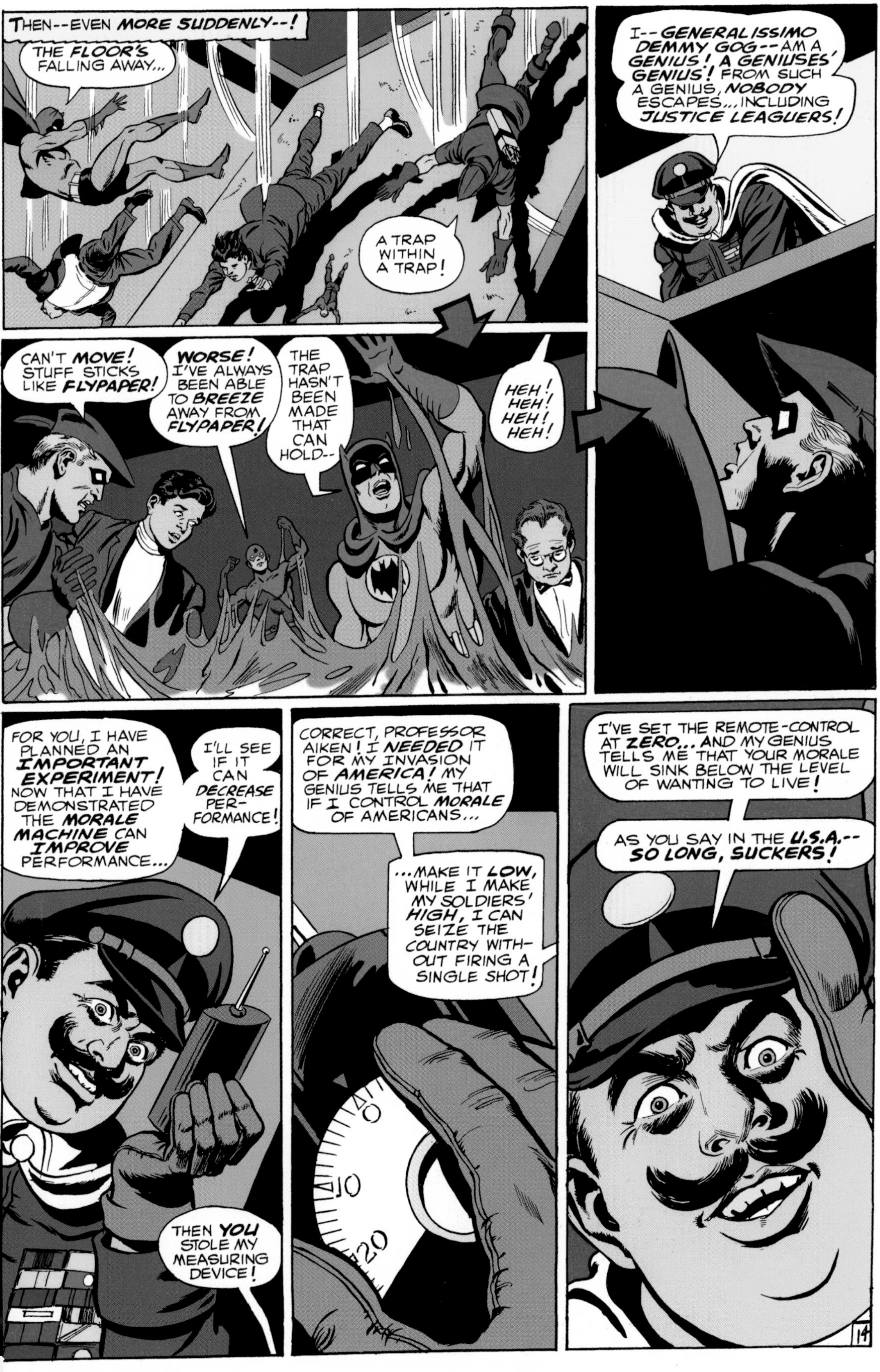
THEN--EVEN MORE SUDDENLY--!
THE FLOOR'S FALLING AWAY...
A TRAP WITHIN A TRAP!
I--GENERALISSIMO DEMMY GOG--AM A GENIUS! A GENIUSES' GENIUS! FROM SUCH A GENIUS, NOBODY ESCAPES... INCLUDING JUSTICE LEAGUERS!
CAN'T MOVE! STUFF STICKS LIKE FLYPAPER!
WORSE! I'VE ALWAYS BEEN ABLE TO BREEZE AWAY FROM FLYPAPER!
THE TRAP HASN'T BEEN MADE THAT CAN HOLD--
HEH! HEH! HEH! HEH!
FOR YOU, I HAVE PLANNED AN IMPORTANT EXPERIMENT! NOW THAT I HAVE DEMONSTRATED THE MORALE MACHINE CAN IMPROVE PERFORMANCE...
I'LL SEE IF IT CAN DECREASE PER-FORMANCE!
THEN YOU STOLE MY MEASURING DEVICE!
CORRECT, PROFESSOR AIKEN! I NEEDED IT FOR MY INVASION OF AMERICA! MY GENIUS TELLS ME THAT IF I CONTROL MORALE OF AMERICANS...
...MAKE IT LOW, WHILE I MAKE MY SOLDIERS' HIGH, I CAN SEIZE THE COUNTRY WITH-OUT FIRING A SINGLE SHOT!
I'VE SET THE REMOTE-CONTROL AT ZERO... AND MY GENIUS TELLS ME THAT YOUR MORALE WILL SINK BELOW THE LEVEL OF WANTING TO LIVE!
AS YOU SAY IN THE U.S.A.-- SO LONG, SUCKERS!
14

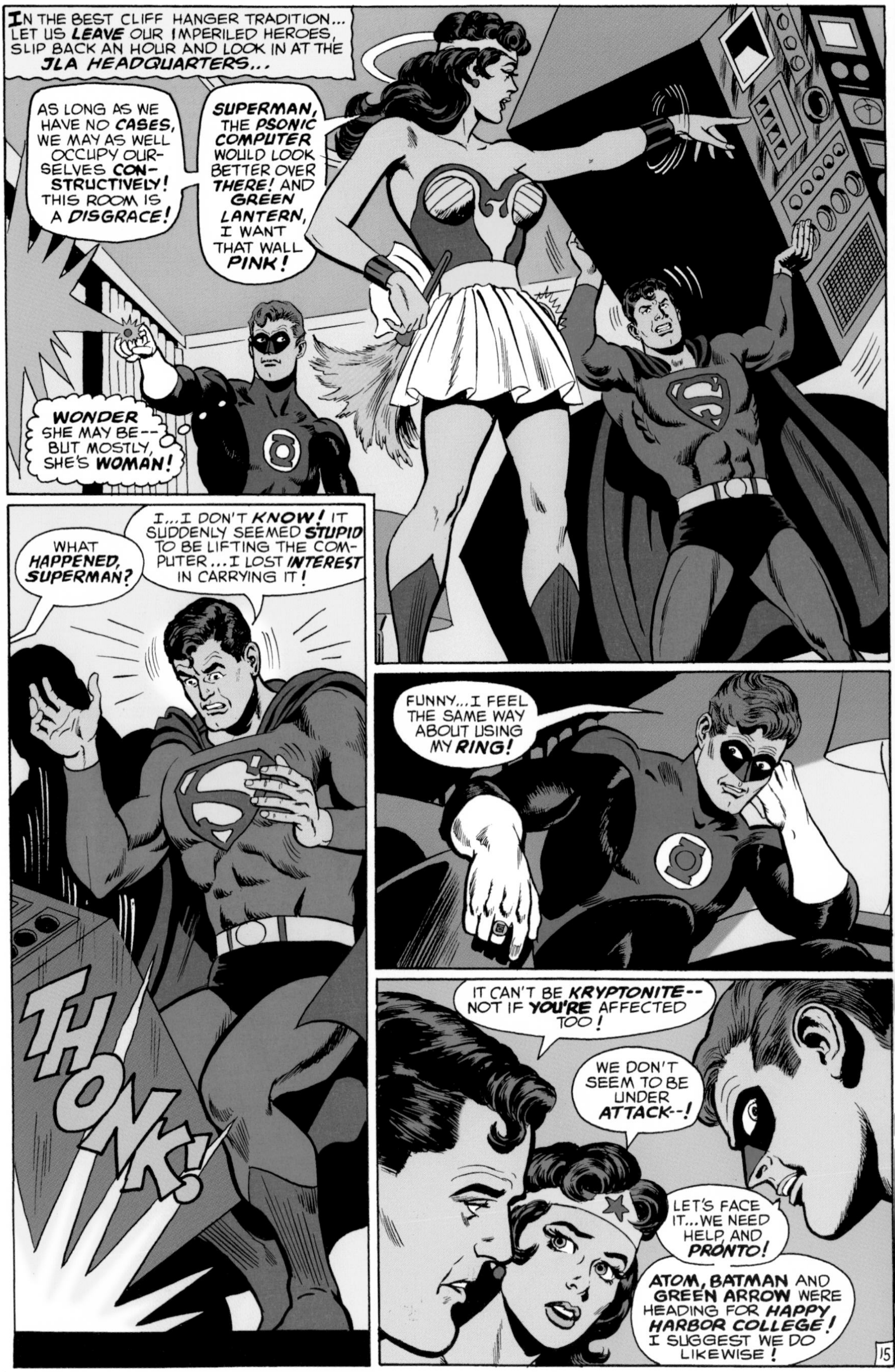
IN THE BEST CLIFF HANGER TRADITION... LET US LEAVE OUR IMPERILED HEROES, SLIP BACK AN HOUR AND LOOK IN AT THE JLA HEADQUARTERS...
AS LONG AS WE HAVE NO CASES, WE MAY AS WELL OCCUPY OURSELVES CONSTRUCTIVELY! THIS ROOM IS A DISGRACE!
SUPERMAN, THE PSONIC COMPUTER WOULD LOOK BETTER OVER THERE! AND GREEN LANTERN, I WANT THAT WALL PINK!
WONDER SHE MAY BE-- BUT MOSTLY, SHE'S WOMAN!
WHAT HAPPENED, SUPERMAN?
I...I DON'T KNOW! IT SUDDENLY SEEMED STUPID TO BE LIFTING THE COMPUTER... I LOST INTEREST IN CARRYING IT!
THONK!
FUNNY...I FEEL THE SAME WAY ABOUT USING MY RING!
IT CAN'T BE KRYPTONITE-- NOT IF YOU'RE AFFECTED TOO!
WE DON'T SEEM TO BE UNDER ATTACK--!
LET'S FACE IT...WE NEED HELP, AND PRONTO!
ATOM, BATMAN AND GREEN ARROW WERE HEADING FOR HAPPY HARBOR COLLEGE! I SUGGEST WE DO LIKEWISE!
15

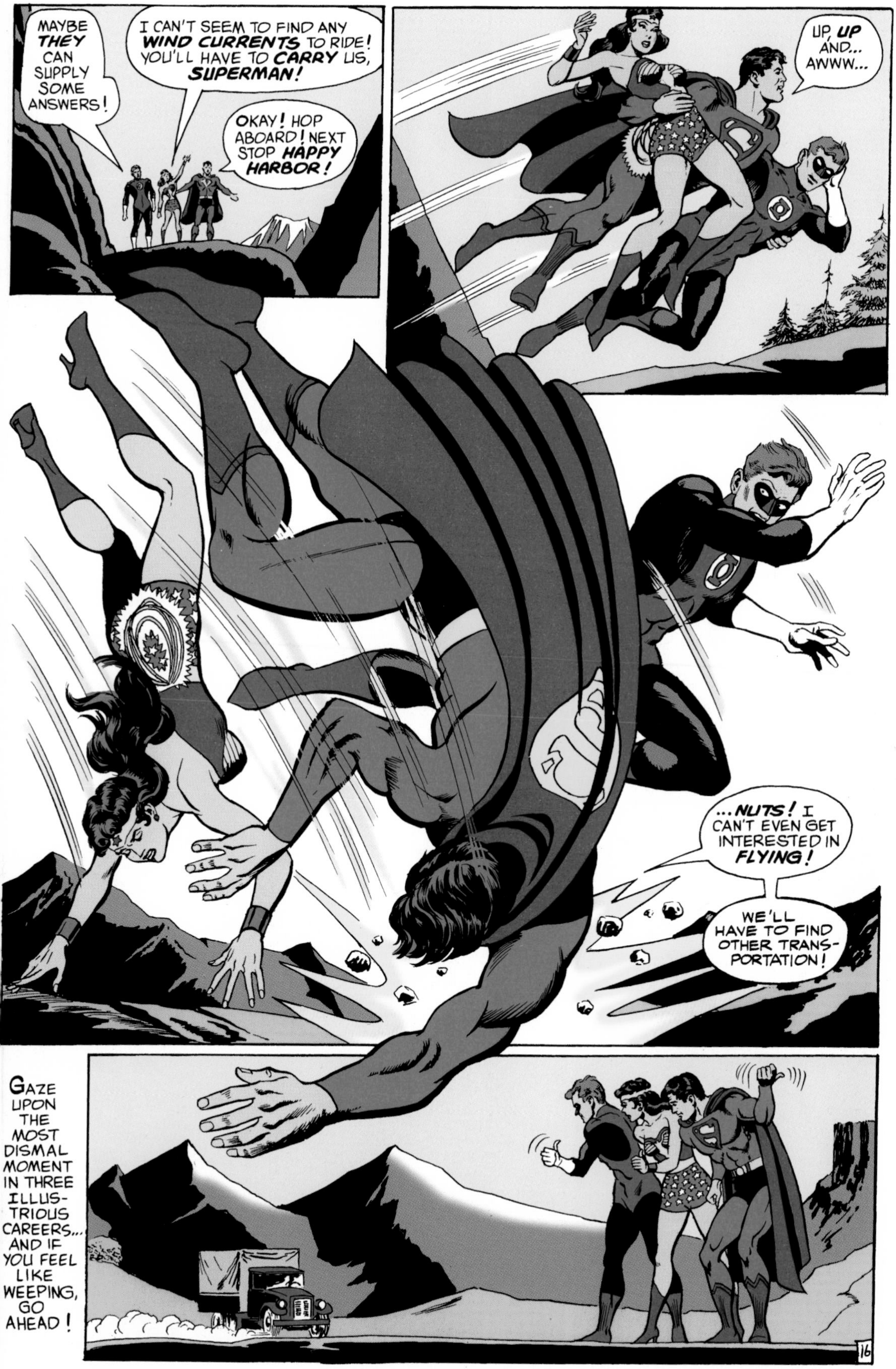
MAYBE THEY CAN SUPPLY SOME ANSWERS!
I CAN'T SEEM TO FIND ANY WIND CURRENTS TO RIDE! YOU'LL HAVE TO CARRY US, SUPERMAN!
OKAY! HOP ABOARD! NEXT STOP HAPPY HARBOR!
UP, UP AND... AWWW...
...NUTS! I CAN'T EVEN GET INTERESTED IN FLYING!
WE'LL HAVE TO FIND OTHER TRANS-PORTATION!
GAZE UPON THE MOST DISMAL MOMENT IN THREE ILLUS-TRIOUS CAREERS... AND IF YOU FEEL LIKE WEEPING, GO AHEAD!
16

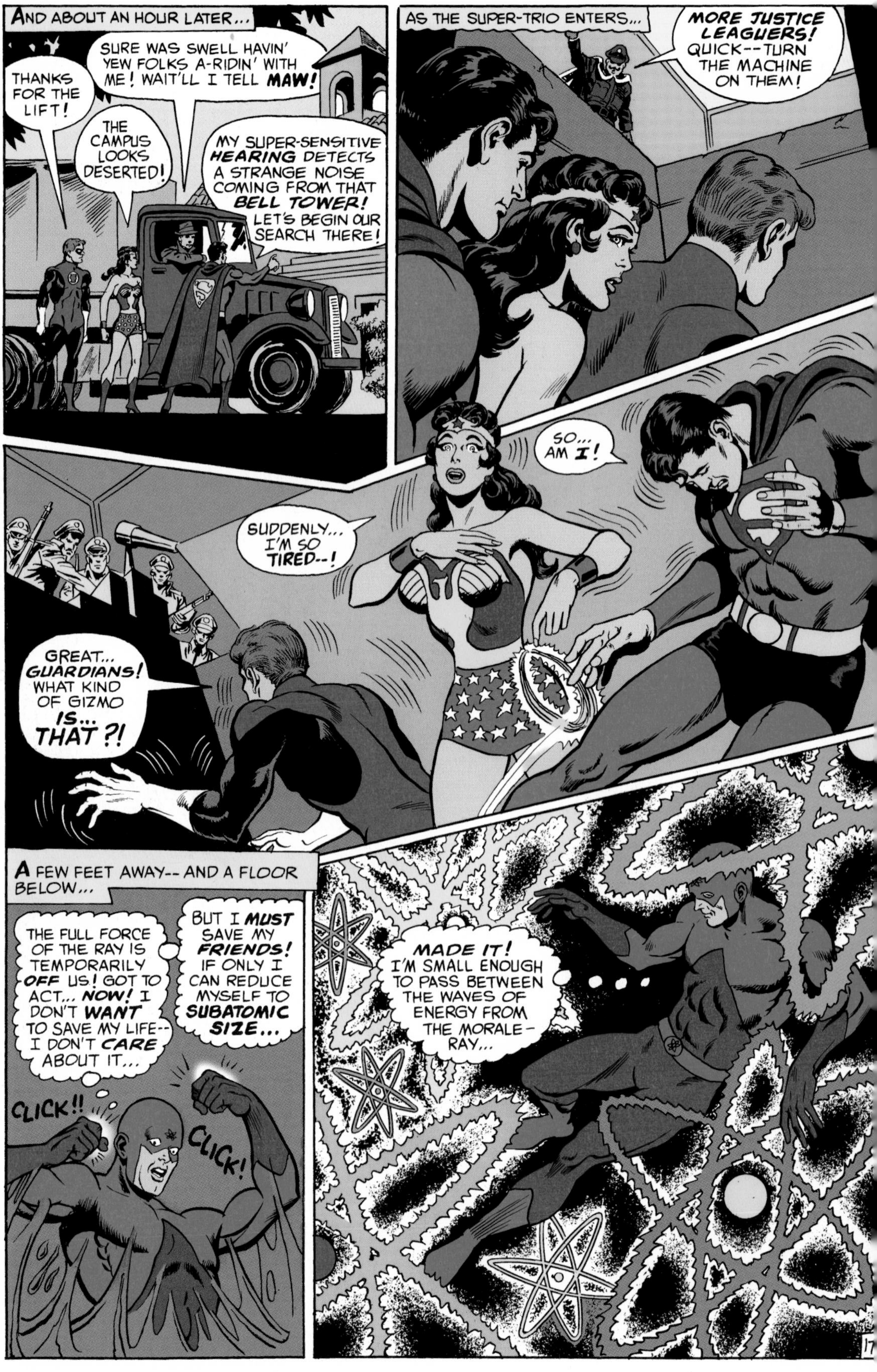
AND ABOUT AN HOUR LATER...
THANKS FOR THE LIFT!
SURE WAS SWELL HAVIN' YEW FOLKS A-RIDIN' WITH ME! WAIT'LL I TELL MAW!
THE CAMPUS LOOKS DESERTED!
MY SUPER-SENSITIVE HEARING DETECTS A STRANGE NOISE COMING FROM THAT BELL TOWER! LET'S BEGIN OUR SEARCH THERE!
AS THE SUPER-TRIO ENTERS...
MORE JUSTICE LEAGUERS! QUICK--TURN THE MACHINE ON THEM!
SUDDENLY... I'M SO TIRED--!
SO... AM I!
GREAT... GUARDIANS! WHAT KIND OF GIZMO IS... THAT ?!
A FEW FEET AWAY-- AND A FLOOR BELOW...
THE FULL FORCE OF THE RAY IS TEMPORARILY OFF US! GOT TO ACT... NOW! I DON'T WANT TO SAVE MY LIFE-- I DON'T CARE ABOUT IT...
BUT I MUST SAVE MY FRIENDS! IF ONLY I CAN REDUCE MYSELF TO SUBATOMIC SIZE...
CLICK!!
CLICK!
MADE IT! I'M SMALL ENOUGH TO PASS BETWEEN THE WAVES OF ENERGY FROM THE MORALE-RAY...
17

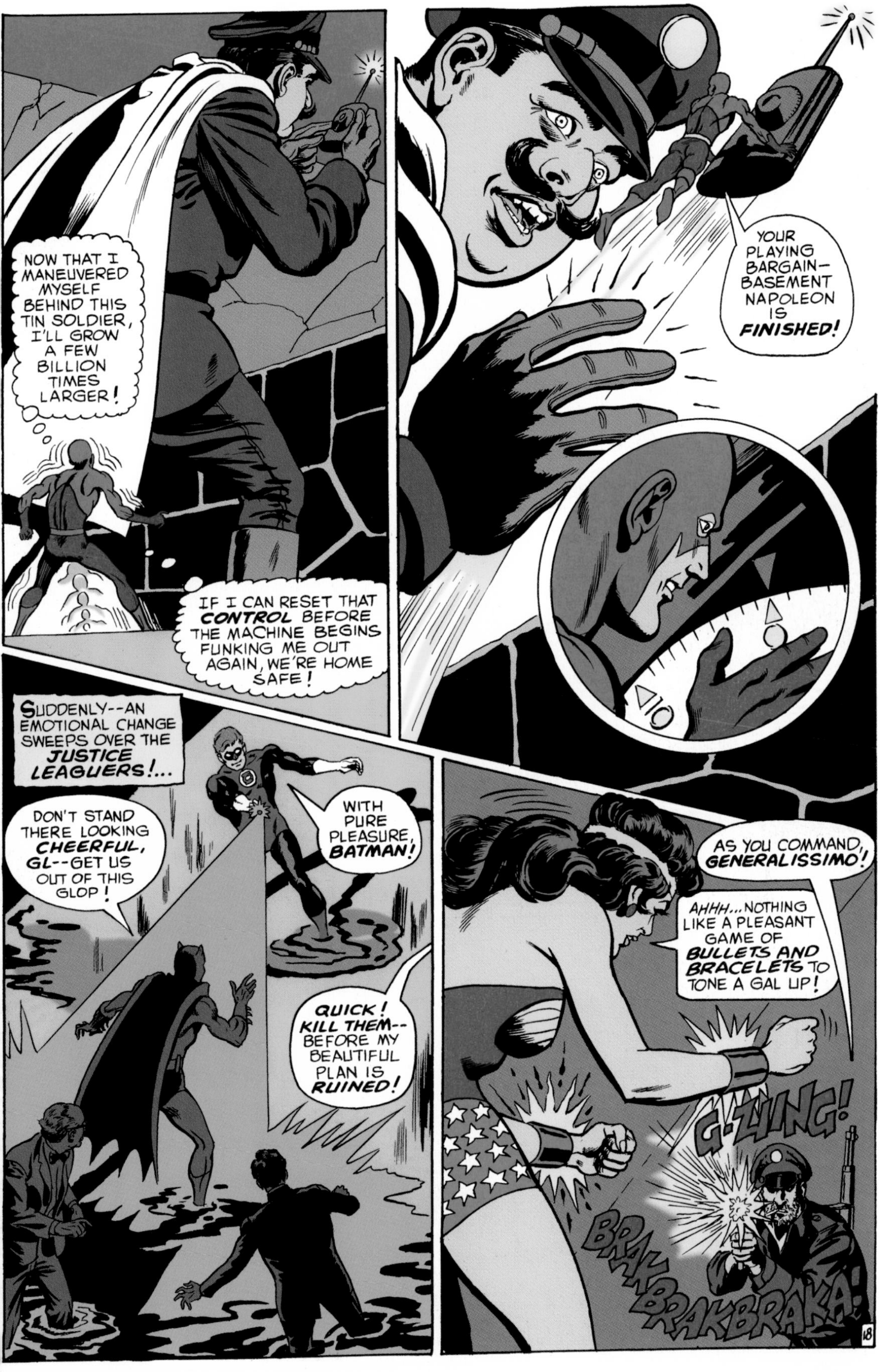
NOW THAT I MANEUVERED MYSELF BEHIND THIS TIN SOLDIER, I'LL GROW A FEW BILLION TIMES LARGER!
IF I CAN RESET THAT CONTROL BEFORE THE MACHINE BEGINS FUNKING ME OUT AGAIN, WE'RE HOME SAFE!
YOUR PLAYING BARGAIN-BASEMENT NAPOLEON IS FINISHED!
SUDDENLY--AN EMOTIONAL CHANGE SWEEPS OVER THE JUSTICE LEAGUERS!...
DON'T STAND THERE LOOKING CHEERFUL, GL--GET US OUT OF THIS GLOP!
WITH PURE PLEASURE, BATMAN!
QUICK! KILL THEM--BEFORE MY BEAUTIFUL PLAN IS RUINED!
AS YOU COMMAND, GENERALISSIMO!
AHHH...NOTHING LIKE A PLEASANT GAME OF BULLETS AND BRACELETS TO TONE A GAL UP!
G-ZING!
BRAKBRAKBRAKBRAKA!
18

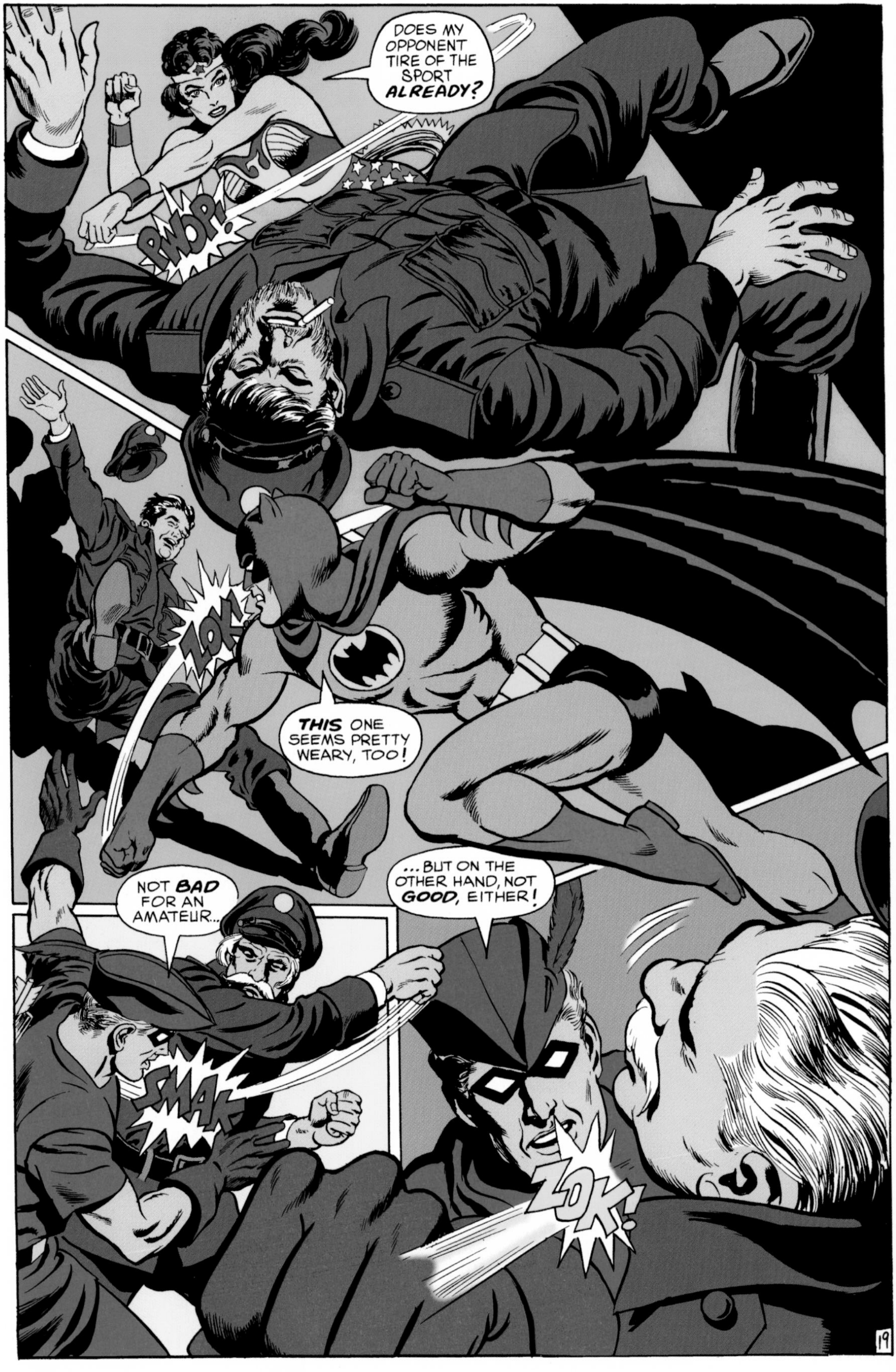
DOES MY OPPONENT TIRE OF THE SPORT ALREADY?
PWOP!
ZOK!
THIS ONE SEEMS PRETTY WEARY, TOO!
NOT BAD FOR AN AMATEUR...
...BUT ON THE OTHER HAND, NOT GOOD, EITHER!
SMAK
ZOK!
19

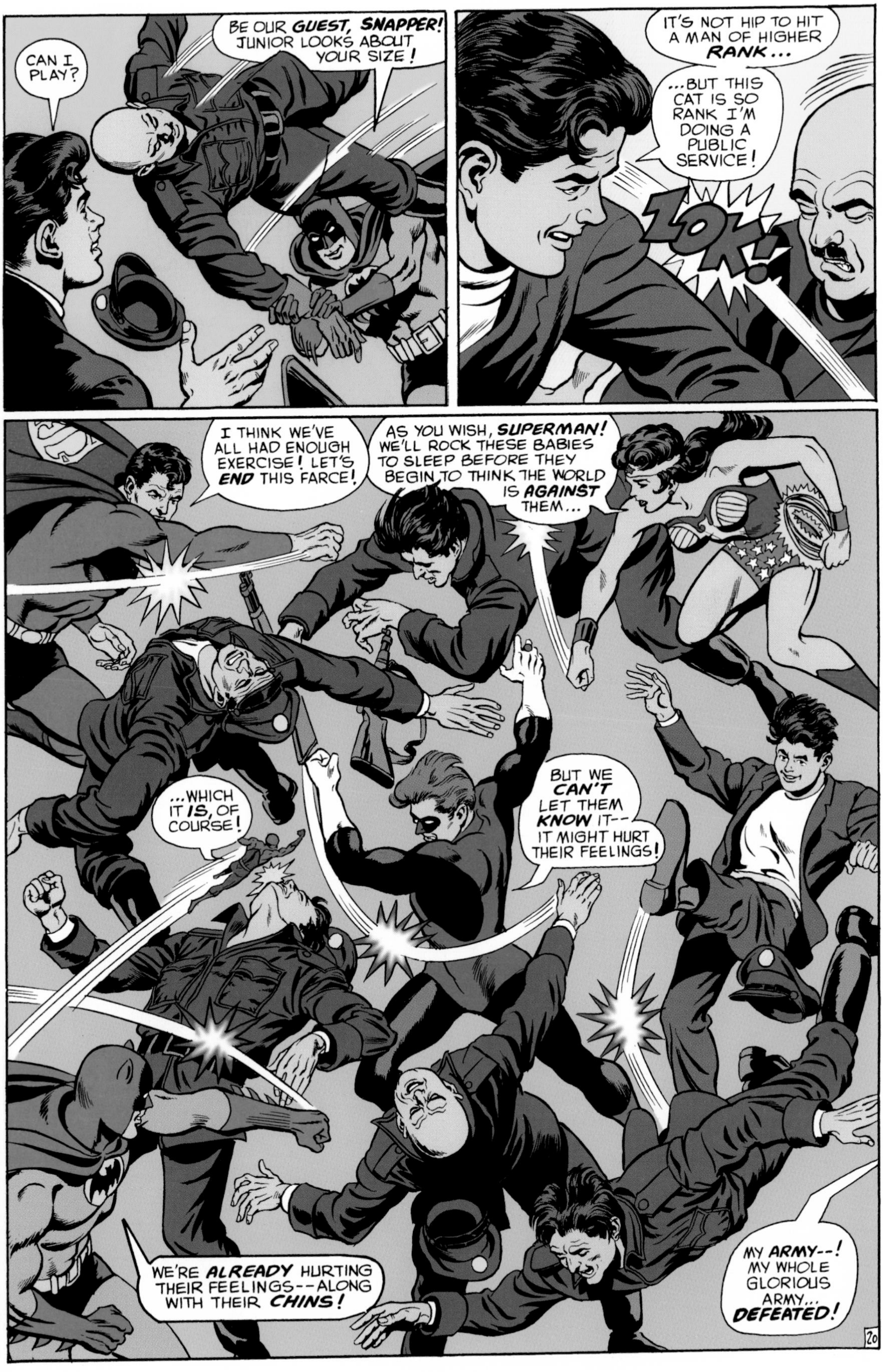
CAN I PLAY?
BE OUR GUEST, SNAPPER! JUNIOR LOOKS ABOUT YOUR SIZE!
IT'S NOT HIP TO HIT A MAN OF HIGHER RANK...
...BUT THIS CAT IS SO RANK I'M DOING A PUBLIC SERVICE!
ZOK!
I THINK WE'VE ALL HAD ENOUGH EXERCISE! LET'S END THIS FARCE!
AS YOU WISH, SUPERMAN! WE'LL ROCK THESE BABIES TO SLEEP BEFORE THEY BEGIN TO THINK THE WORLD IS AGAINST THEM...
...WHICH IT IS, OF COURSE!
BUT WE CAN'T LET THEM KNOW IT-- IT MIGHT HURT THEIR FEELINGS!
WE'RE ALREADY HURTING THEIR FEELINGS--ALONG WITH THEIR CHINS!
MY ARMY--! MY WHOLE GLORIOUS ARMY... DEFEATED!
20

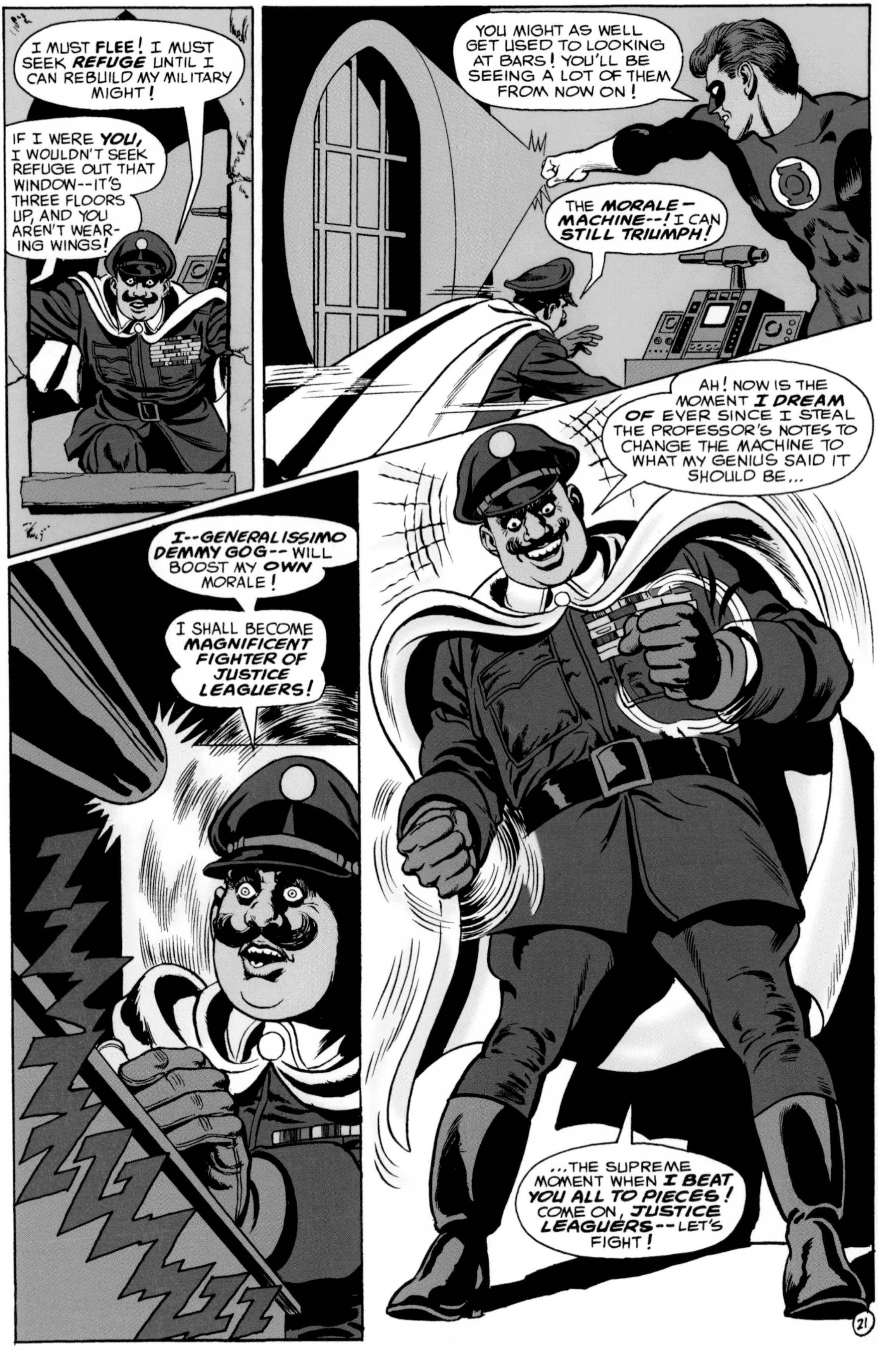
I MUST FLEE! I MUST SEEK REFUGE UNTIL I CAN REBUILD MY MILITARY MIGHT!
IF I WERE YOU, I WOULDN'T SEEK REFUGE OUT THAT WINDOW--IT'S THREE FLOORS UP, AND YOU AREN'T WEARING WINGS!
YOU MIGHT AS WELL GET USED TO LOOKING AT BARS! YOU'LL BE SEEING A LOT OF THEM FROM NOW ON!
THE MORALE-MACHINE--! I CAN STILL TRIUMPH!
I--GENERALISSIMO DEMMY GOG--WILL BOOST MY OWN MORALE!
I SHALL BECOME MAGNIFICENT FIGHTER OF JUSTICE LEAGUERS!
AH! NOW IS THE MOMENT I DREAM OF EVER SINCE I STEAL THE PROFESSOR'S NOTES TO CHANGE THE MACHINE TO WHAT MY GENIUS SAID IT SHOULD BE...
...THE SUPREME MOMENT WHEN I BEAT YOU ALL TO PIECES! COME ON, JUSTICE LEAGUERS--LET'S FIGHT!
21

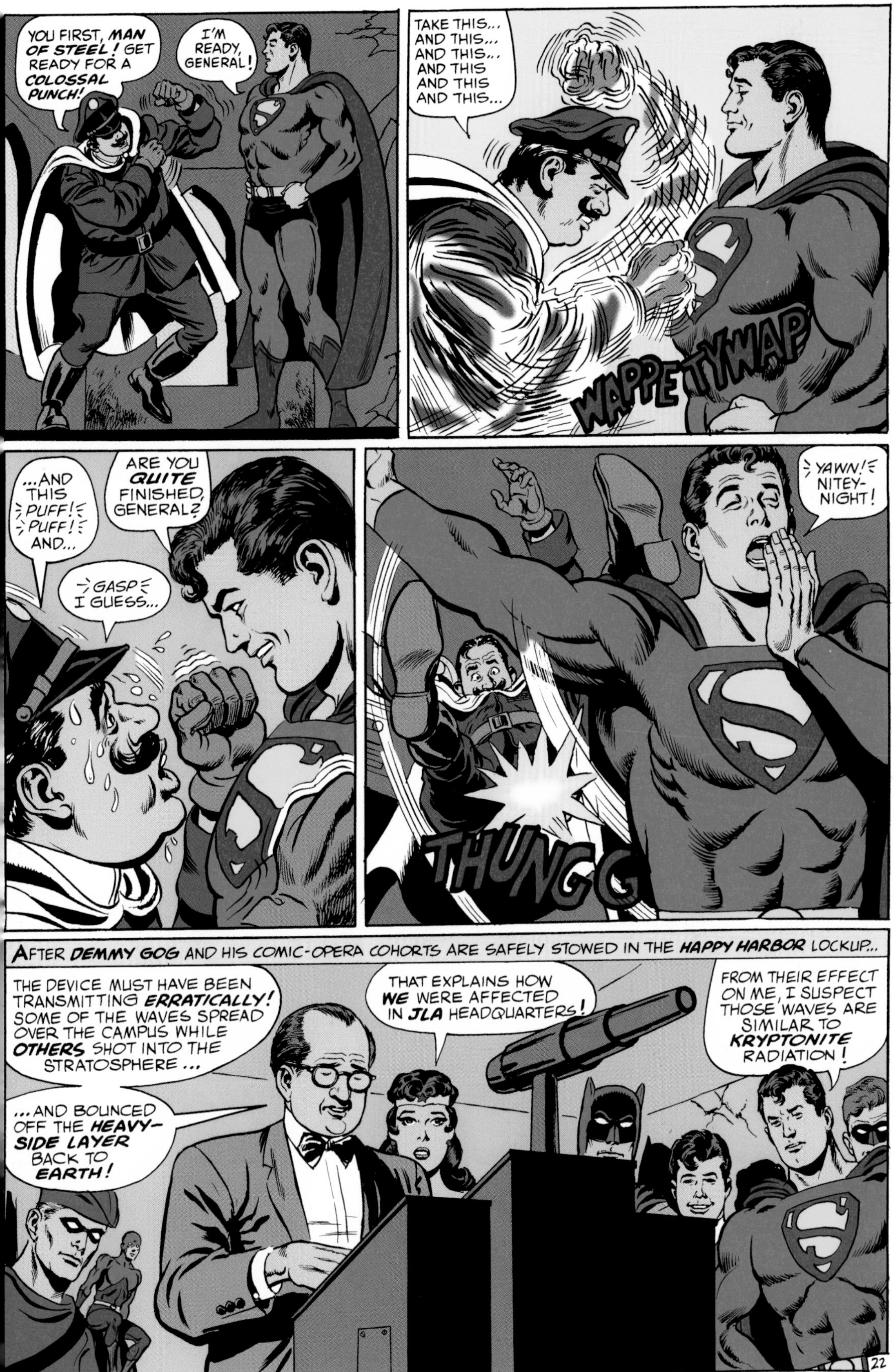
YOU FIRST, MAN OF STEEL! GET READY FOR A COLOSSAL PUNCH!
I'M READY, GENERAL!
TAKE THIS... AND THIS... AND THIS... AND THIS AND THIS AND THIS...
WAPPETYWAP
...AND THIS PUFF! PUFF! AND...
ARE YOU QUITE FINISHED, GENERAL?
GASP I GUESS...
YAWN! NITEY-NIGHT!
THUNGG
AFTER DEMMY GOG AND HIS COMIC-OPERA COHORTS ARE SAFELY STOWED IN THE HAPPY HARBOR LOCKUP...
THE DEVICE MUST HAVE BEEN TRANSMITTING ERRATICALLY! SOME OF THE WAVES SPREAD OVER THE CAMPUS WHILE OTHERS SHOT INTO THE STRATOSPHERE ...
...AND BOUNCED OFF THE HEAVY-SIDE LAYER BACK TO EARTH!
THAT EXPLAINS HOW WE WERE AFFECTED IN JLA HEADQUARTERS!
FROM THEIR EFFECT ON ME, I SUSPECT THOSE WAVES ARE SIMILAR TO KRYPTONITE RADIATION!
22

WELL... WE'RE BACK TOGETHER!
I... UH... I WANT TO **APOLOGIZE** FOR FLYING OFF THE HANDLE BEFORE...
GOG WAS **INSANE!** --BUT NONETHELESS HE NEARLY DEFEATED US!
YES... BECAUSE WE LET PETTY PERSONAL DIFFERENCES BLIND US TO THE FACT THAT WE **NEED** ONE ANOTHER!
The end

JUSTICE LEAGUE of AMERICA

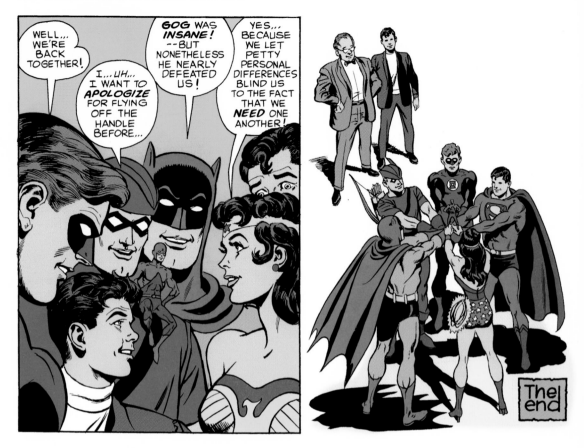

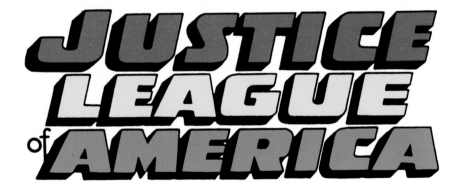

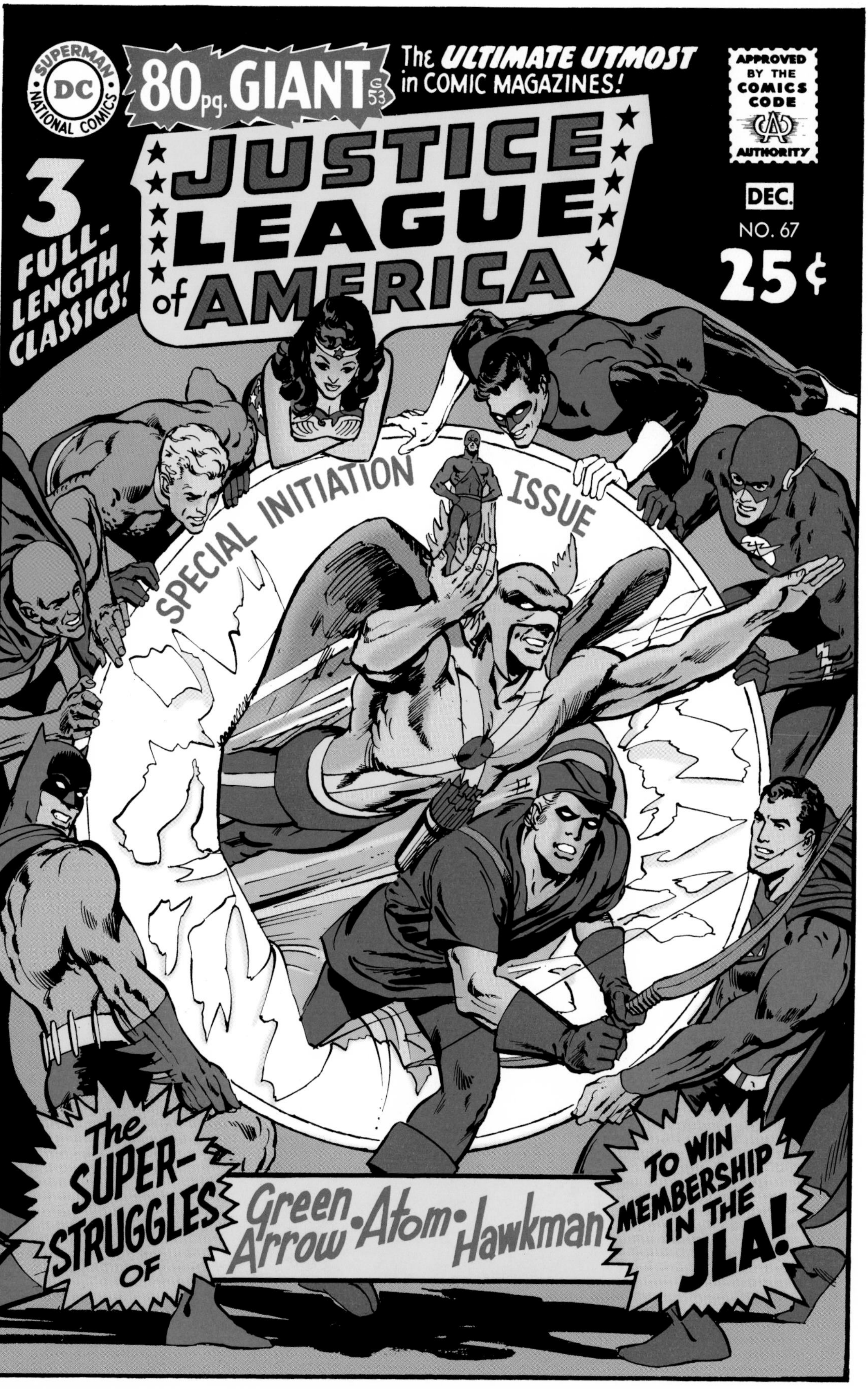
SUPERMAN DC NATIONAL COMICS
80pg. GIANT G 53
The ULTIMATE UTMOST in COMIC MAGAZINES!
APPROVED BY THE COMICS CODE AUTHORITY
JUSTICE LEAGUE of AMERICA
3 FULL-LENGTH CLASSICS!
DEC.
NO. 67
25¢
SPECIAL INITIATION ISSUE
The SUPER-STRUGGLES OF
Green Arrow • Atom • Hawkman
TO WIN MEMBERSHIP IN THE JLA!

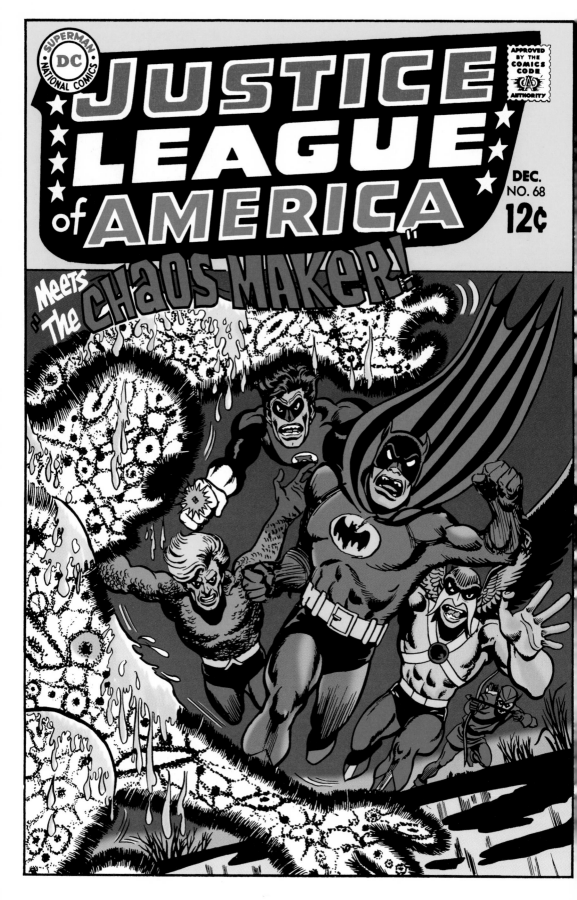

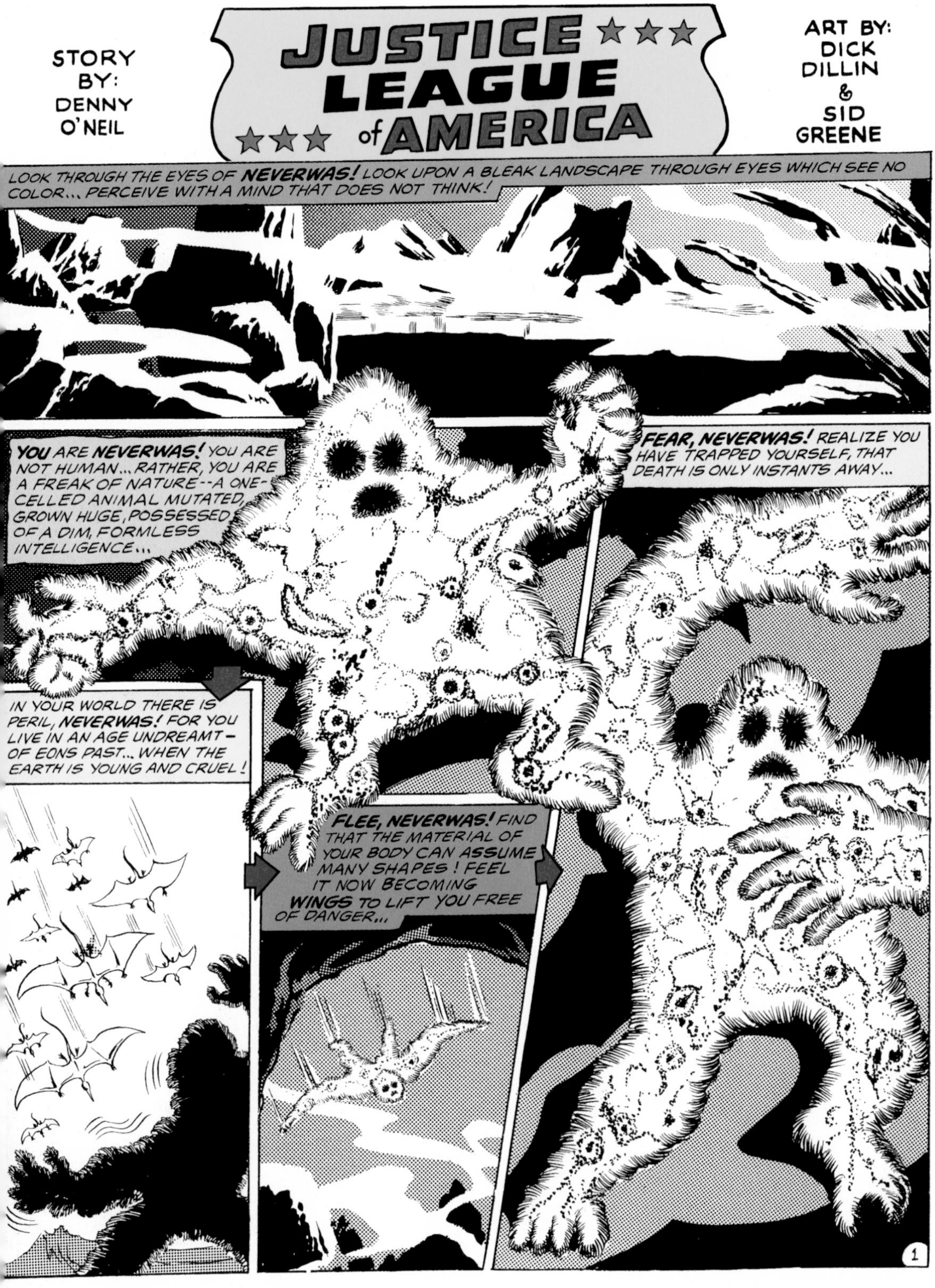
STORY BY: DENNY O'NEIL
JUSTICE LEAGUE of AMERICA
ART BY: DICK DILLIN & SID GREENE
LOOK THROUGH THE EYES OF NEVERWAS! LOOK UPON A BLEAK LANDSCAPE THROUGH EYES WHICH SEE NO COLOR... PERCEIVE WITH A MIND THAT DOES NOT THINK!
YOU ARE NEVERWAS! YOU ARE NOT HUMAN... RATHER, YOU ARE A FREAK OF NATURE--A ONE-CELLED ANIMAL MUTATED, GROWN HUGE, POSSESSED OF A DIM, FORMLESS INTELLIGENCE...
IN YOUR WORLD THERE IS PERIL, NEVERWAS! FOR YOU LIVE IN AN AGE UNDREAMT--OF EONS PAST... WHEN THE EARTH IS YOUNG AND CRUEL!
FLEE, NEVERWAS! FIND THAT THE MATERIAL OF YOUR BODY CAN ASSUME MANY SHAPES! FEEL IT NOW BECOMING WINGS TO LIFT YOU FREE OF DANGER...
FEAR, NEVERWAS! REALIZE YOU HAVE TRAPPED YOURSELF, THAT DEATH IS ONLY INSTANTS AWAY...
1

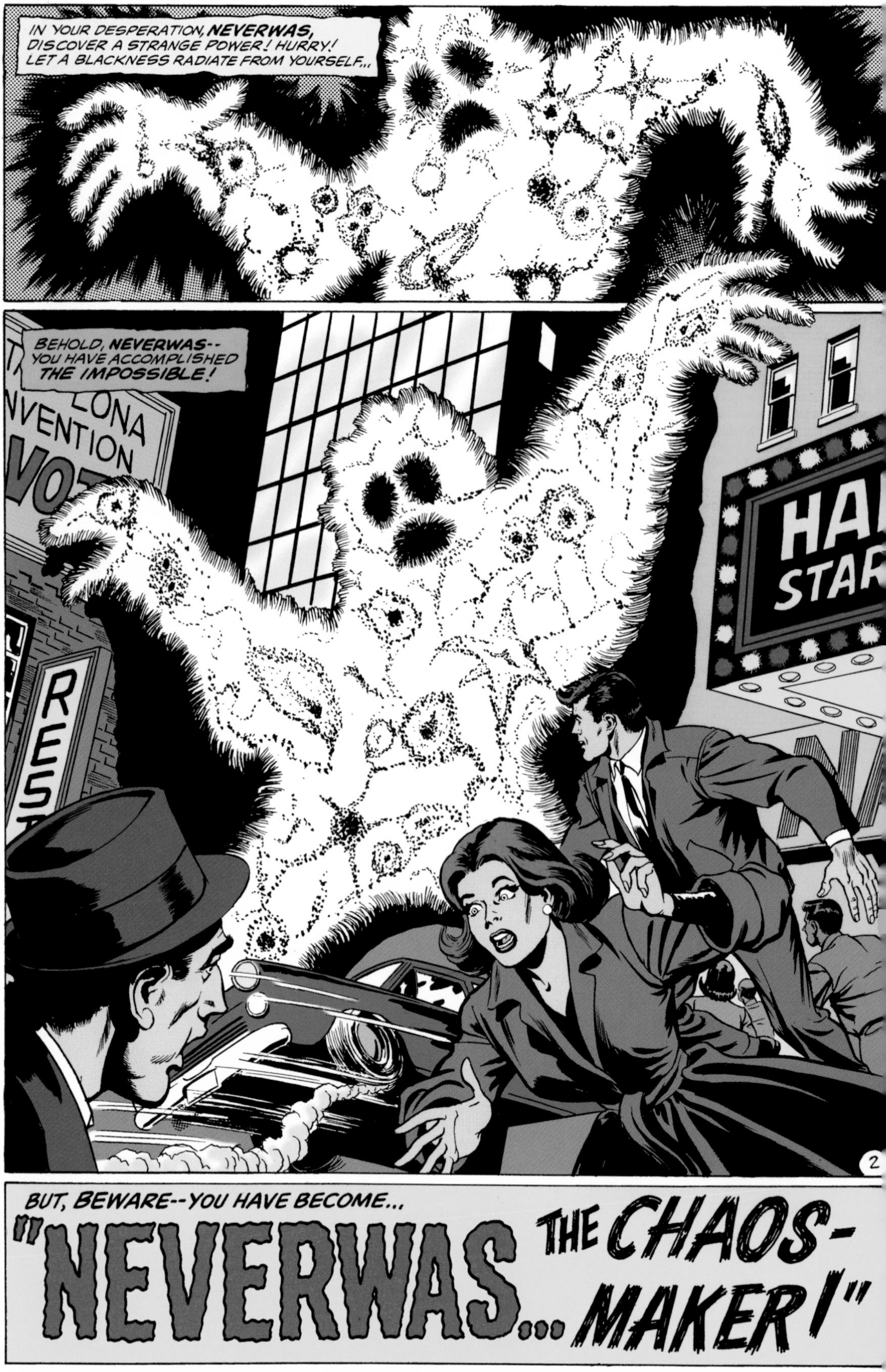
IN YOUR DESPERATION, NEVERWAS, DISCOVER A STRANGE POWER! HURRY! LET A BLACKNESS RADIATE FROM YOURSELF...
BEHOLD, NEVERWAS-- YOU HAVE ACCOMPLISHED THE IMPOSSIBLE!
2
BUT, BEWARE--YOU HAVE BECOME...
"NEVERWAS... THE CHAOS-MAKER!"

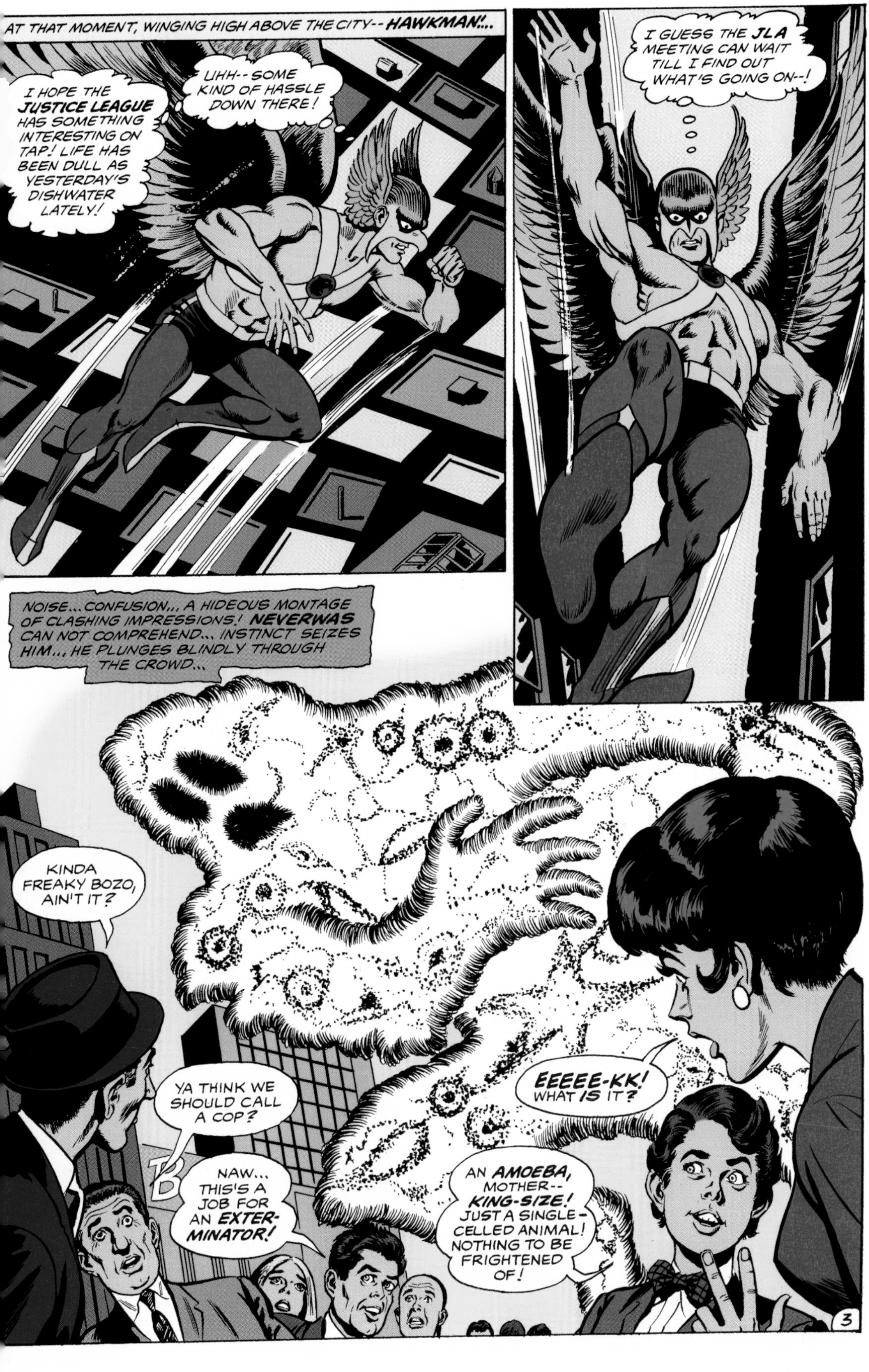
AT THAT MOMENT, WINGING HIGH ABOVE THE CITY-- HAWKMAN!...
I HOPE THE JUSTICE LEAGUE HAS SOMETHING INTERESTING ON TAP! LIFE HAS BEEN DULL AS YESTERDAY'S DISHWATER LATELY!
UHH-- SOME KIND OF HASSLE DOWN THERE!
I GUESS THE JLA MEETING CAN WAIT TILL I FIND OUT WHAT'S GOING ON--!
NOISE... CONFUSION... A HIDEOUS MONTAGE OF CLASHING IMPRESSIONS! NEVERWAS CAN NOT COMPREHEND... INSTINCT SEIZES HIM... HE PLUNGES BLINDLY THROUGH THE CROWD...
KINDA FREAKY BOZO, AIN'T IT?
YA THINK WE SHOULD CALL A COP?
NAW... THIS'S A JOB FOR AN EXTERMINATOR!
EEEEE-KK! WHAT IS IT?
AN AMOEBA, MOTHER-- KING-SIZE! JUST A SINGLE-CELLED ANIMAL! NOTHING TO BE FRIGHTENED OF!
3

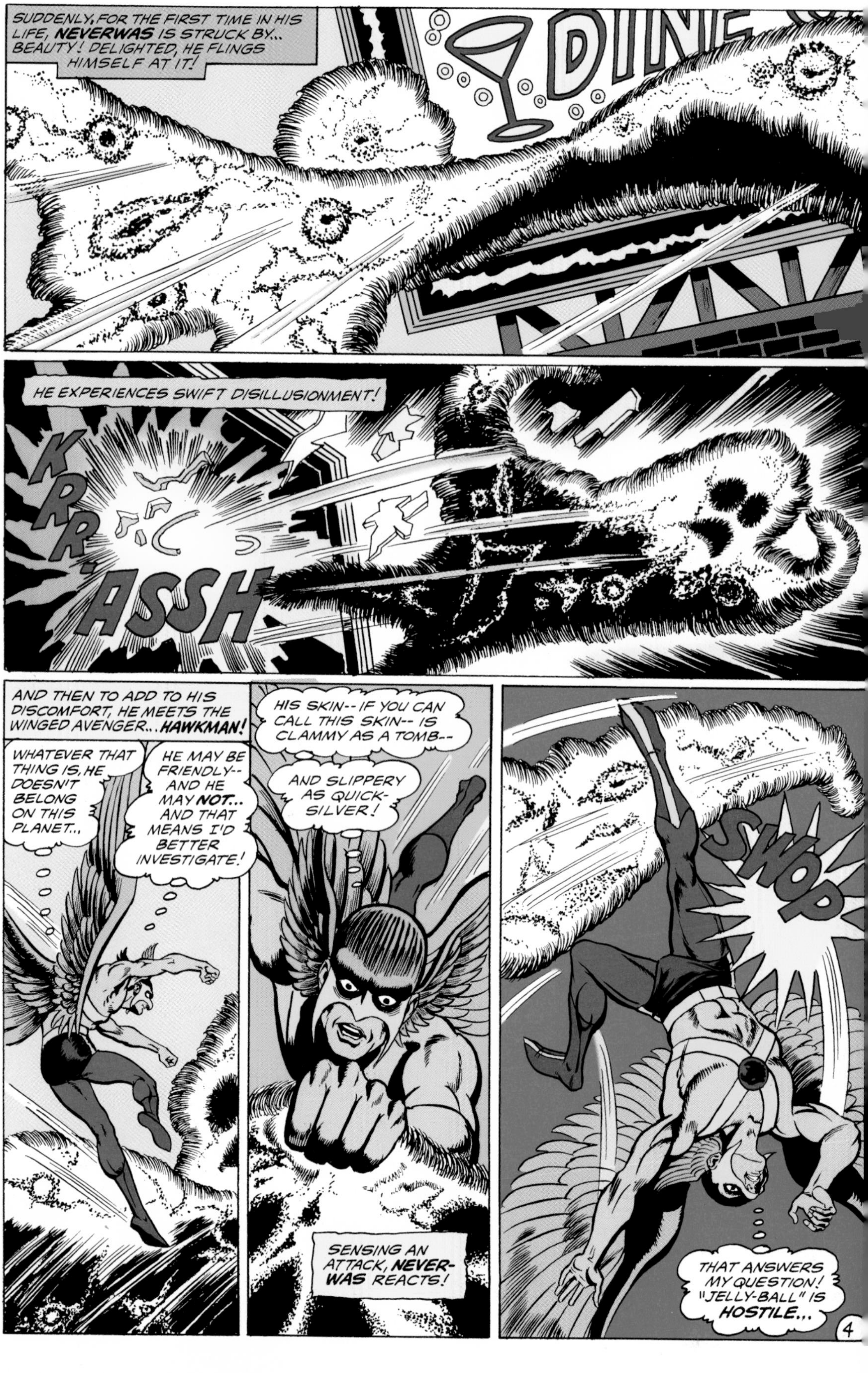
SUDDENLY, FOR THE FIRST TIME IN HIS LIFE, NEVERWAS IS STRUCK BY... BEAUTY! DELIGHTED, HE FLINGS HIMSELF AT IT!
DINE
HE EXPERIENCES SWIFT DISILLUSIONMENT!
KRR-ASSH
AND THEN TO ADD TO HIS DISCOMFORT, HE MEETS THE WINGED AVENGER... HAWKMAN!
WHATEVER THAT THING IS, HE DOESN'T BELONG ON THIS PLANET...
HE MAY BE FRIENDLY-- AND HE MAY NOT... AND THAT MEANS I'D BETTER INVESTIGATE!
HIS SKIN-- IF YOU CAN CALL THIS SKIN-- IS CLAMMY AS A TOMB--
AND SLIPPERY AS QUICK-SILVER!
SENSING AN ATTACK, NEVER-WAS REACTS!
SWOP
THAT ANSWERS MY QUESTION! "JELLY-BALL" IS HOSTILE...
4

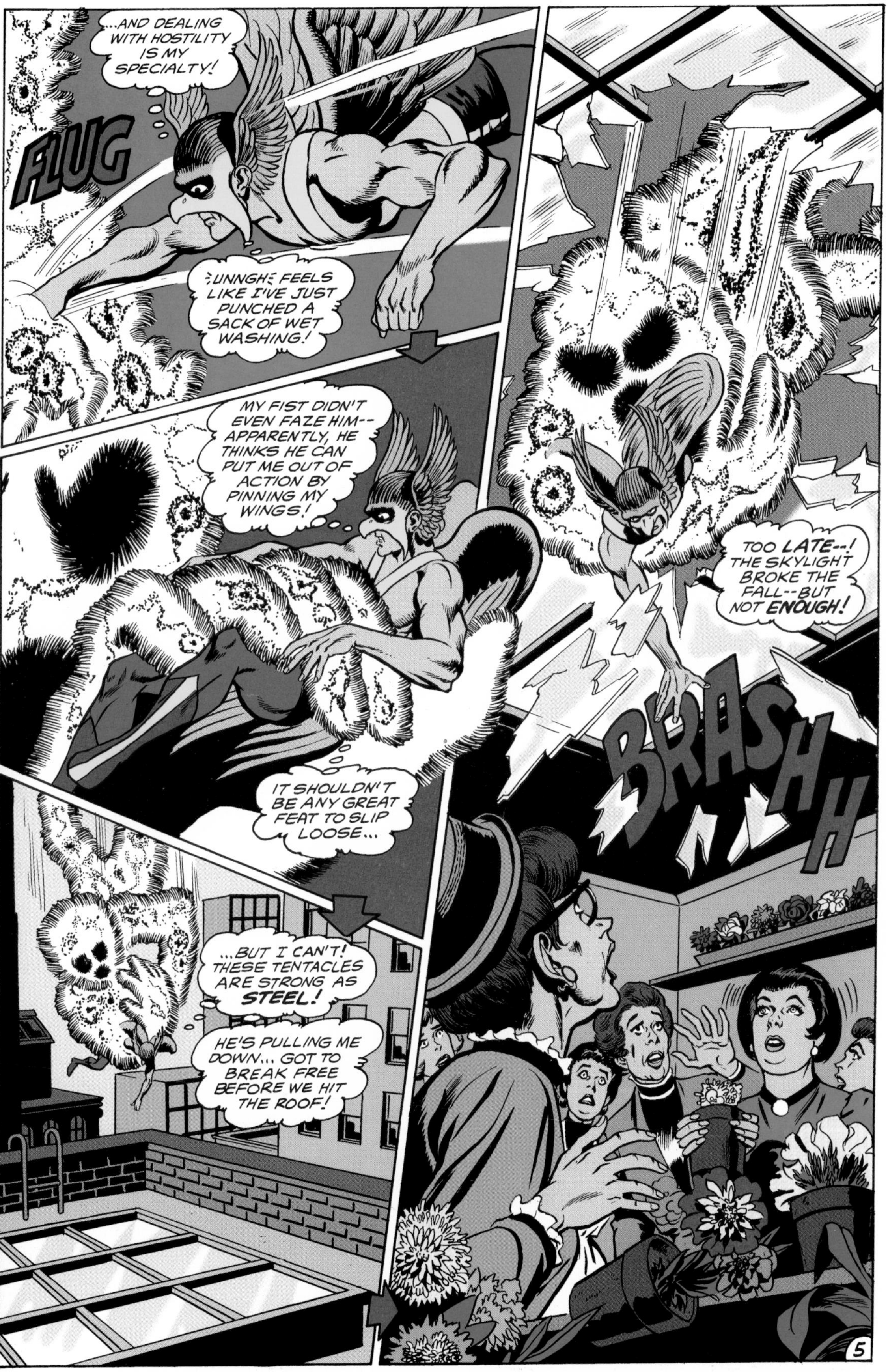
...AND DEALING WITH HOSTILITY IS MY SPECIALTY!
FLUG
UNNGH! FEELS LIKE I'VE JUST PUNCHED A SACK OF WET WASHING!
MY FIST DIDN'T EVEN FAZE HIM-- APPARENTLY, HE THINKS HE CAN PUT ME OUT OF ACTION BY PINNING MY WINGS!
IT SHOULDN'T BE ANY GREAT FEAT TO SLIP LOOSE...
...BUT I CAN'T! THESE TENTACLES ARE STRONG AS STEEL!
HE'S PULLING ME DOWN... GOT TO BREAK FREE BEFORE WE HIT THE ROOF!
TOO LATE--! THE SKYLIGHT BROKE THE FALL--BUT NOT ENOUGH!
BRASHH
5

WITH STUNNING FORCE THE LOCKED COMBATANTS SMASH INTO A TABLE-- AND A BLACK BALL OF PAIN EXPLODES INSIDE *HAWKMAN'S* SKULL!

EEEEEEEEEEEKKK

LADIES GARDEN CLUB

FA-WOMP

AGONIZED INSTANTS LATER, THE *AERIAL ACE* REGAINS CONSCIOUSNESS, AND...

W-WHERE'D HE GO--?

IF YOU MEAN THAT AWFUL NASTY YOU CAME IN WITH-- HE FLEW UP... AND AWAY!

SIR-- YOU HAVE A *NERVE* INTERRUPTING OUR MEETING!

NO CHANCE OF CATCHING HIM NOW! MY BEST BET IS TO CONTACT THE *JUSTICE LEAGUE--* AND QUICK!

I SAY, *HAWKMAN,* WHO'S GOING TO PAY FOR THE FLOWERS YOU RUINED!?

BUT THE MAN OF THE SKIES DOESN'T HEAR THE LADY'S OUTRAGED QUESTION! HE'S ALREADY ON HIS WAY TO *JUSTICE LEAGUE HEADQUARTERS--*

6

JUSTICE LEAGUE of AMERICA

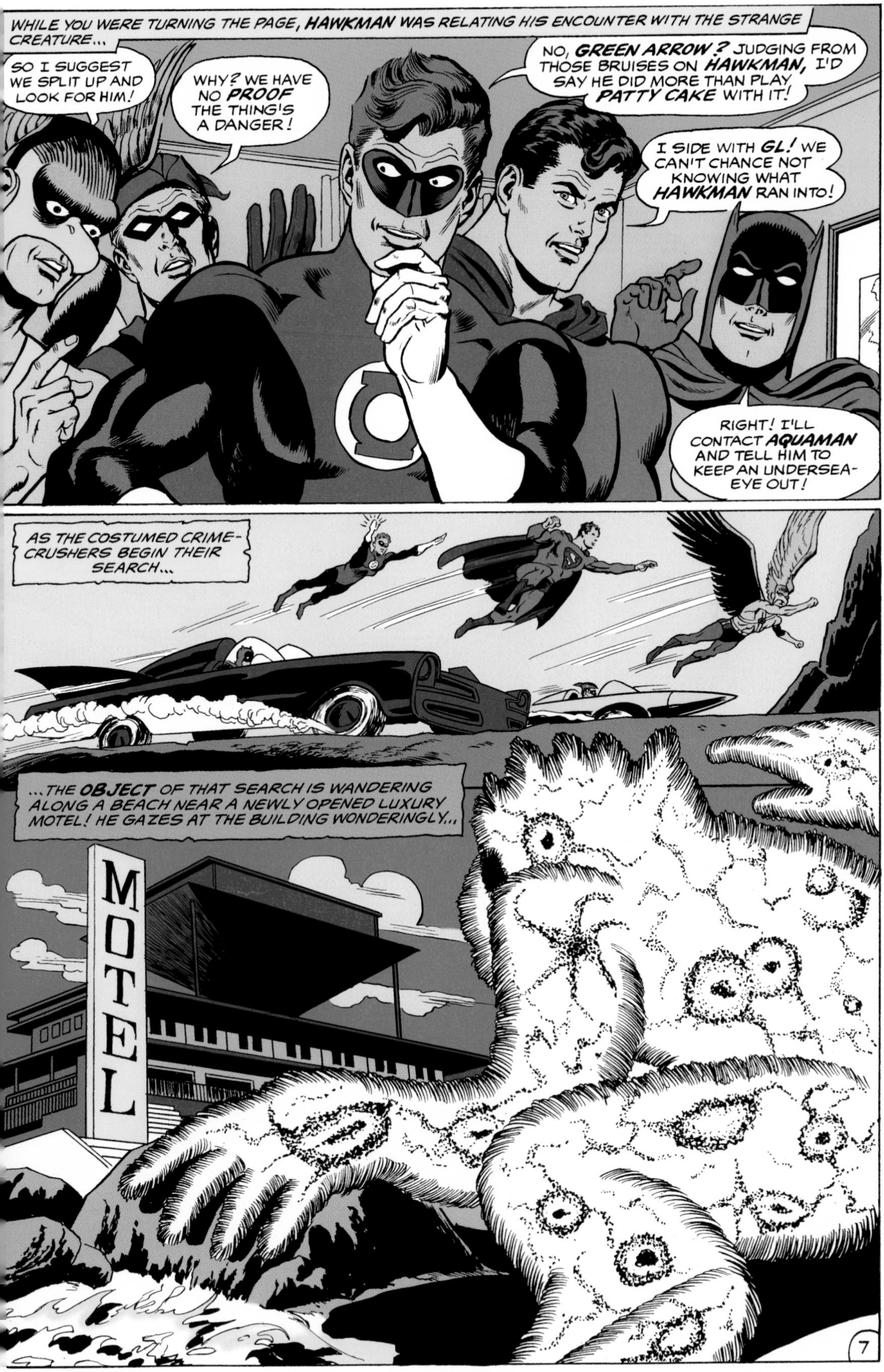
WHILE YOU WERE TURNING THE PAGE, HAWKMAN WAS RELATING HIS ENCOUNTER WITH THE STRANGE CREATURE...
SO I SUGGEST WE SPLIT UP AND LOOK FOR HIM!
WHY? WE HAVE NO PROOF THE THING'S A DANGER!
NO, GREEN ARROW? JUDGING FROM THOSE BRUISES ON HAWKMAN, I'D SAY HE DID MORE THAN PLAY PATTY CAKE WITH IT!
I SIDE WITH GL! WE CAN'T CHANCE NOT KNOWING WHAT HAWKMAN RAN INTO!
RIGHT! I'LL CONTACT AQUAMAN AND TELL HIM TO KEEP AN UNDERSEA-EYE OUT!
AS THE COSTUMED CRIME-CRUSHERS BEGIN THEIR SEARCH...
...THE OBJECT OF THAT SEARCH IS WANDERING ALONG A BEACH NEAR A NEWLY OPENED LUXURY MOTEL! HE GAZES AT THE BUILDING WONDERINGLY...
MOTEL
7

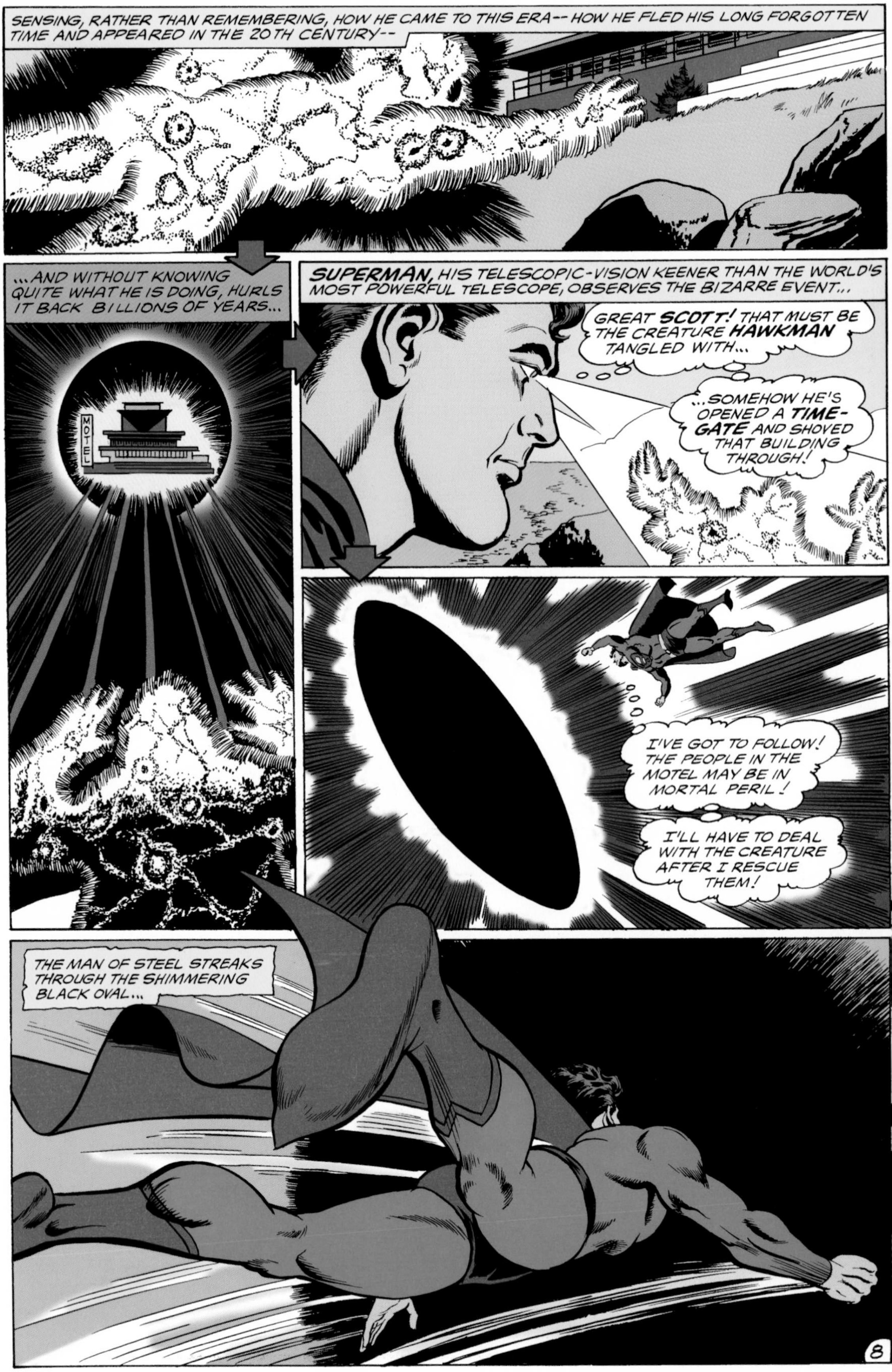
SENSING, RATHER THAN REMEMBERING, HOW HE CAME TO THIS ERA-- HOW HE FLED HIS LONG FORGOTTEN TIME AND APPEARED IN THE 20TH CENTURY--
...AND WITHOUT KNOWING QUITE WHAT HE IS DOING, HURLS IT BACK BILLIONS OF YEARS...
MOTEL
SUPERMAN, HIS TELESCOPIC-VISION KEENER THAN THE WORLD'S MOST POWERFUL TELESCOPE, OBSERVES THE BIZARRE EVENT...
GREAT SCOTT! THAT MUST BE THE CREATURE HAWKMAN TANGLED WITH...
...SOMEHOW HE'S OPENED A TIME-GATE AND SHOVED THAT BUILDING THROUGH!
I'VE GOT TO FOLLOW! THE PEOPLE IN THE MOTEL MAY BE IN MORTAL PERIL!
I'LL HAVE TO DEAL WITH THE CREATURE AFTER I RESCUE THEM!
THE MAN OF STEEL STREAKS THROUGH THE SHIMMERING BLACK OVAL...
8

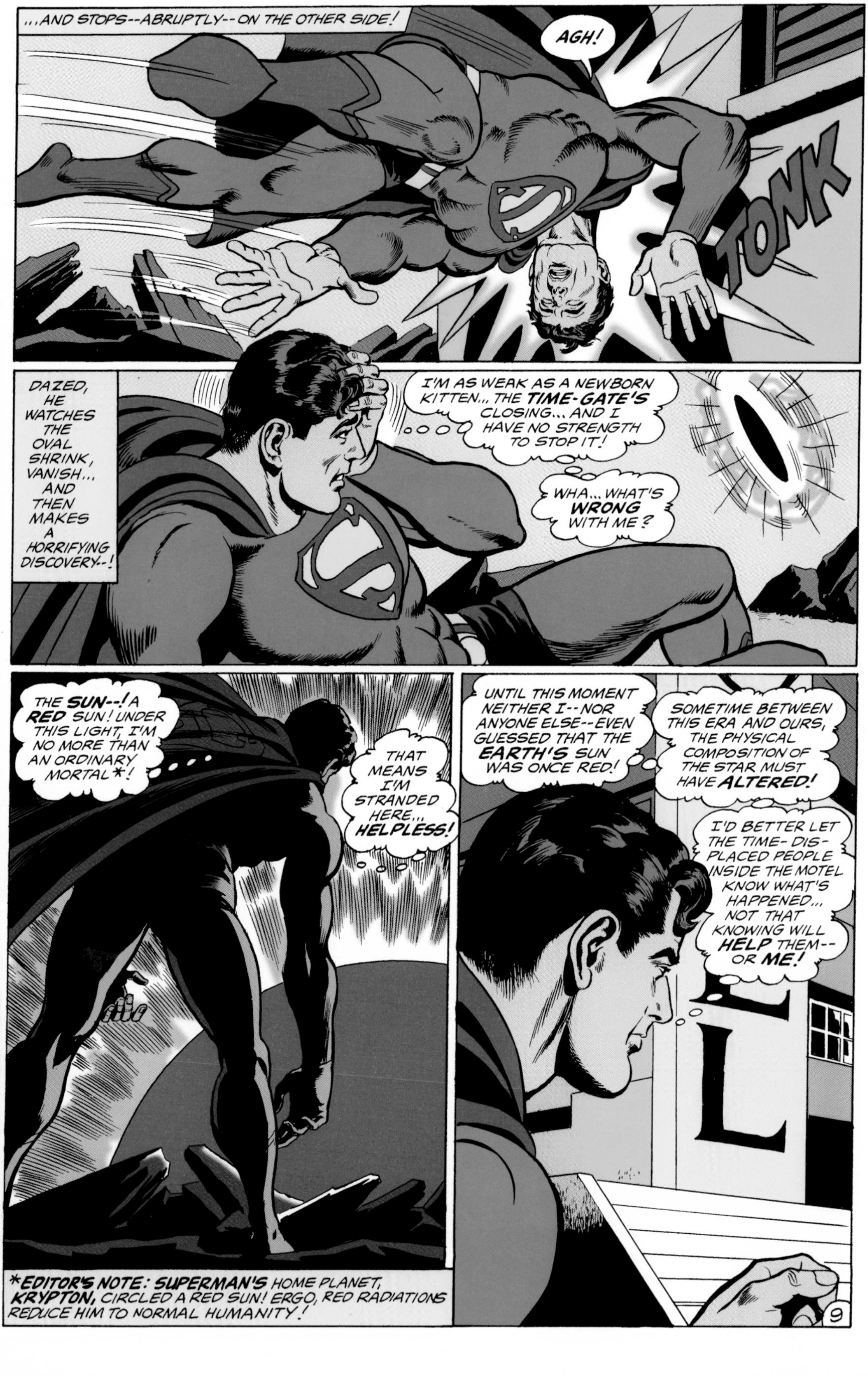
...AND STOPS--ABRUPTLY--ON THE OTHER SIDE!
AGH!
TONK
DAZED, HE WATCHES THE OVAL SHRINK, VANISH... AND THEN MAKES A HORRIFYING DISCOVERY--!
I'M AS WEAK AS A NEWBORN KITTEN... THE TIME-GATE'S CLOSING... AND I HAVE NO STRENGTH TO STOP IT!
WHA... WHAT'S WRONG WITH ME?
THE SUN--! A RED SUN! UNDER THIS LIGHT, I'M NO MORE THAN AN ORDINARY MORTAL*!
THAT MEANS I'M STRANDED HERE... HELPLESS!
*EDITOR'S NOTE: SUPERMAN'S HOME PLANET, KRYPTON, CIRCLED A RED SUN! ERGO, RED RADIATIONS REDUCE HIM TO NORMAL HUMANITY!
UNTIL THIS MOMENT NEITHER I--NOR ANYONE ELSE--EVEN GUESSED THAT THE EARTH'S SUN WAS ONCE RED!
SOMETIME BETWEEN THIS ERA AND OURS, THE PHYSICAL COMPOSITION OF THE STAR MUST HAVE ALTERED!
I'D BETTER LET THE TIME-DISPLACED PEOPLE INSIDE THE MOTEL KNOW WHAT'S HAPPENED... NOT THAT KNOWING WILL HELP THEM--OR ME!
L
L
9

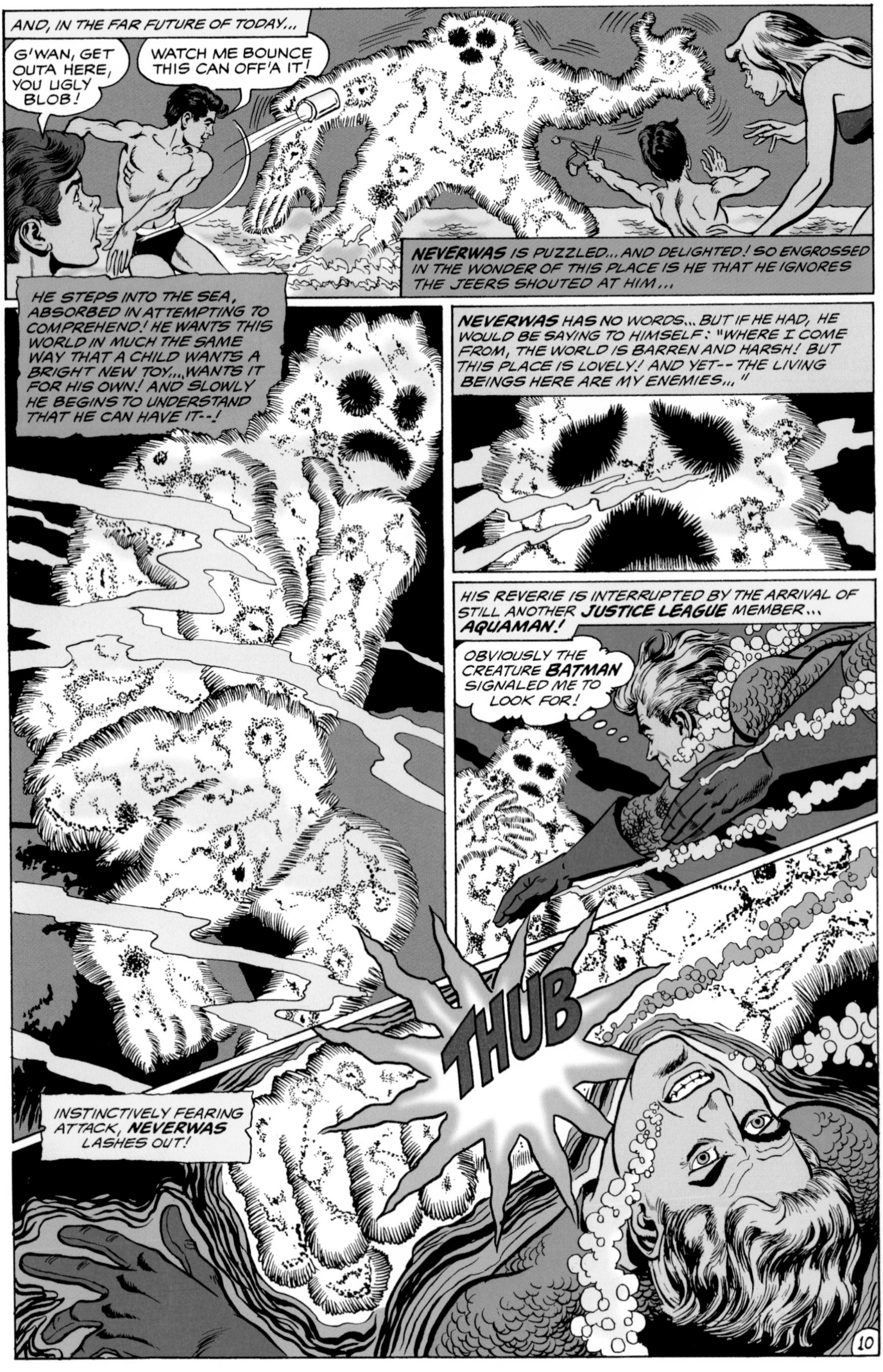
AND, IN THE FAR FUTURE OF TODAY...
G'WAN, GET OUTA HERE, YOU UGLY BLOB!
WATCH ME BOUNCE THIS CAN OFF'A IT!
NEVERWAS IS PUZZLED... AND DELIGHTED! SO ENGROSSED IN THE WONDER OF THIS PLACE IS HE THAT HE IGNORES THE JEERS SHOUTED AT HIM...
HE STEPS INTO THE SEA, ABSORBED IN ATTEMPTING TO COMPREHEND! HE WANTS THIS WORLD IN MUCH THE SAME WAY THAT A CHILD WANTS A BRIGHT NEW TOY,,,WANTS IT FOR HIS OWN! AND SLOWLY HE BEGINS TO UNDERSTAND THAT HE CAN HAVE IT--!
NEVERWAS HAS NO WORDS... BUT IF HE HAD, HE WOULD BE SAYING TO HIMSELF: "WHERE I COME FROM, THE WORLD IS BARREN AND HARSH! BUT THIS PLACE IS LOVELY! AND YET-- THE LIVING BEINGS HERE ARE MY ENEMIES..."
HIS REVERIE IS INTERRUPTED BY THE ARRIVAL OF STILL ANOTHER JUSTICE LEAGUE MEMBER... AQUAMAN!
OBVIOUSLY THE CREATURE BATMAN SIGNALED ME TO LOOK FOR!
THUB
INSTINCTIVELY FEARING ATTACK, NEVERWAS LASHES OUT!
10

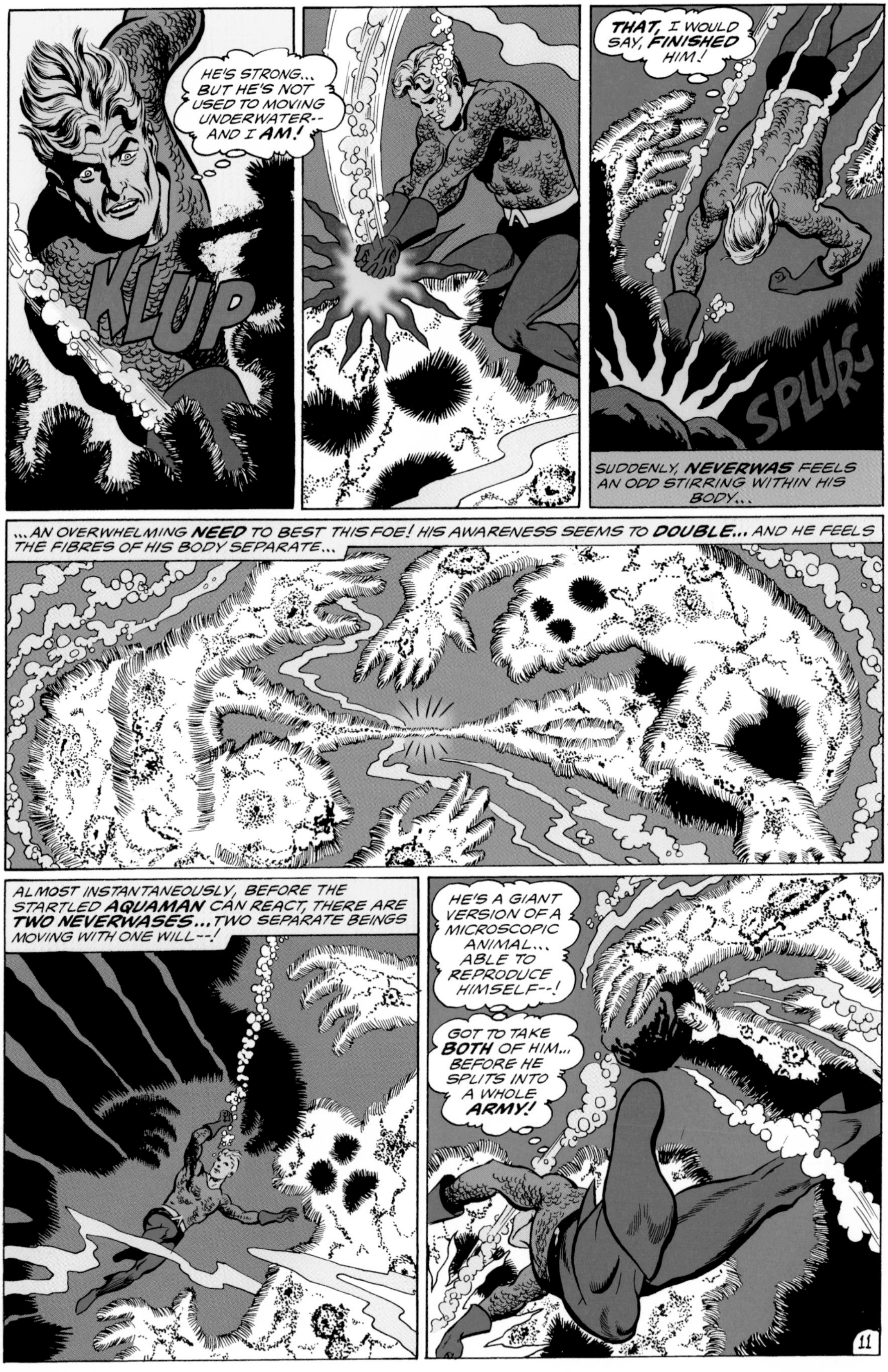
HE'S STRONG... BUT HE'S NOT USED TO MOVING UNDERWATER-- AND I AM!
KLUP
THAT, I WOULD SAY, FINISHED HIM!
SPLURG
SUDDENLY, NEVERWAS FEELS AN ODD STIRRING WITHIN HIS BODY...
...AN OVERWHELMING NEED TO BEST THIS FOE! HIS AWARENESS SEEMS TO DOUBLE... AND HE FEELS THE FIBRES OF HIS BODY SEPARATE...
ALMOST INSTANTANEOUSLY, BEFORE THE STARTLED AQUAMAN CAN REACT, THERE ARE TWO NEVERWASES...TWO SEPARATE BEINGS MOVING WITH ONE WILL--!
HE'S A GIANT VERSION OF A MICROSCOPIC ANIMAL... ABLE TO REPRODUCE HIMSELF--!
GOT TO TAKE BOTH OF HIM... BEFORE HE SPLITS INTO A WHOLE ARMY!
11

SKLUCK
UNNGH!
A SINGLE INTELLIGENCE IN A PAIR OF BODIES--THIS IS NOW NEVERWAS! QUICKLY, HE DRAGS AQUAMAN INTO AN UNDERWATER GROTTO, WHILE HIS OTHER SELF SHOVES A MASSIVE BOULDER OVER THE GROTTO ENTRANCE...
HAVING IMPRISONED THE JUSTICE LEAGUER, THE NEVERWASES LUMBER OFF--NOW FULLY COMPREHENDING THEIR POWER--AND DETERMINED TO USE IT!
12

JUSTICE LEAGUE of AMERICA

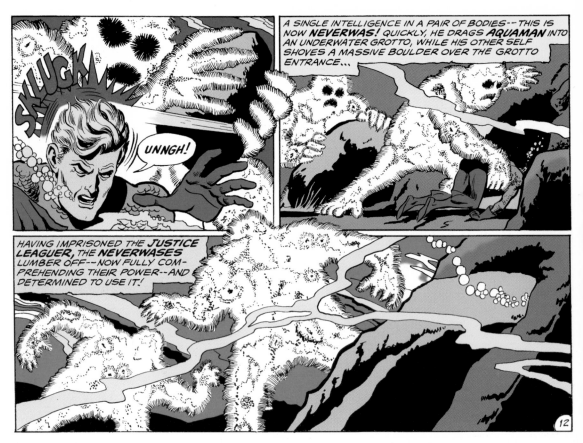

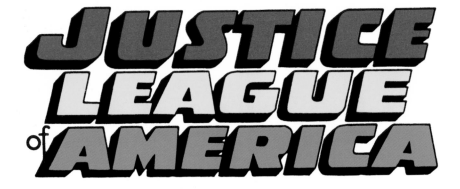

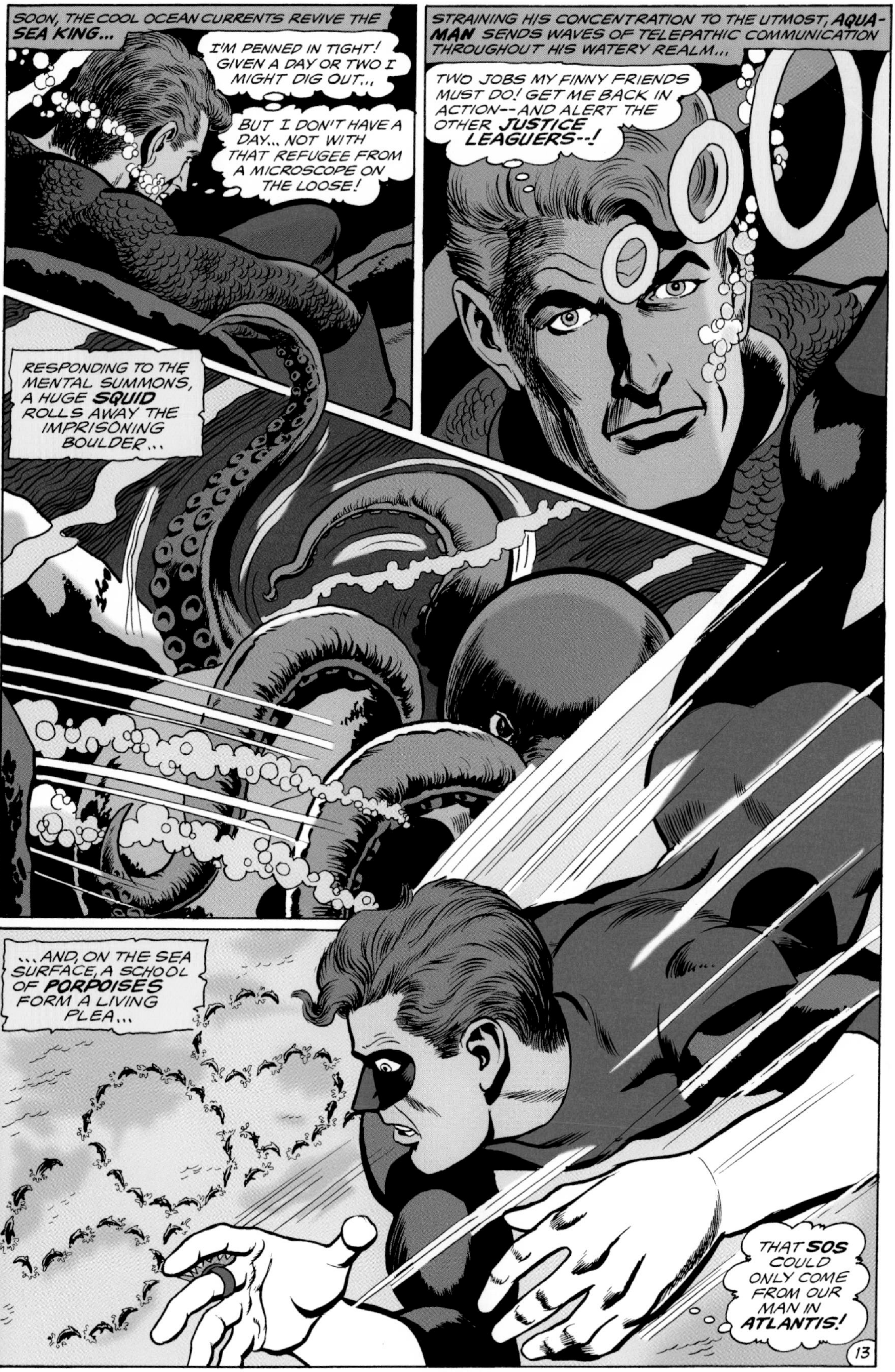
SOON, THE COOL OCEAN CURRENTS REVIVE THE SEA KING...
I'M PENNED IN TIGHT! GIVEN A DAY OR TWO I MIGHT DIG OUT...
BUT I DON'T HAVE A DAY... NOT WITH THAT REFUGEE FROM A MICROSCOPE ON THE LOOSE!
STRAINING HIS CONCENTRATION TO THE UTMOST, AQUAMAN SENDS WAVES OF TELEPATHIC COMMUNICATION THROUGHOUT HIS WATERY REALM...
TWO JOBS MY FINNY FRIENDS MUST DO! GET ME BACK IN ACTION--AND ALERT THE OTHER JUSTICE LEAGUERS--!
RESPONDING TO THE MENTAL SUMMONS, A HUGE SQUID ROLLS AWAY THE IMPRISONING BOULDER...
...AND, ON THE SEA SURFACE, A SCHOOL OF PORPOISES FORM A LIVING PLEA...
THAT SOS COULD ONLY COME FROM OUR MAN IN ATLANTIS!
13

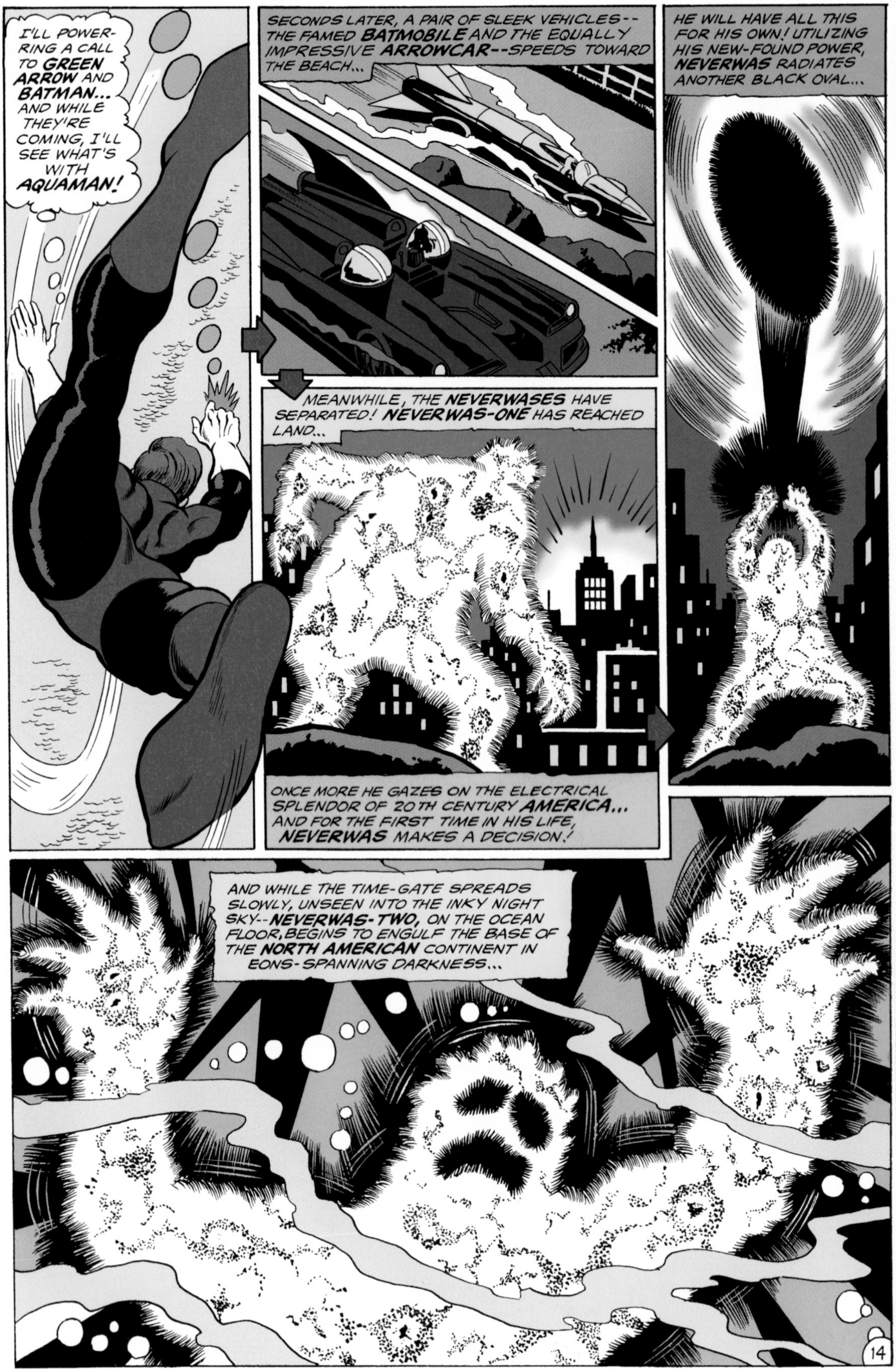
I'LL POWER-RING A CALL TO GREEN ARROW AND BATMAN... AND WHILE THEY'RE COMING, I'LL SEE WHAT'S WITH AQUAMAN!
SECONDS LATER, A PAIR OF SLEEK VEHICLES--THE FAMED BATMOBILE AND THE EQUALLY IMPRESSIVE ARROWCAR--SPEEDS TOWARD THE BEACH...
MEANWHILE, THE NEVERWASES HAVE SEPARATED! NEVERWAS-ONE HAS REACHED LAND...
ONCE MORE HE GAZES ON THE ELECTRICAL SPLENDOR OF 20TH CENTURY AMERICA... AND FOR THE FIRST TIME IN HIS LIFE, NEVERWAS MAKES A DECISION!
HE WILL HAVE ALL THIS FOR HIS OWN! UTILIZING HIS NEW-FOUND POWER, NEVERWAS RADIATES ANOTHER BLACK OVAL...
AND WHILE THE TIME-GATE SPREADS SLOWLY, UNSEEN INTO THE INKY NIGHT SKY--NEVERWAS-TWO, ON THE OCEAN FLOOR, BEGINS TO ENGULF THE BASE OF THE NORTH AMERICAN CONTINENT IN EONS-SPANNING DARKNESS...
14

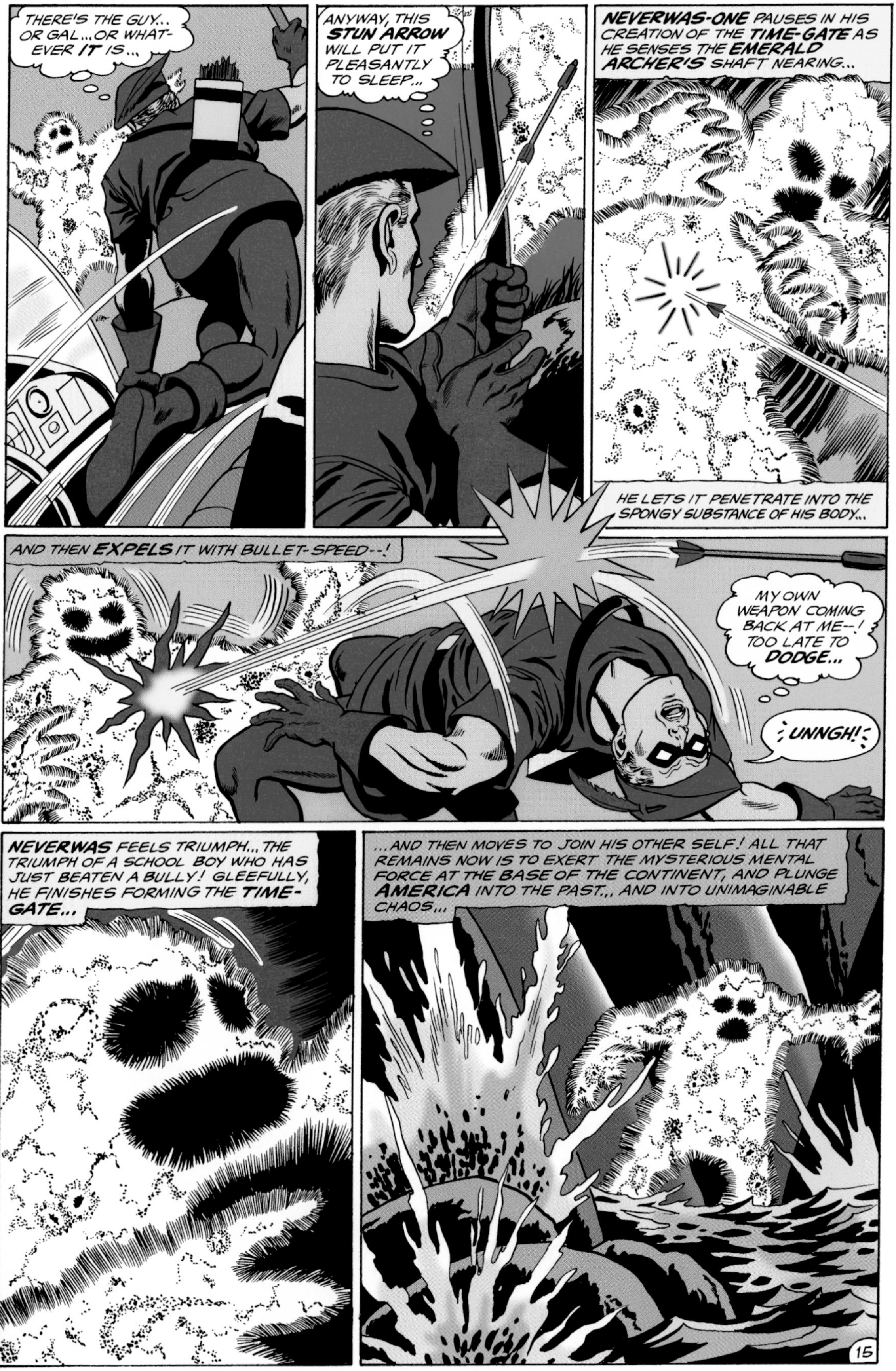
THERE'S THE GUY... OR GAL...OR WHAT-EVER IT IS...
ANYWAY, THIS STUN ARROW WILL PUT IT PLEASANTLY TO SLEEP...
NEVERWAS-ONE PAUSES IN HIS CREATION OF THE TIME-GATE AS HE SENSES THE EMERALD ARCHER'S SHAFT NEARING...
HE LETS IT PENETRATE INTO THE SPONGY SUBSTANCE OF HIS BODY...
AND THEN EXPELS IT WITH BULLET-SPEED--!
MY OWN WEAPON COMING BACK AT ME--! TOO LATE TO DODGE...
UNNGH!
NEVERWAS FEELS TRIUMPH... THE TRIUMPH OF A SCHOOL BOY WHO HAS JUST BEATEN A BULLY! GLEEFULLY, HE FINISHES FORMING THE TIME-GATE...
...AND THEN MOVES TO JOIN HIS OTHER SELF! ALL THAT REMAINS NOW IS TO EXERT THE MYSTERIOUS MENTAL FORCE AT THE BASE OF THE CONTINENT, AND PLUNGE AMERICA INTO THE PAST... AND INTO UNIMAGINABLE CHAOS...
15

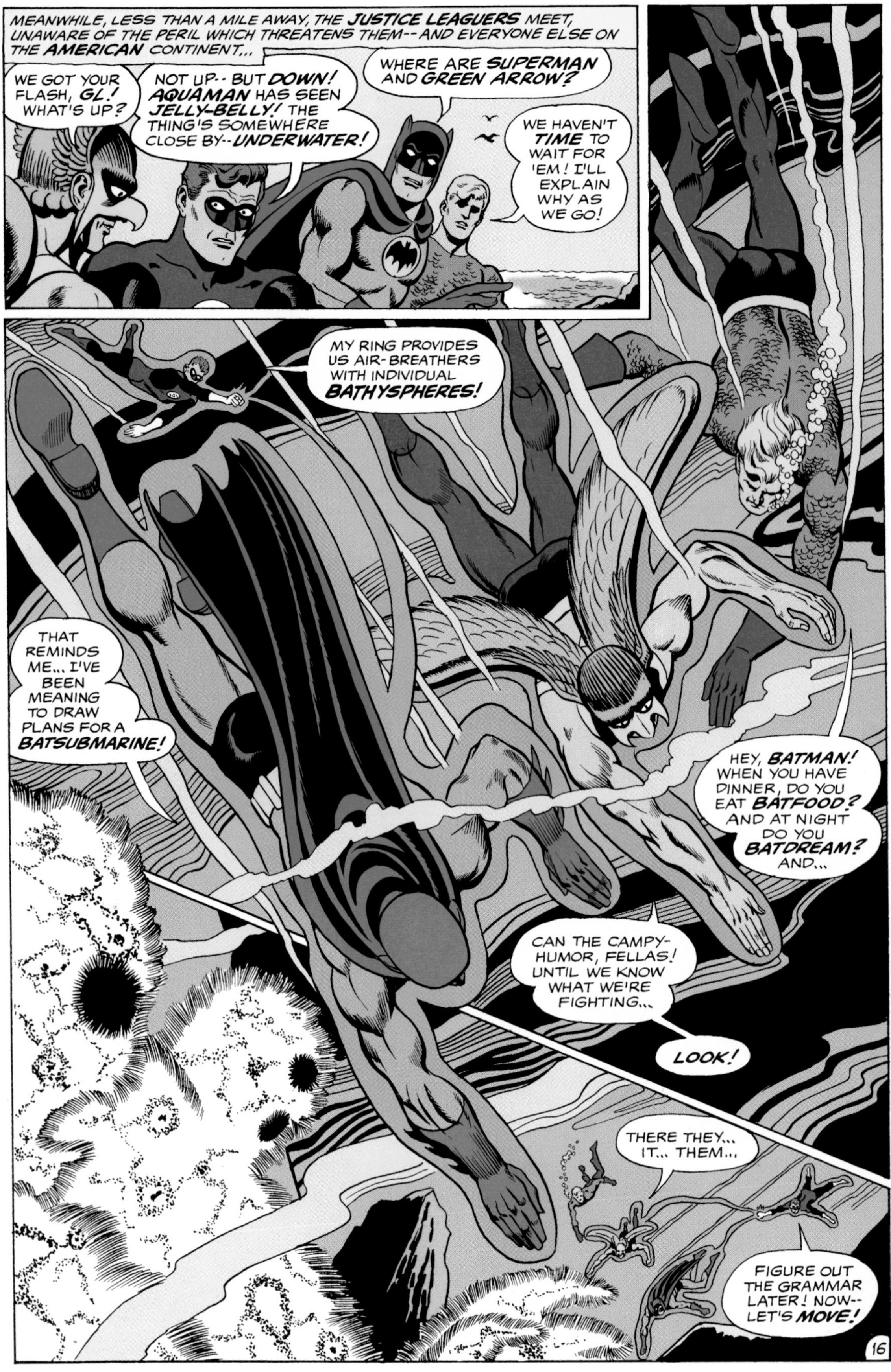
MEANWHILE, LESS THAN A MILE AWAY, THE JUSTICE LEAGUERS MEET, UNAWARE OF THE PERIL WHICH THREATENS THEM-- AND EVERYONE ELSE ON THE AMERICAN CONTINENT...
WE GOT YOUR FLASH, GL! WHAT'S UP?
NOT UP-- BUT DOWN! AQUAMAN HAS SEEN JELLY-BELLY! THE THING'S SOMEWHERE CLOSE BY--UNDERWATER!
WHERE ARE SUPERMAN AND GREEN ARROW?
WE HAVEN'T TIME TO WAIT FOR 'EM! I'LL EXPLAIN WHY AS WE GO!
MY RING PROVIDES US AIR-BREATHERS WITH INDIVIDUAL BATHYSPHERES!
THAT REMINDS ME... I'VE BEEN MEANING TO DRAW PLANS FOR A BATSUBMARINE!
HEY, BATMAN! WHEN YOU HAVE DINNER, DO YOU EAT BATFOOD? AND AT NIGHT DO YOU BATDREAM? AND...
CAN THE CAMPY-HUMOR, FELLAS! UNTIL WE KNOW WHAT WE'RE FIGHTING...
LOOK!
THERE THEY... IT... THEM...
FIGURE OUT THE GRAMMAR LATER! NOW-- LET'S MOVE!
16

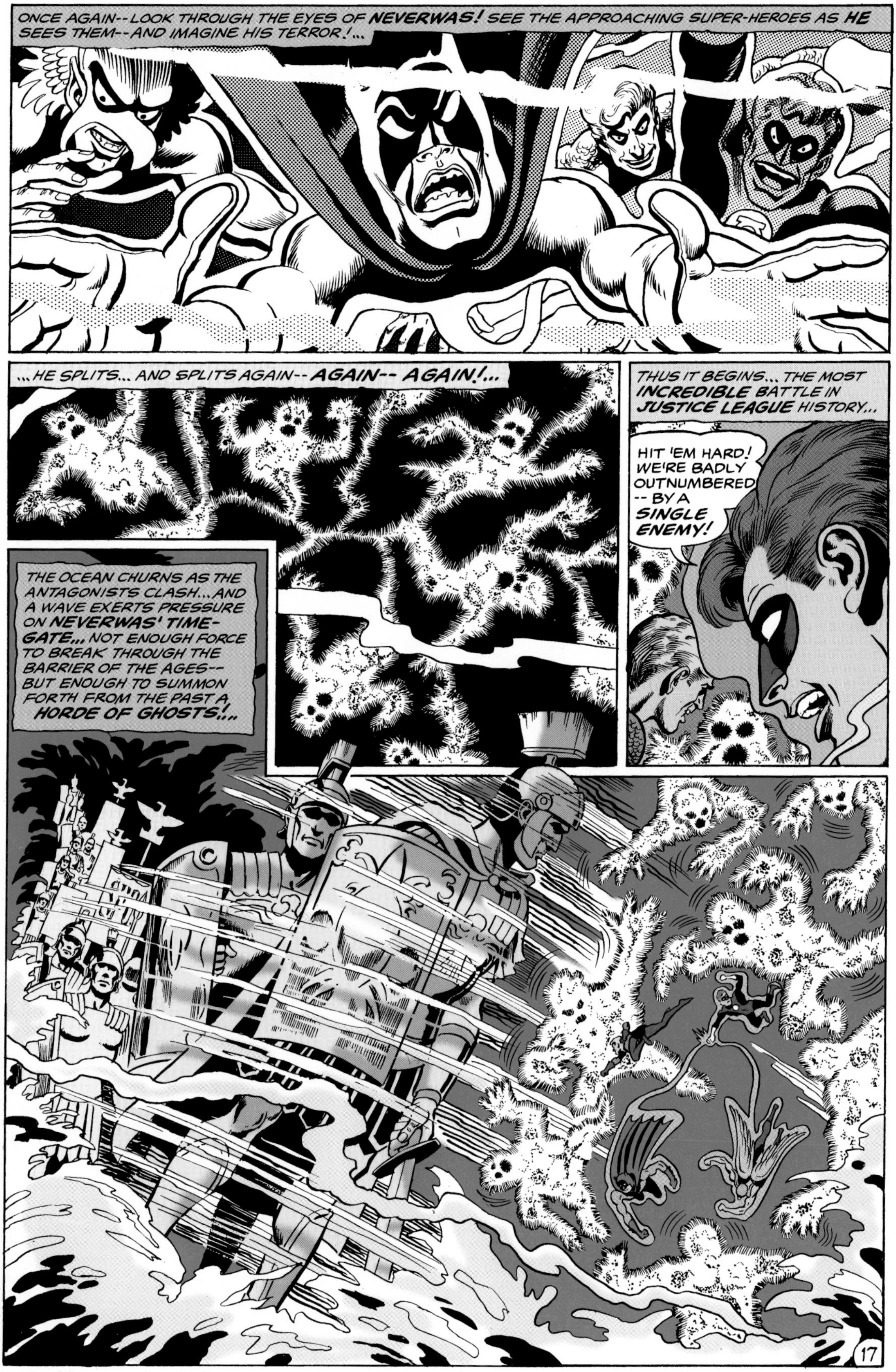
ONCE AGAIN--LOOK THROUGH THE EYES OF NEVERWAS! SEE THE APPROACHING SUPER-HEROES AS HE SEES THEM--AND IMAGINE HIS TERROR!...
...HE SPLITS... AND SPLITS AGAIN--AGAIN--AGAIN!...
THUS IT BEGINS... THE MOST INCREDIBLE BATTLE IN JUSTICE LEAGUE HISTORY...
HIT 'EM HARD! WE'RE BADLY OUTNUMBERED --BY A SINGLE ENEMY!
THE OCEAN CHURNS AS THE ANTAGONISTS CLASH...AND A WAVE EXERTS PRESSURE ON NEVERWAS' TIME-GATE... NOT ENOUGH FORCE TO BREAK THROUGH THE BARRIER OF THE AGES--BUT ENOUGH TO SUMMON FORTH FROM THE PAST A HORDE OF GHOSTS!...
17

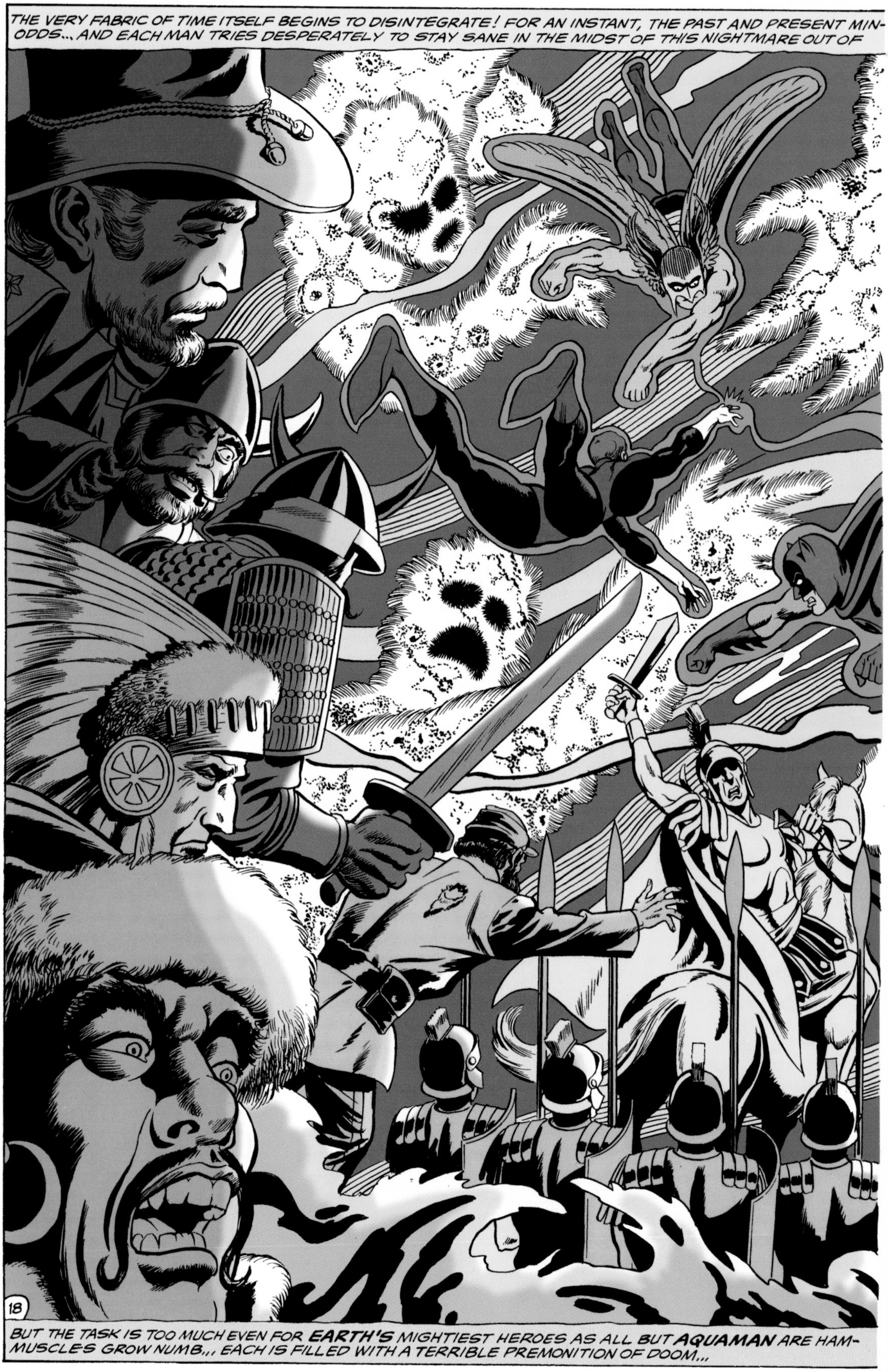
THE VERY FABRIC OF TIME ITSELF BEGINS TO DISINTEGRATE! FOR AN INSTANT, THE PAST AND PRESENT MIN-
ODDS... AND EACH MAN TRIES DESPERATELY TO STAY SANE IN THE MIDST OF THIS NIGHTMARE OUT OF
18
BUT THE TASK IS TOO MUCH EVEN FOR EARTH'S MIGHTIEST HEROES AS ALL BUT AQUAMAN ARE HAM-
MUSCLES GROW NUMB... EACH IS FILLED WITH A TERRIBLE PREMONITION OF DOOM...

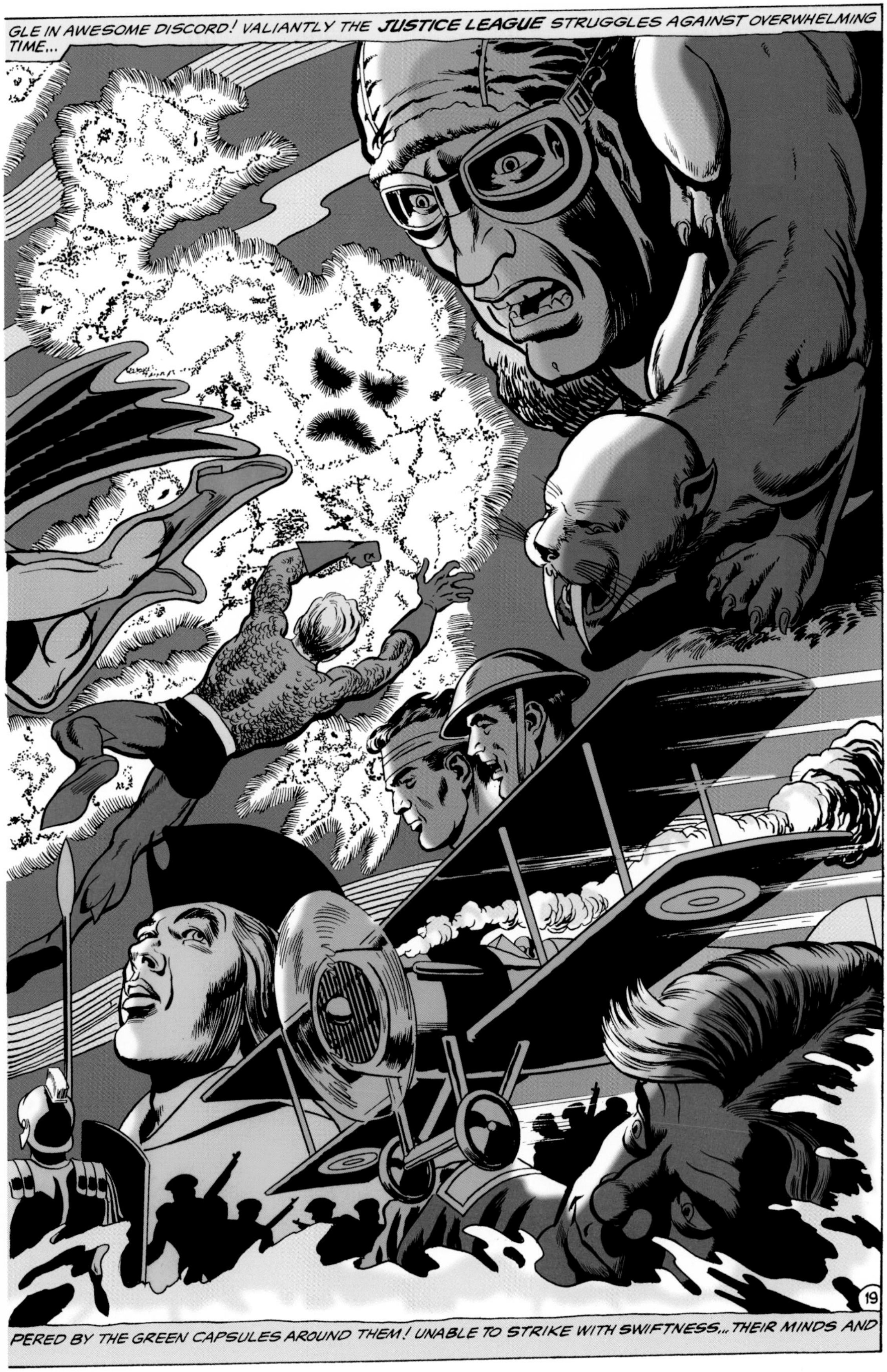
GLE IN AWESOME DISCORD! VALIANTLY THE JUSTICE LEAGUE STRUGGLES AGAINST OVERWHELMING TIME...
19
PERED BY THE GREEN CAPSULES AROUND THEM! UNABLE TO STRIKE WITH SWIFTNESS... THEIR MINDS AND

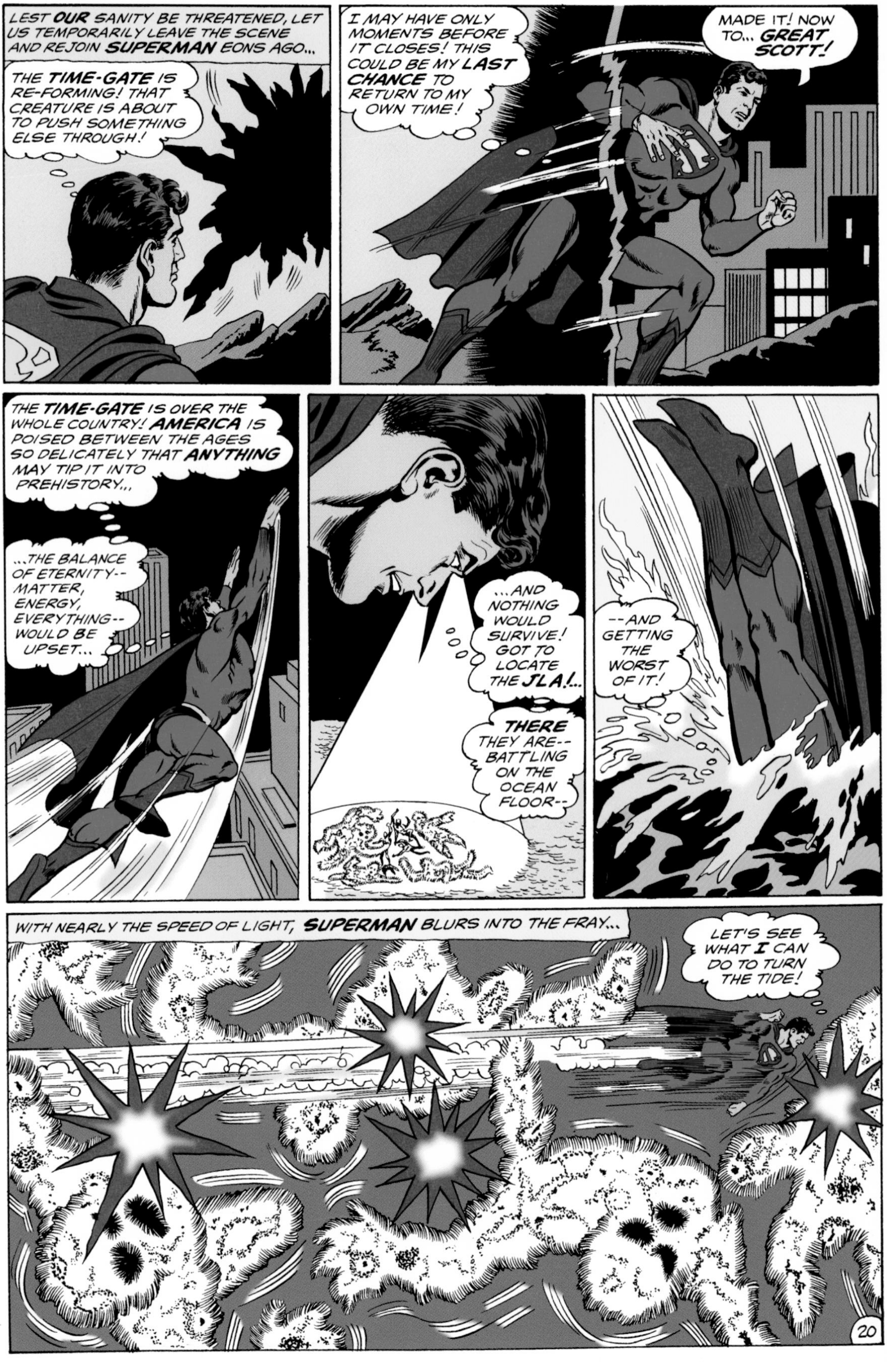
LEST OUR SANITY BE THREATENED, LET US TEMPORARILY LEAVE THE SCENE AND REJOIN SUPERMAN EONS AGO...
THE TIME-GATE IS RE-FORMING! THAT CREATURE IS ABOUT TO PUSH SOMETHING ELSE THROUGH!
I MAY HAVE ONLY MOMENTS BEFORE IT CLOSES! THIS COULD BE MY LAST CHANCE TO RETURN TO MY OWN TIME!
MADE IT! NOW TO... GREAT SCOTT!
THE TIME-GATE IS OVER THE WHOLE COUNTRY! AMERICA IS POISED BETWEEN THE AGES SO DELICATELY THAT ANYTHING MAY TIP IT INTO PREHISTORY...
...THE BALANCE OF ETERNITY-- MATTER, ENERGY, EVERYTHING-- WOULD BE UPSET...
...AND NOTHING WOULD SURVIVE! GOT TO LOCATE THE JLA!...
THERE THEY ARE-- BATTLING ON THE OCEAN FLOOR--
--AND GETTING THE WORST OF IT!
WITH NEARLY THE SPEED OF LIGHT, SUPERMAN BLURS INTO THE FRAY...
LET'S SEE WHAT I CAN DO TO TURN THE TIDE!
20

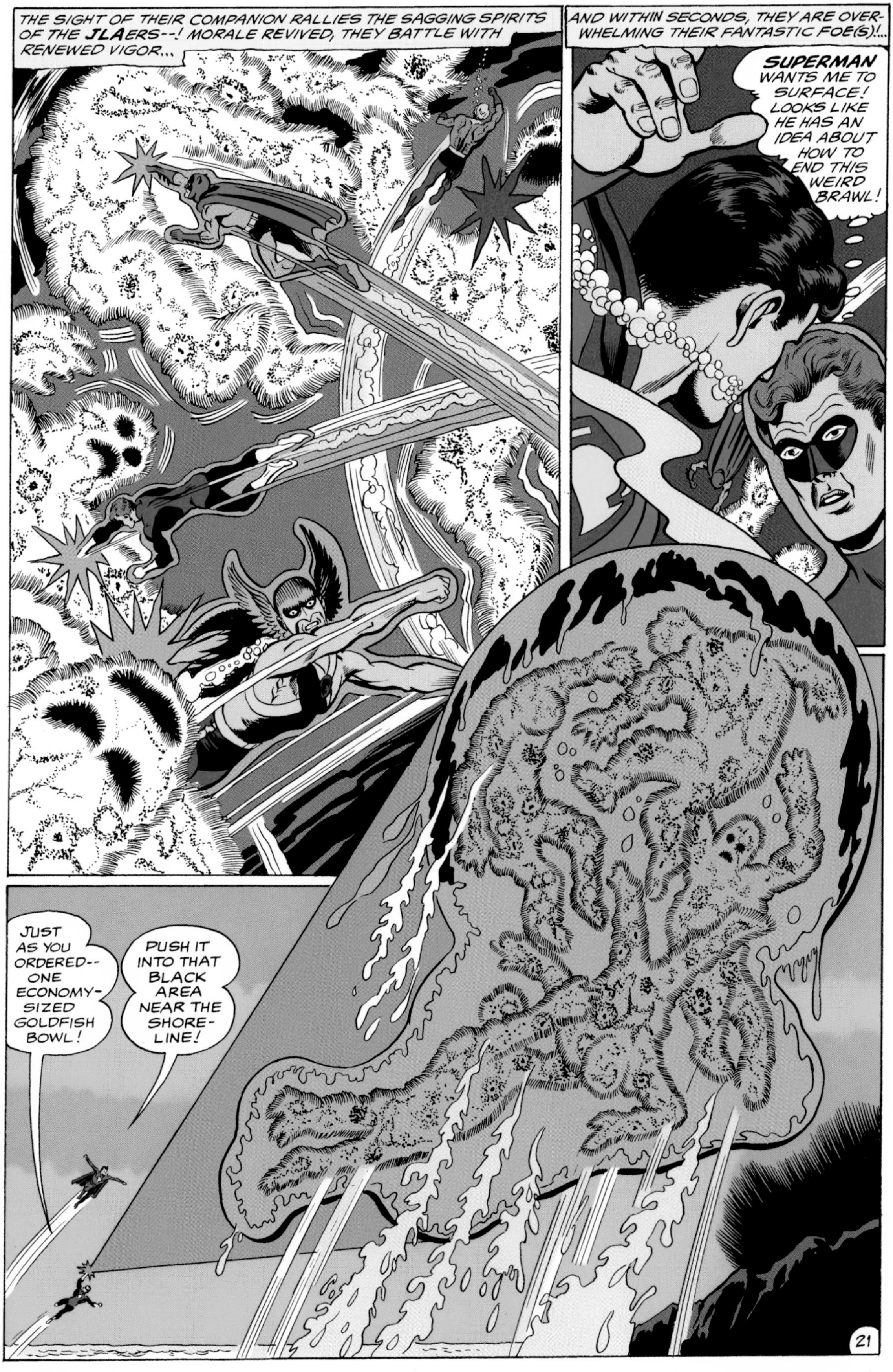
THE SIGHT OF THEIR COMPANION RALLIES THE SAGGING SPIRITS OF THE JLAERS--! MORALE REVIVED, THEY BATTLE WITH RENEWED VIGOR...
AND WITHIN SECONDS, THEY ARE OVERWHELMING THEIR FANTASTIC FOE(S)!...
SUPERMAN WANTS ME TO SURFACE! LOOKS LIKE HE HAS AN IDEA ABOUT HOW TO END THIS WEIRD BRAWL!
JUST AS YOU ORDERED-- ONE ECONOMY-SIZED GOLDFISH BOWL!
PUSH IT INTO THAT BLACK AREA NEAR THE SHORE-LINE!
21

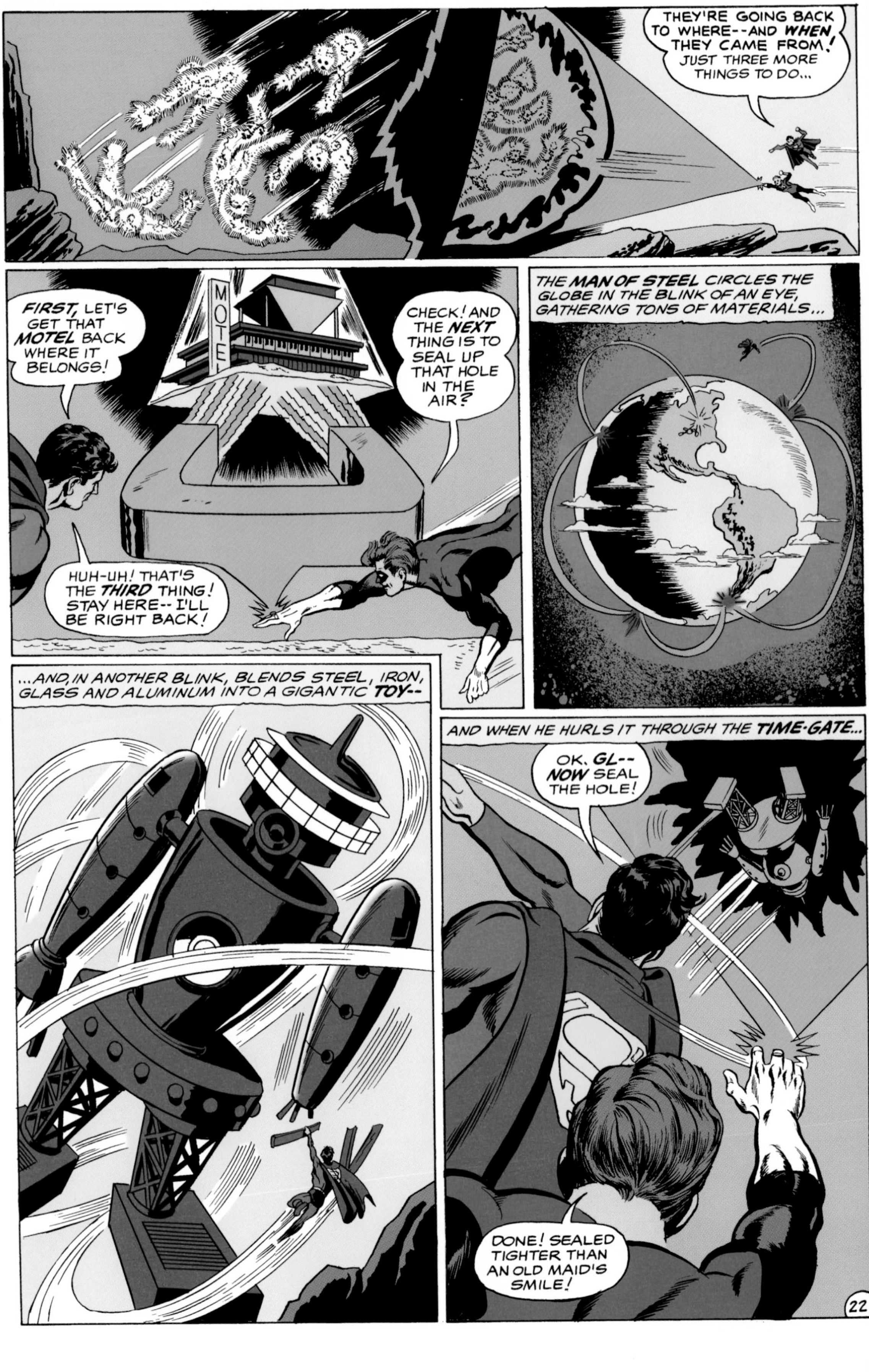
THEY'RE GOING BACK TO WHERE--AND WHEN THEY CAME FROM! JUST THREE MORE THINGS TO DO...
FIRST, LET'S GET THAT MOTEL BACK WHERE IT BELONGS!
MOTEL
CHECK! AND THE NEXT THING IS TO SEAL UP THAT HOLE IN THE AIR?
HUH-UH! THAT'S THE THIRD THING! STAY HERE-- I'LL BE RIGHT BACK!
THE MAN OF STEEL CIRCLES THE GLOBE IN THE BLINK OF AN EYE, GATHERING TONS OF MATERIALS...
...AND, IN ANOTHER BLINK, BLENDS STEEL, IRON, GLASS AND ALUMINUM INTO A GIGANTIC TOY--
AND WHEN HE HURLS IT THROUGH THE TIME-GATE...
OK, GL-- NOW SEAL THE HOLE!
DONE! SEALED TIGHTER THAN AN OLD MAID'S SMILE!
22

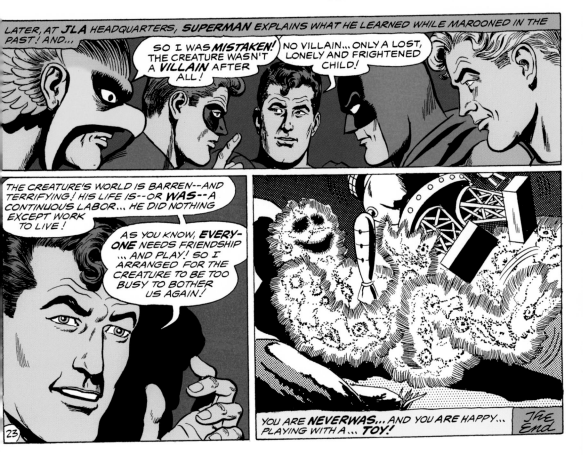

LATER, AT JLA HEADQUARTERS, SUPERMAN EXPLAINS WHAT HE LEARNED WHILE MAROONED IN THE PAST! AND...
SO I WAS MISTAKEN! THE CREATURE WASN'T A VILLAIN AFTER ALL!
NO VILLAIN... ONLY A LOST, LONELY AND FRIGHTENED CHILD!
THE CREATURE'S WORLD IS BARREN--AND TERRIFYING! HIS LIFE IS--OR WAS--A CONTINUOUS LABOR... HE DID NOTHING EXCEPT WORK TO LIVE!
AS YOU KNOW, EVERY-ONE NEEDS FRIENDSHIP ... AND PLAY! SO I ARRANGED FOR THE CREATURE TO BE TOO BUSY TO BOTHER US AGAIN!
23
YOU ARE NEVERWAS... AND YOU ARE HAPPY... PLAYING WITH A... TOY!
THE End

JUSTICE LEAGUE of AMERICA

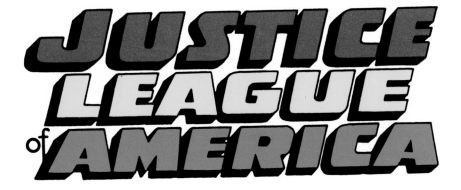

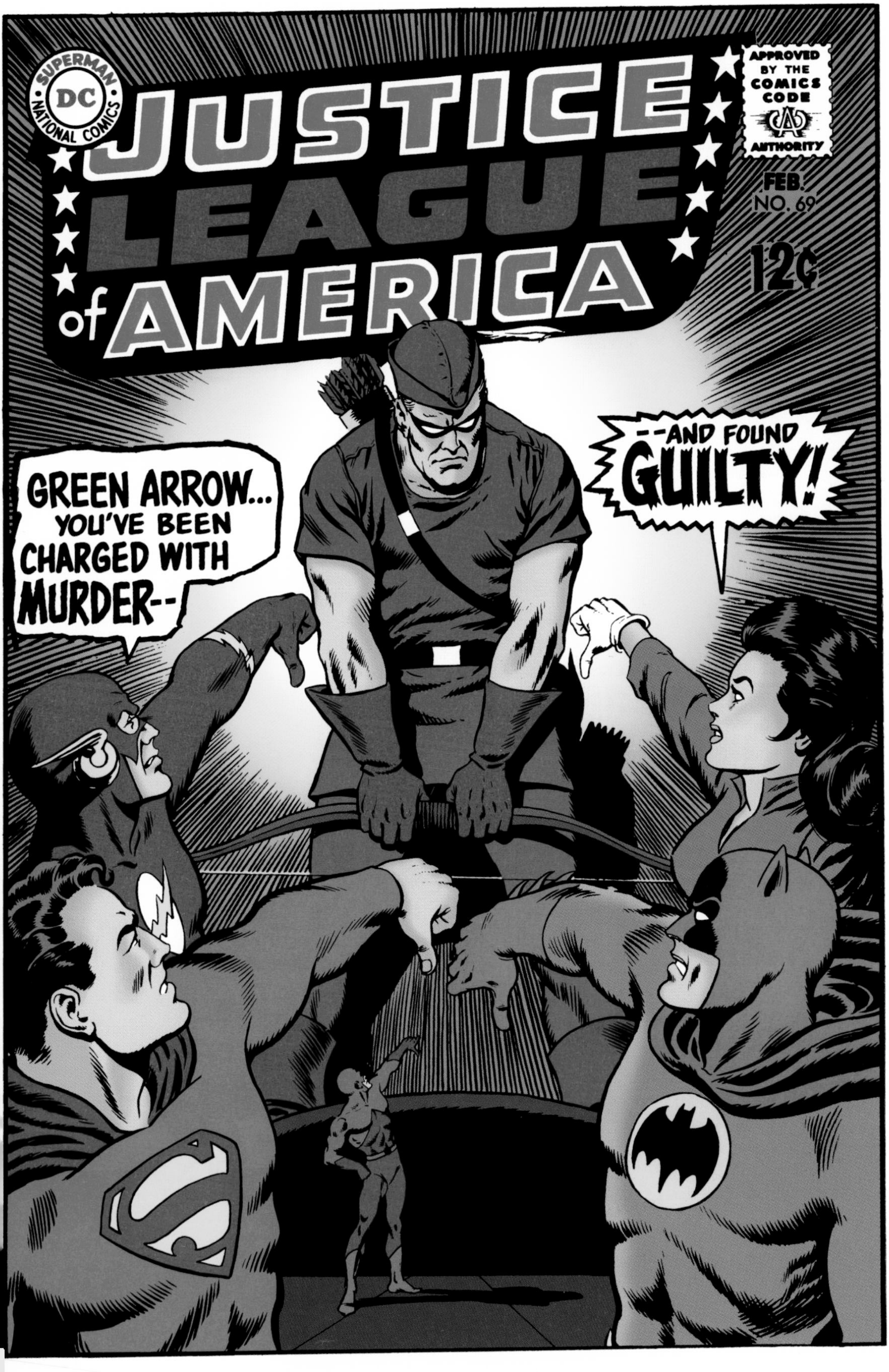
SUPERMAN DC NATIONAL COMICS
JUSTICE LEAGUE of AMERICA
APPROVED BY THE COMICS CODE AUTHORITY
FEB. NO. 69
12¢
GREEN ARROW... YOU'VE BEEN CHARGED WITH MURDER--
--AND FOUND GUILTY!

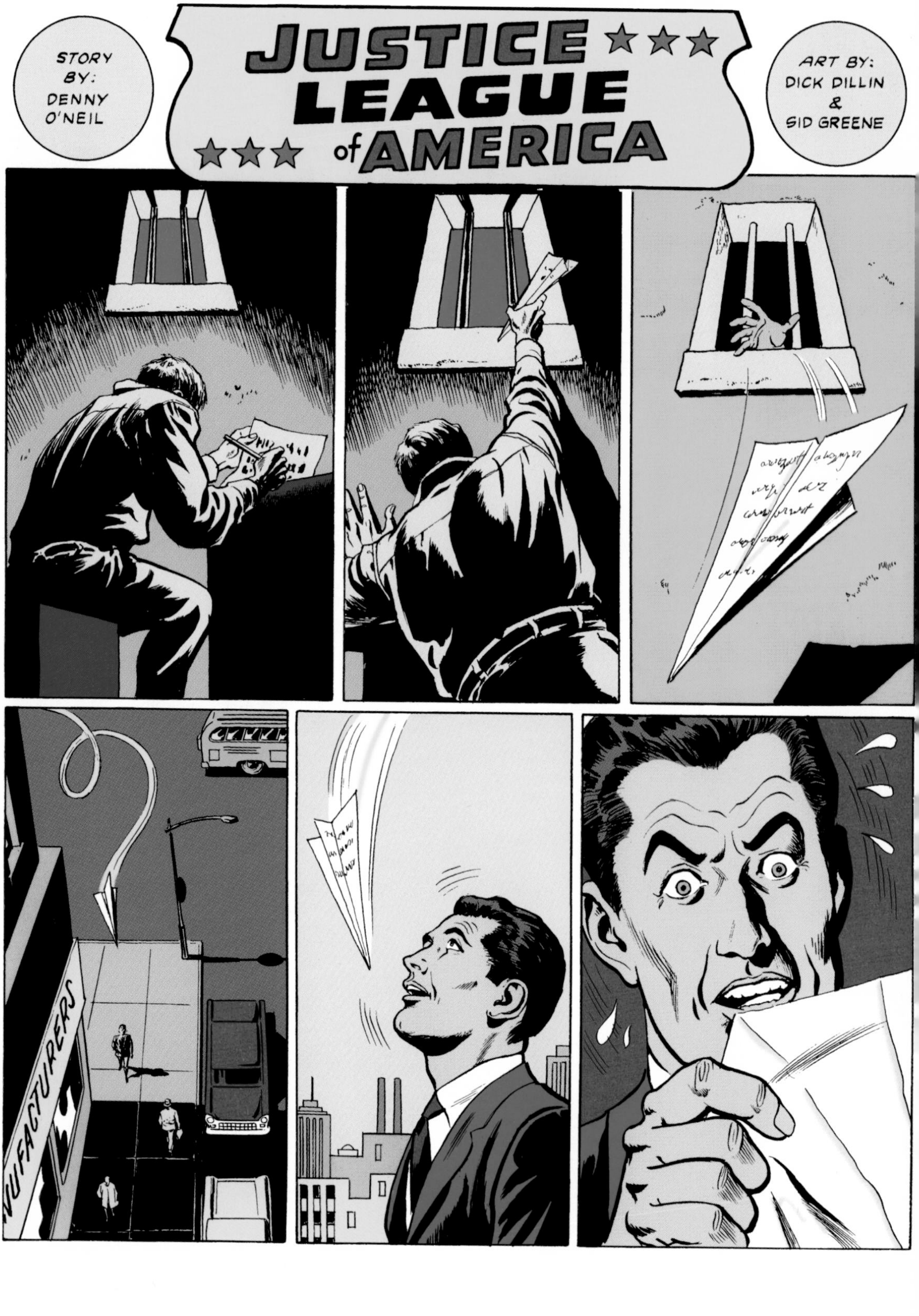
STORY BY: DENNY O'NEIL
JUSTICE LEAGUE of AMERICA
ART BY: DICK DILLIN & SID GREENE
...NUFACTURERS

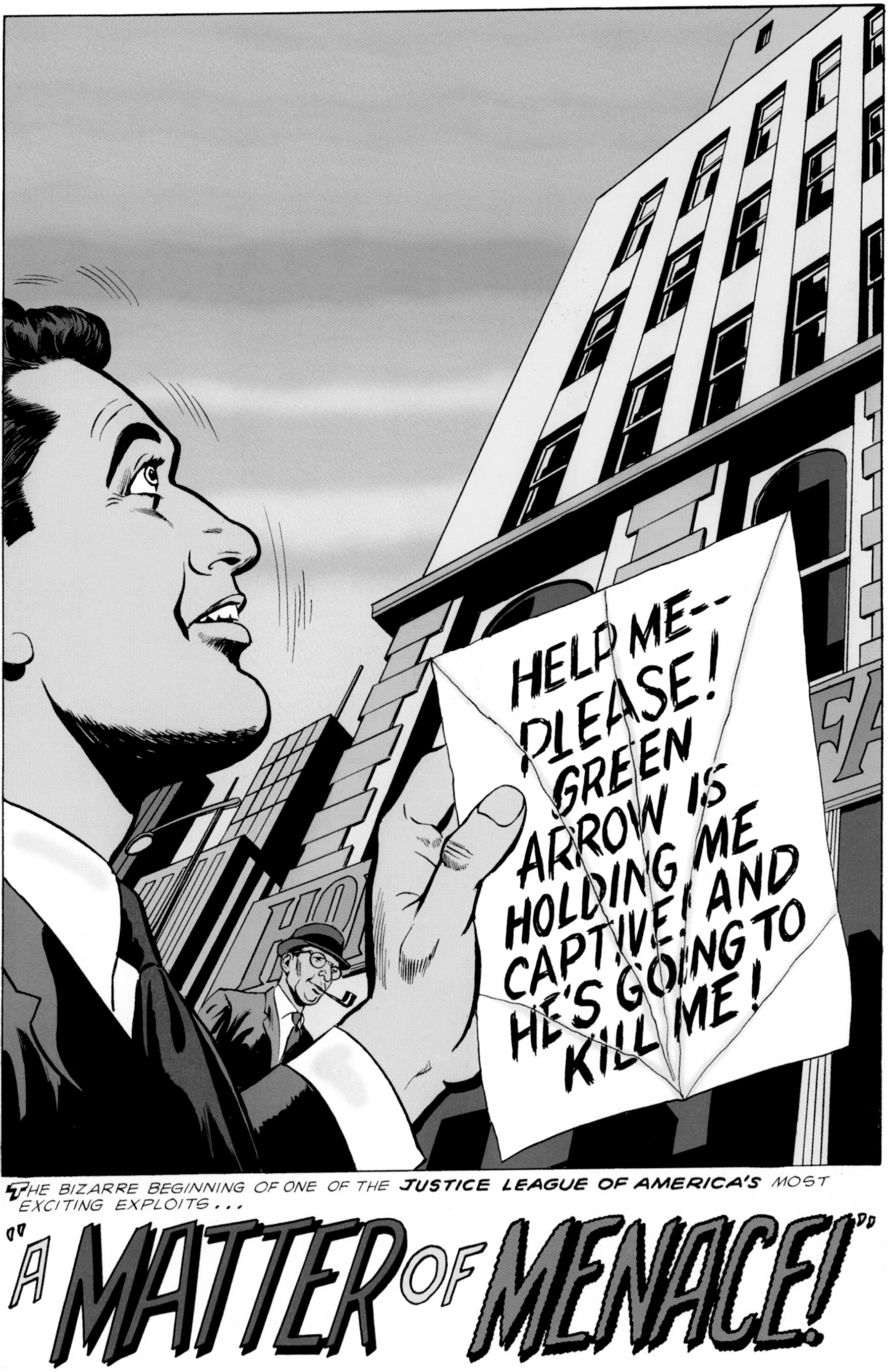
HELP ME--
PLEASE! GREEN ARROW IS HOLDING ME CAPTIVE AND HE'S GOING TO KILL ME!

THE BIZARRE BEGINNING OF ONE OF THE **JUSTICE LEAGUE OF AMERICA'S** MOST EXCITING EXPLOITS...

"A MATTER OF MENACE!"

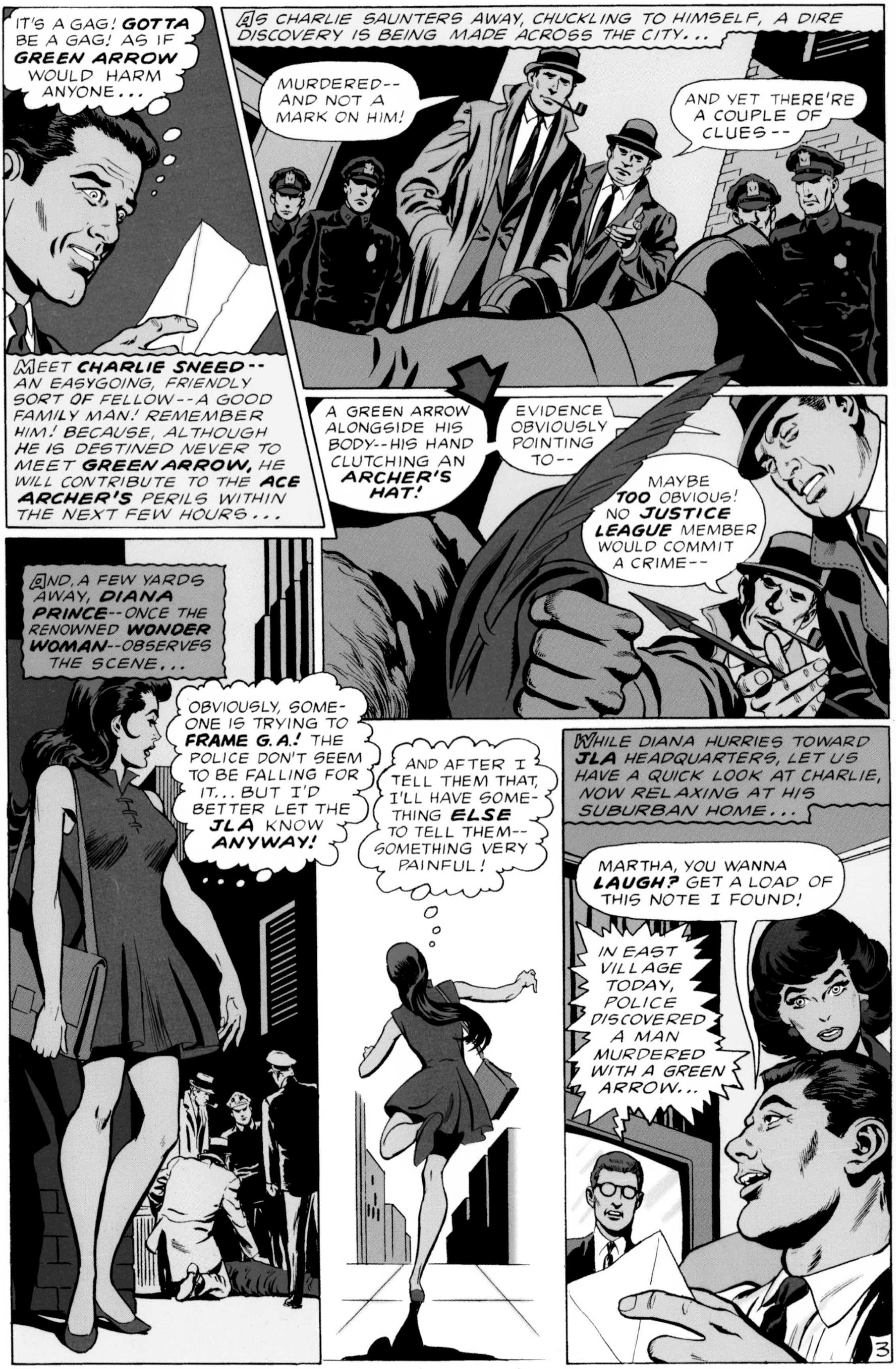
IT'S A GAG! GOTTA BE A GAG! AS IF GREEN ARROW WOULD HARM ANYONE...
MEET CHARLIE SNEED-- AN EASYGOING, FRIENDLY SORT OF FELLOW--A GOOD FAMILY MAN! REMEMBER HIM! BECAUSE, ALTHOUGH HE IS DESTINED NEVER TO MEET GREEN ARROW, HE WILL CONTRIBUTE TO THE ACE ARCHER'S PERILS WITHIN THE NEXT FEW HOURS...
AS CHARLIE SAUNTERS AWAY, CHUCKLING TO HIMSELF, A DIRE DISCOVERY IS BEING MADE ACROSS THE CITY...
MURDERED-- AND NOT A MARK ON HIM!
AND YET THERE'RE A COUPLE OF CLUES--
A GREEN ARROW ALONGSIDE HIS BODY--HIS HAND CLUTCHING AN ARCHER'S HAT!
EVIDENCE OBVIOUSLY POINTING TO--
MAYBE TOO OBVIOUS! NO JUSTICE LEAGUE MEMBER WOULD COMMIT A CRIME--
AND, A FEW YARDS AWAY, DIANA PRINCE--ONCE THE RENOWNED WONDER WOMAN--OBSERVES THE SCENE...
OBVIOUSLY, SOMEONE IS TRYING TO FRAME G.A.! THE POLICE DON'T SEEM TO BE FALLING FOR IT... BUT I'D BETTER LET THE JLA KNOW ANYWAY!
AND AFTER I TELL THEM THAT, I'LL HAVE SOMETHING ELSE TO TELL THEM-- SOMETHING VERY PAINFUL!
WHILE DIANA HURRIES TOWARD JLA HEADQUARTERS, LET US HAVE A QUICK LOOK AT CHARLIE, NOW RELAXING AT HIS SUBURBAN HOME...
MARTHA, YOU WANNA LAUGH? GET A LOAD OF THIS NOTE I FOUND!
IN EAST VILLAGE TODAY, POLICE DISCOVERED A MAN MURDERED WITH A GREEN ARROW...
3

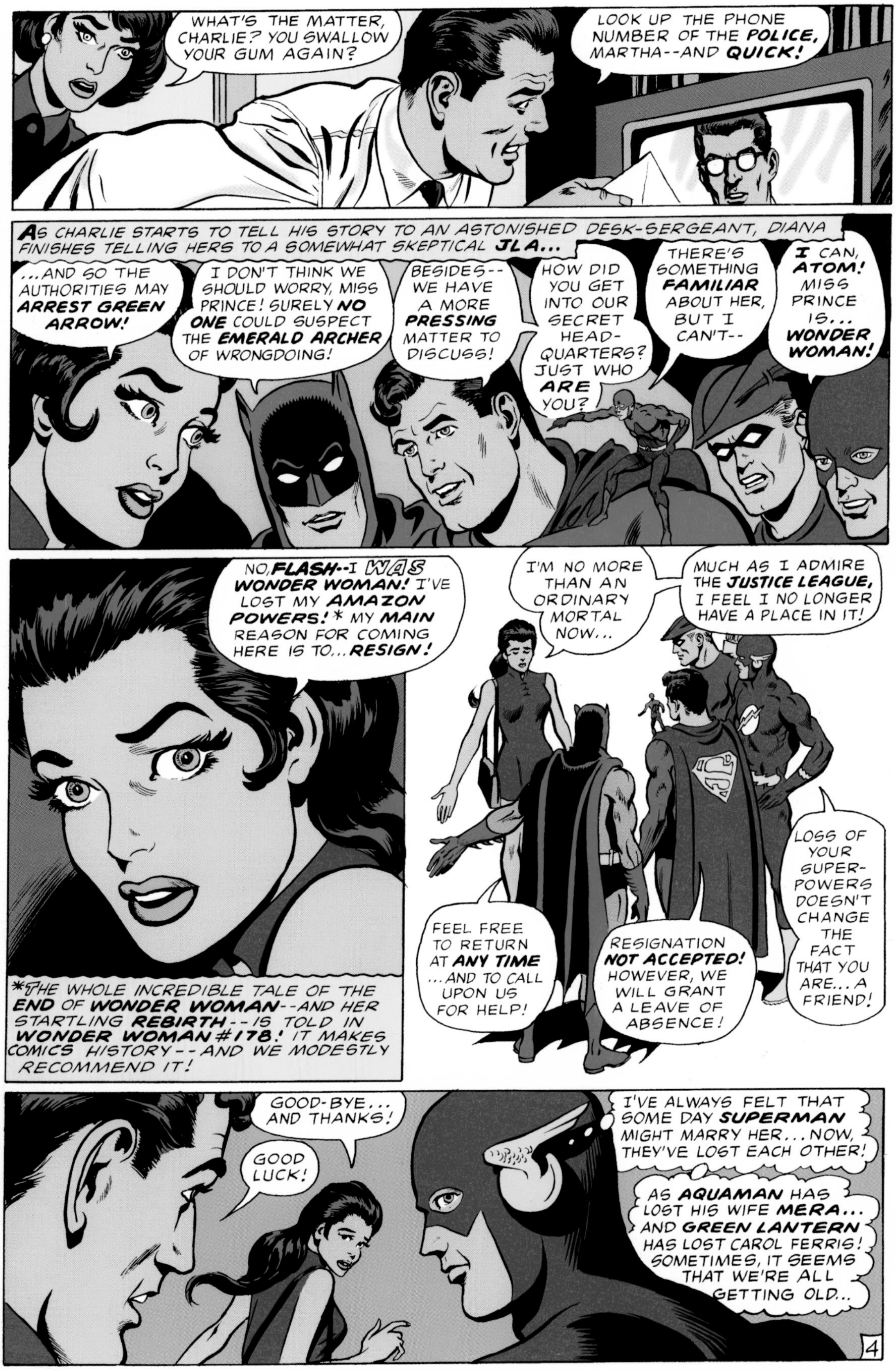
WHAT'S THE MATTER, CHARLIE? YOU SWALLOW YOUR GUM AGAIN?
LOOK UP THE PHONE NUMBER OF THE POLICE, MARTHA--AND QUICK!
AS CHARLIE STARTS TO TELL HIS STORY TO AN ASTONISHED DESK-SERGEANT, DIANA FINISHES TELLING HERS TO A SOMEWHAT SKEPTICAL JLA...
...AND SO THE AUTHORITIES MAY ARREST GREEN ARROW!
I DON'T THINK WE SHOULD WORRY, MISS PRINCE! SURELY NO ONE COULD SUSPECT THE EMERALD ARCHER OF WRONGDOING!
BESIDES--WE HAVE A MORE PRESSING MATTER TO DISCUSS!
HOW DID YOU GET INTO OUR SECRET HEAD-QUARTERS? JUST WHO ARE YOU?
THERE'S SOMETHING FAMILIAR ABOUT HER, BUT I CAN'T--
I CAN, ATOM! MISS PRINCE IS... WONDER WOMAN!
NO, FLASH--I WAS WONDER WOMAN! I'VE LOST MY AMAZON POWERS!* MY MAIN REASON FOR COMING HERE IS TO...RESIGN!
*THE WHOLE INCREDIBLE TALE OF THE END OF WONDER WOMAN--AND HER STARTLING REBIRTH--IS TOLD IN WONDER WOMAN #178! IT MAKES COMICS HISTORY--AND WE MODESTLY RECOMMEND IT!
I'M NO MORE THAN AN ORDINARY MORTAL NOW...
MUCH AS I ADMIRE THE JUSTICE LEAGUE, I FEEL I NO LONGER HAVE A PLACE IN IT!
FEEL FREE TO RETURN AT ANY TIME ...AND TO CALL UPON US FOR HELP!
RESIGNATION NOT ACCEPTED! HOWEVER, WE WILL GRANT A LEAVE OF ABSENCE!
LOSS OF YOUR SUPER-POWERS DOESN'T CHANGE THE FACT THAT YOU ARE... A FRIEND!
GOOD-BYE... AND THANKS!
GOOD LUCK!
I'VE ALWAYS FELT THAT SOME DAY SUPERMAN MIGHT MARRY HER... NOW, THEY'VE LOST EACH OTHER!
AS AQUAMAN HAS LOST HIS WIFE MERA... AND GREEN LANTERN HAS LOST CAROL FERRIS! SOMETIMES, IT SEEMS THAT WE'RE ALL GETTING OLD...
4

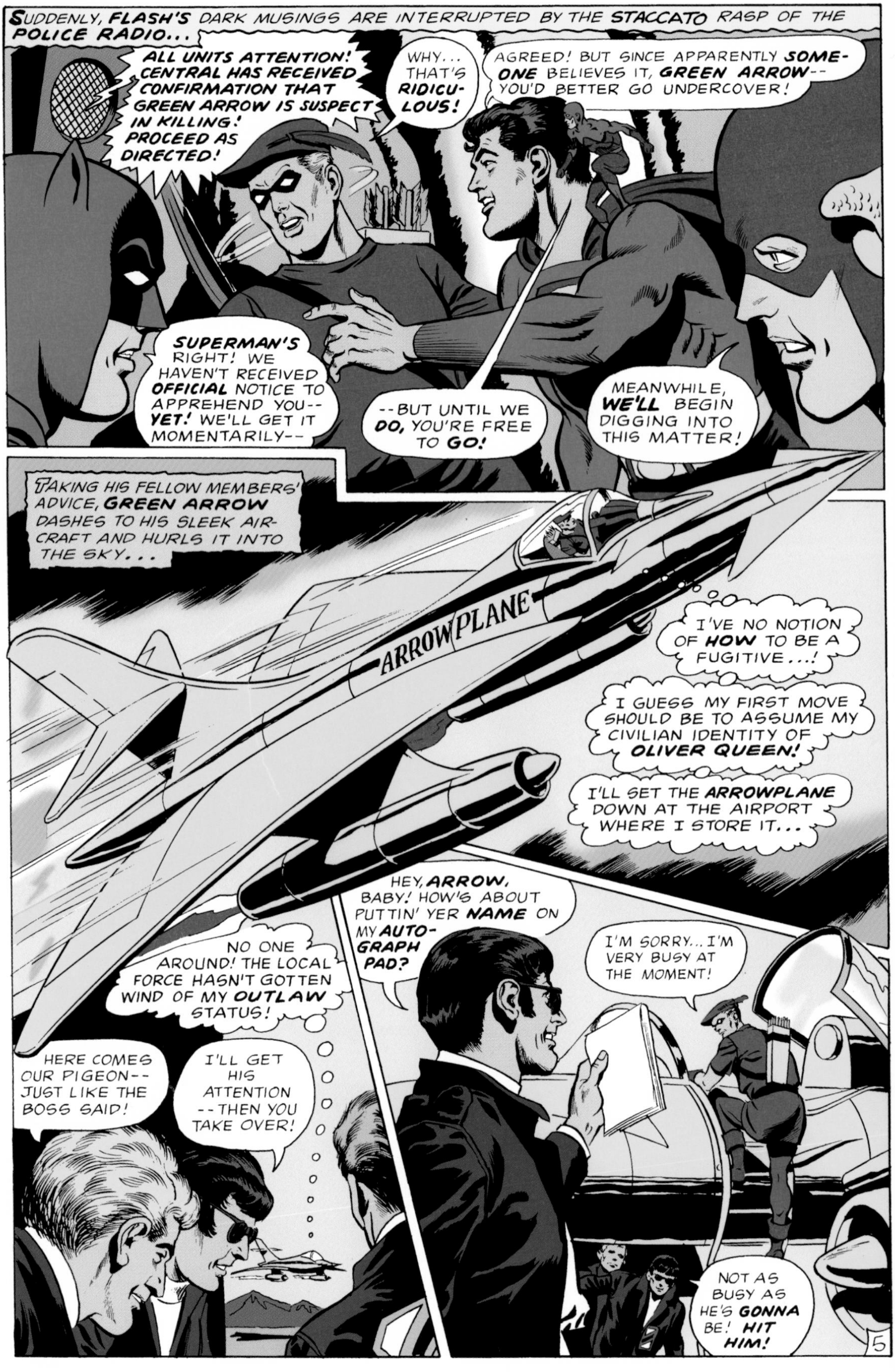
SUDDENLY, FLASH'S DARK MUSINGS ARE INTERRUPTED BY THE STACCATO RASP OF THE POLICE RADIO...
ALL UNITS ATTENTION! CENTRAL HAS RECEIVED CONFIRMATION THAT GREEN ARROW IS SUSPECT IN KILLING! PROCEED AS DIRECTED!
WHY... THAT'S RIDICULOUS!
AGREED! BUT SINCE APPARENTLY SOMEONE BELIEVES IT, GREEN ARROW--YOU'D BETTER GO UNDERCOVER!
SUPERMAN'S RIGHT! WE HAVEN'T RECEIVED OFFICIAL NOTICE TO APPREHEND YOU--YET! WE'LL GET IT MOMENTARILY--
--BUT UNTIL WE DO, YOU'RE FREE TO GO!
MEANWHILE, WE'LL BEGIN DIGGING INTO THIS MATTER!
TAKING HIS FELLOW MEMBERS' ADVICE, GREEN ARROW DASHES TO HIS SLEEK AIRCRAFT AND HURLS IT INTO THE SKY...
ARROWPLANE
I'VE NO NOTION OF HOW TO BE A FUGITIVE...!
I GUESS MY FIRST MOVE SHOULD BE TO ASSUME MY CIVILIAN IDENTITY OF OLIVER QUEEN!
I'LL SET THE ARROWPLANE DOWN AT THE AIRPORT WHERE I STORE IT...
NO ONE AROUND! THE LOCAL FORCE HASN'T GOTTEN WIND OF MY OUTLAW STATUS!
HERE COMES OUR PIGEON--JUST LIKE THE BOSS SAID!
I'LL GET HIS ATTENTION--THEN YOU TAKE OVER!
HEY, ARROW, BABY! HOW'S ABOUT PUTTIN' YER NAME ON MY AUTOGRAPH PAD?
I'M SORRY... I'M VERY BUSY AT THE MOMENT!
NOT AS BUSY AS HE'S GONNA BE! HIT HIM!
5

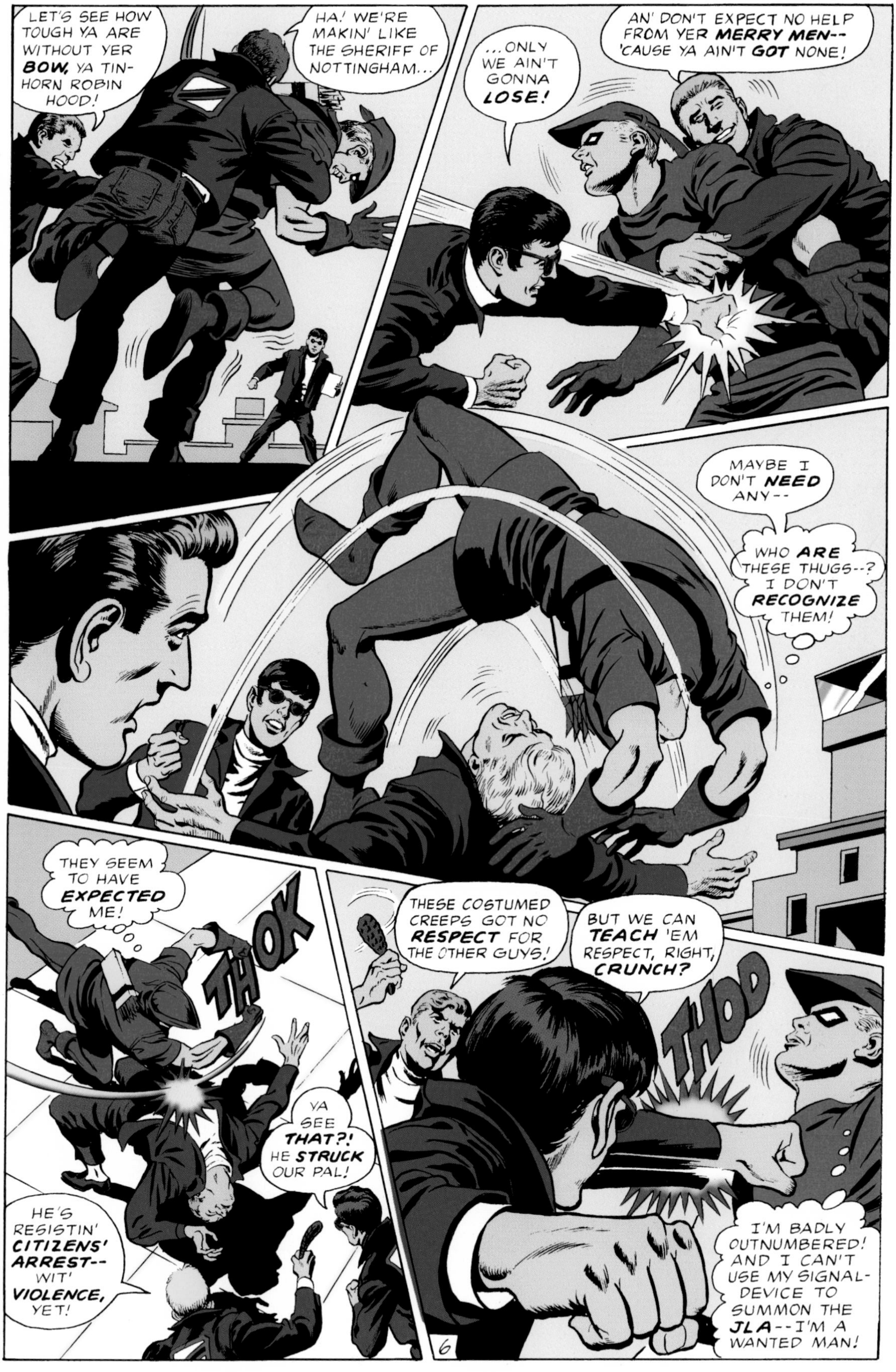
LET'S SEE HOW TOUGH YA ARE WITHOUT YER BOW, YA TIN-HORN ROBIN HOOD!
HA! WE'RE MAKIN' LIKE THE SHERIFF OF NOTTINGHAM...
...ONLY WE AIN'T GONNA LOSE!
AN' DON'T EXPECT NO HELP FROM YER MERRY MEN-- 'CAUSE YA AIN'T GOT NONE!
MAYBE I DON'T NEED ANY--
WHO ARE THESE THUGS--? I DON'T RECOGNIZE THEM!
THEY SEEM TO HAVE EXPECTED ME!
THOK
HE'S RESISTIN' CITIZENS' ARREST-- WIT' VIOLENCE, YET!
YA SEE THAT?! HE STRUCK OUR PAL!
THESE COSTUMED CREEPS GOT NO RESPECT FOR THE OTHER GUYS!
BUT WE CAN TEACH 'EM RESPECT, RIGHT, CRUNCH?
THOD
I'M BADLY OUTNUMBERED! AND I CAN'T USE MY SIGNAL-DEVICE TO SUMMON THE JLA--I'M A WANTED MAN!
6

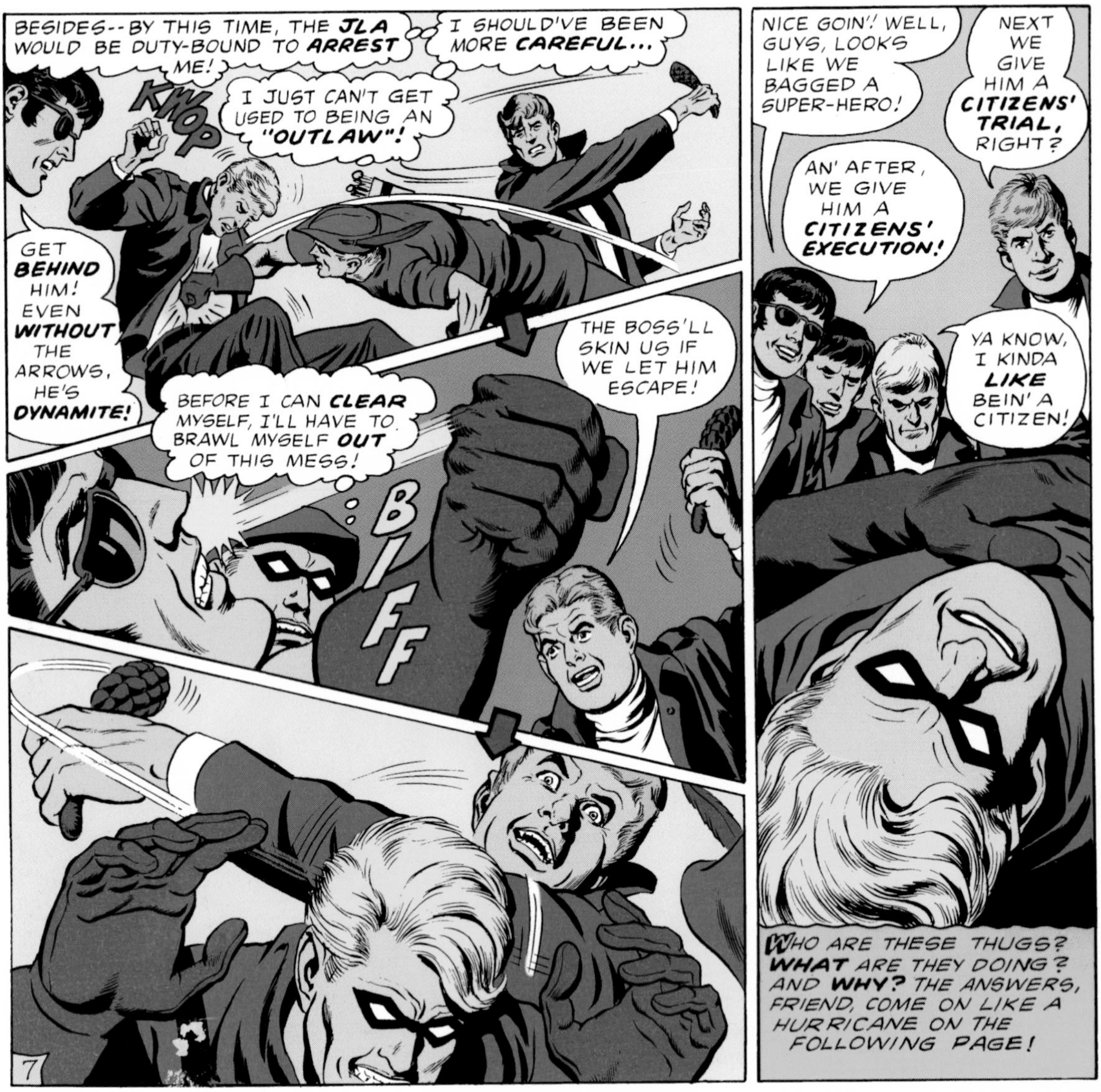
BESIDES--BY THIS TIME, THE JLA WOULD BE DUTY-BOUND TO ARREST ME!
I SHOULD'VE BEEN MORE CAREFUL...
KWOP
I JUST CAN'T GET USED TO BEING AN "OUTLAW"!
GET BEHIND HIM! EVEN WITHOUT THE ARROWS, HE'S DYNAMITE!
BEFORE I CAN CLEAR MYSELF, I'LL HAVE TO BRAWL MYSELF OUT OF THIS MESS!
THE BOSS'LL SKIN US IF WE LET HIM ESCAPE!
BIFF
7
NICE GOIN'! WELL, GUYS, LOOKS LIKE WE BAGGED A SUPER-HERO!
NEXT WE GIVE HIM A CITIZENS' TRIAL, RIGHT?
AN' AFTER, WE GIVE HIM A CITIZENS' EXECUTION!
YA KNOW, I KINDA LIKE BEIN' A CITIZEN!
WHO ARE THESE THUGS? WHAT ARE THEY DOING? AND WHY? THE ANSWERS, FRIEND, COME ON LIKE A HURRICANE ON THE FOLLOWING PAGE!

JUSTICE LEAGUE of AMERICA

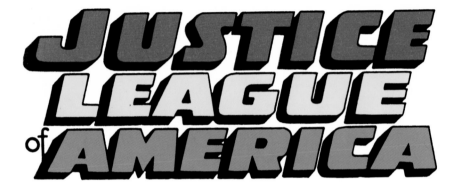

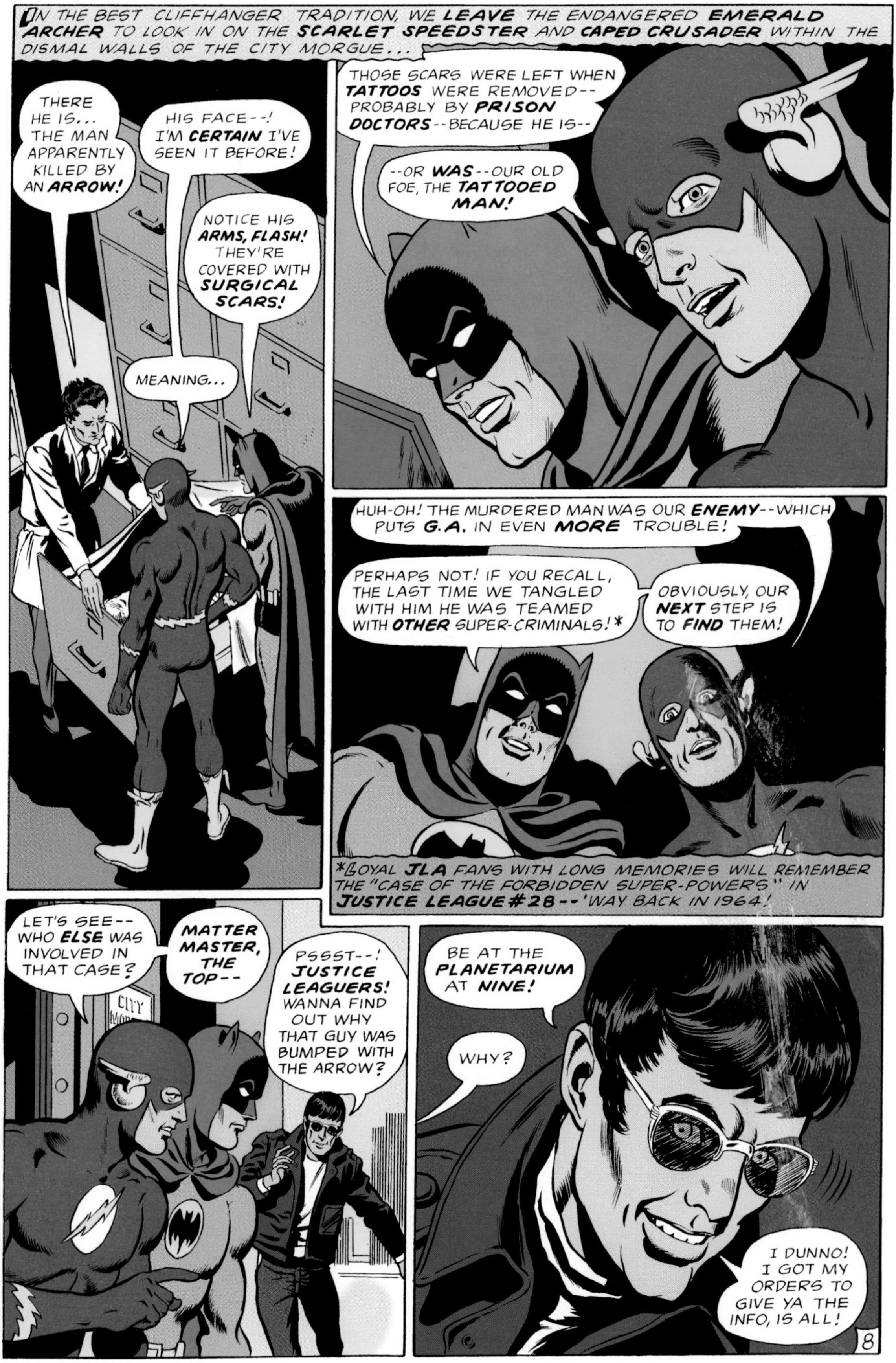
IN THE BEST CLIFFHANGER TRADITION, WE LEAVE THE ENDANGERED EMERALD ARCHER TO LOOK IN ON THE SCARLET SPEEDSTER AND CAPED CRUSADER WITHIN THE DISMAL WALLS OF THE CITY MORGUE...
THERE HE IS... THE MAN APPARENTLY KILLED BY AN ARROW!
HIS FACE--! I'M CERTAIN I'VE SEEN IT BEFORE!
NOTICE HIS ARMS, FLASH! THEY'RE COVERED WITH SURGICAL SCARS!
MEANING...
THOSE SCARS WERE LEFT WHEN TATTOOS WERE REMOVED--PROBABLY BY PRISON DOCTORS--BECAUSE HE IS--
--OR WAS--OUR OLD FOE, THE TATTOOED MAN!
HUH-OH! THE MURDERED MAN WAS OUR ENEMY--WHICH PUTS G.A. IN EVEN MORE TROUBLE!
PERHAPS NOT! IF YOU RECALL, THE LAST TIME WE TANGLED WITH HIM HE WAS TEAMED WITH OTHER SUPER-CRIMINALS!*
OBVIOUSLY, OUR NEXT STEP IS TO FIND THEM!
*LOYAL JLA FANS WITH LONG MEMORIES WILL REMEMBER THE "CASE OF THE FORBIDDEN SUPER-POWERS" IN JUSTICE LEAGUE #28--'WAY BACK IN 1964!
LET'S SEE--WHO ELSE WAS INVOLVED IN THAT CASE?
MATTER MASTER, THE TOP--
PSSST--! JUSTICE LEAGUERS! WANNA FIND OUT WHY THAT GUY WAS BUMPED WITH THE ARROW?
BE AT THE PLANETARIUM AT NINE!
WHY?
I DUNNO! I GOT MY ORDERS TO GIVE YA THE INFO, IS ALL!
8

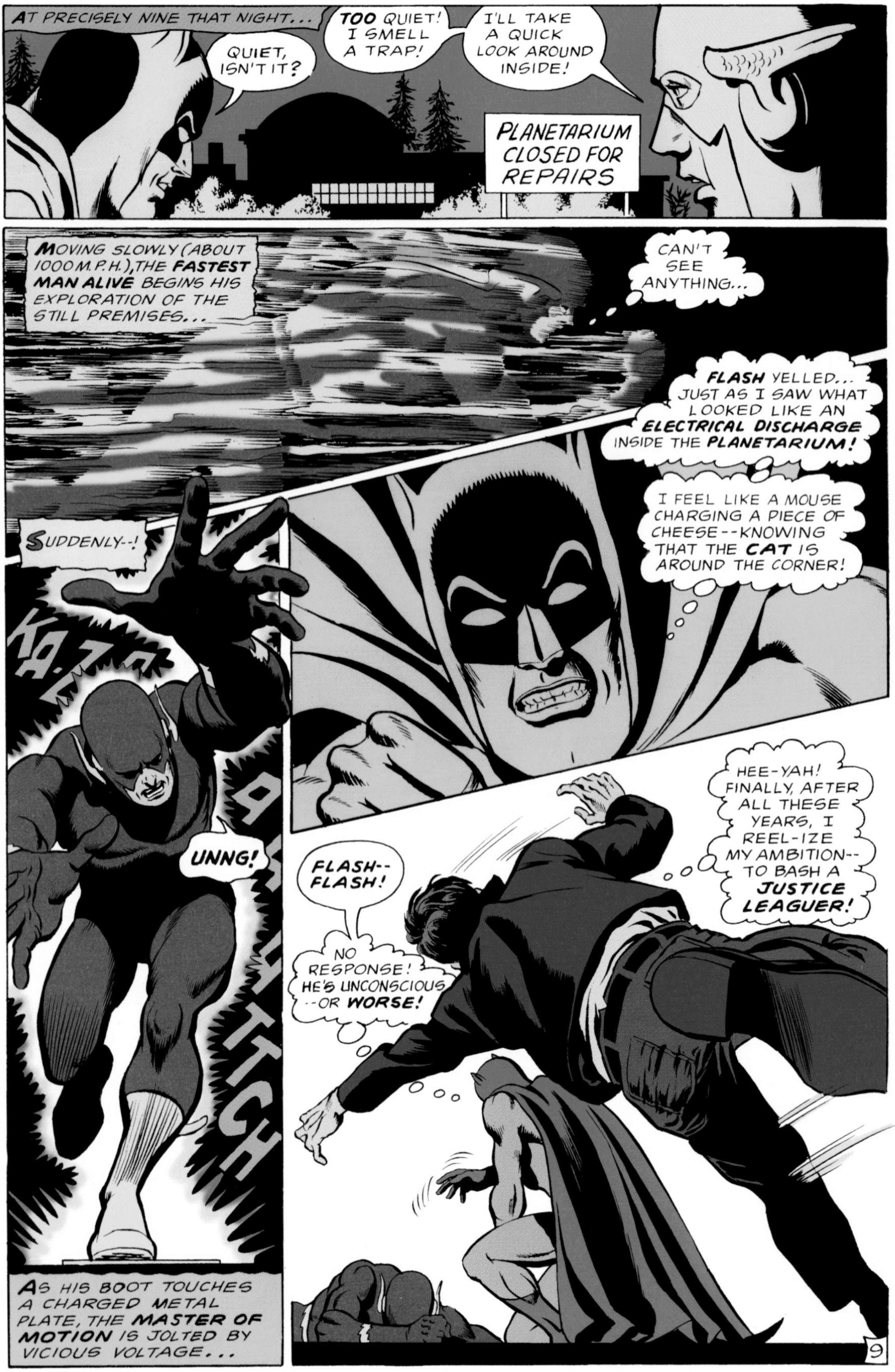
AT PRECISELY NINE THAT NIGHT...
QUIET, ISN'T IT?
TOO QUIET! I SMELL A TRAP!
I'LL TAKE A QUICK LOOK AROUND INSIDE!
PLANETARIUM CLOSED FOR REPAIRS
MOVING SLOWLY (ABOUT 1000 M.P.H.), THE FASTEST MAN ALIVE BEGINS HIS EXPLORATION OF THE STILL PREMISES...
CAN'T SEE ANYTHING...
SUDDENLY--!
FLASH YELLED... JUST AS I SAW WHAT LOOKED LIKE AN ELECTRICAL DISCHARGE INSIDE THE PLANETARIUM!
I FEEL LIKE A MOUSE CHARGING A PIECE OF CHEESE--KNOWING THAT THE CAT IS AROUND THE CORNER!
UNNG!
AS HIS BOOT TOUCHES A CHARGED METAL PLATE, THE MASTER OF MOTION IS JOLTED BY VICIOUS VOLTAGE...
FLASH-- FLASH!
NO RESPONSE! HE'S UNCONSCIOUS --OR WORSE!
HEE-YAH! FINALLY, AFTER ALL THESE YEARS, I REEL-IZE MY AMBITION-- TO BASH A JUSTICE LEAGUER!
9

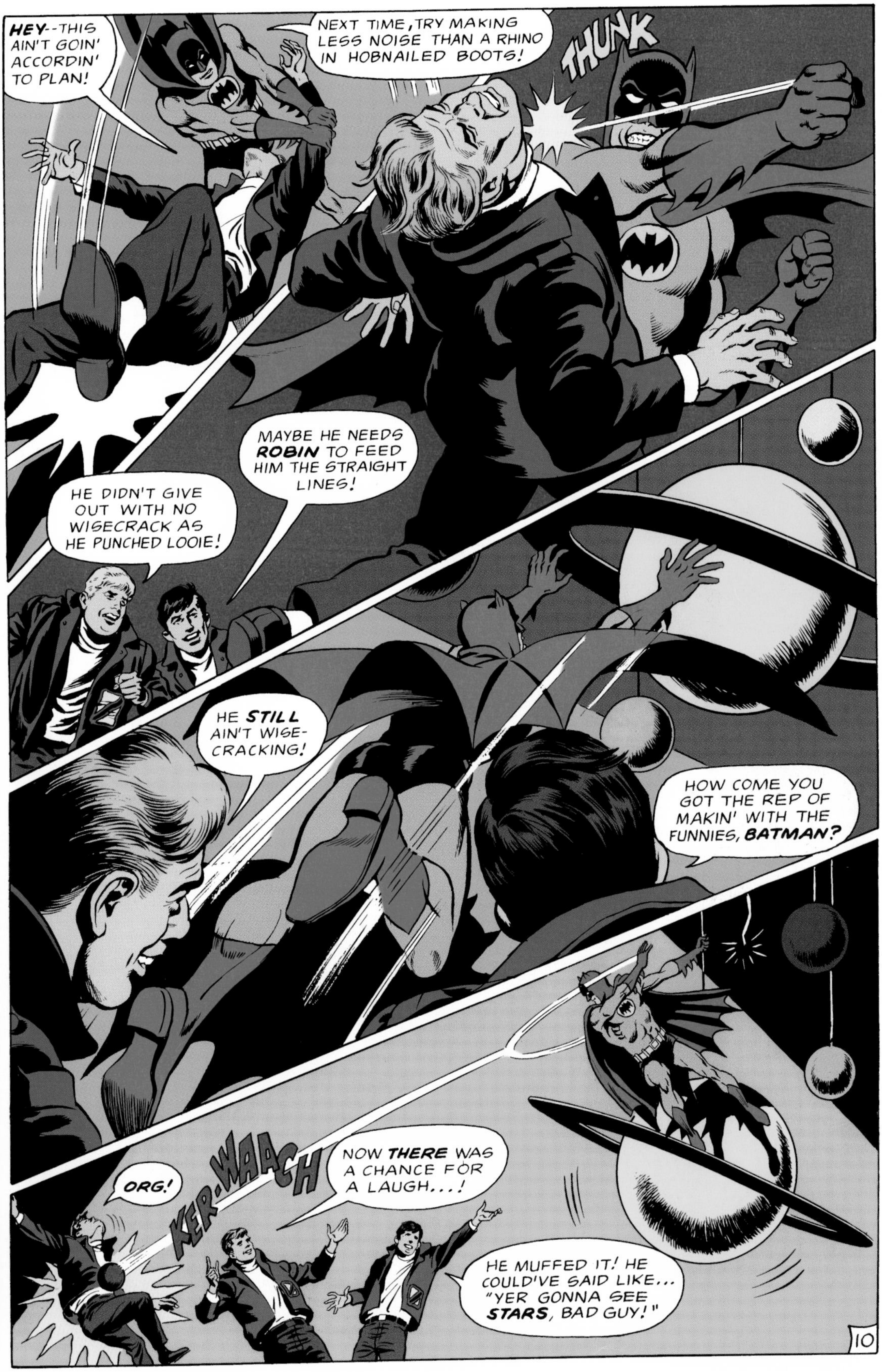
HEY--THIS AIN'T GOIN' ACCORDIN' TO PLAN!
NEXT TIME, TRY MAKING LESS NOISE THAN A RHINO IN HOBNAILED BOOTS!
THUNK
MAYBE HE NEEDS ROBIN TO FEED HIM THE STRAIGHT LINES!
HE DIDN'T GIVE OUT WITH NO WISECRACK AS HE PUNCHED LOOIE!
HE STILL AIN'T WISE-CRACKING!
HOW COME YOU GOT THE REP OF MAKIN' WITH THE FUNNIES, BATMAN?
ORG!
KER-WAACH
NOW THERE WAS A CHANCE FOR A LAUGH...!
HE MUFFED IT! HE COULD'VE SAID LIKE... "YER GONNA SEE STARS, BAD GUY!"
10

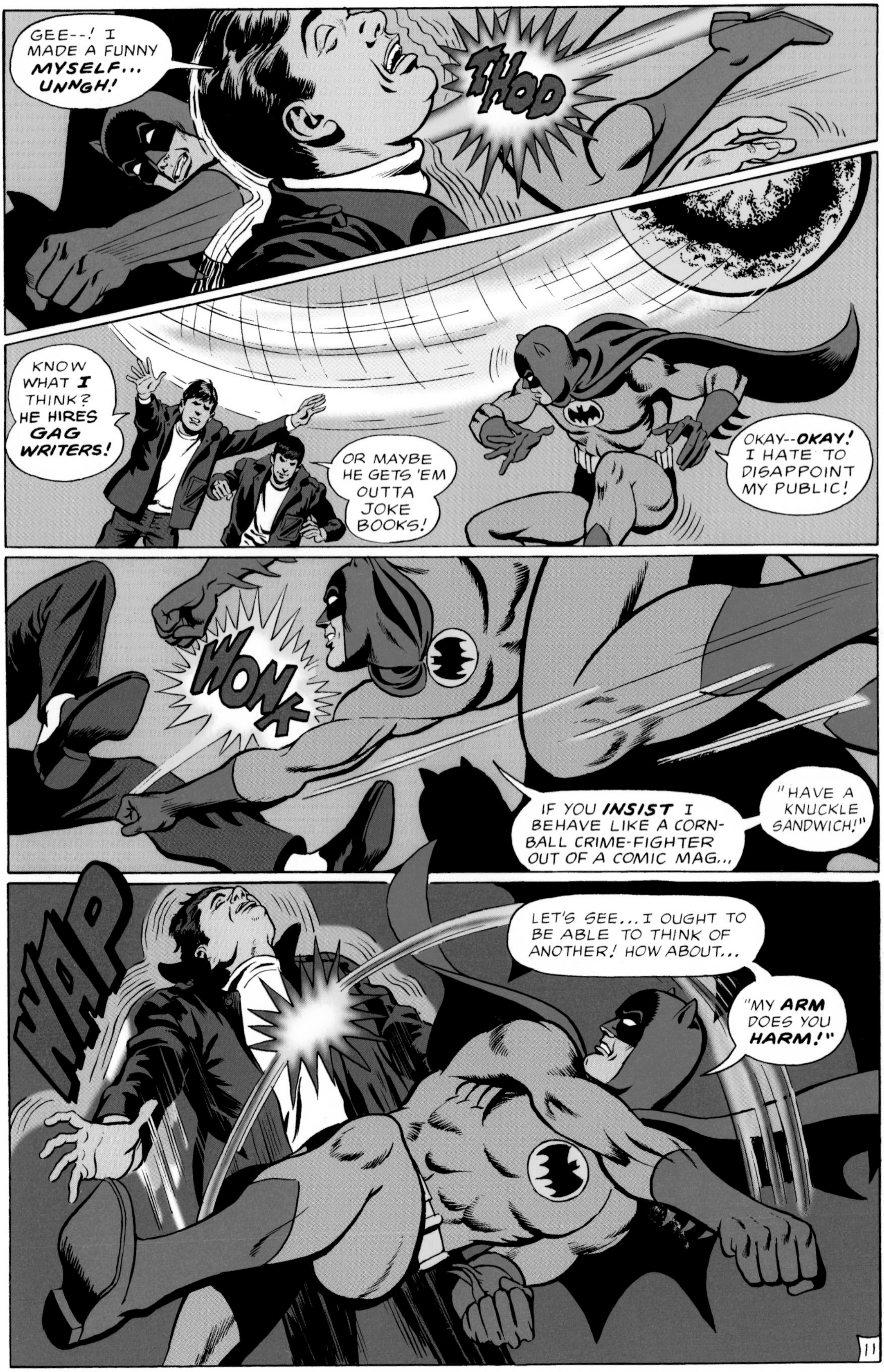
GEE--! I MADE A FUNNY MYSELF... UNNGH!
THOD
KNOW WHAT I THINK? HE HIRES GAG WRITERS!
OR MAYBE HE GETS 'EM OUTTA JOKE BOOKS!
OKAY--OKAY! I HATE TO DISAPPOINT MY PUBLIC!
WONK
IF YOU INSIST I BEHAVE LIKE A CORN-BALL CRIME-FIGHTER OUT OF A COMIC MAG...
"HAVE A KNUCKLE SANDWICH!"
WAP
LET'S SEE... I OUGHT TO BE ABLE TO THINK OF ANOTHER! HOW ABOUT...
"MY ARM DOES YOU HARM!"
11

I HAVE ONE, TOO, BATMAN... "MY GUN STOPS YOUR FUN!"
HIT... BY AN ANESTHETIC DART...
PASSING OUT...
GREEN ARROW... FLASH... AND NOW BATMAN! SOON, I SHALL HAVE ALL THE MEMBERS OF THE CURSED JUSTICE LEAGUE...
AND MY VENGEANCE WILL BE COMPLETE!
12
WITH THIS HIGH-FLOWN THREAT--IN THE BEST TRADITION OF VILLAINOUS BLABBER-MOUTHING--WE LEAVE YOU TO GUESS THE BAD GUY'S IDENTITY AS WE MOVE ON TO THE NEXT PAGE!

JUSTICE LEAGUE of AMERICA

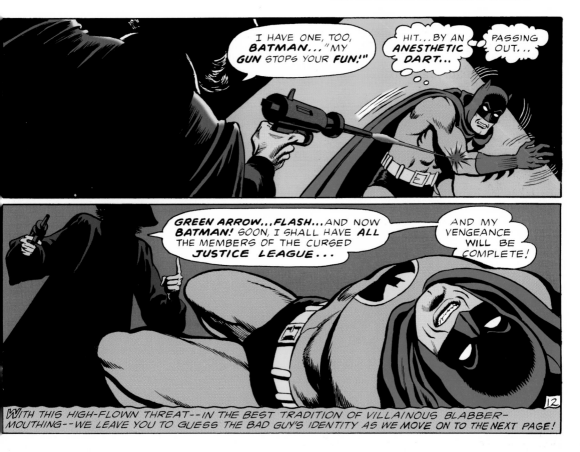

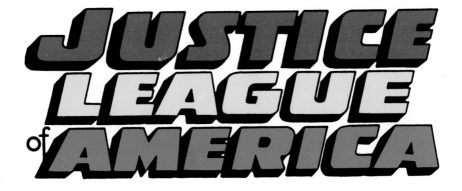

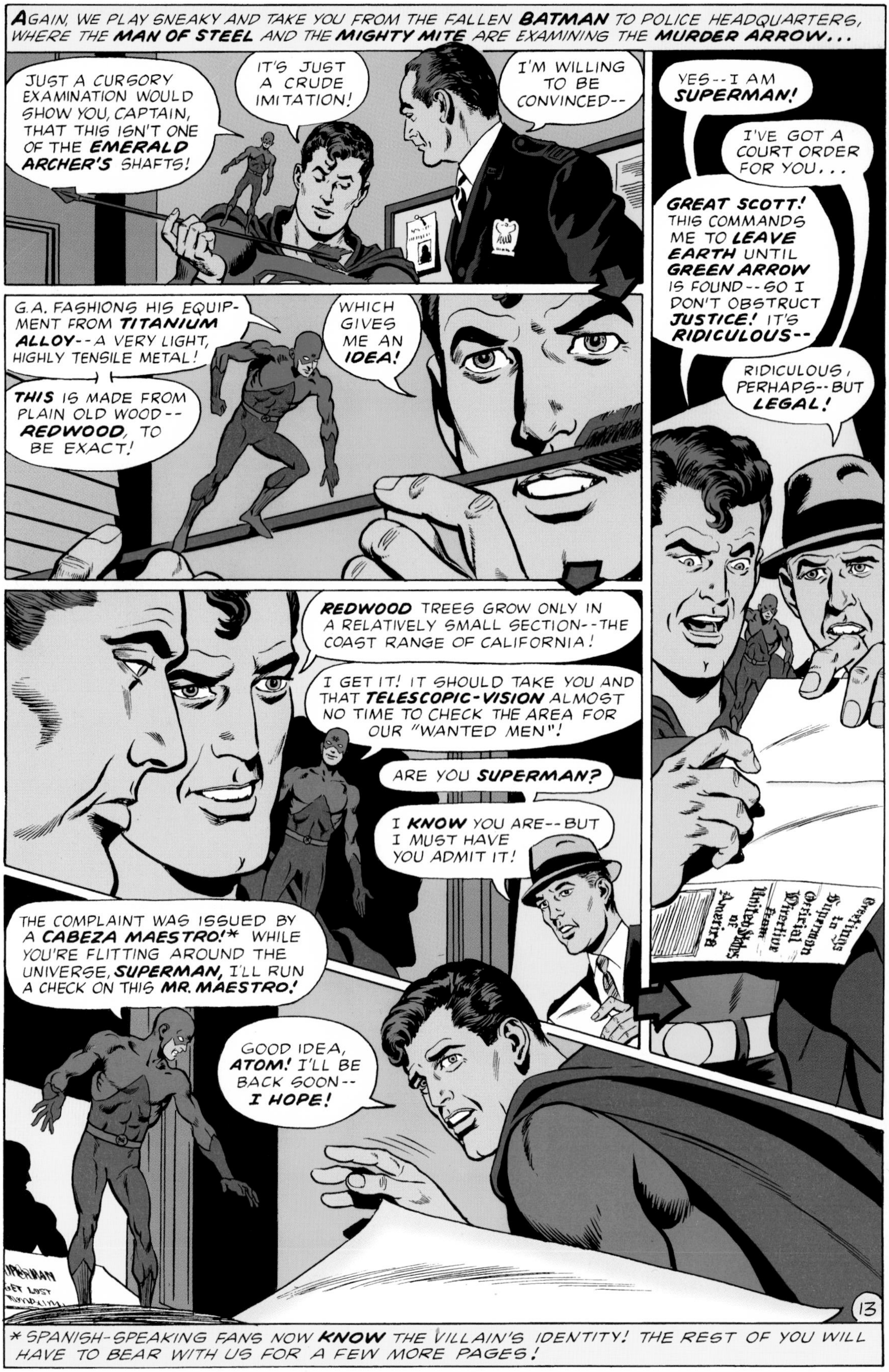
AGAIN, WE PLAY SNEAKY AND TAKE YOU FROM THE FALLEN BATMAN TO POLICE HEADQUARTERS, WHERE THE MAN OF STEEL AND THE MIGHTY MITE ARE EXAMINING THE MURDER ARROW...
JUST A CURSORY EXAMINATION WOULD SHOW YOU, CAPTAIN, THAT THIS ISN'T ONE OF THE EMERALD ARCHER'S SHAFTS!
IT'S JUST A CRUDE IMITATION!
I'M WILLING TO BE CONVINCED--
G.A. FASHIONS HIS EQUIPMENT FROM TITANIUM ALLOY--A VERY LIGHT, HIGHLY TENSILE METAL!
THIS IS MADE FROM PLAIN OLD WOOD--REDWOOD, TO BE EXACT!
WHICH GIVES ME AN IDEA!
REDWOOD TREES GROW ONLY IN A RELATIVELY SMALL SECTION--THE COAST RANGE OF CALIFORNIA!
I GET IT! IT SHOULD TAKE YOU AND THAT TELESCOPIC-VISION ALMOST NO TIME TO CHECK THE AREA FOR OUR "WANTED MEN"!
ARE YOU SUPERMAN?
I KNOW YOU ARE--BUT I MUST HAVE YOU ADMIT IT!
YES--I AM SUPERMAN!
I'VE GOT A COURT ORDER FOR YOU...
GREAT SCOTT! THIS COMMANDS ME TO LEAVE EARTH UNTIL GREEN ARROW IS FOUND--SO I DON'T OBSTRUCT JUSTICE! IT'S RIDICULOUS--
RIDICULOUS, PERHAPS--BUT LEGAL!
THE COMPLAINT WAS ISSUED BY A CABEZA MAESTRO!* WHILE YOU'RE FLITTING AROUND THE UNIVERSE, SUPERMAN, I'LL RUN A CHECK ON THIS MR. MAESTRO!
GOOD IDEA, ATOM! I'LL BE BACK SOON--I HOPE!
13
* SPANISH-SPEAKING FANS NOW KNOW THE VILLAIN'S IDENTITY! THE REST OF YOU WILL HAVE TO BEAR WITH US FOR A FEW MORE PAGES!

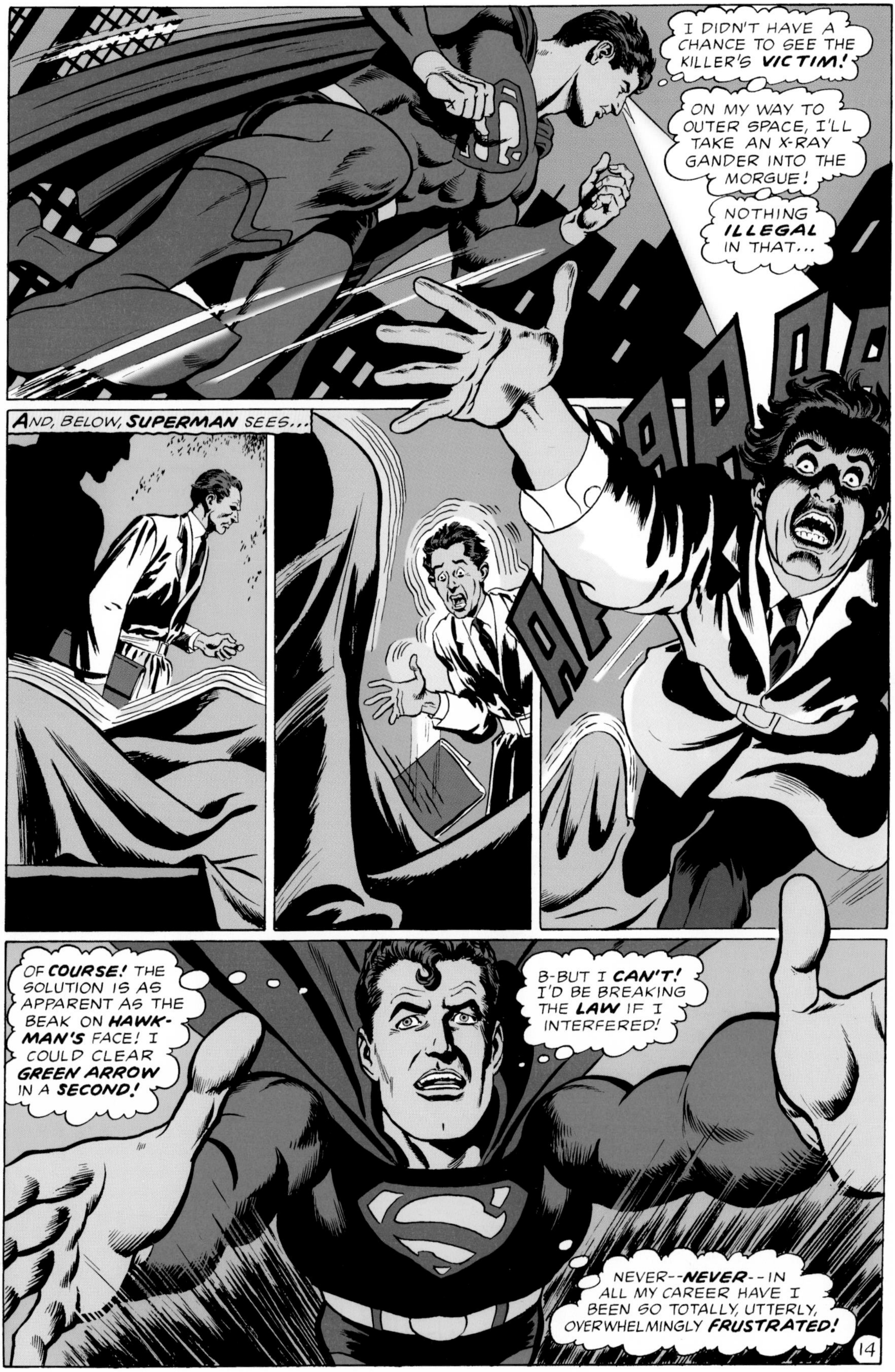
I DIDN'T HAVE A CHANCE TO SEE THE KILLER'S VICTIM!
ON MY WAY TO OUTER SPACE, I'LL TAKE AN X-RAY GANDER INTO THE MORGUE!
NOTHING ILLEGAL IN THAT...
AND, BELOW, SUPERMAN SEES...
OF COURSE! THE SOLUTION IS AS APPARENT AS THE BEAK ON HAWK-MAN'S FACE! I COULD CLEAR GREEN ARROW IN A SECOND!
B-BUT I CAN'T! I'D BE BREAKING THE LAW IF I INTERFERED!
NEVER--NEVER--IN ALL MY CAREER HAVE I BEEN SO TOTALLY, UTTERLY, OVERWHELMINGLY FRUSTRATED!
14

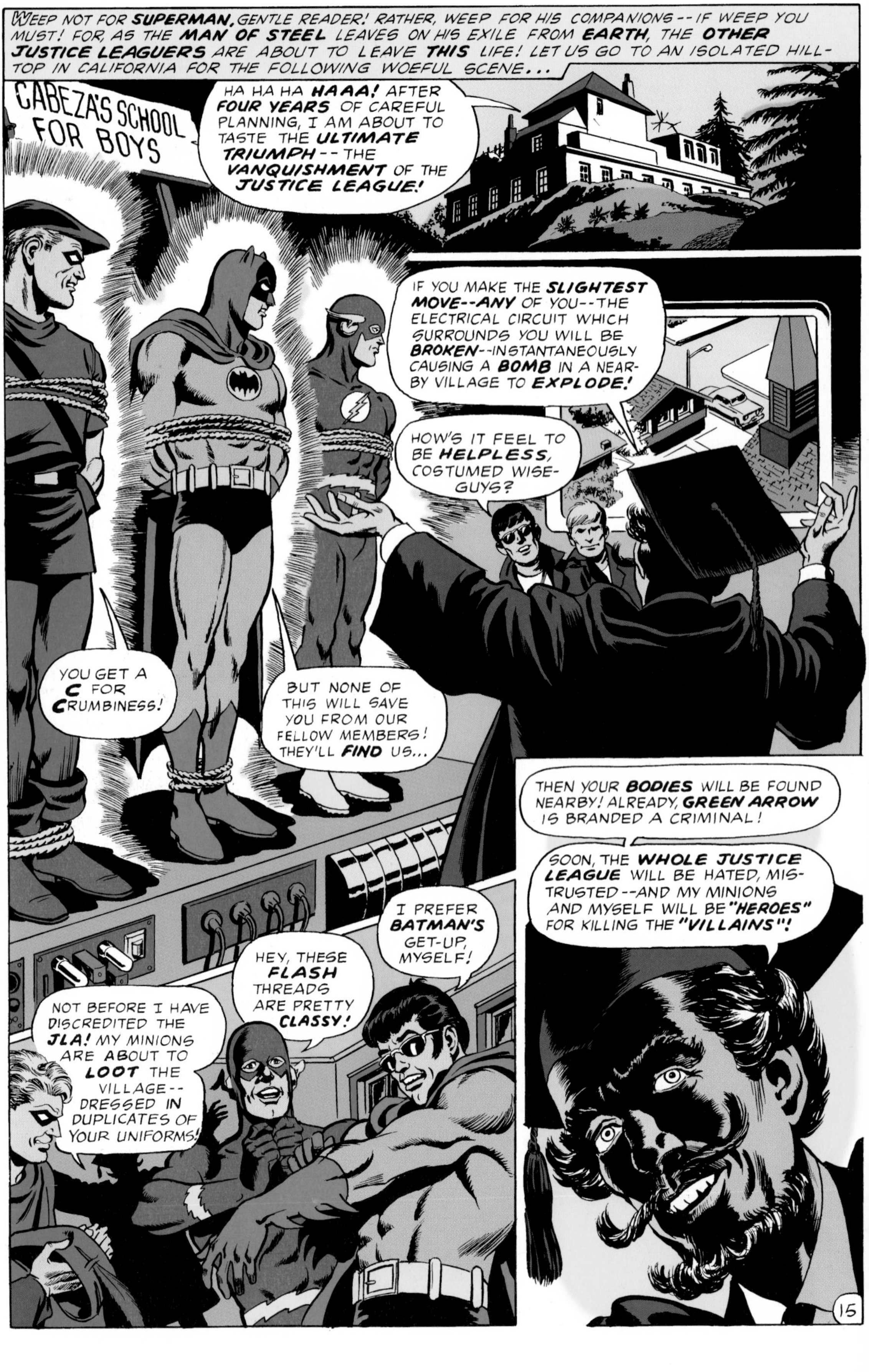
WEEP NOT FOR SUPERMAN, GENTLE READER! RATHER, WEEP FOR HIS COMPANIONS -- IF WEEP YOU MUST! FOR, AS THE MAN OF STEEL LEAVES ON HIS EXILE FROM EARTH, THE OTHER JUSTICE LEAGUERS ARE ABOUT TO LEAVE THIS LIFE! LET US GO TO AN ISOLATED HILL-TOP IN CALIFORNIA FOR THE FOLLOWING WOEFUL SCENE...
CABEZA'S SCHOOL FOR BOYS
HA HA HA HAAA! AFTER FOUR YEARS OF CAREFUL PLANNING, I AM ABOUT TO TASTE THE ULTIMATE TRIUMPH -- THE VANQUISHMENT OF THE JUSTICE LEAGUE!
IF YOU MAKE THE SLIGHTEST MOVE--ANY OF YOU--THE ELECTRICAL CIRCUIT WHICH SURROUNDS YOU WILL BE BROKEN--INSTANTANEOUSLY CAUSING A BOMB IN A NEAR-BY VILLAGE TO EXPLODE!
HOW'S IT FEEL TO BE HELPLESS, COSTUMED WISE-GUYS?
YOU GET A C FOR CRUMBINESS!
BUT NONE OF THIS WILL SAVE YOU FROM OUR FELLOW MEMBERS! THEY'LL FIND US...
THEN YOUR BODIES WILL BE FOUND NEARBY! ALREADY, GREEN ARROW IS BRANDED A CRIMINAL!
SOON, THE WHOLE JUSTICE LEAGUE WILL BE HATED, MIS-TRUSTED --AND MY MINIONS AND MYSELF WILL BE "HEROES" FOR KILLING THE "VILLAINS"!
NOT BEFORE I HAVE DISCREDITED THE JLA! MY MINIONS ARE ABOUT TO LOOT THE VILLAGE -- DRESSED IN DUPLICATES OF YOUR UNIFORMS!
HEY, THESE FLASH THREADS ARE PRETTY CLASSY!
I PREFER BATMAN'S GET-UP, MYSELF!
15

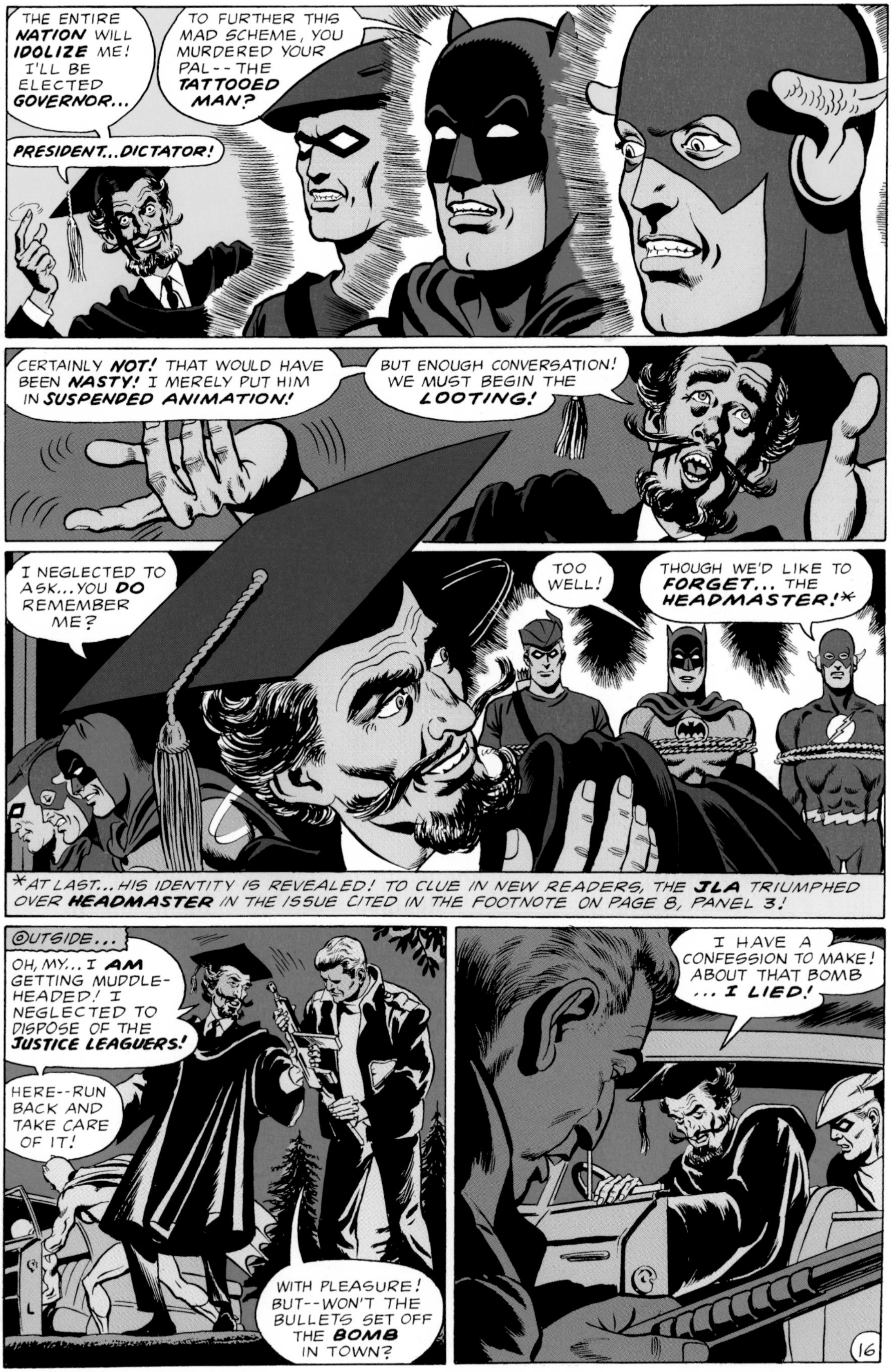
THE ENTIRE NATION WILL IDOLIZE ME! I'LL BE ELECTED GOVERNOR...
PRESIDENT...DICTATOR!
TO FURTHER THIS MAD SCHEME, YOU MURDERED YOUR PAL--THE TATTOOED MAN?
CERTAINLY NOT! THAT WOULD HAVE BEEN NASTY! I MERELY PUT HIM IN SUSPENDED ANIMATION!
BUT ENOUGH CONVERSATION! WE MUST BEGIN THE LOOTING!
I NEGLECTED TO ASK...YOU DO REMEMBER ME?
TOO WELL!
THOUGH WE'D LIKE TO FORGET... THE HEADMASTER!*
*AT LAST...HIS IDENTITY IS REVEALED! TO CLUE IN NEW READERS, THE JLA TRIUMPHED OVER HEADMASTER IN THE ISSUE CITED IN THE FOOTNOTE ON PAGE 8, PANEL 3!
OUTSIDE...
OH, MY... I AM GETTING MUDDLE-HEADED! I NEGLECTED TO DISPOSE OF THE JUSTICE LEAGUERS!
HERE--RUN BACK AND TAKE CARE OF IT!
WITH PLEASURE! BUT--WON'T THE BULLETS SET OFF THE BOMB IN TOWN?
I HAVE A CONFESSION TO MAKE! ABOUT THAT BOMB ... I LIED!
16

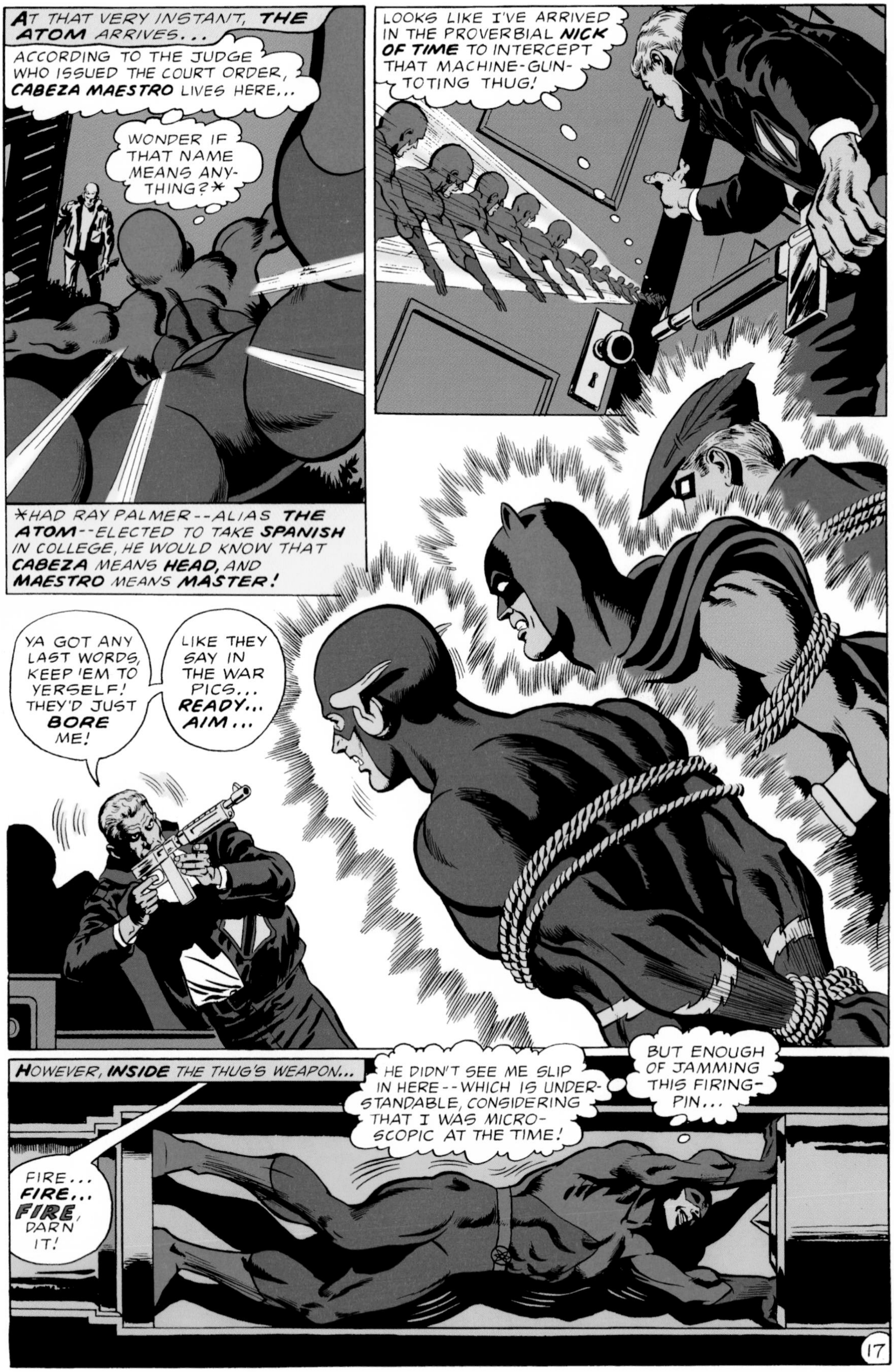
AT THAT VERY INSTANT, THE ATOM ARRIVES...
ACCORDING TO THE JUDGE WHO ISSUED THE COURT ORDER, CABEZA MAESTRO LIVES HERE...
WONDER IF THAT NAME MEANS ANY-THING?*
LOOKS LIKE I'VE ARRIVED IN THE PROVERBIAL NICK OF TIME TO INTERCEPT THAT MACHINE-GUN-TOTING THUG!
*HAD RAY PALMER--ALIAS THE ATOM--ELECTED TO TAKE SPANISH IN COLLEGE, HE WOULD KNOW THAT CABEZA MEANS HEAD, AND MAESTRO MEANS MASTER!
YA GOT ANY LAST WORDS, KEEP 'EM TO YERSELF! THEY'D JUST BORE ME!
LIKE THEY SAY IN THE WAR PICS... READY... AIM...
HOWEVER, INSIDE THE THUG'S WEAPON...
FIRE... FIRE... FIRE, DARN IT!
HE DIDN'T SEE ME SLIP IN HERE--WHICH IS UNDER-STANDABLE, CONSIDERING THAT I WAS MICRO-SCOPIC AT THE TIME!
BUT ENOUGH OF JAMMING THIS FIRING-PIN...
17

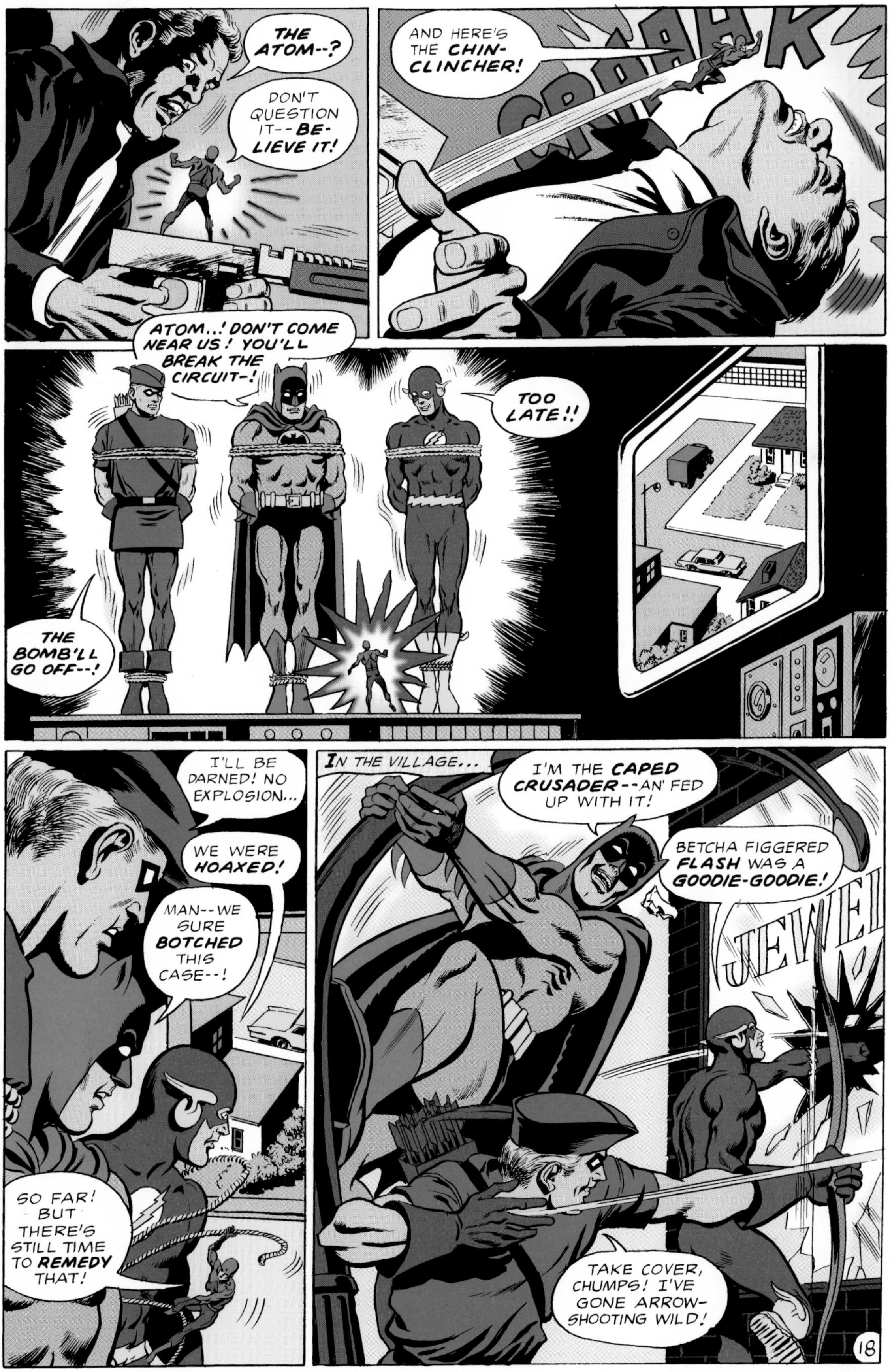
THE ATOM--?
DON'T QUESTION IT--BE-LIEVE IT!
AND HERE'S THE CHIN-CLINCHER!
ATOM..! DON'T COME NEAR US! YOU'LL BREAK THE CIRCUIT-!
TOO LATE!!
THE BOMB'LL GO OFF--!
I'LL BE DARNED! NO EXPLOSION...
WE WERE HOAXED!
MAN--WE SURE BOTCHED THIS CASE--!
SO FAR! BUT THERE'S STILL TIME TO REMEDY THAT!
IN THE VILLAGE...
I'M THE CAPED CRUSADER--AN' FED UP WITH IT!
BETCHA FIGGERED FLASH WAS A GOODIE-GOODIE!
TAKE COVER, CHUMPS! I'VE GONE ARROW-SHOOTING WILD!
18

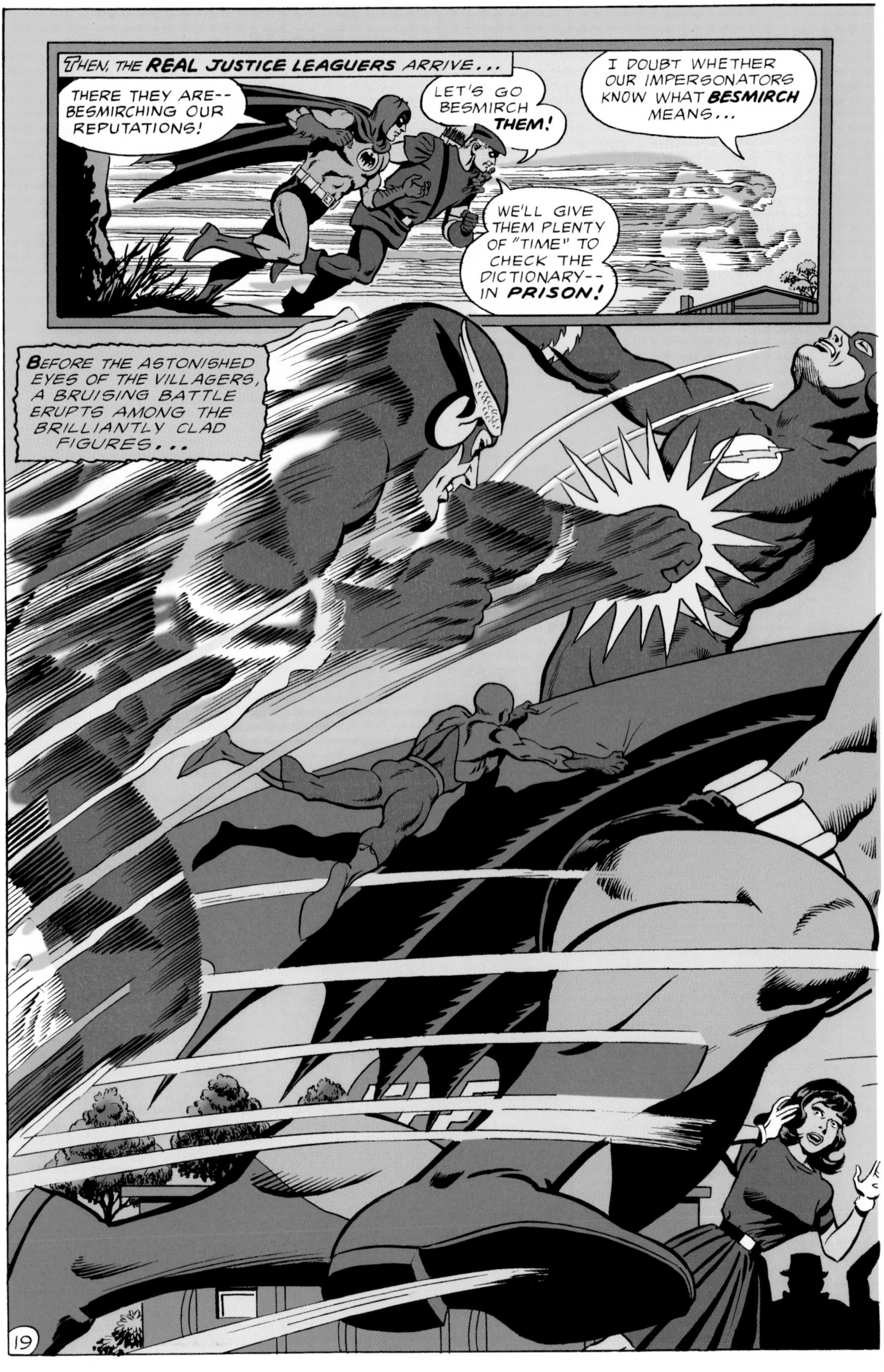
THEN, THE REAL JUSTICE LEAGUERS ARRIVE...
THERE THEY ARE-- BESMIRCHING OUR REPUTATIONS!
LET'S GO BESMIRCH THEM!
I DOUBT WHETHER OUR IMPERSONATORS KNOW WHAT BESMIRCH MEANS...
WE'LL GIVE THEM PLENTY OF "TIME" TO CHECK THE DICTIONARY-- IN PRISON!
BEFORE THE ASTONISHED EYES OF THE VILLAGERS, A BRUISING BATTLE ERUPTS AMONG THE BRILLIANTLY CLAD FIGURES...
19

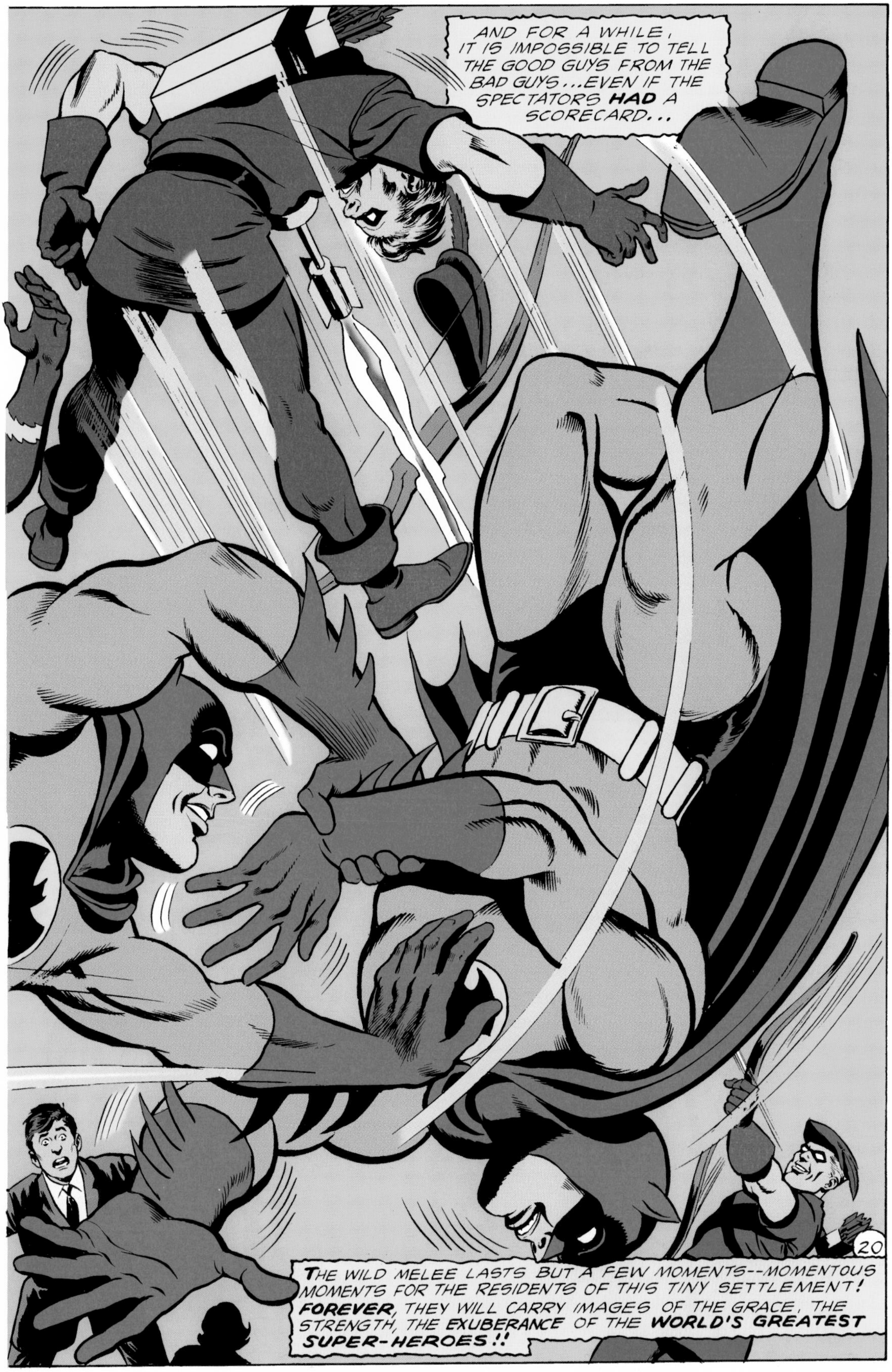
AND FOR A WHILE, IT IS IMPOSSIBLE TO TELL THE GOOD GUYS FROM THE BAD GUYS...EVEN IF THE SPECTATORS HAD A SCORECARD...
20
THE WILD MELEE LASTS BUT A FEW MOMENTS--MOMENTOUS MOMENTS FOR THE RESIDENTS OF THIS TINY SETTLEMENT! FOREVER, THEY WILL CARRY IMAGES OF THE GRACE, THE STRENGTH, THE EXUBERANCE OF THE WORLD'S GREATEST SUPER-HEROES!!

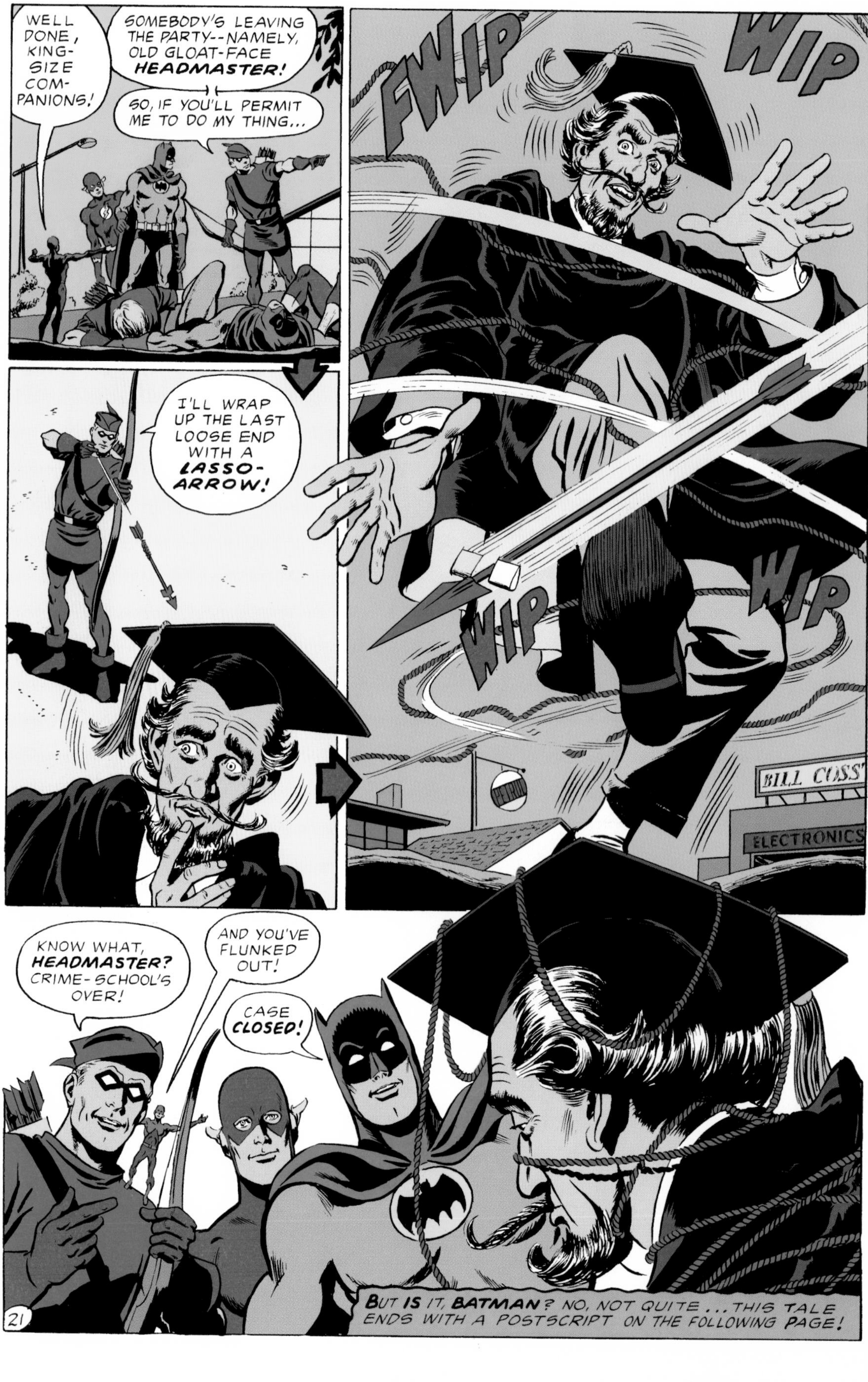

WELL DONE, KING-SIZE COMPANIONS!
SOMEBODY'S LEAVING THE PARTY--NAMELY, OLD GLOAT-FACE HEADMASTER!
SO, IF YOU'LL PERMIT ME TO DO MY THING...
I'LL WRAP UP THE LAST LOOSE END WITH A LASSO-ARROW!
FWIP
WIP
WIP
WIP
PETROL
BILL COSS
ELECTRONICS
KNOW WHAT, HEADMASTER? CRIME-SCHOOL'S OVER!
AND YOU'VE FLUNKED OUT!
CASE CLOSED!
BUT IS IT, BATMAN? NO, NOT QUITE ... THIS TALE ENDS WITH A POSTSCRIPT ON THE FOLLOWING PAGE!
21

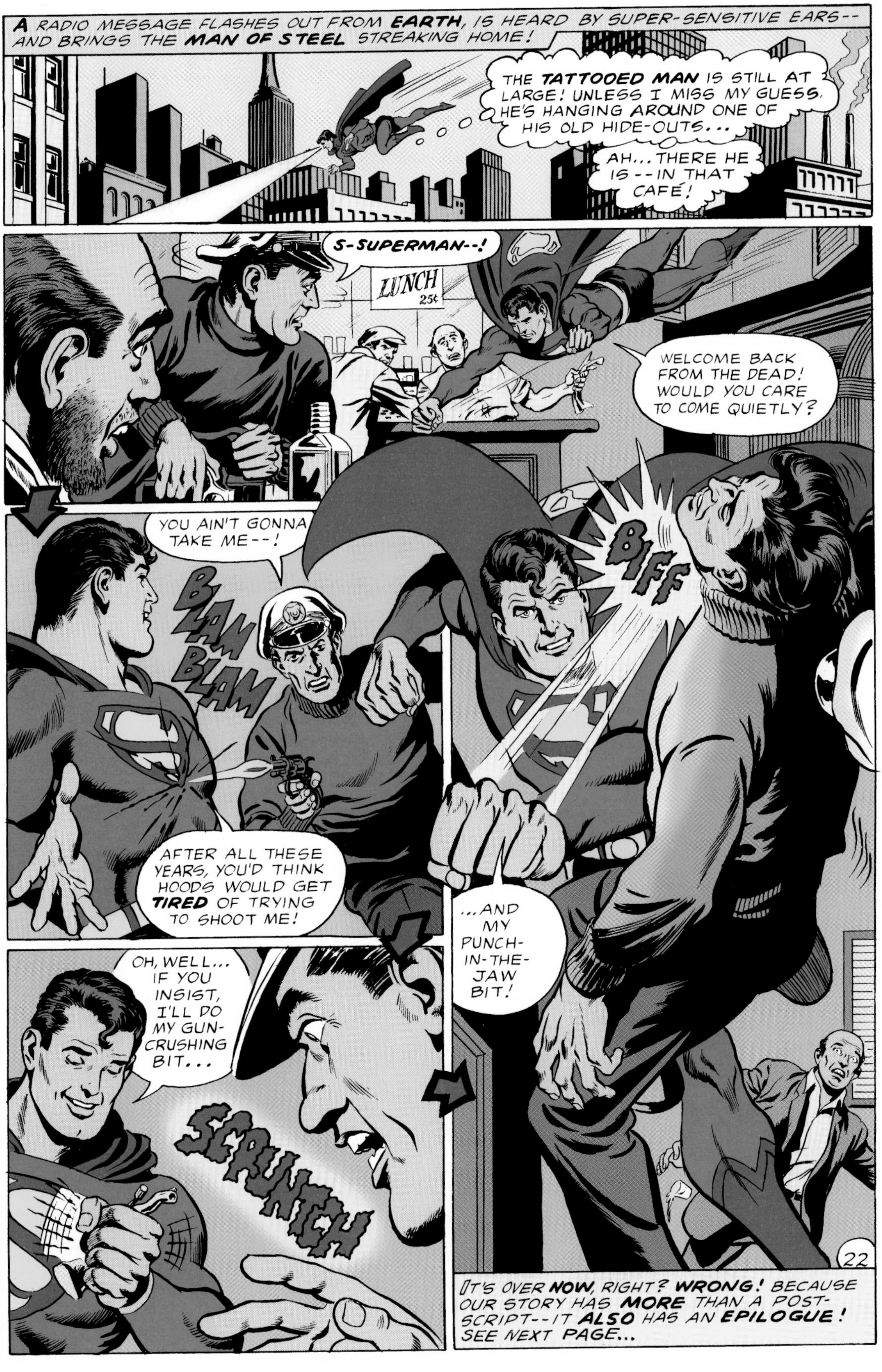
A RADIO MESSAGE FLASHES OUT FROM EARTH, IS HEARD BY SUPER-SENSITIVE EARS-- AND BRINGS THE MAN OF STEEL STREAKING HOME!
THE TATTOOED MAN IS STILL AT LARGE! UNLESS I MISS MY GUESS, HE'S HANGING AROUND ONE OF HIS OLD HIDE-OUTS...
AH...THERE HE IS--IN THAT CAFÉ!
S-SUPERMAN--!
LUNCH 25¢
WELCOME BACK FROM THE DEAD! WOULD YOU CARE TO COME QUIETLY?
YOU AIN'T GONNA TAKE ME--!
BLAM BLAM BLAM
AFTER ALL THESE YEARS, YOU'D THINK HOODS WOULD GET TIRED OF TRYING TO SHOOT ME!
OH, WELL... IF YOU INSIST, I'LL DO MY GUN-CRUSHING BIT...
SCRUNCH
...AND MY PUNCH-IN-THE-JAW BIT!
BIFF
22
IT'S OVER NOW, RIGHT? WRONG! BECAUSE OUR STORY HAS MORE THAN A POST-SCRIPT--IT ALSO HAS AN EPILOGUE! SEE NEXT PAGE...

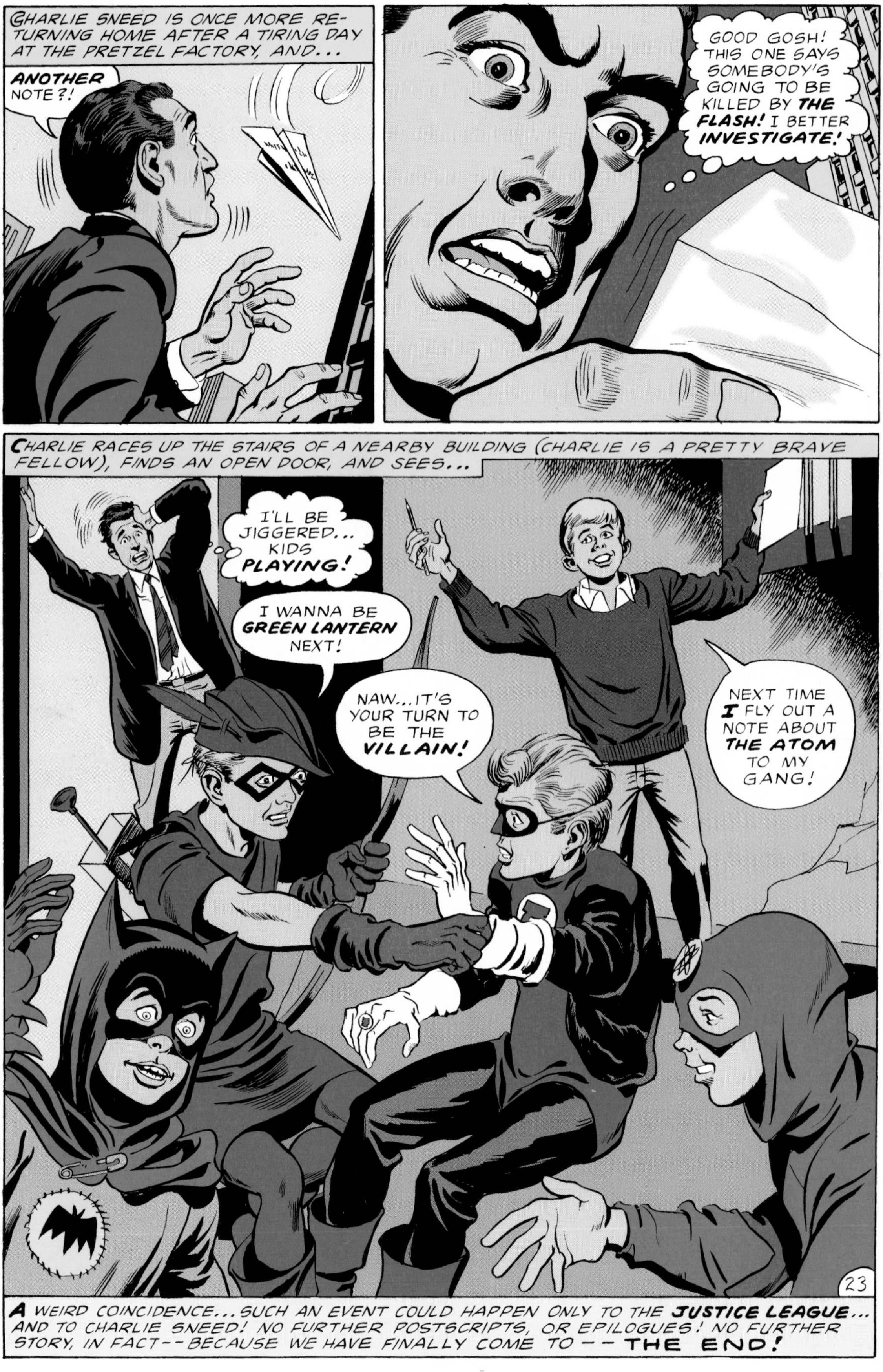
CHARLIE SNEED IS ONCE MORE RETURNING HOME AFTER A TIRING DAY AT THE PRETZEL FACTORY, AND...
ANOTHER NOTE?!
GOOD GOSH! THIS ONE SAYS SOMEBODY'S GOING TO BE KILLED BY THE FLASH! I BETTER INVESTIGATE!
CHARLIE RACES UP THE STAIRS OF A NEARBY BUILDING (CHARLIE IS A PRETTY BRAVE FELLOW), FINDS AN OPEN DOOR, AND SEES...
I'LL BE JIGGERED... KIDS PLAYING!
I WANNA BE GREEN LANTERN NEXT!
NAW...IT'S YOUR TURN TO BE THE VILLAIN!
NEXT TIME I FLY OUT A NOTE ABOUT THE ATOM TO MY GANG!
23
A WEIRD COINCIDENCE...SUCH AN EVENT COULD HAPPEN ONLY TO THE JUSTICE LEAGUE... AND TO CHARLIE SNEED! NO FURTHER POSTSCRIPTS, OR EPILOGUES! NO FURTHER STORY, IN FACT--BECAUSE WE HAVE FINALLY COME TO--THE END!

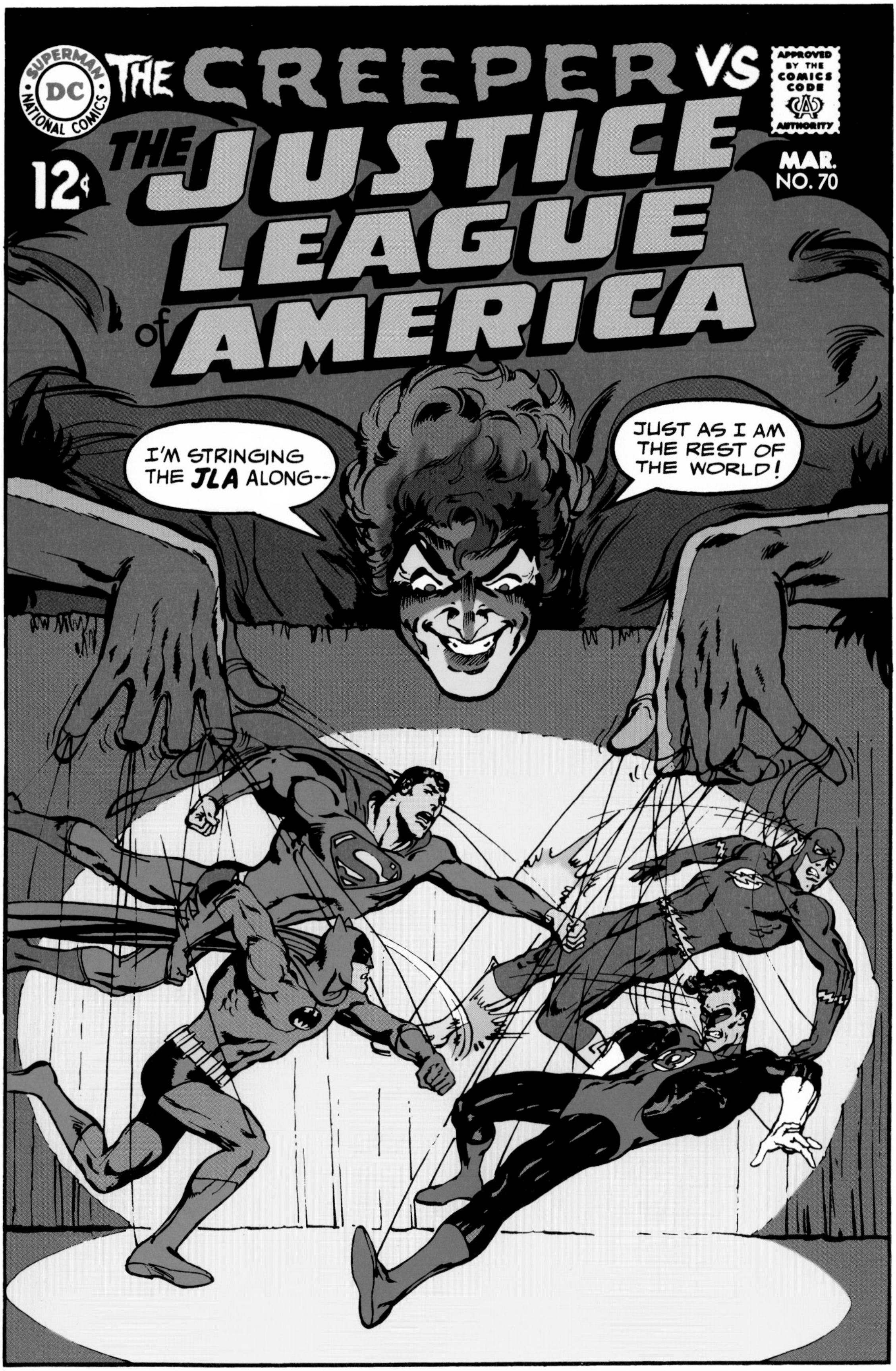
SUPERMAN DC NATIONAL COMICS
THE CREEPER VS
APPROVED BY THE COMICS CODE AUTHORITY
12¢
THE JUSTICE LEAGUE of AMERICA
MAR. NO. 70
I'M STRINGING THE JLA ALONG--
JUST AS I AM THE REST OF THE WORLD!

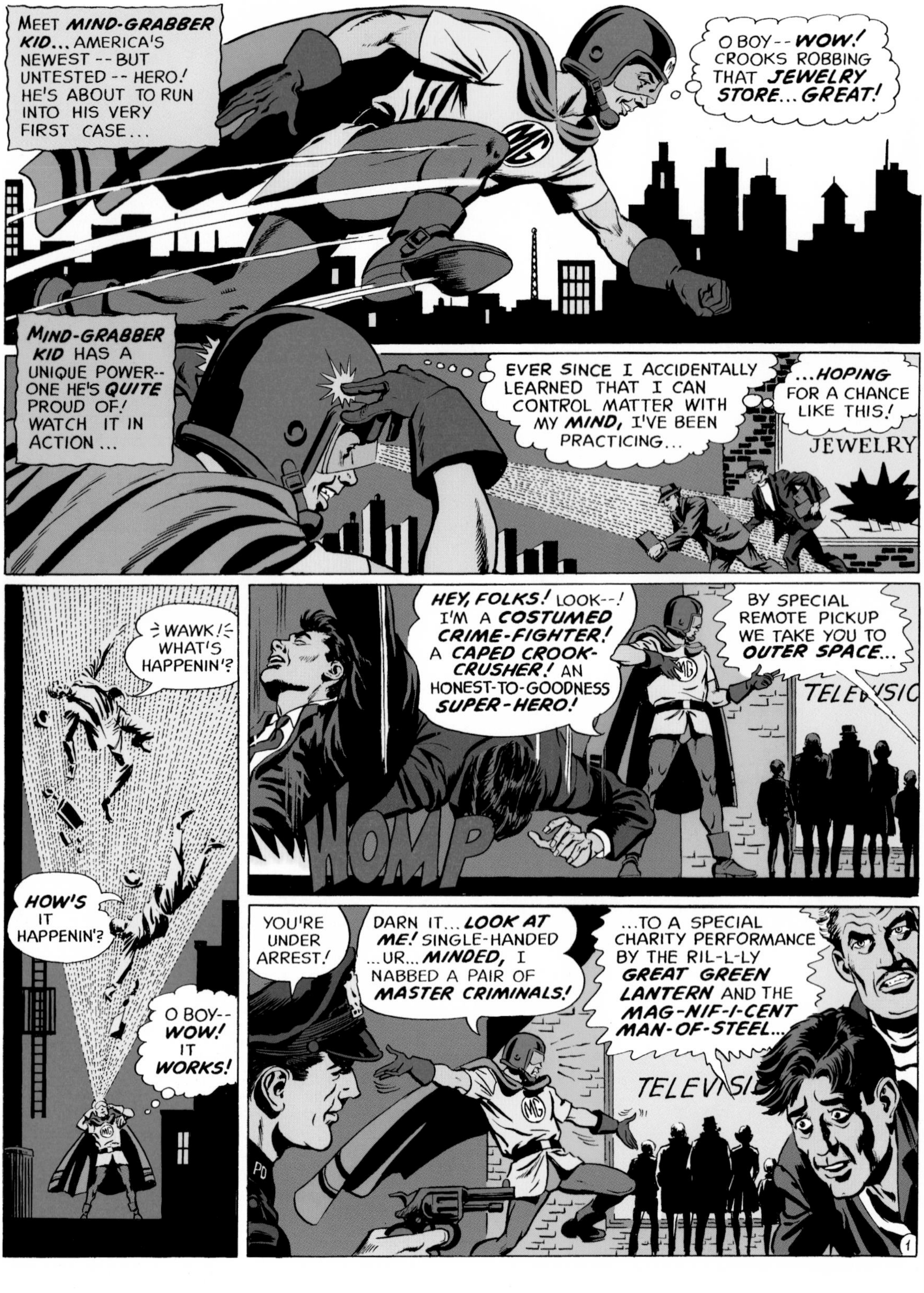
MEET MIND-GRABBER KID... AMERICA'S NEWEST -- BUT UNTESTED -- HERO! HE'S ABOUT TO RUN INTO HIS VERY FIRST CASE...
O BOY -- WOW! CROOKS ROBBING THAT JEWELRY STORE... GREAT!
MIND-GRABBER KID HAS A UNIQUE POWER-- ONE HE'S QUITE PROUD OF! WATCH IT IN ACTION...
EVER SINCE I ACCIDENTALLY LEARNED THAT I CAN CONTROL MATTER WITH MY MIND, I'VE BEEN PRACTICING...
...HOPING FOR A CHANCE LIKE THIS!
JEWELRY
WAWK! WHAT'S HAPPENIN'?
HOW'S IT HAPPENIN'?
O BOY-- WOW! IT WORKS!
HEY, FOLKS! LOOK--! I'M A COSTUMED CRIME-FIGHTER! A CAPED CROOK-CRUSHER! AN HONEST-TO-GOODNESS SUPER-HERO!
BY SPECIAL REMOTE PICKUP WE TAKE YOU TO OUTER SPACE...
WOMP
YOU'RE UNDER ARREST!
DARN IT... LOOK AT ME! SINGLE-HANDED ...UR... MINDED, I NABBED A PAIR OF MASTER CRIMINALS!
...TO A SPECIAL CHARITY PERFORMANCE BY THE RIL-L-LY GREAT GREEN LANTERN AND THE MAG-NIF-I-CENT MAN-OF-STEEL...
PD
1

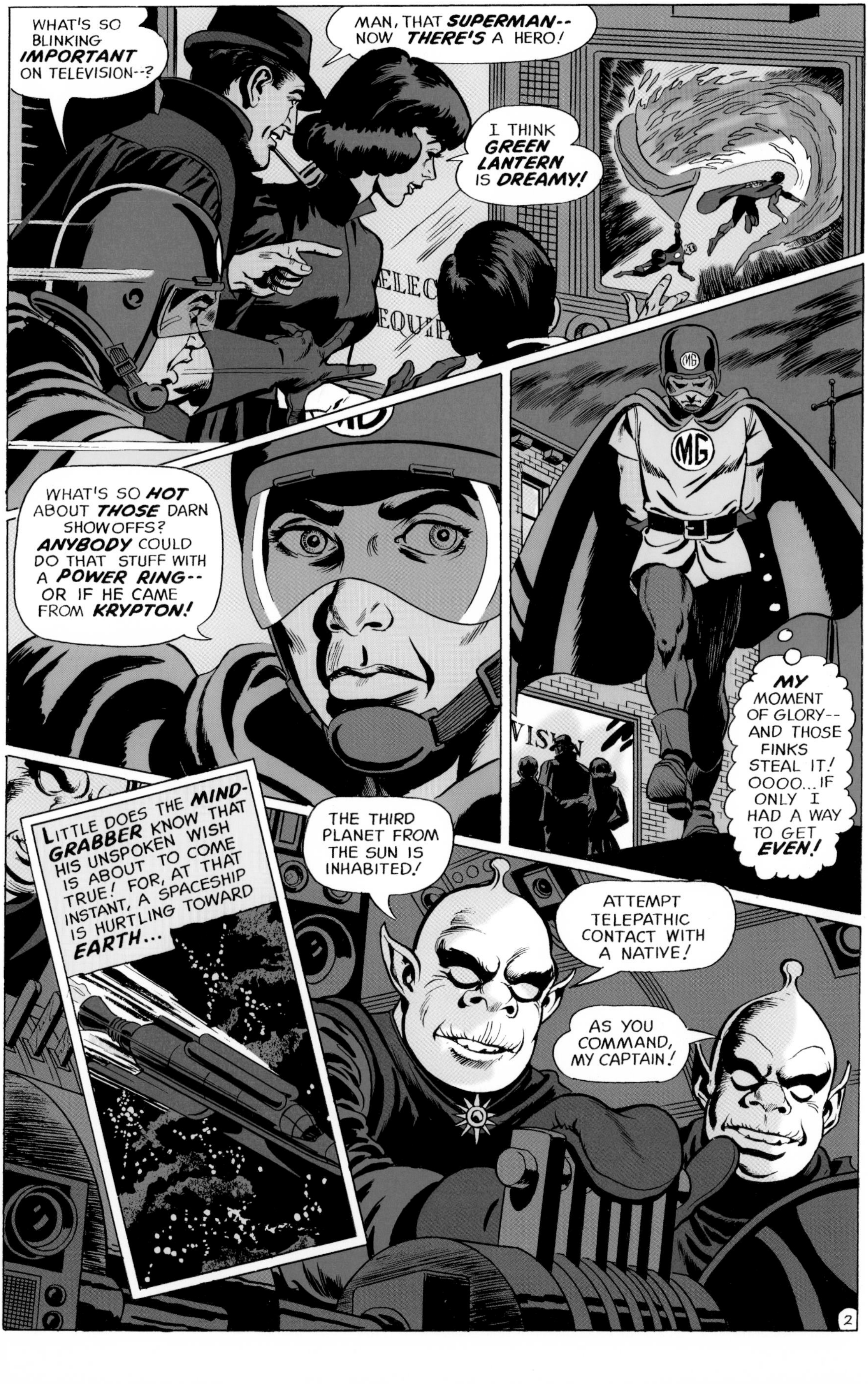
WHAT'S SO BLINKING IMPORTANT ON TELEVISION--?
MAN, THAT SUPERMAN-- NOW THERE'S A HERO!
I THINK GREEN LANTERN IS DREAMY!
WHAT'S SO HOT ABOUT THOSE DARN SHOWOFFS? ANYBODY COULD DO THAT STUFF WITH A POWER RING-- OR IF HE CAME FROM KRYPTON!
MY MOMENT OF GLORY-- AND THOSE FINKS STEAL IT! OOOO... IF ONLY I HAD A WAY TO GET EVEN!
LITTLE DOES THE MIND-GRABBER KNOW THAT HIS UNSPOKEN WISH IS ABOUT TO COME TRUE! FOR, AT THAT INSTANT, A SPACESHIP IS HURTLING TOWARD EARTH...
THE THIRD PLANET FROM THE SUN IS INHABITED!
ATTEMPT TELEPATHIC CONTACT WITH A NATIVE!
AS YOU COMMAND, MY CAPTAIN!
2

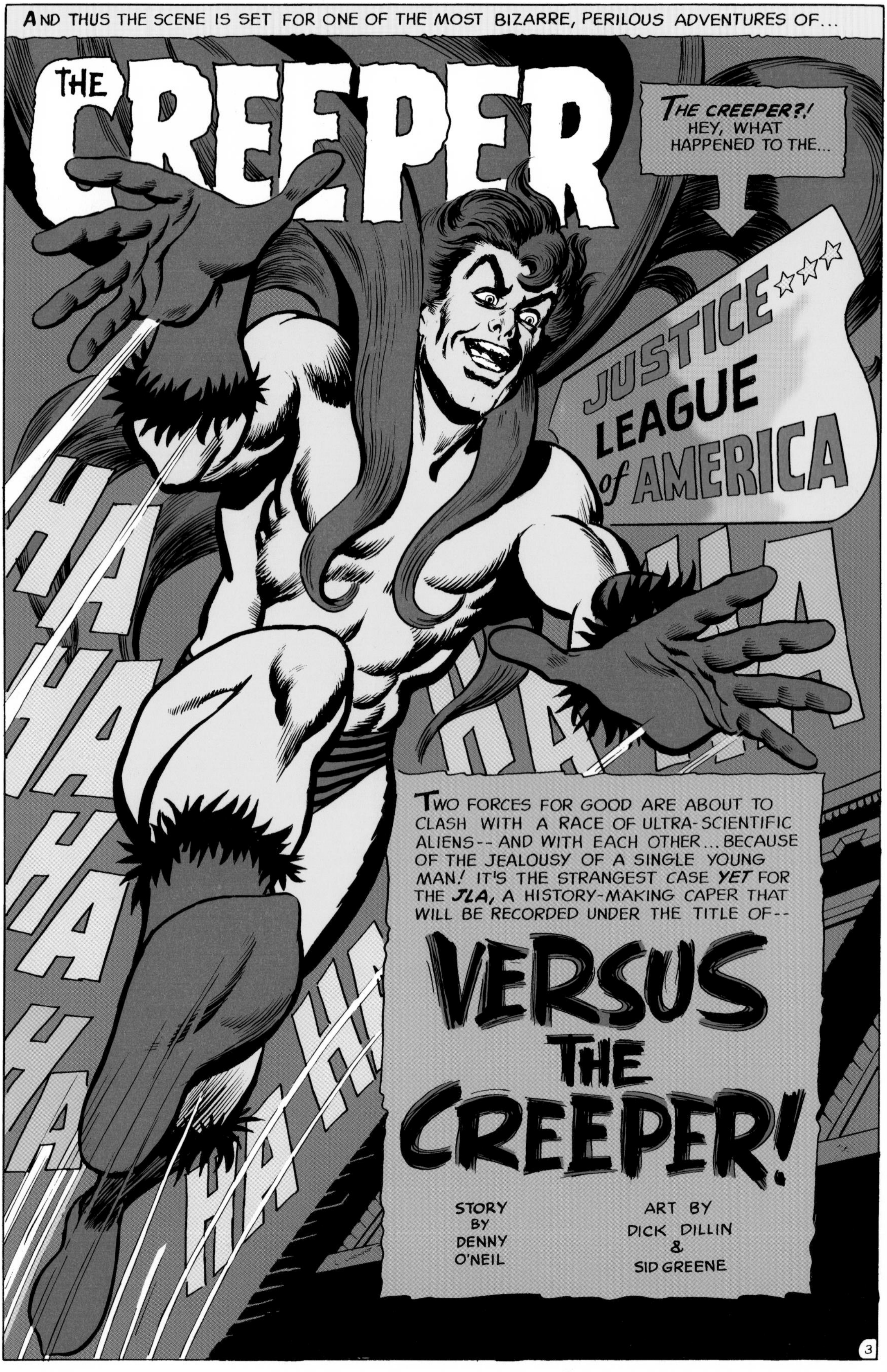

AND THUS THE SCENE IS SET FOR ONE OF THE MOST BIZARRE, PERILOUS ADVENTURES OF...
THE CREEPER
THE CREEPER?! HEY, WHAT HAPPENED TO THE...
JUSTICE LEAGUE of AMERICA
HA HA HA HA HA HA HA
TWO FORCES FOR GOOD ARE ABOUT TO CLASH WITH A RACE OF ULTRA-SCIENTIFIC ALIENS-- AND WITH EACH OTHER... BECAUSE OF THE JEALOUSY OF A SINGLE YOUNG MAN! IT'S THE STRANGEST CASE YET FOR THE JLA, A HISTORY-MAKING CAPER THAT WILL BE RECORDED UNDER THE TITLE OF--
VERSUS THE CREEPER!
STORY BY DENNY O'NEIL
ART BY DICK DILLIN & SID GREENE
3

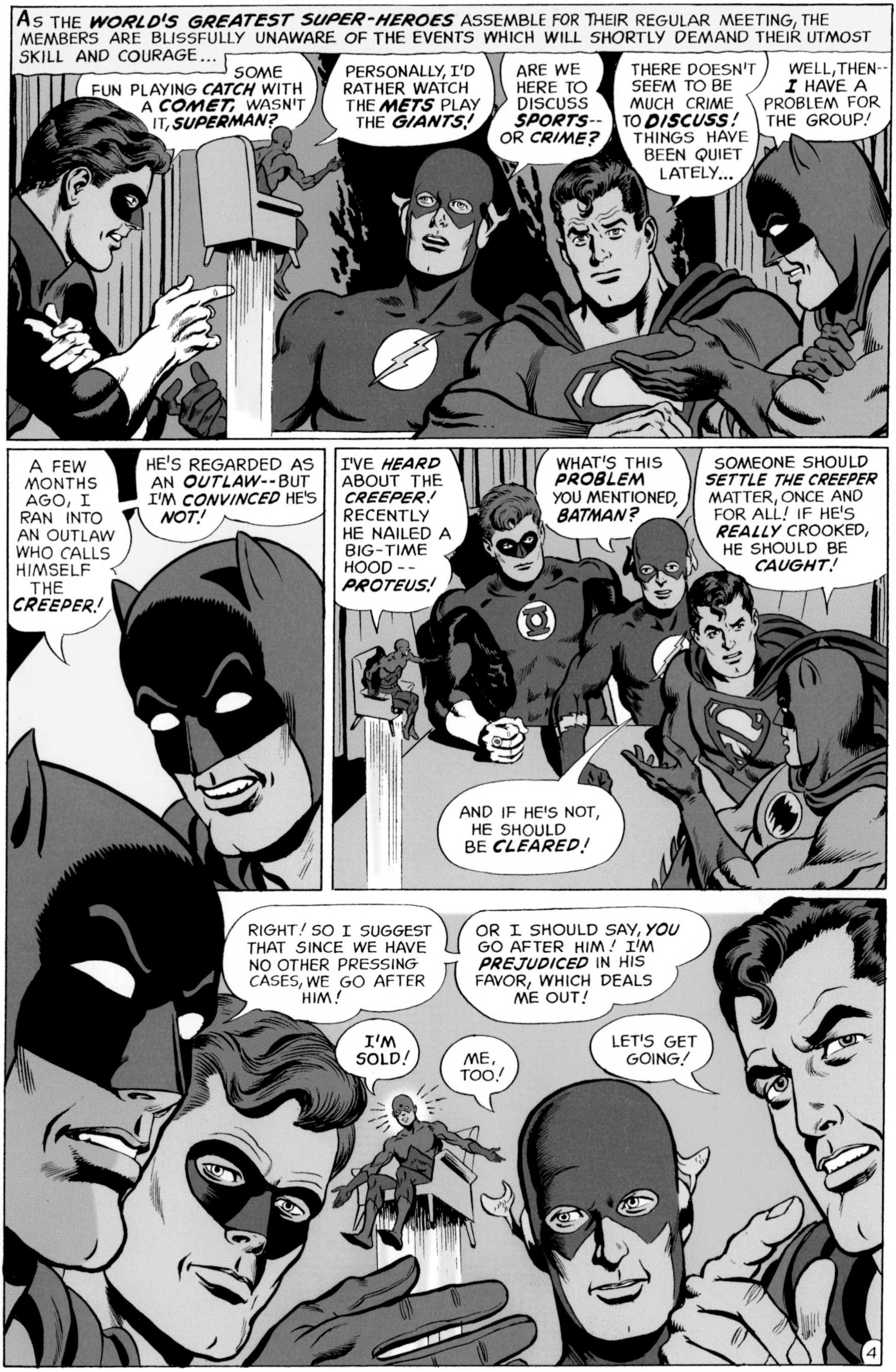
AS THE WORLD'S GREATEST SUPER-HEROES ASSEMBLE FOR THEIR REGULAR MEETING, THE MEMBERS ARE BLISSFULLY UNAWARE OF THE EVENTS WHICH WILL SHORTLY DEMAND THEIR UTMOST SKILL AND COURAGE...
SOME FUN PLAYING CATCH WITH A COMET, WASN'T IT, SUPERMAN?
PERSONALLY, I'D RATHER WATCH THE METS PLAY THE GIANTS!
ARE WE HERE TO DISCUSS SPORTS-- OR CRIME?
THERE DOESN'T SEEM TO BE MUCH CRIME TO DISCUSS! THINGS HAVE BEEN QUIET LATELY...
WELL, THEN-- I HAVE A PROBLEM FOR THE GROUP!
A FEW MONTHS AGO, I RAN INTO AN OUTLAW WHO CALLS HIMSELF THE CREEPER!
HE'S REGARDED AS AN OUTLAW--BUT I'M CONVINCED HE'S NOT!
I'VE HEARD ABOUT THE CREEPER! RECENTLY HE NAILED A BIG-TIME HOOD -- PROTEUS!
WHAT'S THIS PROBLEM YOU MENTIONED, BATMAN?
SOMEONE SHOULD SETTLE THE CREEPER MATTER, ONCE AND FOR ALL! IF HE'S REALLY CROOKED, HE SHOULD BE CAUGHT!
AND IF HE'S NOT, HE SHOULD BE CLEARED!
RIGHT! SO I SUGGEST THAT SINCE WE HAVE NO OTHER PRESSING CASES, WE GO AFTER HIM!
OR I SHOULD SAY, YOU GO AFTER HIM! I'M PREJUDICED IN HIS FAVOR, WHICH DEALS ME OUT!
I'M SOLD!
ME, TOO!
LET'S GET GOING!
4

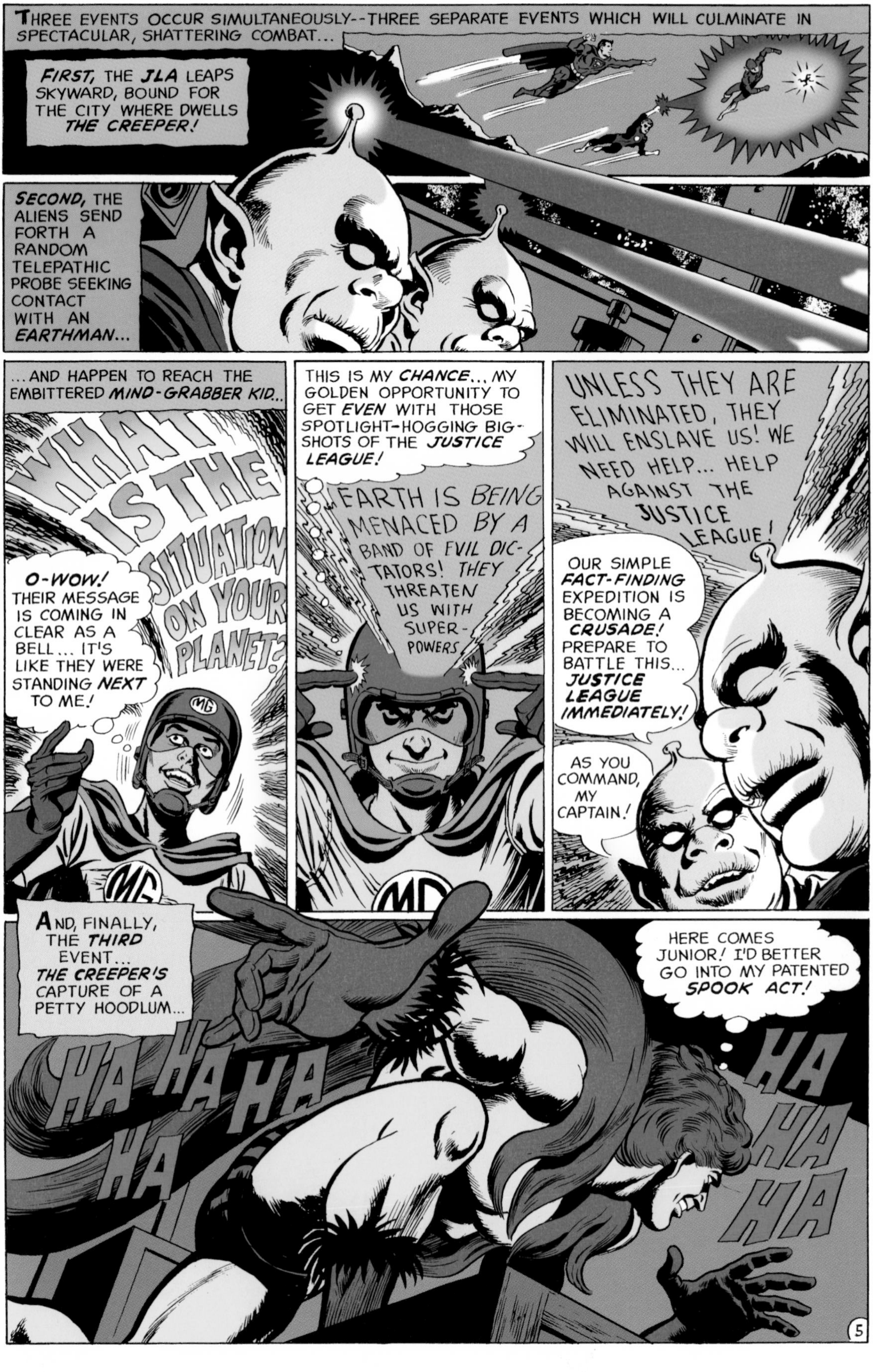
THREE EVENTS OCCUR SIMULTANEOUSLY--THREE SEPARATE EVENTS WHICH WILL CULMINATE IN SPECTACULAR, SHATTERING COMBAT...
FIRST, THE JLA LEAPS SKYWARD, BOUND FOR THE CITY WHERE DWELLS THE CREEPER!
SECOND, THE ALIENS SEND FORTH A RANDOM TELEPATHIC PROBE SEEKING CONTACT WITH AN EARTHMAN...
...AND HAPPEN TO REACH THE EMBITTERED MIND-GRABBER KID...
WHAT IS THE SITUATION ON YOUR PLANET?
O-WOW! THEIR MESSAGE IS COMING IN CLEAR AS A BELL... IT'S LIKE THEY WERE STANDING NEXT TO ME!
THIS IS MY CHANCE... MY GOLDEN OPPORTUNITY TO GET EVEN WITH THOSE SPOTLIGHT-HOGGING BIG-SHOTS OF THE JUSTICE LEAGUE!
EARTH IS BEING MENACED BY A BAND OF EVIL DICTATORS! THEY THREATEN US WITH SUPER-POWERS
UNLESS THEY ARE ELIMINATED, THEY WILL ENSLAVE US! WE NEED HELP... HELP AGAINST THE JUSTICE LEAGUE!
OUR SIMPLE FACT-FINDING EXPEDITION IS BECOMING A CRUSADE! PREPARE TO BATTLE THIS... JUSTICE LEAGUE IMMEDIATELY!
AS YOU COMMAND, MY CAPTAIN!
AND, FINALLY, THE THIRD EVENT... THE CREEPER'S CAPTURE OF A PETTY HOODLUM...
HERE COMES JUNIOR! I'D BETTER GO INTO MY PATENTED SPOOK ACT!
HA HA HA HA HA HA
HA HA HA HA
5

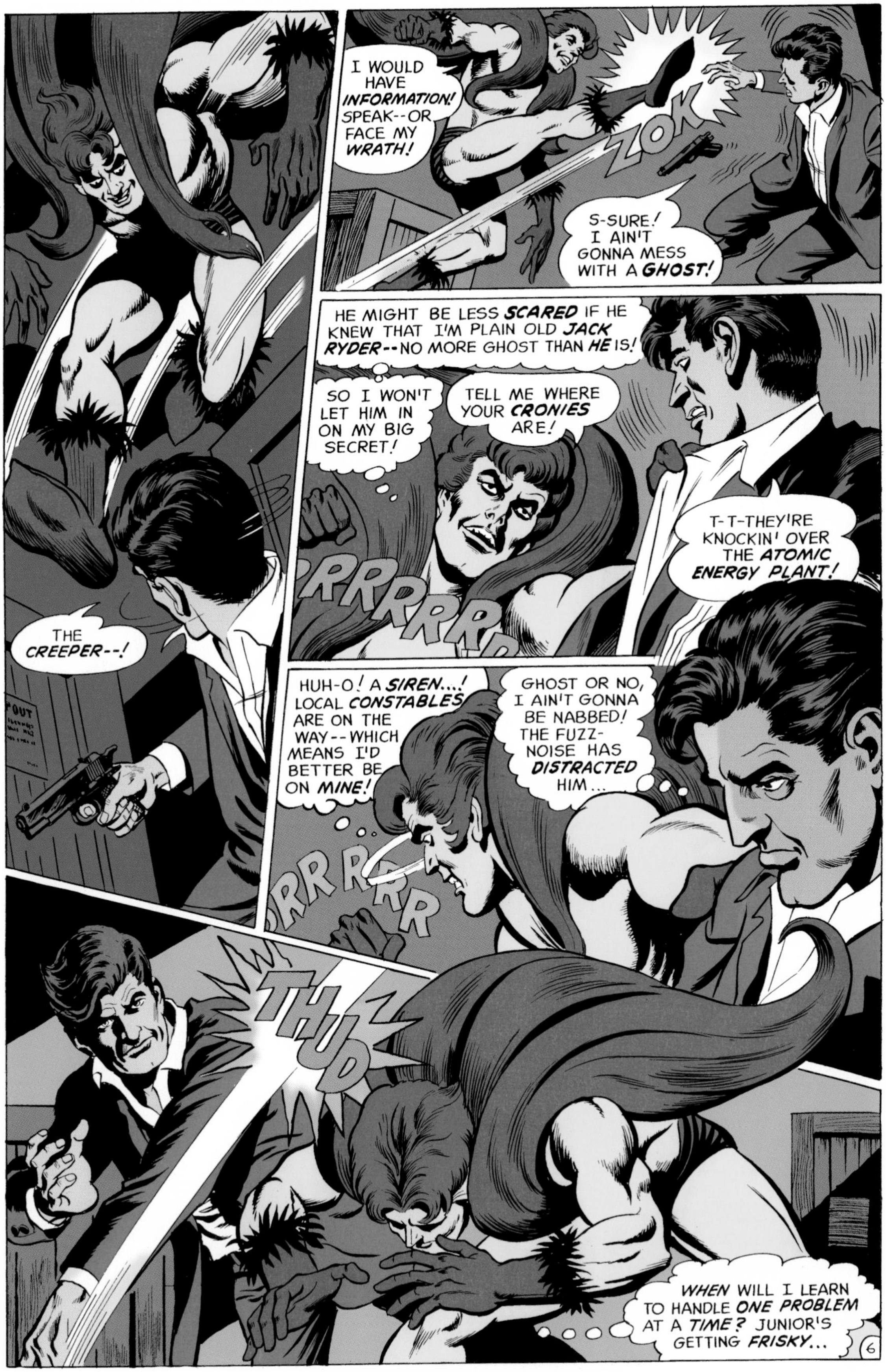
I WOULD HAVE INFORMATION! SPEAK--OR FACE MY WRATH!
ZOK
S-SURE! I AIN'T GONNA MESS WITH A GHOST!
THE CREEPER--!
HE MIGHT BE LESS SCARED IF HE KNEW THAT I'M PLAIN OLD JACK RYDER--NO MORE GHOST THAN HE IS!
SO I WON'T LET HIM IN ON MY BIG SECRET!
TELL ME WHERE YOUR CRONIES ARE!
T-T-THEY'RE KNOCKIN' OVER THE ATOMIC ENERGY PLANT!
RRRRRRRR
HUH-O! A SIREN...! LOCAL CONSTABLES ARE ON THE WAY--WHICH MEANS I'D BETTER BE ON MINE!
GHOST OR NO, I AIN'T GONNA BE NABBED! THE FUZZ-NOISE HAS DISTRACTED HIM...
RRRRRR
THUD
WHEN WILL I LEARN TO HANDLE ONE PROBLEM AT A TIME? JUNIOR'S GETTING FRISKY...
6

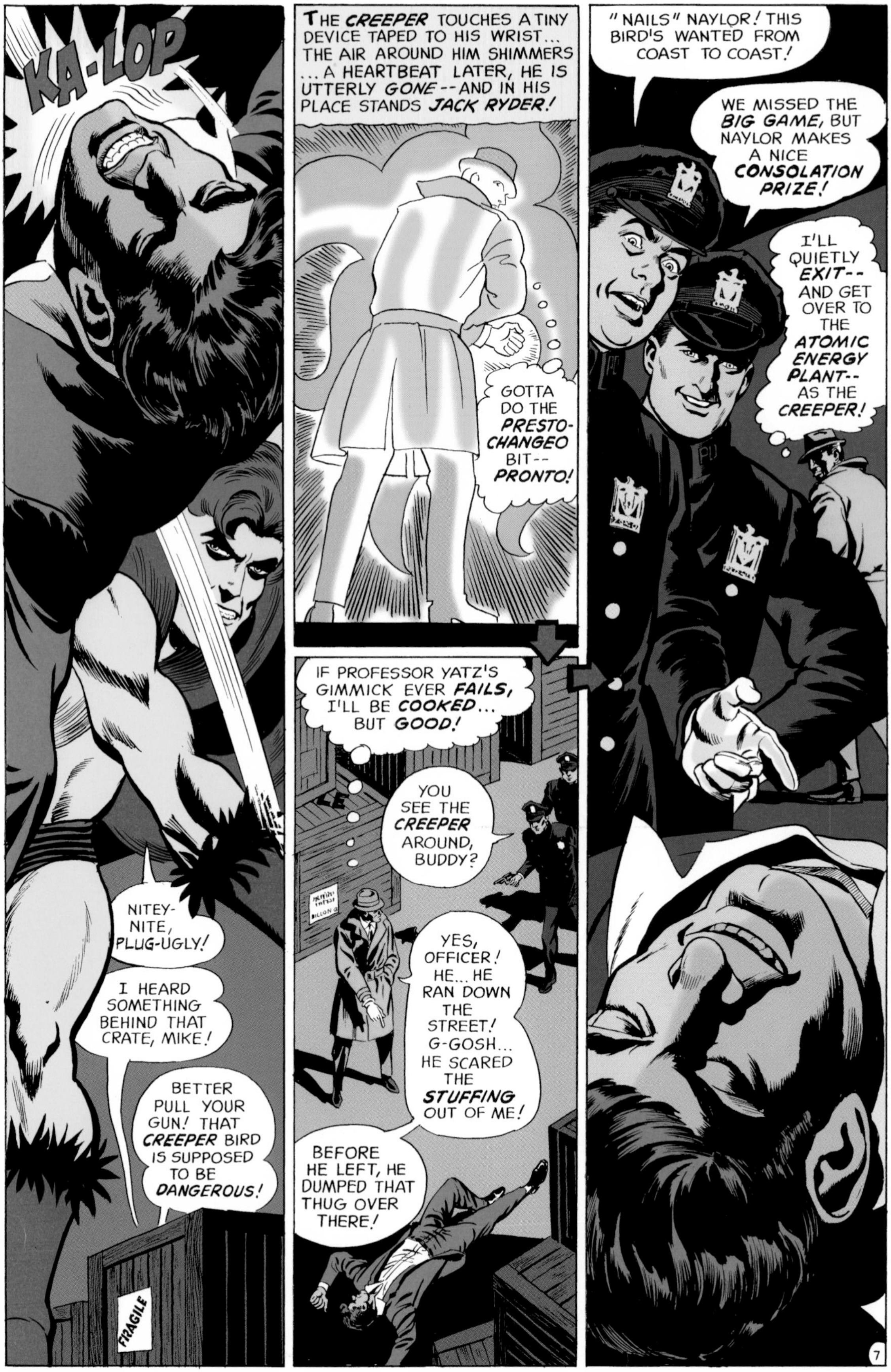
KA-LOP
NITEY-NITE, PLUG-UGLY!
I HEARD SOMETHING BEHIND THAT CRATE, MIKE!
BETTER PULL YOUR GUN! THAT CREEPER BIRD IS SUPPOSED TO BE DANGEROUS!
FRAGILE
THE CREEPER TOUCHES A TINY DEVICE TAPED TO HIS WRIST... THE AIR AROUND HIM SHIMMERS ... A HEARTBEAT LATER, HE IS UTTERLY GONE--AND IN HIS PLACE STANDS JACK RYDER!
GOTTA DO THE PRESTO-CHANGEO BIT--PRONTO!
IF PROFESSOR YATZ'S GIMMICK EVER FAILS, I'LL BE COOKED... BUT GOOD!
YOU SEE THE CREEPER AROUND, BUDDY?
YES, OFFICER! HE... HE RAN DOWN THE STREET! G-GOSH... HE SCARED THE STUFFING OUT OF ME!
BEFORE HE LEFT, HE DUMPED THAT THUG OVER THERE!
"NAILS" NAYLOR! THIS BIRD'S WANTED FROM COAST TO COAST!
WE MISSED THE BIG GAME, BUT NAYLOR MAKES A NICE CONSOLATION PRIZE!
I'LL QUIETLY EXIT--AND GET OVER TO THE ATOMIC ENERGY PLANT--AS THE CREEPER!
7

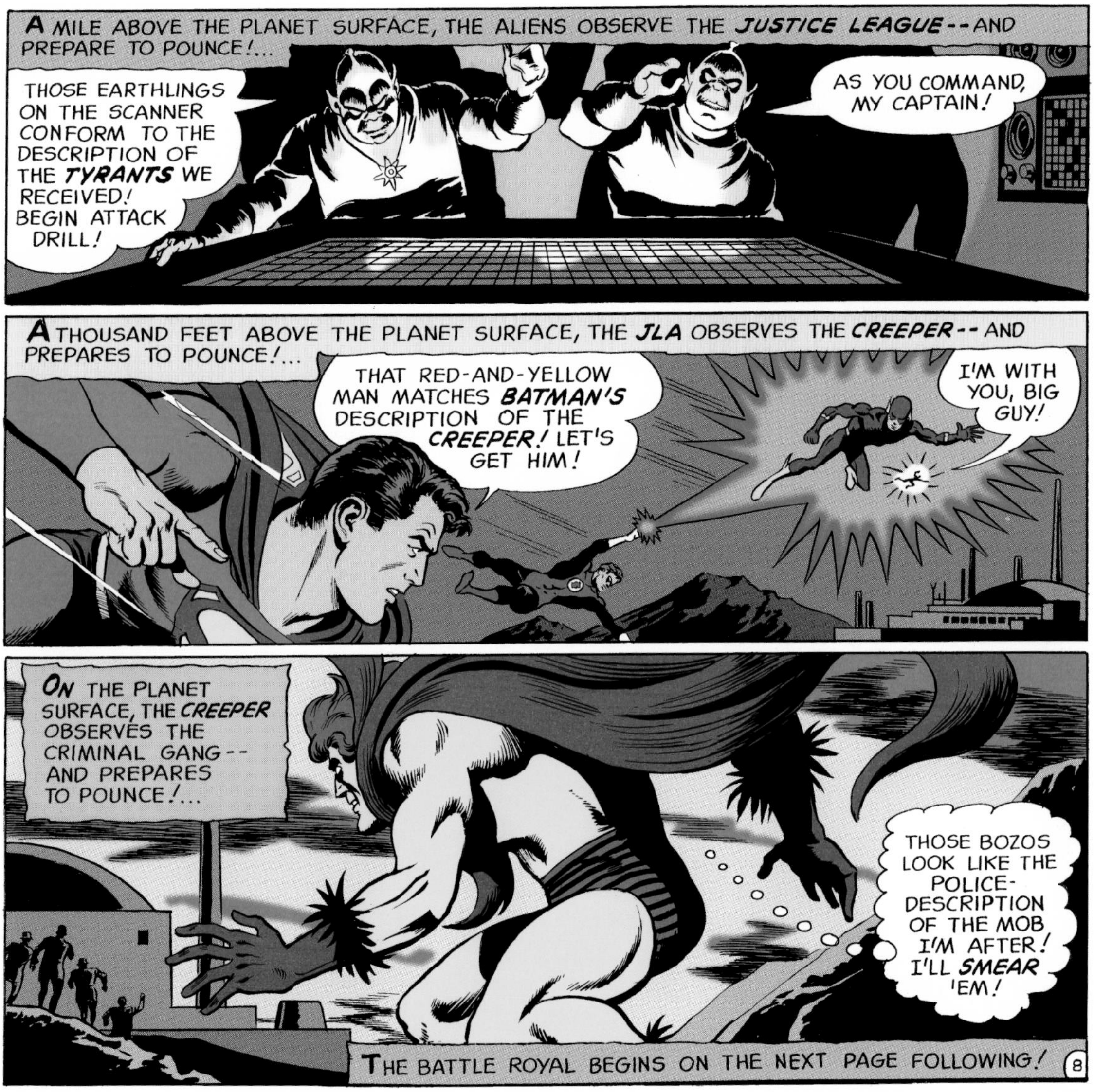
A MILE ABOVE THE PLANET SURFACE, THE ALIENS OBSERVE THE JUSTICE LEAGUE--AND PREPARE TO POUNCE!...
THOSE EARTHLINGS ON THE SCANNER CONFORM TO THE DESCRIPTION OF THE TYRANTS WE RECEIVED! BEGIN ATTACK DRILL!
AS YOU COMMAND, MY CAPTAIN!
A THOUSAND FEET ABOVE THE PLANET SURFACE, THE JLA OBSERVES THE CREEPER-- AND PREPARES TO POUNCE!...
THAT RED-AND-YELLOW MAN MATCHES BATMAN'S DESCRIPTION OF THE CREEPER! LET'S GET HIM!
I'M WITH YOU, BIG GUY!
ON THE PLANET SURFACE, THE CREEPER OBSERVES THE CRIMINAL GANG-- AND PREPARES TO POUNCE!...
THOSE BOZOS LOOK LIKE THE POLICE-DESCRIPTION OF THE MOB I'M AFTER! I'LL SMEAR 'EM!
THE BATTLE ROYAL BEGINS ON THE NEXT PAGE FOLLOWING!
8

JUSTICE LEAGUE of AMERICA

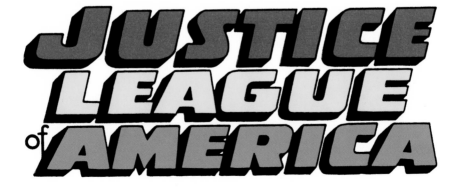

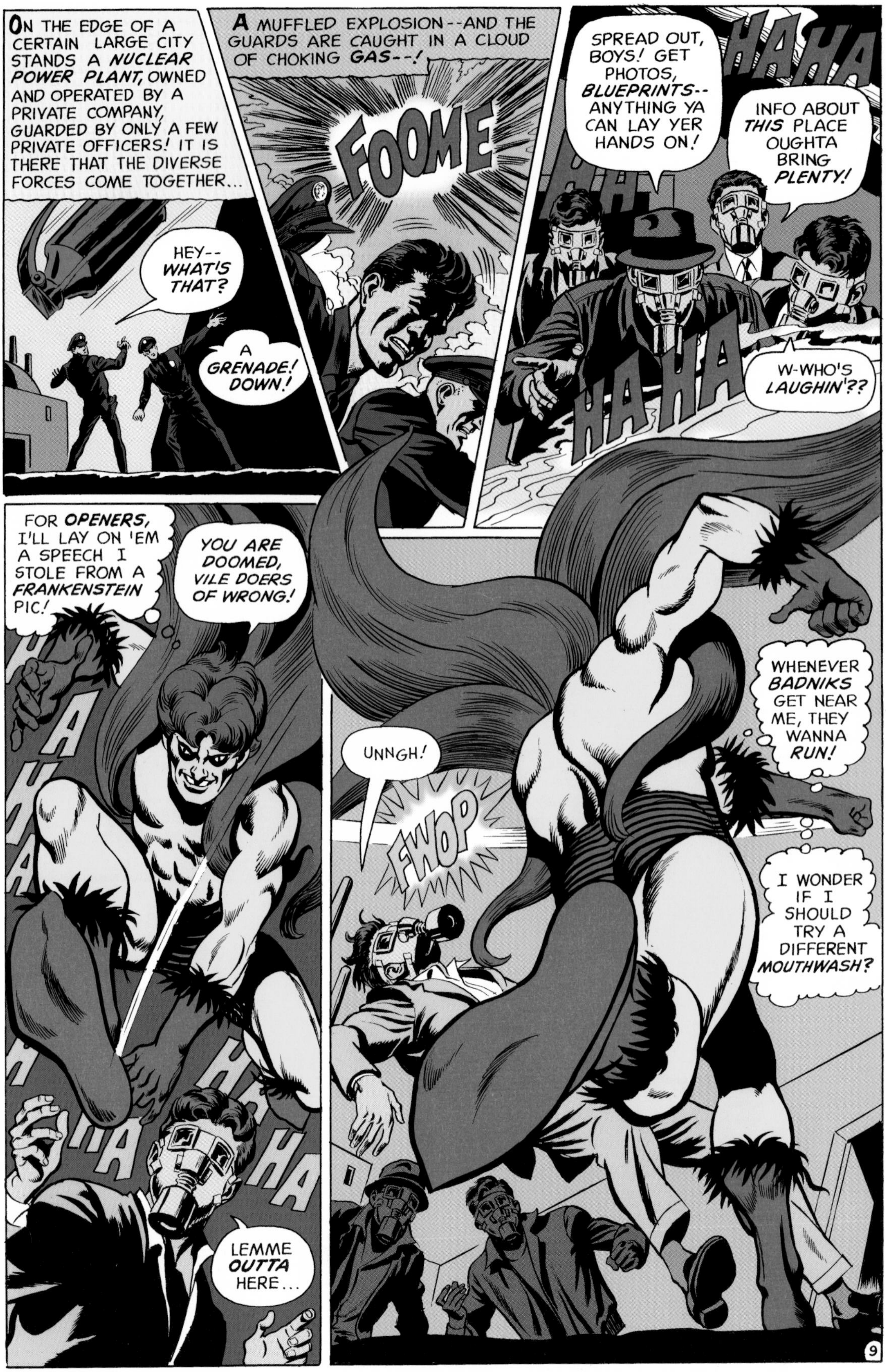
ON THE EDGE OF A CERTAIN LARGE CITY STANDS A NUCLEAR POWER PLANT, OWNED AND OPERATED BY A PRIVATE COMPANY, GUARDED BY ONLY A FEW PRIVATE OFFICERS! IT IS THERE THAT THE DIVERSE FORCES COME TOGETHER...
HEY-- WHAT'S THAT?
A GRENADE! DOWN!
A MUFFLED EXPLOSION--AND THE GUARDS ARE CAUGHT IN A CLOUD OF CHOKING GAS--!
FOOME
SPREAD OUT, BOYS! GET PHOTOS, BLUEPRINTS-- ANYTHING YA CAN LAY YER HANDS ON!
HAHA
INFO ABOUT THIS PLACE OUGHTA BRING PLENTY!
HA HA
W-WHO'S LAUGHIN'??
FOR OPENERS, I'LL LAY ON 'EM A SPEECH I STOLE FROM A FRANKENSTEIN PIC!
YOU ARE DOOMED, VILE DOERS OF WRONG!
LEMME OUTTA HERE...
UNNGH!
FWOP
WHENEVER BADNIKS GET NEAR ME, THEY WANNA RUN!
I WONDER IF I SHOULD TRY A DIFFERENT MOUTHWASH?
9

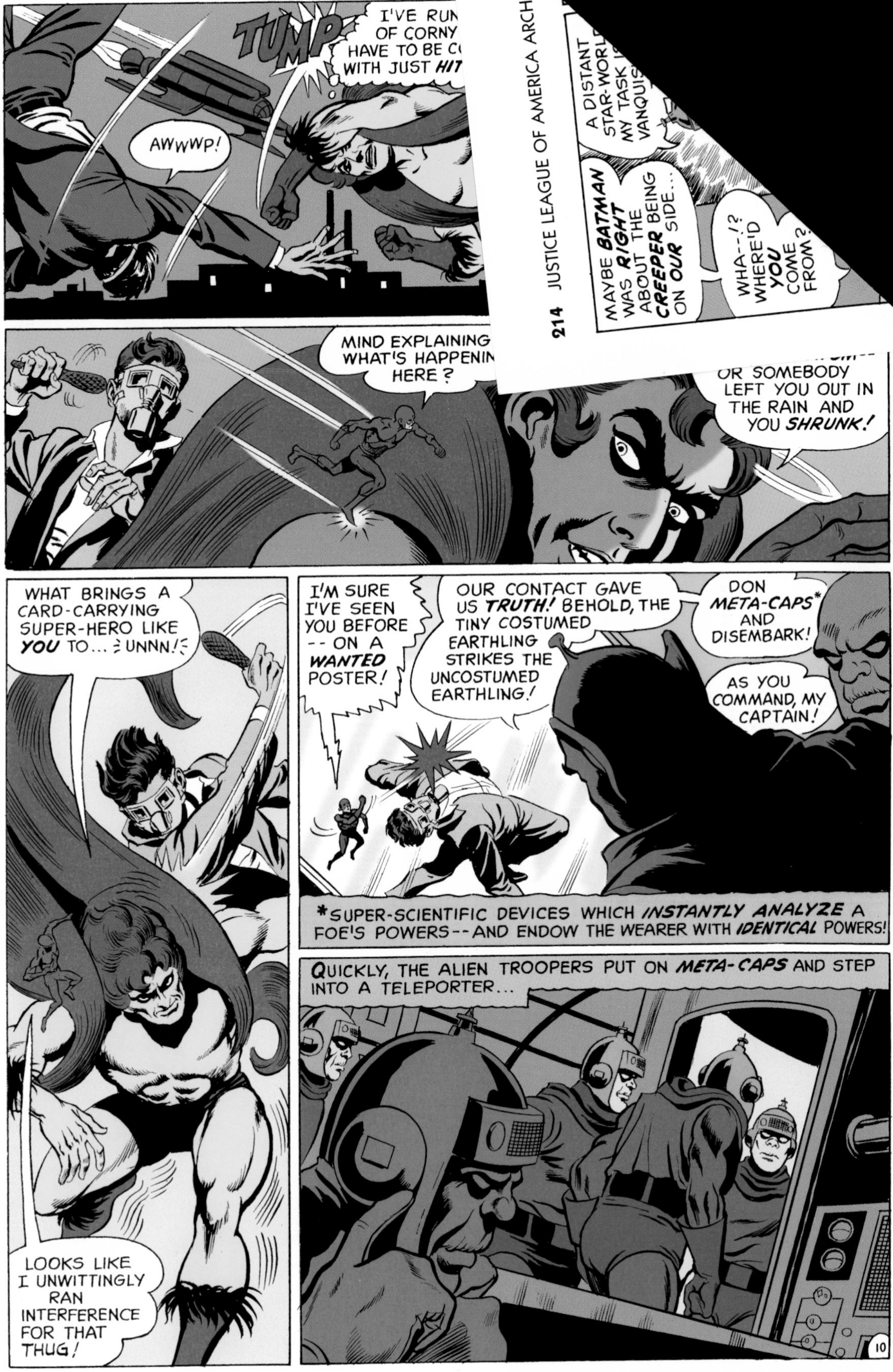
TUMP
I'VE RUN OF CORNY HAVE TO BE C WITH JUST HIT
AWWWP!
MIND EXPLAINING WHAT'S HAPPENIN HERE?
OR SOMEBODY LEFT YOU OUT IN THE RAIN AND YOU SHRUNK!
WHAT BRINGS A CARD-CARRYING SUPER-HERO LIKE YOU TO... UNNN!
LOOKS LIKE I UNWITTINGLY RAN INTERFERENCE FOR THAT THUG!
I'M SURE I'VE SEEN YOU BEFORE -- ON A WANTED POSTER!
OUR CONTACT GAVE US TRUTH! BEHOLD, THE TINY COSTUMED EARTHLING STRIKES THE UNCOSTUMED EARTHLING!
DON META-CAPS* AND DISEMBARK!
AS YOU COMMAND, MY CAPTAIN!
*SUPER-SCIENTIFIC DEVICES WHICH INSTANTLY ANALYZE A FOE'S POWERS -- AND ENDOW THE WEARER WITH IDENTICAL POWERS!
QUICKLY, THE ALIEN TROOPERS PUT ON META-CAPS AND STEP INTO A TELEPORTER...
10

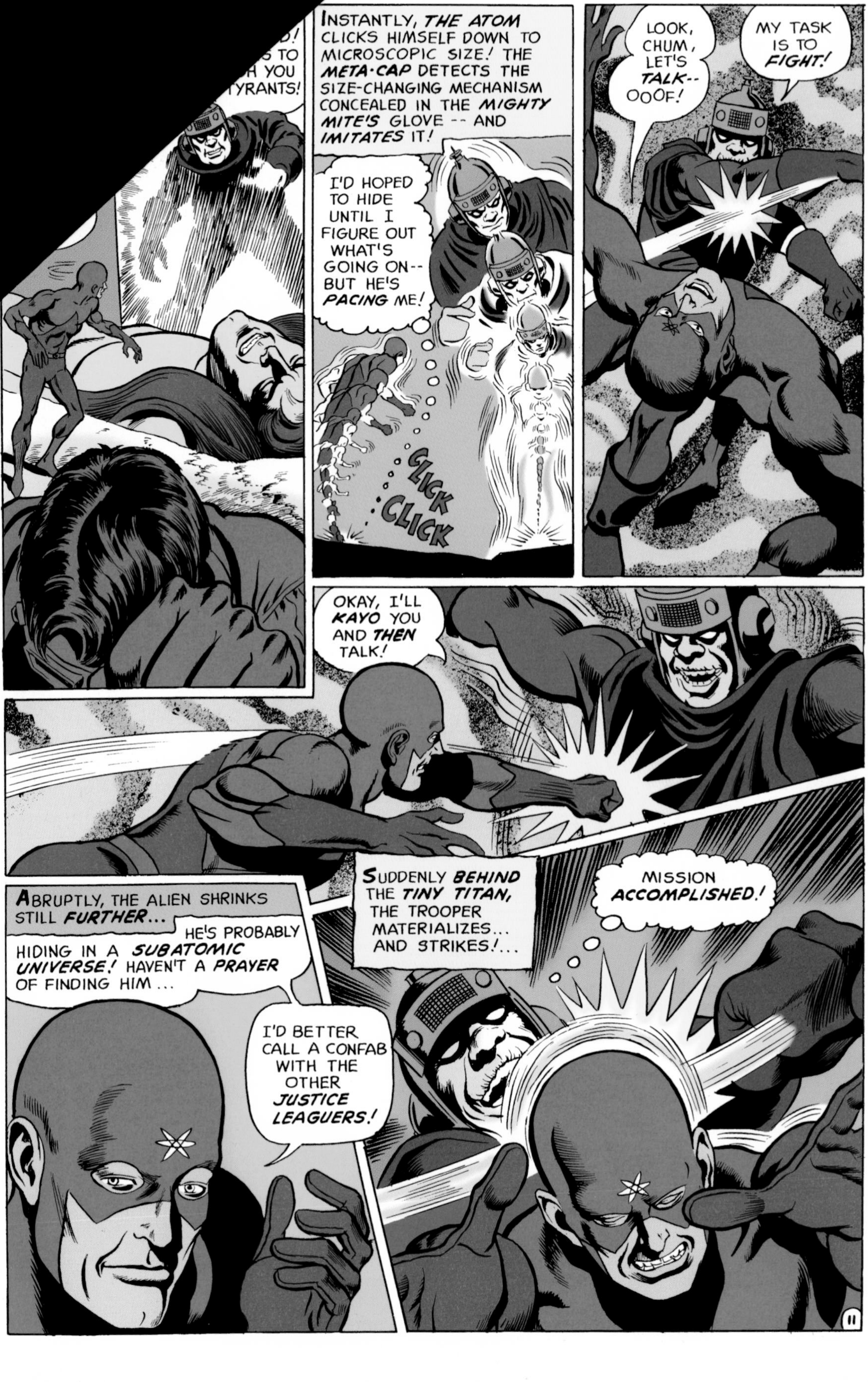

[redacted] TYRANTS!
INSTANTLY, THE ATOM CLICKS HIMSELF DOWN TO MICROSCOPIC SIZE! THE META-CAP DETECTS THE SIZE-CHANGING MECHANISM CONCEALED IN THE MIGHTY MITE'S GLOVE -- AND IMITATES IT!
I'D HOPED TO HIDE UNTIL I FIGURE OUT WHAT'S GOING ON-- BUT HE'S PACING ME!
CLICK
CLICK
LOOK, CHUM, LET'S TALK-- OOOF!
MY TASK IS TO FIGHT!
OKAY, I'LL KAYO YOU AND THEN TALK!
ABRUPTLY, THE ALIEN SHRINKS STILL FURTHER...
HE'S PROBABLY HIDING IN A SUBATOMIC UNIVERSE! HAVEN'T A PRAYER OF FINDING HIM...
I'D BETTER CALL A CONFAB WITH THE OTHER JUSTICE LEAGUERS!
SUDDENLY BEHIND THE TINY TITAN, THE TROOPER MATERIALIZES... AND STRIKES!...
MISSION ACCOMPLISHED!

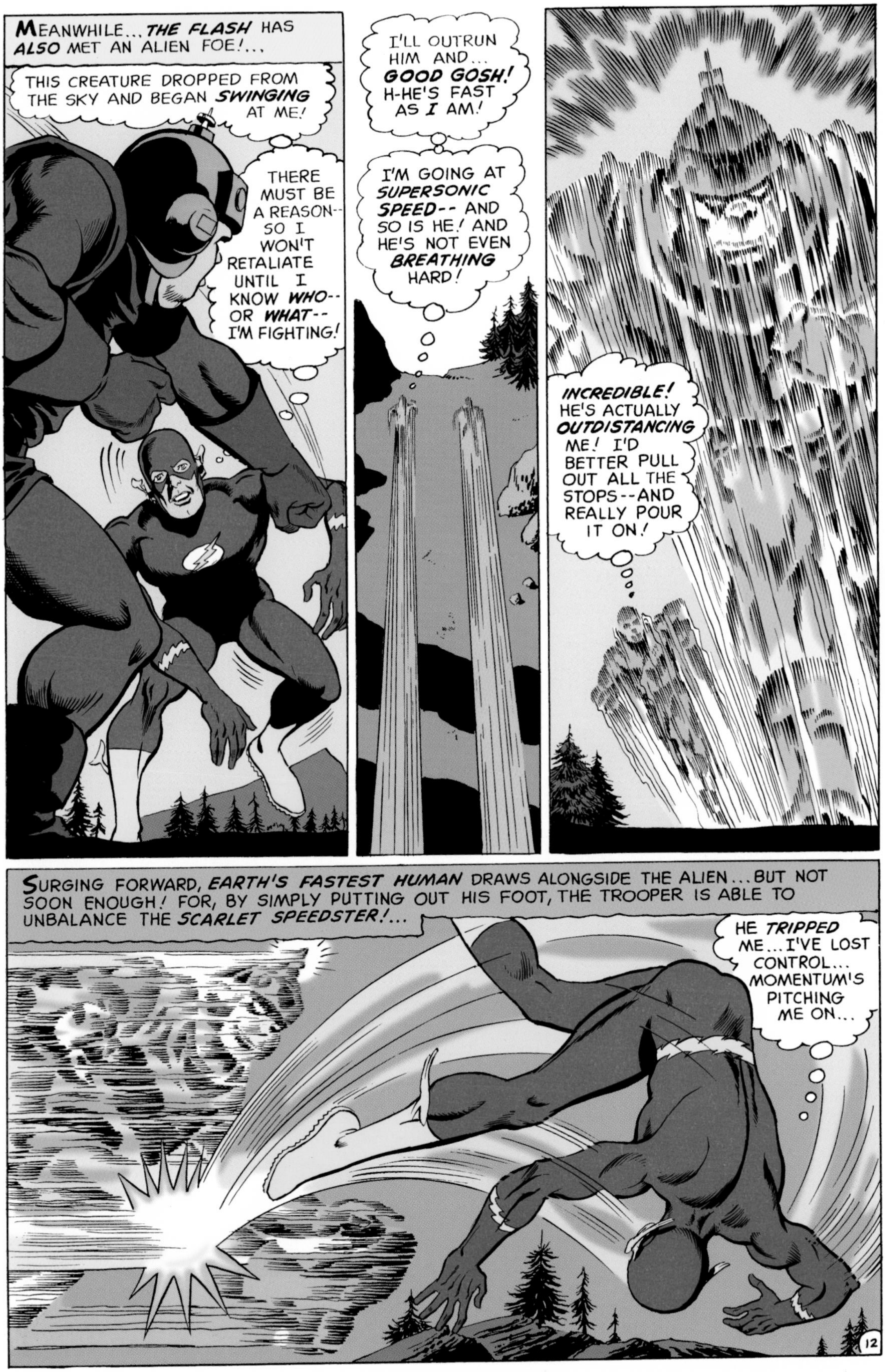
MEANWHILE... THE FLASH HAS ALSO MET AN ALIEN FOE!...
THIS CREATURE DROPPED FROM THE SKY AND BEGAN SWINGING AT ME!
THERE MUST BE A REASON--SO I WON'T RETALIATE UNTIL I KNOW WHO--OR WHAT--I'M FIGHTING!
I'LL OUTRUN HIM AND... GOOD GOSH! H-HE'S FAST AS I AM!
I'M GOING AT SUPERSONIC SPEED-- AND SO IS HE! AND HE'S NOT EVEN BREATHING HARD!
INCREDIBLE! HE'S ACTUALLY OUTDISTANCING ME! I'D BETTER PULL OUT ALL THE STOPS--AND REALLY POUR IT ON!
SURGING FORWARD, EARTH'S FASTEST HUMAN DRAWS ALONGSIDE THE ALIEN... BUT NOT SOON ENOUGH! FOR, BY SIMPLY PUTTING OUT HIS FOOT, THE TROOPER IS ABLE TO UNBALANCE THE SCARLET SPEEDSTER!...
HE TRIPPED ME... I'VE LOST CONTROL... MOMENTUM'S PITCHING ME ON...
12

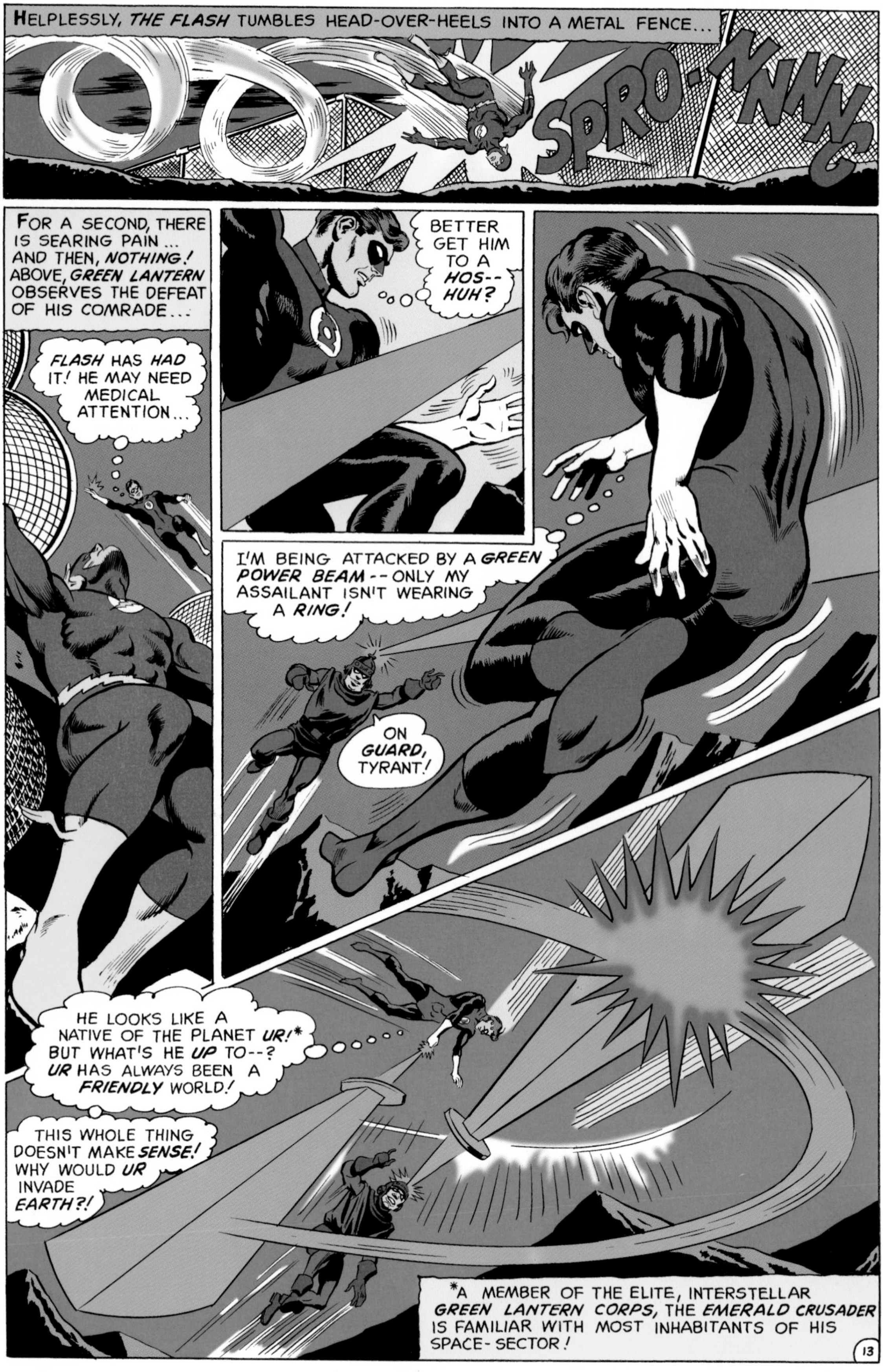
HELPLESSLY, THE FLASH TUMBLES HEAD-OVER-HEELS INTO A METAL FENCE...
SPRO-NNNNG
FOR A SECOND, THERE IS SEARING PAIN ... AND THEN, NOTHING! ABOVE, GREEN LANTERN OBSERVES THE DEFEAT OF HIS COMRADE...
FLASH HAS HAD IT! HE MAY NEED MEDICAL ATTENTION...
BETTER GET HIM TO A HOS-- HUH?
I'M BEING ATTACKED BY A GREEN POWER BEAM -- ONLY MY ASSAILANT ISN'T WEARING A RING!
ON GUARD, TYRANT!
HE LOOKS LIKE A NATIVE OF THE PLANET UR!* BUT WHAT'S HE UP TO--? UR HAS ALWAYS BEEN A FRIENDLY WORLD!
THIS WHOLE THING DOESN'T MAKE SENSE! WHY WOULD UR INVADE EARTH?!
*A MEMBER OF THE ELITE, INTERSTELLAR GREEN LANTERN CORPS, THE EMERALD CRUSADER IS FAMILIAR WITH MOST INHABITANTS OF HIS SPACE-SECTOR!
13

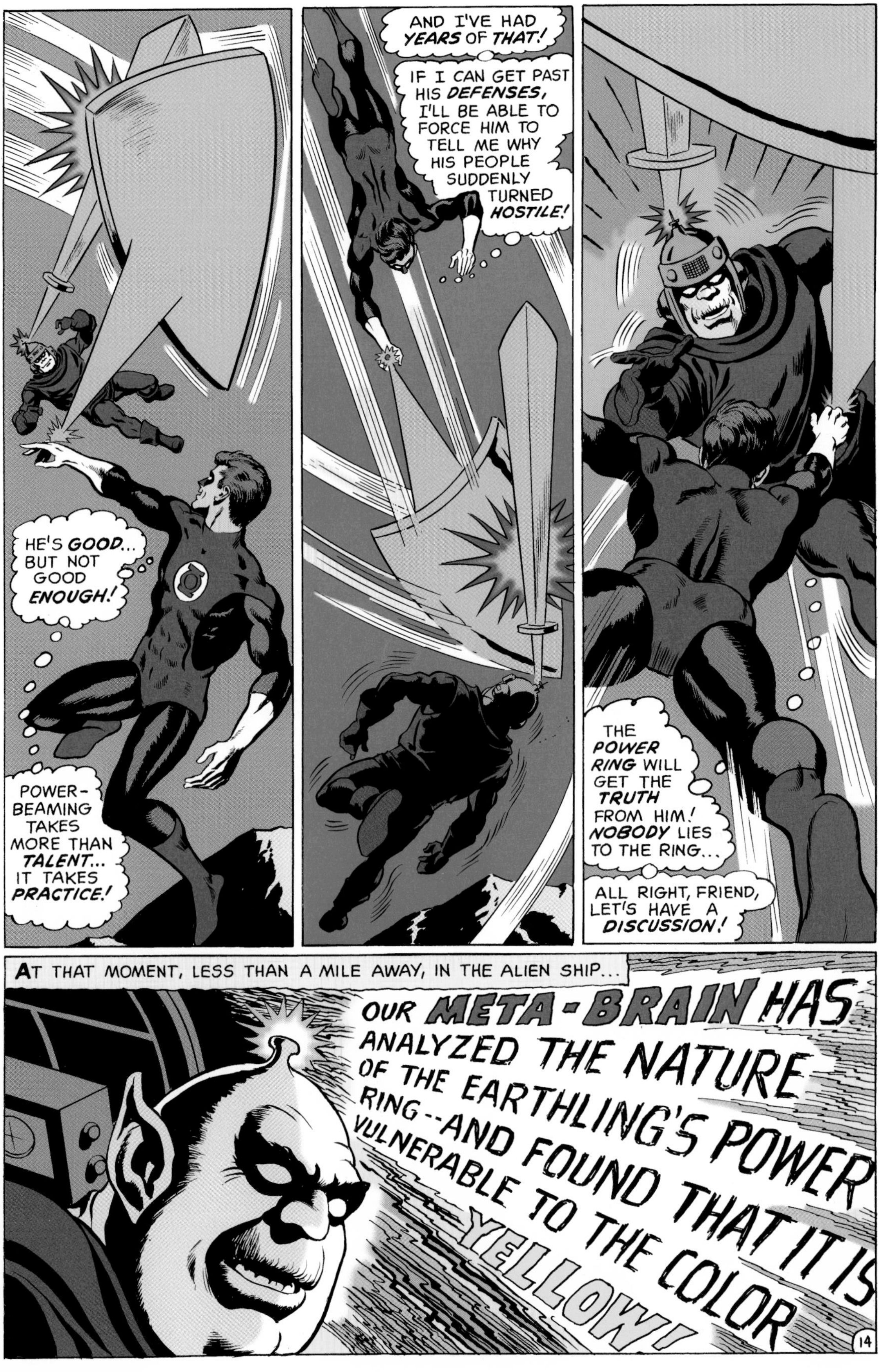
HE'S GOOD... BUT NOT GOOD ENOUGH!
POWER-BEAMING TAKES MORE THAN TALENT... IT TAKES PRACTICE!
AND I'VE HAD YEARS OF THAT!
IF I CAN GET PAST HIS DEFENSES, I'LL BE ABLE TO FORCE HIM TO TELL ME WHY HIS PEOPLE SUDDENLY TURNED HOSTILE!
THE POWER RING WILL GET THE TRUTH FROM HIM! NOBODY LIES TO THE RING...
ALL RIGHT, FRIEND, LET'S HAVE A DISCUSSION!
AT THAT MOMENT, LESS THAN A MILE AWAY, IN THE ALIEN SHIP...
OUR META-BRAIN HAS ANALYZED THE NATURE OF THE EARTHLING'S POWER RING--AND FOUND THAT IT IS VULNERABLE TO THE COLOR YELLOW!
14

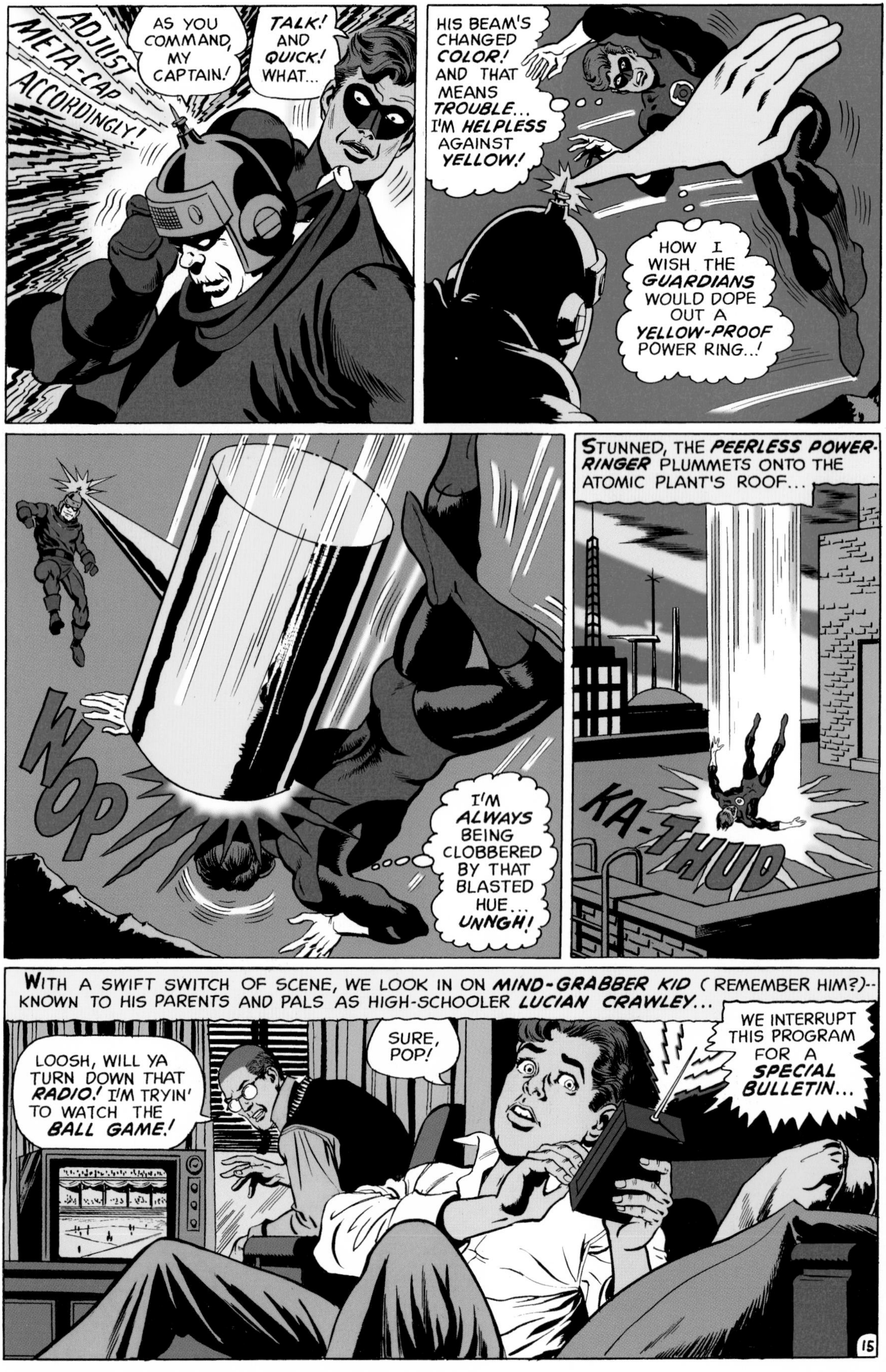
ADJUST META-CAP ACCORDINGLY!
AS YOU COMMAND, MY CAPTAIN!
TALK! AND QUICK! WHAT...
HIS BEAM'S CHANGED COLOR! AND THAT MEANS TROUBLE... I'M HELPLESS AGAINST YELLOW!
HOW I WISH THE GUARDIANS WOULD DOPE OUT A YELLOW-PROOF POWER RING..!
WOP
I'M ALWAYS BEING CLOBBERED BY THAT BLASTED HUE... UNNGH!
STUNNED, THE PEERLESS POWER-RINGER PLUMMETS ONTO THE ATOMIC PLANT'S ROOF...
KA-THUD
WITH A SWIFT SWITCH OF SCENE, WE LOOK IN ON MIND-GRABBER KID (REMEMBER HIM?)-- KNOWN TO HIS PARENTS AND PALS AS HIGH-SCHOOLER LUCIAN CRAWLEY...
LOOSH, WILL YA TURN DOWN THAT RADIO! I'M TRYIN' TO WATCH THE BALL GAME!
SURE, POP!
WE INTERRUPT THIS PROGRAM FOR A SPECIAL BULLETIN...
15

INVADERS FROM A SPACE-SHIP ARE AT THE ATOMIC ENERGY PLANT BATTLING THE JUSTICE LEAGUE!
O BOY-- WOW! THE ALIENS BELIEVED ME!
I'D BETTER CHANGE TO MIND-GRABBER KID!
ANOTHER REPORT HAS JUST COME IN! THE CREEPER WAS SEEN ENTERING THE PLANT SHORTLY BEFORE THE JUSTICE LEAGUE ARRIVED!
I'LL GET ON OVER THERE... GEE! WITH THE JLA AND CREEPER OUT OF THE WAY, I'LL BE THE NUMBER ONE HERO...
WHAT'S THAT KOOKY OUTFIT THE KID'S WEARIN'?
...IN FACT, I'LL BE THE ONLY HERO!
I THINK HE'S IN A SCHOOL PLAY...OR SOMETHING!
KIDS TODAY-- SHEEESH!
16
O BOY-- WOW! WAIT'LL YOU SEE THE CATACLYSMIC CLIMAX OF OUR TALE ON THE NEXT PAGE FOLLOWING...

JUSTICE LEAGUE of AMERICA

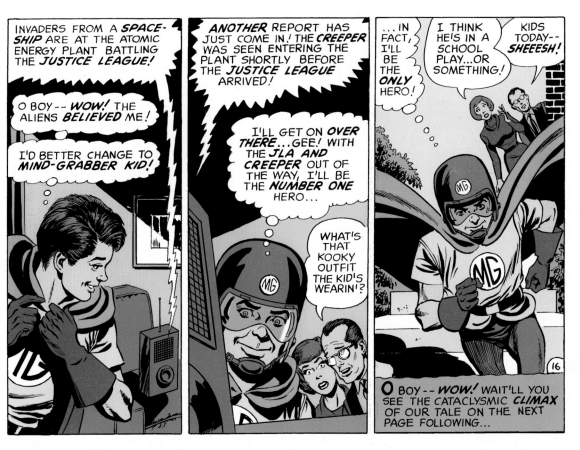

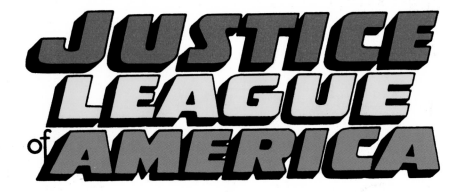

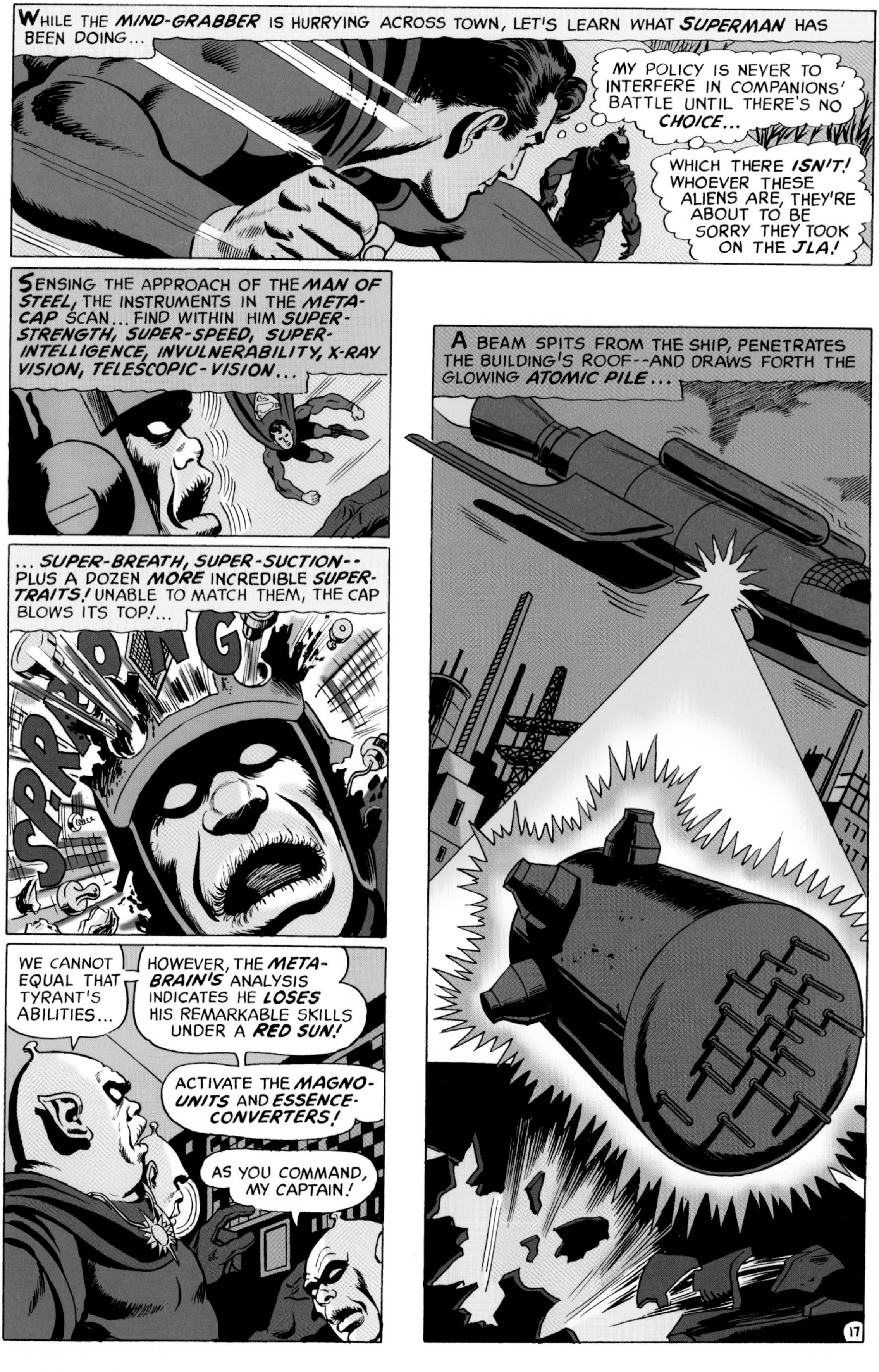
WHILE THE MIND-GRABBER IS HURRYING ACROSS TOWN, LET'S LEARN WHAT SUPERMAN HAS BEEN DOING...
MY POLICY IS NEVER TO INTERFERE IN COMPANIONS' BATTLE UNTIL THERE'S NO CHOICE...
WHICH THERE ISN'T! WHOEVER THESE ALIENS ARE, THEY'RE ABOUT TO BE SORRY THEY TOOK ON THE JLA!
SENSING THE APPROACH OF THE MAN OF STEEL, THE INSTRUMENTS IN THE META-CAP SCAN... FIND WITHIN HIM SUPER-STRENGTH, SUPER-SPEED, SUPER-INTELLIGENCE, INVULNERABILITY, X-RAY VISION, TELESCOPIC-VISION...
... SUPER-BREATH, SUPER-SUCTION-- PLUS A DOZEN MORE INCREDIBLE SUPER-TRAITS! UNABLE TO MATCH THEM, THE CAP BLOWS ITS TOP!...
SPROING!
WE CANNOT EQUAL THAT TYRANT'S ABILITIES...
HOWEVER, THE META-BRAIN'S ANALYSIS INDICATES HE LOSES HIS REMARKABLE SKILLS UNDER A RED SUN!
ACTIVATE THE MAGNO-UNITS AND ESSENCE-CONVERTERS!
AS YOU COMMAND, MY CAPTAIN!
A BEAM SPITS FROM THE SHIP, PENETRATES THE BUILDING'S ROOF--AND DRAWS FORTH THE GLOWING ATOMIC PILE...
17

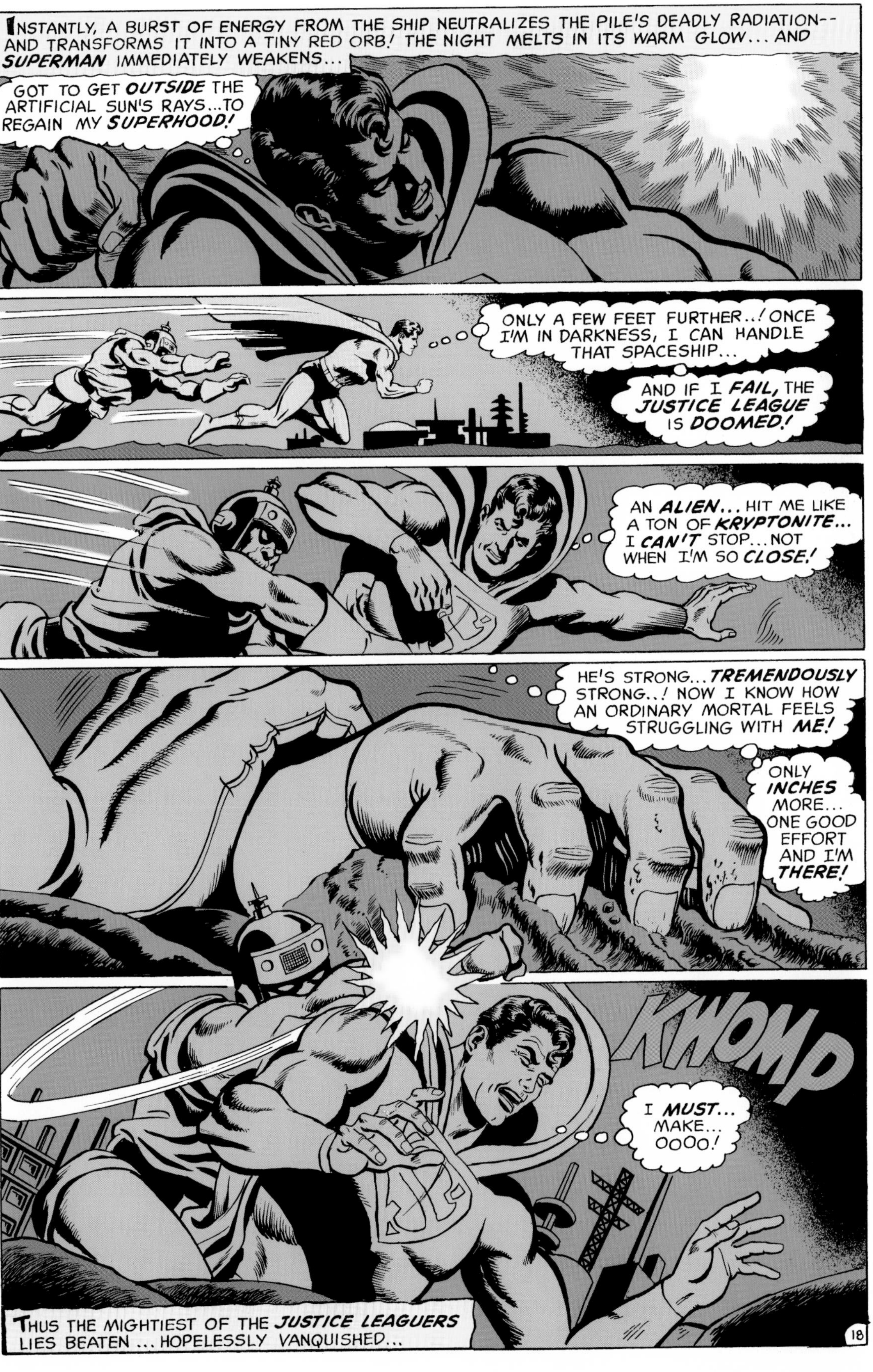
INSTANTLY, A BURST OF ENERGY FROM THE SHIP NEUTRALIZES THE PILE'S DEADLY RADIATION--AND TRANSFORMS IT INTO A TINY RED ORB! THE NIGHT MELTS IN ITS WARM GLOW... AND SUPERMAN IMMEDIATELY WEAKENS...
GOT TO GET OUTSIDE THE ARTIFICIAL SUN'S RAYS...TO REGAIN MY SUPERHOOD!
ONLY A FEW FEET FURTHER..! ONCE I'M IN DARKNESS, I CAN HANDLE THAT SPACESHIP...
AND IF I FAIL, THE JUSTICE LEAGUE IS DOOMED!
AN ALIEN... HIT ME LIKE A TON OF KRYPTONITE... I CAN'T STOP...NOT WHEN I'M SO CLOSE!
HE'S STRONG...TREMENDOUSLY STRONG..! NOW I KNOW HOW AN ORDINARY MORTAL FEELS STRUGGLING WITH ME!
ONLY INCHES MORE... ONE GOOD EFFORT AND I'M THERE!
KWOMP
I MUST... MAKE... OOOO!
THUS THE MIGHTIEST OF THE JUSTICE LEAGUERS LIES BEATEN ... HOPELESSLY VANQUISHED...
18

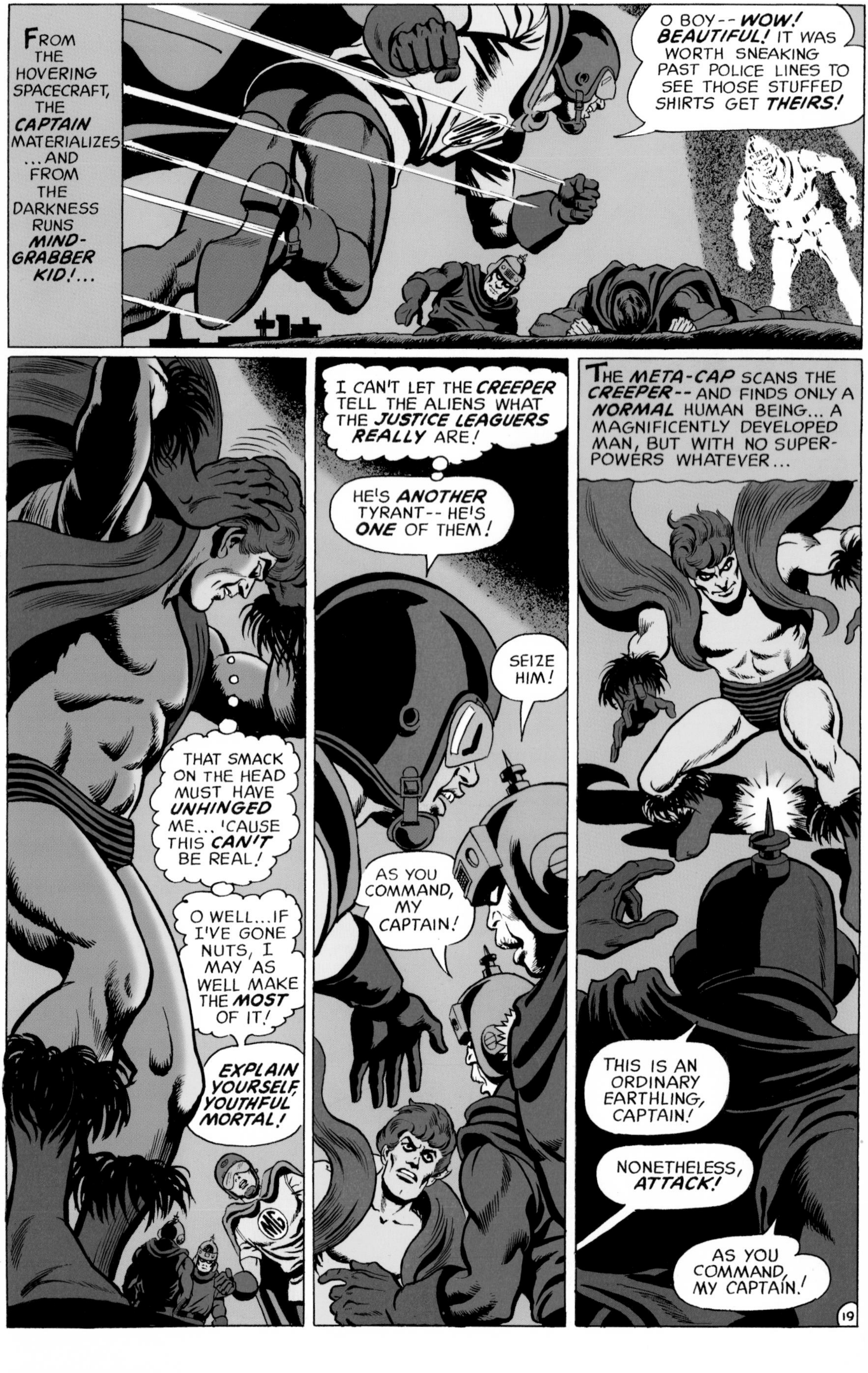
FROM THE HOVERING SPACECRAFT, THE CAPTAIN MATERIALIZES ...AND FROM THE DARKNESS RUNS MIND-GRABBER KID!...
O BOY--WOW! BEAUTIFUL! IT WAS WORTH SNEAKING PAST POLICE LINES TO SEE THOSE STUFFED SHIRTS GET THEIRS!
THAT SMACK ON THE HEAD MUST HAVE UNHINGED ME... 'CAUSE THIS CAN'T BE REAL!
O WELL...IF I'VE GONE NUTS, I MAY AS WELL MAKE THE MOST OF IT!
EXPLAIN YOURSELF, YOUTHFUL MORTAL!
I CAN'T LET THE CREEPER TELL THE ALIENS WHAT THE JUSTICE LEAGUERS REALLY ARE!
HE'S ANOTHER TYRANT--HE'S ONE OF THEM!
SEIZE HIM!
AS YOU COMMAND, MY CAPTAIN!
THE META-CAP SCANS THE CREEPER--AND FINDS ONLY A NORMAL HUMAN BEING... A MAGNIFICENTLY DEVELOPED MAN, BUT WITH NO SUPER-POWERS WHATEVER...
THIS IS AN ORDINARY EARTHLING, CAPTAIN!
NONETHELESS, ATTACK!
AS YOU COMMAND, MY CAPTAIN!
19

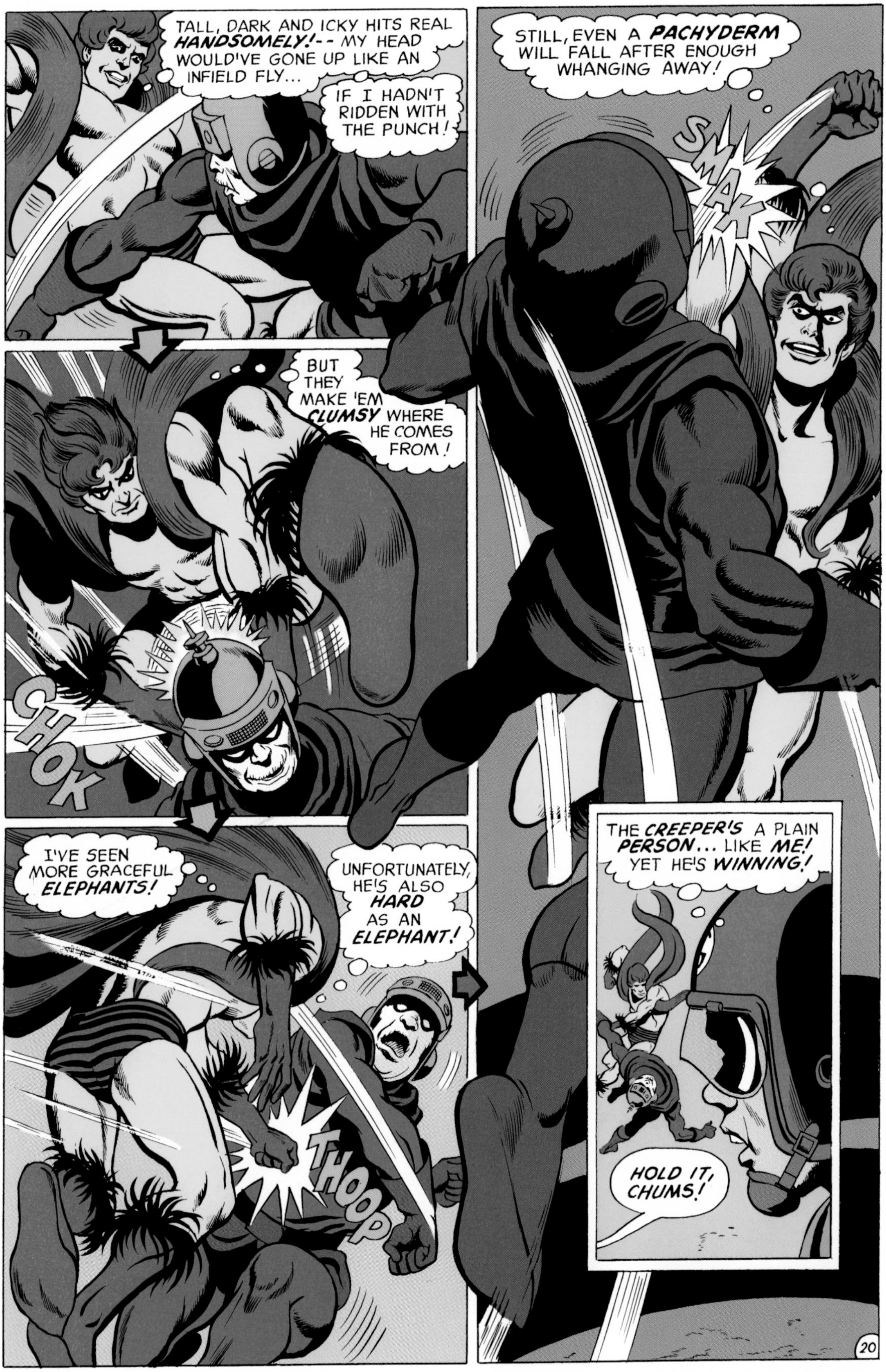
TALL, DARK AND ICKY HITS REAL HANDSOMELY!-- MY HEAD WOULD'VE GONE UP LIKE AN INFIELD FLY...
IF I HADN'T RIDDEN WITH THE PUNCH!
BUT THEY MAKE 'EM CLUMSY WHERE HE COMES FROM!
CHOK
I'VE SEEN MORE GRACEFUL ELEPHANTS!
UNFORTUNATELY, HE'S ALSO HARD AS AN ELEPHANT!
THOOP
STILL, EVEN A PACHYDERM WILL FALL AFTER ENOUGH WHANGING AWAY!
SMAK
THE CREEPER'S A PLAIN PERSON... LIKE ME! YET HE'S WINNING!
HOLD IT, CHUMS!
20

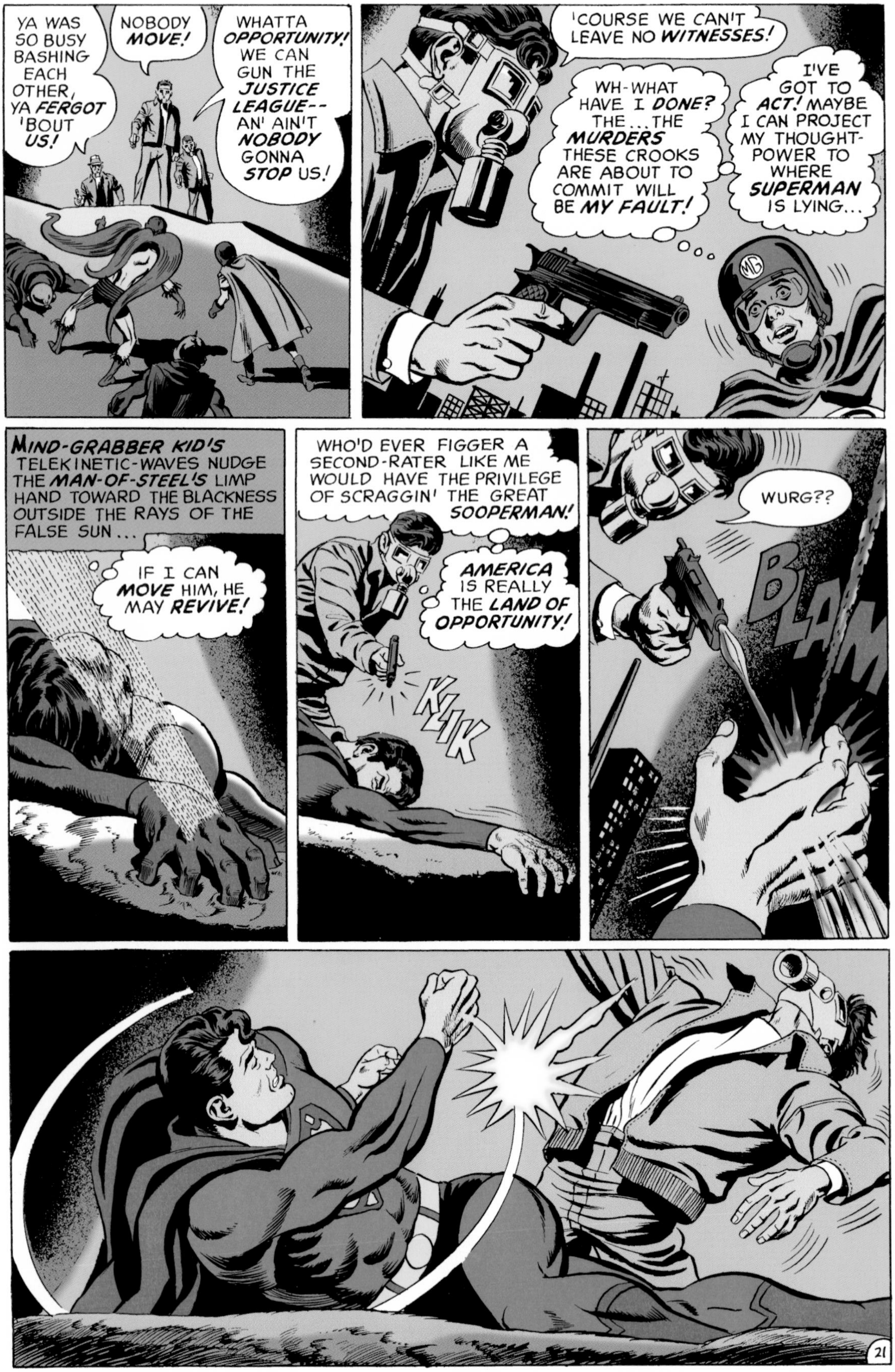
YA WAS SO BUSY BASHING EACH OTHER, YA FERGOT 'BOUT US!
NOBODY MOVE!
WHATTA OPPORTUNITY! WE CAN GUN THE JUSTICE LEAGUE-- AN' AIN'T NOBODY GONNA STOP US!
'COURSE WE CAN'T LEAVE NO WITNESSES!
WH-WHAT HAVE I DONE? THE...THE MURDERS THESE CROOKS ARE ABOUT TO COMMIT WILL BE MY FAULT!
I'VE GOT TO ACT! MAYBE I CAN PROJECT MY THOUGHT-POWER TO WHERE SUPERMAN IS LYING...
MG
MIND-GRABBER KID'S TELEKINETIC-WAVES NUDGE THE MAN-OF-STEEL'S LIMP HAND TOWARD THE BLACKNESS OUTSIDE THE RAYS OF THE FALSE SUN...
IF I CAN MOVE HIM, HE MAY REVIVE!
WHO'D EVER FIGGER A SECOND-RATER LIKE ME WOULD HAVE THE PRIVILEGE OF SCRAGGIN' THE GREAT SOOPERMAN!
AMERICA IS REALLY THE LAND OF OPPORTUNITY!
KLIK
WURG??
BLAM
21

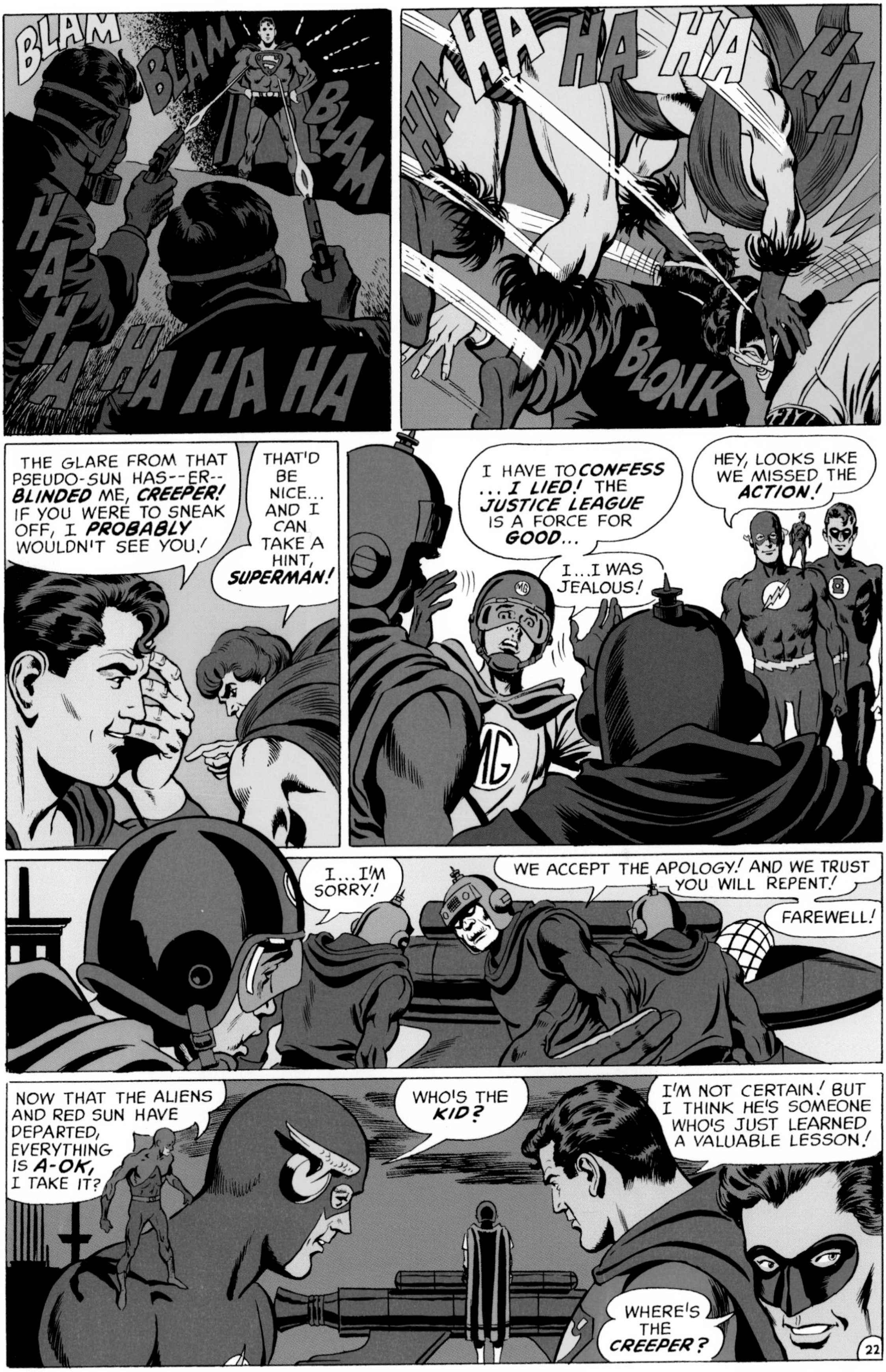
BLAM
BLAM
BLAM
HA HA HA HA HA HA HA
HA HA HA HA HA HA
BLONK
THE GLARE FROM THAT PSEUDO-SUN HAS--ER-- BLINDED ME, CREEPER! IF YOU WERE TO SNEAK OFF, I PROBABLY WOULDN'T SEE YOU!
THAT'D BE NICE... AND I CAN TAKE A HINT, SUPERMAN!
I HAVE TO CONFESS ...I LIED! THE JUSTICE LEAGUE IS A FORCE FOR GOOD...
I...I WAS JEALOUS!
HEY, LOOKS LIKE WE MISSED THE ACTION!
I...I'M SORRY!
WE ACCEPT THE APOLOGY! AND WE TRUST YOU WILL REPENT!
FAREWELL!
NOW THAT THE ALIENS AND RED SUN HAVE DEPARTED, EVERYTHING IS A-OK, I TAKE IT?
WHO'S THE KID?
I'M NOT CERTAIN! BUT I THINK HE'S SOMEONE WHO'S JUST LEARNED A VALUABLE LESSON!
WHERE'S THE CREEPER?
22

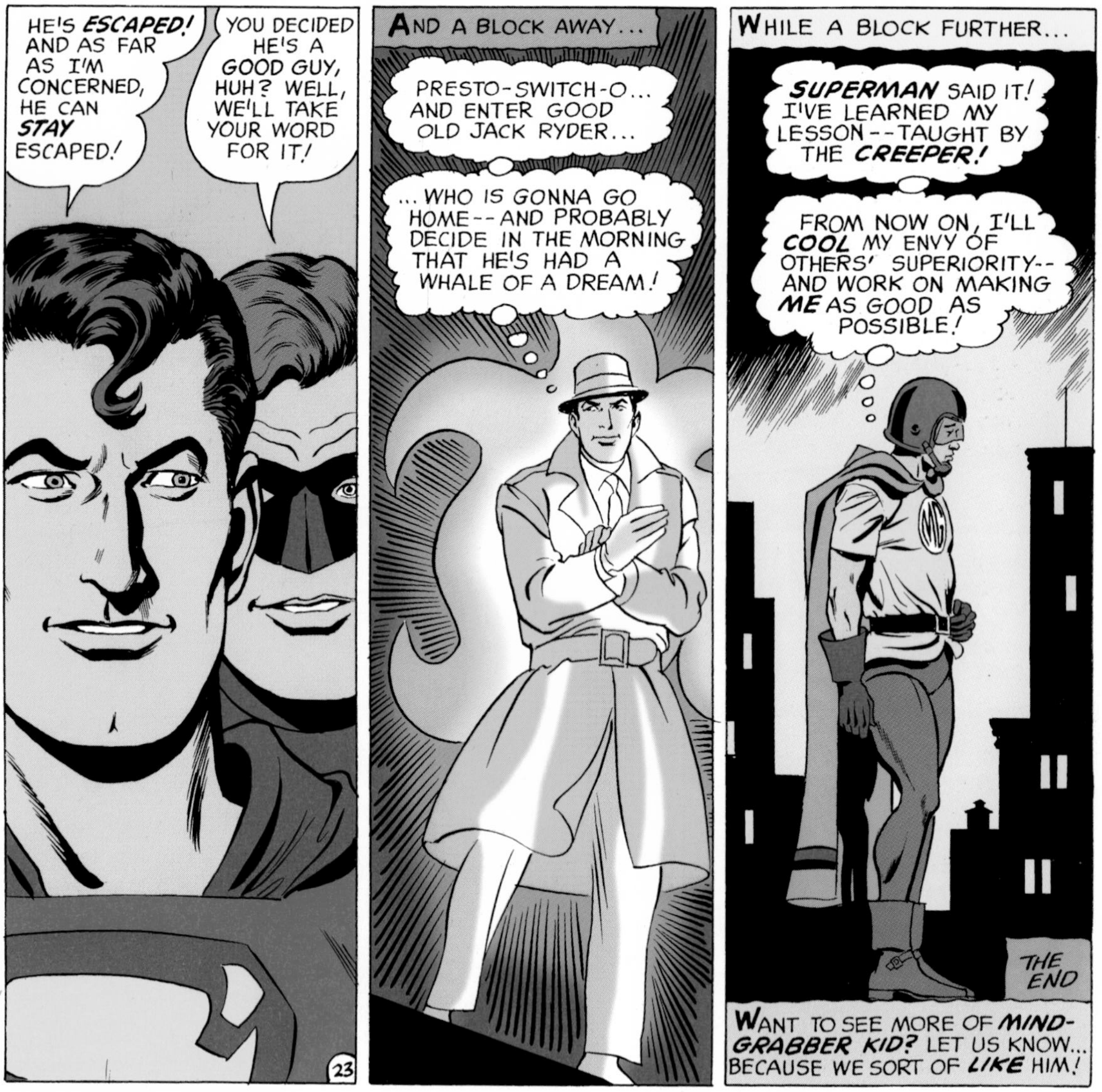
HE'S ESCAPED! AND AS FAR AS I'M CONCERNED, HE CAN STAY ESCAPED!
YOU DECIDED HE'S A GOOD GUY, HUH? WELL, WE'LL TAKE YOUR WORD FOR IT!
23
AND A BLOCK AWAY...
PRESTO-SWITCH-O... AND ENTER GOOD OLD JACK RYDER...
...WHO IS GONNA GO HOME--AND PROBABLY DECIDE IN THE MORNING THAT HE'S HAD A WHALE OF A DREAM!
WHILE A BLOCK FURTHER...
SUPERMAN SAID IT! I'VE LEARNED MY LESSON--TAUGHT BY THE CREEPER!
FROM NOW ON, I'LL COOL MY ENVY OF OTHERS' SUPERIORITY--AND WORK ON MAKING ME AS GOOD AS POSSIBLE!
THE END
WANT TO SEE MORE OF MIND-GRABBER KID? LET US KNOW... BECAUSE WE SORT OF LIKE HIM!

JUSTICE LEAGUE of AMERICA

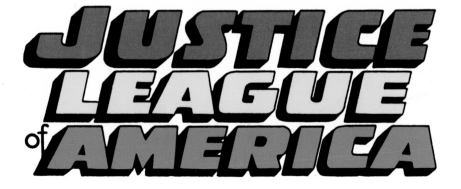

NEAL ADAMS

Born on June 6, 1941 in New York, Neal Adams began his career assisting on and occasionally pencilling the *Bat Masterson* syndicated comic strip. At the same time, Adams did advertising illustration, developing a realistic art style that would become his trademark. From there, Neal went on to a brief stint at Archie Comics and to his own newspaper strip, *Ben Casey*, based on the popular television series. Adams joined DC in 1967 and became an overnight sensation by infusing a new visual vitality into longtime characters. Working closely with Carmine Infantino, Adams quickly became DC's preeminent cover artist during this period, contributing radical and dynamic illustrations to virtually the company's entire line. His work on WORLD'S FINEST COMICS, SUPERMAN, THE SPECTRE, GREEN LANTERN and the Deadman strip made him an instant fan favorite. Adams became one of the most talked-about creator/writer/artist/publishers in the medium and continues to influence, directly and indirectly, today's young comics artists.

MURPHY ANDERSON

Heavily influenced by artists Lou Fine and Will Eisner, Murphy Anderson entered the comics arena in 1944 as an artist for Fiction House. In 1950, he began his life-long association with DC Comics, pulling double duty as both a full illustrator and as an inker over other artists' pencil work. Though he inked only a few of Sekowsky's first Justice League pages, Anderson continued his work on JUSTICE LEAGUE OF AMERICA covers for several years thereafter.

DICK DILLIN

Born in Watertown, New York in 1929, Richard (Dick) Dillin graduated from Syracuse University and spent some years in the field of commercial illustration before embarking on a career in comics. Best remembered for his almost 12-year-long run on JLA, Dillin also had a decades-long association with the character Blackhawk both at Quality Comics and DC. It can be safely said that during the 1960s and '70s there was not a single DCU character that the prolific artist didn't draw at one time or another. Dillin passed away in 1980.

GARDNER FOX

Probably the single most imaginative and productive writer in the Golden Age of comics, Gardner Fox created or co-created dozens of long-running features, among them Flash, Hawkman, Sandman, and Dr. Fate. Working with editor Sheldon Mayer, and later with Julius Schwartz, Fox also penned the adventures of the Justice Society of America, comics' first super-team, during the 1940s. Following the late-1950s revival of the super-hero genre, Fox — again under Schwartz's guidance — assembled Earth's Mightiest Heroes once more and scripted an unbroken 65-issue run of JUSTICE LEAGUE OF AMERICA. Though Fox produced thousands of other scripts and wrote over 100 books, it is perhaps this body of work for which he is best known. Fox passed away in 1986.

JOE GIELLA

Joe Giella began his long career as a comic-book artist in the 1940s, working for Hillman Publications and for Timely, the company that was later to become Marvel Comics. Giella came to DC in 1951 and over the next three decades worked predominantly as an inker, lending his clean, tight line to thousands of pencilled pages and to every major character the company published. During the 1960s, at the height of the TV-fueled "Batmania," Giella pencilled and inked the daily Batman newspaper strip. He continues his syndicated strip work to this day, illustrating the venerable *Mary Worth* feature.

SID GREENE

Brought to JUSTICE LEAGUE OF AMERICA to replace the retired Bernard Sachs, Sid Greene was one of editor Julie Schwartz's most prolific artists and added a new crispness to Mike Sekowsky and Dick Dillin's pencils for three years until his retirement in 1969. Greene died in 1972.

CARMINE INFANTINO

Infantino entered the field of comic-book illustration in the mid-1940s, as the artist on Green Lantern, Black Canary, Ghost Patrol and the original Golden Age Flash. His style graced the pages of a variety of super-hero, Western and supernatural features throughout the 1950s until he was called upon to draw the character he is most associated with — the Flash. While delivering this feature he also contributed to Batman, Elongated Man, and Adam Strange. Infantino became DC's editorial director in 1967 and later its publisher before he returned to freelancing in 1976. Infantino still occasionally contributes to the DC Universe he helped form.

DENNIS O'NEIL

Dennis O'Neil began his career as a comic-book writer in 1965 at Charlton, where then-editor Dick Giordano assigned him to several features. When Giordano moved to DC, O'Neil soon followed. At DC, O'Neil scripted several series for Giordano and Julius Schwartz, quickly becoming one of the most respected writers in comics. O'Neil earned a reputation for being able to "revamp" such characters as Superman, Green Lantern, Captain Marvel — and the Batman, whom O'Neil (with the help of Neal Adams and Giordano) brought back to his roots as a dark, mysterious, gothic avenger. Besides being the most important Batman writer of the 1970s, O'Neil served as an editor at both Marvel and DC. While O'Neil has officially retired as a Group Editor from DC he still remains as prolific a writer as ever.

GEORGE ROUSSOS

George Roussos was hired by Jerry Robinson to assist on Batman by lettering and inking backgrounds. His first work in this capacity appeared in BATMAN #2 (Summer 1940) and he was a mainstay until 1944 when he went freelance. Roussos pencilled, inked and colored Airwave, as well as inking Superman, Johnny Quick, Star Spangled Kid, Vigilante, and other DC characters and titles. From the late 1940s into the 1950s, he worked freelance for a number of comic-book publishers, including Harvey, Hillman, Avon, Ziff-Davis, Fiction House, E.C., Timely, Prize and Pines. In 1963, Roussos also began inking stories for Marvel, including *The Uncanny X-Men*, *The Fantastic Four*, *Captain America* and many others. He left DC around 1970 to work full-time for Marvel and soon became a cover colorist. His career in the comic-book field spans over a half century, and his contributions are numerous. Roussos died on February 19, 2000.

MIKE SEKOWSKY

A tremendously versatile and talented artist, Michael Sekowsky entered the comics field while it was still in its infancy. In 1941, he began work at Timely/Marvel Comics and was soon pencilling some of its top heroes, including Captain America, the Human Torch, and the Sub-Mariner. Sekowsky joined DC in the early 1950s and quickly became known for his dynamic renditions of alien worlds and spacefaring heroes such as Adam Strange, whom Sekowsky co-created with Gardner Fox. Nevertheless, he is best remembered as the penciller of the wildly successful Justice League of America, which was drawn exclusively by Sekowsky for its first eight years. Though never considered one of comics' more polished artists, Sekowsky more than compensated with impeccable and dynamic storytelling. Sekowsky remained active in comics and television animation until his death in 1989.

JULIUS SCHWARTZ

More than any other editor, Julie Schwartz helped shape the face of the comic-book medium as we know it today. Hired as a DC editor in 1944, Schwartz brought an inventiveness and dedication to the craft of storytelling that soon made him a legend in his own right. His true legacy, however, came to flower in the 1950s and early 1960s, when, together with Fox, John Broome, Carmine Infantino and others, he revived and revitalized the all but abandoned super-hero genre, transforming such nearly forgotten heroes as the Flash and Green Lantern into the super-stars that formed the Justice League. Without that timely infusion of energy, comic books might well have gone the way of the penny postcard, the automat and the drive-in movie — faded icons of a bygone era.

Biographical material researched and written by Mark Waid.